Worldwide Destinations: The geography of travel and tourism

Worldwide Destinations: The geography of travel and tourism is a unique text that explores tourism demand, supply, organisation and resources for a comprehensive range of destinations worldwide. The sixth edition is brought up to date with features such as:

- An exploration of current issues such as climate change, recreational preferences, demographic changes and the social impacts of tourism.
- An extended chapter on Asian tourism to reflect developments in the travel industry.
- Improved full colour presentation, packed with helpful teaching suggestions, including discussion points, review questions and assignments to encourage greater student involvement.
- a companion website is available at www.routledge.com/cw/boniface and includes interactive, multiple-choice questions for students to test their own learning.

The first part of the book comprises thematic chapters which detail the geographic knowledge and principles required to analyse the tourism appeal of destinations. The subsequent division of the book into regional chapters enables the student to carry out a systematic analysis of a particular destination, by providing insights on cultural characteristics as well as information on specific places.

Worldwide Destinations: The geography of travel and tourism is an invaluable resource for studying every destination in the world, by explaining tourism demand, evaluating the many types of tourist attractions and examining the trends that may shape the future geography of tourism. This thorough guide is a must-have for any student undertaking a course in travel and tourism.

Brian Boniface, M.A. (University of Georgia) is a tourism consultant.

Chris Cooper is Professor and Director, Christel DeHaan Tourism and Travel Research Institute, Nottingham University Business School.

Robyn Cooper is a graduate student at the University of Leicester.

Worldwide Destinations:
The geography of travel and tourism

Brian Boniface, Chris Cooper and Robyn Cooper

Sixth Edition

Routledge
Taylor & Francis Group

LONDON AND NEW YORK

Sixth edition published 2012
by Routledge
2 Park Square, Milton Park, Abingdon, Oxon, OX14 4RN

Simultaneously published in the USA and Canada
by Routledge
711 Third Avenue, New York, NY 10017

Routledge is an imprint of the Taylor & Francis Group, an informa business

Previous editions published by Heinemann
First edition published as *The Geography of Travel and Tourism* 1985

Previous editions published by Butterworth-Heinemann
Second edition   1994
Third edition   2001
Fourth edition   2004
Fifth edition   2009

British Library Cataloguing in Publication Data
A catalogue record for this book is available from the British Library

Library of Congress Cataloging in Publication Data
A catalog record for this book has been requested

ISBN: 978-0-415-52277-9 (hbk)
ISBN: 978-0-080-97040-0 (pbk)
ISBN: 978-0-080-97041-7 (ebk)

Typeset in Helvetica
by RefineCatch Limited, Bungay, Suffolk.
Printed and bound in Great Britain by Ashford Colour Press Ltd., Gosport, Hampshire.

FSC
www.fsc.org

MIX
Paper from
responsible sources
FSC® C011748

Contents

List of figures

List of tables

Preface

In the mid-1980s when we set out to write the first edition of the *Geography of Travel and Tourism*, we were pioneering new territory, following in the footsteps of a very small band of geographers who had discovered tourism as a field of research. Since then the territory has been well and truly explored by a host of authors writing textbooks, reports and papers for specialist journals. Yet at the same time the focus on tourism is becoming narrower, with most authors specialising in ever-smaller areas of the discipline, and with very few geographers taking a comprehensive approach to travel and tourism.

We hope that the sixth edition has a less Euro-centric approach than its predecessors by giving more space to emerging destinations, particularly in Asia, where a number of countries are now competing with Western Europe and North America as major generators of tourism demand. Nonetheless, we have retained many of the ingredients of previous successful editions. In particular we have retained our comprehensive coverage of every country in the world.

The regional chapters are written to a flexible template which generally consists of the setting for tourism, demand, and the supply-side of tourism, including transport, organisation and resources. As in previous editions we stress the demand side of tourism, particularly where it concerns the world's most important generators of domestic and outbound travel. We make no apology for this comprehensive approach, as we feel it is needed more than ever before in a subject area dominated by increasing specialisation, and our book therefore complements the more detailed treatment of tourism found in the host of textbooks, reports and academic papers that deal with specific themes or destinations. There are moreover a number of differences from its predecessors which we think will improve the appeal of the sixth edition. Each chapter now offers a number of mini-case studies to highlight certain areas or topics, and discussion points to encourage greater student involvement. As in previous editions, each chapter is concluded with a series of summary points.

Supplemented with a good atlas, the book provides a framework for understanding most aspects of travel and tourism. We realise that many students embark on tourism courses without a basic knowledge of locational geography, and it is mainly for their benefit that we have included an appendix on maps and spatial awareness. Geography can make a unique contribution to the study, not only of tourism, but also of those man-made and natural events around the world that make the news headlines. The study of geography provides insights to understand other cultures as well as information on places.

As before, family, friends and colleagues have supported us in writing this edition. Our students, including those on distance learning courses from many countries around the world, have provided invaluable feedback and information on current trends in tourism. We would also like to express our appreciation of Carol Barber for her patience in finalising our work for publication.

Brian Boniface, Chris Cooper and Robyn Cooper,
Poole, Oxford and Leicester,
October 2011

PART **1**

The Geographical Principles of Travel and Tourism

An introduction to the geography of travel and tourism

Learning objectives

After reading this chapter, you should be able to:

- Define and use the terms leisure, recreation and tourism and understand their interrelationships
- Distinguish between tourism, migration, and other types of mobility
- Distinguish between the different forms of tourism, and the relationship of different types of tourist with the environment
- Appreciate the importance of scale in explaining patterns of tourism
- Identify the three major components of the tourism system
- Explain the push and pull factors that give rise to tourist flows
- Appreciate the methods used to measure tourist flows and be aware of their shortcomings

Leisure, recreation and tourism

What exactly is meant by the terms leisure, recreation and tourism, and how are they related? *Leisure* is often seen as a measure of time, and usually means the time left over after work, sleep, household chores and personal obligations have been completed (Figure 1.1). In other words, leisure is free time for individuals to spend as they please. This does, however, introduce the problem of whether all free time is leisure. A good example of this dilemma is whether the unemployed feel that their free time is in fact 'enforced' leisure, or whether volunteers at a sporting event see their activity as

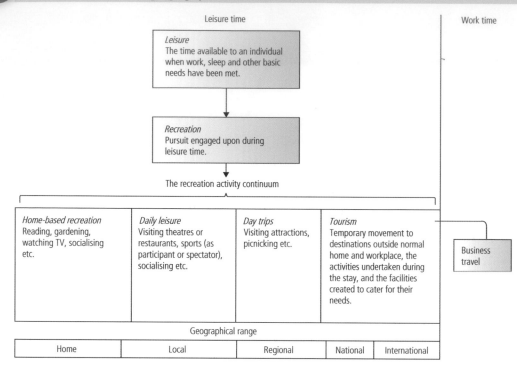

Figure 1.1 Leisure, recreation and tourism

'serious leisure'. This has led to the view that leisure is as much an attitude of mind as a measure of time, and that an element of 'choice' has to be involved. In fact the relationships between work and leisure have changed over the last two centuries in most of the world; the Industrial Revolution brought about a sharp contrast between the home, the workplace, and the leisure environment, which became more widely separated as transport facilities improved. In pre-industrial societies the pace of life is attuned to the rhythm of the seasons rather than being governed by the clock, and personal mobility is limited. In post-industrial countries such as Britain and the USA, one aspect of the so-called '24/7 culture' is the blurring of the boundaries between work and leisure, and the *work-life balance* is increasingly under threat as a result. Highly paid executives are expected to be in contact with the office during their vacations, while some corporate employers provide leisure opportunities based at the workplace.

Recreation is normally taken to mean the variety of activities undertaken during leisure time (Figure 1.1). Basically, recreation refreshes a person's strength and spirit and can include activities as diverse as watching television at home to holidaying abroad. We can make a useful distinction between leisure pursuits that involve the arts, cultural activities and entertainment, and physical activities. We can further distinguish *sports* from other types of physical recreation as they involve competition and participants must follow rules laid down by a recognised authority.

If we accept that leisure is a measure of time and that recreation embraces the activities undertaken during that time, then tourism is simply one type of recreation activity. It is, however, more difficult to disentangle the meaning of the terms recreation and tourism in practice. Perhaps the most helpful way to think about the difference is to envisage a spectrum, with at one end, recreation based at home or the local area, and at the opposite end recreational travel where some distance is involved and overnight accommodation may be needed. This is based on the time required for the activity and the distance travelled, and it places tourism firmly at one extreme of the *recreational activity spectrum* (Figure 1.1). The spectrum also allows us to consider the role of same-day visitors or *excursionists*. These travellers are increasingly a consideration in the geography of tourism – they visit for less than 24 hours and do not stay overnight. In other words, they utilise all tourism facilities except accommodation, and put pressure on the host community and the environment.

Clearly tourism is a distinctive form of recreation and demands separate consideration. In particular, from the geographical point of view, tourism is just one form of temporary or leisure mobility, recognising that technology and changes in society have given people the capacity to travel extensively. In other words we can think of tourism as a form of voluntary, temporary mobility in relation to where people live. International debate as to the definition of tourism still continues, and there are many different interpretations. There are two ways to approach the problem:

1   First we can define tourism from the **demand side**, i.e. the person who is the tourist. This approach is well developed and the United Nations Statistical Commission now accepts the following definition of tourism: 'The activities of persons travelling to and staying in places outside their usual environment for not more than one consecutive year for leisure, business and other purposes.' This definition raises a number of issues:
    - What is a person's usual environment?
    - The inclusion of 'business' and 'other' purposes of visit demands that we conceive of tourism more widely than simply as a recreational pursuit.
    - Certain types of traveller are excluded from the definition. Tourism is only one part of the spectrum of travel, which ranges from the daily journey to work, or for shopping, to migration, where the traveller intends to take up permanent or long-term residence in another area (see Figure 1.2).
2   We can also define the tourism sector from the **supply-side** point of view. Here the difficulty lies in disentangling tourism businesses and jobs from the rest of the economy. After 20 years of debate, the accepted approach is the *tourism satellite account* (TSA), adopted by the United Nations in 2000. The TSA measures the demand for goods and services generated by visitors to a destination. It allows tourism to be compared with other sectors of the economy by calculating its contribution to investment, consumption, employment, gross domestic product (GDP), and taxation.

Discussion point: Defining tourism experiences

Traditional definitions of tourism fail to incorporate the idea of tourism as an 'experience' where in fact, the tourist is as much a creator of the experience as the tourism industry itself. This is known as co-creation of the tourism experience and has been enabled in part by technology whereby tourists construct their own product. Can you devise a new definition of tourism that takes this idea into account?

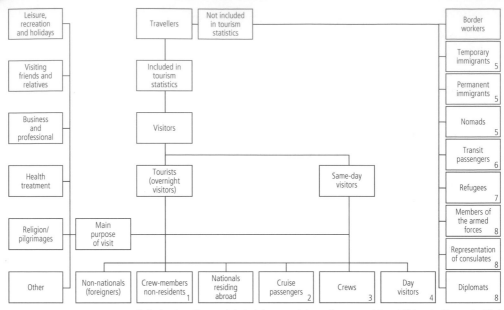

Figure 1.2 Classification of travellers (*Source*: World Tourism Organisation)

1. Foreign air or ship crews docked or in lay over and who use the accommodation establishments of the country visited.
2. Persons who arrive in a country abroad cruise ships (as defined by the International Maritime Organization, 1965) and who spend the night aboard ship even when disembarking for one or more day visits.
3. Crews who are not residents of the country visited and who stay in the country for the day.
4. Visitors who arrive and leave the same day for; leisure, recreation and holidays; visiting friends and relatives; business and professional; health treatment; religion/pilgrimages and other tourism purposes, including transit day visitors en route to or from their destination countries.
5. As defined by the United Nations in the Recommendations on Statistics of International Migration, 1980.
6. Who do not leave the transit area of the airport or the port, including transfer between airports and ports.
7. As defined by the United Nations High Commissioner for Refugees, 1967.
8. When they travel from their country of origin to the duty station and vice versa (including household servants and dependants accompanying or joining them).

Geography and tourism

When we study the geography of travel and tourism, three key concepts need to be considered:

- spatial scale;
- the geographical components of the tourism system;
- spatial interaction between the components of the tourism system.

Spatial scale

Geographers study the spatial expression of tourism as a human activity, focusing on both tourist-generating and tourist-receiving areas as well as the links between them. We can undertake this study at a variety of scales, namely:

- The global or continental scale – the distribution of major climate zones and ecosystems, air and shipping routes and patterns of migration.
- The national scale – the identification of a country's transport networks and tourist regions and population distribution.

- The regional scale – the assessment of tourism resources in part of a country.
- The local scale – the location of particular attractions and the configuration of holiday resorts.

This issue of scale has become important in the global versus local debate. As the tourism sector embraces the tools of globalisation, such as the forging of global airline alliances, we must never forget that the tourism product is delivered at the local scale, often by local people and within a local cultural context.

We have used the idea of scale to organise the material presented in this book because at each scale we can gain a distinctive perspective and insight on tourism. In other words, as a more detailed explanation is required, attention is drawn to increasingly smaller parts of the problem. This idea of scale, or geographical magnitude, keeps in focus the area being dealt with, and can be likened to increasing or decreasing the magnification on a microscope, or the area covered by a map. (To learn more about maps and their many uses for tourism see Appendix.) Flows of leisure tourism in Europe provide a good example of the importance of scale. At the international scale the dominant flow of tourists is from north to south, but at the regional scale a variety of other patterns emerge such as travel between cities, or out of cities to the coast or countryside, while at the local scale we can consider day-trip patterns, with people travelling relatively short distances from their accommodation in the holiday area.

The geographical components of the tourism system

From a geographical point of view tourism has three major components, first the places of origin of tourists, which we call *generating areas*; secondly the tourist destinations themselves or *receiving areas*; and thirdly the routes travelled between these two sets of locations, known as *transit routes* (Leiper, 1979). These components relate to differing economic, environmental and social contexts and in each part of the system the tourist will interact with different parts of the travel and tourism industry. This simple model is illustrated in Figure 1.3 and the components form the basis for Chapters 2 to 5:

1 *Tourist-generating areas* represent the homes of tourists, where journeys begin and end. The key issues to examine here are the features that stimulate *demand* for tourism, and include the geographical location of an area as well as its socio-economic and demographic characteristics. These areas represent the main tourist markets in the world and, naturally enough, the main marketing functions of the tourism industry are found here (such as tour operation and travel retailing). We consider tourist-generating areas in Chapter 2.
2 *Tourist receiving areas* attract visitors to stay temporarily and will have features and attractions that may not be found in the generating areas. The tourism industry located in such an area will comprise the visitor attractions, accommodation sector, retailing and service functions, entertainment and recreation facilities. In our view, destinations deserve more attention than the other two components; not only do they attract the tourist – thus energising the system – but also because the impacts of tourism on the host community and environment explain why the sustainable planning and management of tourism is so important. We examine the features of destinations in Chapters 3 and 4.
3 *Transit routes* are a key element in the system as their effectiveness and other characteristics shape the volume and direction of tourist flows. These routes represent the transport sector of the tourism industry which we consider in Chapter 5.

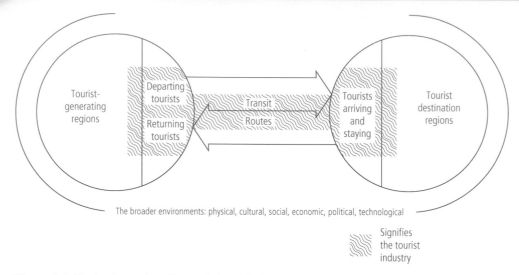

Figure 1.3 The tourism system (*Source*: Leiper, 1979)

The characteristics of each component of the tourism system are determined by the context. For example, a tourism system in a developing country is likely to have a generating component more dominated by domestic travel than would be the case in a developed country of comparable size and population. External factors, such as the international political and economic situation, also affect the tourism system in terms of a range of issues, notably terrorism and security, and this means all components should develop crisis and risk management plans. Tourism is seldom the make-believe world of the holiday brochure, and it is this connection with the real world that makes the geography of travel and tourism such an exciting and vibrant area to study. Of course, change in one part of the system will impact on the other parts – enhanced security arrangements in the transit route, for example, will affect both the demand and supply sides of the system.

Spatial interaction between the components of the tourism system: tourist flows

The consideration of tourist flows between countries or regions is fundamental to the geography of tourism and allows us to see the all-important interrelationships between the three components we have identified. An understanding of tourist flows is critical for managing the environmental and social impacts of tourism, securing the commercial viability of the tourism industry and for planning new developments.

Tourist flows are a form of spatial interaction between two areas with the destination area containing a surplus of a commodity or *resource* (surfing beaches or ski slopes, for example) and the generating area having a deficit, or demand for that commodity. In fact it is possible to detect regular patterns of tourist flows. They do not occur randomly but follow certain rules and are influenced by a variety of 'push' and 'pull' factors:

- **Push factors** are mainly concerned with the stage of economic development in the generating area and will include such factors as levels of affluence, mobility, and holiday entitlement. Moreover an advanced stage of economic development will not only give the population the means to engage in tourism but the pressures of city life will provide the urge to 'get away from it all'. An unfavourable climate will also provide a strong impetus to travel.

- **Pull factors** include accessibility, and the attractions and amenities of the destination area. The relative cost of the visit is also important, as is the effectiveness of marketing and promotion by the destination.

Explaining tourist flows

The movements of people between places are highly complex and are influenced by a wide variety of interrelated variables. A number of attempts have been made to explain the factors that affect tourist flows and to provide rules governing the magnitude of flows between regions. An early attempt by Williams and Zelinsky (1970) selected 14 countries that had relatively stable tourist flows over several years and which accounted for the bulk of the world's tourist traffic. They identified the following factors:

- distances between countries (the greater the distance, the smaller the volume of flow);
- international connectivity (shared business or cultural ties between countries);
- the general attractiveness of one country for another.

The *gravity model* is another way of explaining tourist flows (see Figure 1.4). Push and pull factors generate flows, and the larger the mass (population) of country 'A' or country 'B', the greater the flow between them. The second factor, known as the friction of distance, refers to the cost in time and money of longer journeys, and this acts to restrain flows between the country of origin and more distant destinations. We can also use other models based on travel itineraries.

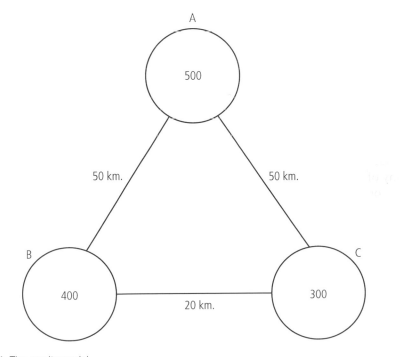

Figure 1.4 The gravity model

Measuring tourist flows

As tourism has become more prominent, national governments and international organisations have introduced the measurement of both international and domestic flows. There are three main reasons why statistics of tourism flows are important:

1 Statistics are required to evaluate the **magnitude of tourist flows** and to monitor any change. This allows projections of future flows to be made and the identification of market trends.
2 Statistics act as a basis of hard fact to allow tourism planners and developers to operate effectively and **plan for the future of tourism**.
3 Both the public (government) and private (business) sectors use the statistics as the basis for their **marketing.**

There are three main categories of tourism statistics. The first one, **volume statistics**, give the number of tourists visiting a destination in a given period of time. Volume statistics also include the length of stay of visitors at their destinations. A variety of methods are available to measure tourist flows.

For volume statistics, tourists can be counted as they enter or leave a country, and immigration control will often provide this information, but measuring domestic travel is very problematic. For destination areas, an alternative method is to enumerate tourists at their accommodation by the use of registration cards. This method is only effective with legal enforcement and normally omits visitors staying in private villas and apartments, or 'VFR' tourists (those visiting and staying with friends or relatives).

Statistics of domestic volume may be obtained by national travel surveys or destination surveys. National travel surveys involve interviewing a representative sample of the population in their homes or on the Internet. People are asked questions on the nature and extent of their travel over a past period, and the results not only provide statistics on volume but may also include information on expenditure. Examples of national travel surveys include the *UK Tourism Survey* (UKTS) and Germany's *Reiseanalyse*. In destination surveys, visitors to a tourist area, specific site or attraction are interviewed to establish the volume, economic value, and characteristics of traffic to that location.

The second category, **statistics of tourist characteristics**, refers to the detailed composition of the tourists themselves. While statistics of volume are a measure of the quantity of tourist flows, this category measures the quality of the flow, including information on the gender, age and socio-economic group of the tourist, the structure of the trip, and attitudes to the destination. It is not uncommon for statistics of tourist characteristics and volume to be collected together.

Surveys of tourist characteristics have evolved from straightforward questioning which gives basic factual information (for example, the age profile of visitors), to surveys which now concentrate on questions that are designed to assist the marketing and management of a destination, or to solve a particular problem. Statistics of tourist characteristics are obtained in a variety of ways. Additional questions can be added to accommodation registration cards, or border checks, but more commonly a sample of travellers is asked a series of questions about themselves, their trip, opinions of the destination, etc. An example of this approach is the *UK International Passenger Survey* (IPS) which measures the volume and economic value as well as the characteristics of inbound and outbound tourism for the United Kingdom.

The third category is **expenditure statistics.** Tourist flows are not simply movements of people but they also have an important economic significance for the tourism system.

Quite simply, tourism represents a flow of money that is earned in one place and spent in another. Thus a major generating country may well have a deficit on its international tourism account (meaning residents spend more on foreign travel than their country receives from tourists), while a developing country will probably have a credit, thereby helping its overall balance of payments. To make comparisons easier, expenditure is usually expressed in US dollars rather than in national currencies. Measurement of tourist expenditure can be obtained directly, by asking visitors how much they have spent on their trip, or indirectly by asking hoteliers and other suppliers of tourist services for estimates of tourist spending. Bank records of foreign currency exchange may be used as another indirect method of obtaining statistics on international expenditure.

Despite the variety of methods that are available to measure tourist flows, it is not easy to produce accurate statistics. In the first place, the tourist has to be distinguished from other travellers, including returning residents, and while internationally agreed definitions of tourists do exist, they are not yet consistently applied throughout the world. At the same time, until recently there has been no real attempt to co-ordinate international surveys. To add to these problems, survey methods change over the years, even within a particular country, making it difficult to compare results over time. A further problem is that surveys count 'events', not 'people', so that a tourist who visits the same country twice in a year will be counted as two arrivals. Those on touring holidays may be counted as separate arrivals in various destinations and will inflate the overall visitor arrival figures. The relaxation of border controls for trade purposes, allowing freedom of movement between countries, makes the statistician's task of enumerating tourists even more difficult. A good example of this is travel within the European Union (EU) under the provisions of the Schengen Treaty.

Forms of tourism

The geographical components of tourism, allied to the idea of scale and tourist flows, combine to create a wide variety of different forms of tourism that we can categorise according to:

* type of destination;
* the characteristics of the tourism system;
* the market;
* the distance travelled.

Type of destination

Here we can make an important distinction between international and domestic tourism. *Domestic tourism* embraces those travelling within their own country, whereas *international tourism* comprises those who travel to a country other than that in which they normally live. We can think of international tourists either as non-residents travelling in a given country, constituting its *inbound tourism* sector, or as residents of a particular country travelling abroad to other countries, which is defined as *outbound tourism*. International tourists have to cross national borders and may have to use another currency and encounter a different language. Clearly, the size of a country is important here. Larger countries are more likely to have a variety of tourist attractions and resorts, and quite simply, the greater physical distances involved in travel may deter international tourism. We can compare, for example, the volume of domestic

Table 1.1 Smith's typology of tourists

Type of tourist	Numbers	Adapt to local destination	Tourist impact decreases	Tourist volume increases
Explorer	Very limited	Accepts fully		
Elite	Rarely seen	Accepts fully		
Off-beat	Unknown, but visible	Adapts well		
Incipient mass	Steady flows	Seeks Western amenities		
Mass	Continuous influx	Expects Western amenities		
Charter	Massive arrivals	Demands Western amenities		

Explorer

These include academics, climbers and true explorers in small numbers. They totally accept local conditions, and are self-sufficient, with portable chemical toilets, dehydrated food and walkie-talkies.

Elite

Travelling off the beaten track for pleasure, they have done it all, and are now looking for something different. While they use tourist facilities, they adapt easily to local conditions—if they can eat it, we can.

Off-beat

Not as rich as the elite tourist, they are looking for an added extra to a standard tour. They adapt well and cope with local conditions for a few days.

Incipient mass

A steady flow of tourists but in small groups or individuals. They are looking for central heating/air conditioning and other amenities, but will cope for a while if they are absent, and put it down to part of the 'experience'.

Mass tourism

Large numbers of tourists, often European or North American, with middle-class values and relatively high incomes. The flow is highly seasonal, with tourists expecting Western amenities and multi-lingual guides.

Charter tourism

This is full blown down-market, high volume tourism. It is totally dependent upon the travel trade. The tourists have standardised tastes and demands, and the country of destination is irrelevant. This type of tourism is less common in developing and undeveloped counties.

Source: Smith, 1978

tourism in the USA (almost 90 per cent of all tourism) with the Netherlands (around 50 per cent) where travel to neighbouring countries is so much easier. Increasingly the distinction between domestic and international tourism is diminishing as restrictions on movement between countries are removed.

Concern for the environmental and social impact of tourism has focused attention on ways of classifying tourists according to their relationship with the destination. For example, Smith (1978) groups tourists along a continuum ranging from explorers, with virtually no impact, to mass tourists where the impact may be considerable (see Table 1.1).

The characteristics of the tourism system

Here we can consider forms of tourism based largely on the destination visited, but also where the nature of the destination will influence the other components of the tourism system, namely the market with its particular motivations to travel, and the means of transport used. In other words the tourism product determines the nature of the tourism system. Thus we can distinguish the following types of tourism:

- rural tourism – focused on the countryside;
- urban tourism – focused on towns and cities;
- spa tourism – travel for health and 'wellness', traditionally based on water sources with therapeutic properties;
- heritage tourism;
- cultural tourism;
- sport tourism – concerned with spectators travelling to sports events as well as the participants;
- ecotourism – based on nature.

Discussion point: Forms of tourism and the tourism system

Each form of tourism might be expected to have distinctive components in each part of Leiper's tourism system. Thinking of ecotourism for example, in the destination area nature will be the main attraction and the ancillary services (accommodation, transport etc.) will be well managed, employ local people, and be 'green' or 'environmentally friendly'. In the generating area the ecotourist will be motivated by responsible attitudes toward the environment and will be educated to an above average level. In the transit zone the ecotourist will seek out locally owned companies who attempt to minimise the environmental impact of their transport operations. Analyse sport tourism in much the same way, giving specific examples for the areas generating the demand, the transit routes and the destinations.

The market

Here we are looking at a section of the population expressing a demand for a particular tourism product or range of products. We can express this in terms of the *purpose of the visit*:

- *Holiday tourism* is perhaps the most commonly understood form, where the purpose of the visit is leisure or recreation. We can broadly classify holidays or vacations as either 'sun, sand and sea' where good weather and beach-related activities are important, or as 'touring, sightseeing and culture' where new destinations and different lifestyles are sought. In addition to the beachgoers and culture-seekers, there is a trend for the more adventurous to seek physical challenge in the world's more remote places, which offer opportunities for adrenalin-fuelled 'extreme sports' that carry a high element of risk. Some see this as a reaction against the comfort and predictability of everyday life in post-modern societies. We should also distinguish the traditional 'long vacation' from *short breaks* lasting less than four nights, and there is now a tendency for people to take several short holidays in the course of the year.
- *Common-interest tourism* comprises those travelling with a purpose shared by those visited at the destination, such as visiting friends and relatives, or for reasons of religion, health or education. Common-interest tourists – especially the VFR category – may make little or no demand on serviced accommodation or other tourist facilities at the destination.

- *Business and professional tourism* includes those attending trade fairs, associate or corporate conferences and those participating in incentive travel schemes. The inclusion of business travel complicates the simple idea of tourism being just another recreational activity. Business travel is work-related and is therefore not regarded as part of a person's leisure time and cannot be thought of as recreation. Yet, because business travellers do use the same facilities as those travelling for pleasure, and they are not permanent employees or residents of the host destination, they must be included in any definition of tourists (Figure 1.1). However the business traveller, unlike the holidaymaker, is highly constrained in terms of where and when to travel. We summarise the differences between business and leisure tourism in Table 1.2.

A further market-based approach is to consider market segments. Here there are two aspects.

1 The nature of the tourists themselves, such as:
   - youth tourism – products geared specifically to the 15 to 25 age group;
   - 'grey' or 'third age' tourism – products geared specifically to older or retired people;
   - gay tourism – which is prohibited or shunned in some parts of the world that have strict moral attitudes to sexual orientation, despite the strength of the 'pink dollar' in spending on leisure products.
2 The type of travel arrangements purchased, such as:
   - an *inclusive tour* where two or more components of the trip are purchased together and one price is paid;
   - *independent travel* arrangements where the traveller purchases the various elements of the trip separately;
   - *tailor-made travel*, which is a combination of the two and increasingly common due to the use of the Internet to purchase travel.

Distance travelled

Here the distinction is between long-haul tourism, which is generally taken to mean travel over a distance of at least 3,000 kilometres (2,000 miles), and short-haul or medium-haul tourism involving shorter journeys. This is important in terms of aircraft operations and for marketing. Because of their geographical location Australians and North Americans are more likely to be long-haul or intercontinental tourists than their counterparts in Europe.

The travel experience

Finally, in describing tourism as a social phenomenon and wealth-creating activity, it is easy to lose sight of the tourist as an individual and the extent to which travel and recreation satisfy the need for self-fulfilment through experiences. All holiday trips have time as well as spatial components, and each phase has specific characteristics:

- In the *anticipation phase* before the trip, perceptions – how we filter the information we receive into an overall 'mental map' of the world – are important in influencing travel decisions.

Table 1.2 Leisure and business tourism			
	Leisure tourism	**Business tourism**	**But.....**
Who pays?	The tourist	The traveller's employer or association	Self-employed business travellers are paying for their own trips
Who decides on the destination?	The tourist	The organiser of the meeting, incentive trip, conference/ convention and trade fair	Organisers will often take into account delegates' wishes
When do trips take place?	During holiday periods and at weekends resulting in seasonal demand	Year-round, no seasonal fluctuations, but less demand at weekends	Peak holiday months are avoided for major events
Lead time (period of time between booking and going on the trip)	Holidays often booked months in advance, short breaks, a few days	Some business trips must be made at very short notice	Major conferences are booked many years in advance
Who travels?	Anyone with the necessary free time or money	Those whose work requires them to travel or members of associations; most business travellers are men, unaccompanied by family members	Not all business trips involve managers on white-collar duties; in the USA women now account for over 50% of all corporate business trips
What kinds of destination, accommodation and transport are used?	Wide choice of destinations–coast, city, mountains and countryside; all types of serviced and self-catering accommodation; wide variety of transport modes	Little choice of destination, except for conferences; largely centred on major cities, using hotels; in transport speed and flexibility are important	Incentive destinations are much the same as for up-market holidays
How important is price in influencing demand?	Sensitive to price, resulting in *elasticity of demand*	Less sensitive to price– time is more crucial	Economic recession can cause a downturn in demand or a switch to cheaper transport (e.g. from business to economy class)

Adapted from Davidson (1994) *Business Travel*

- In the *realisation phase* tourism experiences at the destination are the goal of the trip, but we also need to consider impressions of the outward and return journeys as part of the overall holiday experience (Figure 1.5).
- In the *recollection phase* after the trip, the extent to which the quality of these experiences met expectations will influence future travel decisions.

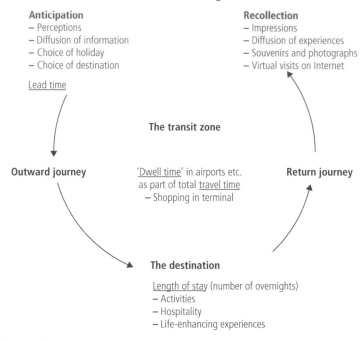

Figure 1.5 The travel experience

Summary

- Leisure has come to be accepted as a measure of free time, while recreation is seen as the activities undertaken during that time.
- Tourism is usually seen as a distinctive form of recreation involving a stay away from home, often involving long distance travel, but it also includes travel for business or other purposes.
- The geography of travel and tourism focuses on three key concepts:
  (i) Tourism is a system comprising tourist-generating areas, tourist-receiving areas and transit routes.
  (ii) We can consider tourism at a variety of scales, from the global to the local, depending on the level of detail required.
  (iii) Tourist flows are the spatial interaction that is generated between the components of the tourism system at different scales. Understanding these flows is fundamental to the geography of tourism, and this includes push and pull factors, and the methods of measuring tourism.
- We can distinguish different forms of tourism, based on the destination, the various components of the tourism system, the market, purpose of visit, the distance travelled, and not least, the nature of the tourists themselves. These all deliver distinctive types of tourist experience.

Assignments

1 How would you classify the following examples of travellers? (NB some may not be tourists!):

   (a) James Pennywise, a computer salesman from Birmingham is visiting Bournemouth to help organise a short training course in the latest information technology.

   (b) Philippa Tease, a travel agent from Miami, Florida, is attending the annual ASTA Convention in Bermuda as a delegate.

   (c) Philippa and her Spanish friend Ramona are planning an 'eco-trip' later in the year to explore the Ecuadorian rainforest 'as far away from tourists as possible'.

   (d) Franco Pirelli from California is visiting Rimini in Italy for a family reunion.

   (e) Ulla Erikson from Stockholm is visiting Santorini in the Greek islands for a few hours as part of a Mediterranean cruise.

   (f) Valentina from Vilnius, a student at an English language school in Poole, England, is travelling to Cherbourg on the 7.30 ferry and returning to Poole at 6.00 the following day.

   (g) Anne-Michelle from Sydney is working as a volunteer on community projects in Thailand, as part of her gap year before starting university.

2 Investigate the ways in which Spanish and Japanese attitudes to work and leisure differ from those prevalent in Britain and the USA.

3 Draw up a chart comparing working hours and paid holiday entitlement (taking account of national holidays) in your own country with other countries in Asia, Europe and North America.

4 Draw up a chart based on Figure 1.5 outlining a recent holiday trip. This should indicate the time spent on various stages of the trip as well as the places you visited and the activities you took part in.

The geography of demand for tourism

Learning objectives

After reading this chapter, you should be able to:

- Explain the term tourist demand and distinguish between effective and suppressed demand
- Understand the concepts of travel propensity and frequency
- Identify the motivations and determinants of demand for tourism
- Explain the influence of stage in economic development, population factors, and political regimes on demand for tourism
- Understand the influence of personal variables on the demand for tourism
- Appreciate the main barriers to travel which lead to suppressed demand

Leisure, recreation, and tourism: a basic human right?

Leisure, recreation, and tourism are of benefit to both individuals and societies. The United Nations (UN) recognised this as early as 1948 by adopting its Universal Declaration of Human Rights, which states that everyone 'has the right to rest and leisure including ... periodic holidays with pay'. More specifically, in 1980 the World Tourism Organisation declared the ultimate aim of tourism to be 'the improvement of the quality of life and the creation of better living conditions for all peoples'. Such statements would suggest that everyone has the right to demand tourism, but more recently the UN and UNWTO have tempered their views with the following considerations:

1 The need to ensure that tourism is consumed in a sustainable manner. The World Tourism Organisation's 'Global Code of Ethics for Tourism' was endorsed by the UN in 1999 and designed to '... minimise the negative impacts of tourism on the environment and on cultural heritage, whilst maximising the benefits for residents of tourism destinations' (WTO 2003).

2 The fact that tourism is perceived as an activity for the privileged and occurs in a socially divided world. The emergence of 'pro-poor tourism' is an attempt to redress this issue.

3 With increased awareness of global climate change, the need for tourists to change their behaviour, not only in terms of the volume of travel, but also in offsetting carbon emissions generated by their demand to travel.

This chapter examines how participation in tourism differs between both nations and individuals and explains why, despite declarations to the contrary, tourism is an activity highly concentrated among the affluent, industrialised nations. For much of the rest of the world, and indeed many disadvantaged groups in industrialised nations, participation in tourism, and particularly international tourism, remains an unobtainable luxury.

The demand for tourism: concepts and definitions

Geographers define tourist demand as 'the total number of persons who travel, or wish to travel, to use tourist facilities and services at places away from their places of work and residence' (Mathieson and Wall, 1982). This definition implies a wide range of influences, in addition to price and income, as determinants of demand and includes not only those who actually participate in tourism but also those who wish to but, for some reason, do not.

We should distinguish between the 'effective' and 'suppressed' demand for tourism:

• **Effective or actual demand** comprises the actual numbers of participants in tourism, i.e. those who are actually travelling. This is the component of demand most commonly and easily measured and the bulk of tourist statistics refer to effective demand.

• **Suppressed demand** is made up of that section of the population who do not travel for some reason. Two elements of suppressed demand can be distinguished.
 (i) First, *potential demand* refers to those who will travel at some future date if they experience a change in circumstances. For example, their purchasing power may increase.
 (ii) *Deferred demand* is a demand postponed because of a problem in the supply environment, such as the disruption to air travel caused by the Icelandic volcanic ash cloud in 2010.
 In other words, both deferred and potential demand may be converted into effective demand at some future date.

• Finally, there will always be those who simply do not wish to travel, constituting a category of **no demand**.

Discussion point: Tourism demand and climate change

To what extent do you think that increasing awareness of climate change will impact upon people's demand for travel and tourism and their behaviour as tourists? For example, will long-haul destinations such as Australia and New Zealand be adversely affected by the realisation that long-haul air travel is potentially a cause of climate change?

Effective demand

Travel propensity

In tourism, a useful measure of effective demand is travel propensity, meaning the percentage of a population which actually engages in tourism. Net travel propensity refers to the percentage of the population who take at least one tourism trip in a given period of time, while gross travel propensity gives the total number of tourism trips taken as a percentage of the population. Clearly, with second and third holidays increasingly important, gross travel propensity becomes more relevant. Simply dividing gross travel propensity by net will give the travel frequency, in other words, the average number of trips taken by those participating in tourism during the period in question (see Box 2.1). The suppressed and no-demand components will ensure that net travel propensity never approaches 100 per cent and a figure of 70 per cent or 80 per cent is likely to be the maximum. Gross travel propensity, however, can exceed 100 per cent and often approaches 200 per cent in some Western European countries with many frequent travellers.

Box 2.1 Calculation of travel propensity and travel frequency

Out of a population of 10 million inhabitants:
3.0 million inhabitants take one trip of one night or more   i.e. $3 \times 1 = 3.0$ million trips
1.5 million inhabitants take two trips of one night or more   i.e. $1.5 \times 2 = 3.0$ million trips
0.4 million inhabitants take three trips of one night or more   i.e. $0.4 \times 3 = 1.2$ million trips
0.2 million inhabitants take four trips of one night or more   i.e. $0.2 \times 4 = 0.8$ million trips
5.1 million inhabitants take at least one trip   **8.0 million trips**

Therefore:

$$\text{Net travel propensity} = \frac{\text{Number of population taking at least one trip}}{\text{Total population}} \times 100$$

$$= \frac{5.1}{10} \times 100 = 51 \text{ per cent}$$

$$\text{Gross travel propensity} = \frac{\text{Number of total trips}}{\text{Total population}} \times 100$$

$$= \frac{8}{10} \times 100 = 80 \text{ per cent}$$

$$\text{Travel frequency} = \frac{\text{Gross travel propensity}}{\text{Net travel propensity}} = \frac{80\%}{51\%} = 1.57$$

A further refinement to the above calculations is to assess the capability of a country to generate trips. This involves three stages. First, the number of trips originating in the country is divided by the total number of trips taken in the world. This gives an index of the ability of each country to generate travellers. Second, the population of the country is divided by the total population of the world, thus ranking each country by relative importance in relation to world population. By dividing the result of the first stage by the result of the second, the 'country potential generation index' (CPGI) is produced (Hurdman, 1979).

$$\text{CPGI} = \frac{(N_e/N_w)}{(P_e/P_w)}$$

where N_e = number of trips generated by country
N_w = number of trips generated in world
P_e = population of country
P_w = population of world

An index of 1.0 indicates an average generation capability. Countries with an index greater than unity are generating more tourists than expected by their population. Countries with an index below 1.0 generate fewer tips than average.

Adapted from: Schmidhauser, H. (1975) Travel propensity and travel frequency, in A. J. Burkart and S. Medlik (eds), *The Management of Tourism*. Heinemann, pp. 53–60; and Hurdman, L. E. (1979) Origin regions of international tourism. *Wiener Geographische Schriften*, 53/54, 43–49.

Determinants of travel propensity

Travel propensity is determined by a variety of factors which, for the purposes of this chapter, can be divided into two broad groups, which demonstrate the importance of 'scale' in considering tourism demand. First, there are the influences that lie at the national level of generalisation and comprise the world view of travel propensity, including economic development, population characteristics, and political regimes. Secondly, we can look at variations in travel propensity from a personal point of view in terms of lifestyle, life cycle, and personality factors. In fact, a third group of factors relating to the supply of tourist services is also important. This group encompasses technology, the price, frequency and speed of transport, as well as the characteristics of accommodation, facilities, and travel organisers. These factors are dealt with in Chapters 3 and 5.

The world view

Stage in economic development

A society's level of economic development is a major determinant of the magnitude of tourist demand because the economy influences so many critical, and interrelated, factors. The economic development of nations can be divided into a number of stages,

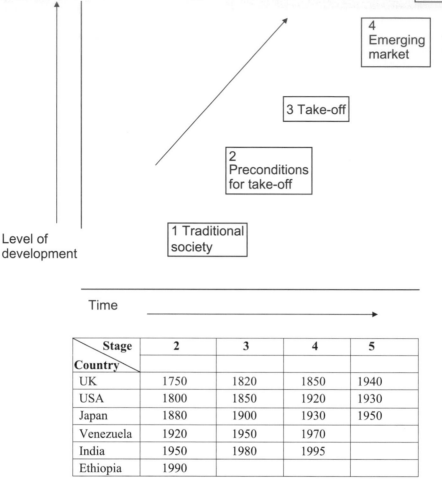

Figure 2.1 Stages in economic growth (*Source:* adapted from Waugh, 2009, p. 615)

as outlined in Table 2.1 and Figure 2.1. This gives a more accurate picture than that presented by the media, which over-simplifies the contrast between the 'First World' developed nations and the 'Third World' of developing countries (the seldom-used 'Second World' referred to the planned economies of the former USSR and other Communist countries in the Cold War era).

As a society moves towards a developed economy a number of important processes occur. The nature of employment changes from work in the primary sector (agriculture, fishing, forestry) to work in the secondary sector (manufacturing) and the tertiary sector (services such as tourism). As this process unfolds, an affluent society usually emerges and numbers of the economically active increase from around 30 per cent or less in the developing world to 50 per cent or more in the high mass-consumption stage of Western Europe or the USA. With progression to an emerging market, discretionary incomes increase and create demand for consumer goods and leisure pursuits such as tourism, as is demonstrated by China, which is forecast to be the leading generator of international tourists by 2020. Development is also characterised by an increase in

Table 2.1 Economic development and tourism

The economic stage	Some characteristics	Examples
Traditional society/Subsistence economy Long-established land-owning aristocracy, traditional customs, majority employed in agriculture. Very low output per capita and productivity, impossible to improve without changing system. Poor health levels, high poverty levels	The least developed countries of the Third World. Economics and social conditions deny most forms of tourism except perhaps domestic VFR. Low levels of transport and other infrastructure also deny tourism	Parts of Africa and Southern Asia
Pre-conditions for take-off Innovation of ideas from outside the system. Leaders recognise the desirability of change and technological breakthroughs facilitate economic development	The more advanced developing countries of the Third World. From the take-off stage, economic and social conditions allow increasing amounts of domestic tourism (mainly VFR)	Parts of South and central America; parts of the Middle East, Asia and Africa
Take-off Leaders in favour of change gain power and alter production method and economic structure. Manufacturing and services expand as economy gains access to overseas aid money and foreign exchange earnings through tourism		Countries such as Mexico and parts of South America
Emerging market Industrialisation continues in all economic sectors with a switch from heavy manufacturing to sophisticated and diversified products which begin to grow an export economy. Considerable government investment in infrastructure and environmental controls	Outbound international tourism is now possible and inbound tourism is often encouraged as a foreign exchange earner. Domestic tourism is well established	The BRIC countries – Brazil, Russia, India and China are in this stage but close to moving into the high mass consumption stage
High mass consumption/technology-based economy Economy now at full potential, producing large numbers of consumer goods and services. New emphasis on satisfying cultural needs to a highly educated and sophisticated market. Information communication technologies permeate and facilitate all economic transactions	The developed world which is a major generator of both international and domestic tourism, facilitated by technology	North America; Western Europe, Japan; Australia; New Zealand and parts of South-East Asia

Source: adapted from Chubb and Chubb, 1981, Cleverdon, 1979 and Rostow, 1959

government investment in infrastructure and a high penetration of technology – both of which encourage tourism.

Other developments parallel the changing nature of employment. The population is healthier and has time for recreation and tourism (including paid holiday entitlement). Improving educational standards and access to technology and the media boost awareness of tourism opportunities, and transportation and mobility rise in line with these changes. Institutions respond to this increased demand by developing a range of leisure products and services. These developments occur in conjunction with each other until, at the high mass consumption stage, all the economic indicators encourage high levels of travel propensity. Clearly, tourism is a result of industrialisation and, quite simply, the more highly developed an economy, the greater the levels of tourist demand, as shown by India's growing outbound tourism activity. For this reason the developing countries only account for a small proportion of the demand for international tourism, although a few – such as Brazil – in the emerging market stage feature among the leading tourist-generating nations. The share of the developing countries in the global tourism market is increasing as more countries reach the emerging market or high mass-consumption stage, while the volume of trade and foreign investment increases and business travel develops. Effectively this means that more countries are joining the 'premier league' of destinations that attract over one million arrivals each year, thereby increasing the worldwide competition for tourists. Business travel is sensitive to economic activity, and although it could be argued that increasingly sophisticated communication systems may render business travel unnecessary, there is no evidence of this to date. Indeed, the very development of global markets and the constant need for face-to-face contact should ensure a continuing demand for business travel.

Population factors

Levels of population growth, distribution, and density affect travel propensity. Population growth can be closely linked to the stages of economic growth outlined in Table 2.1 by considering the demographic transition, where population growth and development is seen in terms of four connected phases (Figure 2.2).

- First, the **high stationary phase** corresponds to many of the least developed countries (LDCs) in the Third World with high birth and death rates keeping population growth at a fluctuating but low level.
- Second, the **early expanding phase** sees high birth rates but a fall in death rates due to improved health, sanitation, and social stability leading to population expansion characterised by young, large families. Clearly, foreign travel is a luxury that most people living in these countries cannot afford, whereas, on the other hand, some governments are developing an inbound tourism industry to earn foreign exchange.
- The **late expanding phase** sees a fall in the birth rate rooted in the growth of an industrial society and advances in birth control technology.

Most developing countries fit into the last two phases of population growth with a transition to the late expanding phase paralleling the emerging market stage.

- Finally, the **low stationary phase** corresponds to the high mass-consumption stage of economic development. Here, birth and death rates have stabilised to a low level. At this stage, it is the changing characteristics of the population which have important implications for tourism demand because:

1 Populations are ageing.
2 These ageing populations have a high discretionary income.
3 The 'baby-boomer' generation (born in the years immediately after the Second World War) are an important population cohort of experienced, discerning travellers exercising 'grey' power and influencing demand.
4 Household composition is changing with increased numbers of single and childless households and fewer families in the traditional sense.

Population density (the number of inhabitants per square mile or kilometre) has little influence on travel propensity compared to the distribution of population between urban and rural areas. Large urban areas normally indicate a developed economy where consumer purchasing power, along with the perceived stress of living in modern

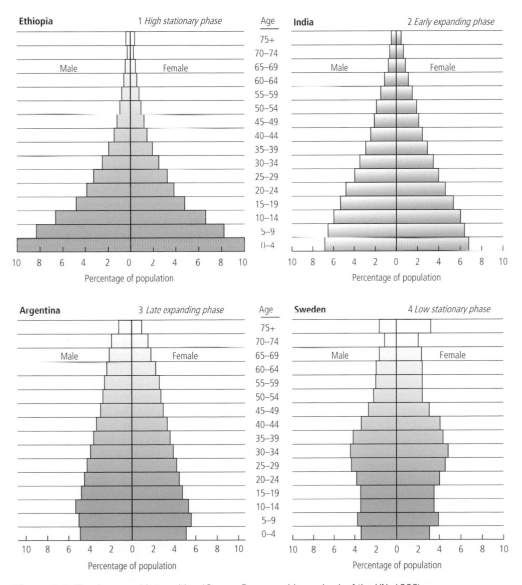

Figure 2.2 The demographic transition (*Source:* Demographic yearbook of the UN, 1992)

cities, give rise to a high travel propensity. Yet the trend to *urbanisation* is even more evident in developing countries, and as a result, after 2005 the world's urban population began to exceed that of its rural areas. Vast numbers of people are migrating from poor rural communities to the major cities, where they live for the most part in peripheral shanty-towns without basic services. Nevertheless, even in such challenging conditions these migrants have greater access to employment, health care and education than before, while the high fertility rates characteristic of subsistence farming communities are likely to decline, resulting in smaller families and eventually less poverty.

The distribution of population within a nation also affects patterns, rather than strictly levels, of tourist demand. Where population is concentrated into one part of the country tourism demand is distorted. This asymmetrical distribution of population is well illustrated by the USA, where two-thirds of the population live in the eastern one-third of the country. The consequent east-to-west pattern of tourist flow (and permanent migration) has placed pressure on the recreation and tourist resources of the western states. At the regional scale concentration of population into cities also has implications for demand patterns, with a recreation and tourism hinterland often developing around the city.

Political influences

Politics affect travel propensities in a number of ways:

* **Political complexion** In democratic nations the degree of government involvement in promoting and providing facilities for tourism varies. Typically, 'conservative' or 'neo-liberal' administrations subscribe to the principles of the free market and act to nurture an environment in which the tourism industries can flourish, rather than the administration being directly involved in tourism itself. Socialist administrations, on the other hand, encourage the involvement of the government in tourism and often provide opportunities for the 'disadvantaged' to participate in tourism. Democracies may also control levels of propensity for travel abroad by limiting the amount of foreign currency that can be taken out of a country. Commonly this occurs when a nation's own currency is weak or the economy faltering. A weak currency will also deter people from travelling abroad. Currency controls are more common in planned economies, where levels of control of international tourism can be considerable. In planned economies tourist organisations are centralised and act as an arm of the administration. The government can also severely restrict its peoples' freedom of movement by controlling access to the Internet and by granting or withholding exit visas. The Chinese government, for example, controls outbound tourism by allowing its citizens to travel only to those countries which have been granted 'approved destination status'.

Discussion point: China's outbound travel

China is set to become one of the world's leading generators of international tourism. To what extent do you think the host countries for these tourists are prepared for them? For example, should hotels be re-designed in accordance with the principles of *feng shui,* and do we understand the needs and preferences of the Chinese tourist when it comes to attractions and activities at the destination? Indeed, should we as hosts modify our way of life to suit our Chinese guests, or any other tourists for that matter?

- **Political groupings** Politics is also influencing tourism demand in terms of political and economic groupings of countries and the increased facilitation of travel between members of such groupings. The member countries of the European Union, for example, are committed to the effective abolition of border controls and the adoption of the euro as the single currency, which has boosted demand for intra-European travel.
- **Deregulation** The political environment for deregulation and privatisation also encourages tourism demand through such initiatives as the deregulation of transportation which can act to reduce fares and thus increase demand for travel; and the increased efficiency of the sector, which again acts to boost demand through lowered prices and higher quality.
- **Political instability** In a more general sense, unstable political environments adversely affect tourism, not simply in specific regimes where civil disorder or war is prevalent, but also with the increased threat of terrorist attacks in this century, tourism demand has been adversely affected across the globe.

The personal view

Two sets of personal factors influence travel propensity and therefore act to condition access to tourism. The first group of factors can be termed *lifestyle* and include income, employment, holiday entitlement, educational attainment, and mobility. A second group comes under the term *life cycle*, where the age and domestic circumstances of an individual combine to affect both the amount and type of tourism demanded. Naturally, these factors are interrelated and complementary. A high-status job is normally associated with an individual in middle age with a high income, above-average holiday entitlement, education, and mobility. The interweaving of these variables, coupled with their rapid growth throughout the latter half of the twentieth century, have combined to make leisure, recreation, and tourism a major force in the developed world. These variables can be used to segment tourism markets, and researchers are now using sophisticated techniques to understand travel behaviour.

Lifestyle determinants

Income

Tourism is a luxury, an expensive activity that demands a certain threshold of income before an individual can choose to take part. The key indicators are:

- **Gross income** – the total amount earned gives little indication of the money available to spend on tourism.
- **Disposable income** – the money that actually reaches the public's hands to dispose of as they please. However, demands on disposable income include essentials such as housing, food, and clothing.
- **Discretionary income** – the most useful measure of the ability to participate in tourism. Discretionary income is the income left over when tax, housing, and the basics of life have been accounted for. Clearly, two households with the same gross incomes may have very different discretionary incomes.

The relationship between income levels and the consumption of tourism is an example of *elasticity of demand*. The demand for business tourism tends to be inelastic, as it is relatively unaffected by changes in the cost of travel, while conventional leisure tourism is sensitive to price. The Americans and the Japanese tend to have a higher elasticity of demand than Europeans on similar incomes, as they are more likely to forego a holiday trip with a downturn in the economy or in their financial situation. A low discretionary income markedly depresses travel propensity. As discretionary income rises, the ability to participate in tourism is associated with the purchase of leisure-oriented goods, until, with a high discretionary income, travel may reach a peak and then level off as the demands of a high-status job, and possibly frequent business trips, reduce the ability and desire to travel for pleasure.

Employment

The nature of employment not only influences travel propensity by determining income and holiday entitlement but also has an effect upon the type of holiday demanded. A more fundamental distinction is between those in employment and those unemployed. The impact of unemployment on the level of tourism demand is obvious, but the nature of demand is also changed, with the threat of job insecurity among the workforce encouraging later booking of trips, more domestic and VFR holidays, shorter lengths of stay, and lower spending levels.

Paid-holiday entitlement

A variety of holiday arrangements now exist worldwide, with most nations having a number of one-day national holidays, as well as annual paid holiday entitlement by law or collective agreements between employers and trade unions. Individual levels of paid-holiday entitlement would seem to be an obvious determinant of travel propensity, but in fact the relationship is not straightforward. However, it is possible to make a number of generalisations:

- Low levels of entitlement do act as a real constraint upon the ability to travel, while a high entitlement encourages travel. This is in part due to the inter-relationship between entitlement and factors such as job status, income, and mobility.
- As levels of entitlement increase, the cost of tourism may mean that more of this entitlement will be spent on leisure at home.
- Patterns of entitlement are changing. Entitlement is increasingly used as a wage-bargaining tool and the introduction of flexitime, work sharing, and long weekends will release blocks of time which may be used for short holiday breaks.

Social status and choice of lifestyle

In pre-industrial and industrial societies an individual's social class or socio-economic group largely determined their use of leisure. In post-industrial countries such as Britain the type of holiday demanded is increasingly related to an individual's choice of a particular lifestyle and the behavioural patterns associated with that lifestyle.

Other personal factors

Level of educational attainment is an important determinant of travel propensity as education broadens horizons and stimulates the desire to travel. Also, the better educated the individual, the higher his or her awareness and susceptibility to information, the media, advertising, and sales promotion. In addition, education enhances the ability to utilise technology and will facilitate demand for travel through access to the Internet. Personal mobility, usually expressed as car ownership, is an important influence on travel propensity, especially with regard to domestic holidays. We will discuss this variable in Chapter 5. Finally, other variables such as gender and belonging to an ethnic minority may condition access to tourism.

Life cycle determinants

The propensity to travel, and indeed the type of tourism experience demanded, is closely related to an individual's age. While the conventional measurement is chronological age, domestic age better discriminates between types of tourist demand and levels of travel propensity. This approach is sometimes referred to as life course analysis. Domestic age refers to the stage in the life cycle reached by an individual and different stages are characterised by distinctive holiday demand and levels of travel propensity (Table 2.2). The concept of domestic age works well for Westernised, industrialised tourist-generating countries and is therefore a useful generalisation for

---

Table 2.2 Domestic age and tourism demand

Adolescence/young adult

At this stage, there is a need for independence and a search for identity. Typically, holidays independent of parents begin at around 15 years, constrained by lack of finance but compensated by having few other commitments, no shortage of free time and a curiosity for new places and experiences. This group has a high propensity to travel, mainly on budget holidays using surface transport and self-catering accommodation. They are seen as opinion leaders and the tourism sector actively seeks their custom hoping to gain their loyalty in later years.

Marriage

Before the arrival of children, young couples often have a high income and few other ties giving them a high travel propensity, frequently overseas. The arrival of children coupled with the responsibility of a home means that constraints of time and finance depress travel propensity. Holidays become more organisational than geographical with domestic tourism, self-catering accommodation and visiting friends and relatives increasingly common. As children grow up and reach the adolescence stage, constraints of time and finance are lifted and parents' travel propensity increases. In the industrialised countries, this post-Second World War 'baby boom' group are the vanguard of the new tourist – discerning, experienced and seeking quality and value for money.

Retirement

The emergence of early retirement at 50 or 55 years is creating an active and mobile group in the population which will demand both domestic and international travel. In later retirement lack of finance, infirmity, reduced personal mobility and often the loss a of partner act to offset the increase in free time experienced by this group. Holidays become more hotel-based and travel propensity decreases.

the leading generators of tourism worldwide. However, it has its critics for these reasons:

- the concept is less well suited to other cultures; and
- in the industrialised world, changing household composition and social norms mean that the concept has to be treated with care.

Discussion point: Tourism and domestic age

To what extent does the idea of domestic age fit the holiday preferences and tourism patterns of members of your family? Also, when thinking about the travel patterns of your family, is there an identifiable 'travel career' demonstrated by anyone in your family or any of your friends?

Personality factors

No two individuals are alike and differences in attitudes, perceptions, and motivation have an important influence on travel decisions. Attitudes depend on an individual's perception of the world. Perceptions are mental impressions of, say, a place or travel company and are determined by many factors, which include childhood, family, and work experiences. As perceptions will be influential in making the decision to travel, it is important for planners and managers in tourist destinations to foster favourable 'images' of their locations in the public's mind.

Attitudes and perceptions in themselves do not explain why people want to travel. The inner urges, which initiate travel demand, are called travel motivators. It is important to understand these motivators as they help explain why some destinations fall in and out of fashion. An individual's personal needs help form motivations – the 'intrinsic' influences; while 'extrinsic' influences such as peer groups and fashion are a second set of influences. Gray (1970) has outlined a classification of travel motivators:

- **Wanderlust** is simply curiosity to experience the strange and unfamiliar. It refers to the basic trait in human nature to see, at first hand, different places, cultures, and peoples. Status and prestige motivators would be included under this heading.
- **Sunlust** can be literally translated as the desire for sunshine and a better climate, but in fact it is broader than this and refers to the search for a better set of amenities for recreation than are available at home.

As tourist consumer behaviour has changed, there has been a shift away from sunlust to wanderlust motivators, partly driven by fears of the effects of exposure to the sun, but also by the desire to fully experience the culture as well as the physical attractions of the destination.

The interaction of personality attributes such as attitude, perceptions, and motivation influence demand in two ways. First, they impact on a tourist's *image* of a destination – an important factor in the decision-making process of whether to visit a particular destination – and second, they allow different types of tourist to be identified. One classification by Cohen (1972) is particularly useful. He uses a classification based on the theory that tourism combines the curiosity to seek out new experiences with the need for the security of familiar reminders of home. Cohen proposes a continuum of possible combinations of novelty and familiarity and, by breaking up the continuum

Table 2.3 Cohen's classification of tourists	
The organised mass tourist	Familiarity
Low on adventurousness, he or she is anxious to maintain his or her 'environmental bubble' on trip. Typically purchasing a ready-made package tour off-the-shelf, he or she is guided through the destination having little contact with local culture or people.	**Institutionalised tourism**
	Dealt with routinely by the tourism industry – tour operators, travel agents, hoteliers and transport operators.
The individual mass tourist	
Similar to the above but more flexibility and scope for personal choice is built-in. However, the tour is still organised by the tourism industry and the environmental bubble shields him or her from the real experience of the destination.	
The explorer	
The trip is organised independently and is looking to get off the beaten track. However, comfortable accommodation and reliable transport are sought, and while the environmental bubble is abandoned on occasion, it is there to step into if things get tough.	**Non-institutionalised tourism**
	Individual travel, shunning contact with the tourism industry except where absolutely necessary.
The drifter	
All connections with the tourism industry are spurned and the trip attempts to get as far from home and familiarity as possible. With no fixed itinerary, the drifter lives with the local people, paying his or her way, and is immersed in their culture.	Novelty

Source: Adapted from Cohen (1972).

into typical combinations of these two ingredients, a fourfold classification of tourists is produced (Table 2.3).

Suppressed demand

Potential demand

Throughout this chapter the concern has been to identify factors which influence effective tourist demand. Yet tourism is still an unobtainable luxury for the majority of the world's population, not just in undeveloped and developing countries but also for many in the developed world. Indeed, the concept of *potential demand* demonstrates that there are considerable inequalities of access to tourism, which are rooted in the personal circumstances of individuals. Lansing and Blood (1960) have identified five major reasons why people do not travel:

- expense of travel;
- lack of time;

- physical limitations (such as ill health);
- family circumstances; and
- lack of interest.

It is not uncommon for individuals to experience a combination of two or more of these barriers. For example, a one-parent family – or a person caring for a disabled relative – may find that lack of income and time will combine with family circumstances to prevent tourism. Obviously it is just these groups who would most benefit from a holiday, and tourism planners are increasingly concerned to identify these barriers and devise programmes to encourage non-participants to travel. Perhaps the best-known example of this is the *social tourism movement*, which is concerned with the participation in travel by people with some form of handicap or disadvantage, and the measures used to encourage this participation. In countries where state intervention is the norm the government and its agencies are largely responsible for social tourism; in some (such as Israel) the labour unions play an important role; while in others the participation of church groups and similar voluntary organisations is more significant.

Deferred demand

Of course, there are also barriers to travel based upon the supply environment, leading to deferred demand. The first decade of the new millennium has seen a series of events that have markedly increased deferred demand around the world and reduced growth rates of international tourism. These events include:

- 9/11 (the terrorist attacks on New York and Washington on September 11, 2001);
- the war in Afghanistan;
- the Bali bombings;
- the outbreak of SARS;
- the Asian tsunami on Boxing Day (December 26) 2004;
- the war in Iraq;
- the Icelandic ash cloud in 2010; and
- increased awareness of climate change.

The effect on demand has been for tourists to either defer travel or to change the nature of their trip and:

- book later;
- travel to 'safer' destinations closer to home;
- use surface transport modes such as trains, which are more 'carbon-neutral' than air transport;
- use 'flexible' booking channels such as the Internet;
- consider the cost and carbon emission impact of travel carefully;
- take shorter trips and avoid travel to long-haul destinations; or
- cease travelling altogether.

The pattern of tourism demand

Determinants of tourist demand, allied to the characteristics of the mosaic of tourism destinations around the world, combine to produce the global rhythms and patterns of

Table 2.4 International tourism demand: the historical trend

Year	International tourism arrivals (millions)	International tourism receipts (US$ millions)
1950	25.3	2,100
1960	69.3	6,867
1970	159.7	17,900
1980	284.8	102,372
1985	321.2	116,158
1990	454.8	255,000
1995	567.0	372,000
2000	696.8	477,000
2001	692.6	463,600
2005	806.0	680,000
2010	940.0	868,400
Forecast for 2020	1,560.0	N/A

tourism. The end of the Second World War represented the beginning of a remarkable period of growth for international tourism, with an annual average growth rate approaching 7 per cent for the second half of the twentieth century (Table 2.4). Until the early years of the twenty first century, international tourism was remarkably resilient to factors that might have been expected to depress growth – recession, oil crises, wars and terrorism. Until September 11, 2001, global tourist demand demonstrated predictable growth and stable regional patterns. In 2008, this stability was further disrupted as the world entered an unprecedented period of economic turbulence.

International tourism arrivals and departures are concentrated into relatively few countries, mainly in Europe and North America. This produces an unbalanced picture that favours developed Western economies and disadvantages the developing world, which is left to compete for the long-haul market – and this accounts for a minor share of the total market. For both generators and destinations of international tourism, as more countries have entered the market, so the dominance of the leading players has been gradually reduced.

- **Generators** The major tourism-generating countries are those in the *high mass-consumption stage* of economic development, although as countries reach the *emerging market stage* they become significant generators of international tourism. For any particular destination country, a typical list of the top generating markets would contain neighbouring states together with at least one from a list containing Germany, the UK, Japan, and the USA. However, it is clear that by 2030 if not earlier, both China and India will become major generating countries.
- **Destinations** The post-war period has been marked by the rapid emergence of the East Asia and the Pacific region (EAP) as an international tourism destination, largely at the expense of the Americas and Europe (Table 2.5).

Table 2.5 International tourism demand: the changing regional picture percentage share of international arrivals by UNWTO region

Region	1950 %	1960 %	1970 %	1980 %	1990 %	2000 %	2005 %	2010 %
Europe	66.5	72.5	70.5	68.4	63.5	57.8	54.8	50.9
Americas	29.6	24.1	23.0	18.9	18.8	18.4	16.6	15.9
East Asia & Pacific (EAP) (including South Asia)	1.0	1.3	3.6	7.8	12.1	16.6	19.3	21.7
Africa	2.1	1.1	1.5	2.5	3.4	3.9	4.6	5.3
Middle East	0.9	1.0	1.4	2.4	2.1	3.3	4.8	6.4

Summary

- Tourism is a major contribution to the quality of life in the twenty-first century, and demand for tourism is made up not only of those who participate but also those who do not travel for some reason.
- Travel propensity is a useful indicator of tourism participation, as it gives the proportion of a population who actually engage in tourism. Travel frequency refers to the average number of trips taken by those participating in tourism during a specified period.
- Travel propensity is determined by a variety of factors that can be viewed at two scales. At the world scale, those countries with a high level of economic development and a stable, urbanised population are major generators of tourism demand. The political regime of a country is also relevant here. At the individual scale, a certain level of discretionary income is required to allow participation in tourism, and this income, and indeed the type of participation, will be influenced by such factors as the type of employment, life cycle stage, mobility, level of educational attainment, and personality.
- Even within the developed world, many are unable to participate in tourism for some reason. Demand for tourism is therefore concentrated in developed Western economies and predominates among those with high discretionary incomes.

Assignments

Using the UNWTO web site, plot the flows of international tourism from the major tourist-generating countries to significant destinations on a world map. Explain the patterns that you see in terms of:

1 short-haul (intra-regional) and long-haul (intercontinental) flows;
2 the reasons for the dominance of developed Western economies in the ten leading generating countries; and
3 the competitive advantages of the 'top ten' world destinations.

How do you think the map will look in the year 2020?

CHAPTER **3**

The geography of resources for tourism

Learning objectives

After reading this chapter, you should be able to:

- Appreciate the nature of resources for tourism
- Distinguish the methods used to classify and evaluate resources for tourism
- Outline the main factors favouring the development of tourism resources
- Understand the way that destinations evolve
- Appreciate the need for tourism planning, marketing and sustainable development
- Match specific types of recreation and tourism to the appropriate resources

Introduction

Technology now allows tourists to reach most parts of the world, yet only a small fraction of the world's potential tourism resource is developed. Nonetheless, with a growing demand for tourism focused on a small resource base, tourist destinations are under pressure. In part this is because tourism does not occur evenly or randomly in time or space; but pressure is focused seasonally and at special and unique places. This demands the effective planning and management of tourism resources and in particular the matching of appropriate types of tourist to particular types of resource. Different types of tourism will have distinctive requirements for growth, and certain sites, regions or countries will be more favourable for development than others. This chapter examines tourism resources on three scales: global, national and local.

The characteristics and management of tourism resources

Characteristics

Tourism resources have three main characteristics:

1 By tourism resources we usually mean tangible features that are considered to be of economic value to the tourism sector. The sector, and indeed the tourist, therefore has to recognise that a place, landscape or natural feature is of value before they can become tourism resources. For example, rugged mountains were viewed by most people in the West as barriers to be feared, rather than as scenic attractions, until the eighteenth century. Similarly, until sunbathing became fashionable in the 1920s, the combination of sun, sand and sea was not seen as a valuable tourism resource, and we are now beginning to see people's perceptions of the beach holiday change due to fears of skin cancer.

2 Most tourism resources are not used exclusively by tourists. Apart from resort areas or theme parks where tourism is the dominant use of land, tourism shares the resource with agriculture, forestry, water management or residents using local services. In many parts of the world beaches continue to be more important as a resource for local fishing communities or the construction industry than for tourism. Tourism is a significant land use but rarely the dominant one, and this can lead to conflict. Tourism, as a latecomer, is 'fitted in' with other uses of land. This is known as *multiple use*, and needs skilful management and co-ordination of users to be successful.

3 Tourism resources are perishable. Not only are they vulnerable to alteration and destruction by tourist pressure but in common with many service industries, tourism resources are also perishable in another sense. Tourist services such as beds in accommodation, or ride seats in theme parks are impossible to stock and have to be consumed when and where they exist. Unused tourism resources cannot be stored, hence the development of yield management systems to maximise the consumption of resources.

Planning

Inevitably tourism is attracted to fragile and unique resources throughout the world. In the period following the Second World War many countries sought international tourism as an ideal solution to economic problems. Tourism was seen as an 'industry without chimneys' which brought economic benefits in employment, income and development. However this economic imperative overlooked the environmental, social and cultural consequences of tourism in many countries. In part, this was due to the ease of measuring the economic impacts of tourism and the difficulty of quantifying other types of impact. There is now an increasing awareness of the need to consider the environment and the host community to complement the economic needs of destinations. Consumer pressure is shunning ethically unsound destinations and environmental impact assessments are being completed for major tourism projects. Since the late 1980s, sustainable tourism development has become the organising framework, as mainstream concepts of sustainability have been applied to tourism. A key priority is to translate the principles of sustainable development into action. For example, in the tourism industry, this is being done in a number of ways:

- Codes of conduct and guidelines – providing the industry with practical measures for say, recycling.
- Accreditation and certification – inspecting and certifying businesses on the basis of sustainable practices.
- Licences – licensing businesses operating in environmentally sensitive areas.
- Best practice dissemination – educating and communicating examples of best practice in sustainable tourism throughout the industry.

Carrying capacity is a key concept of sustainable tourism; in other words, planners determine the levels of use that can be sustained by a resource and manage it to that level (see Table 3.1).

Table 3.1 Carrying capacity

The concept of carrying capacity has a long pedigree. It was originally developed by resource managers in agriculture and forestry to determine the cropping levels that plots of land could sustain without nutrients and other food sources being depleted. In tourism, carrying capacity refers to the ability of a destination to take tourism use without deteriorating in some way. In other words it defines the relationship between the resource base and the market and is influenced by the characteristics of each. One of the best definitions is by Mathieson and Wall (1982, 21): 'The maximum number who can use a site without unacceptable deterioration in the physical environment and without an unacceptable decline in the quality of experience gained by visitors.' This definition raises two key points:

1. Carrying capacity can be managed, and there is no absolute number for any destination. For example, open heathland can appear crowded with very few visitors present, while a wooded area can absorb many more visitors.
2. We can look at carrying capacity in different ways, in terms of the resource itself; from the point of view of the visitor and from the point of view of the host community:
   (a) Physical carrying capacity refers to the number of facilities available, such as aircraft seats or car parking spaces. It is easy to measure and can be calculated on a simple percentage basis.
   (b) Environmental or biological carrying capacity is more difficult to measure and refers to limits of use in the ecosystem. There is increasing interest in the capacity not only of the vegetation cover to take tourism use but also of the animal life, such as tourism based on whale or dolphin watching, or the African game reserves.
   (c) Psychological or behavioural carrying capacity refers to the point at which the visitor feels that additional visitors would spoil the experience. This is less straightforward than may appear at first sight. Completely empty spaces are just as problematic as crowded ones, and the type of tourist also has an effect on perceptions of crowding. To take beaches as our example, the European Union stipulates a density of 0.6 square metres per person as a minimum standard; however, people from Mediterranean cultures are usually prepared to accept much greater levels of crowding than would be acceptable for, say, Scandinavians.
   (d) Social carrying capacity is a measure of the ability of the host community to tolerate tourism. It is a more recent addition to typologies of capacity but is becoming an important issue. Indeed one of the most important tests of a sustainable tourist destination is the level of involvement of the local community in plans and decisions relating to tourism development. Whilst there is a concern that local residents have a lack of knowledge about tourism, new techniques such as 'destination visioning' (where the locals determine the future of tourism) and 'limits to acceptable change' (where they determine levels of future development) are increasingly being adopted and are a form of capacity management.
   (e) Economic carrying capacity refers to the point at which the investment needed to sustain environmental quality becomes prohibitive.

Tourism planning must be central to these issues. Tourism planning has evolved from an inflexible, physical planning approach to a flexible approach which seeks to maximise the benefits and minimise the costs of tourism, while at the same time recognising the holistic nature of tourism, whereby we must plan for the visitor as well as the resource. The benefits of tourism planning are clear (Table 3.2). Ideally, tourism planning is characterised by:

1   a basis in sound research;
2   the involvement of the local community in setting goals and priorities;
3   an holistic approach;
4   implementation by the public sector (government) in partnership with the private sector (business).

Despite the many approaches to tourism planning, the planning progress can be reduced to six basic questions:

1   What type of tourist will visit?
2   What is the scale of tourism?
3   Where will development take place?
4   What controls will be placed on development?
5   How will development be financed?
6   What will be government's role?

The answer to these questions will depend, from place to place, on the government's approach to tourism and the importance of tourism to the economy. The planning process is summarised in Figure 3.1.

Table 3.2 The benefits of tourism planning

For those involved in delivering and developing tourism at the destination, tourism planning:

- provides a set of common objectives for all at the destination to follow;
- co-ordinates the many suppliers of tourism at the destination;
- encourages partnerships between *stakeholders* at the destination (these might include for example, representatives of the local community as well as tour operators and others actually involved in the tourism industry and government);
- encourages effective organisation at the destination; and
- provides an integrating framework for future actions and decisions.

For the destination itself, tourism planning encourages a high-quality tourism environment because it:

- optimises the benefits of tourism to a destination;
- minimises the negative effects of tourism on the economy, environment and host community;
- encourages the adoption of the principles and practice of sustainable tourism;
- provides a plan based on land use for zoning areas for development, conservation and protection;
- encourages design and other standards for the tourism sector to work on;
- encourages careful matching of the development of the destination and its markets;
- allows for the consideration of issues such as manpower and investment;
- upgrades the destination environment; and
- encourages a monitoring system to be implemented at the destination.

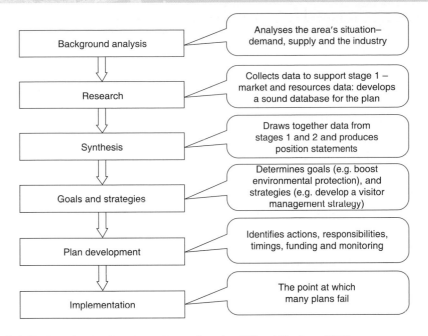

Figure 3.1 Tourism planning flow chart (*Source:* Based on Mill and Morrison, 1985)

For those involved in delivering and developing tourism at the destination, tourism planning:

- provides a set of common objectives for all at the destination to follow;
- co-ordinates the many suppliers of tourism at the destination;
- encourages partnerships between *stakeholders* at the destination (these might include for example, representatives of the local community as well as tour operators and others actually involved in the tourism industry and government);
- encourages effective organisation at the destination;
- provides an integrating framework for future actions and decisions.

For the destination itself, tourism planning encourages a high quality tourism environment because it:

- optimises the benefits of tourism to a destination;
- minimises the negative effects of tourism on the economy, environment and host community;
- encourages the adoption of the principles and practice of sustainable tourism;
- provides a plan based on land use for zoning areas for development, conservation and protection;
- encourages design and other standards for the tourism sector to work to;
- encourages careful matching of the development of the destination and its markets;
- allows for the consideration of issues such as manpower and investment;
- upgrades the destination environment;
- encourages a monitoring system to be implemented at the destination.

Unfortunately, despite the emergence of tourism planning as a profession, many plans for tourism either fail or are opposed. They may fail because policy changes, demand changes, unforeseen competition emerges, investment is not available, or the plan was too ambitious or inflexible in the first place.

If tourism planning does not succeed, these consequences may follow:

* The quality and integrity of the tourism resource are put at risk.
* The role of tourism in multiple land use may be threatened as other uses dominate.
* The tourist suffers from a poor quality experience.

As we have become more sophisticated in the management of tourism, the emphasis has moved from the protection and preservation of resources to the management of visitors, and in particular the need to deliver an enjoyable, worthwhile experience. Figure 3.2 outlines the approaches used to manage visitors.

Discussion point: Valuing tourism resources

The value of a resource cannot always be expressed in terms of money. For example, how can we compare the value of a work of art with a natural attraction such as a waterfall or an area of rainforest threatened by the development of a hydroelectric power plant?

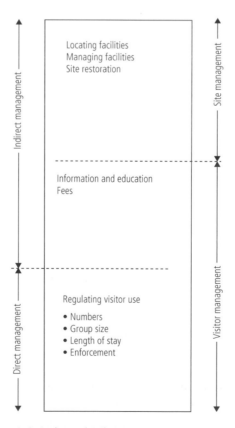

Figure 3.2 Visitor management strategies and actions

Tourism resources at the global scale

Physical features

The Earth's biosphere consists of the atmosphere (air), hydrosphere (water), lithosphere (land) and cryosphere (ice). Nearly three quarters of the Earth's surface consists of sea, including the five oceans – namely the Pacific (by far the largest), the Atlantic, the Indian, the Southern, and the Arctic (which is largely ice-covered). Land makes up the remaining 29 per cent, comprising the seven continents and associated islands, namely Asia (the largest both in terms of population and land area), followed by Africa, North America, South America, Antarctica, Europe and Australasia. (Strictly speaking Europe is part of the greater landmass known as Eurasia.) Almost 40 per cent of the Northern Hemisphere, but less than 20 per cent of the Southern Hemisphere, is made up of land. This uneven distribution of land and sea has important implications for climate, population distribution, economic development, communications, and thus tourism.

The land surface of the Earth is composed of a variety of landforms which we can broadly group into four categories: mountains (areas of elevated, rugged terrain), more gently sloping hill lands, elevated plateaus and lowland plains. Within each category there are features resulting from natural forces such as erosion and variations in the composition of the underlying rock. These physical features provide the focus for the activity known as *geotourism*, and an increasing number of sites of geological interest have been designated by UNESCO as *geoparks*. It is worth looking at some of these features in more detail:

- *Geothermal* features comprise volcanoes, crater lakes and calderas, lava formations, geysers and hot springs; they are caused by disturbances from deep within the Earth's crust. The world's most spectacular mountains are generally associated with geologically unstable areas characterised by earthquakes and volcanic activity. This includes the 'Pacific Ring of Fire' which is situated close to the western and eastern margins of the world's largest ocean. Even in areas where volcanic eruptions have ceased for many millennia, they have left a legacy of hot springs and other water sources rich in minerals. These are thought to have therapeutic properties, and in many instances have given rise to a spa (by this we mean a health resort rather than a facility for health and beauty treatments).
- *Karst* features are found in limestone areas, where surface streams have 'disappeared' underground to carve out impressive gorges, sinkholes and caverns.
- *Glaciated* features are the result of action by frost and slow-moving masses of ice. Most are the legacy of the last Ice Age, which ended in Europe and North America some ten millennia ago. They include spectacular mountain peaks, bowl-shaped cirques at the head of former glaciers, moraines of deposited material in the valleys, lakes and waterfalls. The scenic variety offered by mountains in middle latitudes is particularly attractive for tourism development, and encourages activity and adventure holidays. Most activities involve a limited number of visitors, and are the concern of 'niche' tour operators dealing directly with their customers. In contrast, skiing and snowboarding attract a mass following, and a major winter sports industry has burgeoned in most developed countries, even where suitable resources are in short supply. In summer, regions such as the Alps attract tourists interested in sightseeing for a 'lakes and mountains' holiday.

The sparse population of most mountain regions has made it easier for governments to designate areas as *national parks* for their outstanding natural beauty, unique geological features, wildlife habitats, or their 'countryside capital' – the rural fabric of traditional buildings and landscapes. This last point highlights the fact that very few national parks are areas of pristine wilderness that have remained unaltered by human activity, and many do not satisfy the strict criteria laid down by the World Conservation Union (IUCN). Tourism has to compete with other demands on resources including forestry, pasture for grazing, hydroelectric power generation and mineral extraction. Since mountain areas have a limited carrying capacity, over-development involving the construction of dams, roads and cableways is a matter of growing concern. This has led many authorities to discourage the more popular forms of tourism in favour of activities which are more in harmony with the natural environment, and which will sustain the resource for future generations.

The coast

The coastal zone is where the processes of the sea and the land interact, resulting in a great diversity of landforms and scenery. At least 60 per cent of the world's population are estimated to live on or near the coast, so tourism is but one of many economic activities making demands on its resources.

The quest for the 'perfect beach' is a recurring theme in international tourism. The beach is the world's favourite playground; more than any other environment it appeals to all the physical senses and is associated in people's minds with images of carefree hedonism. In contrast, the 2004 tsunami in the Indian Ocean is a reminder that the sea has always been a potential source of danger. Most coastlines are rugged and indented, so that sandy beaches are restricted to small 'pockets' between headlands. Even where the land is flat and conditions are favourable for large-scale tourism development, coastal sites are sought for industrial use, such as oil refineries and nuclear power stations.

A beach extends from the foreshore to a landward boundary formed by a line of cliffs, protective sand dunes or a man-made feature such as a sea wall. There are significant differences between beaches in terms of texture, from fine-grained sand to coarse shingle, while colours can vary from tan or buff to white and pink (where the sand is derived from fragments of coral), contrasting with black beaches of volcanic origin. The gradient of the beach is important, as this influences the amount of wave energy that reaches the shore. A steeply-sloping beach with waves breaking over an offshore reef is sought by surfers, but is unlikely to provide safe bathing conditions for families with young children.

Although beaches have a high carrying capacity, the same is not true of dunes, where the protective plant cover is highly vulnerable to trampling. Overcrowding and the litter produced by a throwaway society are features of popular holiday resorts in peak season. Furthermore, coastal waters are prone to pollution from a variety of sources. The World Health Organisation reports that industrial waste and faecal contamination from untreated sewage are a serious risk to swimmers on many beaches, particularly in Asia. In response to the pollution threat, a growing number of countries have adopted the 'Blue Flag' scheme, which closely monitors water quality, safety (for example the presence of lifeguards), environmental management to prevent conflict between different types of water-based recreation, and not least, environmental education. Beaches are also severely eroded by winter storms, and

Figure 3.3 Part of South Beach, Miami before and after replenishment in the early 1980s (*Source:* Courtesy of the City of Miami Beach Historical Archives)

this has led many local authorities, with the help of central government, to invest in costly beach replenishment schemes which import material from elsewhere (see Figure 3.3).

Coral reefs are a feature of oceanic islands and most mainland coasts in the tropics, where sea surface temperatures range between 23° and 29°C, the water is clear and of moderate depth. Locations near the mouth of a large river such as the Amazon, or where there is a cold current offshore, are not favourable for their growth. Typically the reef encloses a sheltered lagoon, and slopes steeply as a 'drop-off' to the sea bed. This provides an ideal setting for water sports, particularly snorkelling and scuba diving. Coral reef ecosystems are extraordinarily diverse, but are highly vulnerable, not only to a rise in sea temperature of only 2°C caused by 'global warming', but also a number of other dangers, mostly man-made. These include sediment from beachfront development in places like Florida, over-fishing, pollution from sewage, oil spills, and physical damage by careless holidaymakers. A number of countries have designated *marine reserves* to protect the reefs and sea life in general, but enforcement is problematic, given the scale of commercial fishing worldwide.

Coastal *wetlands,* consisting of estuaries, marshes and swamps, have long been under-valued as a tourism resource, but are now attracting the attention of developers. Although important as natural sea defences, and as habitats for wildlife, including many species of birds – a fact recognised by the Ramsar Convention – the world's wetlands are under threat. In many tropical countries mangrove swamps have been dredged to provide harbours and yacht marinas, or to expand the lucrative shrimp-farming industry. Elsewhere wetlands have been reclaimed for use by airports, industry and intensive agriculture.

Discussion point: Cultural behaviour and tourism resources

The ways in which people use the beach for recreation, and the type of amenities on offer, vary considerably from country to country. This raises the following points for discussion – should some beaches be privately owned, or should access be freely available to everybody? How can we maintain or improve the quality of our beaches? When you have been on holiday in a foreign country, how does the use of the beach differ from your experience at home – is this due to cultural differences, different weather patterns, or other reasons?

Inland water resources

In landlocked countries lakes and rivers provide a substitute for a coastline as a recreational resource; indeed, shallow lakes tend to warm up more rapidly in summer than the sea. We can regard inland water resources for tourism as nodes – namely lakes and reservoirs; as linear corridors – rivers and canals; or simply as landscape features (such as Victoria Falls). Lakes are particularly numerous in recently glaciated areas such as the Alps, northern Europe and North America. Where lakes are accessible to major cities they attract second-home owners and a wide range of recreational activities which may not be compatible (for example, anglers and jet-skiers). Spatial zoning and temporal phasing – planning and resource management that restricts certain activities to a particular area and time – will be necessary to avoid conflict between users. Maintaining water quality is also a major problem, as unlike the tidal nature of the seas and oceans, lakes have no natural cleansing mechanism. Rivers are more widely available than lakes, but usually tourism and recreation have to take second place to the needs of industry, commerce and agriculture. Even so, boating holidays on the inland waterways of Europe are growing in popularity, while rivers previously regarded as unnavigable are sought out by adventurous tourists for the challenge of white-water rafting and canoeing.

Cultural features

A country's resources in the arts, culture and entertainment – the so-called 'creative industries' – are at least as important as its physical resources and sport facilities in attracting tourists. The problem is defining culture, which means different things to specific interest groups. To some it relates to activities that demand intellectual effort, in contrast to most forms of popular entertainment. In the context of tourism, culture in its broadest sense refers to the whole way of life of particular societies. Although only a minority of tourists are primarily culture-seekers, most travellers are interested in the everyday differences between their country of origin and the lifestyle of the people in the countries they visit. These are usually expressed in gastronomy, the performing arts (including dance and music), the visual arts and handicrafts, markets, folklore and festivals.

On a global scale we can recognise a number of cultural regions, where there is a broad similarity in lifestyles, architecture, agricultural systems, and often a shared historical background and religion. These regions rarely correspond to continental boundaries. For example, 'Western' culture since the Renaissance in the fifteenth century has spread well beyond the confines of Europe, as a result of overseas trade, colonial expansion, emigration and advances in technology. Tourism thrives in the absence of barriers to communication, so the existence of a common language is an advantage, although the dominance of English – partly as a consequence of globalisation – poses a threat to minority languages. Nevertheless, in most of Africa and Asia, and parts of Latin America, Western influence is superficial and strong cultural differences persist. This is evident in the Muslim countries of Africa and the Middle East, as well as the countries of south and east Asia where Buddhism has long been the dominant influence. In many countries, indigenous tribal groups continue to live outside the mainstream culture, which often regards them as primitive, backward, or uncivilised. Identified as a 'Fourth World' by some anthropologists (Graburn, 1976), these tribes are increasingly sought as a unique resource by tour operators and included in itineraries, but unfortunately tourism could present another threat to a way of life which is already endangered. Examples of such minority cultures include the hill tribes of Southeast Asia, the Andaman Islanders of India, the Aborigines of Australia, the Koi San (Bushmen) of southern Africa, and the Indians of the Amazon rainforest.

Tourism is a major factor encouraging cultural change in traditional societies. On the other hand, tourism has done much to revive local festivals and handicrafts. Nevertheless in many instances these have been modified to suit the taste of foreign tourists, so that culture becomes just another commodity for sale, losing its authenticity as part of the travel experience. Younger members of host communities are keen to imitate what they see as the desirable lifestyle of the tourist, the so-called 'demonstration effect', often disrupting the community's social cohesion. However the Internet and television, reaching remote villages as yet 'undiscovered' by tourists, may have an even greater impact as a driver of cultural change.

Case study 3.1

Responsible tourist behaviour

As tourists we should respect the differences between our lifestyle and those of the countries we visit. This means being aware of the host community's social conventions, dress codes and taboos to avoid causing offence, and also to minimise the social and cultural impact of tourism. Pressure groups such as Tourism Concern are concerned with such things as a backpacker's code of conduct and 'guilt-free' holidays (see Box 3.1).

Discussion point

The attitude of many holidaymakers is that it is their human right to dress and behave as they are accustomed to do at home, particularly as they have paid good money for a well-earned break. In class, debate these issues, and investigate some 'taboos'.

Box 3.1 Young travellers' code

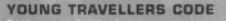

EXPLORING THE WORLD

YOUNG TRAVELLERS CODE

The ideas expressed in this code were developed by and for independent travellers. They show what individuals can do to play their part towards Tourism Concern's goal of more ethical and fairly traded tourism.

Being sensitive to these ideas means getting more out of your travels and giving more back to the people you meet and the places you visit.

THE COST OF YOUR HOLIDAY

→ Think about where your money goes - be fair and realistic about how cheaply you travel. Try and put money into local people's hands; drink local beer or fruit juice rather than imported brands and stay in locally owned accommodation.

→ Haggle with humour and not aggressively. Pay what something is worth to you and remember how wealthy you are compared to local people.

HOW BIG IS YOUR FOOTPRINT? - MINIMISE YOUR ENVIRONMENTAL IMPACT

→ Think about what happens to your rubbish - take biodegradable products and a water filter bottle. Be sensitive to limited resources like water, fuel and electricity.

→ Help preserve local wildlife and habitats by respecting rules and regulations, such as sticking to footpaths, not standing on coral and not buying products made from endangered plants or animals.

Tourism Concern

LEARN ABOUT THE COUNTRY YOU'RE VISITING

→ Start enjoying your travels before you leave by tapping into as many sources of information as you can.

CULTURE

→ Open your mind to new cultures and traditions - it will transform your experience.

→ Think carefully about what is appropriate in terms of your clothes and the way you behave. You'll earn respect and be more readily welcomed by local people.

→ Respect local laws and attitudes towards drugs and alcohol that vary in different countries and communities. Think about the impact you could have. 'The effect on the local community of travellers taking drugs when visiting the hilltribes of Thailand can be devastating. People become trapped into selling drugs to travellers and become addicted themselves, especially young people who want to be like the travellers.'
Jaranya Daengnoy, Thai Tour Organiser

GUIDEBOOKS

→ Use your guidebook as a starting point, not the only source of information. Talk to local people, then discover your own adventure!

PHOTOGRAPHY

→ Don't treat people as part of the landscape, they may not want their picture taken. Put yourself in their shoes, ask first and respect their wishes.

For more information visit: www.tourismconcern.org.uk or call: + 44 (0) 20 7753 3330

This **Tourism Concern** initiative is supported by

Raleigh   EARTHWATCH

STA TRAVEL
www.statravel.co.uk

Source: Courtesy Tricia Barnett, Director, Tourism Concern.

Tourism based on a cultural motivation has a long history. A shared religion can encourage travel between countries, so *pilgrimages* – here defined as journeys with a religious motivation – were arguably the earliest form of organised tourism. Most of the great religions have sacred sites – a shrine, a holy mountain, or a holy city. Pilgrimages tend to be highly concentrated in time as well as space, a notable example being the annual Muslim *hajj* to Mecca (which is a forbidden city to non-believers). Perhaps as a reaction to a secular, materialistic world, *faith tourism* – travel emphasising spiritual values – would appear to be on the increase, as shown by the revival of the pilgrim route to Santiago de Compostela, the greatest Christian shrine of medieval Europe.

Travellers to 'secular shrines', such as the former home of a celebrity, famous writer or national leader, are often called pilgrims, but are more correctly described as cultural tourists, who are also attracted to destinations noted for their art treasures, historic sites and architectural achievements. Such tourists are following in the tradition of those wealthy travellers who undertook the 'Grand Tour' of Europe in the eighteenth century. Thomas Cook, taking advantage of improved means of communication, brought the cultural attractions of Europe and the Middle East within reach of the Victorian middle class. Today's young backpackers taking a gap year from work or college have similar motivations, but the numbers involved are on an altogether vaster scale than was ever the case with the Grand Tour, and their journeys are truly global in scope.

Assignment

Compare the travels of today's Gap Year tourists with those undertaking the Grand Tour in the eighteenth century. See if you can detect any similarities and describe the ways they differ, taking into account the following:

- gender, age and social class
- motivations for travel
- sources of information available
- destinations chosen
- modes of transport used
- documentation required
- types of accommodation used
- activities
- impacts on host communities.

Heritage tourism has grown up with people's curiosity about places, nature and the past (often highly romanticised). It is about much more than an interest in history and old buildings. In effect, legends loosely based on historical fact, mythology, and literary invention play as great a part in creating heritage attractions as actual events and the findings of archaeology. Here the tourist trail spawned by *The Da Vinci Code,* including the hitherto little-known Rosslyn Chapel in Scotland, is one notable example of the influence of the mass media. In its wider sense, heritage includes those natural as well as man-made features that are considered worthy of preservation. Some features are so unique, spectacular or well known that they are of worldwide significance and their loss would affect mankind as a whole. For this reason UNESCO has designated most of these for special protection as World Heritage Sites. While this designation does bring with it management responsibilities, lack of the ability to enforce conservation measures means that some monuments are in a poor state of preservation, or their integrity is threatened by inappropriate development nearby.

Controversies about the recent past are very much part of the growing interest in *dark tourism*. As the name implies, this focuses on places associated with death, suffering and disaster. The best known examples commemorate the sites of the Jewish Holocaust during the Second World War, such as the concentration camp at Auschwitz in Poland. This type of tourism raises moral questions regarding visitor motivation, appropriate methods of interpretation that avoid sensationalism and commercial exploitation, and the extent to which buildings should be preserved or even reconstructed in the pursuit of authenticity.

Finally, many tourists, especially those in the younger age groups, are less interested by a country's past than in its contemporary culture, as reflected in sport, fashion and popular music. Again the influence of the mass media is evident. The national tourism organisation of a country may have a large promotional budget, but this will have considerably less impact than the free publicity and exposure provided by a movie or television series seen by a worldwide audience.

Discussion point: Whose heritage?

In heritage tourism we also need to consider the art treasures and artefacts that form part of national collections like the British Museum and the Louvre. Many of these were acquired from indigenous cultures in, for example, Africa during the period of colonial expansion, or as the spoils of victory in war. Should these museums and art galleries comply with demands that the artefacts should be returned to their countries of origin? To what extent should the need to preserve the integrity of collections for future generations take precedence over the principle of restitution to the 'rightful owners', whoever these might be?

Tourism resources at the national scale

Tourist attractions

Attractions are the *raison d'etre* for tourism; they generate the visit; give rise to excursion circuits and create an industry of their own. The simplest approach to identifying attractions in an area is to draw up an inventory or checklist, by defining the range of attractions, counting them, and either tabulating or mapping the result. Swarbrooke (1995) has classified attractions into the following categories:

- Natural, including beaches, caves, scenic features and wildlife (the flora and fauna).
- Man-made, but not originally designed to attract tourists, such as historic houses, castles and cathedrals.
- Man-made and purpose-built to attract tourists; this includes museums, art galleries, exhibition centres, casinos and a growing range of leisure attractions for a family 'day out' such as theme parks and aqua-parks.
- Special events. These 'event' attractions differ from the others, which are 'site' or 'point' attractions, in that they occur only periodically and in some cases change venues. The latter includes sporting events, notably the football World Cup, the Commonwealth Games, and the Summer and Winter Olympics. These present unique opportunities to promote the host country and have a spin-off effect encouraging other attractions nearby. They also require considerable investment in buildings and infrastructure, planning and organisation to safeguard the health, safety and security of visitors and participants. Cultural event attractions of major international significance would include Rio de Janeiro's Carnival and the Edinburgh Festival.

Quite clearly different forms of tourism are based on different types of attraction. At the risk of stereotyping, we could say that the young tourist is more likely to be

Case study 3.2

Caves as 'natural' tourist attractions

Caves as a recreational resource are usually limited to those with specialist knowledge and equipment. On the other hand caves have been valued in many parts of the world as dwellings and repositories throughout history, partly because they are characterised by only small seasonal variations in temperature.

The subterranean networks of caverns and tunnels in areas of hard limestone are one of the 'last frontiers' of tourism, as only a small fraction have as yet been explored, let alone exploited and made safe for tourists as 'show caves'. Among the features formed by solution and deposition are slender stalactites contrasting with stalagmites rising from the cave floor. In some caves – Drach in Majorca is a fine example – there are underground lakes. Caves have often yielded valuable evidence of early man, including those of the Dordogne region in France and Altamira in Spain. These contain rock paintings dating back to the Ice Age which archaeologists believe may have had religious significance. Deep caves accessible only to divers and speleologists contain life forms that are adapted to an extreme environment. Many caves are therefore sites of scientific importance and subject to strict controls.

Caves differ from most natural attractions in the following ways:

- They are a hidden feature of the landscape.
- Physical alterations to the resource, including roped-off trails and some form of artificial lighting, are necessary to provide access from the cave entrance to the interior 'chambers' containing the most impressive formations.
- Visitors are restricted to guided tours to ensure their safety and to protect this fragile resource from damage. In extreme cases some of the 'painted caves' had to be closed after a few years of public access, to preserve the artefacts from deterioration as a result of exposure to light and the exhaled breath of visitors.

A few caves have the physical capacity to stage event attractions such as concerts – St Michael's Cave in Gibraltar and the Dachstein, high in the Austrian Alps, are good examples. In the area around a show cave there is often demand for facilities and other visitor attractions, some of which may be inappropriate for the setting.

attracted to theme parks with their emphasis on exciting rides, and to demand some vibrant nightlife at their destination. Business travellers will also have different needs. They gravitate toward major commercial centres which offer facilities for conferences and trade exhibitions, as well as a range of services for corporate entertaining.

Tourism development based on a cluster of attractions is more likely to be successful than one based on a single world class attraction. Increasingly tourist attractions and the resource base in general are suffering from intensive use and need effective visitor management. This can only be achieved if these attractions are considered as an integral part of the resource base rather than dealt with in isolation.

A broader view of the tourism resource base

The tourism resource base allows for a multitude of different outdoor recreation activities, ranging from abseiling to zorbing. Some of these activities – notably skiing, golf and yachting – require specialised facilities as well as equipment and skills, whereas others – canoeing, for example – are not associated with development on any scale. All types of sport and outdoor recreation are based on some kind of physical resource that may be natural, man-made or a combination of both. The 'arts, culture and entertainment' sector of tourism focuses more on a destination's human resources.

Clawson provides one of the most useful ways of thinking about the total resource base for tourism (Clawson and Knetsch, 1966). He viewed resources as forming a continuum from intensive resort development at one extreme to wilderness at the other, and his scheme therefore incorporates both resource and user characteristics. Clawson's three basic categories are:

- User-oriented areas of highly intensive development close to population centres.
- Resource-based areas where the type of resource determines the use of the area.
- An intermediate category, where access is the determining factor.

In Table 3.3 we relate a selection of recreation activities to Clawson's classification.

Table 3.3 A classification of recreational resources

User orientated	Intermediate	Resource based
Based on resource close to the user. Often artificial developments (city parks, stadiums, etc.). Highly intensive developments. Activities often highly seasonal, closing in off-peak.	Best resources available within accessible distance to users. Access very important. Natural resources more significant than user-orientated facilities, but these experience a high degree of visitor pressure.	Outstanding resources. Based on their location, not that of the market. Primary focus is resource quality. Often distant from user, the resource determines the activity.

Reproducible ← — — — — — — — → Non-reproducible

Activity paramount ← — — — — — — → Resource paramount

Artificiality ← — — — — — — — → Naturalness

← — — Intensity of development — — →

Proximity ← — Distance from user — → Remoteness

Examples of activities:	Examples of activities:	Examples of activities:
Golf	Yachting	Sightseeing
Tennis	Windsurfing	Mountain climbing
Spectator sports	Boating	Trekking
Visits to theme parks, zoos, resorts, etc.	Camping	Safaris
	Hiking	Expeditions
	Angling	Surfing
	Field sports	Whitewater rafting
	Downhill skiing	Canoeing
	Snowboarding	Potholing
		Scuba dividing

Typical resource:	Typical resource:	Typical resource:
Theme park	Heathland	Unique historical monument National park

Another way of thinking about resources, related to Clawson's ideas, is to distinguish *reproducible* resources (those which can be replaced, such as theme parks) from *non-reproducible* resources which if lost, are irreplaceable, such as elements of the natural and cultural heritage mentioned earlier.

The evaluation of resources for tourism

Measurement of the suitability of the resource base to support different forms of tourism is known as resource evaluation. The main issue here is to match the varied requirements of different users with the characteristics of the resource base. For example, pony trekkers need rights of way, footpaths or bridleways, and attractive scenery. The aim of a resource evaluation system is to satisfy these various needs, which can be plotted on a *recreation opportunity spectrum*. This provides planners with a management tool for matching specific locations in an area to particular types of recreation use.

The tourism product and destination marketing

An area may have tourism potential, with a favourable climate, attractive scenery, hospitable people and a range of resources awaiting discovery, but it will not become a viable tourist destination unless it has:

- at least one attraction that can be promoted as a unique selling proposition (USP);
- support facilities, including accommodation;
- accessibility to a major tourist-generating country;
- favourable preconditions for development, which means the provision of basic infrastructure, a tourist organisation and a measure of political stability.

These elements combine to provide the *tourism product* of a destination. Whilst individual enterprises within the tourism industry supply products to the consumer, notably airlines and hotels, the destination product is the sum of these many parts. Nevertheless, the marketing of places demands a very different approach to the marketing of tangible consumer products such as cars. First, the nature of the product is different. Destination products comprise a set of tangible and non-tangible components based around an activity at the destination. That activity could be a skiing vacation or a spa visit, and for each the mix of components will vary. Using Innsbruck in Austria as our example, we can see that this destination product is made up of the following components:

- The *core destination product* – the winter sports experience.
- The *facilitating destination product* – the transportation services and accommodation in Innsbruck.
- The *supporting destination product* – the high quality shopping and restaurants in Innsbruck.
- The *augmented destination product* – the overall ambience of Innsbruck communicated through the urban design and conservation of the old town. (Kotler et al., 2003)

Secondly, there is a range of stakeholders who feel they should all have a say in the marketing of 'their' destination. Thirdly, destination marketing is commonly done by a public sector agency, though they often lack marketing expertise, and political considerations may override marketing issues. Finally, the real challenge for the marketer is to achieve 'differentiation' – in other words to demonstrate that destination A is truly different from destination B – and create a *brand* that is widely recognised.

Tourism resources at the local scale

For the tourism resource to be developed, someone or some organisation has to act. These agents of development can be either in the private sector, or in the public sector, which includes central government, state-funded organisations acting on its behalf, and local authorities.

The public sector is involved not only in tourism development at the local scale, but at all levels, including the international. Developing countries receive assistance for projects through agencies such as the World Bank or the United Nations Development Programme. Many governments actively encourage in their own countries by providing finance at generous rates and tax breaks to developers. Typically at the national and international levels, government involvement is with the planning and co-ordination of tourism development. At the local level the role of the public sector is usually limited to providing the initial *infrastructure*; this includes all development on or below ground, such as roads, parking areas, railway lines, harbours and airports, as well as the provision of utilities. Adequate water supplies are crucial, bearing in mind that the requirements for a luxury hotel and golf course may be excessive, and conflict with the needs of the local population. Where basic services have failed to keep pace with a spate of hotel building, a destination will suffer bad publicity regarding its standards of health, hygiene and safety. The public sector is also responsible for ensuring adequate security from crime and terrorism. Even an isolated incident affecting tourists can receive widespread coverage by the media in their countries of origin.

As tourism projects are costly, private sector developers typically provide the *superstructure*. This includes the accommodation sector (of which hotels are normally the most important component), entertainment venues, sports facilities, shops, restaurants and passenger transport terminals. Clearly this division of responsibilities reflects the motives of the two sectors; the private sector looks for profit and a return on investment, while the public sector is anxious to provide the basic services in an environment favourable for tourism development. In some developed countries the *voluntary sector*, consisting of non-profit making organisations, has a subsidiary role in the development process. As their main interest is conservation, these organisations are much more likely to oppose large-scale tourism projects than to initiate development. The National Trust is an outstanding British example, but differs from most such organisations in being a major landowner.

At the local scale accessibility is all-important and may be the deciding factor in the success of a tourism project. Resorts in destination areas such as the Mediterranean owe much of their popularity to their location near an airport with direct flights to the major tourist-generating cities in northern Europe. We should point out here that accessibility is a relative term which is determined by cost as well as distance. Exclusive 'up-market' resorts are often located in areas away from the main tourist routes.

Other factors encouraging the development of tourism resources at local level include land availability, suitable physical site attributes (soil, topography), and a favourable planning environment with zoning for tourism use. Normally undeveloped *greenfield* sites are chosen, but there are an increasing number of tourism projects in inner city areas, often utilising a waterfront location previously occupied by dockyards and industry. Such *brownfield* sites usually require costly reclamation treatment before building work can take place.

Finally, tourism development should take place with the consent of the local community. However, in most developing countries (and some developed ones) democratic structures of government are weak at the local level, and even the ownership of land may be the subject of dispute. This became evident in southern Asian fishing communities in the aftermath of the 2004 tsunami, when it was alleged that local people were excluded from the benefits of reconstruction. Local authorities may lack the expertise and financial 'muscle' to take on business interests from outside the region whose activities may have a negative social and environmental impact.

Resorts and other tourist centres

Whereas ecotourism and many outdoor recreation activities are dispersed throughout rural space, most types of tourism are concentrated to some degree in resorts or in centres of population. Resorts are places that are frequented by health and pleasure seekers, and recreational tourism is the reason they came into being. In Britain the term 'resort' usually means a seaside town, while in the USA it denotes a self-contained leisure complex. In our definition, resorts differ from other urban or rural communities in that they have evolved, or been deliberately planned, in response to the needs of tourists. As a result they are distinct in layout and townscape, and are often characterised by eclectic styles of architecture, in contrast to more workaday places. This is not to say that tourism does not play an increasingly important role in a great many towns and cities, particularly those with a long history, regardless of their primary function. Even manufacturing and mining towns, long shunned by tourists, are developing attractions which exploit the growing interest in a country's industrial heritage. We could measure the importance of tourism to a place by reference to the numbers employed in catering to visitors, the type of shops and other facilities, or more simply, by the number of beds available for tourists relative to the population of the host community (Defert, 1967). Defert's tourism function index (Tf) is arrived at by the formula (Tf = $N \times (100/P)$), where N is the number of tourist beds and P is the number of residents. Although the index works fairly well as a measure for holiday resorts, it seriously underestimates the impact of tourism in major cities with a large resident population, or in historic towns such as Bruges that attract large numbers of day visitors.

It is difficult to classify tourist centres, as the categories frequently overlap, and may also change over time (see Table 3.4).

In developing countries many planned holiday resorts are in effect 'tourist ghettos', separated physically and culturally from the support communities that provide the workforce for the hotels. Elsewhere the distinction between 'hosts' and 'guests' is less marked, but typically in resorts we find a concentration of tourist-orientated land and building uses close to the main focus of visitor attraction. This area of tourist-related functions is termed the *recreational business district* (RBD), distinct from the main office and shopping area, which in larger towns is called the central business district (CBD). The RBD develops under the twin influences of the major access route into the resort and the central tourist feature. For example, in seaside resorts the RBD often develops parallel to the beach, behind a promenade or boardwalk, and contains premier hotels and shops. Beyond the beachfront, the intensity of tourist functions and

Table 3.4 **A typology of tourist centres**	
Spa resorts	Reached their peak prior to 1914 as 'watering places' catering for health-seekers; now most visitors are short-stay and attracted for other reasons, including health, fitness and 'wellness' tourism (e.g. Bath, Baden-Baden, Vichy, Hot Springs)
Mountain resorts/hill stations	Mainly established in the colonial era to provide a cool, healthy refuge for expatriates in hot climates; now cater for domestic visitors (e.g. Darjeeling)
Winter sports resorts	Located in mountainous areas with facilities geared to skiing and other snow-based activities; now adapting to the market and climate change to provide all-year sport and leisure facilities (e.g. St Moritz, Aspen)
Seaside resorts	Depend on the quality of their beaches, climate and water sport facilities. Can be categorised as either (a) exclusive, with high class accommodation (e.g Cannes, The Hamptons), or (b) popular, with a wide range of accommodation and many purpose-built facilities (e.g. Blackpool, Benidorm, Atlantic City, Acapulco, Surfers Paradise)
Lake resorts	Appeal based on scenery and access to major cities; attract 'second homers'; facilities for water sports (e.g. Bellaggio)
Gaming and entertainment resorts	Based on market-orientated activities rather than a particular resource, tend to be heavily regulated (e.g. Las Vegas, Sun City)
Service centres	Mainly rural communities providing support facilities for visitors to national parks (e.g. Gatlinburg)
Centres of pilgrimage	Facilities geared to groups of visitors with a religious motivation (e.g. Lourdes, Varanasi)
Cultural and historic centres	Primary function may be education, administration or distribution – tourism has to compete for space; historic towns and cities attract a high proportion of foreign visitors to their heritage or cultural attractions (e.g. Oxford, Florence, Kyoto, Fez)
Primary cities	Usually national capitals; primary function is administration and finance, and tourism is one of many functions; concentration of national culture in theatres, museums and art galleries; business tourism important; tourists typically short-stay, with a high percentage of foreign visitors (e.g. Washington, New York, Madrid, Tokyo)
Industrial centres	Some short-stay leisure tourists attracted by manufacturing or mining heritage (e.g. Bradford, Rio Tinto, Ballarat, Calico)
Ports and border towns	Gateways for tourists in transit; shopping opportunities for cross-border travellers due to price differentials between countries

land values decreases in a series of zones around the RBD (Figure 3.4). In the case of historic tourist centres, the RBD usually corresponds to the ancient core of the town, which in most European examples is focused on a castle, university or cathedral. In practice it is difficult to distinguish the RBD functions from the CBD as they overlap (Figure 3.5). Conservation is of primary concern, and *interpretation*, using costumed guides or re-enactments of historical events, brings the 'heritage experience' to life for the tourist. Nevertheless, 'the attraction may be medieval, but few tourists are prepared

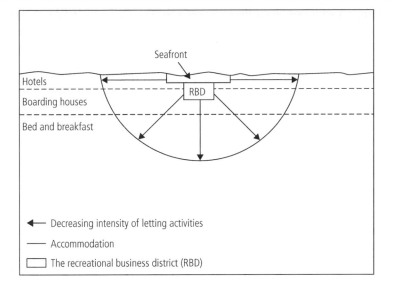

Figure 3.4 The recreational business district (*Source:* Wall, 'Car owners and holiday activities', in Lavery, 1971)

to eat, sleep and travel in medieval conditions' (Ashworth and Tunbridge, 1990). Modern support facilities, while necessary, may be an intrusive feature in the skyline and street scene of the historic city. In large cities, especially national capitals such as London, the tourism function is polycentric. Tourist facilities are widely dispersed

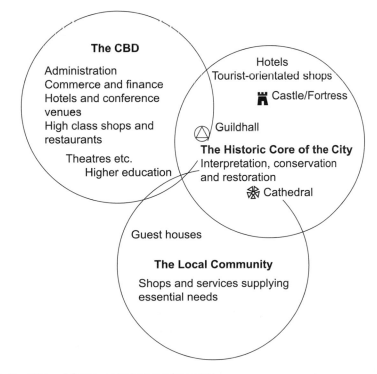

Figure 3.5 The RBD and CBD in an historic tourist centre

between a number of *quarters* or districts catering for recreational or cultural tourism, while the business traveller gravitates to the CBD with its range of financial and commercial services.

The development of resorts over time is an important consideration for geographers concerned with tourism. Butler (1980) has suggested a *tourist area life cycle* where resorts evolve from 'discovery' through development to eventual decline. Although the life cycle approach has its critics – who feel it is difficult to operationalise – the main utility of this approach is a way of thinking about resorts, an explanatory framework for their development, and as a means of integrating supply-side trends with the changing market of a resort. After all, the type of tourist who visits in the exploration phase will be very different from those visiting during consolidation or decline (Figure 3.6). We can summarise the tourist area life cycle as follows:

- Exploration: small number of adventurous tourists; main attraction is unspoilt nature or cultural features.
- Involvement: local initiatives provide facilities and some advertising ensues; larger numbers of visitors, a tourist season and public sector involvement follows.
- Development: large numbers of tourists and control passes from locals to national or international companies. The destination begins to change in appearance. Overuse may begin.
- Consolidation: the destination is now a fully-fledged part of the tourism industry; the rate of growth in visitors is reducing. A recognisable recreational business district has emerged.
- Stagnation: peak visitor numbers have been reached and the destination is now unfashionable with environmental, social and economic problems. Major promotional efforts are needed to maintain visitor numbers.
- Decline: visitors now visit newer resorts as the destination goes into decline. It is dependent on a smaller geographical catchment and repeat visits.
- Rejuvenation: here the authorities attempt to 're-launch' the destination by providing new facilities, attracting new markets and re-investing.

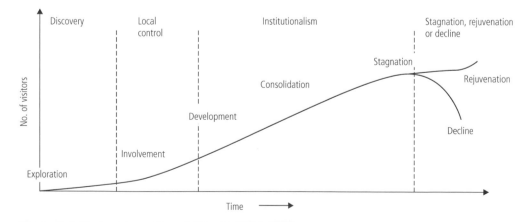

Figure 3.6 The tourist area life cycle (*Source:* Butler, 1980)

Summary

- Certain factors favour the development of tourism resources and this explains why the world pattern of supply is uneven.
- Developed resources are cultural appraisals, considered by society to be of economic value. They are usually shared with other users and are both fragile and perishable.
- As countries realise the negative impacts of tourism, so planning to safeguard these resources has become vital. Planning aims to minimise the costs of tourism and to maintain the integrity of the resource base.
- At the world scale both physical and cultural features are key factors influencing tourism development, with attractive coastlines, mountains and lakes being the most popular locations for recreation and tourism.
- At the national scale, classifications of tourist attractions which include the whole resource base are useful. Evaluations of the potential of the resource base to satisfy tourist's demands allow possible future areas for recreation and tourism to be identified. These evaluations can then be applied at the local scale to resort developments with their distinctive morphology and mix of service functions.
- It is also possible to identify a cycle of resort development.

Assignments

1. Devise a method to increase the capacity of the trails in an area of heathland where excessive numbers of hikers, horse riders and other recreational users have caused severe erosion.
2. Give examples of island destinations where the wildlife resource is vulnerable to even small numbers of visitors, and suggest ways of managing the problem.
3. Devise a method to assess the social carrying capacity of a small fishing community in the early stages of tourism development.
4. There is an increasing trend to involve all stakeholders at a destination in the tourism planning process. How can this be done in a balanced way to ensure that it is not just the loudest and most influential voices that are heard?
5. Sometimes, tourist attractions reach saturation point in terms of capacity and are at risk of deteriorating. How might such attractions introduce 'demarketing' to reduce visitation?

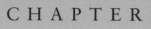

CHAPTER

4

Climate and tourism

Learning objectives

After reading this chapter, you should be able to:

- Understand the importance of latitude and the distribution of land and sea areas in determining climatic differences
- Be aware of the major elements of climate and explain how these affect the various types of recreational tourism
- Understand the problems of classifying world climate zones
- Describe the distribution of world climates and their significance for tourism
- Discuss the possible impact of climate change on tourism patterns

Introduction

Let us start by making a distinction between weather and climate. We can think of climate as a system in which the atmosphere interacts with the hydrosphere, the lithosphere, plant and animal life, and the cryosphere, with the sun as the ultimate energy source. Most of this activity takes place in the atmosphere's lowest layer – less than 16 kilometres (10 miles) in thickness – known as the *troposphere*, which contains the gases essential for life on our fragile planet. Weather is a condition in the troposphere at a given time and place. Climate is the pattern of weather phenomena synthesised over a period of time and we usually base our choices of when and where to go on holiday on climate information. In contrast, outdoor recreation trips are sensitive to changes in the weather, while some are dependent on particular weather conditions, so we need to rely on short-term forecasts.

We can view climate as:

- a resource encouraging the development of tourism;
- a constraint limiting the appeal of a destination; or even
- a consideration in whether or not to travel due to concerns about climate change.

Despite the widespread use of air conditioning and other forms of climate control (as for example in Dubai and Las Vegas), tourists spend some time in an outdoor environment which may be considerably warmer or colder than their country of origin. On a world scale we can see the importance of climate as a 'push' factor in the tourist flows from the colder, cloudier tourist-generating countries to warmer, sunnier destinations; and at a local scale the weather will attract city-dwelling families to a nearby beach on a hot summer day. For a destination, climate largely determines the length of the holiday season (although this is also influenced by other factors such as the timing of school holidays in the generating areas). The providers of leisure goods and services are usually faced with seasonal variations in demand. In most destinations, this problem of *seasonality* influences development and operating costs and therefore profitability and employment in the tourism industry. The relationship between climate and tourism may be changing as evidence linking skin cancer to exposure to solar radiation is publicised, and associated with issues such as 'global warming'. Indeed tourism, particularly where it involves air travel, is itself a major contributor to climate change.

The world climate scene

Tourists usually need information on the *average* rainfall and temperatures they can expect at a particular location, rather than the extreme weather events that make headline news. Nevertheless, in recent years heat waves, storms and floods have become increasingly frequent, and this has been attributed to climate change. For some destinations at least, we should take into account the extremes of temperature we might experience as well as the average for a particular month.

Since the beginning of the twentieth century average temperatures for the world as a whole have risen by 0.6°C and the rate of change appears to be accelerating. Most scientists link this global warming to the emissions of carbon dioxide (CO_2), methane (CH_4) and nitrous oxides into the atmosphere, resulting from the burning of fossil fuels since the Industrial Revolution. It is known that CO_2 is largely responsible for the 'greenhouse effect' that prevents excessive radiation of heat from the earth's surface back into space. On the other hand sceptics argue that episodes of warming and cooling have occurred throughout history, as shown for example, by the retreat and advance of glaciers in the Alps. These were almost certainly due to natural cycles, such as sunspot activity, rather than human interference with the environment. Whatever the causes of climate change, the impact of rising temperatures is potentially very significant and is already being felt in some parts of the world. This presents the tourism industry with a formidable challenge, and some of the responses to climate change are shown in Box 4.1.

Climate is determined by three main factors:

1 latitude or distance from the Equator;
2 the distribution of land and sea; and
3 relief.

Box 4.1 **The response to climate change**

The tourism sector is responding to climate change in two ways. The first is to attempt mitigation of the effects of climate change by altering behaviour, through reducing the carbon footprint of travellers, for example. The second is in terms of adaptation, where destinations develop strategies to cope with the realities of climate change, as in the following chart:

Adaptation approach	Coastal and small island destinations	Mountain and winter destinations
Examples of technological adaptation approaches	Development of new weather-independent attractions including theme parks, casinos and sports facilities. Development of new facilities for business, particularly conferences. Development of facilities to support niche markets, such as food and wine, adventure and marine tourism.	Ski slope development to reduce snow needs. Snow-making equipment. Development of ski facilities at higher altitudes. Development of facilities for year-round tourism such as trails, nature-based attractions, spa facilities, and year-round accommodation. Landscaping with native vegetation and reforestation.
Examples of business model adaptation approaches	Scenario planning to review competitive positioning for 'beach-plus' tourism. Market diversification strategies away from beach tourism. Season extension strategies, including event programmes. Development and marketing of non-weather dependent products. Visitor education. Withdrawal from tourism.	Scenario planning to review competitive positioning for year-round tourism. Market diversification to attract those not participating in winter sports. Season extension strategies, including festival and event programmes. Development of non-weather dependent products such as hiking, health and spa facilities. Withdrawal from tourism.

Partly adapted from Abegg, B (2006) Climate Change and Winter Tourism, OECD Wengen Workshop, OECD, Paris

Latitude is the primary factor, as this determines the angle of the sun's rays at any given time of the year; if this is too oblique the sun's heating power will be limited. Due to the Earth's rotation the Northern Hemisphere is tilted towards the sun in June, when it is overhead at noon on the Tropic of Cancer (latitude 23.5° North). At high latitudes north of the Arctic Circle (66.5° North) there is daylight for at least 24 hours at midsummer, while Antarctica (south of 66.5° South) is experiencing continual darkness. By December, the sun's overhead path has moved south of the Equator to the Tropic of Capricorn (latitude 23.5° South). This marks the onset of summer in the Southern Hemisphere, and in contrast a period of continuous cold and darkness north of the Arctic Circle. The low latitudes between the Tropics of Cancer and Capricorn enjoy a warm climate all year round, as the sun is high in the sky for most of the day, with only a very brief period of twilight before nightfall. The result of increasing distance from the Equator is a shorter summer, a greater difference in day length between the seasons, and a longer period of twilight.

The simple model of a steady decrease in temperature from the Equator to the poles is complicated by the fact that most of the world's landmass is concentrated in the Northern Hemisphere. Land surfaces heat and cool more rapidly than large areas of water. The oceans therefore act as a reservoir of warmth, so that windward coasts and islands have a *maritime* climate which is equable. Furthermore, warm ocean currents, notably the Gulf Stream and the North Atlantic Drift, distribute some of the warmth of tropical seas to higher latitudes (see Figure 4.1). As a result, Britain and Ireland have a much milder climate than their position relatively near the Arctic Circle would suggest. Cold currents have a chilling effect, the most well known example being the Labrador Current off the east coast of Canada (icebergs carried by this current caused the 1912 *Titanic* disaster). The Pacific Ocean, because it is so much larger than any other body of water, has a worldwide influence on climate as shown by the El Niño phenomenon. The heartlands of Eurasia and North America, at similar latitudes to the British Isles, are far removed from the influence of the sea and experience a *continental* climate, characterised by extreme variations in temperature.

In many parts of the world where there are high mountains, *relief* has a major effect on weather patterns. Climbers are well aware that air temperatures are considerably lower on the summit of a mountain. As a rough guide, the temperature falls by 6.5°C per 1,000 metres of altitude (equivalent to 3.5°F per 1,000 feet). There is also a reduction of barometric pressure with increasing altitude; at 5,000 metres the density of the air is less than 60 per cent of its sea level value. The thinner atmosphere at such altitudes means that, although more solar radiation reaches the ground by day, heat is lost more rapidly to the sky at night. Because there is less oxygen in the air, physical exertion becomes more difficult. Great contrasts in temperature, moisture and sunshine are found within short distances in mountain regions, providing a variety of habitats or *life zones* for plants and animals. Mountain barriers profoundly modify the climates of adjacent lowlands since moist air from the sea is forced to rise over them, becoming drier and warmer as it descends. At a local scale, the position of a slope or valley in relation to the direct rays of the sun has important consequences for land use and resort development, as in the Alps for example.

Again at a local scale, the energy consumption of large cities results in a climate that is appreciably warmer than the surrounding rural areas, the so-called *heat island* effect. Most of the acute problems that occurred in Europe's cities during the heatwave of August 2003 – such as 11,000 deaths in France alone – were attributed to very warm nights with minimum temperatures over 25°C, 5 to 10°C above the summer average. As a consequence the demand for air conditioning is now set to approach American levels, which in itself would be a significant contributor to climate change.

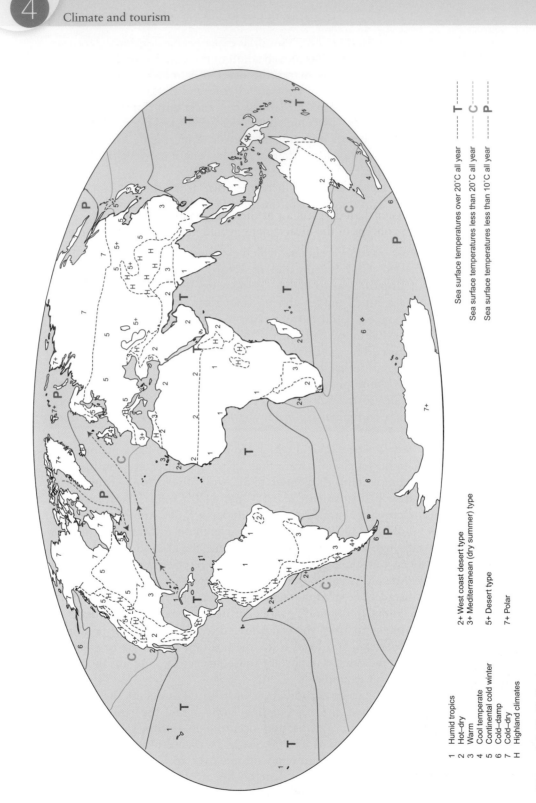

Figure 4.1 World climate zones

1 Humid tropics
2 Hot–dry
3 Warm
4 Cool temperate
5 Continental cold winter
6 Cold–damp
7 Cold–dry
H Highland climates

2+ West coast desert type
3+ Mediterranean (dry summer) type
5+ Desert type
7+ Polar

Sea surface temperatures over 20°C all year ----- T
Sea surface temperatures less than 20°C all year ----- C
Sea surface temperatures less than 10°C all year ----- P

Climate elements and tourism

Temperature is the element of climate which has the greatest influence on tourist activity and the amount of clothing necessary for comfort (see Figure 4.2). Here we are mainly concerned with average *maximum* (daytime) temperatures. Significant numbers of people participate in beach activities and sunbathing only when the maximum temperature exceeds 18°C (65°F). Even if the air temperature is well above this figure, the sea surface temperature in summer is often 5°C lower. Away from tropical shores, a *wetsuit* providing insulation is essential for surfers, replaced by a *drysuit* when the water is really cold (below 12°C). This is because water chills the body through conduction thirty times faster than dry, still air at the same temperature.

The young beachgoer's concept of the ideal climate would probably not be shared by older tourists interested in sightseeing. The comfort zone for most people, wearing standard business clothing, is a narrow band of temperature, varying slightly between winter and summer, where the air is neither excessively dry nor too humid. 'It's not the heat, but the humidity' is a complaint often made about summer weather. This acknowledges the importance of *relative humidity*, which is a measure of the moisture content of the air as a percentage of the total amount it could hold at a given temperature. Thus tropical air at 35°C can hold nine times more water vapour than cold air at 0°C. A dry heat, where the relative humidity is less than 30 per cent, is widely recognised as more tolerable than the humid heat typical of many tropical countries. When moisture levels in the air are nearing saturation it is difficult to keep cool despite profuse sweating, and

OSLO	PARIS	ALICANTE	TENERIFE	BARBADOS
2.0 clo.	1.6 clo.	1.2 clo.	0.8 clo.	0.1 clo.

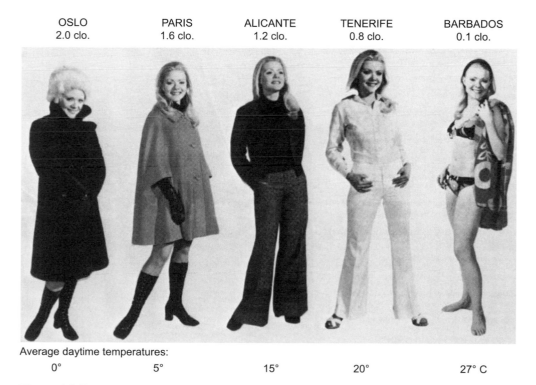

Average daytime temperatures:

0°	5°	15°	20°	27° C

Figure 4.2 Temperature and clothing for holiday travel in January

failure to maintain the body's heat balance will result in heat exhaustion or, in extreme cases, heatstroke. A more common problem, due to the wearing of unsuitable clothing, is the skin condition known as 'prickly heat'. We can express the effect of humidity on heat perception as the *effective temperature* which also takes into account air movement, or more simply, as the *apparent temperature* shown in the bioclimatic chart (Figure 4.3). You can see the importance of this for human well-being by comparing the *climographs* for Delhi and Aswan. These graphs use as co-ordinates the average daytime temperature and relative humidity for each month of the year. August in Delhi would feel more uncomfortable than in Aswan where the actual air temperature is 5°C higher.

Tourists do vary considerably in their ability to acclimatise, according to their age, gender, body mass index, rate of metabolism and ethnic origin. The human body can adapt fairly readily to tropical conditions through an increase in the sweat rate and the supply of blood to the skin, but much depends on how we modify our lifestyle and patterns of behaviour. The body responds to cold mainly by shutting off the blood supply to the hands and feet to maintain the core temperature at 37°C (98°F). In cold climates physiological adaptation is therefore much less effective. Radiant heat from the sun and air movement also influence comfort levels.

Sunshine is particularly important at the beach, where ultraviolet light is reflected from the water surface and the sand, adding to the heat load which the exposed skin is receiving from the sky. The British Isles, despite the advantage of long summer days, experience a cloudy climate compared to southern Spain, where the sun shines brightly

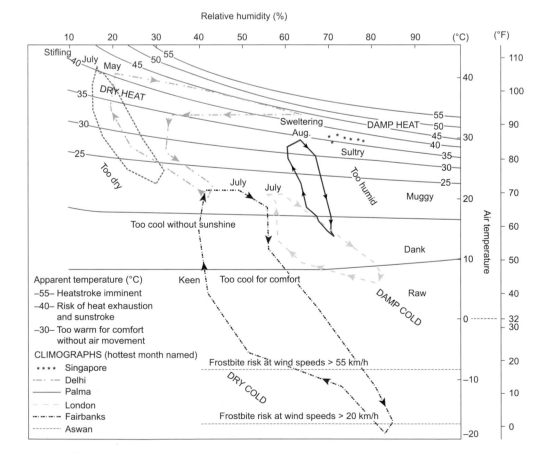

Figure 4.3 Bioclimatic chart

for as much as 80 per cent of the daylight hours. Ultraviolet (UV) radiation is even more intense in tropical latitudes, although skies are often overcast and the duration of bright sunshine is usually less than in the Mediterranean. The UV Index is a simple numerical scale that measures the ultraviolet radiation reaching the Earth's surface in terms of its potential for skin damage. It can be incorporated into local weather forecasts to warn people about the risk of sunburn. Sunscreen preparations protect the outer skin from the short-wave UVB rays, which cause sunburn, but allow through the long-range UVA rays to stimulate melanin production for a sun tan. Prolonged exposure to UVA radiation will, however, result in premature ageing of the skin. Skiers, trekkers and mountain climbers at high altitudes are particularly at risk from sunburn, since the air is clear and sunlight is strongly reflected from snow and bare rock. Such 'incident radiation' can provide considerable warmth to the skin, allowing sunbathing and skiing to take place in the same location.

Case study 4.1

The pros and cons of sunbathing

In Britain and other northern countries there are scare stories in the media over skin cancer and premature ageing, the penalty for indulging in the sun's rays after a long, dark winter. On the other hand there is ample evidence that a moderate amount of exposure allows the skin to produce the vitamin D that is necessary for health and wellbeing. Indeed, in the early part of the twentieth century medical opinion positively encouraged sunbathing in the fight against tuberculosis and rickets, a bone disease resulting from a deficiency of vitamin D. This was common among children living in large cities who were deprived of sunlight as a result of overcrowding and the blight of industrialisation.

Like much else in tourism, sunbathing is subject to the vagaries of fashion. Throughout recorded history, the leisured elite in most civilisations have valued a pale complexion and avoided the sun, whereas a tan was the characteristic of those who had to perform outdoor manual work. This changed in the 1920s, following the First World War, partly as a reaction against Victorian attitudes. The French Riviera was reinvented as a summer destination by artists, writers and the designer Coco Chanel, who did so much to make *le bronzage* fashionable. The cult of sunbathing soon spread to the rest of Europe and the Americas. However, it was not until the 1950s, following the Second World War, that holidays in sunny, exotic destinations came within the reach of most North Europeans and North Americans. Here too, France was a driver of social change, with the 'invention' of the bikini and the Club Méditerranée holiday village concept based on sun, sea, sports, food and wine. This epitomised the cult of the body, free from the constraints of social class, and represented an escape to a pre-industrial 'Polynesian' lifestyle. By the 1970s a deep 'mahogany' tan had become a status symbol, and the manufacture of sun creams a major industry.

This began to change in the 1980s, particularly in Australia, where the Queensland Cancer Society raised awareness of the risks of excessive exposure through their SunSmart campaign. The industry's response has been to shift the emphasis from tanning to skin protection, marketing sunscreens with a high sun protection factor (SPF) that indicate the damage caused by both UVA and UVB radiation, and making 'fake tans' fashionable.

On a global scale the discovery of an 'ozone hole' in the stratosphere, increasing the risk of cataracts and skin cancer, led to international action to ban CFCs. The effects of the thinning of the ozone layer are particularly evident in Southern Hemisphere countries such as Chile, New Zealand and Australia. Fair skinned visitors need to be aware of the increased risk of sunburn, by wearing clothing with a high SPF, as a standard T-shirt offers little protection.

Discussion point

With climate change, do you think that sunbathing will once again become unfashionable, particularly among young people?

Winds are influenced in their direction and strength by the Earth's rotation, by topography, and by the gradient between high and low pressure areas (shown by the spacing of isobars on a weather map). A world view of air circulation shows that in tropical latitudes the trade winds are blowing in an easterly direction. This simple model is greatly modified, particularly in the Northern Hemisphere, by the great seasonal contrasts in temperature and pressure between the continents and the oceans. These result in notable shifts in wind direction in West Africa and much of Asia, where the monsoon is the dominant feature of the climate. At the local scale, mountain and valley winds are characteristic of many highland regions, while onshore sea breezes during the day and weaker offshore land breezes at night are a feature of many coastal areas during periods of warm, settled weather. Coastal locations with a particularly windy climate tend to be shunned by holidaymakers, but this is changing with the growth in popularity of aerial and water sports, notably windsurfing and kite surfing. Tarifa at the southern tip of Spain and Dakhla in the Western Sahara are two such examples. In the case of surfing, although the swells are the result of storms in mid-ocean, local offshore winds provide a smooth face for surf riders by holding off the incoming waves.

Onshore sea breezes moderate the humid summer heat of the Mediterranean and tropical islands like Singapore, resulting in cooler effective temperatures at certain times of the year. At high latitudes, and in middle latitudes during the winter months, strong winds combined with low temperatures have a pronounced chilling effect on exposed skin, leading in extreme cases to frostbite. Even in the relatively mild conditions typical of maritime locations such as the British Isles, this *wind-chill* factor is a major constraint on outdoor recreation.

While many tourists from the Arabian Peninsula find rainy weather appealing, people generally regard **precipitation** in its various forms of rain, hail, sleet and snow as a constraint, although much depends on its intensity, duration and seasonal distribution. In the tropics there is usually a well-defined division of the year into 'wet' and 'dry' seasons, where the rain typically falls in short, heavy downpours following strong convectional heating of the air and the build-up of cumulus clouds during the afternoon. In contrast, most of the rain that falls in the British Isles is cyclonic in origin; it may be smaller in total amount but is spread over many more rainy days.

We can view snow as an expensive hazard for transport or as a valuable recreational resource. Suitable locations for winter sports resorts are found mainly in accessible mountain regions, where there is snow cover to a depth of 30 cm or more for at least three months of the year. As the provision of facilities for skiers is costly, the resort operator needs accurate information on the local climate, including temperature (with average minima below $-2°C$), sunshine, wind speeds and relative humidity. The type of snow cover is important and skiers favour *powder* (loose, low-density snow). Such is the demand for skiing that artificial 'snow domes' have proliferated even in countries where snowfall never occurs, such as Dubai. Although the introduction of winter sports has brought economic benefits to remote mountain communities, it has also led to environmental degradation, especially in the Alps. Deforestation to create ski runs has increased the risk of avalanches, while the use of snow-making equipment to guarantee snow cover inhibits the growth of delicate alpine plants. Many ski resorts, such as those in Scotland and Australia, are climatically marginal and therefore vulnerable to the impact of global warming.

Unlike other elements of the climate, fog invariably has a negative effect on tourist activities. As a natural phenomenon fog is a feature of many coastal areas and enclosed valleys in mountain regions, but human interference with the environment has greatly aggravated the problem. Due to pollution, the monitoring of **air quality** is increasingly crucial as part of the concern about environmental issues and the quality of life generally. The motor vehicle is widely regarded as a major polluter, emitting nitrous oxide, hydrocarbons and ground level ozone (not to be confused with the ozone in the upper atmosphere). More recently attention has focused on the growth of air transport, and frequent fliers are being encouraged to reduce their 'carbon footprint' in response to the threat of climate change. An older problem in most of the world's large cities, especially in those countries undergoing rapid development, is the emission of sulphur dioxide from 'smoke-stack industries'. Smogs, or episodes of severe air pollution are particularly common in regions where anticyclonic conditions, inhibiting air movement, prevail for much of the year. Examples would include the Mediterranean countries and California in summer, and the continental heartlands of North America and Eurasia in winter. An unpleasant cocktail of gases and particulates poisons the air of our cities, reducing visibility, blighting vegetation, eroding historic buildings and monuments, and threatening the health of people suffering from respiratory problems. Prior to the enforcement of strict clean air regulations, 'acid rain' degraded forests and lakes in many areas downwind of sources of industrial pollution in Europe and North America. Now the Arctic is under threat from pesticides and other pollutants carried north by winds and ocean currents; as these are slow to break down at low temperatures, the snow is contaminated, with disastrous consequences for the food chain.

World climates

Classifying climates

Even in a small country like Britain, temperatures, rainfall and exposure to wind or sunshine vary a good deal, resulting in many local climates. However, these differences are less significant on a global scale than those between, say, the south of England and the French Riviera. It is also true that areas of the world separated by vast distances have such similar features that we regard them as belonging to the same climate zone. Thus the climate of California resembles that of Spain, and the South Island of New Zealand shows broad similarities to England, once we appreciate that the seasons are reversed in the Southern Hemisphere.

It is relatively simple to draw a series of world maps showing the various elements of climate, but much more difficult to synthesise this information in order to determine the best overall conditions for tourism. A number of attempts have been made to classify climates from a human rather than a botanical standpoint:

- Of particular relevance is the work of Lee and Lemons (1949), who devised a scheme relating temperatures to clothing requirements.
- Terjung (1966) utilised data on temperature and relative humidity to produce a 'comfort index' for each month of the year for both daytime and night-time conditions. This was further refined, where the data were available, to take account

of the effects of wind-chill and solar radiation. Terjung's classification is the most comprehensive, but produces an excessive number of climate zones, even when the features of the comfort index are summarised for the year as a whole.

- An approach which is gaining wide acceptance is the 'tourism climatic index' (TCI) devised by Mieczkowski (1985) which uses values for temperature, relative humidity, sunshine, precipitation and wind speeds.

The bioclimatic chart (Figure 4.3) is the starting point for our classification scheme. We can think of the world's climates as a continuum, from hot, humid conditions at one extreme to cold and dry at the other. However, most parts of the world have climates which lie somewhere between these extremes, and which are characterised by distinct seasonal variations. This is shown by the *climographs* for Delhi, Palma, London, and in an extreme form, for Fairbanks, Alaska. Such climates are conventionally described in terms of their temperature and rainfall characteristics. We have grouped them into seven major zones that can be related more closely to human comfort and clothing needs. Figure 4.1 shows the world distribution of these zones, but you should be aware that the boundaries drawn on the map indicate wide areas of transition rather than abrupt changes.

The humid tropics (zone 1)

The tropical climates have perhaps the greatest potential for tourism development. Here the main problem is keeping buildings and their occupants cool, as temperatures tend to remain above 20°C throughout the year even at night, while humidity is generally high. Buildings should be designed to take advantage of any breezes, so usually an open plan is adopted with rooms having access to a veranda. Sometimes buildings are elevated on stilts to capture any air movements above the vegetation. Clothing for the tourist should be lightweight, of open texture and made of absorbent materials. Most of the diseases for which the tropics are notorious are mainly due, not to the climate, but to the poor standards of sanitation prevailing in many Third World countries. Nevertheless, the hot, moist environment does favour the growth of harmful bacteria and parasites, while diseases such as malaria are carried by insects that cannot thrive in cold temperatures. Tourists can protect themselves from malaria by taking prophylactic drugs and by preventative measures, for example by 'covering up' in the evenings when the mosquitoes are active. For other tropical diseases such as yellow fever, vaccination is essential.

With the exception of some areas near the Equator, the tropics have a dry season of varying length when conditions are not unfavourable for tourism. Here we can distinguish between the trade wind climate of many tropical islands and coastal areas, and the tropical wet–dry climate which is characterised by much greater seasonal variations in rainfall, temperature and humidity. It is during the long dry season that the savanna grasslands, typical of much of Africa, provide the best conditions for game viewing or 'safari tourism'. In the Caribbean, West Africa and Southern Asia the dry season coincides with the winter months in North America and Europe, so these destinations are well placed to attract winter-sun seekers from the main tourist-generating countries. Tropical countries south of the Equator are less favoured, as their best months for beach tourism coincide with the summer in the countries of the Northern Hemisphere.

The exuberant vegetation and diversity of species of the tropical rainforest is nowadays perceived as a unique resource for ecotourism. Most natural habitats in fact are threatened by the growing pace of development in the tropical 'South', which is still perceived primarily as a source of raw materials for the industrialised countries of the 'North'. The destruction of the rainforests of the Amazon Basin and Indonesia are two well known examples. The environmental consequences may well be serious, not just for the tropical zone but for the Earth as a whole, in terms of loss of biodiversity. The problem of erratic rainfall, however, hits the least developed economies hardest.

Tropical highland climates

Health resorts have been developed in mountain areas in the tropics which enjoy a cooler climate and are malaria-free. Tropical highland climates occur wherever mountains or plateaus rise more than 1,500 metres above sea level, as this is the altitude at which the effects of reduced air pressure become perceptible. Many cities in Latin America, East Africa and Asia are situated at altitudes of between 2,000 and 4,000 metres, where it is advisable for the tourist and business traveller to spend a few days adjusting to the rarefied air. At higher altitudes further acclimatisation becomes problematic, and some visitors are likely to experience the symptoms of acute mountain sickness.

At high altitudes in the tropics the air temperature is considerably cooler than at the coast, particularly at night, although the seasonal rhythm is similar (see Figure 4.4). We can think of the arrangement of climate zones in tropical mountain regions as a series of layers, corresponding to the mean annual temperature at different altitudes. For example, in Mexico, Central America and the Andes of South America these climate zones are generally recognised:

1 the *tierra caliente*, or tropical zone up to 1,000 metres;
2 the *tierra templada* or sub-tropical zone between 1,000 and 2,000 metres, where coffee is one of the main crops;
3 the *tierra fria* between 2,000 and 4,000 metres; and
4 the *tierra helada* above 4,000 metres.

Ascending a high mountain in the tropics has been compared to a journey towards the poles, but with one important difference. Unlike the polar regions, high altitude locations are exposed to intense solar radiation throughout the day all year round. Notable examples of a 'cold region where the sun is hot' would be Tibet, and the Altiplano of Bolivia, where the Indian poncho provides protection from sun, shade and strong winds. Mountain summits above cloud level in the tropics have been likened to 'islands in the sky' containing some unusual vegetation adapted to a daily freeze–thaw regime. These ecosystems are particularly vulnerable to climate change due to the very restricted area of the habitat. One such example is Kilimanjaro, where the snow cap of this iconic mountain is in danger of disappearing. This may also be true of glaciers in the Peruvian Andes and the Himalayas, which has consequences for the water supply of many cities in South America and the Indian subcontinent.

The hot dry climates (zone 2)

Areas of constant drought account for over a quarter of the Earth's land surface, and the threat of *desertification* affects many countries outside the arid zone. The 'hot deserts' in tropical and subtropical latitudes occur wherever the air is dry as a result of subsidence from the permanent high pressure belts. The hot dry regions can claim the sunniest places on earth – both Upper Egypt and Arizona receive more than 4,000 hours of bright sunshine annually. They are also subject to great extremes of temperature. Due to the intensity of solar radiation, air temperatures in the shade often reach 45°C by mid-afternoon in the summer but fall rapidly after dusk as a result of

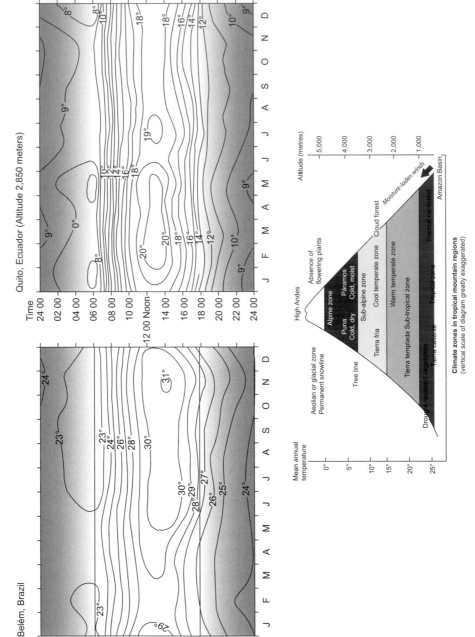

Figure 4.4 Tropical lowland and highland climates. The thermoisopleths (lines of equal temperature) on the charts for Belém and Quito indicate average variations in air temperature (° C) during the day throughout the year. As both cities are situated on the Equator, seasonal variations in temperature are very small compared to the differences between day and night. This is evident in the chart for Quito (upper right), where the close spacing of the thermoisopleths indicates a rapid rise in temperature after sunrise. (*Source:* Adapted from Trewartha (1954): 243, 271)

radiation from the ground to the clear night sky; during the winter months frost may occasionally be recorded before dawn. The relative humidity is generally very low during the daytime (see the *climograph* for Aswan in Figure 4.3). The main exceptions are coastal areas, particularly those adjoining an enclosed sea where humidity is high due to evaporation from the water surface. Very little of this moisture is able to rise to produce rainfall, so that summers in places like Aden and Bahrain are particularly oppressive. The western coasts of continents in these latitudes, flanked by cold ocean currents, normally experience much milder temperatures and a good deal of mist; the rainless Atacama and Namib Deserts are striking examples. Here the *upwelling* of cold water from the ocean depths is associated with strong offshore winds. These provide world-class conditions for surfing, although sea temperatures may be 20°C lower than air temperatures on the beaches.

In the heat of a desert summer, the dryness of the air, aggravated by strong dust-laden winds, results in the rapid evaporation of moisture from the skin. To prevent dehydration, a high daily intake of water is necessary, ranging from 5 litres when at rest in the shade to an impressive 24 litres for hard physical activity while exposed to the sun. The intense glare from the sky can cause eye disorders. The clothing most suited to the climate is loose fitting, to allow evaporative cooling from the skin; the material should be of close texture and moderate thickness. It should also be light in colour to reflect radiation, and cover as much of the body as possible. A variety of shading, cooling and insulation devices have traditionally been used by architects in hot dry regions to even out the daily variations of temperature and reduce the impact of solar radiation.

Areas of sand dune devoid of vegetation in fact account for only a small proportion of the desert regions, which support a surprising variety of plant and animal life adapted to drought conditions. Strong winds and flash floods after the sporadic rains have, over the millennia, produced many spectacular landforms by erosion. In the places where ground water is available the vegetation can be luxuriant, and some of these oases can support large urban communities on the basis of complex irrigation systems.

The more accessible areas of the deserts are increasingly sought after by tourists, who value the space, the winter sunshine, and the scenery which they can offer. At night, the stars shine with a clarity no longer experienced in Europe, where 'light pollution' from brightly lit urban areas and motorways is the norm. Some dry regions such as Arizona are perceived to have a healthy climate free of respiratory diseases, whereas in the irrigated areas of the Sahara and parts of the Middle East there is a substantial risk of malaria. Tourism development has taken place in those regions where adequate supplies of water and power can be provided at reasonable cost and where good external communications are available from the main tourist generating countries. Coastal areas generally have the best prospects as water can be obtained from the sea by desalinisation, although this could be prohibitively expensive for countries deficient in exportable resources such as petroleum.

The warm climates (zone 3)

Situated mainly between latitudes 25° and 40°, these regions come under the influence of air masses of tropical origin in summer and the westerly winds of middle latitudes in winter. Unlike the tropics, there is a definite cool season, but winters are rarely cold enough to prevent outdoor activities such as golf and tennis from being enjoyed in comfort. One standard layer of clothing (or 1 clo of thermal resistance, equivalent in insulation value to a business suit) is sufficient for average winter temperatures that range between 10°C and 20°C. Most of the zone is actually too cool for beach tourism in winter, despite the impression given by some 'winter sun' holiday brochures. The main exceptions are the Canary Islands, Madeira, southern Florida and Bermuda, which can be described as 'subtropical'.

Within this zone the Mediterranean climate, with its dry summers and abundant sunshine, acts as a strong 'pull' factor, since it offers the best all-round conditions for most types of tourism and outdoor recreation. As the name implies, this climate is best developed around the Mediterranean Sea, which allows the influence of the Atlantic Ocean to penetrate as far as south-west Asia. It is also found in California and to a lesser extent, in equivalent latitudes of the Southern Hemisphere. During the autumn and winter months these regions lie in the path of depressions which bring a good deal of rain. The summers are very warm, although the afternoon heat is moderated by sea breezes and fairly low humidity, while the nights are pleasantly cool. Lack of rain causes problems in ensuring adequate water and power supplies to meet the needs of agriculture, local communities and tourism, aggravated by the growing demand for golf courses, aqua-parks, and for second or retirement homes. The dry evergreen vegetation characteristic of these climatic conditions is vulnerable to devastating fires. With climate change, more frequent episodes of extreme summer heat, combined with the effects of air and water pollution, will probably make the Mediterranean resorts much less attractive for foreign holidaymakers from northern Europe, although prospects for tourism in the 'shoulder season' months in spring and autumn might improve.

On the eastern margins of the continents in these latitudes, the warm temperate, humid summer climate zone differs from the Mediterranean in having adequate rainfall throughout the year. In some regions, notably southern China and Japan, summer is the rainy season and winters are relatively dry, thanks to the monsoon. Summers can be oppressive due to the high humidity, and there is generally more cloud cover than in the Mediterranean. If less than ideal for tourism, the prevailing warm moist conditions are very favourable for agriculture.

Case study 4.2

Mega-fires: Symptom of climate change or man-made disaster?

A lethal combination of high temperatures (over 30°C), high winds (exceeding 30 kilometres per hour) and low humidity (under 30 per cent) breeds devastating wildfires that have grown in ferocity and frequency in recent years. Some claim the fires that occurred in Portugal in the summer of 2006 and in Greece in August 2007 are symptomatic of global warming. Similar fires on a much larger scale are a big problem in the western USA. Here imported grasses have replaced much of the natural scrub vegetation which easily regenerated itself after fire. In the Mediterranean region, tourism and the building of second homes for city-dwellers must share part of the blame. It is even alleged that many of the fires have been set deliberately, to clear land designated as forest for development. In the USA and Australia environmentalists could share some of the responsibility. Conservation practices now discourage the controlled burning of forests, allowing a vast quantity of tinder-dry vegetation to accumulate.

The cool temperate and continental cold winter climates (zones 4 and 5)

Countries in middle latitudes are significant mainly as generating areas for sun-seeking tourism. Yet it was in the cool temperate zone that the beach holiday was invented in the nineteenth century, although sea temperatures rarely exceed 20°C during the summer months. Nowadays many of these 'cold water' destinations, such as the Isle of Man, are re-inventing themselves to meet the challenge of warmer, sunnier climates, by diversifying their tourism product and investing in all-weather attractions. Climate change should result in a longer and more reliable holiday season, particularly benefiting domestic tourism.

The main difference between the maritime climates on the western margins of the continents and the continental climates of their heartlands and eastern margins in these latitudes is the relative mildness of winter in the west compared to its severity elsewhere. In Europe the prevailing westerlies and their associated depressions can penetrate far to the east, in the absence of any significant north-to-south mountain barrier. It is therefore difficult to draw any meaningful boundary between the maritime climate of Western Europe, best exemplified by the British Isles, and the continental climate of Eastern Europe. Indeed, anticyclones centred over Scandinavia can occasionally block the westerlies and bring spells of very cold winter weather to parts of Britain. In North America high mountains run parallel to the west coast, shutting out the moderating influence of the Pacific Ocean and confining mild, moist climatic conditions to a narrow coastal strip. You may find it surprising that the coastal margins of eastern North America and East Asia have a severe winter climate, but this is because the prevailing winds are offshore, bringing very cold air from the continental heartlands. The Atlantic and Pacific Oceans do have a slight warming effect, and this is sufficient to trigger heavy snowfalls in the mountains of New England and northern Japan. The situation is quite different at equivalent latitudes in the Southern Hemisphere where there are vast expanses of ocean, interrupted only by the peninsula of Patagonia and the islands of Tasmania and New Zealand. These experience a maritime climate which is generally milder, more equable and certainly less prone to air pollution than the British Isles.

In the maritime or cool temperate zone average winter temperatures range from 0°C to 10°C, and there is little snowfall except on high ground. Two standard layers of clothing (1.6 clos) are normally sufficient for these conditions. However, the mild temperatures are often associated with overcast skies, drizzle, fog and strong winds. Due to the continual progression of warm and cold fronts, the weather is very changeable. Rainfall is generally adequate at all seasons, and it is often excessive on west-facing coasts and mountain slopes. Summers tend to be rather cool and cloudy, with maximum temperatures rarely exceeding 25°C. Such a climate is invigorating, and is better suited to the more active forms of outdoor recreation.

Continental climates in mid-latitudes show much greater seasonal contrasts in temperature. Winter temperatures are below 0°C (32°F) for several months, so that snow, icy roads and frozen waterways are to be expected – and dealt with – as a matter of course. Buildings are well insulated and in some regions have traditionally been designed to withstand heavy snowfalls. Winter clothing consists of three standard layers (equivalent to 2 clos) separated by 6 mm of trapped insulating air. An overcoat, adequate head covering and protection for the extremities are essential at these low temperatures. However the winter weather is generally more settled, due to the prevailing anticyclonic conditions, than in the cool temperate zone. This provides opportunities for a variety of snow-based activities such as cross-country skiing and snowmobiling. Summers are appreciably warmer than in the British Isles with maximum temperatures often exceeding 25°C; nevertheless a good deal of rain falls during this season and hailstorms are frequent. Autumn in forested areas is a colourful season and is characterised by crisp, stimulating weather.

The continental heartlands of North America and Asia have little or no rainfall due to the 'rain shadow' effect of mountain barriers. These mid-latitude deserts, such as the

Gobi of Mongolia, differ from those of the hot dry zone in the severity of the winter climate.

Mid-latitude highland climates

In middle latitudes both the permanent snowline and the tree line in mountain regions such as the Alps and Rockies are at much lower altitudes than is the case in the tropics, providing favourable conditions for skiing. The upper ski slopes are generally located in the alpine zone above the tree line, and while those resorts situated above 1,500 metres in the forested sub-alpine zone have a reliable snow season, many in the Alps are at much lower altitudes. During the winter months, the upper mountain slopes are often much warmer and sunnier than the valleys, due to the temperature inversions that occur under anticyclonic conditions in mountain regions.

The cold damp climates (zone 6)

Small in terms of land area, these maritime climates are dominated by the permanent low pressure belts over the North Atlantic, North Pacific and Southern Oceans, which generate a great deal of stormy weather throughout the year. The islands situated here receive less sunshine than any other part of the world, while temperatures rarely fall below −5°C in winter or rise much above 10°C in summer. The climate is too cold and windy for tree growth and there is much boggy terrain due to the constant precipitation. Rain and wet snow can easily penetrate clothing, removing its insulating qualities. Heat loss also occurs from the feet if these are not adequately protected from the waterlogged ground, causing serious skin damage or 'trench foot'. Suitable clothing for these bleak conditions consists of material with small air spaces that prevents heat loss due to the wind and at the same time allows the skin to 'breathe' freely, plus a water-repellent layer that can be easily removed. Despite the unfavourable climate, the rich bird and marine life of the Faeroes, Aleutians and the islands of the Southern Ocean offer potential for ecotourism.

The cold dry climates (zone 7)

Until the late twentieth century the polar regions were the frontier of tourism; while the 'Near Arctic' fringes in northern Scandinavia and Alaska had been developed to an extent, the 'High Arctic' and Antarctica remained the preserve of scientific expeditions.

Cold climates, where the mean annual temperature is below 0°C, account for a third of the Earth's land surface, including 10 per cent (mainly in Antarctica and Greenland) which is permanently ice covered. Although temperatures in the sub-arctic regions of North America and Eurasia can reach 25°C during the brief summers, the length, darkness and extreme severity of the winters is the dominant fact of life in high latitudes. In the polar regions the sun's rays are oblique even in summer, but expeditioners must guard against the risk of snow blindness due to the strong incident radiation. In the Southern Hemisphere, Antarctica has an even colder climate than those northern lands adjoining the Arctic Ocean. Although the icy seas of both polar zones are surprisingly rich in marine life, their ecosystems are distinct. The Arctic islands support a variety of land mammals as well as marine species, with the polar bear at the top of the food chain. In contrast, the interior of Antarctica is virtually sterile and only its coastal fringes provide a habitat for penguins and other bird life.

Provided the weather is calm, temperatures as low as −40°C are bearable, as the air is very dry. However this causes dehydration, as moisture is lost from the body to the atmosphere in exhaled breath, and this, together with heat emitted from vehicles and buildings, produces 'human habitation fog', as in the urban areas of Siberia. Extreme cold has a punishing effect on people and materials; for example steel becomes brittle and shatters like glass. Under blizzard conditions exposed flesh can freeze in less than a minute. The extremities have to be protected from frostbite; the ears by a fur-lined hood and the hands and feet by two insulating layers. Such cold weather clothing tends to be bulky as several layers are needed under a wind-proof parka, and with physical exertion large quantities of sweat are produced. The clothing should therefore fit fairly loosely when active, but can be drawn in when at rest to trap insulating air. However, no amount of clothing will keep an inactive person comfortable for long at temperatures much below −15°C, and high energy foods are essential (over 5,000 calories a day may be needed).

Throughout the Arctic and most of the sub-arctic regions the summers are not warm enough to thaw the ground to more than a shallow depth, so that the moisture beneath this 'active layer' remains frozen year-round. This condition, known as *permafrost*, presents costly engineering problems. Buildings and even utilities must be insulated from contact with the ground, otherwise the permafrost would melt and the structure subside. Because moisture cannot drain down, there is much waterlogged ground in summer, attracting swarms of biting insects. The southern part of the sub-arctic zone is dominated by vast, rather sombre forests of spruce, birch, or larch, trees that can withstand a short growing season and poor soils. As summer temperatures decrease these are replaced by the stunted vegetation of the tundra and the polar deserts of the High Arctic.

Fur trapping has long been the only source of income for the native peoples of Alaska, northern Canada, Greenland and Siberia. Tourism offers them alternative employment as guides and outfitters to groups of hunters, anglers and expeditioners from the south. There is also a growing demand for ecotourism in the polar regions, particularly from the USA. Although the market for this continues to be small, there is evidence that even minimal numbers of tourists can have a damaging effect on the fragile ecosystems, even where their movements are strictly controlled, as in Antarctica. This is a problem simply because the ecosystem takes such a long time to recover from any damage.

Polar ecosystems are also under threat from climate change, particularly in the Arctic, where temperatures have risen by twice the world average. The icecaps of Greenland and Antarctica, together with the year-round floating pack ice of the Arctic and Southern Oceans, make up most of the Earth's *cryosphere* and as such, form an important part of the global climate system as they reflect solar energy rather than absorbing it. The decline in the thickness and extent of the Arctic sea ice in summer means that greater expanses of open water are exposed to the warming influence of direct sunlight, causing further melting. Glaciers in Alaska and northern Canada have retreated considerably since the 1970s, while the flow of melt water from the Greenland icecap has increased significantly. Furthermore, much of the permafrost of Alaska and Siberia is thawing, releasing methane and CO_2 into the atmosphere and amplifying the 'greenhouse effect'. In Antarctica the evidence for climate change is less apparent, with the exception of the Antarctic Peninsula.

Summary

* At the world scale, climate is one of the key factors influencing tourism development and holiday travel.

- In developed countries with cold winters and unreliable weather, climate is more likely to be a 'push' factor for recreational tourism than a 'pull' factor. Climatic conditions are determined by latitude, altitude, and the interrelationship of coasts and mountains.
- Climate is made up of several factors, of which temperature and humidity are most significant for human well-being, while others strongly influence particular types of recreation activity.
- Seasonal variation is an important characteristic of most climates and this is used as a basis for classification, so that useful comparisons can be made between different destinations.
- The optimal climate for tourism is the Mediterranean type, but this is particularly vulnerable to the impact of global warming.
- Tour operators are increasingly seeking out 'exotic' locations where conditions are much less favourable. The hot climates, formerly regarded as unhealthy, are now highly regarded as destinations for beach holidays, cultural tourism and ecotourism. The cold climates of high latitudes and high mountain regions are attracting the more adventurous tourists who value the unpolluted natural environment despite its hazards.
- Like other tourism resources, climate is subject to change. It remains to be seen whether these changes will be beneficial to the tourism industry, or to tourists themselves. Some destinations will gain as a result, whereas others, dependent on beach tourism, will lose out. It is certain that tour operators and tourism generally will have to adapt, as the climate is beyond human control.

Assignments

1 Design a chart to compare the length of the beach holiday season (where applicable), and the best months for specific types of outdoor recreation, in the following destinations:
   (a) The Costa del Sol, Spain
   (b) Cornwall, England
   (c) Kenya
   (d) St Moritz, Switzerland
   (e) Napier, New Zealand
   (f) Atlantic City, USA
   (g) Thunder Bay, Canada
   (h) Rio de Janeiro.
2 Design a leaflet giving climate advice and information to a mixed-age group planning to climb Mount Kilimanjaro.
3 Investigate the costs and benefits of developing attractions which depend entirely on creating an artificial climate. Examples might include the 'Tropical Islands' indoor beach complex near Berlin in Germany (website www.my-tropical-islands.com) and 'Ski Dubai' (www.skidxb.com).
4 Discuss how the various stakeholders in tourism, particularly the hotel sector and the airlines, can alleviate the effects of climate change in various parts of the world.

CHAPTER 5

The geography of transport for travel and tourism

Introduction

In Chapter 1, three components of tourism were identified: the tourist-generating area, the tourist destination area and the linkages between them. This chapter introduces some of the basic principles of transport geography and illustrates their application to tourism.

Tourism and transport are inseparable. Tourism is about being elsewhere and transport bridges the gap between origin and destination. We need to consider transport for these reasons:

- In an historic sense transport has developed hand in hand with tourism. Improvements in transport have stimulated tourism and in turn, tourism demand has prompted such transport developments as the growth of charter air services to serve the leisure market.
- Transport renders tourist destinations accessible to their markets in the tourist-generating areas. All tourism depends on access. Indeed accessibility, or the lack of it, can make or break a destination.
- Transport for tourism involves considerable public and private investment and represents a major sector of the tourism industry in terms of employment and revenue generated. Tourism then, is transformed by, and has helped to transform, the world communications map.
- Yet transport also has significant environmental implications – particularly in terms of carbon emissions, and it is important that tourists understand the consequences of their transport choices.

Moreover, transportation is a major industry in its own right, with concerns extending well beyond tourism and influencing most aspects of everyday life. In effect, transport is essential to civilisation.

Principles of interaction

In Chapter 1 the basic principle of spatial interaction between two places was outlined in terms of a supplying area containing a surplus of a commodity and a generating area having a demand for that commodity. In geography this is known as spatial differentiation, with transport linking the two areas. Ullman (1980) has suggested that three main factors are necessary for spatial differentiation and transport development:

1 **Complementarity.** This is a way of saying that places differ from each other and that in one place there is the desire to travel and in the other the ability to satisfy that desire. This complementarity of demand and supply will produce interaction between areas and a transport system will be required. Examples of complementarity are the flows of tourists from north-eastern states of the USA to Florida, or from north west Europe to the Mediterranean.
2 **Intervening opportunities.** While Ullman's idea of complementarity makes interaction possible there may be competing attractions. To take an example, for a resident of Munich wishing to take a summer holiday in a Spanish resort, mainland Spain is closer than one of the Canary Islands. Mainland Spain is therefore an intervening opportunity, even though perfect complementarity exists between Munich and the Canary Islands.
3 **Transferability** or the friction of distance. This refers to the cost (in time and money) of overcoming the distance between two places. If the cost of reaching a destination is too high then even complementarity and lack of intervening opportunities will not persuade movement to take place.

The elements of transport

If interaction does take place a transport system will be needed. Faulks (1990) has identified four basic physical elements in any transport system:

- the way
- the terminal
- the carrying unit
- motive power.

For each *mode* or form of transport the characteristics of these elements vary and it is therefore useful to examine them in turn.

The way

The way is the medium of travel used by the various transport modes. It may be artificial, such as roads, railways, tramways and cableways; it may be a natural way i.e. the air, the sea, lakes and rivers; or it can be a combination of the two, such as inland waterways. The following distinctions are important:

- If the way has to be provided artificially a cost is incurred.
- The cost of the way is influenced by a second distinction: whether the user shares the way with others (for example roads), or has the sole use of a specialised way (such as railways).
- Vehicles on roads and boats on inland waterways are controlled almost exclusively by their drivers or operators. In contrast the movement of aircraft, trains and to some extent shipping is subject to traffic control, signalling or some other navigational aid.

The way is usually the responsibility of an organisation that is independent of transport operators such as the airlines and bus companies. (Examples in the UK would include the Civil Aviation Authority and the Highways Agency.)

The terminal

A terminal gives access to the way for the users, while a terminus is the furthest point to which that system extends – literally the end of the line. Terminals can also act as interchanges where travellers transfer from one mode to another (for example from aircraft to coach/train at an airport, or in the case of the Channel Tunnel, from coach or car to the shuttle train). Terminals vary considerably in size, layout and the amenities they provide, as these are determined by the length and complexity of the journey, and the expectations of passengers. A terminal for riverboat passengers in a Third World country might be little more than a landing stage. International airports on the other hand are often showpieces of modern engineering design, although the traveller rarely experiences a 'sense of place' because of standardisation. A century ago, the monumental railway stations of London, Milan and New York, and the Cherbourg terminal for the great ocean-going liners were the national showpieces of their time.

Table 5.1 The historical development of transport and tourism

Mode of transport	Pre-industrial era	1840–1920	1920–1940	1950	1960–1970	1980–2000	The future
Air			Propeller technology; civil aviation begins; travel is expensive and limited; airships enjoy a brief period of acceptance; basic terminal facilities	Speeds of 400 km/h	Jet aircraft (B707); speeds 800 km/h; cheap fuel; rapid expansion of charter services; development of CRS and GDS	Wide-bodied jets (B747); extended range; fuel efficiency; no increases in speed except for Concorde; extensive terminal services	Hypersonic aircraft; space tourism; global alliances of airlines; new generation jumbo jets with large capacity; increased deregulation
Sea	Sailing vessels	Steamships and packet boats	Ocean liners and cruisers; little competition from air; short sea ferry speed less than 40 km/h with very basic facilities; no increase in speed for passenger liners		Air overtakes shipping on North Atlantic routes; hovercraft and hydrofoils being developed	Fly-cruise established; larger and more comfortable ferries; fast catamarans developed	Amphibious 'ground effect' craft; submarine tourism; themed cruising
Road	Horse-drawn carriages; unpaved roads		Cars achieve speeds of 55 km/h but remain unreliable; coaches develop from charabancs		Cars improve in speed and performance, 100–115 km/h; cars increasingly used for domestic tourism in place of public transport; roads improve; motorways introduced	Speed limits in USA; steep rise in car-ownership rates; urban congestion; green fuel; improved coaches; re-introduction of trams	Urban gridlock; automated road systems; personal rapid transit; demand-responsive transport; resurgence of road-based public transport
Rail		Steam locomotive	'Golden age' of rail; speed exceeds that of cars		Electrification of rail networks; continuous welded tracks	High-speed networks develop in Europe; business products offered; dedicated rail tourism products developed based on nostalgia for steam	Development of medium-haul tourism products; enhanced motive-power technology

Source: Adapted from Cooper et al. (1998, 277)

The carrying unit

Each type of way demands a particular type of carrying unit – aircraft; ships and smaller vessels for waterways; cars, buses/coaches and other vehicles for the roads; and rolling stock for the railways. Aircraft have to be designed to particularly high specifications to ensure safety and comfort, and are therefore costly. Aircraft, ships and road vehicles are flexible to operate compared to trains, monorails and trams, where breakdowns on the track cause extensive delays.

Motive power

The historical development of motive power technology reads almost like a history of tourism, with a marked acceleration of the pace of change after the 1950s (see Table 5.1). Motive power combines with the 'way' and the carrying unit to determine the speed, range and capacity of the transport mode in question.

The motive power for most transport modes is now dependent on petroleum as the energy source. Geology determines that this natural resource is unevenly distributed, with the Middle East supplying almost two-thirds of the total world output. We are facing the possibility of an energy crisis even more severe than that of the early 1970s. Oil reserves are being depleted by competing demands not only from transport but the rest of the global economy. The USA is the world's largest consumer of petroleum, importing 50 per cent of its requirements, and is concerned to secure the flow of oil from the effects of political turmoil in the Middle East by tapping alternative suppliers in the Caspian Basin and the Gulf of Guinea. Heavy oil sources such as the tar sands of northern Canada are becoming commercially viable, but this would release unacceptably high levels of carbon dioxide into the atmosphere. In the meantime Japan and the EU are seeking to harness alternative energy sources, notably hydrogen, but as yet this is not a realistic prospect for transport on a large scale. Another alternative – the development of biofuels, is becoming a controversial issue as there is a danger that the diversion of agricultural land for this purpose will raise food prices.

In terms of the capacity of a transport system, the most important consideration is to find the combination of carrying unit and motive power that can hold the maximum number of passengers while still allowing sufficient utilisation of the transport system. Increasing size does bring its own problems; larger aircraft such as the Airbus A380 for example require reconfigured airport access.

Transport costs and pricing

Transport costs and pricing are fundamental to the geography of tourism. The distinctive cost structure of each mode influences consumer choice and thus determines the volume of traffic on a route. There are two basic types of transport cost:

1 **Social and environmental costs**. These costs are not paid for by the transport operator or user but are borne by the community. An example would be the unquantifiable cost of aircraft noise to residents living near an international airport or the carbon emissions from cars.
2 **Private costs**. Those who operate the transport system pay private costs which are then passed on to the customer as fares. A basic distinction needs to be made here between fixed and variable costs:

(a) Fixed costs (or overheads) are incurred before any passengers are carried or indeed before a carrying unit moves along the 'way'. These costs are 'inescapable' and include items such as interest on capital invested in the system and depreciation of assets. The most important feature of fixed costs is that they do not vary in proportion to the level of traffic on a route, the distance travelled or the numbers of passengers carried. For example the railway track and bed has to be maintained irrespective of the number of trains that use it.

(b) Variable or running costs do depend on the level of service provided, distance travelled and the volume of traffic carried. Here costs include fuel, crew wages and maintenance. These costs are escapable because they are only incurred when the transport system is operating and can be avoided by cancelling services.

Because each mode has a different ratio of fixed to variable costs, the distinction is a very important one. Railways for example have to provide and maintain a track. This means that a railway system has to sustain a high proportion of fixed costs whereas for road transport the fixed costs are low. The outcome is that the cost per passenger-kilometre decreases rapidly for rail but more slowly for road transport. In other words railways are uneconomic if they are only carrying a few passengers, as each one has to make an unacceptably large contribution to fixed costs.

On the other hand road transport is much more competitive as the greater part of the costs are variable, and fleets of buses, coaches or taxis can be deployed more readily to meet changes in demand.

It is interesting to note that the success of low cost carriers in the air transport business is due to their distinctive business model which allows them to significantly reduce the fixed costs of operating (paperless tickets and internet booking for example) whilst also reducing the variable cost by cutting out many services to passengers such as free catering.

In fact the distinction between fixed and variable costs is blurred; for example costs of staffing and equipping a terminal may increase with the volume of traffic. These costs are known as semi-fixed. While we could say that wages are a variable cost, in reality crew have to be retained and paid irrespective of the utilisation of the transport system in the short term. In the longer term staffing can normally be adjusted to the volume of business.

The ratio of fixed to variable costs is an important consideration for transport operators in the tourism business. Compared to many activities, transport has a high proportion of fixed costs. The product is also perishable, because if a seat is not sold on a flight it cannot be stored and sold at a later date. This means that operators must achieve a high utilisation of their systems – if carrying units are idle for long periods they do not make a contribution to fixed costs. Finally, it is important to achieve a high *load factor* (i.e. the number of seats sold compared to the number available).

The link between load factor and pricing is clearly illustrated by the *marginal cost principle*. Using an air-inclusive tour as our example, marginal cost is the additional cost incurred by carrying one extra unit of output (in this case a passenger). The operator determines a load factor that covers the fixed costs of the journey and the variable cost of each passenger carried. If the flight is budgeted to break even at a load factor of 80 per cent, then every passenger carried over this level will incur a small marginal cost, because variable costs are low, and this represents a substantial profit for the tour operator. Unfortunately for the tour operator the opposite also applies – for every passenger below the 80 per cent level a loss will be incurred.

A related problem is the fact that tourism demand tends to be highly peaked on a daily, weekly and annual basis. This means that airline fleets may only be fully utilised at certain times of the year. Both in Europe and North America one solution to this was the creation of the winter holiday market in the late 1960s to utilise idle aircraft and make a contribution to fixed costs. Another solution is to use *differential pricing*. Here operators offer low fares for travel in the off-peak period to increase the traffic at those times. The trend in all transport modes is for fares to match distinctive market segments, each of which have their own travel requirements.

Transport modes, routes and networks

Modes

Each transport mode has different operational characteristics, based on the different ways in which technology is applied to the four elements of any transport system (Table 5.2). Technology determines the appropriateness of the mode for a particular type of journey. It also ensures that some modes overlap in their suitability for the needs of travellers, and this may lead to competition between airlines and surface transport operators on some routes, such as London to Paris. In other cases transport modes are complementary, for example the road or rail links between airports and city centres. Another example would be fly-drive holidays, where the tourist has the advantages of air transport to reach the destination and the convenience of a hired car for touring the holiday area.

> ### Discussion point – environmental considerations and choice of transport mode
> Carbon emissions are a recognised source of global warming, and transport modes used by tourists – particularly cars and aircraft – are known polluters. The question for the future will be whether some forms of transport that are not as polluting, trains for example, will be favoured by tourists over aircraft or the car. The choice is complicated by the fact that companies now offer 'carbon offsetting' services where tourists can purchase say tree planting or low energy light bulbs for the developing world, to 'offset' the carbon they have used during their flight. At the same time, governments may also influence the decision by applying green taxes to cars and aircraft, effectively increasing the cost of their use. In other words, transport choice is both a victim and a vector of climate change.

Routes

Transport routes do not occur in isolation from the physical and economic conditions prevailing in different parts of the world. Mountain ranges, extensive hilly terrain, deep river valleys, waterlogged ground and climatic factors influence their direction, as do the locations of major cities and political boundaries. However, not all modes of transport are equally affected by these factors. For example, mountains do not deflect air transport routes although they will influence the location of airports. In contrast, railways are very much influenced by topographical features. These factors, combined with considerations of technology and investment, ensure that transport routes remain relatively stable channels of movement.

Table 5.2 Characteristics of transport modes

Mode	Way	Carrying unit	Motive power	Advantages	Disadvantages	Significance for tourism
Road	Normally a surfaced road, although 'off road recreational vehicles' are not restricted	Car, bus or coach; low capacity for passengers	Petrol or diesel engine; some use of electric vehicles	Door-to-door flexibility; driver in total control of vehicle; suited to short journeys	Way shared by other users leading to possible congestion	Door-to-door flexibility allows tourist to plan routes; allows carriage of holiday equipment; acts as a link between terminal and destination; acts as mass transport for excursions in holiday areas
Rail	Permanent way, with rails	Passenger carriages; high passenger capacity	Diesel engines (diesel/electric or diesel/hydraulic); also electric or steam locomotives	Sole user of the way allows flexible use of carrying units; suited to medium or long journeys, and to densely populated urban areas; non-polluting	High fixed costs	In mid-nineteenth century opened up areas previously inaccessible for tourism; special carriages can be added for scenic viewing etc. trans-continental routes and scenic lines carry significant volume of tourist traffic
Air	Natural	Aircraft; high passenger capacity	Turbo-fan engines; turbo-prop or piston engine	High speed and range; low fixed costs; suited to long journeys	High fuel consumption and stringent safety regulations make air an expensive mode; high terminal costs	Speed and range opened up most parts of the world for tourism; provided impetus for growth of mass international tourism
Sea	Natural	Ships; can have a high degree of comfort; high passenger capacity	Diesel engine or steam turbine	Low initial investment; suited to either long-distance or short ferry operations	Slow; high labour costs	Confined to cruising (where luxury and comfort can be provided) and ferry traffic

The fact that some modes of transport have a restricted 'way', namely roads, railways and canals, will automatically channel movement. For navigational purposes those modes which use natural ways – the air or the sea – are also channelled and movement does not take place across the whole available surface of the Earth. We can look at transport route systems at a variety of scales:

- At the world scale there is a network of inter-continental air routes, and those countries with a coastline are also linked by the long-haul sea routes (line routes) nowadays used mainly by oil tankers and to transport freight.
- At the regional scale, many countries have nationwide bus, coach and rail services.
- At the local scale there are excursion circuits based on a particular city or resort.

Networks

Each transport network is made up of a series of links (along which flows take place) and nodes (terminals and interchanges). The accessibility of places on a network is of particular interest to geographers as once a node is linked to another it becomes accessible. Scale is important here; at a local scale many places may be highly accessible, but when viewed at the world scale they become relatively inaccessible.

Geographers analyse these networks in a variety of ways:

- The most straightforward technique is a flow map, which shows the volume of traffic on each route. Examination of the map gives a rough indication of major nodes and links.
- A more accurate approach is to analyse the network using *graph theory*. However before this can be done the transport network must be reduced to its basic structure of nodes and links on a *topological* map. Although such a map retains contiguity of relationships, it is not true to scale like the familiar topographic map of an area. A well-known example is the map of the London Underground system, where the different lines are colour coded and straightened out, diagonals are featured, and where the distance between stations is much less important than their relationship to each other on the route network. The principle can be applied to other modes of transport (see Figure 5.1). In theory, the more links there are in a network, the greater the connectivity of that network. In fact even dense transport networks can be badly connected, making some cross-city or cross-country journeys difficult. For example, London south of the River Thames is poorly served by the Underground compared to the central area and the north.

The remainder of this chapter provides a detailed consideration of transport systems for each mode and their relationship to tourist demands.

Air transport

Developments in civil aviation have done most to bring about far-reaching changes in the nature of international tourism and the structure of the travel industry since the Second World War. Few parts of the world are now more than 24 hours flying time from any other part, and it is estimated by the UN World Tourism Organisation that around 20 per cent of international tourists use air transport. The jet aircraft has opened up many formerly remote areas as holiday destinations. Here it is instructive to

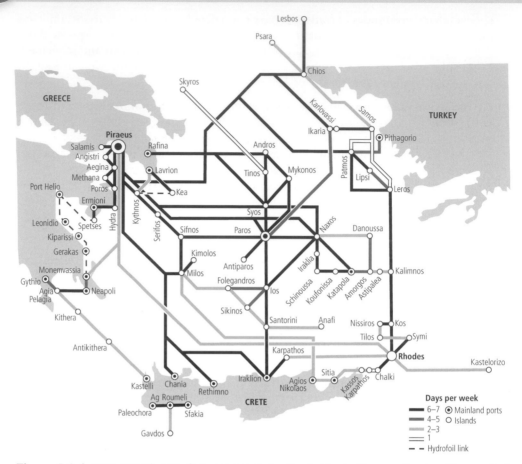

Figure 5.1 A route network map: ferry services to the Greek islands (*Source*: Courtesy Thomas Cook Publishing.)

compare 'Concorde' with the Boeing 747. Although the supersonic airliner captured the public imagination in the last quarter of the twentieth century, it had limited range and capacity, and the high fares ensured that it accounted for only a small share of the market for air travel compared to wide-bodied jets. Concorde was in the last analysis unsustainable for environmental as well as economic reasons. Despite the current massive growth in air travel it is true to say that only a small percentage of the world's population have experienced flying, and even in developed countries surface modes of transport carry much greater volumes of traffic than the airlines. This situation is however changing as low cost carriers make air travel a real option on short haul routes that used to be the preserve of surface transport.

The following are the main advantages of the air transport mode:

- The way allows the aircraft a direct line of flight unimpeded by natural barriers such as mountain ranges, oceans, deserts or jungles.
- Superior speeds can be reached in everyday service.
- Air transport has a high passenger capacity and is ideally suited to journeys of over 500 kilometres, travel over difficult, road-less terrain (as in Papua-New Guinea), and journeys between groups of islands separated by stormy seas from the mainland (such as the Shetlands of Scotland).

Air transport does however have disadvantages:

- It needs a large terminal area that may be some distance from the destination it serves.
- It is expensive due to the large amounts of power expended and the high safety standards demanded.
- Payload restrictions mean that vehicles cannot be carried, in contrast to sea-going ferries and some rail services.
- It has negative environmental impacts. The true cost of air travel for the airlines and their passengers has been masked by the fact that the airlines, unlike other business enterprises, are exempt from certain taxes. The continued rapid growth of air traffic may not be sustainable, given the contribution of aircraft emissions to climate change. It has been estimated that a passenger on a single trans-Atlantic flight contributes as much to global pollution as a motorist driving 16,000 kilometres (10,000 miles) a year.
- Air transport is particularly vulnerable to terrorism and to fluctuating fuel prices.

The world pattern of air routes

The shortest distance between two places lies on a great circle, which drawn on the surface of the globe, divides it into equal hemispheres. Aircraft can utilise *great circle routes* fully because they can ignore physical barriers, with the improvements in range and technical performance that have been achieved since the Second World War. For example the great circle route between Britain and the Far East lies over Greenland and the Arctic Ocean. Aircraft can fly 'above the weather' in the extremely thin air, uniformly cold temperatures and cloudless conditions of the stratosphere at altitudes of between 10,000 and 17,000 metres. In middle latitudes pilots take advantage of westerly winds in the stratosphere that attain speeds as high as 450 kilometres per hour. These *jet streams* reduce the flying time from California to Europe by over an hour compared to the journey in the opposite direction.

However, air routes are influenced not only by the operational characteristics of jet streams but also by safety and security factors. The movement of aircraft, particularly over densely populated countries, is channelled along designated airways. The development of commercial routes is determined by:

- the extent of the demand for air travel;
- adequate ground facilities for the handling of passengers and cargo;
- international agreements.

The Chicago Convention of 1944 defined five freedoms of the air that are put into practice by bilateral agreements between pairs of countries (Figure 5.2). These freedoms are:

- The privilege of using another country's airspace.
- To land in another country for 'technical' reasons.
- The third and fourth freedoms relate to commercial point-to-point traffic between two countries by their respective airlines.
- The fifth freedom allows an airline to pick up and set down passengers in the territory of a country other than its destination.

In many parts of the world these freedoms are greatly affected by international politics, but with the ending of the Cold War commercial considerations have become even more

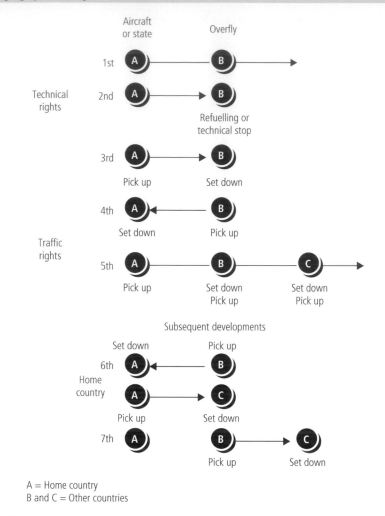

Figure 5.2 The five freedoms of the air

important. For example, as Russia and some other countries have tried to compete with established airlines to gain foreign exchange, new freedoms have emerged. The sixth and seventh freedoms allow an airline to pick up in a country other than the country of origin, take passengers back to its home base or 'hub' and then take them on to another destination. For example, the German airline Lufthansa may pick up passengers in London, then fly them back to their Frankfurt hub where they change planes and are taken on to say, Singapore. This is known as 'hub and spoke' operations and has encouraged the development of hub airports at a regional and intercontinental scale.

International agreements are becoming less important with the deregulation of the air transport system. This means that governments are no longer allowed to control routes, fares and volumes of traffic on flights within and across their borders. The first major country to deregulate was the USA in the late 1970s followed by the EU in the 1990s. Deregulation:

- Encourages competition among airlines.
- Has led to the building of strategic alliances between airlines such as the 'Star Alliance' and the 'One World' alliance.

- Encourages the growth of regional airlines and regional airports.
- Has favoured the development of 'budget' or low cost carriers (LCCs) on busy routes because it not only allows competition on the routes, but also opens up the possibility of using smaller regional airports.

Nevertheless, many countries have yet to agree to an 'open skies' policy for reasons of military security, or to protect the national 'flag-carrier' – usually state-owned and heavily subsidised – from foreign competition.

Discussion point – the impact of low cost carriers on transport routes and choices

Low cost carriers (LCCs), sometimes known as budget, or no frills carriers, have changed the pattern of air transport. By significantly lowering fares they have opened up air travel as an option to markets that otherwise would have used surface transport. In Australia for example, the advent of LCCs has significantly reduced the long haul overland bus services beloved of backpackers. In deregulated skies, the LCCs are able to fly point-to-point to regional airports, so opening up new destinations for tourism. Of course, while this may sound like an advantage for tourist and destination alike, we must remember that more aircraft in the sky has environmental implications.

In class, debate the case for the expansion of low cost carriers.

The routes and tariffs of the world's scheduled international airlines are, to an extent, controlled by the International Air Transport Association (IATA) to which most belong. IATA has divided the world into three Traffic Conference Areas for this purpose (see Figure 5.3).

Most of the world's air traffic is concentrated in three main regions – the eastern part of the USA, Western Europe and East Asia. This is due partly to market forces originating from their vast populations and partly because of the strategic location of these areas. The situation of London is particularly advantageous as it is at the centre of the earth's 'land hemisphere' in which over 90 per cent of the world's population – and an even greater proportion of the world's industrial wealth – are concentrated.

The 'air bridge' between Europe and North America across the North Atlantic is the busiest intercontinental route, linking the greatest concentrations of wealth and industry in the world. The capacity provided by wide-bodied jets and vigorous competition between the airlines has brought fares within reach of the majority of the population of these countries, while the Atlantic has shrunk, metaphorically speaking, to a 'pond' that can be crossed in a few hours.

Time zones

International travel usually necessitates a time change if the journey is in any direction other than due south or north. These differences in time result from the Earth's rotation relative to the sun; at any given moment at one locality it is noon, while half the world away to the east or west it is midnight. The sun appears to us to be travelling from east to west and making one complete circuit of the Earth every 24 hours. Viewed from space, the Earth is in fact making a complete turn on its axis through 360 degrees of longitude. This means that for every 15 degrees of longitude the time is advanced or put back by one hour; places that lie to the east of the Greenwich Meridian have a later hour, those to the west an earlier hour due to this apparent motion of the sun.

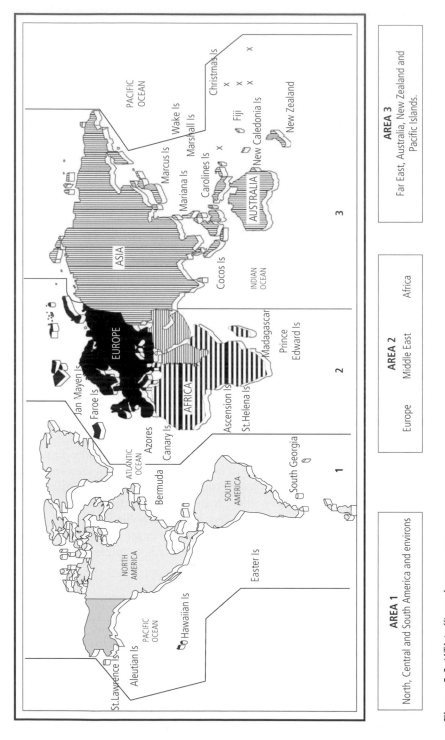

Figure 5.3 IATA traffic conference areas

AREA 1
North, Central and South America and environs

AREA 2

| Europe | Middle East | Africa |

AREA 3
Far East, Australia, New Zealand and Pacific Islands.

Nowadays we take satellite navigation for granted to fix our position, so it is difficult to appreciate the problems that sailors faced until the invention of a reliable timepiece – the chronometer – in the eighteenth century. This made it possible to determine longitude accurately, and was as important as any technological advance in making possible the development of travel and tourism across the globe.

Theoretically every community could choose its own local time. The development of the railways made standardised timetables essential, using an international system of time zones based on the Greenwich Meridian. Since 1884 the world has been divided into 24 time zones in which standard time is arbitrarily applied to wide belts on either side of a particular meridian which is usually a multiple of 15 degrees. Often these correspond to political units rather than strictly following the meridians (for example Paris is one hour ahead of London despite being on the same longitude). A number of countries are too large for one standard time to be conveniently acceptable. Russia has the greatest west to east spread of any country, with no less than eleven time zones, followed by Canada with six, while the contiguous USA (excluding Alaska and Hawaii) has four, namely Eastern, Central, Mountain and Pacific. (In contrast China applies Beijing time to all its territory.) Countries in the Western Hemisphere have time zones that are designated with a minus number as so many hours 'slow' behind Greenwich Mean Time (GMT), which is the standard time on the Greenwich Meridian passing through London. Countries in the Eastern Hemisphere have time zones designated with a plus number as so many hours 'fast' on GMT. Only when it is noon on the Greenwich Meridian is it the same day worldwide; at all other times there is a 24 hour difference between each side of the 180° meridian. In 1884 the International Date Line (IDL) was established as the boundary where each day actually begins at midnight and immediately spreads westwards across the globe. By coincidence the IDL passes conveniently through the world's largest ocean and corresponds to the 180° meridian, except where deviations are necessary to allow certain territories and groups of Pacific islands to have the same calendar day. The calendar on the western (Asian) side of the IDL is always one day ahead of the eastern (American) side.

Whereas travellers by road or rail simply adjust their watches by one hour when crossing time zone boundaries, long-haul air travel presents more of a problem. For example, the time difference between London and Singapore is eight hours, and this needs to be taken into account when calculating the *elapsed flying time* (how long the flight actually takes between London and Singapore). Jet travel across a large number of time zones also causes disruption to the natural rhythms of the human body, which respond to a 24-hour cycle of daylight and darkness. The effect of *jetlag* varies considerably between individual travellers and appears to be more disruptive on long west–east flights than on westbound journeys.

Case study 5.1

Crossing the International Date Line

	When it's 21.00 (9 pm) GMT on Sunday 6 June:	
WEST	International Date Line	EAST
Auckland GMT +12 hours		Los Angeles GMT – 8 hours
Monday 7 June 0900		Sunday 6 June 1300
Earth's rotation -----------------------------		--→

Case study 5.1

The time difference between New Zealand and California is 20 hours. This should explain why you take a day from the calendar (you 'gain' a day) when travelling from west to east across the IDL, and add a day to the calendar (you 'lose' a day) when travelling from east to west.

Now answer the following questions:

1 On Monday 7 June a cruise liner crosses the IDL from east to west en route from Tahiti to Tonga. The calendar should be changed to which new day?
2 At 1200 noon local time on Monday 7 June a patrol aircraft takes off from the Chatham Islands and flies east. Five minutes after crossing the IDL, the pilot reports a vessel engaged in illegal whaling in the Pacific Ocean. Give the approximate time, the day and the date of the incident.

The location of international airports

A major international airport acts as the primary *gateway* to a country for most foreign visitors, so first impressions are important. Such an airport needs several passenger terminals, a cargo terminal, hotels with conference facilities, and convenient interchange with long-stay car parks, bus and rail transport. It provides thousands of jobs in the retail, catering and transport sectors, and has all the problems associated with a large urban area. Also, security has been given a higher profile since 9/11. At the same time passenger terminals increasingly resemble shopping malls, providing a stream of revenue to the airport authorities, and with a captive market of travellers faced with a lengthy 'dwell time' due to delayed or cancelled flights.

The largest jet aircraft in operation need runways at least 3,000 metres in length. In tropical countries, and especially at high altitudes, runways have to be even longer, as the lower density of the air means that jets have to make longer runs to obtain the lift to get airborne. A major airport therefore requires a great deal of land. The physical nature of the site is important; it should be as flat as possible with clear, unobstructed approaches. Such land is not abundant in the small islands that are popular with holidaymakers, or for that matter near many of the world's cities. In Rio de Janeiro, Osaka and Hong Kong airports have been built on land reclaimed from the sea. Runways are aligned so that aircraft can take off against the prevailing wind and airports are located up-wind of large concentrations of industry, which cause smog and poor visibility. The local weather record is therefore important.

At the same time the airport must be in a location that is readily accessible to the large centres of population it is primarily meant to serve. However most are 20 to 30 kilometres distant, while Narita is 50 kilometres from the centre of Tokyo. Investment is needed to construct or improve rapid surface transport links with the city centre to minimise total travel time. This is particularly important for business travellers on short-haul flights. Generally there is a motorway link or in densely populated areas a dedicated high speed railway, separated from the main network.

The growth of air traffic has meant that many airports are now reaching, or have exceeded, their passenger and aircraft capacity for safe and efficient operation. This is beginning to pose a real constraint on the development of air transport. Yet, despite their importance for tourism and the national economy, proposals for new airports, or for airport expansion, are fiercely opposed in developed countries. This is mainly due to the problem of noise pollution and because land is scarce, particularly in Western Europe. Consequently on short and medium haul routes there is a definite role for short take-off and landing (STOL) aircraft. Helicopters require minimal ground facilities but are noisy and expensive to operate, and have only a limited range and capacity. The helicopter is however widely used for premium business travel, and in North America for sightseeing flights, or to reach mountain areas for hiking and skiing that would otherwise be inaccessible. On environmental grounds there is scope for new versions of seaplanes and airships. Airships are slow but are ideally suited for luxury cruising, and unlike their ill-fated predecessors in the 1930s, they would use helium for motive power.

Case study 5.2

The impact of a natural disaster on air transport

The eruption of the Icelandic volcano Eyjafjallajökull in April 2010 is a reminder of the vulnerability of mankind to the raw forces of nature, and the dependence of a global economy on air transport. A plume of fine silica ash was ejected high into the atmosphere, and then carried into the path of the jet stream at an altitude of 8,000 metres over western and northern Europe. This was an unprecedented event, and the International Civil Aviation Authority (ICAO) had recommended a 'zero tolerance' approach to volcanic ash, as even minute quantities of the silica can cause serious damage to jet engines. Following the advice of the UK Meteorological Office, most of European airspace was closed for several days, causing massive disruption to airline operations. According to IATA, this cost the industry 1,700 million dollars, with Lufthansa as one of the airlines most affected. Some smaller airlines, already struggling as the result of the global financial crisis, may yet face bankruptcy. The loss of working hours by well over a million travellers who were delayed in airports around the world would have a significant economic impact. However, this should be compared to the hardships faced by farmers in developing countries such as Kenya who were unable to export their produce to British supermarkets. The effect on the tourism sector of various European countries, such as Spain, was soon felt. The impact was made more severe as a consequence of globalisation, the dependence of countries, particularly Britain, on air transport, and the weak European economy. Other aspects of the shutdown include:

- The piecemeal response by governments in resuming services demonstrated the need for a Europe-wide air traffic control system to replace the existing 27 national systems.
- A reassessment of the risk to aviation by determining safe levels of volcanic ash. The shutdown had been criticised by the airlines as an over-reaction by governments and as a symptom of a risk-averse culture. In the USA, for example, the authorities do not close airspace after volcanic eruptions in Alaska, but allow the airlines to make decisions on the basis of ash forecasts.
- Ferries, car hire companies and rail transport were the main beneficiaries of the crisis as stranded passengers sought alternative ways of getting home.
- Plans for airport expansion, for example at Heathrow, may be put on hold. During the shutdown scientists were able to determine from the decrease in nitrogen oxide emissions that London's airports, rather than its road traffic, are the main factor causing air pollution levels that already exceed EU limits.

A volcanic eruption on a much larger scale – as has occurred several times in Iceland since the eighteenth century – is a distinct possibility, with catastrophic consequences if the ash cloud persists for several months, through its impact on global weather patterns, agriculture and the wider economy.

Land transport

Unlike air transport, which is truly worldwide in its scope, travel by road or rail is constrained to some extent by national boundaries. Although few borders are 'no go areas' like the Iron Curtain of the Cold War era, neither do they provide open access. Following '9/11' surface transport was perceived as safe from terrorism, but this changed with the bombings of the rail networks in Madrid and London when the authorities realised that to implement security measures for surface transport is, if anything, more difficult than it is for air transport. Road and rail transport is subject to a greater degree of control by national governments than the airlines, and is therefore described in more detail in the regional chapters.

Road transport

The main advantage of road transport is the possibility in ideal conditions of door-to-door flexibility, and travel by other transport modes almost invariably begins and ends with a road journey. This, combined with the fact that road vehicles can only carry a small number of passengers and have a relatively low speed, makes them particularly suitable for short to medium distance journeys. Also, the development of recreational vehicles (RVs) allows a form of motorised accommodation. The main disadvantage of road transport is that many users share the way and this can lead to congestion at periods of peak demand. As tourism is subject to annual and weekly peaks this can be a major handicap. Since the Second World War the private car has become the dominant transport mode for most types of tourism, while coach travel accounts for a much smaller share of the holiday market (note that 'coach' means economy class air travel in the USA). Coach operations differ from scheduled bus services in that they are very much part of the tourism industry and provide higher standards of comfort and service. Coach travel not only provides a transfer service at airports and other terminals, but is also used for excursions from resorts, and for touring holidays as a product in its own right.

The main impetus toward an international system of highways has come about through the demands of an increasingly motorised population and the development of long distance coach services and road haulage. The popularity of the car is due to the fact that it can provide comfort, privacy, flexibility in timing, the choice of routes and destinations, and door to door service. The demands of the private car have resulted in a tourism landscape of motels and other drive-in facilities dedicated to personal mobility.

Current trends suggest that there will be around a billion cars worldwide by 2030, with the largest increases taking place in India, China and other Third World countries. Nevertheless, car ownership in most developing countries is a luxury and public transport systems are often rudimentary. Passenger service vehicles may be improvised from former American school buses, jeeps or even trucks. Climatic conditions also affect road transport systems and the type of vehicles that may be used. In large areas of the tropics there are fairly extensive networks of roads made from the laterite subsoil; these are viable during the dry season but impassable after the rains. In sub-arctic regions highways have a gravel surface which is less damaged by frost and thaw than tarmac. Many developing countries have by-passed 'the age of the locomotive', investing heavily in road building to achieve national unity and economic progress. Brazil is one such example, with an extensive network of long-distance bus and coach services on offer. International road projects include the Pan-American Highway system in Latin America and trans-continental routes in Africa and Asia that can be used, when the political situation allows, by overland expeditions and the more adventurous traveller.

In Western Europe and North America a network of motorways or freeways – limited access highways – connects most major cities and industrial areas, though holiday resorts are sometimes less well served. Motorways have shortened journey times and appreciably reduced accident rates. Roads designed especially for sightseeing have been built in scenically attractive coastal and mountain areas. However too much road building, and the development that invariably goes with it, can destroy the very beauty the tourist has come to see.

The private car has brought about greater individual freedom, but at a cost to both society and the environment. Some allege that the West is already characterised by 'hypermobility', implying that many trips for shopping or recreation are unnecessary and could be reduced by a change in lifestyle. Car ownership is unlikely to decline in democratic countries, but car *use* can be reduced in urban areas in a number of ways (for example 'park and ride') by improving access to bus and train services. It is clear, however, that more drastic measures are needed to curb car use in the world's major cities, such as road pricing or congestion charges, if traffic gridlock and episodes of severe air pollution are to be avoided. In the Third World, antiquated diesel buses, 'collective taxis' and taxi-motorcycle combinations (such as the trishaws of South-East Asia) add to the traffic problems. Civic authorities worldwide are investing in 'rapid transit' – automated light railways with a high passenger capacity – such as Bangkok's 'Skytrain' – rather than building urban motorways. The environmental cost of road transport is increasingly understood and governments in some countries are taxing cars according to their carbon emissions whilst manufacturers are now designing 'zero' emission and hybrid cars.

Car use can also be controlled in national parks and other attractions in rural areas by imaginative traffic management schemes. However, the most sustainable forms of transport are cycling and horse riding; these are growing in popularity as activity holidays, although artificial motive power is still needed to reach the destination area and provide logistical support to tour groups. In Europe a network of 'green routes' is being developed for the use of hikers, cyclists and riders; one such example is the revival of the medieval pilgrim route to Santiago de Compostela. In some of the remote mountain regions of the Third World tourists on horseback are arguably preferable to those using four-wheel drive vehicles in terms of their impact on host communities.

Rail transport

In contrast to the road, the railway track is not shared and extra carriages can be added or removed to cope with demand. This is particularly important in holiday areas where special trains may be run. Also special facilities can be provided on rolling stock such as dining cars or viewing cars on scenic routes. The railway's main disadvantage is that the track, signalling and other equipment has to be maintained and paid for by the single user of the way. Providing railway track is particularly expensive as the train can only negotiate gentle gradients. This means that engineering work for railway cuttings, viaducts and tunnels is a major cost consideration, especially on long routes and in mountain regions. Railways are therefore characterised by high fixed costs and a need to utilise the track and rolling stock very efficiently to meet these high costs. The railway's speed and capacity to move large numbers of passengers make it suitable for journeys of 200–500 kilometres between major cities.

In the nineteenth century the introduction of railways revolutionised transport and enabled large numbers of people to travel long distances relatively cheaply. The great trans-continental railways were built before 1914, when there was no serious competition from other modes of transport. The first was the Union Pacific between Chicago and San Francisco, completed in 1869, which opened up the American West to settlement and tourism. The introduction of the Pullman car at the same time allowed long distance journeys to be made in comfort. The Canadian Pacific was built for political as well as economic reasons, as to a large extent was the Australian Trans-continental linking Perth to Sydney. The world's longest line – the Trans-Siberian linking Moscow to Vladivostok – took fifteen years to complete (1891–1905) and still remains the vital lifeline of Siberia.

After the Second World War the railways came under increasing competition from the airlines for long distance traffic and from the private car for short journeys. New railway construction virtually ceased in most countries, but improvements were made to track and steam was replaced as motive power by diesel fuel or electricity. The decline in passenger rail transport has been greatest in the Americas. In France, China and Japan, on the other hand, there has been considerable government investment in applying new technology to the development of high-speed trains and upgrading the trunk lines between major cities. In Western Europe the Channel Tunnel between England and France has encouraged the development of rail-based tourism products such as the 'Eurostar' service between London and Paris/Brussels. There is also a niche market for luxury travel based on nostalgia for the 1920s, with products such as the revived 'Orient Express'. The growth of environmentalism and concern at a future energy crisis may yet prompt a modal switch from congested airspace and roads. It is perhaps ironic that high speed trains – namely the TGV in France – have themselves been opposed by environmentalists.

In mountain regions, specially designed railways have long been used, as in Switzerland, to overcome the problem of steep gradients, and these are tourist attractions in themselves. However, aerial cableways are more versatile and cost-effective, as well as being faster in transporting large numbers of skiers and other tourists.

Water-borne transport

Voyages by sea are slow compared to air travel – an aircraft can make 20 crossings of the Atlantic in the time a ship makes one return journey. By the late 1960s most of the long-haul market on the North Atlantic routes had been lost to the airlines. Also many travellers are badly affected by the six types of motion that characterise a ship in heavy seas. However the advantage of this mode is that:

- Ships expend relatively little power.
- Ships can be built to much larger specifications than any vehicle or aircraft, to carry as many as 10,000 passengers and crew at a time over long distances. Increasing size does bring safety and pollution problems, and few of the world's ports are equipped to accommodate very large ships.
- Ships can also provide a high degree of comfort. This has led to the development of the cruise market, which is travel for travel's sake in 'floating resorts'.
- Ships can be designed as roll-on roll-off ferries accommodating large numbers of motor vehicles – in effect 'floating bridges'. This has led to marketing directed

at motorists using the short sea routes, such as those crossing the English Channel.

Technological advances are beginning to overcome some of the natural disadvantages of sea transport. For example a conventional vessel has to displace a volume of water equivalent to its own weight. This can be partly overcome by vessels using the hydrofoil principle, where the hull is lifted clear of the water by submerged foils acting like aircraft wings, or hovercraft, where the entire vessel uses a cushion of air to keep it clear of the water. So far neither hydrofoils nor hovercraft are used on long ocean voyages due to their vulnerability in rough seas and strong winds, as well as their limited capacity and range of operation. They are successful on short sea crossings where their speed (up to three times that of a conventional ship), manoeuvrability, and fast turn-round in port give them the advantage. Wave-piercing catamarans have proved to be more versatile than hydrofoils or hovercraft on some routes. As a result, hovercraft are being phased out of car ferry services, but their amphibious characteristics are well suited for specialist roles, such as transport in areas of marshy terrain. Hydrofoils cannot carry vehicles, but they have proven advantages operating on lakes such as those of northern Italy, and on the wide waterways of Russia. There is obvious potential for ocean-going high speed craft, combining the advantages of air and sea modes, currently under development.

The world pattern of sea routes

We must make a distinction between the long-haul or line routes plied by shipping and the short sea routes, especially those of Europe and the Mediterranean, where ferries provide vital links in the international movement of travellers by road and rail. Cruising is a separate category as it is essentially a type of holiday and not a point-to-point voyage.

Long-haul routes

Despite having the advantage of the freedom of the high seas outside a country's territorial waters, ships rarely keep to great circle routes. Instead they ply sea-lanes determined by the availability of good harbours en route and which avoid sea areas characterised by storms and ice hazards.

Discussion point

Piracy on the high seas is no longer a subject just for writers of historical adventure stories. How big a threat is piracy to tourism on the world's shipping routes and how should it be dealt with?

Economic considerations are foremost; the most important routes are those linking Europe with its main trading partners. Many ports on the long-haul routes, including Liverpool and Valparaiso, have declined as a result of changing patterns of trade. Tourists and legal emigrants now account for only a small fraction of the business due to competition from the airlines and the high labour costs involved in operating a passenger liner. (Some cargo liners do take up to twelve passengers, and voyages on these ships attract a significant niche market in the USA.) The Panama and Suez Canals are vital links between the oceans on the line routes, avoiding a much longer voyage around Cape Horn or the Cape of Good Hope. Generally speaking, international regulations on shipping have been less effective than for civil aviation. Many ship owners operate under 'flags of convenience' to avoid strict adherence to safety standards and labour laws in their countries of origin.

Short sea routes

Passenger traffic on the short sea routes is increasing rapidly throughout Western Europe largely as the result of the popularity of motoring holidays and the growth of trade between the countries of the EU. The introduction of roll-on roll-off facilities has enabled ports on these routes to handle a much greater volume of cars, coaches and trucks, and most ferries now operate throughout the year with greatly improved standards of comfort and service. The opening of the Channel Tunnel in 1994 caused shipping companies to transfer investment to the western English Channel. Ferries are often the only transport option available to groups of small or remote islands where airports may be few and far between. In the case of the Aegean Islands of Greece, a popular holiday destination, large capacity ferries provide a link to the mainland ports, while smaller vessels offer an inter-island service, especially during the peak summer season. Services making greater use of hydrofoils connect the many islands along the Adriatic coast of Croatia. In the case of Hawaii, however, inter-island ferries have long been replaced by air services. In island nations of the Third World such as the Philippines, ferries are popular due to their low fares, although safety standards are below those considered acceptable in Western countries. Ferries are not widely used by business travellers for whom time is money; one notable exception is the jetfoil service linking Hong Kong to Macau.

Discussion point

Western countries are too dependent on air transport. In the near future people may re-discover the benefits of 'slow travel' by train, ship, seaplane or airship, where the journey becomes a positive and enjoyable part of the travel experience, in much the same way as 'slow food' is now an important part of the dining experience. In class, debate this proposition.

Cruising

The chartering of ships for inclusive tours began in the 1860s. Prior to the Second World War such cruises typically lasted for several months and catered exclusively for upper income groups with abundant leisure and wealth. The sea voyage, often undertaken for health reasons, was more important than the places visited. Faced with increasing competition from the airlines in the 1950s, ship owners diversified from operating passenger liners into cruising, although this was not an easy transition as the ships were often unsuitable. Few ports of call can accommodate 30,000 tonne vessels.

The introduction of *fly-cruising* in the 1960s was important as it allowed the cruise ship to be based at a port in the destination region, so that clients no longer had to make a long, possibly stormy voyage from a port in their home country. The cruise market has proved resistant to recession with a loyal, repeat clientele. There has been massive investment in large purpose-built cruise ships, designed with a great deal of open deck space for warm water voyages. As well as a high standard of service and accommodation, a variety of sports, activities and entertainment are available. At the same time prices have fallen and there are more passengers in the younger age groups, so that cruising is less of a 'grey market' than in the past. Themed and special interest cruises are increasingly promoted as the ship provides an ideal viewing platform. For example, there are an increasing number of cruises to Antarctica and the Arctic Ocean, and whale and dolphin watching are popular activities in many parts of the world, but these are controversial in view of their possible ecological impact.

The Caribbean is the most popular cruising destination, due to its location close to the North American market, the warm climate and the wide variety of scenery offered by the islands. The two other main cruising destinations are the Mediterranean and the Far East/Pacific. The North European market dominates cruising in the Mediterranean, where many ports of great cultural, historic and natural interest can be visited on shore excursions. The western Pacific and South China Sea are mainly popular with the Australians and the Japanese.

Areas for summer cruises include the Baltic and Norwegian coast in northern Europe, and the even more spectacular coastline of British Columbia and Alaska in North America.

Ports

There are relatively few seaports with deepwater harbours, and most are located on river estuaries where improvements are necessary to accommodate modern shipping. For example the English Channel port of Poole boasts one of the world's largest natural harbours and has shown impressive growth as a container port and ferry terminal. However shipping is restricted to a narrow channel less than 10 metres in depth that requires constant dredging. Ports need considerable investment in terminal facilities and improved transport links with major cities in the hinterland. The popularity of leisure sailing may involve conflicts of use, justifying the development of purpose-built marinas, where yachts can be safely moored and serviced in a location separate from the commercial activities of the port.

Inland waterways

In pre-industrial times rivers were used wherever possible by merchants and other travellers in preference to the hazards of the road. Improvements to these natural waterways, and the development of canals in the eighteenth century, provided cities located in the interior with a commercial route to the sea, but locks and other engineering devices were needed to ensure constant water levels. Most inland waterways are now used as a recreational resource (such as the narrow canals of Britain). Waterbuses have an important role in a few places with an extensive river or canal waterfront. At the regional scale the world's great rivers serve as a lifeline for many communities. Cruises on the Rhine, Danube and the Nile have been part of the international tourism scene since the nineteenth century, and in recent years the Volga, Yangtze, Mekong and Amazon have been promoted as river cruise destinations.

Transport integration

Travellers on complex journeys suffer from the lack of co-ordination between transport operators as regards timetables and the siting of terminals, and this causes frequent delays. An integrated transport system would make travel much more convenient. In a wider sense transport needs to be more closely integrated with other issues affecting tourism in policy making. At the international scale airlines are seldom concerned with the environmental impact of their operations, although British Airways' 'Tourism for Tomorrow' awards are a notable exception. At the national scale few countries have an agency that co-ordinates policies on say, highway planning with the demands from the tourism industry. At the local scale transport facilities should be designed as part of the leisure environment; the monorail serving Darling Harbour in Sydney is a good example.

Summary

- Transport satisfies a need for spatial integration between two places, which can be explained by the principles of complementarity, intervening opportunity and transferability.
- A transport system consists in general terms of four basic physical elements: a way, a terminal, a carrying unit and motive power.
- There are as yet few alternative sources to petroleum as an energy source.
- Increased mobility is an advantage to the individual and the economy, but transport development takes place at a cost to the community. The fixed and variable costs of the transport system are borne by the operators and the users, while the cost structure determines the suitability of a particular transport mode for different types of journey.
- Transport routes are determined by economic considerations, the nature of the way, or navigational convenience.
- The development of rapid means of communication, especially in civil aviation, has done much to revolutionise the scale and structure of the travel industry.
- It has also meant that almost all countries have adopted a system of time measurement based on the Greenwich Meridian.
- Airports are closely integrated with surface forms of transport, but the expansion of major international airports leads to demands on scarce land, energy and human resources that are increasingly difficult to resolve.
- Airlines and shipping are part of worldwide networks that are based on market forces and which need to be examined on an international scale. This is less true of road and rail transport operators which are subject to more scrutiny by national governments and therefore best dealt with on a country by country basis.
- The private car is the dominant mode in domestic tourism, while coaches and some forms of rail transport have significant roles in reducing the environmental impact of car use.
- In shipping we need to distinguish between the long-haul routes that have long ceased to carry much passenger traffic, and the short sea routes used mainly by holiday motorists.
- Some forms of transport such as the hydrofoil have highly specialised roles, while cruising is a type of holiday rather than a means of transport in the true sense.

Assignments

1 Explain why airport expansion in developed countries with a democratic form of government is often a controversial issue.

2 Suggest transport solutions for the following situations:
   - A method of crossing a deep ravine in a forested mountain region in the tropics.
   - A system capable of moving very large numbers of people efficiently in a densely populated metropolitan area.
   - A system capable of operating efficiently in a region where winter temperatures regularly fall below −30° C in winter and rise above 20° C in summer.

3 Describe the elements of transport as applied to a particular ferry route. (A diagram might be useful.)

4 Compare the advantages and disadvantages of the car with public transport in satisfying the demand for specific types of outdoor recreation (such as surfing, for example).

PART 2

The Regional Geography of Travel and Tourism

Europe

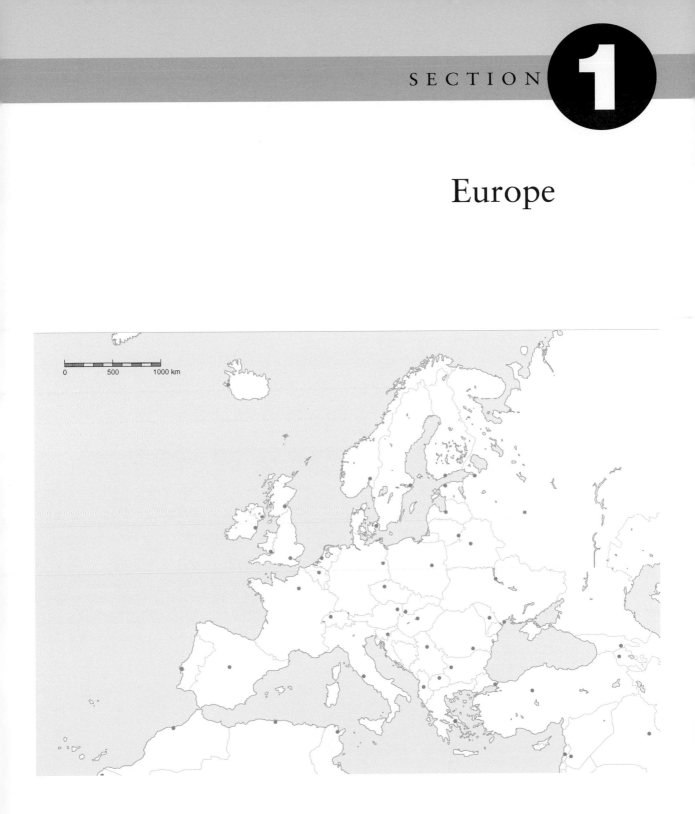

CHAPTER 6

An introduction to the tourism geography of Europe

Introduction

Within relatively narrow physical confines, Europe is a continent of immense economic, social and cultural diversity. In part this diversity explains why Europe has long been a crucible of conflict, culminating in two world wars in the twentieth century, which ended with a civil war in the Balkan region. On the other hand, the devastation of the Second World War brought about a movement towards economic and political integration which is still in progress. Europe is now under economic pressures from both North America and the newly industrialising BRIC countries (Brazil, Russia, India and China), and this is reflected in its failure to maintain market share in international tourism:

- in 1960 Europe accounted for 72 per cent of international tourism arrivals; and
- by 2010 this share had fallen to almost 52 per cent.

Nonetheless, Europe continues to dominate world tourism, despite accounting for only 11 per cent of the world's population and an even smaller share of the total land area. In 2010 it received 477 million of the world's 940 million international tourist arrivals, and accounted for 47 per cent of the world's receipts from international tourism. The strong economies in the region still account for most of the world's top tourist generating countries, dominating the outbound flow of international travel, and also generates massive demand for domestic trips.

Europe is pre-eminent in the world's tourism system for the following reasons:

- Most of the region's economies are in the high mass-consumption stage. The population, though ageing, is in general affluent, mobile, and has a high propensity to travel.
- Europe consists of a rich mosaic of languages, cultural resources and tourist attractions of world calibre.

- The adoption of the single European currency, the Euro, in many European countries has facilitated tourism.
- Europe comprises many relatively small countries in close proximity, encouraging a high volume of short international trips.
- The region's climatic differences are significant, leading since the 1950s to a considerable flow of sun-seeking tourists from northern Europe to the south.
- Europe's tourism infrastructure is mature and of a high standard.
- The tourism sector throughout most of the region is highly developed, and standards of service – though not the best in the world – are good.
- Most European governments have well-funded, competent tourist authorities with marketing and development powers.

With a few striking exceptions, Europe's political and economic structures are stable, providing a safe environment for investment in tourism. Since the 1980s, the dismantling of the Iron Curtain and the opening up of Eastern Europe, along with the advent of the Single European Market and the adoption of the Euro, have removed barriers to tourism movement within Europe. With the admission of ten former Eastern Bloc countries since 2004, the European Union now includes most of the continent.

Physical features

Physically, but not culturally, Europe is a western extension of Asia, a peninsula surrounded on three sides by sea. Its eastern boundary is rather indeterminate, and is in fact straddled by two important nations – Russia and Turkey. Within Europe we can distinguish two major physical/climatic divisions – north and south – separated by a series of mountain ranges such as the Alps.

The dominant feature of Northern Europe is a plain, crossed by many rivers, and extending from southern England to the Urals in Russia, with the remnants of worn-down mountain systems along its periphery. It is on this plain that the major industries and cities are located, and therefore it acts as the source of many tourists to the rest of Europe. Southern Europe on the other hand is hilly or mountainous, containing only small pockets of fertile lowland, and with few inland waterways of any length.

Europe's mountain ranges act as a major influence on weather systems, in the past were barriers to communications, and nowadays are seen as a recreational and tourism resource for both winter sports and 'lakes and mountains' summer holidays. The most important are:

- The **Alps** – a series of high mountain ranges extending in an arc from south-eastern France to Austria and Slovenia. Their great height is due to geologically recent earth movements, while the valleys were widened and deepened by glaciers during the last Ice Age. A number of large lakes were formed as a result of moraines – accumulations of glacial debris – blocking the valleys.
- The **Pyrenees** – the mountain ranges extending from the Bay of Biscay east to the Mediterranean, and forming the boundary between France and Spain.
- The **Balkan Peninsula** consists of a complex system of mountain ranges in south-eastern Europe bordered by the Adriatic, Aegean and Black Seas. Earthquakes are frequent in this region. There is a striking contrast between the coastlands that enjoy a Mediterranean climate, and the interior that experiences harsh winters.
- The **Carpathians** – a series of mountain ranges forming a crescent around the Danubian Plains in the heart of Europe.

- The **Caucasus** lie far to the south east, between the Black Sea and the Caspian (which is not really a sea, but a vast, partially saline lake). These mountains rise to even greater altitudes than the Alps.
- The Kjolen Mountains form the spine of the **Scandinavian Peninsula**. They differ from the other ranges in being geologically stable, the remnants of a much older mountain system than the Alps, and over the ages they have been worn down to a series of high plateaus rather than forming rugged mountain peaks.

Europe's seas also deserve consideration in view of the importance of coastal tourism – in most countries with a coastline more than two thirds of the accommodation stock is found at the seaside. Tourism is however only one of many uses of the coast, with the result that pollution and degradation of the marine ecosystems are serious problems.

This is especially true of the **Mediterranean**, which is virtually an inland sea. Not only are there a number of large industrial cities on the coast but the Mediterranean also attracts over 160 million holidaymakers each summer, far in excess of any other body of water of similar size. In other words, the Mediterranean accounts for only 0.7 per cent of the world's sea area but its shoreline attracts almost 20 per cent of the world's international tourism arrivals. Over 500 rivers flow into this enclosed sea, carrying all manner of pollutants. The natural cleansing action of the sea is reduced by the weakness of the tides, and the water is changed only once in every 90 years, through the Mediterranean's only outlet – the Straits of Gibraltar – to the Atlantic Ocean. The scope for international co-operation to mount clean-up operations and prevent further pollution is limited, as less than half of the shoreline belongs to EU countries. The Mediterranean's reputation for calm weather is a misconception, as it is frequently disturbed by strong regional winds, such as the Sirocco (blowing from the Sahara) and the Mistral.

The importance of the **Baltic Sea** as a major focus for summer tourism is likely to increase as a result of climate change. Like the Mediterranean it is almost enclosed, but the water is brackish rather than saline, and it is rather shallow, so its northern reaches are often ice-covered in winter. It is also the repository of many rivers and much industrial waste, particularly from the countries of the former Eastern Bloc, where environmental controls are less stringent than those of Germany and Scandinavia.

Climatically, Europe is very varied – on the western fringes of the European plain Atlantic influences keep the climate mild, but unpredictable, whilst the further east one travels, the more extreme are the temperatures in both summer and winter. In the mountains long periods of high pressure bring clear skies and excellent visibility, while the Mediterranean climate is judged to be just about perfect for most tourism activities, with hot sunny summers and mild winters. Nonetheless, Europe has not escaped the effects of climate change with many winter sports resorts suffering from a lack of snow and countries in the south of the region experiencing prolonged heat waves in summer.

Cultural features

Europe has resisted the trend toward homogenisation, with national and even regional cultures, languages, and traditions continuing to flourish. These cultural differences are rooted in history and partly determined by language and religion. The most striking differences in life styles, cultural traits and perhaps national temperaments are:

- Those between northern Europe and the 'Latin' south-west, so called because its languages – notably French, Italian, Portuguese and Spanish – are derived from

Latin, the language of the Roman Empire, which once dominated southern Europe, and later the language of the Roman Catholic Church. Whereas the Protestant Reformation of the sixteenth century came to dominate most of northern Europe, it failed to take root south of the Alps.

- Between Western and Eastern Europe the differences go much further back in time than the Cold War division of Europe between Russia and the Western powers between 1945 and 1989. Whereas Roman Catholicism dominated Western Europe in the Middle Ages, the eastern part of the continent was much more influenced by the Orthodox version of Christianity based at Constantinople. In the east, subsequent political and economic development was also disrupted by invaders from Asia. The differences between east and west are shown in their starkest form in the conflict between Catholic Croats, Orthodox Serbs, and Muslims in Bosnia-Herzegovina. In contrast, in Western Europe, the tensions between Catholics and Protestants that culminated in the Thirty Years War (1618–1648), have to a large extent disappeared, with the notable exception of Northern Ireland.

- Many of the mountain regions of Europe contain communities that are culturally different from those of the surrounding lowlands. Their former isolation helped preserve traditional lifestyles, but these are now increasingly under threat, partly as a result of tourism and second-home development by affluent city-dwellers.

A complex history of interaction between the different cultures spanning more than two millennia has left a rich architectural heritage throughout Europe that is now an important tourism resource (see Box 6.1).

Box 6.1 Stages in Europe's cultural development

Timescale	Major developments	Cultural features	Examples
20000 BP	Culmination of the Palaeolithic hunting culture	Cave paintings	Altamira, Lascaux
10000 BP	End of the last **Ice Age**		
5000 BP	Introduction of agriculture and later, metal-working in the **Bronze Age**	Megalithic monuments Minoan civilisation in Crete and Aegean Islands	Stonehenge, Skara Brae, Newgrange, talayots of Minorca Knossos
3000 BP	**Iron Age** **Rise of Classical Greece,** extending throughout the western as well as the eastern Mediterranean	Celtic hill forts Overland trade route in amber linking Baltic to the Mediterranean Temples, theatres	Maiden Castle, Dorset Acropolis, Athens, Taormina, Sicily
30 BC	**Rise of the Roman Empire,** extending literacy and order beyond the Mediterranean to the Rhine and Danube in the north	Road system, bridges, aqueducts, public baths, military fortifications, arenas	Pont du Gard, Nîmes, Alcantará, Ephesus, Hadrian's Wall, Coliseum, the Pantheon Rome, Hadrian's villa at Tivoli

Timescale	Major developments	Cultural features	Examples
500 AD	**The Dark Ages** – a period of cultural regression in western Europe, following the invasion of barbarian tribes from the north and east and the break-up of the Roman Empire.	Romanesque architecture, characterised by churches and monasteries of a simple but robust design.	Sutton Hoo treasure Viking longships The churches on the pilgrim route to Santiago
	In the eastern Mediterranean civilisation continued, based on **Constantinople**	The more elaborate Byzantine style of architecture, which eventually spread to Russia and other parts of eastern Europe	Santa Sophia
1100 AD	**High Middle Ages** – triumph of Catholicism in the West, the Crusades	Gothic style of architecture, originating in northern France, emphasising the vertical (notably soaring spires and an abundance of stained glass) Castles and walled towns, the first universities	Chartres Cathedral
1500 AD	**The Renaissance** – the rediscovery of classical learning – starting in Italy, followed by the global expansion of European power during the Age of Discovery	Classical architecture inspired by the design of ancient Greek and Roman temples, followed by the Baroque style that emphasised colour and exuberant ornamentation	St Peter's, Rome, Vicenza, Versailles
1800 AD	**The Industrial Revolution**	Technological changes resulting in the use of mass produced building materials. Engineering achievements, particularly applied to transport, impressive civic buildings	
2000 AD	**Post-industrial**	Social as well as technological changes have led to a great emphasis on individuality of design in architecture and experimentation in new materials, often expressed in airports and other public buildings	Guggenheim Museum, Bilbao, Millau Viaduct

EUROPE

The Council of Europe based in Strasbourg is the organisation that has been most active in the search for a common European heritage, with a membership that extends beyond the European Union to embrace the entire continent, including Russia. It has designated a number of cultural itineraries or themed routes spanning a number of countries, such as the pilgrim routes to Rome and Santiago de Compostela.

Within contemporary Europe there are striking regional differences in economic development. Geographers have identified a core region extending from Birmingham to Milan where there is a pronounced concentration of industrial wealth, aided by excellent communications. The contrast between this central axis and the peripheral regions may become less evident in the future, and a secondary axis of development is already in evidence along the 'sunbelt' – the north shore of the Mediterranean from Barcelona to Genoa.

Tourism demand

Europe's population exceeds 700 million people and represents a major tourism market for both the region and elsewhere in the world. There are a number of demographic trends impacting upon tourism:

- decreasing propensity to marry;
- increasing diversity of lifestyles and living arrangements;
- a trend to marrying later in life;
- a decline in fertility;
- an increase in the number of divorces;
- an increase in immigration from less developed countries outside Europe, where fertility rates are much higher.

This means that the traditional family holiday will no longer be the norm in many countries, the elderly will become an important consideration in tourism, and also that the European market is not growing as fast as other regions of the world. To some extent, the rise of the eastern European market will offset the slower growth characteristic of Western Europe.

These social and demographic factors have resulted in a complex pattern of tourism demand in Europe, although the methods of collecting tourism statistics do differ between countries, making comparisons difficult. Western Europe takes the lion's share of international tourism with around one third of arrivals, followed by southern Europe, with a share of over a quarter. However, there are clear signs that the traditional flow of tourists from the northern industrial areas to the south is diminishing for the following reasons:

- consumers are tiring of the inclusive-tour format;
- the Mediterranean is becoming increasingly polluted;
- traditional 'sun, sea and sand' holidays are less popular, as people become more aware of the risk of skin cancer;
- competing destinations for other forms of tourism have become increasingly available;
- new destinations are opening up in the east of Europe;
- long-haul destinations are growing in popularity; and
- the adoption of the Euro making what had been reasonably-priced destinations, such as Spain, more expensive.

The bulk of tourism in Europe is generated from within the region and only the USA is a major market from outside it. Most countries are important destinations in their own right but Spain, Italy, and France are clearly in the lead, not just for the region but also for the world as a whole. Estimates suggest that two-thirds of European international tourism is for leisure purposes, around 20 per cent is business travel and 15 per cent is VFR. The car is the dominant mode of transport because of the many short, cross-border trips, followed by air travel.

International tourism is an important feature of the European economy with a redistribution of wealth from north to south, which varies in significance from country to country. For example, in Spain and Portugal tourism is a significant source of export earnings in the form of foreign exchange, yet for the major generators of tourism (such as the Netherlands and Germany) tourism represents only a small percentage of the expenditure on imports, despite the volume of outbound travel. Tourism is therefore a vital ingredient in Mediterranean economies and the fall in arrivals is a major problem for these countries, demanding imaginative solutions. It is also these countries in southern Europe – particularly Portugal, Spain, and Greece – which still have low levels of holiday taking by populations who are less urbanised, and more family-centred than other parts of Europe. Seasonality is a major issue in European tourism, fuelled not only by climate but also by traditions. Although beach tourism (increasingly augmented by sports and activities) still dominates the European product, other sectors of tourism are on the increase. These and other trends include:

- Europeans will continue to take more, but shorter tourism trips;
- short-break city and cultural tourism is growing rapidly;
- traditional north–south holidays are still a significant feature of European tourism, but east–west and west–east travel is growing rapidly;
- significant market segments for the growth of tourism will be those aged over 55 years, and those aged under 25 years of age;
- intra-regional flows of tourism dominate Europe's international tourism, but their share is decreasing;
- the market is moving increasingly towards holidays which involve active pursuits, and/or exposure to local society and culture;
- the popularity of the car for leisure-based trips is decreasing, with an increase in the use of air travel encouraged by the growth of the low cost carriers;
- demand for business tourism in Europe will continue to be strong despite the growth of communication technologies; and
- capacity ceilings are being reached in some Western European countries, whereas countries in eastern and southern Europe have considerable growth potential.

Supply of tourism

Transport

The transport sector in Europe has been heavily influenced by deregulation.

For air transport, deregulation has encouraged the development of regional airports and airlines and is taking pressure from the very busy routes between major cities, and from the north to southern holiday destinations. There are three key trends evident in the air transport sector in Europe:

- the rapid growth of low cost carriers is one result of deregulation and increased competition on routes and they are taking passengers away from the traditional charter airlines;
- congestion in the skies over Europe is likely to become acute, necessitating a more unified system of air traffic control; and
- the impact of 9/11 was severe on Europe's national scheduled airlines.

Discussion point

Some travel commentators have asserted that low cost carriers, and the wide choice of city breaks that are available as a result, have done more to increase a cultural awareness of Europe in countries such as Britain than any number of directives from the European Union. Discuss whether there is any truth in this assertion.

Although deregulation also applies to surface modes of transport, its impact is less obvious, but other events are significant. The cross-Channel ferry industry, for example, has moved its activities to the western Channel to counter the effect of the Channel Tunnel; the European rail network is investing in high-speed routes which will eventually link the major European countries and could conceivably extend into Eastern Europe. Indeed, the continued investment in rail transport will see a gradual switch from road and air to rail travel. Although this is being done partly for environmental reasons it is not clear whether these lines will be cost-effective and they may even create their own pollution problems. For road transport, the disappearance of border controls, which will extend across the region as more countries are drawn into the European Union, will encourage international travel. There is already a network of Continental highways bearing the 'E' designation (for example, E1 running from Le Havre to Sicily and E2 from Paris to Warsaw via Nuremberg). Mountain ranges act as a constraint on overland transport, although the Alps separating northern and southern Europe are no longer a formidable barrier, with a number of tunnels, bridges and passes allowing year-round travel. However, any further road developments in the Alps will exacerbate the environmental problems which are already acute.

Tourist attractions

The range of natural and man-made attractions is impressive and many are of a high quality. Despite the drive to a unified Europe, very significant differences exist between the constituent countries, and this diversity is, in itself, a major part of Europe's attraction to tourists.

- Southern Europe is the most climatically favoured area, characterised by a *pleasure periphery* of resorts in almost every country fringing the Mediterranean with an extension along the Black Sea. Add to this the cultural and heritage attractions of many of these countries – for example, Greece and Italy – and the classic mix of a tourist destination is created. It is therefore doubly tragic that the pollution and low-cost development in much of the Mediterranean has detracted from these natural and cultural attractions.
- The mountains of Europe, extending from the Pyrenees to the Carpathians, are also a major summer and winter destination. They are complemented by the uplands

of northern Europe which tend to cater for a regional or local, rather than an international, market for outdoor recreation.

- The lowlands of Europe offer fewer natural attractions for tourism, but a large number of major cities provide cultural and business opportunities. Theme parks and other market-based attractions have also developed in response to demand from the urban populations of north-western Europe.

Discussion point

Visitors from Asia are mainly attracted to Europe's heritage and cultural attractions, despite the wealth of other resources that are available. Yet many Asian visitors perceive Europe as 'an expensive museum'. Suggest ways in which this perception may be changed, to the benefit of those tourists and the host cities which they visit.

Accommodation

The accommodation and catering sectors are mainly characterised by small businesses throughout Europe; in the UK over one-half of accommodation establishments are independently owned, and in the Netherlands two-thirds have less than 16 rooms. There is however a trend towards dominance by large hotel chains such as the French group Accor. These can take advantage of the opportunities offered by globalisation and an expanding EU to extend their operations all over Europe, including the former Eastern Bloc countries.

The organisation of tourism in Europe

The organisation of tourism in Europe is complex. Each country has its own distinctive administration and traditions that influence both the public and private sector in tourism. Every country in Europe has a national tourism organisation, supported by both regional and local organisations. Generally, the functions of these organisations are to develop and promote tourism, although in some cases their powers are more wide ranging and include the registration and grading of accommodation as well as education and training. There is an identifiable trend towards devolution of tourism powers from the national level to regions, and a move to involve the private sector in the activities of the tourist boards. The individual organisations and their powers are described in the relevant chapters, but since the early 1980s, the European Union has also become involved in the organisation and administration of tourism.

Summary

- Europe is pre-eminent in world tourism representing half of international world arrivals, and has a large outbound and domestic tourism industry. This is because most of the region's economies are either in the high mass-consumption stage or the drive to maturity, so the population, though ageing, is in general affluent, mobile, and has a high propensity to travel.

- Europe also comprises many relatively small countries in close proximity, encouraging a high volume of short international trips.
- The region's climatic differences are significant and have led to a flow of tourists from the industrialised countries of northern Europe to the south.
- In terms of the organisation of tourism in Europe, most governments have well-funded, competent tourist authorities with marketing and development powers and, as the region attempts to compete with other world destination regions, the role of the EU will become increasingly important to tourism.
- Europe's tourism infrastructure is mature and of a high standard, with a fully developed transport network.
- The tourism industry is also highly developed, with the largest regional concentration of accommodation in the world.
- Europe's rich mosaic of culture and physical features produces many tourist attractions of world calibre.

Assignment

Investigate the principle of subsidiarity in the European Union and its application to the tourism sector. Discuss the possible effect of EU regulations on employment, health and safety etc. on the ability of European countries to compete with other destinations.

CHAPTER 7

An introduction to the tourism geography of Britain

Introduction

Geographically, Great Britain and Ireland are the two largest islands in the group known as the British Isles, lying off the north-west coast of Europe. They include two sovereign states – the United Kingdom of Great Britain and Northern Ireland (UK) and the Republic of Ireland. *Britain* comprises the three nations of England, Scotland and Wales, and so excludes Northern Ireland that we cover along with the Republic in Chapter 9. The islands of Guernsey, Jersey, and the Isle of Man are semi-independent states associated with the UK.

Although only a narrow stretch of water separates Britain from the continent of Europe, this has been sufficient to give the British the following characteristics:

- A strong maritime outlook with interests in all parts of the world, while the heritage of the Royal Navy in the defence of the realm, protection of the seas, and exploration, is an important part of Britain's identity and tourist appeal.
- A cultural identity quite different from other west Europeans. The North Sea and English Channel are often stormy, and in the past have acted as a barrier against unwelcome invaders from the mainland of Europe.

The British, with their long tradition of travel and exploration invented holidays in the modern sense, since Britain was the first country to experience the consequences of the Industrial Revolution. The importance of tourism is clearly illustrated by these statistics for 2006:

- overseas arrivals to the UK approached 30 million;
- the British took 59 million trips abroad;
- the British took around 120 million domestic trips; and
- tourism was estimated to support over 2.3 million jobs directly and indirectly, and contribute almost 4.5 per cent of gross domestic product (GDP).

The physical setting for tourism

Britain has a large population relative to its area, although over 85 per cent of this is concentrated in England. Only 11 per cent of the country is actually classified as urban, thanks to strict planning controls. Britain offers great scenic variety, but we can recognise three landscape zones as the physical setting for tourism:

- **The highland zone** includes Central and North Wales, the Southern Uplands, and the Highlands and Islands of Scotland. Here rocks are older, often impermeable, and high rainfall gives leached, infertile soils. The population is thinly scattered and land use is dominated by livestock rearing.
- **The upland zone** includes Exmoor, Dartmoor, the Brecon Beacons, the Black Mountains, and the Pennines; and in Scotland, Caithness, Sutherland, and the Orkneys. Here the rocks are younger, landforms more rounded, and distinctive regional differences are apparent (contrast the Yorkshire Dales with Dartmoor). Britain's national parks are mainly in the highland and upland zones where they have been designated for their natural beauty and characteristic landscapes.
- **The lowlands** nowhere exceed 300 metres in altitude and encompass much of southern and eastern England. The lowlands are warmer and drier, with intensive agriculture and sprawling conurbations dominating land use.

The coasts are of major importance, particularly for domestic tourism. The western coasts are deeply indented and rugged, with sandy coves and many offshore islands, in contrast to the east and south, where smooth, low-lying coasts are typical, with long beaches, spits, chalk cliffs, or dunes. Most of the more attractive stretches of coastline have been given protection as 'Heritage Coasts' and there are plans to designate areas of the sea and sea bed as marine conservation areas.

Climate and weather

The latitudinal extent of the British Isles (from 50° to 60° North) gives a diversity of climatic influences and conditions. The location off the coast of mainland Europe does mean that the climate is tempered by maritime influences, especially in the south-west of England, where moist, mild conditions predominate. The British Isles are a battleground of different air masses and conditions are dependent upon either the nature of the dominant air mass at the time or the wet and stormy weather which results from the 'fronts' where the air masses meet. Low-pressure systems are constantly coming in from the Atlantic, and the western highlands and uplands bear the brunt of these systems, sheltering the lowland zone.

In winter, temperatures are lowest in the north-east of the British Isles and mildest in the south-west, but in summer the gradient changes to west–east, with cooler air temperatures in the west, although bathers should note that sea temperatures are often lower along the North Sea coast, as the prevailing westerly winds are offshore. In the summer, too, sunshine figures are a source of keen competition between resorts. The south coast has the highest average duration of bright sunshine, with the number of sunshine hours decreasing inland, to the north, and with altitude.

If sunshine is the goal of many holidaymakers, precipitation is to be avoided (apart from snow in winter sports resorts). The highest precipitation is found in the higher ground of the west (the Lake District, Wales, and the Scottish Highlands) which, at

2,500 millimetres per year, is about four times as much as parts of eastern England. Precipitation falling as snow is more common in the highland and upland zones, and the colder east. In the Cairngorms in Scotland snow can lie for more than 100 days of the year and this has led to a major development of winter sports in the Aviemore area. Climate statistics can be deceptive and the variety of influences upon weather in the British Isles means that there are considerable differences from the average experience.

Changes in British society since the Second World War

Demand for tourism and recreation in Britain has grown at a phenomenal rate since 1945, not only in terms of volume but also in variety. The cause of this growth is rooted in the social and economic development of Britain since the Second World War; specifically, two major influences can be identified: social/economic and technological.

Social and economic influences

Social and economic changes in Britain have combined to boost demand for both domestic and international tourism. Since 1945 rising per capita incomes have brought higher purchasing power. The 1960s were a particularly prosperous period of high employment in which the first real stirrings of mass demand for holidays abroad were experienced. The following decades suffered the setbacks of energy crises, recession, and unemployment, but even so, real household disposable incomes per head have increased steadily, fuelling demand for tourism.

The dramatic increase in *car ownership* has played its part in revolutionising holidaying habits. Car ownership has increased rapidly over the period and, in 2009, stood at almost 30 million vehicles, and facilities for motorists have grown accordingly. For example, the length of British motorway exceeds 3,500 kilometres bringing many holiday destinations within reach of the conurbations. As a consequence of these developments, the number of passenger-kilometres driven increased considerably. However, rising concerns about the environmental impact of traffic have slowed government road building schemes and attempts are being made to curb the use of the car, especially in the cities, as in London with the introduction of a 'congestion charge' in 2003. Environmental taxes on motorists are also designed to reduce the use of the car and this will impact upon its leisure or non-essential use.

Increased affluence and personal mobility have been paralleled by an increase in both educational levels and access to education, and as a consequence there has been a heightened awareness of opportunities for tourism. In 2009 2.4 million students were in full-time higher education.

The *time available* for holidays has also grown with increased holiday entitlement, three-day weekends, and various flexible-working arrangements providing blocks of time for trips away from home. Through the 1960s, for example, industry and services (such as retailing and banking) moved towards a five-day working week. This in itself is significant for the shorter-holiday market, but for the traditional long holiday, it is the annual entitlement that matters, and this has greatly increased since the Second World War. Since the 1990s, legislation at the European level has increased workers' entitlement to holiday and leisure time.

Perhaps surprisingly, the increase in demand for tourism and recreation has come more from changes in society brought about by the above factors, than by any large increase in the population itself. Indeed, between 1951 and 2001 the population in Britain grew by less than 20 per cent, despite large-scale immigration. More important to tourism is the changing composition of the population. For example, the post-Second World War baby boom produced a generation that demanded tourism and recreation from the late 1970s onwards. Similarly, people are healthier and living longer than previous generations, and almost one third of the population will be over the present retirement age (60/65) by 2030. Given the problem of pensions, most older people may not be able to afford an active, leisured and affluent lifestyle, and the options available to government and society generally, faced with the situation of a declining birth rate and fewer economically active citizens, are limited.

Technology

These changes in society have gone hand in hand with technological innovations (aside from transportation, which we looked at in Chapter 5). For example:

- Breakthroughs in product design have brought a range of leisure goods within reach of the majority of the population (such as fibreglass boats, mountaineering equipment and specialist outdoor clothing).
- Technology, too, through the media and the Internet, has brought awareness of holiday and recreational opportunities to all, specifically through newspaper and magazine travel sections, television and radio programmes featuring holiday opportunities, the guidebooks produced by tourist boards and motoring organisations, and many web sites featuring tourism destinations.
- The Internet and computer reservation systems have empowered both the tourism industry and the consumer to allow the assembly of tailor-made travel itineraries, the formation of on-line travel communities and review sites and rapid response to consumer demand.
- Finally, not only has technology released the work-force from mundane tasks as microprocessors and robot engineering are introduced, but labour-saving devices have also helped to reduce the time spent on household chores and released that time for leisure and tourism.

Discussion point

Since 1990 the growth of the Internet has transformed both the demand for, and supply of tourism in the UK. In addition it has provided destinations and companies with a cheap and effective promotional and information tool. It is interesting that technology experts feel that the technology is running ahead of the tourism sector's ability to design and create content for web sites. Looking at web sites for destinations that you are familiar with, do you agree with this statement?

Demand for tourism in Britain

Overseas visitors

Britain is a major recipient of international tourists in the global scene while nationally tourism is an important earner of foreign currency. Overseas visitors come to Britain for heritage, culture, the countryside, and ethnic reasons. The ebb and flow of tourist movements in and out of Britain is due to the relative strength of sterling against other currencies, the health of the economy, special event attractions, the impact of international and national crises, and the marketing activities of both public and private tourist organisations.

The historical trend

The 1960s. The early 1960s saw between 3 and 4 million overseas visitors coming to Britain, but with the devaluation of sterling in 1967 Britain became a very attractive destination.

The 1970s. The number of overseas visitors had increased to almost 7 million visits by 1970. By the mid-1970s the weakness of the pound against other currencies made Britain the 'bargain basement' of the Western world and arrivals leapt to 11 million. This boom in inbound travel easily outpaced the depressed demand for overseas travel by British residents, and Britain enjoyed a surplus on its balance of payments travel account. In other words, spending by overseas visitors to Britain was greater than spending by British residents overseas. This was compounded by the Queen's Silver Jubilee in 1977, which increased arrivals to 12 million. By 1978 sterling was a stronger currency and Britain was experiencing high inflation.

The 1980s. These latter two factors had the effect of increasing the real price of tourism services and goods in Britain and increased taxation on goods in the early 1980s led to a 'price shock' for overseas visitors. Britain was no longer a cheap destination and both visitor numbers and spending (in real terms) declined accordingly. This led to a deficit on the balance of payments travel account, the first for many years. World economic recession also depressed visits in the early 1980s but an upturn began in 1982, caused by a weaker pound and allied to economic recovery in the main generating areas of Western Europe and North America. Only in 1986 was this growth rate checked by the Pan-Am bombing over Lockerbie, the Chernobyl disaster and the weakening of the US dollar.

The 1990s. This period saw significant events that have profoundly influenced the trend of tourism to the UK. The opening of the Channel Tunnel changed the mode of transport of visitors to the UK and took market share from both air and sea arrivals, whilst deregulation of air travel within Europe and the emergence of budget airlines encouraged the growth of arrivals to regional gateways.

The new millennium. At the beginning of the new millennium, world events – notably 9/11 and the bombing of the London transport system – depressed international travel, while the outbreak of foot and mouth disease in the British countryside also had a negative impact. As a result, overseas visits to the UK fell back to 23 million. Recovery began in 2002 with over 24 million arrivals and by the end of the decade the number approached 30 million. In the new millennium we can recognise the following trends for incoming tourism:

- The origin of overseas visits to Britain is changing. Not only are the sources of travel becoming more diverse, but also visits from all major source areas have increased steadily. Visits from Western Europe form the majority of the market at around two thirds of the total, but are declining. Visits from North America have remained relatively stable at between 15 and 20 per cent of the total whilst new markets such as Eastern Europe have made a major contribution to arrivals over the decade. In the rest of the world, the major markets are Australia, New Zealand, the Middle East, and Japan.

- Length of stay is decreasing.
- Independent travel is increasing.
- Visitor spend is increasing.

Visitor characteristics

Aggregate figures conceal variations in the different segments of incoming tourism:

- Holiday visits grew rapidly up until 1977 (to almost half of total arrivals), but have declined slowly since that date, with considerable annual fluctuations, to reach 32 per cent by 2006.
- Visiting friends and relatives is a reliable and growing segment that has reached a plateau at 29 per cent of total arrivals. This is a particularly important sector of the Scottish market.
- Business travel has also grown steadily over the decade but recession has impacted upon visitation which fell to 22 per cent of total arrivals in 2008.

Within the UK, both the geographical and seasonal distribution of overseas visitors is very concentrated. Geographically, almost 90 per cent of visitors are to England, with Scotland (9 per cent) and Wales (2 per cent) taking much smaller shares. Even within England, the pattern is concentrated on London, which as the capital, international gateway, and world business centre receives almost half of all overseas visits, especially first-time arrivals. However, tourist authorities are anxious to spread the benefits of this spending to other areas by encouraging motoring and touring holidays (especially from Western Europe). Equally, encouraging traffic through the English Channel and North Sea ferry terminals, the Channel Tunnel, and use of regional airports by low cost carriers may reduce the dominance of London. Indeed, there is evidence that these measures are meeting with some success, with Glasgow and Edinburgh increasing their share of overseas visits. Seasonality is less of a problem than before, but the third quarter of the year still accounts for the highest percentage of overseas visitors to Britain.

Around 75 per cent of visitors to Britain arrive by air and 15 per cent by sea, with 10 per cent arriving through the Channel Tunnel. The share of seaborne visits is declining due to:

- competition from the Channel Tunnel;
- growth of budget airlines and regional air services; and
- deregulation of Ireland/UK air services.

British residents' demand for tourism

Britain's tradition of tourism has led to a high level of travel propensity in the population. Around 60 per cent of the British take a holiday in any one year, but, taken over a period of 3 years, this figure rises to 75 per cent as some enter and others leave the market in a particular year. Even so, there is a hard core of those who do not travel, especially the poor and the elderly.

The main growth in tourism has been overseas travel at the expense of the domestic long-holiday market. For the British tourism market as a whole the underlying factors fuelling growth – leisure spending, holiday entitlement, and mobility – continue to rise. However, while outbound tourism continues to grow, domestic tourism can only share in this growth through the trend towards leisure day trips and shorter holidays.

Domestic tourism in Britain

Although domestic tourism accounts for about 6 per cent of consumer spending, it contrasts sharply with international tourism out of Britain in the following ways:

- the length of stay is shorter;
- the level of spending is lower; and
- it is more difficult to measure – in 1989 the four UK national tourist boards launched the United Kingdom Tourism Survey (UKTS), replacing previous surveys.

The historical trend

Holidays in Britain are inextricably linked with disposable income and general economic health:

The 1970s. The decade began with strong demand for domestic holidays in Britain. However, over the decade demand fluctuated and, in the face of changing economic factors, the share of domestic tourism experienced an absolute decline as that of overseas tourism by British residents increased.

The 1980s. Recessions adversely affected demand for domestic tourism and a number of factors came into play. First, domestic tourism is dominated by those in the lower socio-economic groups who are more sensitive to price and changes in income or economic circumstances. Second, the industrial heartlands of the North, the Midlands, Scotland, and South Wales, which traditionally generated high levels of demand for domestic holidays, were particularly badly hit by the recessions. As a consequence, demand for holidays in Welsh and northern resorts fell. Finally, not only did inflation push up the cost of a domestic holiday but also, at the same time, recession bred uncertainty about employment and holiday decisions were delayed. The mid 1980s saw a significant upturn in domestic tourism due to the increased cost of travel overseas, a weak pound, and vigorous promotion of holidays in Britain. Hopes for the continuation of this increase were dashed in the late 1980s/early 1990s as recession and the Gulf War severely reduced domestic volumes and spending across the whole of the UK.

The 1990s and the new millennium. Whilst world events in the new millennium might have been expected to keep the British to holidaying at home, the outbreak of foot and mouth disease rendered large parts of the British countryside out of bounds and the bombing of the London transport system was a deterrent to visit the capital. Nonetheless, the volume of domestic trips grew to over 123 million in 2006. Since the 1990s there have been important structural changes in the domestic tourism market:

- a continued decline in length of stay;
- growth in the market for short holidays;
- growth of business and conference tourism;
- a shift away from traditional coastal destinations towards towns and countryside;
- a response by the coastal resorts to upgrade and reposition their facilities;
- the impact of the financial crisis from 2008 onwards, boosting the appeal of the 'staycation'; and
- an increased volume of trips to friends and relatives.

Visitor characteristics

Aggregate totals do disguise differences between the various sectors in Britain, but an important distinction in the domestic market is between a long holiday (four nights or more) and a short holiday (one to three nights). For some time, the general trend has been a gradual decline in domestic long holidays and an increase in short, often additional, holidays. Clearly, many short holidays are taken as 'additional' holidays to complement the 'main' holiday (which may be taken in Britain or overseas). The generation of domestic holiday trips is broadly proportional to the distribution of population across the British Isles. However, some areas have a relatively high holiday-taking propensity (London and the South-east of England) while others are comparatively low (Scotland, the North-west of England).

England is the dominant domestic holiday destination for the UK with 80 per cent of mainland trips in 2006. Scotland accounts for 11 per cent of trips and Wales 8 per cent, with Northern Ireland approaching 2 per cent of the market. Within England, the West Country is by far the most popular destination. Britain's holiday islands – Guernsey, Jersey, the Isle of Man, and the Isles of Scilly – together account for over 2 million trips a year from the mainland.

Of course, holiday choices are difficult to explain and are subject to the vagaries of changing tastes and fashion. However, the basic principle of spatial interaction is in operation in the domestic market, with a supplying area containing a surplus of a commodity and the tourist-generating area possessing a demand for that commodity. For example, the South of England and the West Country are perceived to be sunny and warm, with their added advantages of an attractive coast, established resorts with a range of amenities, and opportunities for touring. But set against these attractions is the problem of overcoming distance to reach the holiday destination from home.

Domestic tourism demonstrates a clear pattern in time as well as space. The trend towards short, additional holidays has gone some way towards reducing the acute seasonal peaking of domestic holidays, rooted in the timing of school and industrial holidays. Around two-fifths of long holidays begin in July or August, but for short holidays, this figure falls to one-fifth.

The business and conference sector of the domestic market has grown steadily representing 12 per cent of total trips, but 15 per cent of total expenditure. Resorts, towns and cities hotly compete for this lucrative sector across Britain for these reasons:

- it is not concentrated in the summer peak;
- business and conference tourists tend to use serviced accommodation; and
- this type of visitor spends much more per capita than the average holidaymaker.

Demand for overseas travel

The UK consistently features among the world's top five tourist-generating countries. Indeed, the greatest market growth in tourism has been in trips overseas which approached 60 million trips in 2009. Since the 1950s, the holiday sector in particular has exhibited strong growth, especially inclusive tourism to short-haul (mainly Mediterranean) destinations. This growth has been fuelled by:

- competitive pricing of inclusive tours;
- the growth of budget airlines;

- a strong consumer preference for overseas destinations; and
- an increasingly experienced outbound market which can manipulate the Internet to book and create their own trips.

In the future, growth in the market will be by an increase in travel frequency, rather than through newcomers to overseas travel attracted by the low fares offered by budget airlines.

Discussion point

A succession of warm summers, escalating fuel costs and concerns over the impact of travel on the world's climate, allied to fears over terrorism, could mean a renaissance for the UK's tourism destinations. In class, debate whether they are prepared for this and whether they can deliver.

The historical trend

Growth in the holiday sector stems from economic factors, but the activities of the travel trade since the 1950s have brought a holiday overseas within reach of a large percentage of the population. What has happened is that the increased organisation of the travel industry coupled with the growth of travel intermediaries, such as travel agents and tour operators, has taken much of the responsibility of organising a holiday away from the tourist. Add to this sophisticated marketing, pricing, reservations systems and the Internet, and it is clear that the travel industry has done much to convert suppressed demand for a foreign holiday into effective demand. Taking the critical twenty years when growth was at its height, in 1970 only one-third of the population had ever taken a holiday overseas; by 1990 this figure was well over two-thirds. Clearly, this has implications for both products and destinations as the market matures.

The 1970s. Between 1965 and 1972 the real price of inclusive tours fell by 25 per cent, due to increased use of jet aircraft, fierce price competition, and the increased availability of winter holidays. This encouraged demand, only to see it dashed by the oil crisis of 1973/1974 and the bankruptcy of a major tour operator. The mid 1970s saw fluctuations in the numbers of holidays taken overseas as higher oil prices, weak sterling, economic recession, and higher holiday prices took their toll. In the late 1970s, a strong pound, cheaper holidays/air fares, and vigorous marketing increased demand to a growth rate of 20 per cent per annum. At the same time, high inflation pushed up the price of a domestic holiday, and with the British beginning to view the annual holiday as a priority, overseas holidays grew in popularity.

The 1980s. The decade of the 1980s saw virtually uninterrupted growth in overseas holiday trips. Four key underlying causes can be identified:

1 Thanks partly to North Sea oil, Britain was a wealthier country with a relatively strong currency vis-à-vis popular holiday destinations.
2 Real discretionary income rose for those sections of the population with a preference for overseas travel (the young, the upwardly mobile and the higher socio-economic groups).
3 A sophisticated tour operation and distribution system, allied to high spending on promotion, made overseas travel accessible also to lower socio-economic groups.
4 Competitive pricing of inclusive tours.

The 1990s and the new millennium. The market continued to grow into the twenty-first century, despite the setbacks of '9/11' and other world events leaving a considerable deficit on the UK's travel account. The outbound market is influenced by a number of factors:

- acquisition and merger in the tour operator/travel agency sector leading to an increased concentration of capacity in the hands of a few companies;
- the deregulation of European airlines, blurring the distinction between charter and scheduled services and allowing the growth of budget airlines;
- opening of the Channel Tunnel leading to a response by the ferry companies in terms of new ships and routes in the western English Channel;
- effective devaluation of the pound in 1992 when the UK left the European Monetary system;
- introduction of green taxes such as those on air passenger departures;
- introduction of the Euro as European currency;
- increasing use of the Internet to evaluate and book travel; and
- competitive pricing of long-haul destinations such as Florida and the Far East.

Visitor characteristics

The level of spending on overseas trips confirms the high priority given to overseas travel by the British. Examining the reason for the visit, holiday tourism is growing, representing two thirds of trips; business tourism accounts for 15 per cent; and VFR for 12 per cent of trips.

In total, almost three quarters of trips are by air, compared to 16 per cent of trips by sea while almost 10 per cent use the Channel Tunnel. The modal split changed in the 1990s due to the influence of the Channel Tunnel (which provided the first fixed link to the Continent) and European airline deregulation. Holiday arrangement – inclusive tour or independent – has also changed with a growth in independent travel, as the relative share of inclusive tours shrinks and the boundary between the two forms of travel blurs as travellers use the Internet to create their own travel. The fact that a large majority of the British population has experienced a holiday overseas has led to an increased number who feel confident to travel independently. For these travellers, France is the most important destination. However, this new breed of experienced travellers now travels further and to a greater range of countries.

In the new millennium the most popular destinations continue to be Spain, France, Ireland, North America, Italy, and Greece. Clearly, Western Europe dominates, with the USA the only non-European country with considerable drawing power. In line with this and recent trends worldwide, long-haul destinations are a sector showing considerable growth. Business trips have remained buoyant over the decade and trade with EU member states generates a significant volume of surface travel for business purposes.

Key influences that will determine the volume and nature of the UK market for travel overseas in the future are:

- prospects for the UK economy, particularly the financial crisis which began in 2008;
- the UK's relationship with Europe and the Euro;
- changes in consumer habits and attitudes, particularly with regard to green issues; and
- the growing maturity of leisure markets in terms of the products offered and the response of consumers.

The supply of tourism in Britain

The components of tourism

This section examines the various components of tourism in Britain from a geographical viewpoint. Those involved in the industry now have an organisation – the Tourism Alliance – that can represent their views to the government.

Resources

Britain's tourism resource base is remarkably diverse, including a number of national parks and other areas subject to varying degrees of protection under planning law. In England and Wales national parks are required both to preserve their landscapes and to enhance their enjoyment by the public. It is not always easy to balance these objectives, as unlike those of North America and Africa, Britain's national parks contain sizeable communities, most of the land is in private ownership, and to a large extent the landscape has been modified by farming and mining activities over the centuries. Multiple use is also characteristic of the areas managed by the British Forestry Commission, whose primary aim is to reduce the country's dependence on timber imports. The Commission is charged with opening up the forests for recreation and tourism, and it has developed self-catering cabins in holiday areas for this purpose. 'Community forests' have also been designated on the edge of conurbations on land previously used for agriculture and industry. Widening public access to the countryside and Britain's waterways is a controversial issue, with Scotland favouring legislation, whereas England places more emphasis on voluntary agreements with landowners.

Britain also boasts many scenic lakes and reservoirs, but demand for their recreational use outstrips supply. This has led to intensive management of lakes such as Windermere and Lake Bala as well as the Norfolk Broads. Other linear features include rivers and canals, both of which are extensively used for recreation, as are the Heritage Coasts and national hiking trails, such as the Pennine Way. Government provision for tourism and recreation is complemented by conservation trusts and charities, notably the National Trust which has purchased extensive areas of attractive coast and countryside, as well as a large number of historic buildings.

Britain's built heritage includes:

- many ancient monuments, of which Stonehenge is the best known;
- medieval castles, abbeys and cathedrals;
- the great country houses of the landowning class (many of these 'stately homes' are now major attractions with a much wider appeal than simply history-based tourism);
- the examples of Georgian and Regency architecture from the eighteenth and early nineteenth centuries in Britain's spas, seaside resorts, market towns and cities;
- the legacy of the Industrial Revolution. The art and architecture of Victoria's reign are now widely appreciated after a period of neglect, along with its engineering achievements.

Separate government agencies are involved in the protection of the countryside and the conservation of historic buildings and ancient monuments, namely Natural England and English Heritage and their equivalents in Wales and Scotland.

EUROPE

Assignment

Britain's battlefield sites are an important but neglected part of the national heritage as a window on a violent past which includes the Norman Conquest, the Scottish wars of Independence, the Wars of the Roses and the English Civil War. There are often problems of access, inadequate interpretation, and a lack of even basic facilities for visitors. This is not due to a lack of interest in history, as shown by the popularity of staged tournaments and the re-enactment of Civil War battles by volunteer enthusiasts.

1   Plot the location of what you consider to be the most significant battlefields in British history, starting with Stamford Bridge (1066) and ending with Culloden (1746). Give reasons for your choice.
2   Discuss how battlefield sites could be improved as tourist attractions, using specific examples in England, Scotland and the Welsh border country.

Regional landscapes and character feature in the novels of British writers and the marketing of a particular area often capitalises on these literary associations; for example South Tyneside has been promoted for many years as 'Catherine Cookson Country' and Carmarthenshire in Wales as 'Dylan Thomas Country'. However, association with a celebrity (for example Bedfordshire as 'Glenn Miller Country'), a well-known TV series, or a feature film are perhaps less easy to justify. Nevertheless, 'film tourism' is now a major factor in attracting visitors to a number of country houses and other historic places. One example would be tourists following the locations of the Harry Potter films throughout Britain.

In concentrating on heritage, which many criticise as nostalgia for an imagined past in 'theme park Britain', we could easily overlook the major economic contribution made by contemporary Britain's creative industries and achievements in art, music, the media and sport. These are increasingly appreciated worldwide, thanks in part to the status of English as a world language.

Attractions

It is in areas such as national parks and the hinterlands of major cities and resorts that the most successful tourist attractions lie. Since the 1990s, tourist attractions in the UK have received a major funding boost from the Heritage Lottery and Millennium funds, which have directed money to develop new attractions and improve many existing ones. Indeed, these initiatives have begun to transform the leisure landscapes of Britain. The UK has some 6,400 tourist attractions and their very diversity of size, type, and ownership makes classification difficult but, Patmore (1983) identified three basic types:

1   Many attractions simply result from the opening of an existing resource – an ancient monument, stately home or nature reserve.
2   Some attractions have begun to add developments (such as the motor museum and monorail at Beaulieu Palace) to augment the attraction and broaden their appeal. The varying shades of provision in the English and Welsh *country parks* mean that they should also be included in this second category.
3   The third type of attraction is one artificially created for the visitor, including theme parks such as Alton Towers, the London Zoo, or heritage attractions such as the London Dungeon. The government and the tourist boards are anxious to

improve the professionalism of tourist attractions and to diversify the range on offer – which now include coal-mining museums – capitalising on Britain's rich industrial heritage.

Accommodation

Although the major cities account for much of the stock of serviced accommodation, around two-fifths of beds in hotels and guest houses are located at the seaside, especially on the south and south-western coasts of England, and in North Wales. However, much of this accommodation is in outmoded Victorian and Edwardian buildings – establishments that do not meet the aspirations of contemporary holidaymakers. Both the public and private sectors are trying to remedy this problem and ensure that accommodation supply matches demand. The real change in holiday tastes has been for self-catering accommodation; between 1951 and 2001 the proportion of main holidays in England based on self-catering rose from 12 to over 30 per cent. Self-catering developments were initially in holiday camps, later in caravan parks, and more recently in purpose-built leisure complexes with provision for a range of sports and other activities. The first of these all-weather complexes was opened by the Dutch company Centre Parcs in Sherwood Forest. This company has since expanded its operations as well as attracting competitors such as the Oasis holiday village in Whinfell Forest on the edge of the Lake District National Park. At the same time the holiday camps, pioneered by Butlin before the Second World War, have had to upgrade their facilities and reposition themselves in the marketplace as tastes have changed. In major towns and cities, demand from business and overseas travellers keeps bed occupancy rates high. Here provision tends to be in the larger, expensive hotels (often with more than 100 bedrooms).

Accommodation is also dispersed along routeways and in rural areas. Initially, board and lodging for travellers was found on stage-coach routes and later, during the nineteenth century, at railway termini and major seaports. More recently, airports and air terminals have attracted the development of large, quality hotels (as at Heathrow and in west London) and motorway service areas now also offer budget accommodation – the equivalent of the old coaching inns. This heralded the growth of large budget chain hotels – such as Travel Lodge and Premier Inn – across the UK. In rural areas accommodation is concentrated in south-west England, Scotland and Wales. There is a growing demand for farm holidays, self-catering cottages, and 'time-share' developments. It is also the rural areas that bear the brunt of second-home ownership, with social consequences for declining village communities.

Transport

Travellers entering Britain can do so through a variety of gateways, but in fact both air and surface transport networks focus on the south-east of England.

Air. Over 80 per cent of international passengers travelling by air are channelled through the London airports and the major airlines are reluctant to move out from these gateways. Manchester has been identified as the UK's second major airport and Glasgow's international status has stimulated major growth. Airports on Guernsey, Jersey and the Isle of Man complete the network, and although holiday traffic to these islands is not inconsiderable, it has a highly seasonal pattern. Overall, Britain's major airports handled almost 220 million passenger movements in 2009.

Sea. For sea traffic, there is again a concentration of passengers in southern England due to the dominance of cross-Channel ferry routes. Elsewhere there is a diversification of routes such as those from Hull and Harwich on the east coast. A second concentration of routes is from the west coasts of mainland Britain to the Republic of Ireland and Northern Ireland. On the sea routes the upgrading of ships and the introduction of high speed 'catamarans' is a response both to the threat of the Channel Tunnel and the rise in the expectations of travellers.

The Channel Tunnel. The 'Chunnel' opened in 1994 and has not only stimulated new traffic, but also taken traffic from both air and especially sea services to Europe. Its impact is expected to continue as high-speed rail links are developed on the English side of the Tunnel. Interestingly, the response of ferry operators to develop routes in the western English Channel has been less successful than hoped. Other responses have been mergers on the short sea routes, closure of some routes (Newhaven to Dieppe for example) and price competition.

Land Transport. In the domestic holiday market, and for overseas travellers touring Britain, road transport dominates. Since the Second World War the use of the car has become more important than either rail or coach services, as road improvements have been completed and the real cost of motoring has fallen. The 1980 Transport Act revolutionised bus/coach operations in the UK by deregulating services. Coach travel poses a very real alternative to the railways on journeys of up to 400 kilometres and the new generation of luxury coaches have increased passenger numbers for this type of public transport. Privatisation of British Rail in the mid-1990s resulted in train services being operated by a multiplicity of companies while the permanent way and terminals remained the responsibility of a separate organisation. There has been much private sector investment, particularly on some inter-city routes and those serving coastal and inland holiday areas. There are also over 40 small private railways outside the network which are tourist attractions in themselves, trading on nostalgia for the 'age of steam'.

Organisation

Public agencies with responsibility for tourism in Britain play a vital role in shaping the tourist 'product', through their promotional activities and advice to business enterprises. Increasingly, government is 'devolving' these functions from national level to regional and local organisations.

National level

In Britain the 1969 Development of Tourism Act formed three statutory national tourist boards, (English, Scottish, and Wales Tourist Boards) and the British Tourist Authority (BTA) which was given sole responsibility for overseas promotion and any matters of common interest between the national tourist boards. The Scottish and Wales Tourist Boards (STB and WTB) reported to the Scottish Office and the Welsh Office respectively. The Northern Ireland Tourist Board predates these bodies, having been created in 1948.

In the 1990s the administration of tourism throughout mainland Britain was reorganised as a result of changes in the perception of the role of the public sector, and with the devolution of power to Scotland and Wales in 1999 their tourist boards could undertake overseas promotion. In England, the focus has been changed to be more strategic and less operational, with the creation of the English Tourism Council (ETC) from the English Tourist Board, followed by the merger of the ETC with the BTA in 2003 to form VisitBritain, which is primarily a marketing agency for both domestic and international tourism. At ministerial level the Department of Culture, Media and Sport oversees the work of VisitBritain. Guernsey, Jersey, and the Isle of Man each continue to have small, relatively independent boards reporting directly to their island governments.

Regional and local level

The increasing emphasis on devolution is shown by the regional development agencies, which receive tourism funding for development, and across the UK there is a structure of regional tourist boards (RTBs). There are ten RTBs in England, and three regional tourism companies in Wales. In Scotland, a major restructuring at the regional level has given rise to Area Tourist Boards, with enterprise agencies taking responsibility for development. At the local level throughout Britain, county and district councils have considerable powers that they can use for tourism promotion and development. In the next chapter we describe in more detail the tourism resources and attractions for each of Britain's component countries, regions and offshore islands.

Summary

- Britain is a major generator of both domestic and international tourism. Demand for tourism has grown rapidly since the Second World War for social and economic reasons.
- Around 60 per cent of the British population now take a holiday in any one year, but, even so, there is a hard core of those who do not travel.
- The long-established pattern of domestic holidays spent at the seaside is changing with the trend towards shorter holidays.
- The demand by residents of Britain for holidays abroad has increased steadily since the Second World War and the UK is consistently one of the world's top tourist generators. A combination of economic circumstances and the response of the travel industry has converted suppressed demand into effective demand for holidays abroad.
- Britain is a major recipient of overseas tourists on the global scene and this demand is influenced by the relative strength of currencies, the health of the economy, special events, external world events such as '9/11', and the marketing activities of tourist organisations.
- Britain offers a rich variety of landscapes and weather conditions, but the climate is everywhere tempered by maritime influences.
- The main components of tourist supply in Britain are a diversity of attractions from national parks to purpose-built theme parks; a wide accommodation base focused on the coasts and the major cities; and a comprehensive internal transport network, as well as international gateways of global significance, including the major innovation of the Channel Tunnel.
- Tourism in Britain is administered by a newly reorganised structure of organisations involving the private as well as the public sectors.

Assignments

1 Explain how changes in British society since the 1950s have influenced leisure, outdoor recreation and the choice of holiday destination.
2 Describe the various ways the public, private and voluntary sectors protect Britain's coast and countryside.

CHAPTER 8

The regional geography of tourism in Britain

England

England's great variety of scenery is partly due to differences in geology – for example the contrast between chalk downlands, sandstone or limestone ridges, and clay vales. These have not only influenced the shape of the countryside but also the traditional building materials used in rural communities. However, much of the English countryside we see today was the creation of the Enclosure Acts of the eighteenth century. This important resource is increasingly under threat from development pressures and changes in farming practices, such as the removal of hedgerows.

Tourism resources

For convenience we have divided England for tourism purposes into a number of geographical regions. These are broadly based on the areas covered by the regional tourist boards, but sometimes regional boundaries are arbitrary and the historic counties have greater significance for both visitors and local communities.

The South

Aside from London, two regional tourist boards – Tourism South East and South West Tourism – cover the south of England. The South is the UK's main gateway region for all modes of transport, and is also a major concentration of population, wealth and commercial activity. As a consequence this part of England suffers more than other regions from the problems of economic growth, including congestion on air and surface transport routes. These problems are particularly evident in London and the adjacent Home Counties for the following reasons:

1   London is the focus of national communications, including the main railway termini, the Channel Tunnel terminal, a major coach interchange, and the busiest motorways. It is circled by airports (Heathrow, Gatwick, Stansted, London City Airport, and Luton) which are fundamental to the international network of air services.

2   London is one of the world's great cosmopolitan cities with a population of 7.5 million, attracting overseas and domestic tourists as well as day visitors. The capital offers the ceremonial and architectural heritage of Britain's imperial past, world-class tourist attractions, shopping and nightlife. As well as the great showpieces of Church and State – notably St Paul's Cathedral, the royal palaces and the Houses of Parliament – most of the nation's leading museums and art galleries are located here. Since the 1990s a range of new attractions have been developed, some as a result of Millennium funding, including:

–   the FA Premier League Hall of Fame, showcasing soccer;
–   the London Aquarium;
–   Churchill's Cabinet War Rooms, commemorating his leadership in the Second World War;
–   Rock Circus;
–   the London Eye (like the Eiffel Tower in Paris a century earlier, this was not originally meant to be a permanent attraction, but very soon became a feature of the city's skyline);
–   the Millennium Bridge, enhancing the appeal of the River Thames; and
–   London Zoo's Millennium Conservation Centre.

Tourism does add to the capital's traffic problems, especially in the central area, where most of the attractions and quality hotels are situated. This area includes:

•   The City of London, which was the original trading nucleus on the north bank of the Thames, and is now a major centre of international finance. Since it has only a small resident population, it is almost traffic-free at weekends. The annual Lord Mayor's Show is a reminder of the traditions of 'The City' and its separate identity.
•   The City of Westminster, which was once the seat of royal power, and is now the nation's administrative centre; it includes most of the 'West End', where luxury trades and entertainment originally developed to serve the court and the aristocracy.
•   The Royal Borough of Kensington and Chelsea, with its quality shopping and world-class museums.

Tourist pressure is a particular problem for London's historic buildings, but set against this is the fact that tourism contributes to London's economy through spending and jobs. It also helps to support the West End theatres, department stores and other amenities that Londoners enjoy.

Following the abolition of the Greater London Council in 1986, it was difficult to co-ordinate the tourism policies of the 33 London boroughs. With the formation of the Greater London Authority (GLA) in 1999 there is once again a single body, with an elected London Assembly and mayor, to implement strategies for tourism and transport covering the metropolitan area. Here the London Development Agency, which is responsible for promotion and 'Visit London' play an important role. Even so the GLA has a limited budget for tourism compared to say, New York City. A congestion charge was imposed in 2003 to price out non-essential traffic from the central area, and Trafalgar Square was partly pedestrianised. Efforts have been made to 'spread the load' of tourist pressure to lesser-known attractions outside central London, such as Islington, Greenwich and the former dock area to the east. London Docklands is one of the world's largest examples of inner city regeneration, the redevelopment of almost 27 kilometres of waterfront for residential or commercial use. There are facilities for water sports, and attractions based on London's historic role as a great port. To the waterfront west of London there is a cluster of well-established attractions, including Hampton Court, Kew Gardens (now a World Heritage Site), the Thames at Richmond, and the London Wetlands Centre.

London is the setting for many special events in the sporting and arts calendar which draw hundreds of thousands of visitors (notably the 2012 Olympics, Notting Hill Carnival, Wimbledon, Twickenham, soccer finals and cricket test matches). London was the first city to stage an international exhibition (in 1851), and continues to attract business and conference tourism on a vast scale. While there are a number of purpose-built facilities – ExCel, the Barbican Conference Centre, the Queen Elizabeth II Conference Centre, Olympia, and Earl's Court – much of the activity takes place in the capital's larger hotels that have world class facilities for meetings. Even with more than 200,000 beds presently available, there is a shortage of accommodation in London. There are new developments to address this problem, notably in the expanding budget hotel sector and in converted buildings such as the former County Hall.

The countryside of the Home Counties has been protected by a 'green belt' from the sprawl of Greater London. This includes two Areas of Outstanding Natural Beauty (AsONB) – the Chilterns to the north west of London and the North Downs in Surrey – where country parks, picnic sites, and trails focus visitor pressure. The range of tourist attractions includes:

- St Albans Cathedral;
- 'stately homes' such as Blenheim Palace (Churchill's birthplace), Clandon Park, Knebworth, Luton Hoo, Polesden Lacey, and Woburn Abbey – one of the first to appeal to the mass market by providing additional attractions to the house and gardens;
- Whipsnade Wild Animal Park; and
- the Grand Union Canal, one of England's most popular waterways.

The Thames flows through several towns which feature prominently on the *milk run* – the standard excursion circuit for foreign tourists. In Oxford the university's historic colleges, libraries and museums are the main attraction; here the conflict between tourist pressure and the historic townscape is recognised but as yet unresolved. Windsor further downstream is a classic example of the tension between tourism and local interests. Windsor's key attractions – associated with royalty over the centuries – are the castle and St George's Chapel. This small town is inundated with coaches in the summer months and has introduced a strict management regime. Henley is famous for its regatta, in an area noted for boating activities celebrated in the town's Museum of River and Rowing. Other attractions in the Thames Valley include the historic site of Runnymede, Ascot racecourse and new developments such as the Lookout Discovery Centre and the Roald Dahl Gallery. A number of theme parks – Legoland, Thorpe Park and Chessington World of Adventures – have been located in the Windsor/north Surrey area to take advantage of the motorway ring around London and the access this provides to a major concentration of demand. The city of Guildford is also well situated as a focus for business tourism and tourism education.

To the south-east of London, **Kent** is both the 'Garden of England' – with its orchards, hop farms and country houses – and the historic gateway for visitors from the Continent. As a result this county has been the focus of considerable development pressure in association with the Channel Tunnel and its rail link to London. It is also the focus of the demand for 'out of town' shopping, with the Bluewater leisure and shopping centre – the largest in Europe. The Channel ports, notably Folkestone, have declined in the face of severe competition from the Channel Tunnel. To mitigate the loss of jobs, Dover is highlighting its dual role as gateway and fortress from Roman times to the Second World War. Although many of the coastal towns of Kent are attractive centres of tourism (Broadstairs, Ramsgate, Whitstable, Herne Bay) or historic and important resorts (Margate), the industrialisation of the south side of the Thames estuary conflicts with tourism, while the improvement in communications is a mixed blessing, as the area now faces competition from northern France as a destination for Londoners. The Historic Dockyard at Chatham is an example of how England's naval heritage has been adapted to become a popular tourist attraction. Rochester has capitalised on its associations with Charles Dickens, although the 'Dickens World' theme park based on his novels is located at Chatham.

Kent boasts many historic buildings, of which the most famous are Hever Castle and Leeds Castle – a major heritage attraction and conference venue. The following market towns are important tourist centres:

* Ashford – now given added importance as a Channel Tunnel rail terminal;
* Tonbridge with its Norman castle;
* Royal Tunbridge Wells with its chalybeate spa; and
* Canterbury, which is the spiritual capital of England and the worldwide Anglican community. The cathedral and the themed 'Canterbury Tales' exhibition, recalling its importance as a centre of pilgrimage in medieval times, are a major attraction for domestic and overseas visitors.

Westwards along the coast in Sussex, historic towns such as Rye compete for attention with the large well-established resorts of Eastbourne, Brighton, Hove, Littlehampton, Worthing, and Bognor Regis. Brighton in particular has been successful in attracting a younger clientele while other resorts have declined. It has good transport links to London, and is arguably more sophisticated than other English seaside resorts, with a readiness to accept alternative lifestyles. Brighton has the usual holiday attractions (except for a good beach) but it can also offer a unique architectural fantasy (the Royal Pavilion), a purpose-built marina and conference centre, and it is the stage for cultural events such as the Brighton Film Festival. In a bid to attract new markets, Hastings has developed themed attractions – the 1066 Story, Smugglers' Adventure, the Shipwreck Museum, and the Blue Reef Aquarium. Although much of the Sussex coastline has been overdeveloped, significant natural features such as the Seven Sisters are protected by the National Trust and through designation as Heritage Coast. A short distance inland, the South Downs AONB, finally designated a national park in 2010, owes its character as open, rolling grassland to centuries of farming practice. Opponents of the national park have long argued that the area's new status would increase visitor impacts and antagonise local farmers. Historic towns in the area include Chichester with its cathedral and Festival theatre, and Arundel which features a castle and a cathedral in a spectacular setting.

The counties of Dorset and Hampshire form a major part of the vaguely defined region known as **Wessex,** which is loosely based on the Anglo-Saxon kingdom of that name and the novels of Thomas Hardy. The two counties offer a variety of resources for tourism, including:

- A number of harbours with facilities for sailing, such as Christchurch, Lymington, Poole, and Cowes – with its famous yachting Regatta. The Solent separating the Isle of Wight from the mainland is one of Europe's finest coastal waterways.
- Large areas of unspoiled countryside, particularly Cranborne Chase and the much-visited New Forest. The New Forest is an environmentally sensitive area with a unique landscape under severe pressure from tourism and recreation. Today, the landscape, flora and fauna are conserved under a variety of pieces of legislation, underlined in 2005 with the granting of national park status. Visitor pressure in the Forest arises from the adjacent Bournemouth and Southampton conurbations, and the fact it is easily accessible through the national motorway network. Managing the growing numbers of visitors is vitally important, given their possible impact on local communities and the sensitive wildlife habitats that visitors find so appealing. This will be achieved by the tourism strategy for the New Forest.
- The Dorset coast is a classic fieldwork area for geographers and geologists, attracting many educational visits to the fossil beds near Lyme Regis, Chesil Beach and Lulworth Cove, which has gained international recognition as a World Heritage Site and re-branding as the 'Jurassic Coast'. Careful management is needed to reduce the impact of visitors on the Dorset Coastal Path and at popular sites such as Studland and Lulworth Cove.
- Portsmouth is a major gateway to France and the Channel Islands. Here, England's naval heritage is the focus of a maritime leisure complex regenerating the harbour area, where visitors can inspect historic ships from different eras, namely Henry VIII's *Mary Rose*, Nelson's *Victory* and *HMS Warrior* overlooked by the spectacular viewing platforms of Spinnaker Tower. The adjoining seaside resort of Southsea has invested in attractions such as the Blue Reef aquarium, the Pyramids leisure pool, and the D-Day Museum which highlights Portsmouth's role in the Second World War.
- Southampton also has an important maritime heritage relating to the era of the great ocean liners, but this tends to be eclipsed by the city's role as a regional administrative and shopping centre.
- The Bournemouth conurbation (embracing Poole and Christchurch) is the region's major holiday destination with one of the largest concentrations of tourist accommodation outside London. It is also a major provider of English language schools, so that the spend of foreign students contributes significantly to the local economy. Bournemouth has successfully adapted to change, updating its former genteel image to attract the youth market with a vibrant club scene and an artificial surfing reef. At the same time the resort has retained its appeal to the family market and senior citizens. Although Bournemouth's beachfront remains less commercialised than other major resorts, the council has invested in a major international conference centre among other attractions, and has been foremost in launching sports events and festivals. To some extent Poole has been overshadowed by Bournemouth, partly because its beach is far from the town centre; however the redevelopment of the historic quay should raise its tourism profile significantly.
- Weymouth is both a historic seaport and one of England's oldest seaside resorts. Regeneration initiatives include the 'Timewalk' exhibition and speciality shopping at Brewer's Quay, while the sailing events of the 2012 Olympics provide a new role for Portland Harbour.
- Swanage is a small family resort in an attractive setting backed by the Purbeck Hills.

- Winchester is the most important of the region's historic towns. At one time a royal capital, with a famous castle and cathedral, it has moved with the times as shown by INTECH 2000 – an interactive learning centre. Other tourist centres include Dorchester, with its Thomas Hardy associations, Wimborne, Sherborne and Bridport.
- The Isle of Wight is an important holiday destination in its own right, offering a choice of family resorts such as Ryde, Shanklin and Ventnor, and is responding to the challenge of its competitors with attractions based on local finds of dinosaur fossils. The island is linked to Lymington, Portsmouth and Southampton by car and passenger ferry services.

The West Country

The area covered by South West Tourism includes the counties of Cornwall, Devon, Somerset, west Dorset, Gloucestershire and Wiltshire. The South West Peninsula corresponds geographically to the major part of the region, offering two attractive coastlines, fine scenery – including two national parks – and a mild, relatively sunny climate (which has given rise to such advertising slogans as 'The Cornish Riviera' and more recently 'The English Riviera'). The M5 motorway and increased car ownership have made the region much more accessible and ensured its continued popularity with the domestic market. Tourism is important for employment and income generation in a largely rural region with few alternative industries, although seasonality is a problem. The countryside is a major tourism resource throughout the region, encouraging farm stays and activity holidays. Many of the picturesque villages with their craft workshops are linked by themed routes for cycling, hiking or riding. Perhaps the best known of these is the 'Tarka Country' trail in north-west Devon which is held up as a classic example of sustainable tourism. As the West Country largely escaped the Industrial Revolution, many of the market towns have preserved a rich architectural heritage and some now act as regional tourism centres – for example Truro, Barnstable, Taunton, Marlborough and Salisbury. However the coast of the South West Peninsula is the best known feature, through the experiences of successive generations of British holidaymakers since Victorian times. Most of this varied and often beautiful coastline is protected by National Trust ownership or Heritage Coast policies, which effectively prevent the encroachment of industry or insensitive tourism development. The coast provides many recreational opportunities, notably surfing off the more exposed beaches, sailing in the sheltered estuaries, and long distance paths for hiking.

Cornwall epitomises the beach tourism product of south-west England, but it is different in character from other parts of the region, with its granite cliffs and Celtic heritage, where the Cornish language is recalled by the distinctive place names. As a peninsula, Cornwall has the advantage of both an Atlantic and Channel coastline, but a peripheral location is also a disadvantage in terms of accessibility and possibilities for touring. A new airport at Newquay has nevertheless enhanced Cornwall's appeal to up-market tourists. The county faces high unemployment with the decline of its traditional mining and fishing industries, while the growth of second-home ownership has aroused controversy. A number of attractions are based on this maritime and industrial heritage, while the small fishing ports of the south coast, such as Fowey, Looe, Mevagissey and Polperro have preserved much of their character. Cornwall's tourism resources also include:

- the surfing beaches along the Atlantic coast, focusing on the resorts of Bude, Newquay and Polzeath;
- the large family resorts of Falmouth and Penzance;
- the impressive coastal features of Land's End and St Michael's Mount;
- the mild climate that has made possible an ambitious garden restoration project – the Lost Gardens of Heligan with their sub-tropical vegetation;
- the Eden Project, backed by Millennium funding, is another example of reclamation – in this case a former china clay pit has been transformed into a series of climate-controlled 'biodomes' representing the world's major ecosystems;
- Tintagel and Bodmin Moor are associated with the legends of King Arthur; and
- the county's dramatic landscapes and seascapes have been an inspiration to writers and artists; St Ives in particular is a well-established 'artists' colony', with a branch of the Tate Gallery and the Barbara Hepworth Museum attracting many visitors.

With the exception of Dartmoor, Devon and Somerset are characterised by a gently undulating, more wooded landscape, where dairy farming is the predominant land use. Areas of Outstanding Natural Beauty account for a large part of the two counties, while the two national parks differ greatly in character. Dartmoor is a bleak, treeless moorland punctuated by granite masses known as 'tors'. Exmoor is visually appealing and has been romanticised for tourism promotion as 'Lorna Doone Country'.

The maritime heritage includes reminders of the Elizabethan age of overseas expansion, in which the small ports of north Devon – Appledore and Bideford – played an important role as well as Bristol, Dartmouth and Plymouth. There is a wide choice for beach holidays; in south Devon the large resorts around Torbay – Brixham, Paignton and Torquay – are distinct in character and cater for different market segments, yet are promoted together as the English Riviera. They have been the focus of a tourism development plan and share the English Riviera Conference Centre, with the purpose of diversifying their product to attract new clients. East Devon includes part of the 'Jurassic Coast' and a number of smaller resorts such as Exmouth that cater for the traditional family market. The north Devon coast offers more spectacular scenery and good surfing beaches, with Ilfracombe as the major resort. Clovelly is an example of a picturesque village that has become a popular 'honeypot' for swarms of day-trippers, and where a new visitor centre should ensure that residents are less exposed to the tourist gaze. Further along the Bristol Channel in Somerset, Minehead has the themed accommodation development of Somerwest World, based on a former Butlin's holiday camp, while Weston-super-Mare has invested in new initiatives such as the controversial Tropicana development.

Other major tourism resources include:

- Bath, which reached its zenith as a spa resort in the eighteenth century, although the Romans first recognised the value of a geothermal resource unique in Britain. Spa tourism is expected to revive with a new state of the art facility, but Bath is mainly visited for its cultural heritage, fine Georgian architecture (earning UNESCO designation as a World Heritage City), event and shopping attractions.
- Bristol, on the other hand, is a major commercial centre with a functioning port at Avonmouth. Its tourism industry is based on business travel; transport heritage – particularly that associated with the great Victorian engineer, Brunel; the city's role in the expansion of the British Empire; and contemporary museums (for example the 'Explore at Bristol' hands-on science centre and Science World).
- Wells is a small historic town noted for its cathedral and other medieval buildings.

- The Mendips nearby offer impressive limestone scenery, featuring the Cheddar Gorge and show caves such as Wookey Hole with their stalagmite and stalactite formations;
- Glastonbury has been regarded as a sacred site since ancient times, when the imposing hill known as Glastonbury Tor was an island amid the marshes of the Somerset Levels. In the Middle Ages the abbey attracted pilgrims as the burial place of King Arthur. The town has now become a destination for 'New Age' devotees and the Glastonbury music festival also attracts a wide youth following.
- Exeter is the county town of Devon, featuring an imposing cathedral and Roman remains among its attractions.
- Plymouth promotes its naval heritage, focusing on the Hoe, the historic Dockyard and the *Mayflower* connection. The large natural harbour of Plymouth Sound is ideal for sailing, while the Aquarium is a long-established tourist attraction.

The chalk downland of Salisbury Plain is a dominant feature of Wiltshire. This part of Wessex is particularly rich in prehistoric remains, the best known being Avebury and Stonehenge – both World Heritage Sites and subject to tourist pressure. Responsibility for Stonehenge is shared between English Heritage and the National Trust, while much of the rest of Salisbury Plain is used by the Ministry of Defence for military training. For Stonehenge to retain its mystique it needs effective traffic and visitor management. Contrasting attractions in Wiltshire include Longleat – a stately home with a popular safari park attached; the National Trust village of Lacock Abbey (which is associated with one of the pioneers of photography); and the restored Kennet and Avon Canal.

Discussion point

Some of Britain's iconic attractions, such as Stonehenge, are suffering from excessive tourist pressure. In class, discuss how this pressure might be relieved by promoting and developing alternative attractions.

East Anglia

Facing the North Sea and within easy reach of London, East Anglia is well placed to attract Continental visitors through Stansted Airport and the ports of Harwich and Felixstowe. In medieval times the region was the most prosperous part of England thanks to the wool trade with the Low Countries, and this explains the rich architectural heritage of small towns such as Lavenham. East Anglia largely escaped the developments of the Industrial Revolution and has preserved much of its rural character. Predominantly low-lying, the landscape is nonetheless varied, including the former marshlands of the Fens to the north west, the sandy heaths and forests of Breckland in west Suffolk, and the fertile countryside along the River Stour in east Suffolk, an area made famous by Constable's paintings. We can consider the following as important tourist centres:

- Cambridge, where the university's historic colleges are located in a beautiful riverside setting;
- Ely, famous for its cathedral dominating the Fens;
- King's Lynn – once a major port, now featuring the 'North Sea Haven';
- Norwich is the regional capital with many historic buildings; and
- Colchester with a heritage dating back to Roman times.

The north Norfolk coast with its low cliffs of boulder clay, and the sandy coast of east Suffolk are quite different in character. Both have been designated as Heritage Coasts, and the latter boasts an internationally renowned bird reserve. North Norfolk has a number of small resorts – Cromer, Hunstanton, Sheringham and Holt – which are linked by a coastal steam railway. The Essex coast is characterised by marshes and river estuaries, on which are situated the yachting centres of Burnham on Crouch and Maldon. Essex resorts illustrate different approaches to tourism; for example, Clacton has developed to attract the mass market, while neighbouring Frinton has banned any commercialisation of its seafront. Southend, boasting the world's longest pier, is primarily a day trip destination for Londoners.

Great Yarmouth is one of eastern England's largest and oldest resorts, and is also the gateway to the Norfolk Broads. These shallow lakes of medieval origin are Britain's best-known area for water-based recreation and holidays. There are over 200 kilometres of navigable waterways and over 2,000 powered craft are available for hire. However, the commercial success of tourism has been achieved in competition with agriculture, which makes heavy demands on water supplies in an area with a relatively low rainfall, and at a cost to the environment, for example:

- detergents, human sewage, discarded fuel, and a lowered water table have upset the ecological balance;
- banks are eroded and wildlife disturbed by the wash from the boats; and
- the sprawl of boatyards and other development despoils the landscape.

In an effort to balance the conflicting demands of tourism, agriculture, and wildlife this unique wetland area is now carefully managed by the Broads Authority as a national park in all but name.

The Midlands

The Midlands are usually associated more with manufacturing than with tourism, presenting the tourist boards covering the west and east of the region with an image problem. However imaginative themeing of short breaks, investment in attractions and accommodation, and effective marketing is attracting tourists and day visitors to the countryside, historic towns, and industrial heritage of the region. The Midlands boasts one of Britain's most popular theme parks – Alton Towers – which takes advantage of the national motorway network. For both domestic and overseas tourists, the Cotswolds are famous for their mellow limestone buildings in tourist centres such as Broadway and Chipping Campden. In comparison, Cannock Chase scarcely ranks as a tourist destination but is an important recreational resource for the region, as it is located near the West Midlands conurbation. Other countryside areas in the west Midlands include the Malverns and the Shropshire Hills, while the Wye Valley near the Welsh border attracts canoeing and other activity holidays.

Of the many historic towns, the best known is Stratford-on-Avon, which is popular with overseas visitors for its literary associations, underlined by the redeveloped Royal Shakespeare Theatre. Other important tourist centres in the west Midlands are:

- the cathedral cities of Gloucester, Hereford and Worcester, which host the Three Choirs Festival celebrating the music of Elgar;
- the elegant spa town of Cheltenham;
- Warwick and its castle, now a major themed attraction; and

- Shrewsbury and Ludlow in the Middle Ages were fortress towns of the Welsh Marches (the border country with Wales) and preserve a rich architectural heritage. Ludlow is also noted for its quality restaurants.

The industrial heritage of the West Midlands is undergoing radical change, with the restoration of canals for recreation and a new breed of museum such as:

- the Ironbridge complex which interprets the beginnings of the Industrial Revolution;
- the Potteries Museum at Stoke-on-Trent and 'Ceramica' at Burslem showcase the ceramics industry of north Staffordshire; and
- the Black Country Museum at Dudley portrays life and work in this former area of heavy industry.

Modern engineering industries are still thriving in the West Midlands conurbation, which includes Birmingham, Coventry and Wolverhampton. The National Exhibition Centre and National Arena at the heart of the motorway system enhance Birmingham's importance as a centre for business tourism and event attractions. This is complemented by the redeveloped Bull Ring shopping complex in the city centre, the Jewellery Quarter focusing on Birmingham's speciality trades, and new attractions such as 'Think Tank' (an interactive discovery museum), Cadbury World of Chocolate, and the National Sealife Centre. For many people Coventry and its cathedral symbolise urban recovery after the Second World War, but the city's museums also celebrate its contributions to transport technology, while Millennium Place is a new outdoor arena.

The East Midlands region includes the Lincolnshire coast, with the resorts of Skegness, Mablethorpe and Cleethorpes providing traditional seaside recreation for the industrial cities of Derby, Leicester and Nottingham. Lincoln is a major tourist centre with a magnificent cathedral dominating the city's skyline. Nottingham has exploited its association with the legendary Robin Hood, while Leicester has downplayed its heritage in favour of the National Space Centre. Countryside areas for recreation include Charnwood Forest, the Vale of Belvoir and Sherwood Forest, while the artificial lake known as Rutland Water is an important resource for water sports.

The North

The northern part of England, which includes four regional tourist boards, is one of contrasts, from industrial heartlands, through the spectacular scenery of national parks, to its bustling resorts. The region also forms an important gateway to Britain for Scandinavian, German, and Dutch tourists who enter through the ports of Newcastle and Hull. The scenery of the area is evidenced by the fact that it contains five national parks – which are the focus of tourism and day trips – and a number of areas of outstanding natural beauty, such as the Solway Firth – noted for its golf courses – and the Eden Valley and North Pennines – which are popular with anglers.

In many rural upland areas EU and British regional funds are supporting the development of farm-based tourism. Tourism and recreation brings income and jobs, supports rural services, and stems depopulation, but herein also lie seeds of conflict, as some argue that tourism interferes with farming operations and destroys the very communities that tourists visit. This may occur through the purchase of second homes and the reorientation of rural services towards weekend and summer visitors. The opportunities for outdoor recreation and the threats from tourist pressure are greatest in the national parks.

The **Lake District** is intensively managed for tourism and recreation with 'honeypot' areas designed to take pressure, for example Ambleside and Bowness, along with traffic management and car-parking schemes. Access to the park from the north is through the market town of Penrith, and from the south through the historic town of Kendal. Keswick is the major service centre for the park and there is an interpretation facility at Brockholes. There are attractions based on the literary associations with Wordsworth and Beatrix Potter, but the Lake District is mainly popular for active tourism and recreation – walking, water sports, outdoor pursuits, and mountaineering. In the past these activities have interfered with the upland farming regime of the area, but management schemes run by the park's authorities have solved many of these problems. The landscape is on a human scale with attractive towns and villages, *fells* (low moorland hills), and lakes, each with its own character. Windermere, for example, is intensively used, while remoter lakes and tarns are little visited.

The **Yorkshire Dales** National Park is characterised by a gentler landscape than the Lake District. It is criss-crossed by limestone walls and dotted with field barns (some converted to shelters for walkers). Touring centres in the park include Richmond, Skipton, and Settle, and popular villages such as Malham with its cove and tarn which are spectacular relics of the Ice Age. In and around the park are literary sites linked to the Brontes and also locations associated with a popular series on British television. Like its southern neighbour, the Peak District National Park, the Dales are popular for outdoor pursuits and field studies. The Settle/Carlisle Railway is a major scenic route linking two national parks.

The **Peak District** is the most visited of Britain's national parks due to its proximity to the industrial cities of both the North and the Midlands, with some valleys, notably Dovedale, experiencing visitor pressure. The White Peak is the southern and central area of limestone dales and crags with important centres such as Matlock and Castleton. The Dark Peak in the north is a more rugged and spectacular area with a number of lakes and reservoirs. Some caverns and mines are open to visitors and the industrial heritage is featured in attractions such as the Crich National Tramway Museum. At Matlock Bath the Heights of Abraham is a country park with theme park attractions. The main touring centres are Bakewell, Ashbourne, Matlock, and Holmfirth – home of another popular television series. The spa town of Buxton has revived its opera house and conference facilities. Hardwick Hall in Chesterfield is one of Britain's foremost Elizabethan country houses, while Chatsworth is one of its most visited stately homes.

The **North York Moors** National Park is characterised by heather-covered, rolling countryside with picturesque villages. It also offers a spectacular coastline, summits such as Roseberry Topping, and natural features such as the Hole of Horcum, popular with hang gliders. The North Yorkshire Moors steam railway runs through the park from Pickering to Grosmont.

The **Northumberland** National Park lies on the Scottish border and contains Kielder Forest and Kielder Water, both recent additions to the landscape. Hadrian's Wall to the south is of unique historic interest as a Roman military achievement, with associated archaeological attractions, but in places under intense tourist pressure. Hadrian's Wall runs from Hexham westwards to Carlisle, which is an important regional centre and historic gateway to Scotland.

Discussion point

The designation of national parks in the UK began in the 1950s, and then stalled for many years until the New Forest was granted this status in 2005. Nevertheless, national park designation is not universally welcomed by local residents. Devise a list of the key stakeholders in a selection of national parks and identify their main concerns. Where might the main areas of conflict be?

Photo 8.1 Scarborough beach

The coasts of northern England include both major resorts and areas of scenic interest that have been conserved as Heritage Coast or as wildlife sanctuaries, such as Spurn Head and the Farne Islands. Many of the North's resorts have faced the problem of declining traditional markets in nearby industrial cities by investing in new facilities, upgrading accommodation, and marketing aggressively to attract new market segments. Holidaymakers have the following choice of resorts:

- Blackpool's 'Golden Mile' is a classic example of a recreational business district (RBD), where the famous Tower is jostled by a townscape of tourist facilities and small guest-houses. The Pleasure Beach is one of the most visited attractions in Britain. Blackpool introduced 'The Illuminations' as an early attempt to extend the holiday season, and has constantly developed new attractions such as the Sandcastle Centre, but has so far failed in its bid to become Britain's main gambling resort.
- Scarborough is one of Britain's oldest resorts, an elegant town between two bays, offering a Sealife Centre among its modern attractions. The redeveloped Spa Conference Centre adds a business dimension to its market.
- There is a range of smaller resorts, such as Bridlington, Hornsea, Whitby, and Filey on the North Sea coast and Morecambe on the less bracing Irish Sea coast.
- Day-trip resorts close to conurbations include New Brighton and Southport serving Merseyside, and Whitley Bay for Newcastle. Southport has been re-branded as 'England's Classic Resort', and with seven championship courses in the vicinity, as the capital of 'England's Golf Coast'

The North of England is mainly known for its great industrial cities and their role in sport and popular culture, but the region can also boast many historic buildings and sites of national importance, which increasingly attract overseas tourists as well as day visitors. These include:

1   A large number of castles, particularly in areas close to the Scottish border – Alnwick and Bamburgh are good examples.
2   Reminders of pre-Reformation England in ruined abbeys such as Fountains and Rievaulx in Yorkshire, and the pilgrimage centre of Holy Island off the Northumberland coast.
3   Great country houses such as Castle Howard, which has been used as a location for costume dramas.
4   More modest buildings from different parts of the region have been brought together on one site at the Beamish North of England Open Air Museum in County Durham.
5   The spa towns of Buxton, Ilkley and Harrogate – now a major conference venue.
6   The historic centres of Beverley, Chester, Durham, Lancaster and York. Chester has significant Roman remains, but tourism focuses on 'The Rows', which are medieval shopping arcades. Durham boasts an impressive castle and Romanesque cathedral, reflecting the power of its prince-bishops in the Middle Ages. However **York** is outstanding for these reasons:
     – It has retained its medieval walls, city gates and street pattern;
     – York Minster is one of Europe's largest Gothic churches; and
     – The Jorvik Viking Centre has transformed an archaeological site into a visitor attraction featuring 'authentic' sights, sounds and smells.

York has also exploited its part in the Industrial Revolution through the National Railway Museum, although the industrial heritage is more obvious in larger, less historic cities. Bradford for example has shown an imaginative approach to tourism based on its woollen textile industry, but also utilising its proximity to 'Bronte Country' and the contribution of the large Asian community to contemporary culture, particularly food. Indeed the resurgence of tourism, sport and leisure-related projects on 'brownfield' sites reclaimed from industrial use characterises most northern cities. Regional centres such as Hull, Leeds, Newcastle, Liverpool and Manchester have major tourist developments leading their drive for reinvestment. For example in Merseyside the Liverpool Garden Festival and Albert Dock schemes were designed to attract investment in other sectors of the economy. As a result the city now features the Tate Liverpool Art Gallery and museums celebrating its maritime and musical heritage, as well as an impressive collection of civic buildings from the Victorian era. Manchester raised its international profile by hosting the Commonwealth Games in 2002 and its city centre was redeveloped following an IRA terrorist attack. At Castlefield there is now an urban heritage park and a new exhibition venue – the GMex Centre. Further along the Ship Canal there is the Lowry Centre at Salford Quays, celebrating one of the region's most famous artists. Manchester has set out to attract particular markets – for example, sport tourism, music lovers, youth tourism with a vibrant club scene, and gay tourism. Developments elsewhere in the North West include Wigan Pier – a themed heritage attraction based on life in Victorian England – and at Preston, the National Football Museum and the Riversway marina docklands.

On the other side of the Pennines, Newcastle has expanded its leisure and shopping attractions, while 'The Baltic' in Gateshead is at the cutting edge of the contemporary arts scene. In Yorkshire and Humberside the following tourism developments are significant:

•   Wakefield's National Coal Mining Museum in a former colliery, celebrating one of England's major industries prior to the 1980s;
•   the Royal Armouries Museum and the Thackray Medical Museum in Leeds;

- Sheffield is developing special event tourism and boasts the Meadowhall leisure and shopping complex – one of Europe's largest – and the Ski Village with dry slopes and other facilities for winter sports;
- Rotherham's 'Magna' is a visitor attraction based on the achievements of British industry; and
- Hull hosts 'The Deep Aquarium', an exhibition interpreting the life of the oceans and the nineteenth century whaling industry. Similarly Grimsby's trawlermen are celebrated in the national Fishing Heritage Centre. These attractions have helped to alleviate the loss of jobs and income caused by the decline of the North Sea fishing industry.

Scotland

Scotland, Wales and the Isle of Man are situated in the rugged north and west of Britain, and form part of the 'Celtic fringe' of western Europe. Neither the Romans in the second century AD, or Edward I of England in the thirteenth century, succeeded in conquering Scotland, and it remained an independent country until the Act of Union in 1707. However, a form of the English language became dominant except in the more remote western and northern parts of the country, where the Gaelic language and culture still survive. The Scots developed a separate legal system, and with the Reformation in the sixteenth century their own Church, which placed a high value on education. Styles of architecture were influenced by France rather than England. There is a strong sense of national identity, expressed in sport, music and dance, food and literature, and with devolution in 1999, Scotland has regained most of its former independence.

Outside the conurbations of Glasgow and Edinburgh, Scotland is a much less crowded country than England, with plenty of space for outdoor recreation. Two-thirds of the country is mountainous, and the Highlands are one of the largest areas of unspoiled mountain and lake scenery in Europe. Many potential visitors are deterred by the reputation of the climate such that, outside of the Central Lowlands, leisure tourism is very seasonal. In fact the west coast of Scotland with is fine beaches enjoys more spring sunshine than most parts of Britain. Apart from the scenery, Scotland can also offer a wealth of folklore and a romantic history – re-interpreted by Hollywood films in the 1990s.

Scottish tourism is administered by the Scottish Tourist Board (VisitScotland), EventScotland and a range of regional and local agencies, while the Scottish Tourism Forum represents the industry to government. Tourism is important economically, directly supporting almost 200,000 jobs and accounting for 5 per cent of GDP. The Scottish tourism product is delivered primarily by small businesses and this places a question over the quality of the product at times, and has also held back investment in the sector; for example there are few all-weather developments. Scottish tourism is based on scenery, cultural heritage, and the large ethnic market formed by the descendants of emigrants, especially in Canada. Special interest and activity holidays are also important – particularly those based on fishing, whisky, and golf. Scotland's tourists come mainly for leisure purposes, as the country was a late entrant into the conference and exhibition market. The overseas market has remained healthy for Scotland, with North America (around a quarter of arrivals) and Continental Europe (almost two thirds of arrivals) providing most of the demand. Most visitors arrive by air, as there is only one port (Rosyth) providing a ferry service to mainland Europe. Scotland also attracts domestic tourism, of which around one–half originate from within the country. Increasingly, Scotland faces a dilemma: the traditional image of lochs, tartan, and heather is inappropriate for the newer forms of tourism, based on short city-break products as developed in Glasgow and Edinburgh.

Tourism resources

We can identify three main tourism regions in Scotland, based mainly on differences of geology:

- the Southern Uplands, mainly high moorlands with only a few pockets of lowland;
- the Central Lowlands, which is actually a rift valley formed between two faults or lines of weakness in the Earth's crust (although this region occupies only 10 per cent of the total area, it contains 80 per cent of Scotland's population of 5 million); and
- the Highlands and Islands of the north and north-west, where ancient rocks form rugged mountains and a magnificent coastline, and the nearest there is to true wilderness in the British Isles.

The Southern Uplands

The Southern Uplands lie between the Cheviots on the English border and the southern boundary fault of the Central Lowlands, which approximates to a line drawn between Girvan in Ayrshire to Dunbar. Granite is the rock most commonly found in Galloway in the west, forming a rugged landscape. To the east of Dumfries the hills are more rounded and broken up by areas of lowland, the most extensive being the Merse of the Tweed valley. The Southern Uplands as a whole are thinly populated, the towns are quite small, and the main lines of communication with England keep to the valleys.

This area forms the gateway to Scotland and tourist developments at Gretna have exploited this, although the centuries of border battles and cattle raiding are still much less well known outside Scotland than the clan warfare of the Highlands. The main tourist attractions in the Border Country to the east include:

- the abbeys at Jedburgh, Kelso, and Melrose, immortalised by the great Romantic novelist Sir Walter Scott;
- the spa town of Peebles; and
- the textile weaving towns of Hawick and Selkirk.

On the route west to Galloway, Dumfries has a 'Burns Trail' celebrating its associations with Scotland's national poet. Galloway has a milder climate and gardens are an attraction. The area has facilities for sailing and other activity holidays, and there are important archaeological sites and the Galloway Forest Park. Stranraer is a major ferry port for Northern Ireland.

North of Galloway the Ayrshire coast has notable seaside resorts such as Girvan, and Ayr has one of Scotland's few all-weather facilities at Haven Holiday Park. There are also golf courses, as at Troon.

The Central Lowlands

Despite the name, the Central Lowlands include a good deal of high ground, since the formation of this rift valley was accompanied by extensive volcanic activity. The isolated 'necks' of long-extinct volcanoes can still be seen, the crag on which Edinburgh Castle stands being a good example. The Ochils and Sidlaws to the north of the estuary known as the Firth of Forth, and the Pentland Hills to the south, rise to 500 metres – high by English standards. Parts of the eastern Lowlands are quite fertile, notably the Carse of Gowrie in Fife and the Lothians around Edinburgh. The western part of the Lowlands has a damper climate. The coastline is deeply indented by three great estuaries – the Firths of Forth, Clyde, and Tay – on which are situated Scotland's major ports, Leith (for Edinburgh), Glasgow with its outport at Greenock, and Dundee.

The Central Lowlands contain by far the greater proportion of Scotland's industry and population. The main centres – Glasgow, Edinburgh, Dundee, and Stirling – are linked by a good communications system, which has involved bridging the Forth and Tay. Here too are the main international and domestic air gateways to Scotland. Both Edinburgh and Glasgow have shuttle services to London, while Glasgow Airport has developed international services since the deregulation of air services in Scotland and the demise of Prestwick. Budget airlines also operate to Dublin, Luton and regional airports in the British Isles.

The region is dominated by the two rival cities of Glasgow and Edinburgh. Both are significant cities for tourism but have very different products and approaches. Each has its own tourist board and tourism strategy.

Edinburgh as the capital of Scotland, is home to the Scottish Parliament, and is a major cultural centre, attracting a large number of overseas visitors especially to the International Festival and Military Tattoo. The old city is built on a narrow ridge on either side of the 'Royal Mile' connecting the castle to the palace of Holyrood House, and is crammed full of picturesque buildings. It is separated from the 'New Town' to the north by the Norloch Valley, now occupied by public gardens and the Waverley railway station. The New Town, built according to eighteenth-century ideas of planning and architecture, contains Princes Street, a major shopping area, but other speciality shopping streets now compete with Princes Street's multiple stores. In particular, the area to the north of Princes Street, the Grassmarket area in the old town and Stockbridge abound with restaurants and speciality retailing. Edinburgh has a wealth of historic buildings and national attractions, such as the Royal Scottish Museum and the newly developed 'Dynamic Earth' story of the planet. The Edinburgh International Conference Centre has been a major boost to business tourism. There are also many attractions on the outskirts, including:

- Edinburgh Zoo;
- the Forth road and rail bridges;
- Dirleton, Tantallon and Crichton Castles;
- Linlithgow Palace, associated with Mary Queen of Scots;
- the restored Royal Yacht Britannia;
- Ocean Terminal at Leith; and
- the Scottish Mining Museum.

Discussion point

The traditional image of Scotland is of tartan, heather, lochs and mountains, bagpipes and shortbread. Yet for the cosmopolitan cities of Edinburgh and Glasgow some argue that this image is counterproductive. These two cities have tourism markets based upon short breaks, conference and business tourism – markets that are not attracted by Scotland's 'traditional' image. How can this 'clash' of communication be resolved?

Across the Forth Estuary lies Dunfermline, a former capital of Scotland. The Fife coast has a string of picturesque fishing villages – amongst them Elie and Crail – and the historic university town of St Andrews with its golf course. Dundee is the regional centre and has the twin attractions of the royal research ship *Discovery* at Discovery Point and a Science Centre. Perth is another former Scottish capital and acts as the gateway to the Highlands.

Glasgow is a much larger city than Edinburgh, and has acquired a much grittier image. It developed mainly during the nineteenth century as Scotland's major port and industrial centre. Glasgow's renaissance as a city was well publicised in 1990 with its selection as European City of Culture. With the vision of the local authority and the Greater Glasgow and Clyde Valley Tourist Board, a fine Victorian city now has a wealth of attractions, accommodation, restaurants and tourist facilities.

Assignment

Investigate why Glasgow was chosen as European City of Culture, and why this was important for Glaswegians. In your research evaluate what the city has to offer, including cultural attractions such as the Burrell Collection, the Glasgow Science Centre, sports facilities, exhibition venues, heritage attractions, entertainment, and shopping opportunities. How does Glasgow compare in these respects with, say, Liverpool?

Stirling, with its strategically located castle, played a major role in the Scottish Wars of Independence during the thirteenth and fourteenth centuries, and was given worldwide recognition by the film *Braveheart*.

The Highlands and Islands

Geologically speaking, the Highlands include the whole of Scotland to the north of a line drawn from Helensburgh on the Firth of Clyde to Stonehaven on the North Sea coast, which represents the northern boundary fault of the Central Lowlands. The region is made up of very old, highly folded rocks, and was severely affected by glaciation during the Ice Age, which formed its landscape of rugged mountains (the highest in the British Isles), lochs, and broad, steep-sided glens. Most of the forests of Scots pine which formerly covered much of the Highlands have disappeared, with the significant exception of the Cairngorms area, leaving a treeless, heather-covered landscape.

The Highlands are divided into two by Glen More, the great rift valley extending right across Scotland from Fort William to Inverness, which is followed by the Caledonian Canal. The North-west Highlands to the west of Glen More are more rugged than the Grampians to the east. The Atlantic coast from Kintyre to Sutherland is deeply indented by sea lochs and is fringed by innumerable islands, with very little in the way of a coastal plain. Along the North Sea coast the coastline is more regular and less spectacular; there are fairly extensive lowlands in the north-east 'shoulder' of Scotland between Aberdeen and the Moray Firth, where the climate is drier and better suited to farming.

By comparison with other mountain regions of Europe such as the Alps, most parts of the Scottish Highlands are sparsely populated, for historical reasons. Despite a difficult climate and poor soils, the glens, the coastal lowlands and islands once supported substantial communities whose way of life was quite different from that of the Lowlands. The Highlanders spoke Gaelic and had a strong feeling of loyalty to the clan or tribal group. In the nineteenth century many such communities were evicted in the Clearances to make way for large private sheep farms and reserves for field sports. Traditionally, many Highlanders have gained a living from 'crofting' – a self-sufficient type of agriculture on smallholdings supplemented by fishing. In some localities weaving and whisky distilling have been important activities.

Tourism has become an important source of income and provider of jobs. In 1965 the Highlands and Islands Development Board was set up by the British government to encourage public and private investment in the seven 'crofting counties' (Argyll, Inverness, Ross and Cromarty, Sutherland, Caithness, Orkney, and Shetland). In the past this area was very short of quality accommodation, so the Board financed new hotels and self-catering accommodation. In 1991 it became the Highlands and Islands Enterprise (HIE) which is also concerned with investigating ways of extending the short tourist season, and ensuring that tourism does not damage the beauty of the scenery.

The main tourism centre for the Highlands is Inverness, where the majority of accommodation and services are found. South of this university town, Loch Ness has a tourist industry based on the world famous 'monster' with visitor centres at Drumnadrochit.

Transport is a problem in the Western Highlands on account of the deeply indented coastline; so wide detours have frequently to be made to get from one place to another. With the exception of Skye, which now has a bridge to the mainland, the Hebrides are not easily accessible, although some of the small scattered communities are linked by 'air taxi' services and ferry connections. The ports of Ullapool, Kyle of Lochalsh, Mallaig, and Oban are the main bases for visiting the Hebrides. Islands have a great attraction for holidaymakers, despite in this instance the unpredictable weather and lack of facilities:

- Skye is popular because of its historical associations with the clans, and the 1745 Jacobite rising to restore the Stuart dynasty, as well as the magnificent mountain scenery of the Cuillins.
- Iona is a place of pilgrimage.
- Staffa is noted for its basalt sea caves.
- Crossing the Minch, the Outer Hebrides or Western Isles have a bleaker environment. Harris is noted for its tweed, cloth hand woven into distinctive patterns, while Lewis has a major prehistoric site at Callanish. The remote islands of St Kilda, uninhabited since 1930, are a World Heritage Site.
- The Orkneys and the Shetlands, separated from mainland Scotland by some of the stormiest seas in Europe, were once ruled by Norway – and in the Shetlands the Scandinavian influence remains strong even today (one manifestation being the 'Up Helly Aa' festival in Lerwick). The Orkneys are fairly low-lying and fertile, and contain unique prehistoric sites at Skara Brae and Maes Howe. The magnificent harbour of Scapa Flow was once an important naval base. The Shetlands lie 140 kilometres further north and are bleaker and much more rugged. Oil has brought wealth to a community where fishing has traditionally been the mainstay of the economy and the distinctively small, hardy island sheep and ponies are reared. These northern islands are linked by regular air services from Edinburgh and Glasgow as well as ferries from Scrabster (near Thurso) and Aberdeen.

The scenic attractions of the Grampians are more readily accessible to the cities of the Lowlands than the Western Highlands. This part of Scotland was made fashionable as a holiday destination by Queen Victoria, and the Dee Valley west of Aberdeen is particularly associated with the British royal family, More recently Hollywood films based on Scottish heroes have also stimulated renewed interest in the area. During the nineteenth century a number of hotels were built, notably on the shores of Loch Lomond, in the Trossachs (an area of particularly fine woodland and lake scenery now designated as a national park), and at Gleneagles near Perth, which is a noted centre for golf. The Spey Valley (famous for its whisky and salmon fishing) was another area that particularly benefited from Victorian tourism. It has good road and rail communications to Glasgow and London. After the 1960s, this area became important for winter sports, since the Cairngorms can provide a suitable climate and terrain.

Case study 8.1

Tourism versus conservation in the Cairngorms

The Cairngorms are unique in Britain as an example of an arctic-alpine ecosystem, one of the reasons for the designation of these mountains as a national park. However there is scope for conflict here with the growing winter sports industry, which demands sophisticated infrastructure and facilities. The ski fields lie in the Coire Cas, a corrie or cirque that acts as a 'snowbowl', located high above the treeline on the northern slopes of Cairngorm Mountain. The season is from December to April, but climate change means that snow-cover can be reliable. The Aviemore Centre in the valley below is a purpose-built resort offering a full range of services. Conferences are held in spring and autumn, while in summer the Centre is used as a base for activity holidays, including pony-trekking, mountain biking, gliding and nature study – for which the Cairngorms nature reserve is probably unrivalled in Britain. Unlike other Scottish resorts, Aviemore has a year-round season and adequate wet-weather facilities, so that it can take full advantage of tourism. However, proposals to expand ski facilities have received considerable opposition from environmentalists, concerned about the fragile nature of the mountain ecosystems.

Elsewhere in the Scottish Highlands, winter sports facilities have been developed near Fort William and at Glen Shee.

Wales

Wales was able to maintain a separate national identity thanks to centuries of successful resistance to the Anglo-Saxon invaders who took over the rest of Roman Britain, but the last of the principalities into which the country was divided was conquered by King Edward I in the thirteenth century. Despite this and the 1536 Act of Union with England imposed by Henry VIII, who was himself of Welsh descent, Welsh cultural traditions continued to flourish. Welsh national identity is evidenced by:

* the vigour of Welsh as a living language, especially in the mountainous north and west of the country;
* the Celtic heritage, expressed in a strong literary and musical tradition, and the national gatherings known as *eisteddfods*;

- the strength of Nonconformist Christianity, with simple chapels featuring in the landscape rather than imposing cathedrals;
- the world famous choirs; and
- the importance of rugby football as a focus for national pride.

In the course of the twentieth century, the Welsh language and culture have been encouraged by the British government, although Wales has not yet achieved the same degree of devolution as Scotland. Overall tourism policy and product development is the responsibility of the Wales Tourist Board (VisitWales), a public body reporting to the Welsh Assembly.

Tourism resources

We can divide Wales into three tourist regions on the basis of geography and culture.

North Wales

North Wales, consisting of the counties of Gwynedd and Clwyd, is scenically the most interesting part of the country. Gwynedd is the most important tourist region in Wales. It is often regarded as the cultural 'heartland' of Wales, where the people continue to speak Welsh as their first language. The traditional culture has persisted partly because the region is isolated to some extent by the rugged mountains of Snowdonia, which rise abruptly from the coast. North Wales contains Britain's largest national park and impressive castles dating from Edward I's conquest of Gwynedd in the thirteenth century. A number of these castles – Conwy, Harlech, Beaumaris, and Caernarfon – are World Heritage Sites.

The mountains of Snowdonia form the core of the Snowdonia National Park. They have a craggy appearance quite different from the rounded outline of the Cambrian Mountains to the south and the Hiraethog or Denbighshire moors to the east. Radiating from Snowdon itself are a number of deep trough-like valleys carved out by the glaciers of the Ice Age – examples include the Llanberis Pass and Nant Ffrancon, which contains a number of small lakes. In such a valley is Lake Bala, offering facilities for water sports and fishing. The beautiful scenery has encouraged touring and activity tourism in such centres as Beddgelert, Llangollen, and Betws-y-Coed. For the less active, the Snowdon Mountain Railway takes visitors to the summit of the highest mountain of Wales from Llanberis, but visitor pressure has caused serious erosion.

Tourism dominates the economy of North Wales and takes advantage of both the rural and industrial heritage. Most of the high land in North Wales is of little agricultural value. In the upper valleys there are isolated sheep farms, with their characteristic stone buildings and small irregular fields separated by roughstone walls. As in northern England, hill farms cater for tourists as a way of supplementing their incomes. The other major industry is based on mineral resources; large areas near Bethesda, Llanberis, and Ffestiniog are the sites of slate quarries, some of which have become important tourist attractions – as at Llechwedd. In Llanberis the Welsh Slate Centre interprets this once important industry for the tourist. Other industrial features that are now tourist attractions are the narrow-gauge railways, promoted as 'the Great Little Trains of Wales'. Today, Wales is a source of both power and water for England and these resources are also used for tourism, as the power stations welcome visitors. In contrast to these examples of Victorian and modern industry, the Centre for

Alternative Technology at Machynlleth is an important attraction with true 'green' credentials.

Discussion point

There is no doubt that national parks such as Snowdonia are under increased visitor pressure. One management approach to this problem is to 'spread the load' to ensure that visitor pressure is not focused at particular points; the other is to use the 'honeypot' approach where visitors are focused and funnelled into particular areas, which are then intensively managed to cope with the increased visitor load. In class, debate the pros and cons of each approach.

The coastline of North Wales is particularly attractive and easily reached from the conurbations of Merseyside and Manchester. There are a number of popular seaside resorts along the coast east of the estuary of the Conwy:

- Llandudno is perhaps best known as a conference venue, but boasts a fine beach situated between two headlands – the Great and Little Orme;
- Colwyn Bay is the site of the Welsh Mountain Zoo; and
- Rhyl pioneered all-weather tourism facilities with its 'Sun Centre' and Sea Life Centre, as part of a substantial redevelopment programme. Much of the narrow coastal strip around Rhyl accommodates large caravan sites.

These resorts, and particularly Llandudno, have benefited from the upgrading of the A55, traditionally the route from the conurbations of North-West England, although this does mean that day visitors now easily outnumber staying holidaymakers.

Anglesey and the Lleyn Peninsula are less commercialised, with smaller resorts, such as Pwllheli, devoted to sailing or other 'activity' holidays. Bardsey Island off the coast is a nature reserve. In parts of North Wales the purchase of country cottages as 'second homes' by visitors from outside the region is controversial (partly because it is felt to weaken the Welsh language and culture). Although some villages (for example, Abersoch on the Lleyn peninsula) are dominated by second homes, others argue that the rural area benefits economically by bringing business to local suppliers. Holyhead, with its marina and important ferry service to Ireland, is the only significant commercial centre.

Mid Wales

Mid Wales is also mountainous and thinly populated, except for the narrow coastal plain around Cardigan Bay, and the upper valleys of the Wye and the Severn. Around Cardigan Bay Welsh culture is strong, while much of Powys has been English speaking for centuries. North–South communications are difficult, especially by rail, and there are no large towns. There are a number of small seaside resorts on Cardigan Bay, such as Aberdovey and the university town of Aberystwyth, which are popular with visitors from the English Midlands. Inland, there are some small market towns, such as Newtown, Llanidloes, and Welshpool, and a number of former spas, such as Builth Wells. These have become centres for touring the Cambrian Mountains, but are important historic towns in their own right; Montgomery, for example, has many Georgian buildings. Other attractions in Mid Wales include Powis Castle, Lake Vyrnwy, and the Glywedog Gorge.

South Wales

South Wales contains the majority of the Welsh population of almost three million and most of the industries. The region is separated from the rest of Wales by the Black Mountains and the Brecon Beacons, but is easily accessible from southern England via the two Severn road bridges. In the centre of the region lies the South Wales coalfield, which is crossed from north to south by a number of deep narrow valleys, including those of the Taff, Rhondda, and Rhymney. Mining communities straggle almost continuously along the valley bottoms, and the landscape was formerly disfigured by spoil heaps, tips, and abandoned workings. Both British and European Union initiatives have transformed this landscape of dereliction with:

- landscaped country parks;
- the development of a museum of coal mining at Big Pit, Blaenavon; and
- the Rhondda Heritage Park.

A similar transformation has occurred in the two main urban centres of Wales. In Swansea dockland areas have been redeveloped as a maritime quarter with water sports, retailing, restaurants, and hotels. West of Swansea, the Gower Peninsula is an Area of Outstanding Natural Beauty with good beaches. Cardiff owes its growth as a major city to the Industrial Revolution and was not officially designated as the capital of Wales until 1955. Now the seat of the Welsh Assembly, Cardiff is the location of major developments such as:

- the Millennium Stadium;
- the Wales Millennium Centre for the Performing Arts; and
- the large-scale redevelopment of Cardiff Harbour and the former dock area with museums (such as Techniquest), restaurants and hotels, and international exposure as the location for a science fiction TV series.

The capital has good international links through Cardiff Wales Airport. The city centre is dominated by Cardiff Castle, which despite appearances is largely a Victorian creation rather than a medieval fortress, and the National Museum and Art Gallery of Wales. On the outskirts of the city is another national institution – the Welsh Folk Museum at St Fagans and Castell Coch, a Victorian fantasy castle. Penarth is a small seaside resort, while Barry Island boasts a major pleasure park.

Historically, the region has a great deal to offer. There are important Roman remains at Caerwent and Caerleon, and in the eleventh century the Normans, following their conquest of England, built many castles to control the coastal plain and the valleys leading into the mountains of Mid Wales. Near the Welsh border, Tintern Abbey, Monmouth – with its fortified bridge – and Chepstow Castle are notable examples of heritage attractions.

The Brecon Beacons National Park rises to over 900 metres at Pen-y-Fan, while to the west is the old hunting ground of Fforest Fawr, in the north-east the broad valley of the River Usk, and to the south spectacular waterfalls and caves. Hay-on-Wye is the touring base for the park, the centre for the second-hand book trade and inspiration for the 'book city' concept. On the Usk, Abergavenny is also a touring and trekking centre. East of Brecon, Llangorse Lake is developed for water sports and is an important centre for naturalists.

In Dyfed in the south-west, the National Botanic Garden for Wales is an attraction of international significance. The Pembrokeshire Coast National Park is Britain's only linear national park, extending from Pen Camais in the north to Amroth in the south.

It includes some offshore islands, such as Caldey, famous for its monastery, and the bird sanctuaries of Skokholm and Skomer. The most important cultural attraction is the small city of St David's, whose cathedral was a major place of pilgrimage in medieval times. A coastal path around the park links a number of attractions such as the resorts of Tenby and Saundersfoot, Manorbier Castle, the lily ponds at Bosherston, and Pendine Sands, where attempts on the world land speed record have taken place.

Assignment

Eating out is an important part of the tourism experience and although standards in restaurants and hotels have improved considerably in recent years throughout Britain, there are skills shortages and other problems in these sectors. Discuss how Wales can draw on locally sourced food specialities and its cultural traditions to give visitors, such as a group of foreign language students based in Bournemouth, or a Japanese tour group, an authentic 'Taste of Wales'.

The offshore islands

Britain's offshore island destinations include the Channel Islands, which are geographically much closer to the Cherbourg Peninsula in France than to southern England, the Isles of Scilly lying some 60 kilometres to the south west of Cornwall in the Atlantic Ocean, and the Isle of Man, situated in the Irish Sea, midway between England, Scotland and Ireland.

The Channel Islands

The Channel Islands capitalise on their favourable climate (they enjoy more sunshine than other parts of the British Isles), their Norman-French traditions, and their culinary attractions. Jersey and Guernsey are officially dependencies of the British Crown, with their own parliaments, postal services, and fiscal systems offering low rates of tax, which attracts business visitors, an influx of retired people, and duty-free shoppers. The islands have attractive coastal scenery and fine beaches (although the strong tides are hazardous to bathers). The Channel Islands were the only part of the British Isles to be occupied by Germany during the Second World War, and the Occupation from 1940 to 1945 features in a number of heritage attractions. Tourist facilities are well developed, with a range of accommodation (other than camping). Jersey and Guernsey are linked by air, fast ferry and shipping services to ports in northern France and southern England. Tourism has helped to boost an economy once largely dependent on dairy farming and horticulture, but hotels depend to a large extent on imported labour and visitors' cars add to the pressure of traffic on the road networks of the islands.

- **Jersey's** tourist centre is the capital, St Helier, which features Elizabeth Castle in the bay and the Fort Regent Leisure Centre above the town. The waterfront includes a marina development, illustrating the importance of the yachting market. The island's history is interpreted at a number of sites, particularly the Living Legend themed attraction. Other key attractions are Jersey Zoo, beaches such as St Brelade's and the sweep of St Ouen's Bay, and a number of secluded coves. Jersey has lost market share to Mediterranean destinations; however, the island's tourist board has developed an imaginative strategy to claw back tourists, facilitated by the introduction of budget-priced air services.

- **Guernsey's** tourism industry is on a smaller scale than that of Jersey but offers similar attractions. These include a number of craft centres and museums based on the island's literary associations, while the introduction of gambling casinos may attract higher spending visitors. The focus of tourism is the capital, St Peter Port.
- The smaller Channel Islands can be visited on day excursions from Guernsey or Jersey. Sark boasts spectacular coastal scenery, and along with Alderney, Herm and Jethou, can offer a limited amount of accommodation.

The Isles of Scilly consist of 200 small islands, of which five are inhabited. They belong to the Duchy of Cornwall, and tourism, along with other matters affecting the islanders, is the responsibility of the Council of the Scillies based at Hugh Town on the island of St Mary's. The main attractions are the mild climate (as shown by the subtropical gardens of Tresco), the unspoilt maritime scenery and bird life, and the many shipwreck sites awaiting investigation by scuba divers. St Mary's provides boat services to the other islands, and is linked to Penzance on the mainland by air and shipping services.

The Isle of Man

The Isle of Man – 50 kilometres long and 20 kilometres wide – is often described as 'northern England' in miniature, but it is administratively and culturally distinct, with a Celtic and Viking heritage. It has its own language, postal service, parliament (Tynewald), and an independent fiscal system which has allowed it to develop as an offshore finance centre. In Victorian times holidaymakers reached the Isle of Man by steamship, sailing out of Liverpool, Heysham, Belfast and Dublin. In recent years fast catamarans have also been introduced, and the island's airport, Ronaldsway, is linked to many regional airports in the UK, Ireland and the Channel Islands with carriers such as Flybe and Manx2.Com. The island can provide a variety of attractions:

- **Douglas and other coastal resorts.** Douglas, with its sweeping Victorian promenade of guest houses and terraced hotels, is the capital and major seaport of the Isle of Man, featuring the Manx Museum and 'The Story of Mann' exhibition. It represents the main concentration of bed spaces, and offers a range of restaurants and entertainment facilities that are used by residents and visitors alike, such as the Summerland casino and leisure centre. Other coastal towns, each with a range of small visitor attractions, craft workshops and accommodation, include Port Erin, Peel, Ramsey and Castletown.
- The **cultural heritage** includes many historic buildings, for example the castle and cathedral in Peel and Castle Rushen at Castletown, which was the former capital. The best known feature is the world's largest working waterwheel at Laxey. There are a number of museums and craft centres, while the Cregneash Folk Village interprets the crofting way of life of islanders in the past.
- The **natural heritage** provides the setting for special interest holidays, and both walking and cycling trails are available.
- The **transport heritage** includes horse-drawn trams and narrow gauge railways, but the most famous attraction is the annual Tourist Trophy (TT) motorcycle races, which started in 1904 as a way of extending the holiday season. This event takes place on a road circuit around the northern half of the island and fills hotels to capacity during 'TT Week' in June.

The Isle of Man has a varied accommodation base ranging from luxury country house hotels to value-for-money guesthouses. The Manx government has a long-standing scheme to assist the accommodation sector both to adjust to the demands of the contemporary holidaymaker, and to attract new accommodation stock. The tourism authorities also operate a compulsory registration and grading scheme for accommodation. The thriving business tourism market has encouraged a range of excellent restaurants.

The Tourism and Leisure Department has responsibility for both the promotion and development of tourism on the island as well as leisure and public transport. The Isle of Man has had to adapt its tourism product to the tastes of twenty–first century holidaymakers. The island's traditional markets sought an English seaside product, and while this still forms part of the island's appeal, other elements of the destination mix are now seen as more important in attracting visitors. The Isle of Man is therefore an excellent example of a destination that has successfully repositioned itself to become more competitive.

EUROPE

Summary

- England, Scotland, Wales and the larger offshore islands are well endowed with most types of tourist attractions, and an increasingly professional approach to their management is evident.
- We can identify a number of common themes that include (1) the growth of heritage attractions, often based on declining industries; (2) the increasing use of rural resources for tourism and recreation, and (3) the growth of what we may broadly call cultural as well as recreational tourism to cities that until recently were associated solely with commerce and industry.
- The resorts that traditionally provided a British seaside holiday are re investing in improved facilities to attract new markets.
- With devolution, Scotland, Wales and the Isle of Man have much greater scope for product development, marketing and promotion than hitherto.

Assignments

1 Compile a map to show places associated with the 'greats' in British literature, music and painting.

2 Explain why Britain's industrial heritage is an important part of its tourism appeal.

3 Following the success of a recent movie on this theme, a group of Australians wish to visit places associated with Britain's naval heritage. Arrange a tour route to meet their requirements.

4 Discuss the strengths and weaknesses of London as a venue for a major international sport event.

5 Explain the rise of the British seaside resort and its decline since the 1950s. Suggest how particular resorts could be revitalised.

The tourism geography of Ireland

Introduction

As an island situated on the western periphery of Europe, Ireland is geographically isolated from the rest of the EU and the world's main tourist-generating countries, with the exception of Britain. Since 1921 it has also been a divided island. The 26 predominantly Catholic counties that made up Eire (later the Republic of Ireland) chose the path of independence after centuries of English rule, and neutrality in the Second World War, whereas six out of the nine counties of Ulster opted to remain part of the UK as the Province of Northern Ireland. This partition never achieved widespread support among the Catholic community of Northern Ireland, who were subjected to economic and political discrimination by the Protestant majority. The differences between the two communities even extended to sport, with Catholics supporting Gaelic football and hurling, while Protestants favoured soccer. The outbreak of violence in Northern Ireland in 1969 proved detrimental to both its tourism industry and that of the Republic, with considerable disruption to cross-border communications. The division of Ireland remains an unresolved problem, but on-going peace initiatives since the mid-1990s have made considerable progress toward ending 'the troubles' and have led to the co-ordinated development of tourism, with an 'all-island' agency – 'Tourism Ireland' – funded by the Irish Government and the Northern Ireland Executive.

After centuries of relative poverty, between the 1980s and the 2008 global financial crisis, the Republic of Ireland experienced substantial economic growth, due to EU membership, attractive investment opportunities for foreign companies, and a highly educated workforce, to become the so-called 'Celtic Tiger'. Many feared that the traditional lifestyle and countryside were threatened by runaway development, materialism and large scale immigration during the boom years at the beginning of the twenty first century. Northern Ireland experienced less growth, despite considerable investment by the British government.

Nevertheless, Ireland remains more rural than other West European countries, with few major cities. There is generally less pressure on resources, although some parts of the coastline have been adversely affected by unplanned development. The low population density, uncrowded roads, unspoiled countryside and slower pace of life make Ireland a destination which is particularly well suited to rural tourism. The people have a reputation for hospitality and conviviality and the legendary *craic* is itself an attraction. It is therefore no accident that Irish 'themed' pubs are now found all over the world, while Irish music and dance have gained an international following.

The central feature of Ireland is a low-lying plain, dotted with drumlins (rounded hills of glacial origin), lakes and expanses of peat bog. These lowlands are almost encircled by mountains, which are not particularly rugged, and breached by both the valley of the Shannon in the west and the coast around Dublin in the east – traditionally the gateways for visitors. Ireland's reputation as the 'Emerald Isle' is due to the mild, damp climate, which favours the growth of lush dairy pasture throughout the year, and in the south-west, sub-tropical vegetation. However, the unpredictable weather, particularly cool cloudy summers, is one of Ireland's weaknesses as a holiday destination.

Ireland is poor in natural resources compared to Britain, and from the seventeenth century onwards, many of its young people emigrated to seek greater economic opportunities, including enlistment in the British and foreign armies. The Protestant 'Scots-Irish' from Ulster played a major role advancing the frontier of settlement in North America. Following the Great Famine of 1845–1848 much larger numbers, mainly from the Catholic south and west, were forced to emigrate overseas. The descendants of those emigrants in the USA, Canada, Australia and Britain are now many times more numerous than the population of Ireland itself. Ethnic tourism and genealogy (tracing family roots) is therefore a lucrative business in both the Republic and Northern Ireland. The epic theme of emigration also plays a major role in the heritage attractions of both countries.

Ireland's heritage is an important part of its tourism industry, though Catholics and Protestants in Northern Ireland interpret this differently. We can identify the following themes:

- **The Ireland of myth and legend.** Ireland is particularly rich in archaeological sites from the Neolithic period, the Bronze Age and Iron Age, which probably had ritual or religious significance. These include many stone circles, the passage graves at Newgrange north of Dublin, the hill fort of Navan near Armagh, and the Hill of Tara in Meath, capital of the high kings of Ireland in pre-Christian times.
- **Religion in Ireland as the 'Land of Saints and Scholars'.** Many of Ireland's religious monuments – Celtic crosses, monasteries and 'round towers', together with works of Celtic art such as the Book of Kells – date from the centuries following the collapse of the Roman Empire, when Ireland was a centre of Christian missionary endeavour to the rest of Europe. The monastic cells clinging to the remote, rugged Skellig Islands and the Rock of Cashel in County Tipperary are remarkable examples of this religious heritage.
- **Nation building.** The Gaelic language and Celtic heritage in music and dance are seen as central to Ireland's national identity. Nevertheless, the Vikings contributed by founding Dublin, Limerick and Cork. Moreover the great majority of the

population are English-speaking, due to the long period of rule by England, starting with Henry II in 1170, but not consolidated until the sixteenth and seventeenth centuries, with the imposition of English law, the Anglican Church, and an influx of settlers from other parts of the British Isles. The Anglo-Irish landowning class left a legacy of castles and great country houses that are now important tourist attractions, but which were viewed at the time by the dispossessed Catholic peasantry as symbols of oppression. The struggle for land and freedom, particularly the 1798 rebellion, is a major theme in heritage interpretation.

- **The literary and artistic heritage**. Ireland has produced many of the great writers and dramatists of the English-speaking world, and tourist trails and guides are available.

Transport

The mode of travel to Ireland has changed since the 1970s as low cost carriers and aggressive marketing have seen air transport increase at the expense of the ferry services. The only direct sea routes to Ireland from the Continent are:

- Cork/Roscoff;
- Rosslare/Cherbourg; and
- Rosslare/Roscoff.

There is a wide choice of sea routes from Britain:

- Rosslare/Fishguard or Pembroke;
- Dun Laoghaire/Holyhead;
- Dublin/Liverpool, Douglas or Holyhead;
- Belfast/Liverpool;
- Belfast/Douglas and Heysham; and
- Belfast/Stranraer, Troon or Cairnryan.

On many of these sea routes operators are investing in state of the art vessels, including high-speed catamarans, and are also cutting fares in a bid to regain market share from the airlines. Deregulated airlines have also reduced fares, sparking a price war, and opened up access to Ireland's regional airports. Ryanair for example, pioneered the low cost carrier as a business model and the development of regional airports – supported by EU funding – namely Waterford, Kerry (Farranfore), Galway, Sligo, Donegal (Carrickfinn), and Horan International (formerly Knock). The four main airports are Belfast, Dublin, Shannon and Cork. Dublin is the international gateway to the Republic of Ireland, and the hub for Aer Lingus, the national carrier. Belfast City Airport is the gateway to Northern Ireland, and is well served by routes to the rest of the UK (including a shuttle service to Heathrow) and the Continent. The expansion of air services has encouraged the growth of business and conference traffic. Ireland's location on the western periphery of Europe does give it the advantage of uncongested skies and, with the development of route networks between European regional airports, the authorities intend that Ireland will become less isolated from its tourist markets. Road transport is much more important for domestic tourism than the limited rail network. There has been a substantial increase in car ownership since the 1990s, and Dublin is now the focus of a national motorway network. Some measure of integrated travel is possible through Coras Iompair Eireann (CIE) which operates rail and bus services throughout the Republic, closely linked to transport providers in Northern Ireland.

Discussion point

Account for the success of Ryanair as a low cost carrier. Investigate the impact of Ryanair on tourist routes and tourism development in Ireland and continental Europe.

The Republic of Ireland

Domestic and outbound tourism demand

The propensity for, and frequency of, holiday taking has increased in recent years particularly for overseas travel. The growth of the Irish economy allied to airline competition has encouraged outbound tourism, and over 7 million trips overseas are made each year. The most popular destinations are the United Kingdom (around half of all trips) and mainland Europe, but with budget and charter flights to long-haul destinations, a greater range of destinations is now available. There is also a substantial volume of cross-border traffic by road and rail between the Republic and Northern Ireland. Factors differentiating the nature of tourism demand in Ireland from that in Britain include:

- a much higher proportion of young people in the population (35 per cent are under 25 years of age), resulting in an expanding market for family holidays; and
- although the role of the Roman Catholic Church has diminished since the 1980s, pilgrimages to shrines such as Lourdes continue to have great popular appeal. The most important of these in Ireland itself is Knock in County Mayo, which has its own airport.

Nonetheless, domestic tourism remains the mainstay of Irish tourism with over 7 million trips in 2009. The south-west is the most popular region, and holiday trips are growing at the expense of business trips and VFR.

Inbound tourism demand

In contrast to the UK, Ireland achieved only very slow growth in overseas arrivals over the decade of the 1970s, and high inflation and unfavourable exchange rates led to slight reductions in arrivals in the early 1980s. However, deregulation of Ireland/UK air services and the development of regional airports has increased arrivals to approach 7 million in 2009. Substantial investment in the Irish tourism product, improved marketing and the prospects for peace in Northern Ireland have boosted arrivals – particularly from North America. Features of the Irish inbound market include:

- heavy dependence on the British market, which accounts for almost 60 per cent of arrivals;
- the increasing domination of the airlines, leading to a response by the ferry companies to improve quality and introduce faster services;
- acute seasonality; and
- the high percentage of 'ethnic' visits, especially from Britain and the USA. Dependence on the US market leaves Ireland vulnerable to external crises such as '9/11'.

The Republic of Ireland's tourism industry employs six per cent of the economically active population, and is characterised by small businesses. The tourism sector has received considerable assistance from the government and the European Union, providing Ireland with a competitive edge in the twenty first century.

In the Republic the policy-making body for tourism is the Department of Arts, Sport and Tourism, supported by the national tourist organisation – Tourism Ireland. This is responsible for promoting the whole of Ireland as a destination overseas, with new markets emerging in Japan, Eastern Europe, South Africa and the Middle East. The original tourist board for the Republic, Bord Fáilte, was established in 1955 with promotion (both domestic and overseas) and development functions. Unlike the situation in most of the UK, hotels and guesthouses are classified under a statutory registration scheme, while the government's business expansion scheme supports tourism enterprises. In the 1980s the Irish government re-evaluated the importance of tourism to their economy, leading Bord Fáilte to contract out much of its operational work to focus on international marketing. At the same time, a five-year planning framework for tourism was put in place with the aim of increasing both tourist volume and spending. The review was closely integrated into a successful bid for investment from the European Regional Development Fund and the European Social Fund. These were applied to programmes to extend and upgrade the range and quality of tourist facilities.

The injection of money into the tourism sector has led to greater professionalism, widened the product range and improved quality generally. It has also had the effect of changing the distribution of tourism across Ireland. While tourism is more evenly spread than in most other European countries, the west and the south-west have lost market share to Dublin.

With the new millennium and the apparent success of the peace process in Northern Ireland, 'Fáilte Ireland', an all-island marketing body was created in 2003. The functions of the new body comprise:

* domestic marketing;
* product development and promotion;
* improving the quality of accommodation; and
* managing the tourism product development scheme.

In the wake of the peace process local authorities on both sides of the Irish border are co-operating in tourism development, aided by considerable investment from Interreg (the European Structural Fund's assistance for border regions) and other EU schemes.

Tourism resources

The Republic's tourism resource base includes a long coastline with many unspoiled surfing beaches facing the Atlantic Ocean and the Irish Sea, six national parks, a number of forest parks, and an extensive system of inland waterways. Among the most important linear attractions are the Grand Canal and the Wicklow Way, a long distance footpath.

The following tourism products are available:

* Rural tourism that not only supports the local economy and helps to stem depopulation from the more remote parts of the country, but also keeps alive traditions and handicrafts such as embroidery and knitwear.

- Activity holidays, including fishing in the many unpolluted lakes and rivers, golf (with ample space for development), sailing, canoeing and horse riding.
- Cultural activities based on the theatre, folk museums, and international festivals.
- Ethnic activities based around the many centres of genealogy.
- English language schools in competition with the UK.
- Culinary activities sourcing local produce and characterised by high standards of service.

Although the Republic of Ireland is organised in five regional tourist boards, we prefer to divide the country for tourism purposes into three main regions, based on the historic provinces of Leinster, Connacht and Munster:

1 Dublin and the east;
2 Western Ireland; and
3 The South-west.

Dublin and the east (Leinster)

Dublin is not only the capital of the Republic of Ireland and home to a third of its population, but has also become one of the world's great tourist cities, with a major airport and ferry access through the port of Dun Laoghaire. The Dublin region has seen the largest growth of tourism in Ireland, so that by 2006 the city received 5.8 million overseas visitors and almost a million domestic tourists, supporting 25,000 full-time jobs.

The main tourism resources of Dublin are linked by a series of themed trails and include:

- The city's role in Irish history, recalled by Dublin Castle (the seat of government under British rule), Kilmainham Gaol, and the General Post Office (associated with the 1916 Easter Rising). This history is brought to life in the multi-media exhibition at City Hall and a number of museums.
- Literary heritage showcased in the Dublin Writers' Museum, featuring the lives and works of Joyce, Sheridan, Wilde and other celebrities, and the Abbey Theatre where many of their plays were first performed.
- The architectural heritage of fine eighteenth century buildings and squares.
- The Genealogical Office, an important resource for the ethnic tourist market retracing their Irish roots.
- The Guinness Storehouse, a themed experience based on Dublin's most famous product.

The river Liffey divides the city into the *northside* and the *southside* and was the focus for city-wide initiatives to celebrate the millennium. The southside of Dublin contains Trinity College, Ireland's oldest and most famous university, and Temple Bar, an exciting 'left bank' district that has emerged since the early 1990s. This is now one of the city's most popular tourist areas, offering a wide range of leisure facilities and entertainments. The northside includes O'Connell Street, Phoenix Park, and a cluster of cultural attractions.

The capital is a good base for tourism circuits that include some of the most attractive scenery of eastern Ireland – the granitic Wicklow Mountains with their steep-sided glens, now designated as a national park. The narrow coastal plain is fertile, with a relatively dry and sunny climate. The Vale of Avoca is famous for the beauty of its landscape, and the village of Avoca attracts many visitors as the setting for a well-known TV series. The main tourist centres include the holiday resorts of Bray and Tramore; Waterford, which is world famous for its glassware; and Wexford, which hosts an international opera festival. New Ross is one of many small towns that have capitalised on ethnic links with the USA – in this case the Kennedy family. Kilkenny has a fine medieval heritage, also supported by international festivals.

Western Ireland (Connacht and Donegal)

The Irish government has encouraged tourist facilities to locate in the west, which is a much poorer region economically with a high dependence on traditional peasant farming. Special incentives are available in the Gaeltacht – those areas where the people still speak the Gaelic language as their mother-tongue. This is because the west is regarded as the true repository of Irish national culture, epitomised by the *ceilidh*, rather than the Anglicised south and east. Local communities have encouraged tourism with farmhouse holidays and by providing self catering accommodation in the form of traditional style cottages.

> **Discussion point**
>
> Tourism is often blamed for threatening the survival of ancient languages, but it can also be a force for their revival, as language is an attraction in itself. In class, debate the two sides of this argument.

Galway is the recognised capital of the west and its airport has developed rapidly in line with Ireland's other regional airports. It is the southern gateway to the Connemara area and, with its adjoining resort Salthill, is an important centre for touring holidays and conferences. The main touring circuits are:

- the Great Western Lakes – Corrib, Mask, and Caarra – to the north; and
- to the west is a superb indented coastline and the Twelve Bens, mountains that are included in the Connemara National Park.

In the south-west, the Aran Islands – famous in Irish literature and folklore – can be reached by sea or air.

Donegal in the north-west is geographically part of the historic province of Ulster, but is largely Gaelic-speaking. Here a rugged coastline is interspersed with fine beaches and a number of attractive fishing harbours such as Killybegs, while the lake and mountain scenery of Glenveagh National Park is popular with visitors.

The South-west (Munster)

The South-west includes the most attractive scenery in Ireland. County Clare boasts the spectacular cliffs of Moher and the Burren area of limestone scenery, which is of great interest to botanists as well as geologists. A modern visitor centre interprets this heritage, helping to reduce the impacts of tourism on this sensitive natural area which is now a national park. Three of Ireland's most important tourist centres are located in the South-west:

- **Killarney** was recognised as a holiday resort of international significance in the nineteenth century. Nowadays it is an ideal touring centre, including the famous scenic road known as the 'Ring of Kerry'. Killarney has the largest concentration of bedspaces outside the capital, and its airport at Farranfore is positioned to attract the short break market from the UK. Nearby are the lakes and mountains of the Killarney National Park, Muckross House and some of the best golf courses in Europe.
- Tralee is famous for its festival, largely created by Bord Fáilte to attract participants claiming Irish descent from all over the world.
- **Cork** is the second city of the Republic and the centre of a development zone that includes:
    - Kinsale – a long-established and important sailing and fishing centre, finding a niche market in culinary short-breaks;
    - Blarney – world famous for its castle, featuring the stone which confers the gift of eloquence; and

Photo 9.1 The Cliffs of Moher facing the Atlantic: western Ireland offers some of the most spectacular coastal scenery in Europe (istockphoto.com/ kelvinjay)

- Cobh was historically important before the jet era as the principal staging point for passenger liners and millions of emigrants to the United States, most of whom would have travelled in steerage class. The quayside has been restored with attractions recalling its role in Ireland's social and transport history, including the voyage of the *Titanic*.
- **Limerick and the Shannon** area offers high quality accommodation and provides good access to other areas. Shannon Airport until the 1960s was a compulsory stop on trans-Atlantic flights and pioneered the 'duty free' concept of airport shopping shortly after the Second World War. The River Shannon is now more important as a tourism resource for sailing and fishing than as a commercial waterway, with Athlone and other smaller centres providing facilities. North-west of Limerick is Bunratty Castle, which pioneered the medieval banquet theme so popular with North Americans. Bunratty has now expanded its heritage attractions into a folk park and shopping complex.

Case study 9.1

The horse as a focus for tourism

In a post-industrial society it is difficult to appreciate the central role the horse played in European and American history until well into the twentieth century, with the selection of different breeds for their suitability in warfare, hunting, agriculture, transport and racing. There is still a widespread interest in horse-related leisure activities, known as equestrianism (from *equus*, the Latin word for horse). Horse-riding is an important part of countryside-based recreation, but has received less attention from policy-makers than hiking or cycling. Riding makes few demands on resources and provides income for significant numbers of farmers and small businesses, such as tack shops supplying specialist equipment. The environmental impact includes trail erosion and trampling of vegetation in areas with the greatest recreational demand, for example Epping Forest with its heavy clay soils close to the Greater London conurbation. Equestrian tourism is a relatively neglected field of study, bringing together a wide spectrum of horse-related activities for tourists or day visitors. These involve:

- Active participants in recreation, where the visitor does the riding or driving. This includes trail riding, hacking, trekking, show jumping, and touring by horse-drawn caravan (an Irish speciality).
- Spectators at events where the visitor watches others display their skills. This includes horse races, horse fairs, horse shows, gymkhanas, eventing competitions, rodeos, and polo matches.
- Visitors to attractions that breed and train horses, or where the history of the horse is showcased along with other elements of the rural heritage.

With its mild climate and largely rural setting, Ireland is well suited to this type of tourism. The Irish have traditionally excelled in horsemanship, rider training and horse breeding, and in few other countries is there such widespread interest in riding and racing (the Republic with a population of only 4 million boasted 25 racecourses in 2007, compared to Britain's 59). This interest is part of the national psyche and may date back to pre-Christian times when the horse was regarded as sacred by the Celtic tribes. Connemara ponies and Irish hunters are two native breeds that are renowned internationally. Events such as the Dublin Horse Show and race meetings attract many visitors from Britain and contribute significantly to the national economy. Riding holidays attract 37,000 overseas visitors a year, with a spend of $42 million. As for facilities, in 2007 Ireland offered 254 riding centres approved by the Association of Irish

Riding Establishments (AIRE). Some of these are large purpose-built facilities, whereas many are attached to working farms and others form part of resort hotels. Ireland's rolling countryside of lowland heath, grassland and woods provides an attractive resource base, with less road traffic than in most parts of western Europe. Along the Atlantic coast there are wide stretches of almost empty beaches for trail riding.

The Irish government has taken a close interest in the horse industry, establishing the Irish Horse Board in 2006 to co-ordinate the sporting, breeding and leisure aspects of this sector of the economy. Nevertheless, equestrian tourism has played only a minor role in the promotion of Ireland's image as a destination. Like other rural activities, riding suffered from the foot and mouth crisis of 2001, which closed access to much of the countryside, and was slow to recover from the effects of '9/11'. This may be due to the following reasons:

- Ireland has become more urbanised, with demands from city dwellers for more recreational opportunities conflicting with the interests of farmers, who fear damage to property and litigation.
- With the exception of areas managed by Coillte (the forestry service) and the National Parks and Wildlife Service, most of the countryside is privately-owned farmland, holdings are often fragmented, and there are few legally recognised rights of way.
- The providers of the riding or race-going experience have lacked an overall vision for this sector of tourism.

In response Fáilte Ireland has set out a strategy for equestrian tourism that identifies target markets and co-ordinates the activities of the stakeholders in the industry, with the aim of positioning Ireland as 'The Land of the Horse', where riding and race-going become part of a broader cultural experience.

Case study 9.1

EUROPE

Assignments

1 Identify the barriers that may prevent greater participation in riding as a recreational activity, and suggest ways in which demand might increase in the future.
2 A tour operator based in southern England has identified riding holidays as a niche product. This means investigating the advantages and disadvantages of Ireland as a destination for their clients. Other destinations being considered are Spain, Hungary, Argentina, Kentucky and Arizona, which many see as offering serious competition. You should take account of climate, resources, facilities, alternative activities for members of a group or family who are not horse-lovers, and 'après-ride' (the equivalent of après-ski in winter sports).

Northern Ireland

The Province is often referred to as Ulster, which in fact includes three of the Republic's border counties – Cavan, Monaghan and Donegal. It is much smaller than the Republic, with a third of its population of 1.8 million living in Belfast. Northern Ireland has frequent air and shipping services to Scotland and England, and a good road and railway network. Tourism marketing within the Province and product development are the responsibility of the Northern Ireland Tourist Board (NITB), which is overseen by the Department of Enterprise, Trade and Investment. The NITB works closely with

Fáilte Ireland and VisitBritain. There are also a number of regional tourist associations. Nevertheless, tourism contributes much less to Northern Ireland's GDP than is the case for other parts of the UK or the Republic.

Tourism resources

Northern Ireland boasts the largest inland body of water in the British Isles – Lough Neagh – at the centre of a network of rivers and lakes that provide a valuable recreational resource, including a canoe trail extending from Lough Erne in the west to Strangford Lough in the east. The scenery of limestone uplands, lakeland, and basalt cliffs is an important part of the country's tourism appeal. There are a number of forest parks and country parks providing facilities for recreation. Visitors are mainly attracted to the coast, with the National Trust playing an important role in conservation. Here Northern Ireland is at a disadvantage compared to the Republic, as there are as yet no national parks to attract overseas visitors. Many feel that the present designation of the Antrim Glens and the Mountains of Morne as AONBs is too low a profile for destination marketing, which since 1998 has been carried out by an all-Ireland agency, and also gives these key attractions insufficient protection against development. We will now look at the six counties in more detail, starting with the capital.

Belfast

Belfast is the seat of the Northern Ireland Assembly and Executive. The city owes its growth in the nineteenth century to the Industrial Revolution, when it became an important port and shipbuilding centre, thanks to its location on a deep, sheltered estuary. Linen manufacture here and at nearby Lisburn was also of major importance, so the industrial heritage (including the launching of the *Titanic*) is a significant part of Belfast's appeal. From 1969 to 1994 sectarian strife and the threat of terrorism caused a steep decline in tourist arrivals, especially from Britain. Since the 1998 Good Friday power sharing agreement the city has received an increasing number of visitors and is attracting investment, assisted by the formation of the Belfast Visitor and Convention Bureau in 1999. Belfast remains a deeply divided city, with 'peace walls' separating Catholic and Protestant communities. Even at the height of 'the troubles' the sectarian murals attracted sensation-seeking groups of foreign tourists. More conventional attractions include the redeveloped area around the cathedral, which now rivals Dublin's Temple Bar district for shopping and nightlife; the Odyssey Project – a large scale education, science, entertainment and sport development; and ECOS – an environmental education centre. Belfast also hosts a variety of international events such as the Cutty Sark Tall Ships Race. Attractions on the outskirts of the city include Hillsborough Castle, Carrickfergus Castle, and the Ulster Folk and Transport Museum at Cultra.

Antrim

North of Belfast lies the Antrim Plateau where the basalt rock gives rise to impressive scenery, including:

- The Giant's Causeway, Ireland's most famous natural attraction, and because of its unique character, a World Heritage Site, but one which is under considerable tourist pressure.

- The nine glens of Antrim – deep wooded valleys sloping down to the sea which were carved out of the basalt by fast-flowing streams. Glenariff is the best-known of these, and at the foot of the glen one of the many *feiscanna* (festivals) of the region is held.
- The spectacular coastline between Larne and Portrush. Portrush, Ballycastle, and Coleraine are the main resorts on the Antrim coast which are popular with day trippers. They have reinvested to improve facilities for family holidays and golf tourism.

Derry and Tyrone

Londonderry (Derry) is the main tourist centre in the west of the Province, set on a hill on the banks of the Foyle Estuary. This is also a divided city for sectarian reasons, with the Protestant community occupying the walled town that withstood a historic siege in 1689. South-east of Londonderry are the touring circuits of the Sperrin Mountains, where attractions include the Sperrin Heritage Centre, Springhill House, and the historic town of Moneymore. To the south is the Ulster-American Folk Park of Omagh, one of the increasing number of folk museums in the Province, which explores Scots-Irish links with the USA.

Fermanagh lakeland

Here the river Erne links a number of large lakes to provide an important resource for water-based recreation, nature lovers, and fishing holidays, which have long been popular with Dutch and German tourists. Castle Archdale on Lough Erne is the main centre for sailing and hire cruising, while Marble Arch is the best known of a number of caves in this limestone area. Castle Coole and Florence Court are significant attractions run by the National Trust. Enniskillen is an historic garrison town, noted for its associations with the British Army.

Armagh and County Down

This area includes the historic city of Armagh which is the spiritual capital of Ireland with two cathedrals serving the Catholic and Anglican communities. South Armagh is a former problem area on the border, where EU funding has benefited rural tourism initiatives by farmers' co-operatives. To the south-east rises the granite mass of the Mournes, rounded mountains sweeping down to the sea, and because of this area's closeness to the Belfast conurbation, subject to considerable pressure from a variety of outdoor recreation activities. On the coast, Newcastle is a seaside resort and a sailing and golf centre. Other resorts at the foot of the Mourne Mountains are lively Warrenpoint and the quieter Rostrevor, both on Carlingford Lough. The Ards Peninsula is a scenic area within easy reach of the resort of Bangor and the city of Belfast. Attractions on the peninsula include Castle Ward, Mount Stewart, and Kearney Village. The Ards Peninsula is separated from the rest of County Down by the inlet of Strangford Lough, now a marine reserve and bird sanctuary. It is also the setting for the Strangford Stone, erected for the Millennium. Around the Lough are the abbeys of Inch, Grey, and Comber, and to the south, the cathedral town of Downpatrick with a visitor centre interpreting the legacy of St Patrick as the bringer of Christianity to Ireland in the fifth century.

Summary

- Despite the political and religious divisions, Ireland is well endowed with many types of tourist attractions.
- It can be divided geographically into a number of tourist regions, each with a particular blend of natural and cultural resources.
- We can however identify a number of common themes. These include (1) the use of European funds to develop tourism; (2) the growth of themed heritage attractions, particularly those stressing the Celtic contribution; (3) the increasing use of rural tourism to encourage the economy in remoter areas – often based on farm stays; and (4) the growth of urban tourism in terms of both short holidays, based on cultural attractions, and business trips.
- The unified development of tourism across Ireland is a significant innovation that should benefit both countries.

Assignments

1 Describe the resources and facilities available in Ireland for various types of outdoor recreation.
2 Evaluate the importance of Irish culture and tradition to its tourism industry.
3 Explain why historical ties to the USA and other countries largely determine tourist flows to Ireland.

CHAPTER 10

The tourism geography of Scandinavia

Introduction

Geographically speaking, Scandinavia is a peninsula in the north of Europe that for most of its history has been somewhat isolated from the rest of the continent. In addition to Norway and Sweden, Scandinavia as a cultural and political entity includes Denmark, Finland, Iceland and the Faroe Islands. All these countries are members of the Nordic Council (Norden) which is responsible for a high level of co-operation in policies affecting transport, tourism, education and the environment. The Scandinavian airline SAS, which is jointly owned by the governments of Denmark, Norway and Sweden is one such example of international co-operation, and was the first to develop transpolar routes to North America and the Far East.

Until well into the twentieth century, the Scandinavian countries were relatively poor and the source of large-scale emigration to North America. The disadvantages of infertile soils, a rigorous climate and a peripheral location have been overcome by hard work, discipline, skill, ingenuity and a strong sense of civic responsibility. As a result, the Scandinavian countries have achieved a high level of economic prosperity based on advanced technology, combined with health and social welfare services that are among the best in the world. The region also boasts some of the most striking examples of modern architecture. High environmental standards are maintained, both in the cities, which are free of litter and graffiti, and in the countryside. Compared to the crowding which afflicts most of Europe, Scandinavia can offer vast areas of sparsely populated coast and countryside, with almost unrestricted access to a range of recreational resources, which in Norway and Sweden is guaranteed by law. Although car ownership levels are high, public transport systems are usually integrated and provide a viable alternative for touring in the more populated areas.

The Scandinavian landscape still bears the imprint of the glaciers of the last Ice Age. The glaciers eroded the valleys of western Norway into deep troughs, which were later invaded by the sea to form the fjords, and scraped bare the ancient plateau surfaces of Finland and Sweden. Here the ice sheets left masses of boulder clay, which are now covered by coniferous forest dotted with lakes and outcrops of rock. The climate varies from cool temperate in Jutland to sub-arctic in northern Scandinavia. Most of the region has a continental climate with severely cold winters and warm summers. The main negative feature affecting the development of tourism is the shortness of the summer season and the darkness of winter, due to the northerly latitude.

The Scandinavian countries have shared similar cultural features since the Viking era (approximately 750 to 1100). The Viking heritage has perhaps been over-emphasised with a view to international tourism, compared to less widely-known aspects of the region's history. In the medieval and early modern periods Denmark, and later Sweden, dominated the whole of Scandinavia – with the result that they now have a more impressive heritage of historic buildings than the other three countries. Also, the Lutheran Church has provided a measure of cultural unity since the Reformation in the sixteenth century. Nevertheless, each country has developed a strong national identity and the differences extend to international politics and attitudes towards immigration. Sweden for example has pursued a policy of neutrality for the last two centuries, but has welcomed large-scale immigration, in contrast to the restrictions imposed by Denmark since the 1990s. Both countries are members of the EU along with Finland, whereas Norway and Iceland have decided that their best interests lie in a looser trade association with Europe.

Perceptions of Scandinavia fostered by the media include its supposed ethnic homogeneity, whereas the cities are now home to many ethnic minorities as a result of immigration. In the 1960s and 1970s Sweden and Denmark were renowned for their permissive attitudes to sexual liberation and the absence of censorship, but the differences with the rest of Europe in this respect are much less evident today.

The Scandinavian countries have a total population of approximately 25 million, which is mainly concentrated in the towns and cities of the southern part of the region. The climate as well as social and economic conditions combine to make Scandinavia one of the major generating areas in the world for holiday tourism, especially to winter sun destinations. The people enjoy a high standard of living, but at the same time place great emphasis on leisure, active participation in outdoor recreation, and the quality of life; levels of education are also high and typical annual leave entitlement is five weeks or more. Add to this a well-developed and efficient travel trade throughout the region, and it is no surprise that levels of both domestic and foreign holiday-taking are much higher than the average for Europe. Holidays abroad represent around one-third of all holidays taken by residents of Norway, Sweden and Denmark and, in consequence, these countries have a substantial deficit on their international travel account. A large percentage of these holidays are to other countries in the region, facilitated by the abolition of passport controls for inter-Scandinavian travel. This does mean, however, that statistics for international travel between Scandinavian countries are not collected, making it difficult to measure regional tourism flows. In domestic tourism there is a growing trend for short second holidays, especially those based on winter sports and other types of outdoor recreation.

On the other hand, the relatively high cost of living, high levels of taxation and strong currencies combine to make Scandinavia an expensive destination for foreign visitors. The majority of tourists are from other parts of Europe, especially Germany. There is a widespread perception that Scandinavia is not only more expensive but also less accessible than other destinations, involving long journeys by road and car ferry, or expensive air travel. The completion of a number of bridges and tunnels connecting the

Danish islands to the mainland is greatly improving transport by road and rail between Scandinavia and the rest of Europe. With deregulation under the EU, air fares are falling, while Copenhagen is rapidly becoming a major hub for long-haul as well as inter-regional air services. Inbound tourism to Scandinavia should also increase as interest in 'green tourism' gathers momentum. The tourism products offered by the Scandinavian countries pay more than lip service to environmental issues. They include:

* camping and self-catering holidays in the countryside; and
* a range of activity and 'wilderness adventure' holidays.

The climate and topography of the Scandinavian countries, with the exception of Denmark, have encouraged the development of winter sports, particularly 'Nordic' or cross-country skiing, which has much less impact on the environment than alpine skiing. As a cold-water destination, beach tourism is largely limited to the domestic market, but the more southerly and sheltered parts of Scandinavia may soon be 'discovered' by summer sun-seekers from outside the region as the result of climate change.

Denmark

The smallest and most densely populated of the Scandinavian countries, Denmark lacks wilderness areas and spectacular scenery (the highest point is only 170 metres above sea level). Denmark's appeal lies in its neat, gently rolling countryside and picturesque towns and villages, while the national tourist icon is the 'Little Mermaid' on the Copenhagen waterfront, immortalised by Hans Christian Andersen. Consisting of many islands and the Jutland Peninsula which has only a short land border with Germany, no part of the country is far from the sea. It is therefore not surprising to find that sailing is a popular pastime and that the Danes have the highest rate of yacht ownership in Europe. They also have one of the highest rates of ownership of second homes (known locally as 'summer houses'). Much of the demand is generated from the capital, Copenhagen, where most families live in apartments. Cycling is also very popular – the topography is ideal even if the weather is unpredictable – and this greenest of transport modes is encouraged by a nationwide system of bikeways. Danes have the reputation for being more informal and 'continental' than other Scandinavians, with a quality of life expressed by the Danish word *hygge* (roughly translated as 'cosy'). This is experienced in the traditional inns, as drinking laws are more relaxed than elsewhere in Scandinavia. Copenhagen is particularly renowned for its exuberant nightlife and tolerance of different lifestyles.

The demand for tourism

Domestic and outbound tourism

Danes enjoy up to five weeks annual holiday entitlement and two-thirds of the population take a holiday away from home every year. People prefer to stay with friends and relatives, in owned and rented 'summer houses', or use camping sites in preference to serviced accommodation. Along with other Scandinavian countries, Denmark encourages the principle of 'tourism for all' or social tourism for those people who for various reasons find it difficult to take a holiday; for example, retired people on limited incomes can even take state-subsidised holidays in the Canary Islands during the winter months, which at least reduces the cost of heating bills. In 2008 the Danes took 6.1 million holiday trips, of which 64 per cent were abroad. Other Scandinavian countries are less popular than Spain and Germany.

Inbound tourism

With over 4 million arrivals annually, Denmark is heavily dependent upon Germany and the rest of Scandinavia for its income from tourism. International arrivals are highly seasonal with most concentrated between May and September.

The supply of tourism

Transport

Apart from Kastrup, serving Copenhagen, there are an increasing number of low cost carriers offering flights to regional airports such as Aarhus, Esjberg and Billund. Surface transport links are also excellent with good road, rail and ferry links to the UK and the rest of Europe. Transport within Denmark is mainly by private car using a well-developed internal and international road system with ferry connections between the islands. Stena and DFDS Seaways operate international ferry services to the rest of Scandinavia, Germany and the UK. However the ferries will decline in importance as a result of the completion of a number of bridge and tunnel projects. These must rank as some of the world's most spectacular engineering feats; they include the Great Belt Bridge linking the islands of Funen and Zealand, and the Oresund Bridge and Tunnel connecting Zealand to Sweden. The Oresund link, positioned close to Copenhagen, is already enhancing the city's role as the gateway to Scandinavia. Another project – the Fehmarn Belt Tunnel – will provide a more direct route between Copenhagen and north Germany.

Accommodation

The majority of Denmark's accommodation capacity is self-catering, including summer homes and campsites, and this is where most of the growth has occurred. Hotels, inns and youth hostels are widely available, with the highest occupancy levels in Copenhagen, and, during the summer peak, on the island of Bornholm. Stays on Danish farms are popular with British families, often as part of a package deal with the ferry operators.

Organisation

The Danish Tourist Board (VisitDenmark) is the national body responsible for the marketing and travel trade development of Denmark as a destination, while domestic tourism is the responsibility of the regional and local authorities.

Tourism resources

We can divide Denmark for convenience into the Jutland Peninsula and the islands of the Danish archipelago to the east, but the scenic 'Marguerite Route' allows the visitor to see virtually all the key attractions of this compact country in the course of one short touring holiday. The dominant natural feature of Jutland is a moraine formed in the last Ice Age, which is partly covered with pine forest and large tracts of heathland.

These are interspersed with peat bogs which have yielded fascinating evidence about ways of life in the Bronze and Iron Ages. Interest in Denmark's archaeological heritage is widespread, forming the basis of a number of folk museums where buildings and traditional crafts are preserved in an authentic setting, or in reconstructed villages, where students re-enact the lifestyles of the remote past. The preserved 'old town' of Aarhus is another heritage attraction, which can be enjoyed alongside a vibrant modern city. Denmark is well equipped with activity parks for children known as 'Sommerlands', but the most popular attraction is undoubtedly Legoland at Billund. Jutland's west coast has fine sandy beaches backed by dunes, but bathing is often unsafe due to the changing winds and tides. The fishing port of Esbjerg is a major centre with ferry connections to Harwich in England and the islands of Fanø and Romø. It is also close to the medieval town of Ribe with its Viking Centre. Artists have long been attracted to the fishing community of Skagen at the northern tip of Jutland.

The islands of the Danish Archipelago offer different landscapes and attractions:

- Bornholm, situated in the Baltic Sea 200 kilometres east of Copenhagen, is particularly appealing with its rocky granite scenery, but is somewhat remote from the rest of the country.
- Funen, known as the 'Garden of Denmark' is especially well equipped for tourism. The city of Odense attracts many American tourists as the birthplace of Hans Christian Andersen.
- Zealand is the largest of the islands and probably the most interesting for the foreign visitor. At Roskilde there is much evidence of Denmark's Viking past and 'longship cruises' are even available. There are a number of important historic buildings, the best known being Frederiksborg Castle and Kronborg Castle at Helsingor, famous as the setting for Shakespeare's *Hamlet*. Above all, Zealand contains Copenhagen, which is a long-established short break destination. With its copper-sheathed roofs and spires, harbour and pedestrianised shopping streets, the Danish capital has a wide appeal. Specific attractions include the Tivoli Gardens, Europe's oldest amusement park, with its theatres and summer festivals, the Danish Royal Ballet, the Louisiana Museum of Modern Art; the Amalienborg Palace and the Carlsberg Brewery. Unlike most European capitals, Copenhagen has fine beaches and resort attractions within easy reach by public transport from the city centre.

Discussion point

In the early twentieth century Denmark pioneered farmers' co-operatives, which have proved successful in boosting the country's food exports. Nowadays, as elsewhere in western Europe, farmers are under increasing pressure to diversify into rural tourism. Discuss the benefits and costs of farmstays in Denmark from the viewpoint of both the host farmer and his guests, in this case a middle income professional English couple with young children.

Norway

Of all the Scandinavian countries, Norway is probably the best known. Since the nineteenth century, tourists have visited the fjords in the western part of the country, attracted by the breathtaking combination of mountain and coastal scenery.

The land is rugged and only 3 per cent can be cultivated; so Norwegians throughout their history have turned to the sea for their livelihoods. Norway has the longest coastline in Europe, deeply cut by the fjords, with chains of small offshore islands known as the *skerryguard* providing a sheltered coastal waterway for shipping. Norway has a substantial merchant navy and is a dominant player in the cruise market, while sailing is a popular pastime for Norwegians. The heritage of seafaring and exploration, from the Viking longships to Amundsen and Thor Heyerdahl (of *Kon Tiki* fame), along with the controversial whaling industry, is greatly valued. The former isolation of many areas, separated by mountain and fjord, explains why Norway has retained much of its traditional culture, including the wearing of colourful regional costumes on special occasions. Norway's huge resources of hydro-electric power are vital to the economy, but concern about the impact of the power industry on the environment has led to demands for more areas to be set aside as national parks. The nation's recent prosperity is, however, largely based on its huge reserves of oil and natural gas. The foreign exchange earnings from this mineral wealth are invested in infrastructure that will benefit Norwegian society as a whole, rather than in showpiece projects.

There are substantial variations in climate in such an elongated country – the North Cape is almost 2,000 kilometres by air from Kristiansand in the south. Temperatures on the coast are much milder than might be expected for such high latitudes, due to the influence of the Gulf Stream, so that the fjords and shipping lanes remain ice-free in winter, even as far north as Kirkenes on the Russian border. To experience true Arctic conditions, you need to go even further north, to Svalbard. It is worth emphasizing that you can only see the midnight sun in summer, weather permitting, north of the Arctic Circle; at the North Cape there is continuous daylight from mid-May to the end of July. Exposed coastal areas like Bergen receive an excessive amount of rain, while the sheltered heads of the fjords are much drier, sunnier and warmer in summer - but cold in winter. In the mountainous interior, heavy snowfalls are frequent, making it possible to ski year-round in areas like the Hardangervidda plateau east of Bergen. The Norwegians claim to have invented skiing - although as a means of travel rather than as a sport - and they probably have the world's highest participation rate in skiing, with ski trails even in cities such as Oslo.

The demand for tourism

The prosperity of the Norwegian economy explains why travel propensities are high. However, holiday patterns are changing as the traditional long summer holiday gives way to shorter, more frequent trips:

Domestic and outbound tourism

Norwegians took 21.2 million trips in 2009, of which 70 per cent were within their own country. This is largely because of the widespread ownership of holiday chalets, known as *hytte*. Many of these are situated in the *saeter*, the high summer pastures above the treeline, and are a reminder of the pastoral lifestyle of the past. Hiking is a popular activity in summer and skiing in winter. With over 5 million foreign trips by Norwegians, there is a deficit on the country's travel account. Only a small percentage of trips are to other Scandinavian countries, as Norwegians prefer overseas travel to the UK, southern Europe, North Africa and the Canary Islands.

Inbound tourism

Norway experienced a growth of inbound travel following the Lillehammer Winter Olympics in 1996, followed by a gradual decline. There was a recovery during the first years of the twenty first century, and 7.5 million overnight stays by foreign tourists were recorded in 2009. Norway's foreign visitors come largely from Denmark, Germany and Sweden, but those from outside Scandinavia, such as the British and Americans, tend to stay longer and spend more. There is a pronounced peaking of demand during the short summer season.

The supply of tourism

Transport

In such a mountainous and elongated country, getting around can be a problem – it takes over a week to travel the length of Norway by car – so air transport is important. International air passengers are served by Oslo's two airports, boosted in recent years by low cost carriers such as Ryanair, Sterling, Norwegian Airlines and Color Air. Domestic air services – such as those operated by Widerøe – link almost 50 destinations. However, the majority of foreign visits and domestic trips are by private car, taking advantage of the improved road network, with numerous tunnels supplementing the ferry links across major fjords, as these tend to be crowded during the summer peak. The rail network run by Norwegian State Railways is more limited, since it terminates in Bodø, leaving northern Norway without a rail service. The Bergen to Oslo railway does offer the tourist one of Europe's most scenic journeys, and it played a major role in opening up Norway for tourism. Traditionally it is the shipping services that have provided the country with a lifeline, notably the Hurtigruten fleet which serves a large number of coastal communities from Bergen to Kirkenes, taking on or unloading passengers and cargo throughout the year. The round trip takes 12 days, and is an interesting alternative to the summer holiday cruises available to the western fjords and 'the Land of the Midnight Sun'. Large numbers of visitors also use the ferry services which link Norway to the UK and Denmark through the ports of Bergen, Stavanger, Oslo and Kristiansand.

Accommodation

In the peak season the majority of accommodation is in camping, although other types of self-catering have grown in popularity, leading to a shortage in the supply of holiday cabins. Other accommodation is available on farms and in *rorbus* – fishermen's winter cabins built on stilts over the water's edge. Relatively few tourists, other than business travellers, use hotels although these are generally open year-round. Even so, there is an acute shortage of accommodation capacity in the popular tourist areas in the peak summer and Easter periods.

Organisation

The Norwegian government recognises the importance of the industry in aiding rural communities, transport operators and the accommodation sector, and has therefore attempted to reduce the acute seasonal and geographical concentration of visits. In an attempt to boost the volume of tourism in Norway and to develop professionalism in the sector, the Norwegian Tourist Board (VisitNorway) has been created as an independent, commercial agency, jointly supported by the Norwegian government and the tourism industry. It is licensed by the Ministry of Trade and Industry.

Tourism resources

We can divide Norway for convenience into western, southern and northern regions.

The **Western Fjords** is the most popular area for foreign visitors since it includes the five most spectacular fjords (Hardanger, Sogne, Nord, Geiranger and Romsdal), the highest mountains of Scandinavia, and Jostdalsbreen, the largest glacier in mainland Europe. Less well known is a cultural resource unique to Norway – the *stave* churches, built entirely of wood and with Viking features in their design. The region is easily accessible by air, with airports at Trondheim, Alesund, Bergen and Stavanger. The historic port of Bergen, situated between the two longest fjords – the Hardanger and the Sogne – is the gateway for exploring this region by ship, road or rail. The Geiranger Fjord is generally recognised to be the most attractive, with its towering rockfaces and myriad waterfalls. Of the many villages lining the shores of the fjords, Laerdal, Olden and Ulvik are the most popular resorts, while Balestrand has retained much of the ambience which attracted British tourists in Victorian times. A short distance inland lies the Jotunheim National Park, consisting of an extensive plateau above the tree line. It is Norway's most visited wilderness area, and a favourite with hikers and climbers. Alesund, with its art nouveau architecture, and Stavanger are growing in popularity as tourist centres for the UK market. Close to Stavanger is the Lysefjord and the spectacular

Photo 10.1   Pulpit Rock, often regarded as Norway's most iconic landmark (©istockphoto.com/ Harald Tjøstheim)

Pulpit Rock, often regarded as Norway's most iconic landmark. Trondheim in the north of the region is an historic cathedral city and former capital of Norway.

Southern Norway offers a gentler coastline of sheltered coves and beaches that are popular with domestic holidaymakers. Although a modern city compared to Bergen, Oslo is an established destination for cultural tourists. The main attractions are the museums celebrating Viking and maritime heritage, and the Vigeland sculpture park. Oslo is the gateway to Norway's main skiing areas, and a number of resorts have developed along the railways linking the capital to Bergen and Trondheim. Lillehammer, venue for the 1996 Winter Olympics, is the most important.

Northern Norway is the part of Norway lying within the Arctic Circle and has a distinct character, not least because the interior is occupied by people of an age-old, distinct culture – the *Sami* (formerly known as Lapps). Lapland also includes part of northern Sweden, Finland and Russia, but the Sami of Finnmark have retained their semi-nomadic way of life, based on reindeer herding, to a greater extent than elsewhere. Tourism provides a welcome source of income but as with all such indigenous peoples, represents a potential disruption to a culture which is in delicate balance with the harsh environment.

Case study 10.1

Tromsø: Tourism development in Europe's far north

Tromsø, with its far northerly island location, and a winter climate characterised by two months of darkness, would appear to be an unlikely tourist destination. Yet clever marketing, good communications and a positive attitude to their environment by the local community have turned these natural disadvantages into attractions. This is no remote Arctic outpost, but a bustling modern city with 65,000 inhabitants (over 70,000 if nearby communities in Troms County are included).

Photo 10.2 Telegraph Bay, a beach warmed by the North Atlantic Drift 300 km (200 miles) north of the Arctic Circle (courtesy of VisitTromsø © Bard Løken)

EUROPE

Case study 10.1

Thanks to the influence of the Gulf Stream, Tromsø has a much milder climate than its location 300 kilometres inside the Arctic Circle would suggest. It is possible to grow fruit and vegetables and raise dairy cattle. Winter temperatures are much higher than places at the same latitude in North America, Greenland and Siberia, while summers are warm enough for a variety of outdoor recreation, including sunbathing on the beaches of Troms County (see Figure 10.1). On the other hand, at this latitude the sun is below the horizon from November 21 to January 21, with only a few hours of twilight to relieve the darkness of the 'polar night'. Yet Tromsø, which is a university city with as many as 10,000 students, keeps seasonal affective disorder (SAD) at bay with constant partying and a vibrant music and arts scene, culminating in the international film festival held in January each year. The city's most iconic building – the Tromsdalenkirke, known as the 'Cathedral of the Arctic Ocean' celebrates the theme of light in its design.

The outdoor activities on offer during the winter include the following.

- 'Chasing the Northern Lights'. Tromsø, because of its latitude, accessibility and modern amenities, is probably the best place in the world for tourists to view the aurora borealis (Northern Lights) in the night sky between October and May. However these spectacular displays are unpredictable, and a number of specialist operators, using various modes of transport, enable tourists to follow sightings.
- Cross-country and downhill skiing, following floodlit trails.
- Dog-sledding with teams of Alaskan huskies.
- Horse-drawn sleigh rides.
- Snowshoe trekking.
- Snowmobile rallies.
- Ice fishing on the lakes and rivers of the interior.

As the regional capital of northern Norway, Tromsø has an international airport and is also one of the country's largest cruise ports. Tourism plays a significant role in the local economy. The city's hotels have a capacity of 3,300 bed spaces, while cabins and campsites in Troms County are available for small numbers of visitors. Tromsø's historic role as the 'Gateway to the Arctic' is featured in the Polar Museum, commemorating the Norwegian explorers Nansen and Amundsen, who used the city as the base for their expeditions. The city continues to be a centre for scientific research, while the Polaria exhibition allows the visitor to experience the Arctic environment in safety and comfort.

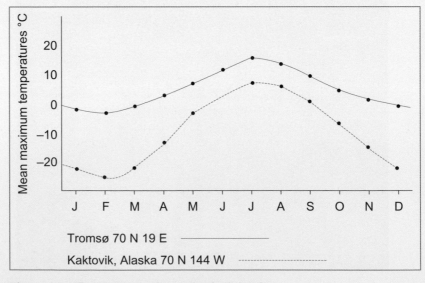

Figure 10.1 Tromsø compared to another Arctic location

Table 10.1	Tourist overnights in Troms County, 2010 (data supplied by Kyle Parsonage, Visit Tromsø)						
	January	**February**	**March**	**April**	**May**	**June**	**July**
Foreign	8,518	10,286	10,744	6,937	13,423	46,972	63,478
Norwegian	39,680	43,019	45,462	42,448	52,150	72,691	75,083
	August	**September**	**October**	**November**	**December**	**Total**	
Foreign	40,341	11,494	6,663	6,186	6,372	231,414	
Norwegian	72,414	64,938	56,674	56,560	41,928	663,047	

The coastal communities, such as those on the spectacularly rugged Lofoten Islands, largely depend on the fishing industry and tourism is of secondary importance. The North Cape ranks as a mass tourism destination by Arctic standards, attracting several thousand visitors daily during the summer.

Assignments

1 A city has features that distinguish it from lesser towns. Justify Tromsø's claim to be the world's most northerly city, with reference to its population characteristics, service functions and facilities.
2 Draw a bar graph to interpret the tourism statistics in Table 10.1, which shows that domestic and foreign patterns of tourism differ substantially. Try to account for these differences.

Svalbard

Norway's Arctic archipelago lies 1,000 kilometres north of the Norwegian mainland. Spitzbergen, the largest island, is noted for its dramatic landscape of fjords, ice-sculpted mountains and glaciers, as well as for the variety of wildlife that has adapted to an inhospitable environment. Svalbard is situated in the High Arctic north of 75° latitude, where winter is characterised by several months of continuous darkness as well as extreme cold. In summer temperatures rarely rise above 10°C despite continuous daylight from April to August, and the weather is also highly unpredictable. West Spitzbergen is much more accessible than the rest of the archipelago, which is hemmed in by pack ice year-round. It is visited by over 20,000 cruise passengers each summer, who are attracted by the scenery, the heritage of the former whaling industry at Magdalen Fjord, and Ny Alesund, which was the base for a number of expeditions to the North Pole.

Although the islands are under Norwegian sovereignty, they are regarded by treaty as an international zone for commercial activities, and this explains the presence of two Russian communities based on a coal mining industry which is no longer competitive. Apart from their appeal to ecotourists, the extreme environment provides a challenge for adventure-seekers. Such tourists are usually aware of the risks, which include the possibility of attack by polar bears. Nevertheless the Norwegian government has imposed a comprehensive system of regulations on tour operators as well as independent expeditioners, to ensure the protection of fragile Arctic ecosystems.

Sweden

Although it is the largest of the Scandinavian countries in area, population and GNP, Sweden lacks the clearly defined image presented by Norway and Finland. The country is known mainly for its mineral resources, the quality of its manufactured products, particularly motor vehicles and furniture, and its contribution to popular music and the film industry, rather than for any specific tourist attractions. This may change as a result of literary associations with the novels of Steeg Larsen. Most of the population live within the Stockholm–Gothenburg–Malmö triangle which is the economic and cultural focus of the nation.

The demand for tourism

Domestic tourism

The Industrial Revolution came late to Sweden, and most city-dwellers have rural roots and a strong love of nature. By 1900 the growing middle class regularly spent summers in the countryside, or in fishing communities along the west coast. They stayed in modest boarding houses, or in 'summer houses' where families catered for themselves, and the large fashionable hotels typical of continental Europe did not become a dominant part of the resort scene. It was not until the late 1930s, with the coming to power of the Social Democrats and the introduction of a statutory two week vacation, that working class families were able to stay at the seaside, usually in campsites. The development of a prosperous economy after the Second World War made it possible for the Swedes to have one of the highest travel propensities in the world (75 per cent). The majority of the working population have at least five weeks holiday entitlement, and they are more likely to take a second holiday than the citizens of other European countries. Self catering is still the favoured type of accommodation, and over a quarter of Swedish households own a cottage or 'summer house' in the country. Sweden has one of the highest rates of second home and pleasure boat ownership in Europe. The majority of holiday trips are taken by car, although escalating costs and a faltering economy since the late 1990s have reduced the amount of touring. Domestic business travel is focused on the cities of Stockholm, Gothenburg and Malmö.

Outbound tourism

Sweden is among the world's leading generators of international tourism, with over 12 million trips taken annually. Destinations popular with Swedish holidaymakers include other Scandinavian countries, Germany, Spain, the UK, Italy, France, and Greece. Long-haul travel is also increasing to destinations such as Malaysia.

Inbound tourism

There are around 11 million overnight visitors to Sweden annually, but a much larger number of day trips from other Scandinavian countries. For overnight visitors, the main generating countries are the rest of Scandinavia, Germany, the UK, the Netherlands, and the USA, where there is a large ethnic market.

The supply of tourism

Transport

International air transport is served by Stockholm Arlanda, Gothenburg and Malmö Airports, and domestic flights are operated by SAS to some 20 destinations. However most holiday tourists arrive by car, using the ferry or hovercraft for the sea crossings on the main routes from Denmark and Germany. Car travel is expensive in Sweden and government policy is to favour public transport by imposing controls on car use. Swedish railways have therefore received considerable public investment to provide high-speed routes between the major cities. There is also a nationwide system of cycle routes.

Accommodation

Sweden's serviced accommodation stock has grown since 1997, though it is still dominated by small businesses. Demand for hotel accommodation by domestic tourists is small, with the exception of business travellers. In the past, acute shortages of suitable hotels in cities like Stockholm has led to the development of company apartments. Self-catering accommodation in the form of summer cottages and log cabins is in demand for holiday tourism; timeshare and multi-ownership schemes are being developed, as are high quality campsites.

Organisation

In 1992, the state-owned Swedish Tourist Board was replaced by a private sector initiative, the Swedish Travel and Tourism Council. The Council is jointly owned by the private sector and the Swedish government, and its mission is to promote Sweden as a tourist destination. It is supported by an independent network of 22 regional organisations. Another agency – the Swedish Tourism Authority – is publicly funded and has the remit of co-ordinating tourism activity in Sweden.

Tourism resources

Sweden shares the Kjolen Mountains with Norway, but the scenery tends to be less spectacular on the eastern slopes. With 50 per cent of its area under forest, and boasting innumerable lakes, rivers and rapids, Sweden has the largest area of unspoiled wilderness in Europe. Sweden's tourism resources also include a varied coastline on two seas and a network of inland waterways. Sweden was the first country in Europe to develop a system of national parks to protect its wilderness areas from exploitation by the powerful mining, timber and wood pulp industries. Public access to the countryside is guaranteed by the traditional law known as *Allemansrätt* (every man's right), which allows the visitor to camp overnight, hike, ride, cycle and picnic on private land. Although winters are severely cold with abundant snow, summers are warm and sunny, especially along the Baltic coast. Midsummer Day is the occasion for festivities throughout the country, when the formality characteristic of much of public life is relaxed.

Sweden's cultural resources include prehistoric rock carvings at Tanum on the west coast, the heritage of the copper mining industry, the historic university towns of Lund and Uppsala, and reminders of the period in the seventeenth and eighteenth centuries when Swedish military power controlled the Baltic under leaders such as Gustavus Adolphus and Queen Christina.

The main tourist areas are found in the south, along the Baltic and North Sea coasts, and in the central lake district west of Stockholm. These three areas are linked by the Göta Canal. This scenic waterway is a linear attraction, 190 kilometres in length, which connects Gothenburg to Stockholm and the three largest lakes – Vänern, Vättern and Mälaren. The canal was built in the nineteenth century to provide a short cut for shipping. Although it has lost most of its significance as a commercial waterway, some of the original vessels have been adapted for summer cruises.

The North Sea coast

Gothenburg is Sweden's major North Sea port but offers many cultural attractions and the Liseberg theme park, one of the largest in Scandinavia. The 'golden coast' of Bohuslän nearby is popular with Swedish families, especially the resort of Tanum Strand, which is an excellent base for exploring the many offshore islands. Scania in the extreme south of Sweden has lowland landscapes similar to those of Denmark and its capital Malmö, now linked to Copenhagen, is a major business centre.

The Baltic coast

Here the island of Gotland with its white sandy beaches and strange rock formations is a major destination. The well-preserved medieval city of Visby is a World Heritage Site as well as being a summer holiday resort offering a vibrant nightlife.

The Central Lake District

Lying close to the Norwegian border, the provinces of Värmland and Dalarna offer scenic lake and forest landscapes, and are ideal for activity holidays, including fishing, canoeing, and whitewater rafting in summer. Mora on Lake Siljan has hosted international downhill ski events, but is mainly noted for the Vasalöppet, a cross-country ski race which attracts thousands of participants each March. Dalarna is regarded as the cultural heartland of Sweden, offering picturesque folk customs, heritage museums and innumerable handicraft outlets which attract large numbers of domestic tourists. The most interesting place for the foreign visitor is undoubtedly Stockholm. The capital is attractively situated on a number of islands at the entrance to Lake Mälaren, while thousands more islands scattered along the Baltic coast provide ideal sites for summer homes. The well-planned modern city contrasts with heritage attractions such as Gamla Stan (the preserved old town), the Vasa Ship Museum, and Skansen, Scandinavia's oldest folk museum, which has given its name to similar attractions in other countries.

Case study 10.2

Stockholm: A role model of sustainability

Stockholm Visitors Board actively promotes the capital as a 'green city' by hosting a number of festivals and other events with an environmental theme. Significantly, the city was chosen as the 'European Green Capital' for 2010 by the European Commission. This annual award is presented to the city which has:

- a proven track record of environmental achievement;
- ambitious goals for further improvements; and
- the ability to promote best practice in sustainable development to other cities.

Stockholm is a green city in the literal sense, as almost half its area is given over to parks which are well maintained and highly valued by Stockholmers. The largest of these is Ekoparken, established in 1994 as a conservation area to protect biodiversity. There are many beaches, where the water quality is maintained to the highest standards.

Stockholm has been a pioneer in encouraging *sustainable transport*. Every effort is made by the civic authorities to encourage cycling through a very extensive network of cycleways, and a programme which allows pass-holders to use a large number of 'borrow and return a bike' sites. Largely as a result, the number of cyclists grew by 70 per cent between 2005 and 2010. Public transport is efficient and is used daily by 80 per cent of the city's residents, so that car use, which is discouraged by a congestion charge, is much lower than in other European capitals.

Stockholm is also notable for the progress it has made in developing a *sustainable hospitality* sector. The city's hotels follow strict environmental guidelines, using district heating based on renewable energy sources, and maintaining advanced standards of waste separation, energy-efficient insulation and measures to conserve water. Scandia, a leading hotel chain in Scandinavia which is based in Stockholm, has succeeded in reducing CO_2 emissions by 80 per cent, energy consumption by 31 per cent and water consumption by 22 per cent. Sustainability has become part of company culture, and Stockholm residents are 'very keen on all things eco' (Jezovit, 2010). Hotels and restaurants are committed to use locally-sourced produce, and many have been certified by the Nordic Swan eco-label, which calls for particularly high standards.

EUROPE

The North

Norrland, the sparsely populated northern half of Sweden, includes part of Lapland. Tourism in Swedish Lapland began in the late nineteenth century, and is growing in importance because of the demand for ecotourism and adventure holidays. It is one of the largest areas of unspoiled wilderness in Europe, including six national parks. It is Europe's most northerly developed ski area, offering skiers and snowboarders the novelty of practising their sport until late June under the midnight sun. The area is guaranteed heavy snowfalls, with less risk of avalanches than in the Alps. On the other hand the season does not start until mid-February, due to the short period of winter daylight. Riksgransen, located on the railway linking the mining city of Kiruna to the Norwegian port of Narvik, is the main winter sports resort. It offers extensive trails for ski touring and telemarking, but with a vertical descent of only 400 metres, Riksgransen's slopes have less appeal for downhill skiers. Other winter activities include ice-fishing, snow-scooter 'safaris' and sledging with a team of

Case study 10.3

The Ice Hotel concept

One of Swedish Lapland's major attractions is the Ice Hotel at Jukkäsjarvi, promoted as the 'world's largest igloo'. The rooms and furniture are made from 30,000 tons of ice and compacted snow, which is taken each November from the frozen River Torne, and the structure is used until it melts, usually in early May. The temperature inside the hotel is kept at a constant –7°C, whereas outside it may fall to –35°C. Bed furnishings are made from reindeer hides and skins which provide insulation against the cold, but most tourists prefer to use the adjoining wooden chalet-style huts. There is also an open air theatre modelled on Shakespeare's Globe, but made entirely of ice, and where the plays are performed in the Sami language.

Discuss the claim that the Ice Hotel is an excellent example of sustainable tourism, given that the concept has been widely copied, not only in Scandinavia, but in countries outside the region. Why does it appeal to certain types of tourist, including honeymoon couples from Japan?

huskies. Tourists also visit to experience the Sami (Lapp) culture, centred on Jukkasjärvi and Jokkmokk, where the old ways continue to flourish and silver and leather handicrafts are sold.

Finland (Suomi)

Culturally, Finland is different from the other Nordic countries due to its non-Germanic language and the cultural links with Russia to the east, which ruled here for over a century until the 1917 Revolution. However, the country was for much longer under the rule of Sweden, so that Swedish and Finnish are the official languages. Finland offers the visitor vast expanses of lakeland blending almost imperceptibly with forest, a unique landscape associated with the music of Sibelius. The marketing campaigns of the Finnish Tourist Board emphasise unspoiled nature and the absence of air and water pollution, although the majority of the population live in the cities of the south west. Of the total area no less than 10 per cent is inland water – lakes, marshes, rivers and rapids – while forests of conifers and birch make up another two-thirds. Eskers, long sinuous ridges of material laid down by glaciers in the last Ice Age, separate the lakes and are a distinctive feature in a landscape which is for the most part lowland. Winters are long and severe, but the Finns are adept at dealing with them; fleets of icebreakers keep open the shipping lanes and a whole range of winter sports, including ice hockey and snowmobile rallies are popular during the cold season.

Although high-tech industries, represented for example by Nokia, now play a leading role in the economy, Finland's prosperity is based on its seemingly inexhaustible forest resources which make up 75 per cent of the country and which provide timber, wood pulp and furs. The exploitation of these in the past has caused concern among environmentalists, but as in Sweden, the timber is now harvested on a sustained yield basis. The forests and lakes are much valued as a recreational resource by city dwellers. Many families in Helsinki own a lakeside cabin as a weekend retreat, usually with a sauna attached. In Finland the sauna is as much a social institution as a means of relaxation.

The demand for tourism

Around 50 per cent of the population take a holiday of four nights or more away from home. The proximity of Finland to the weak economies of the countries of the former Soviet Union, allied to devaluations of the Finnish mark, meant that the tourism sector suffered from overcapacity in the 1990s. In turn this led to reductions in prices and a formerly expensive destination became much more affordable. Finland therefore experienced considerable increases in inbound travel in the 1990s, and volumes have stabilised to around 5.5 million arrivals annually with an additional 2.2 million day trips. As Finland recovered from this economic crisis and began to share in the EU's prosperity, including adoption of the Euro, outbound tourism has grown to 3.6 million trips annually. Domestic tourism however remains more important for the Finns, who own substantial numbers of second homes at the coast and beside the lakes.

The supply of tourism

Transport

Geographically Helsinki is not only a northerly capital, but is further east in longitude than Athens, so that distance is an important factor in planning a trip from the UK. Swedish and Norwegian visitors arrive mainly by sea through the ports of Helsinki, Turku, and Maarianhamina, in preference to the long road journey around the Gulf of Bothnia. Visitors from other west European countries can take the more direct ferry route from Travemunde in north Germany. Air transport has grown steadily in importance, with Helsinki acting as the gateway and Finnair as the national airline. Domestic transport arrangements are excellent, with broad all-weather highways, an improved rail system and a network of domestic air services to over 20 destinations.

Accommodation

Motels and hotels are concentrated in the major cities (Helsinki, Turku and Tampere) where business travel means they can maintain a high annual bed occupancy rate (up to 75 per cent in Helsinki). Finland can also provide low-density holiday villages, concentrated in the central lakeland area, holiday cottages, farm accommodation and campsites. Seasonality is high, the majority of foreign tourists arriving between May and October with a peak in July. In consequence, roughly one-quarter of the accommodation stock is only open for part of the year. A conscious effort has been made to extend the season by developing conference and winter sports tourism. Partly because of Finland's post-Second World War neutrality in world politics, Helsinki has become a major international conference centre, offering facilities such as Finlandia Hall and first class hotels.

Organisation

Finland has pursued an aggressive tourism policy, spearheaded by the Finnish Tourist Board (VisitFinland), which reports to the Ministry of Trade and Industry. Tourism is seen as a means for regional development in the rural areas, and also for diversification of Helsinki's economy.

Tourism resources

Finland's appeal to foreign visitors lies in its uncrowded natural resources and it has capitalised fully on the growth of ecotourism. We can broadly divide the country for tourism purposes into northern, south-eastern and coastal regions

Finnish Lapland

Northern Finland especially offers scope for wilderness adventure holidays, both for independent travellers and for package tourists. Summer activities include rafting, canoeing, gold panning and mountain-biking – while in winter 'reindeer safaris' involving a stay in a Sami encampment, and dog-sled expeditions are on offer. Charter flights are available in December from Britain to Rovaniemi, the main tourist centre, which has been promoted with considerable success as 'the home of Santa Claus' and now has a theme park –'Santa Park'. As a result Finland has a larger share of winter visitors from the UK than any other Nordic country. Skiing 'under the midnight sun' is available in the far north near Lake Inari, where the forest at last gives way to barren fells and tundra.

Saimaa Lake District

The best opportunities for outdoor recreation are to be found in the Saimaa Lake District in the south-east of the country. The lakes offer no less than 50,000 kilometres of shoreline and are forested down to the waters' edge; not surprisingly, this is a popular area in summer. The main tourist centres are Lapeenranta for summer cruises, and the spa town of Savonlinna which has an international opera festival. The Karelia forest region bordering Russia is culturally distinct, as shown by the many Orthodox churches.

The coasts

Both the southern and western coasts of Finland are characterised by clusters of offshore islands which provide opportunities for sailing. Seafaring traditions are particularly important in the Aland Islands which are Swedish-speaking and have the status of an autonomous region. For this reason they are popular with Swedish as well as Finnish holidaymakers, not least for the duty-free shopping available on the ferries. Other destinations include:

* the resort of Hanko, favoured by the Russian aristocracy prior to the 1917 Revolution;
* the Moominland theme park at Nantaali;
* Helsinki, which is noted more for its fine modern architecture than for historic buildings, but along with other cities in Finland is promoting festival tourism; and
* Turku, the former capital of Finland and university town, which shared the status of 'European capital of culture' with Tallinn (Estonia) in 2010.

Iceland

Promoted as 'a land of ice and fire', exposed to the raw forces of nature, Iceland is unique. This large island is a geological 'hot spot' located on one of the major fault lines in the Earth's crust and contains over 200 volcanoes – major eruptions and earthquakes occur on average every five years. Although one-fifth of the country is covered by glaciers, Iceland is by no means as cold as its western neighbour Greenland, thanks to the warming influence of a branch of the Gulf Stream. Nevertheless, its location close to the Arctic Ocean does mean that Iceland has historically been vulnerable to climate change and the weather is highly unpredictable. The tourist season is short, even by Scandinavian standards, and summer temperatures rarely exceed 20°C, but the air is unpolluted and remarkably clear. Iceland's abundant geothermal resources supply a third of its energy requirements and are harnessed to heat swimming pools, buildings and greenhouses. One well-known tourist attraction is the so-called 'Blue Lagoon' outside Reykjavik, which is actually an effluent reservoir from a power plant. Agriculture is largely restricted to sheep farming and the landscape is for the most part treeless. Nearly all the population lives on or near the coast, while the interior is made up of desert-like lava plateaux, rugged mountains and the vast Vatnajokull ice sheet. Some of the local food specialities, and the traditional farmhouses covered with turf for insulation, are reminders of the harsh conditions that Icelanders had to endure until well into the twentieth century.

Since the Second World War living standards have greatly improved, but as the population of Iceland is only 300,000, the demand for outbound tourism is small by international standards. Nevertheless, Icelanders are well-travelled and the country has a substantial deficit on its tourism account.

With few resources other than the dominant fishing industry, Iceland is anxious to encourage tourism. Promotion is the responsibility of the Icelandic Tourist Board assisted by the national carrier Icelandair. Because Iceland is an expensive destination and relatively difficult to reach, the volume of inbound tourism is small, at around 350,000 arrivals a year, though growing and significant, given the country's sparse population. Visitors come mainly from the other Nordic nations, USA, Germany and the UK.

The bulk of the air transport services from Western Europe and Scandinavia are provided by Icelandair, Iceland Express, and SAS, while the international airport at Keflavik is often used as a stopover on transatlantic flights. Access by sea is much less convenient and comprises ferry services from Bergen, the Shetlands and Esbjerg. There is an extensive domestic air network which is necessary in view of the fact the Iceland has no railways and most of the roads, particularly in the interior, are suitable only for four-wheel drive vehicles. Iceland's accommodation stock comprises hotels, guesthouses, youth hostels, farms and campsites.

Iceland's tourism appeal lies in its unspoiled natural scenery and the scope this provides for ecotourism, as well as for 'soft' and 'hard' adventure. The demand for extreme sports in the rugged interior is likely to grow as life in post-industrial societies such as Britain becomes safer and more predictable. Pony trekking is a successful product utilising the native breed of horse which is small and uniquely adapted to the broken volcanic terrain. Skiing facilities on a modest scale are available near Reykjavik and Akureyri. Bird-watching and whale-watching are popular, but Iceland's green credentials have been called into question by the decision in 2003 to resume commercial whaling, and the project for an aluminium smelter in the north east of the country. Most Icelanders would argue that the need to diversify the economy, particularly after the financial crisis of 2009, and to stem rural depopulation are more pressing concerns than wilderness conservation.

The most popular tourist attractions are located in the 'Golden Circle' east of Reykjavik, including the Gullfoss waterfall, the Great Geyser and the Thingvellir

National Park – a spectacular natural amphitheatre where Iceland's parliament was held in Viking times. Another cluster of natural attractions in the north of the country includes Lake Myvatn and Dettifoss, Europe's largest waterfall. Man-made attractions are few, and found mainly in Reykjavik, but Iceland has made a remarkable contribution to European culture in the form of the Viking sagas, and nowadays in architecture, fashion and popular music. Unlike most capitals, Reykjavik is a small city and close-knit community characterised by low-rise, brightly painted wooden buildings. It does contain 60 per cent of the country's population and most of its stock of hotel accommodation. Thanks to its strategic location, the city has hosted a number of international conferences, including the 2005 G8 Summit. Reykjavik is also promoted to the youth tourism markets of western Europe as a destination for 'clubbing' and is noted for its uninhibited nightlife.

The Faroes

The Faroes consist of 18 inhabited islands in the stormy North Atlantic, halfway between the Shetlands and Iceland. They are a self-governing nation within the Kingdom of Denmark, but have opted to stay outside the EU. As yet, tourism is much less important than the fishing industry, which may explain why the Faroese have rejected calls from the world's environmentalists that they should give up their whaling traditions. The excessively wet and windy climate is a major constraint on tourism, but the islands can offer some of Europe's most spectacular cliff scenery and vast colonies of seabirds. The capital, Thorshavn is accessible by scheduled flights from Copenhagen and by summer ferry services from Esbjerg, Bergen and Iceland.

Summary

- Scandinavia has a degree of political and cultural unity, and was historically distinct from the rest of Europe, but the differences between the component countries of the region, for example in landscapes, are as important as the similarities.
- Scandinavia's climate is a push factor, making the region a major generator of holiday tourism.
- The physical legacy of the last Ice Age is still evident in the landscapes, particularly the fjords and mountains of Norway and Iceland.
- The Industrial Revolution came late to the countries of Scandinavia, so most city dwellers have rural roots and a love of nature and the outdoor life.
- The social and economic development that took place in the twentieth century has enabled Scandinavians to have one of the world's highest propensities for travel.
- Outbound tourism is more significant than inbound tourism, such that Scandinavian countries have large deficits on their travel accounts.
- Travel within the region has been facilitated by the abolition of passport controls.
- Although the region has good air transport links with other parts of the world, the majority of international tourists arrive by car, using the ferry services that are available. Inter-city transport services by rail, road and sea are good, and set to improve.
- Accommodation capacity in the short summer season is dominated by the self-catering sector, as serviced accommodation is in short supply.

* The most important of Scandinavia's tourism resources are the uncrowded, unpolluted countryside and coastlines, the spectacular scenery of the mountains, the lakes and forests, and the unpretentious culture of the capitals and major cities of the region.

Assignments

1 What are the significant differences and similarities between the countries of Scandinavia in terms of their landscapes and other physical features?
2 Is the reputation of the Scandinavian countries for 'green' (environmentally-friendly) tourism always justified? Provide evidence from different countries and cities in the region.
3 How would you summarise the cultural attractions of the countries of Scandinavia, including their associations with art, music and literature?
4 Climate is both a constraint on tourist activity and a resource for particular types of tourism. Discuss this with examples from Scandinavian countries.

11

CHAPTER

The tourism geography of the Benelux countries

Introduction

Three small countries in Western Europe – Belgium, the Netherlands and Luxembourg – have a much greater economic, cultural and political significance than we might expect from their size. Historically known as the Low Countries, the Netherlands and most of Belgium are made up of lowland plains adjoining the North Sea, while flat-topped uplands are characteristic of southern Belgium and Luxembourg. Areas of heathland separate the coastal lowlands from the uplands of the Ardennes, which rise to just over 600 metres above sea level. The region has a cool maritime climate similar to that of England. Near the coast the cloudy weather is unpromising for tourism with moderate rainfall throughout the year, whereas inland the maritime influence begins to fade; winters are colder, with enough snow in the Ardennes for skiing, while summers are warmer.

Culturally the Benelux countries are interesting for their heritage of historic buildings and art treasures, a reminder that the region has played a major role in European history. However their economic prosperity has frequently led to conflict with powerful neighbours, with the result that after the Second World War Belgium, the Netherlands and Luxembourg led the way to European unity with the formation of a customs union. This means that restrictions on movement between the three countries are minimal. With a combined population of 27 million, the Benelux states are the most densely populated countries in Europe. Not only does this lead to intense competition for land use, but it also places pressure on the environment to the extent that any proposed tourism developments are very closely scrutinised. The economies of the three countries have grown steadily since the Second World War, giving rise to increasing demands for both domestic and foreign tourism. Expenditure on outbound tourism exceeds the receipts from inbound tourism. Annual holiday entitlement averages five or more weeks and a typical working week is less than 40 hours.

The Netherlands

The Netherlands is better known as 'Holland', although the name strictly applies to just two of the eleven provinces that united to resist Spanish rule in the sixteenth century. Holland has a strong identity; its landscapes and cultural features are known worldwide. The Dutch contribution to art, with its emphasis on scenes from everyday life, seascapes and landscapes, has been outstanding. This reflected the tastes of middle class patrons rather than those of monarchs, aristocrats and cardinals. Dutch achievements in seamanship, agriculture and engineering have also been remarkable. Much of the country, especially in the west, is made up of flat *polderlands* reclaimed from the sea. The story of this reclamation and the constant battle against the sea is proudly told in exhibitions and museums, as well as in the many engineering works (such as the Delta Plan) which are tourist attractions in themselves. The countryside is criss-crossed by dykes and canals, although relatively few windmills now survive along with the *meers* (lakes) resulting from early drainage schemes. However much of the east and south of the Netherlands is scenically different, with extensive areas of heath and woodland.

The Netherlands can also offer cultural diversity. For centuries the Dutch ruled a major overseas empire, with colonies in the Caribbean, South America, South Africa and Asia. The influence of their most important former colony – Indonesia – is evident for example in the buffet-style *rijstaffel*. More recently, the Netherlands has attracted a greater number of immigrants, in relation to its size, than any other European country. Perhaps because of their maritime outlook and the pressures of living in a small, crowded country, the Dutch have a reputation for both tidiness and tolerance, and it is probably this which has attracted young tourists from all over the world. In contrast, some of the formerly isolated fishing communities around what was once the Zuider Zee (now the Ijsselmeer) have retained a strong religious outlook, along with the wearing of the traditional costumes that attract tourists. Contrary to its image, the Netherlands is a major industrial nation, boasting centres of advanced technology such as Eindhoven. High living standards, urban pressures, excellent transport systems, and an unpredictable climate have combined to encourage the development of theme parks, zoos and innovative ideas in leisure. The best known examples are the De Efteling Family Leisure Park near Breda, and the Center Parcs accommodation concept, which uses advanced technology to create an all-weather leisure environment in an attractive woodland setting.

The demand for tourism

The level of economic development has fuelled the demand for leisure and tourism. Generally, although domestic tourism remains healthy, the Dutch take more foreign holidays, so that the Netherlands has a growing deficit on its tourism account.

Domestic tourism

Domestic holidays (particularly short trips) and day excursions are an important sector of the Dutch tourism industry and recreation is becoming a major part of the Dutch lifestyle. In the new millennium the Dutch took between 17 and 18 million domestic holidays annually. The majority of these holidays are concentrated in July and August, leading to congestion in popular holiday areas. A nationwide programme to stagger holidays was introduced in 1983 to help ease seasonal congestion, while a trend to take more winter holidays may also help combat the problem. Most people taking domestic holidays use the private car and tend to stay in self-catering accommodation (such as 'summerhouses', caravans, campsites, or holiday villages) rather than in hotels. Despite the prevalent use of the private car, the Dutch rarely take touring holidays, preferring instead single-centre stays in their small and crowded country. Business and conference tourism is an important sector of the domestic market. Good-quality conference facilities are dispersed throughout the country in both purpose-built centres and in hotels, motels, and holiday villages. International conferences are seen as a growth area, especially given the Netherlands' central position in Europe.

Outbound tourism

As the Dutch have one of the highest holiday propensities in Europe – they take more holidays abroad than in their own country – the Netherlands is a major generator of international tourists on a world scale. The small size of the country encourages day excursions and cross-border trips, often for shopping, while a generous social welfare system enables all levels of society to travel abroad. There is an increasing trend for the Dutch to take winter sun and skiing holidays. In the first decade of the twenty first century the Dutch took around 18 million outbound trips annually.

Inbound tourism

With the new millennium inbound tourism to the Netherlands suffered, with totals of between 9 and 10 million visitors annually, leaving a substantial deficit on the travel account. The majority of these tourists are from Western Europe, dominated by arrivals from Germany. The international short-break market is important in the Netherlands with most foreigners only staying for two to three nights on average. However, in contrast to the domestic market, they tend to use serviced accommodation. In consequence, hotels and foreign visitors are concentrated into a few centres; Amsterdam alone accounts for around 50 per cent of the commercial bednights spent in the country.

The supply of tourism

Transport

Schiphol, Amsterdam's international airport is not only the major gateway to the country, but also a serious competitor to London Heathrow as an inter-continental hub and now, with a fifth runway, its services are expanding. Likewise KLM, the national carrier, is one of the world's leading airlines and dominates the industry in the Netherlands. It serves both domestic passengers and those travelling to neighbouring countries, with an aggressive pricing policy encouraging European short breaks. Martinair and Transavia are the main tourist charter airlines. Other international gateways are Maastricht Airport and the ferry terminals at Vlissingen, Europort, and the Hook of Holland, mainly handling passengers from the British Isles. Surface transport arrangements are excellent throughout the Netherlands and also into neighbouring countries, with 137,000 kilometres of road and a comprehensive intercity rail network. There is a fully integrated public transport network of buses, trams, and trains. Cycling is encouraged with a nationwide system of dedicated routes.

Accommodation

Accommodation in the Netherlands is dominated by self-catering with campsites, holiday villages, and a network of 'trekkers' huts' for cyclists and walkers. This sector of the accommodation market is well developed to meet the demand for inexpensive family holidays, but with increased affluence preferences are switching to hotels and motels. Also, given the extensive water resources of the Netherlands, marinas are important in providing accommodation.

Organisation

Tourism promotion, both domestic and international, is the responsibility of the Netherlands Board of Tourism and Conventions. The Board is backed by the provincial and local authorities, as well as by the Netherlands Congress Bureau. The government is improving tourist infrastructure by investing in 'bungalow parks', hotels, marinas, and tourist attractions. Promotional themes focus on the country's waterland setting, its cultural heritage, cities, the seaside and event attractions such as the 'Floriade' flower show.

Tourism resources

Each of the provinces of the Netherlands has a special appeal for foreign visitors (except maybe for Flevoland, which consists almost entirely of polders reclaimed from the Zuider Zee in the 1930s). Most foreign tourists are attracted to the western half of the country, particularly to the cities of the **Randstad**. This is a ring of urban development that contains almost half the population of the Netherlands, but on just 15 per cent of its land area. Development in the Randstad is therefore carefully planned to preserve

Photo 11.1 Amsterdam is one of the world's top five tourist cities (©istockphoto.com/Waltraud Ingerl)

its 'green heart', an area of attractive countryside inside the ring that includes the world-famous bulbfields between the historic towns of Haarlem and Leyden. The Randstad includes Amsterdam and the following major tourist centres:

- The Hague (Den Haag), the diplomatic capital of the Netherlands. Attractions nearby include Madurodam – 'Holland in miniature'; Delft which is famous for its ceramics and associations with Vermeer; and the resort of Scheveningen.
- Utrecht – a University town celebrated for its music festivals, and a major centre for trade fairs.
- Rotterdam – Europe's largest port at the mouth of the Rhine. Whereas other Dutch cities tend to promote their heritage attractions, Rotterdam was rebuilt after the Second World War and tourism focuses on its modern architecture, shopping and sport.

Case study 11.1

Amsterdam: images of an historic city

Amsterdam is the commercial capital of the Netherlands, and one of the world's top five tourist centres. Most of the historic area dates from Amsterdam's 'Golden Age' in the seventeenth century, when the city was the hub of a vast trading empire, and there was little expansion or rebuilding in the long period of subsequent decline. The merchant's houses, with their intricate brickwork, stepped gables, and narrow frontage along tree-lined canals, now form one of the world's most picturesque urban landscapes.

Amsterdam boasts an excellent transport infrastructure that includes the famous trams, a network of cycleways and a metro system that provides improved access to Schiphol Airport. The *Grachtengirdle* – the concentric ring of canals – is now mainly used for sightseeing excursions.

Compared to London or Paris, Amsterdam has few individual buildings that are internationally renowned as iconic tourist attractions. The floating flower market on the Singelgracht, and the Ann Frank House – a reminder of the city's important Jewish community – are among those 'must-see' attractions for foreign visitors. Art lovers are attracted to the Rijksmuseum with its paintings by Dutch masters such as Rembrandt and Vermeer, and the Van Gogh Museum. However, the main appeal of Amsterdam lies in its street life, shops, cafes and entertainment facilities. These include the theatres around the Leidseplein, the smoke-filled *brown bars* of the Jordaen district, and the De Wallen area near the Eastern Docks which has a long-established sex industry.

Amsterdam faces a number of problems in competing with other European cities as a tourist destination, namely:

- tourism development is often given a low priority by the city government, whose policies are aimed at maintaining a large resident population in subsidised housing in the historic centre;
- long-established perceptions of the city relate to a particular time period – the seventeenth century – which make change and diversification difficult; whereas
- since the 1960s a very different image of Amsterdam as a city of drugs and sex has become deeply ingrained in the popular culture, especially among young tourists. This has led in some areas to an ambience of sleaze, litter and drug-related crime that provides an unwelcome contrast to the traditional Dutch obsession with cleanliness and public order.

The North Sea coast with its sandy beaches backed by dunes is served by a string of resorts, which attract large numbers of German holidaymakers (mainly from the Ruhr conurbation), as well as the Dutch themselves. The busiest resorts are:

- Zandvoort – noted for its motor racing circuit;
- Noordwijk – renowned for its flower gardens; and
- Scheveningen – Holland's best known seaside resort.

After a long period of decline, Scheveningen was transformed by an ambitious scheme of re-investment in exciting new leisure facilities, and it has become a major conference venue, as well as a classic example of the rejuvenation stage of the tourism area life cycle. Between the resorts there are conservation areas where further development is strictly prohibited. This is because the dunes, which play a vital part in Holland's coastal defences, are very vulnerable to visitor pressure. To the south lies the province of **Zeeland**, originally a group of islands at the mouth of the Rhine, now connected by the Delta Plan to create an environment suitable for a wide range of water sports. In contrast, the medieval towns of Middelburg and Veere have much to attract the heritage tourist.

In the north east, the province of **Friesland** offers a more tranquil environment of small rural communities where the Frisian language is still spoken. The main attraction here is the Frisian Lake District around the resort of Sneek that offers facilities for boating and sailing. Separated from the mainland by the extensive mudflats of the Wadden Sec, the Frisian Islands such as Texel provide fine beaches, self-catering accommodation and a number of important nature reserves.

Gelderland in the east of the country is under-populated by Dutch standards, and large expanses of heath and woodland have been designated as the Hoge Veluwe National Park. The city of Arnhem was the scene of a major battle in the Second World War, and now offers a number of museums and attractions focusing on the region.

The province of **Limburg** in the extreme south is the only part of the Netherlands that can be described as hilly. Partly for this reason the resort of Valkenburg, with its casinos and golf courses, is very popular among domestic tourists. The attractive city of Maastricht has taken advantage of its location on the borders of three countries to become an important venue for international conferences.

Belgium

It can be difficult to define the tourism product of Belgium compared to neighbouring France, Germany and Holland. This is largely because the country is divided in language and culture between the Dutch-speaking Flemings in the north and the French-speaking Walloons in the south. In the past the Walloons were dominant in politics, society and the economy, but this has changed with the decline of industry in the Sambre-Meuse

Valley. There is also a German-speaking minority in the border districts of Eupen and Malmedy in the east. Scenically too, the flat farmlands of Flanders and the heaths of the Kempen are quite different in character from the hills and forests of the Ardennes. Moreover Belgium as an independent nation did not exist until 1830. In the Middle Ages, cities such as Bruges, Ghent, Antwerp and Liège were to a large extent independent, and grew wealthy on the profits of the cloth trade. However, lack of political unity led to the region being dominated by the great powers of the time, namely Burgundy, France, Spain, and the Austrian Empire. Unlike the Dutch, the Belgians were generally ready to accept foreign rule and remained strongly Roman Catholic in religion after the Reformation in the sixteenth century. This is shown by the abundance of religious art and impressive Baroque architecture in cities such as Brussels.

Case study 11.2

Battlefield tourism in Belgium

Belgium has been called the 'cockpit of Europe' on account of the numerous wars that have taken place on its soil. The following conflicts would interest amateur military historians:

- The Wars of Spanish Succession, provoked by the aggressive policies of Louis XIV of France, with Britain at the head of a mainly Protestant coalition. The most important battles were Ramillies and Oudenaarde (1708), won by the Duke of Marlborough.
- The French Revolution and the subsequent Napoleonic wars (1793–1815). This conflict ended with Wellington's victory at the battlefield of Waterloo, just south of Brussels. Ironically Napoleon is given greater prominence in the heritage attractions commemorating the battle than the victorious British and Prussian armies.
- The First World War (1914–1918) which caused even greater devastation and loss of life. Sites include the cemeteries and war memorials around Mons and Ypres, where the Menin Gate and Flanders Fields exhibition feature on many tourist itineraries.
- The Ardennes campaign (1944–1945), in the closing stages of the Second World War, is commemorated in the 'Battle of the Bulge' museum at Bastogne in the Ardennes, which is of particular interest to American tourists.

Assignment

Draft an itinerary that would include the most significant battlefield sites as well as visitor attractions likely to interest a group of British college students on an escorted tour of Belgium and Luxembourg.

Although it can offer beaches, attractive waterways, and fine scenery, Belgium's appeal is mainly cultural, in the widest sense. Like the French, the Flemish and Walloons take food and drink seriously, and it is worth noting that the country produces little wine but over 400 different kinds of beer! As this is a predominantly Catholic nation, the tourist can also enjoy many interesting festivals, although by no means all are religious in character. As in the Netherlands, theme parks are popular, which attract large numbers of tourists from neighbouring countries such as France.

The demand for tourism

Belgian travel propensities are very high, with 80 per cent of the population taking a holiday in any one year and the rise in the number of holidays abroad has outstripped growth in the domestic market; equally expenditure on travel abroad is greater than receipts from inbound tourists.

Domestic tourism

For domestic holidays the car is the most popular form of transport, and self-catering accommodation (holiday villages, caravans, and camping) is increasingly used, as serviced accommodation declines in popularity. Social tourism is important in the Belgian domestic market. The Ardennes and the coast are the most popular holiday destinations.

Outbound tourism

Belgium is an important generator of international tourists with the majority of main holidays taken abroad. Most trips are to neighbouring countries, but Italy and Spain are also important destinations. As in the Netherlands, the high number of trips abroad leaves a deficit on the travel account.

Inbound tourism

The performance of Belgium as an international tourist destination is modest with around 7 million arrivals in 2009. The majority of foreign visitors are from other European countries, particularly the Netherlands. However, visits from neighbouring countries tend to be short compared to those from, say, the UK or the USA. Business trips are concentrated in Brussels (particularly as it hosts the European Commission), and Antwerp. International conferences are attracted to the seaside resorts of Ostend and Knokke, as well as to new facilities in Liège and Bruges. Apart from these business travel centres, visits elsewhere in the country tend to be for holiday purposes.

The supply of tourism

Transport

Both external and internal transport links are highly developed. Brussels is the gateway to Belgium for the great majority of air travellers, although the airports at Antwerp, Liège and Ostend do have some international services. More significant from the viewpoint of price-conscious British tourists are the ferry services to Ostend and Zeebrugge, including a fast catamaran connection. The Channel Tunnel is providing competition for the ferry operators and the airlines, so that the Eurostar fast train service from London to Brussels has gained a large share of the lucrative business travel market. The *Thalys* service between Bruges and Paris also plays an important role, but overall the Belgian railway network is less convenient for touring the country, as it is focused on Brussels. Belgium has over 1,250 kilometres of motorway, which is an extensive network for such a small country. The environmental impact of this has been considerable, but it does mean that no part of the country is more than three hours drive from the coast, and Belgium's traditional role as 'the crossroads of Europe' has been enhanced.

Accommodation

In the serviced accommodation sector low occupancy rates mean that few new hotels are being built and, despite government assistance schemes, little investment is occurring in the existing hotel stock. Most hotel guests are business travellers while demand for self-catering accommodation comes from holidaymakers. Campsites, holiday villages, chalets, and apartments are available.

Organisation

The small size of the tourism industry in Belgium has meant that government policy for tourism is low on the priority list and lacks clear objectives. There are separate promotional commissions for the French-speaking and Flemish regions, both with head offices in Brussels, while the Belgian Tourist Office oversees the promotion of Belgium abroad.

Tourism resources

Belgium's strength has been the diversity of its cultural resources, and it has been less active than neighbouring countries in protecting the rural environment. The first national park was designated in 2006, not, as you might expect, in the scenic Ardennes, but in the Kempen, an area of heathland with derelict quarries and coal mines in the densely populated north-east. Belgium's main tourism resources can be categorised as:

* the coastal resorts;
* the art cities of northern Belgium; and
* the Ardennes.

The **North Sea coast,** like that of Holland, is sandy, flat and backed by dunes. However flooding has been less of a problem in the past than the silting up of ports such as Bruges, which now lies a considerable distance inland. The coast is only 60 kilometres in length and it has suffered from over-development and lack of planning, as shown by the ribbon development of high rise apartments and holiday villas. However the beaches are well maintained, colourful windbreaks provide protection from the constant breezes, while the resorts provide many amenities. A tramway linking all the resorts offers a safe alternative to the car in an area where traffic can reach saturation point in peak season. In addition to domestic tourists, the coast is popular with Germans, while Ostend has long been an established favourite with the British. The resorts differ a good deal in size and character:

* De Panne with its wide expanse of beach can offer sand yachting as an activity for the young affluent visitor;
* Zeebrugge caters more for families;
* Ostend and Blankenberge are the busiest resorts, providing a sophisticated holiday product including casinos; and
* Knokke-Heist near the Dutch border is definitely up-market.

The main destinations for foreign tourists are the **art cities**, mostly situated in Flanders within easy reach of the coast. These are ideal for short breaks, or as part of an extended tour taking in Northern France and the Rhineland. The heritage of Gothic and Renaissance art and architecture is a reminder, not only of the power of the Church, but also the wealth and prestige of the merchant guilds from the fourteenth to the sixteenth centuries.

- Bruges (Brugge in Flemish) is one of the best-preserved medieval cities of northern Europe. For this reason it has become a popular short-break destination as well as a long-established attraction on European touring circuits. Unlike modern conurbations, the townscape of Bruges is on a human scale, a picturesque composition of red-brick gabled buildings, church spires, cobblestone streets and squares, and tranquil waterways set in the green Flemish countryside. Bruges is often described – somewhat misleadingly – as the 'Venice of the North'.
- Ghent is perhaps more typical, as it has moved with the times and remained a major centre of commerce.
- Antwerp on the River Scheldt is Europe's second port and rivals Brussels in its nightlife and range of museums and exhibition centres. It was the birthplace of the painter Rubens and was designated European City of Culture in 1995. The important diamond industry owes a great deal to the city's close links with Belgium's former colony in the Congo.
- Brussels has the advantage of being the capital, not only of the Flanders region and of the country, but also, in a sense, of the European Union. Flemish, French – and increasingly English – are in use throughout the city. It contains the European Commission that has spawned a high-spending bureaucracy and encouraged many multinational corporations to set up their head offices near the centre of power. This has encouraged significant levels of business tourism. Brussels boasts one of the finest groups of Baroque buildings in Europe – around the Grand Place, and in contrast, the modernistic Atomium. But, not having a river as a focus, it lacks the visual appeal of most European capitals.
- Liège is the most important city in French-speaking Wallonia and is famous for its glass and gun-making industries. It is close to the Ardennes holiday region. Much of the Sambre-Meuse Valley to the west was blighted by heavy industry in the nineteenth century, but is now undergoing economic regeneration.
- Namur, in an attractive setting at the confluence of the rivers Meuse and Sambre, is the official capital of Wallonia.

The **Ardennes** uplands, with their forests, limestone gorges, winding river valleys, and picturesque chateaux, are Belgium's scenic resource; in the past much of the region was remote and sparsely populated. Field sports were historically important, but nowadays a wide range of activities are catered for such as riding, cycling, rock-climbing, caving and canoeing. The Ardennes attract large numbers of Dutch tourists as well as domestic visitors, but this popularity has put increasing pressure on its resources. In the areas most accessible to the conurbations of Belgium, the Netherlands, and Germany, the unplanned proliferation of second homes has caused social and environmental problems.

Many of the villages and market towns of the region have become resorts, the most important being Dinant, in an attractive setting on the River Meuse. Specific tourist attractions include the caves at Han-sur-Lesse, the castle at Bouillon, and Orval Abbey, which is noted for its beer. One other resort deserves special mention, as it has given its name to similar attractions elsewhere; this is Spa, where the mineral-rich springs set the fashion for 'taking the waters' to the rest of Europe. Like other health resorts it offers a range of cultural and sporting activities, and is the venue for the Belgian Grand Prix motor racing event.

Discussion point

In Belgium even beauty competitions involving Flemish speakers and Francophones can be controversial. Discuss whether the language and cultural differences between Flanders and Wallonia could be promoted as a strength and an opportunity for developing Belgium's tourism product, rather than being perceived as an obstacle to national unity. Try to look at this from the viewpoint of a variety of tourists, such as a British motorist touring the country on a family holiday, a group of American college students, and a Japanese businesswoman attending conferences in Liège and Bruges.

Luxembourg

The Grand Duchy of Luxembourg is the smallest member of the European Union, but the largest of the six 'mini-states' of Europe, which are survivals from medieval times. Since 1839 it has been closely linked with Belgium and the Belgian franc is legal tender. Due to its size (slightly less than Dorset or Rhode Island), inbound tourism is of far greater importance to Luxembourg than it is to Belgium. The annual number of visitor arrivals is almost double the resident population, but the impact of tourism is less than you might expect for two reasons; the length of stay is short, and many visitors are business travellers to Luxembourg City. Others are transit passengers taking advantage of Luxembourg's low cost international flights from Findel Airport, while most holidaymakers tend to be campers from the neighbouring conurbations in France, Belgium, the Netherlands, and Germany. Tourism has a major impact on the economy and is Luxembourg's third foreign currency earner after financial services (banking and insurance), and steel exports. The majority of visitors are from Europe with almost half originating from Belgium and the Netherlands. Seasonality is high, with most tourists arriving between June and September.

Most of Luxembourg's accommodation capacity is on campsites. Although more nights are spent in campsites than in hotels, it is the latter which are most important in terms of tourist spending. However this is affected by the nature of the business travel market, which can afford the high tariffs.

Tourism is the responsibility of the Ministry of Tourism backed by the National Tourism Office. The promotion of conference tourism is given a high priority; helped by the fact that the country has three official languages and its people are proficient linguists and supporters of European co-operation.

Luxembourg's tourist appeal lies in its capital city and attractive countryside:

- **Luxembourg City** is an important financial centre as well as hosting the Secretariat of the European Parliament and other EU organisations. The city has a picturesque setting among hills and valleys linked by viaducts. Although most of the massive fortifications were torn down and replaced by boulevards long ago, enough remains to explain why Luxembourg was once called 'the Gibraltar of the North'.
- The country's other attractions lie mainly in the **Oesling** region in the north, which forms part of the Ardennes. They include Vianden, a noted beauty spot with an impressive castle; Clervaux, famous for its abbey; and Echternach, a pilgrimage centre, which is of unique interest for its Whitsun dancing processions. The Germano-Luxembourg Nature Park nearby is an outstanding example of international co-operation in conservation. The **Bon Pays/Gutland** region in the south of the country is less impressive scenically, but it does contain the spa town

of Mondorf-les-Bains, which has been rejuvenated to meet contemporary leisure demands.

Summary

- Physically, the Benelux countries comprise three regions – the lowlands of the coast, the intermediate plateaux zone, and the uplands.
- The Benelux countries were joined by a customs union in 1947 and are an outstanding example of close European integration and co-operation.
- Demand for tourism and recreation is high, but this does place pressures on the environments of these small, densely populated countries.
- In each country demand for overseas travel is high and there is a deficit on travel accounts.
- The majority of foreign tourists are from other countries of Western Europe.
- Transport facilities are comprehensive and the region's position in Europe attracts many transit passengers.
- Accommodation provision is dominated by self-catering capacity, particularly campsites and holiday villages, although growing affluence is seeing a shift in preference towards hotels.
- There are three main areas of tourist attraction. First, the facilities and cultural resources of the historic towns and cities attract business and holiday tourists alike; second, the resorts of the North Sea coast are major holiday and day-trip centres; and third, the uplands and countryside are important holiday destinations for campers.

Assignments

1 This region of the world contains many small historic and cultural towns and cities such as Bruges. Devise a sustainable transport plan for the centre of one of these towns to ensure that the visitor experience is enhanced and that local residents can still go about their daily lives.
2 Assess the impact on the host community of the Formula 1 Grand Prix at Spa Francochamps in Belgium.

12

The tourism geography of Germany, Austria and Switzerland

Introduction

Germany, Austria and Switzerland occupy a key position in the centre of Europe. Germany and Austria have played pivotal roles in European history, and share a similar heritage through their association in the Holy Roman Empire, which for centuries was ruled by an Austrian dynasty, the Habsburgs. Switzerland remained on the sidelines, a small country with a strategic location astride the major passes over the Alps. German is the dominant language throughout the region, but in Switzerland French, Italian and Romansch are also official languages. Nevertheless, as a result of large-scale immigration from southern and eastern Europe, there is a trend toward greater cultural diversity. The large Turkish communities in the cities of Austria and Germany are often seen as a problem rather than as an opportunity, and these two countries have opposed the admission of Turkey to the EU.

Apart from Germany's short North Sea and Baltic coasts, the area under consideration in this chapter is landlocked. Three major physical regions can be identified:

1 the North German Plain and the coast are of relatively limited importance for international tourism;
2 the Central Uplands, which include areas such as the Rhineland and the Harz Mountains in Germany, the Mittelland plateau in Switzerland, and the Danube Valley in Austria, are more significant; and
3 the mountainous Alpine region is of major importance for international tourism. It includes most of Austria, half of Switzerland and the south of Bavaria in Germany.

With the exception of the North Sea coast the region has a continental climate, with winters getting colder, not only as we travel further east, but also as a result of altitude. In the mountains the climate is bracing with clean air and brilliant sunshine, but the weather varies with aspect and altitude and fogs are frequent in some valleys during the winter. The cold winters bring the snow which made possible the development of winter sports, yet the resorts on the shores of the more southerly lakes bask in almost Mediterranean temperatures. The *Föhn* wind frequently blows down some of the south-facing valleys of the Alps bringing unseasonal warmth and excessive dryness during the winter months.

Despite their very different historical backgrounds, all three countries are federal republics, with considerable devolution of powers (including tourism responsibilities) to the *länder* (states) in Germany, provinces in Austria, and cantons in Switzerland. Major population concentrations include the Rühr conurbation of Germany, Vienna in Austria, and in Switzerland, Zürich, though not the capital, is the largest city.

The economies of the three countries are highly developed and industrialised with a high standard of living and a strong interest in 'green' issues. This is reflected in the widespread demand for environmentally sound tourism. Both Germany and Austria are members of the European Union, while Switzerland – in line with its historic tradition of neutrality – has no political affiliation. A central geographic location and good communications mean that levels of outbound tourism are high in all three countries. However, high prices do limit the number of inbound tourists. In Germany and Switzerland the annual holiday entitlement is 4 weeks or more, and in Austria entitlement is 5 or more weeks. In Austria there is a 35 to 40 hour working week, in Germany 35 to 37 hours is the norm, but in Switzerland working hours are relatively high and attempts arc being made to reduce them.

Event attractions play an important role in tourism in all three countries, notably music festivals and sport. For example, Austria and Switzerland jointly hosted the Euro 2008 football championship.

Germany

Unlike Austria or Switzerland, Germany lacks a well-defined tourism image, and is often regarded as a destination for business rather than holiday travel. This is not surprising as Germany is Europe's leading industrial nation and its largest economy. However, in 2007 the tourism sector, excluding business travel, generated 3.2 per cent of Germany's GDP. The country is well endowed with a variety of beautiful scenery and cultural attractions, particularly those based on music and the applied arts and sciences.

The Cold War political division of Germany between East and West has tended to obscure the long-standing physical and cultural differences between the Protestant northern part of the country and the predominantly Catholic south and west. Strong regional identities are also a reminder that for most of its history Germany was a patchwork of kingdoms, duchies, prince-bishoprics and free cities owing nominal allegiance to the Holy Roman Emperor. Many of the rulers of these states were generous patrons to artists and musicians. As a result, Berlin, which became the capital of the new united Germany in 1871, has strong rivals in several other major cities, which act as world class cultural and business centres.

The development of tourism in Germany has also been complicated by the fact that from 1945 to 1990 the country was divided, along with the city of Berlin. The two Germanies that resulted from this division had widely differing political and economic structures:

- West Germany, officially known as the Federal Republic of Germany (BRD) prospered under a democratic style of government and a free market economy; while:
- East Germany, officially called the German Democratic Republic (DDR) was compelled by its Soviet regime to adopt Communism and a centralised command economy. Tourist enterprises such as hotels were nationalised and the whole industry was subject to state control. East Germans were discouraged from visiting other countries, with the exception of those in the Eastern Bloc, such as Romania and Hungary. Visits from West Germans were virtually prohibited while tourism from other Western countries was subject to many restrictions.

The structure changed rapidly after 1989 with the removal of the Berlin Wall, and the reunification of Germany a year later. A united Germany could offer a range of new tourism products and domestic markets for tourism. For example there has been a flood of West German tourists into East Germany, attracted by the low cost of accommodation. Yet East Germans have a lower propensity than West Germans to travel abroad, due to the continuing legacy of half a century of repression and a lack of financial resources. The economy of the former DDR was badly depressed because it was based on industries that could not compete with foreign products without the protection of state subsidies, a pattern repeated in other countries of the former Eastern Bloc. The cost of reunification also contributed to the downturn in the German economy as a whole after the late 1990s. The former West Germany comprises 80 per cent of the population, and dominates both tourism supply and demand in the new Germany.

Unlike many countries that have experienced dictatorial regimes, Germany has not sought to cover up or deny the crimes perpetrated by the National Socialists between 1933 and 1945, and the abuses of human rights later committed by the *Stasi* (secret police) in the Communist DDR. A number of cities, notably Berlin, Munich and Nuremberg, have museums and exhibitions confronting these issues and the phenomenon of 'dark tourism' with sensitivity.

The demand for tourism

Domestic tourism

The Germans have been among the world's greatest spenders on travel and tourism for many years and they attach great importance to their annual holiday, even in times of recession. Generous holiday entitlement means that travel frequencies are high and holiday propensities reach almost 75 per cent, though this does vary according to age, socio-economic status, and place of residence. The domestic market accounts for the great majority of bed-nights and so dominates the industry; in 2007 Germans made 368 million overnight stays, and one in three Germans took a holiday within their own country. Domestic holidays are concentrated seasonally in the summer months and geographically in the south of Germany and on the coast. Business travel is important in the domestic market.

Germans are very health-conscious and over 200 spa resorts, based on abundant mineral springs, have developed to meet this demand, some of which were internationally famous in the nineteenth century as resorts for the European elite. These now cater for a wide cross-section of the population, and have been supported by generous state-sponsored health insurance schemes. Most spas are located in the uplands of the Mittelgebirge in the central part of the country. Germans have long been renowned for 'wanderlust', here with its original meaning of 'love of walking' and the country is well provided with a network of waymarked hiking and cycling trails. Germany also initiated the youth hostel movement in the early 1900s. By way of contrast, since the 1980s there has been considerable investment in theme parks, such as Phantasia near Cologne, and visitor attractions focusing on science and technology, for example, the Bremen Space Centre and those associated with the Volkswagen assembly plant at Wolfsburg.

Outbound tourism

Germany vies with the USA as the world's leading generator of international tourism, spending over US $80 billion annually on foreign travel. The majority of trips are to Germany's neighbours (particularly Austria) and to Mediterranean countries (particularly Italy and Spain). Many trips are package tours sold by the highly organised travel industry that has grown up to meet the demand for holidays abroad. Spain is by far the most important package holiday destination, but whereas Germans take roughly the same number of holidays in Spain as the British, they are much more likely to take a second holiday in their own country. Long-haul travel is also important to a wide range of destinations.

Inbound tourism

The high volume of travel abroad keeps Germany's travel account in considerable deficit even though, in 2009, there were around 23 million arrivals. The main countries of origin are Germany's neighbours, and there is a significant volume of daily cross-border traffic. Around 56 million overnight stays were recorded in 2010, but generally average lengths of stay are short at around two days, and this does mean that foreign visitors contribute only a small percentage of the bed nights in the country. Business travel, including visits to trade fairs and exhibitions, is important in the inbound market, exceeding the volume of holiday traffic from abroad. Thanks to the links with industry and government encouragement in the past, Germany is noted for its world-class venues for motor racing. A number of international sports events have been instrumental in raising the country's international image and tourism profile, notably the Olympic Games hosted by Berlin in 1936 and Munich in 1972, and the FIFA World Cup in 1974 and 2006.

Case study 12.1

Trade fairs in Germany

Germany accounts for a third of the European demand for trade fairs and exhibitions. As for supply, the country outstrips Italy, France and the UK in the number of large exhibition centres. Every major town has its *messe* (trade fairground), financially supported by local and state governments, rather than operated as a profit-making business by the private sector. Exhibitors (who are primarily there to make a sale) and visitors (who are mainly attending for work-related reasons) create a high level of demand for accommodation, catering and travel services, and thus benefit the local economy. Major venues for international trade fairs include Berlin and the following cities:

Case study 12.1

- Hanover, hosting the *Deutschesmesse*, reputedly the world's largest trade fair;
- Cologne, noted for the biennial exhibition on photography – Photokina;
- Düsseldorf, noted for its fashion shows;
- Essen, for cars;
- Frankfurt, for books;
- Nuremberg, the largest international fair for toys and games; and
- Leipzig, where two annual fairs were held as far back as medieval times. After the Second World War these served as the showpiece for the industrial achievements of the DDR and the Eastern Bloc countries generally.

Germany now faces increasing competition in this sector of business tourism and a possible over-supply of exhibition capacity. Financial constraints are forcing local and state governments to contract out some services to the private sector, and there is a trend toward greater diversification, to make more efficient use of exhibition floor space throughout the year.

Assignment

1 The Internationale Tourismus-Börse (ITB) hosted by Berlin is the world's largest travel trade show. How does it compare with similar events in Britain and other European countries in terms of the capacity of the exhibition centre, the number and type of exhibitors, and the number and type of visitors?
2 Discuss the ways in which a medium-sized exhibition centre can make more cost-effective use of its floor space by hosting events other than trade shows. Is diversification necessarily better than specialisation in a particular type of industrial product?

The supply of tourism

Accommodation

Domestic business travellers and most foreign visitors are accommodated in hotels in towns and cities. Demand for self-catering accommodation exceeds supply, as does that for most types of accommodation in the peak season. There is a concentration of hotels and guesthouses serving the holiday market in Bavaria and Baden-Württemburg, and a shortage of accommodation throughout most of the former DDR, although many hotel chains are now developing properties in this part of Germany. Holiday parks – groups of chalets around a pool and other leisure facilities – are popular with German families.

Transport

The car is the most important form of tourist transport. The road network is excellent with *autobahns* (motorways without an imposed speed limit), and also specially designed scenic routes for visitors. A major problem is seasonal congestion both on the access routes and in the popular holiday areas. Rail travel is the second most popular form of travel with promotional fares and inclusive package holidays available; plans for a high-speed train network (ICE) are well advanced. The larger cities have a fully integrated public transport system of trams, buses, 'U' Bahn (underground), and 'S Bahn' (fast suburban trains). Air travel is served by ten international airports, all well connected by rail with the urban areas they serve. The national carrier, Lufthansa, is based at the main gateway and hub at Frankfurt. Tourists arriving by sea can use ferries from Harwich to Hamburg, from Trelleborg in Sweden to Sassnitz, and from Roby Havn in Denmark to Puttgarten. Cruises are popular on the Rhine and the other major rivers, the canals that link these natural waterways, and on the Boden See (Lake Constance).

Organisation

Tourism in Germany suffers from a long history of having no representation at senior level in the federal government. Tourism responsibilities are in the hands of the state governments which have considerable independence to promote and develop tourism, but this does result in considerable fragmentation. There is for example, no national tourism policy as tourism is low on the list of government economic priorities, and the little federal aid that is available for the industry is mainly used to boost accommodation in less-developed areas and to stimulate farm tourism. The states provide funds for both upgrading accommodation and for season-extension developments (such as indoor swimming pools) in resorts. The German National Tourist Board (Deutsche Zentrale für Tourismus – DZT) is the major marketing agency for Germany, with responsibilities for both domestic and international promotion. It is mainly financed by the federal government and aims to boost visitor arrivals and revenue, and to reposition Germany as a multi-faceted, attractive destination.

Tourism resources

Forests cover almost a third of Germany, and as a managed resource are an important part of its national image and tourism appeal. The country is a leader in green issues, and there are 14 national parks protecting a great diversity of landscapes. The many small historic towns with their half-timbered buildings in a variety of styles are also an important cultural resource. Germany's cities have world-class facilities for music and the performing arts. These are becoming more prominent for international tourism, as the generous state subsidies to cultural institutions were scaled down owing to the stagnation of the economy in the 1990s.

Northern Germany

This region includes the states of Schleswig-Holstein, Lower Saxony, Hamburg, Bremen, along with Mecklenburg-West Pomerania in the former DDR. In this part of Germany the main tourist attractions are found in the historic cities or on the coast. Inland, there are large areas of forest, heathland, and lakes – such as those of Holstein and Mecklenburg. The rivers of the region are linked by the valleys of glacial origin known as *urstromtaler* trending from east to west, that have been utilised by a number of canals. These features offer some variety in the otherwise low-key landscapes of the North European Plain and provide opportunities for activities such as canoeing.

The North Sea is colder and rougher than the Baltic, and the coast is low-lying, with large areas of mudflats exposed at low tide. However, the North Frisian Islands have fine beaches, the most popular being those of Sylt, which is linked to the mainland by a causeway. The resort of Westerland attracts fashionable holidaymakers as well as German families, and it was here that naturism – known in Germany as *freikorpskultur*

(FKK) – first appeared on the holiday scene in the 1920s. The tideless Baltic coast is scenically more attractive, with sandpits enclosing extensive lagoons. With the exception of Kiel – a major yachting centre – and Travemünde, most of the Baltic resorts were situated in the former DDR. These flourished serving a captive domestic market, but their outdated facilities and substandard service practices left them ill-equipped to face the competition following German reunification and the introduction of a free market economy. They are now being 'rediscovered' by West German holidaymakers, who are attracted by the lack of commercialisation, ironically caused by decades of neglect under Communism.

This is particularly true of the island of Rügen, with its chalk cliffs, deeply indented coastline, beaches and beautiful countryside, which attracted Romantic artists such as Casper Friedrich and the German elite in the nineteenth century. Here the National Socialist regime developed the resort of Prora as a regimented form of 'tourism for the people' in the 1930s as part of the 'Strength through Joy' movement. After 1945 the East German government, with a different ideology but adopting a similar policy, used these facilities for the rest and recreation of selected workers and the Communist Party elite. Resorts on the mainland near the port of Rostock include Heiligedamm and Warnemünde. Heiligedamm was the first resort in Germany to adopt the English fashion of sea bathing; its fashionable reputation has been revived in recent years, and in 2007 it was chosen as the location for the G8 Summit meeting. A characteristic of the beach at many German resorts is the proliferation of *strandkörbe*, a type of mini-cabin that can be easily moved to take advantage of the sun while providing protection from the wind.

Many of the cultural attractions of northern Germany date back to the Middle Ages, when the powerful Hanseatic League of merchants from Hamburg and other cities dominated trade throughout northern Europe. This heritage is exploited for tourism in the picturesque port of Lübeck, with its well-preserved city walls and gates, church spires and red-brick merchants' houses. Similar examples, but less commercialised, can be found in Rostock, Wismar and Stralsund.

The major cities of the region – Hamburg, Bremen and Hanover – are primarily business centres with tourism playing a secondary role. Hamburg deserves special mention for the following reasons:

- it is one of Europe's major ports, with worldwide trading connections, and a special economic role in relation to Eastern Europe and the countries of the former USSR;
- it is a major cultural centre, with publishing as one of its major industries;
- the picturesque setting of the old city, between the harbour and the Alster Lakes, appeals to visitors; and
- the vitality of its nightlife, centred on the Saint Pauli district and the notorious Reeperbahn.

Central Germany

To the south of the North German Plain rise the forested uplands of the Mittelgebirge. For the most part they are not high or rugged enough to be regarded as mountains, but they are ideal hiking country. The towns of the state of Hesse and the Weser Valley are rich in legendary associations, notable examples being Hamelin and the castle at Sababurg immortalised by the brothers Jakob and Wilhelm Grimm. The German Tourist Office has promoted a tourist route from Bremen south to Marburg based on these resources as the 'Fairy-Tale Road'.

To the east, the Harz Mountains are renowned for their beautiful scenery and picturesque medieval towns such as Goslar and Quedlinburg. During the Cold War division of Germany this region was bisected by the Iron Curtain, which severely disrupted all communications to the detriment of its tourism industry. The minefields and other barriers have long gone, to be replaced by nature reserves and hiking trails.

The Rhineland

This part of Germany has long been popular with foreign visitors. Its people tend to be more pleasure-loving and *Fasching* (Carnival) is an important festive event in many of the towns and cities. The Rhine has been a major commercial artery since Roman times, and the cities on its banks featured prominently on the Grand Tour. From about 1800 the most picturesque stretch of the river, between Bingen and Koblenz, became a focus of the Romantic Movement in art, literature and music, and a tourist attraction in itself. (Romanticism was inspired by a love of nature, landscape and the heritage, much idealised, of the Middle Ages.) In the Rhine Gorge the river, followed closely by the autobahn and railway, meanders between terraced vineyards on south-facing slopes, and steep crags crowned by the picturesque castles which feature prominently in German legend. The northern Rhineland is less attractive as it includes the heavily industrialised Rühr Valley conurbation. This area is now undergoing regeneration, with the transformation of polluting factories and mines into heritage museums, theme parks and leisure centres, and much has been done to 'green' the landscape. There is also scenic countryside within easy reach, notably in the Sauerland, which is promoted internationally by a tourist association. The many tourist centres in the Rhine Valley include the following:

- Rüdesheim hosts the most popular of the wine festivals in the region.
- Düsseldorf is the commercial hub of the region and is a 'must' for the serious shopper as well as business travellers.
- Cologne (Köln) is one of a number of cities in the Rhineland that have Roman origins. It boasts Germany's most famous cathedral.
- Bonn was a small university town, famous as the birthplace of Beethoven, when it was chosen as the capital of the new Federal Republic in 1949, a status it lost after reunification.
- Aachen (known to the French as Aix la Chapelle) lies close to the border with Belgium and the Netherlands, and is an example of international city promotion, in partnership with Liège and Maastricht. It is historically important as the place, noted for its healing springs, that Charlemagne chose to be the capital of the Holy Roman Empire, and where his chapel, once a major place of pilgrimage, can still be visited.
- Trier in the wine-producing Moselle Valley, is rich in historical monuments dating back to the fourth century, when it was an imperial capital, strategically located near the Rhine frontier of the Roman Empire.

Other important historic cities in the Rhine Valley are Mainz, Wörms and Speyer, similarly located near vineyards. In contrast, Frankfurt on the River Main emphasises its modern role as one of the world's great financial centres, rather than any particular heritage attractions. Its airport is one of the world's busiest, and it lies at the 'crossroads' of the autobahn network.

Southern Germany

Southern Germany comprises the states of Baden-Württemberg and Bavaria. This region vies with Italy in its wealth of Baroque churches, monasteries and palaces. Baden-Baden is Germany's most famous spa resort, while the old university town of Heidelberg is a 'must' on the international tourist circuit. In contrast, Stuttgart is the centre of the German motor vehicle industry and attracts a good deal of business travel for this reason.

The **Black Forest**, a scenic area of pine-covered uplands, waterfalls and picturesque villages rising to the east of the Rhine, offers ideal opportunities for skiing in winter and hiking in summer, with the world's oldest long-distance waymarked trail – the *Westweg*. The region is also famous for its folklore and clock-making industry, carried on in small towns such as Triberg.

Bavaria is the most popular state with domestic and foreign tourists, since it can offer a great variety of scenery and is noted for its folklore. A shortlist of specific attractions in Bavaria would include the following:

* Munich, the capital of Bavaria, has a wealth of Renaissance architecture and is a favourite with art and music lovers. Its beer gardens and annual *Oktoberfest* attract many foreign visitors.
* Nuremberg, the birthplace of the painter Albrecht Dürer, is another major cultural centre, containing the German National Museum.
* The **'Romantic Road'** is Germany's best-known tourist route linking a number of well-preserved medieval towns, including Würzburg, Bamberg, and Rothenburg.
* Regensburg on the Danube a former capital of the Holy Roman Empire.
* Bayreuth is celebrated for the annual Wagner music festival.
* Friedrichshafen on the Boden See is important in the history of aviation as the base for the Zeppelin airship flights.

The Bavarian Alps

Although not as high as the mountains in Austria and Switzerland, the Bavarian Alps offer spectacular lake and mountain scenery. Neuschwanstein is the best-known of the

Case study 12.2

The Oberammergau Passion Play

The small town of Oberammergau in the foothills of the Bavarian Alps is famous for its community involvement in a religious drama held every ten years. Passion plays depict the events leading to the Crucifixion and are a genre that originated in the 'miracle plays' of pre-Reformation Europe, and which have been adapted for modern film audiences. The Oberammergau Play originated in 1634 at the height of the Thirty Years War, a time when Germany was devastated by foreign armies and bubonic plague. It is not the oldest Passion Play, but it is certainly the largest, with performances running from May to October and involving over 2,000 participants. These are all established members of the community who provide not only the cast of players, choristers and musicians but also the costumiers and stage designers. The 2010 event attracted half a million visitors from all over the world, with performances taking place in a purpose-built auditorium holding 4,700 spectators. Over the decades there has been a tendency toward greater professionalism, but also commercialisation, with the sale of kitsch souvenirs.

Between events, Oberammergau continues to be a major tourist destination, thanks to its appealing frescoed buildings, traditional handicrafts such as woodcarving, and a variety of attractions in the surrounding area.

romantic castles built by Wagner's patron, King Ludwig II of Bavaria. The resort of Garmisch-Partenkirschen is Germany's major winter sports centre.

Discussion point

1 Compare the Oberammergau Play with the religious events that take place during Holy Week in other Catholic countries such as Spain, for example, the *Passió* in the Catalan village of Olesa de Montserrat,
2 Explain why the Oberammergau Play has attracted controversy.

Eastern Germany

Prior to 1990 this region, consisting of the states of Brandenburg, Saxony, Saxony-Anhalt, and Thuringia formed the bulk of the DDR. It is crossed by the River Elbe, and cruises are now available from Hamburg to the scenic area known as the 'Saxon Switzerland' near the border with the Czech Republic. Unfortunately, much of Saxony south of the Elbe has suffered severe pollution from obsolescent heavy industrial plant using low-grade coal. Investment on a vast scale was necessary to bring environmental standards up to the level of those in the former West Germany. In contrast, the state of Thuringia is a forested upland region and has more tourist appeal. Eastern Germany offers the visitor a number of towns and cities that have played an important role in German history. These include:

* Weimar, an example of the German Enlightenment, associated with Göethe, Germany's greatest poet, and the composer Franz Liszt;
* Eisenach and Wittenburg, where Martin Luther initiated the Protestant Reformation;
* Leipzig, the leading commercial centre of Saxony, associated with the composer J.S. Bach; and
* Dresden, the capital of Saxony and a beautiful Baroque city with important art collections that was destroyed by Allied bombing in 1945, and now substantially restored (Dresden porcelain is actually made 30 kilometres away in the town of Meissen).

Berlin exerts a special fascination for tourists because of its place in recent history. The city first became important in the eighteenth century under Frederick the Great as the capital of Prussia, the most militaristic of the German states. In the 1920s Berlin was notorious for its cabarets. During the Cold War era, the Berlin Wall and 'Checkpoint Charlie' epitomised the confrontation between NATO and the Soviet Union. West Berlin was a cosmopolitan 'island' of democracy and free enterprise surrounded by Communist East Germany (although it was heavily subsidised by the federal government in Bonn), whereas East Berlin was the capital of the DDR. West Berlin's shopping and nightlife contrasted with the greyness and restrictions of life in East Germany. Shortly after the fall of the Berlin Wall, the administrative functions of a re-united Germany gradually moved from Bonn to Berlin, a process symbolised by the opening of the new *Reichstag* (Parliament Building) in 1998, and East Berlin became the focus of one of the world's greatest urban regeneration projects. Berlin offers the cultural tourist a number of world-class museums and music venues, while the legacy of Frederick the Great includes the Brandenburg Gate, the elegant avenue known as the *Unter den Linden*, and the royal palaces at Charlottenburg and Potsdam.

Discussion point

Most of the media coverage of the 2006 FIFA World Cup showed Germany as the host nation in a favourable light, and had a spin-off for tourism by publicising some of the country's attractions. On the other hand some journalists claimed that the trafficking in female immigrants for sex tourism (prostitution is legal in Germany) increased as a result. Compare the World Cup with other sports events that have been held in Germany and assess the extent to which they improved the country's image.

Austria

Austria is a small country with an outsize capital, due to the historical fact that Vienna ruled the vast Hapsburg Empire until its break-up in 1918. The lavishly decorated Baroque churches, monasteries and palaces are part of that heritage. Austrian composers – notably Mozart, Haydn, Schubert and Mahler – made an immense contribution to the world of music and are now celebrated through music festivals. But for most people, the abiding image of Austria is its scenic countryside of lakes and mountains, while its reputation as one of the world's major winter sports destinations has tended to overshadow the many cultural attractions the country can offer.

Tourism plays a major role in Austria's economy, accounting for 10 per cent of the country's economic output. Austria has the benefit of both a summer and a winter season; the winter sports market has grown steadily since the late 1950s, and is now more significant in terms of tourist spending than summer tourism, although it remains smaller in volume. Skiing helped to restore national pride following the disaster of two World Wars, and ski-racing is a major spectator sport. For many years Austria was in the top position as a skiing destination, having overtaken Switzerland in the 1950s, but more recently France has relegated it to second place. Much of the resort development took place in the years following the Second World War as part of the reconstruction of Austria's economy.

The demand for tourism

Domestic and outbound tourism

Over two-thirds of the Austrian population take a holiday, with domestic holidays accounting for over half of all trips. There is a growing move towards taking more than one holiday, particularly in the form of short breaks to event attractions in Austrian cities, and this is spreading the holiday pattern away from July and August. Farmhouse stays have been successfully promoted to encourage tourism throughout the rural areas, but there is still a concentration of holidays in the Tyrol, creating considerable congestion with visitors outnumbering the inhabitants in many villages. Austria is a major generator of international tourists on a world scale, though the majority of trips are to neighbouring countries, emphasising Austria's favourable location in Europe. The majority of holidays abroad are to Mediterranean countries – particularly Italy, Greece, Spain and Croatia.

Inbound tourism

Austria attracted around 21 million international visitors in 2009, giving Austria a surplus on its tourism account. The majority are on a holiday visit and there is no doubt that proximity to Germany is important to Austria as that market accounts for just under half of all arrivals. The next two countries, the Netherlands and the UK, are also important sources of tourists but together only account for a small proportion of overnights. New markets in Eastern Europe, coupled with marketing initiatives also mean that Austria is receiving an increasing number of visits from this region. In addition to their proximity, Germans are attracted to Austria with its more relaxed lifestyle and absence of language barriers. This reliance on one market does leave Austria vulnerable in times of recession and the concentration of visits determined by holiday periods in Germany causes congestion at the borders. In popular holiday areas many resorts become totally geared to the German market.

The supply of tourism

Transport

With the German market so dominant, the majority of tourists arrive by car on the 18,000 kilometre road network (including 2,000 kilometres of tolled motorways and expressways) and experience traffic congestion at the beginning and end of the main holiday periods. The tortuous nature of some of the roads emphasises the difficulty of transportation in this elongated and mountainous country, yet the network reaches into the most remote parts, and includes Europe's highest road to the summit of the Gross Glockner. There are over 6,000 kilometres of railway including 20 private railway companies, and these are well integrated with rural bus services reaching the most remote communities. With six airports of international standard in Austria, this is the main mode of travel for outbound tourism, although some argue that a restrictive policy on inbound flights to Vienna in the past has held back the development of the tourism industry and compounded Austria's dependence on the German market. On the other hand Austrian Airlines is renewing its fleet and expanding its international network, with Vienna as the hub.

Accommodation

The majority of Austria's bedspaces are in serviced accommodation and except in the cities, these are mainly small, family-run hotels and guesthouses. The authorities are improving the quality of accommodation as a means of boosting both domestic and foreign tourism. Although business travel is relatively unimportant in Austria, the small conference market is being developed, particularly in Vienna, Linz, Salzburg, Innsbruck, Graz, and Villach, as well as in the larger *schlosshotels* – castles and palaces formerly owned by the aristocracy - which have been converted into hotels.

Organisation

Each of the nine Austrian provinces has responsibility for tourism administered by the provincial government and a tourist board. At national level tourism is the responsibility of the Ministry of Economic Affairs. Promotion of Austria is the responsibility of the Austrian National Tourism Office, a joint public/private agency with funding from the government and the Chamber of Commerce. The organisation has undergone a restructuring to ensure an overtly marketing focus in the face of stagnant demand from the international market. The tourism authorities in Austria are upgrading tourist infrastructure generally, particularly in the area of sports and facilities for activity holidays, and extending the network of ski lifts and funiculars. Nevertheless some

EUROPE

resorts (such as Mayrhofen) have halted further development in line with Austria's green image and this may have persuaded potential skiers to choose France instead.

Tourism resources

Austria contains 35 per cent of the area covered by the Alps (compared to Switzerland's 15 per cent) and the country is famed for its lake and mountain scenery, winter sports facilities, and picturesque towns and villages. Trending east – west across the country and separated by the deep valley of the River Inn, the mountains are Austria's main attraction. Here tourism is often the only economic land use and its development is seen as a means of stemming the migration of young people from rural communities. However, this is not without environmental costs, such as forest hillsides and meadows scarred from ski-lift development or villages marred by insensitive building.

Each of the Austrian provinces can offer distinctive attractions:

- **Tyrol** is by far the most popular destination for foreign visitors, containing the most spectacular Alpine scenery and the greatest number of ski resorts. Tyrolean folklore and costumes are the best known of Austria's traditional cultures. Most of the resorts have been developed from farming villages situated in the tributary valleys of the River Inn – the Ötztal and Zillertal for example – at altitudes of between 1,000 and 1,800 metres. Traditional building styles, based on the chalet that is well adapted to heavy winter snowfalls, provide a pleasant ambience for holidays. Summer activities in the Tyrol include hiking and gliding, while most villages are equipped with a swimming pool and facilities for tennis and other sports. The region also offers a number of scenic trails and wine routes. Tourist centres include the following:
  - Innsbruck is not only the capital of the Tyrol but an important cultural centre, a reminder of its former role as a summer residence for the Hapsburg emperors; this explains the many Renaissance buildings. Along with the ski resorts on the slopes nearby, the city has twice hosted the Winter Olympics.
  - St Anton, Kitzbuhl, Söll, Seefeld and Mayrhofen are ski resorts of international significance.
- **Vorarlberg** to the west of the Arlberg mountains was historically isolated from the rest of Austria and has some affinity with neighbouring Switzerland. Lech and Zurs offer up-market skiing, while Bregenz on the Boden See is a popular lake resort and a venue for music festivals. At this point we should include the tiny independent principality of **Liechtenstein**, which is better known as a tax haven than as a winter sports destination. It has strong historical ties to Austria but uses the same currency as Switzerland.
- The province of **Salzburg** and the **Salzkammergut** area (so called because of the historically important salt mining industry) offer gentler lake and mountain scenery. St Wolfgang is the most popular of the resorts in summer, but its entertainment scene is subdued compared to Söll or Kitzbühl in winter. Other attractions include the Krimml waterfalls in the Höhe Tauern National Park, the Dachstein ice caves, the picturesque old town of Hallstatt, and the spas of Bad Ischl and Bad Gastein.
- **Styria**, the forested 'green province' is mainly visited by domestic tourists, although its capital, Graz is Austria's second largest city and a major cultural centre, which played a key role in the defence of the Habsburg Empire against the Ottoman Turks.

- **Carinthia** is increasingly popular with foreign visitors as a summer holiday destination, where the warm sunny climate and lakes such the Wörther See, offering many facilities for water sports, are the main attractions.
- The remaining provinces of Austria, occupying the Danube Valley, are scenically less attractive, with large areas of lowland supplying most of the country's agricultural needs. The Burgenland is similar in its steppe landscapes to neighbouring Hungary (to which it belonged prior to 1918), while the shallow Neusiedlersee is an important nature reserve. Both the provinces of Upper and Lower Austria contain vineyards, monasteries (such as Melk) and castles (such as Durnstein) and it is possible for the tourist to see these on a Danube river cruise from Vienna.

Whereas Graz, Linz and Innsbruck are important regional centres, only two of Austria's cities – Vienna and Salzburg – attract huge numbers of visitors from all over the world, thanks to their heritage of music and architecture:

- **Vienna** is full of reminders of its imperial past. These include the monumental buildings lining the Ringstrasse encircling the old city, and the art treasures housed in the former palaces of the Hofburg, Belvedere and Schönbrunn. Music and dance are as much a part of the city's social and entertainment scene as they were in the time of the 'Waltz King' (Johann Strauss) in the nineteenth century. The State Opera House and St Stephen's Cathedral are also part of this musical heritage. Although Vienna trades on nostalgia and the café lifestyle for its tourist appeal, the city is an efficiently run modern conference venue, with an international role as a United Nations centre, while geographical location makes it the recognised gateway to Eastern Europe.
- **Salzburg** has a flourishing tourism industry based on:
  - the summer music festival, which was further boosted in 1991 by the Mozart bicentenary celebrations (during festival time, accommodation in this relatively small city is at a premium);
  - the *Sound of Music* connection means that classical music lovers are outnumbered by those tourists who are attracted to the city (and the scenic countryside of lakes and mountains nearby), through their associations with this popular film; and
  - it's unique heritage of Baroque architecture – probably unrivalled outside Spain or Italy – which was brought into being by the powerful prince-bishops who once ruled Salzburg.

Discussion point

In Europe the 'second city' of a country is usually not a tourist centre of international significance, unlike the national capital. Yet Graz was chosen as the 'European capital of culture' for 2003, and its old town is recognised by UNESCO as a World Heritage Site. Assess how effective these designations have been in raising the tourism profile of Graz, and suggest ways in which the city could be marketed more effectively in the UK.

Switzerland

Switzerland is poor in natural resources and contains a diversity of languages and cultures. Yet its people have achieved a degree of political stability and economic prosperity that is envied by the rest of the world. Swiss industrial products, based on a high input of skill in relation to the value of the component raw materials, have an international reputation for quality. Similarly, the country's scenic attractions – arguably the most spectacular in Europe – have been intelligently exploited by a hospitality industry that is renowned for its professionalism and training institutions. Historically, the country developed as a confederation of cantons – small mountain states – fighting to preserve their independence from foreign domination, yet at the same time exporting mercenaries to join foreign armies. In many respects the cantons still play a more important role in Swiss politics than the federal government in Berne. At the local level the communes also determine tourism planning and development to a large extent, in line with the Swiss tradition of direct citizen participation in politics and national defence.

Tourism in Switzerland has a long history, and the industry was already well established in the late nineteenth century. Its development came about as a result of a number of factors:

- From early times, Switzerland was a transit zone for invading armies, merchants and pilgrims, and later had to be crossed by wealthy travellers undertaking the Grand Tour. The Swiss were in demand as guides, as there were no serviceable roads and the Alpine passes were often hazardous. Accommodation was also needed for travellers, the most famous example being the hospice on the St. Bernard Pass.
- As a result of the Romantic Movement in art and literature at the close of the eighteenth century, the mountains were no longer perceived as a barrier to be feared, but as a resource to be valued. For example, Byron and Shelley stayed for a considerable time by Lake Geneva, and summer resorts gradually developed for well-off tourists around other lakes in Switzerland.
- From the middle of the nineteenth century the demand for tourism in Switzerland grew as the result of the Industrial Revolution in Western Europe, the improvement in road and rail communications and the growth of the middle class, particularly in countries like Britain, where Thomas Cook did much to popularise the country. The more adventurous tourists sought the challenges of mountain climbing, following Whymper's ascent of the Matterhorn in 1865. More remote areas of the Alps were progressively opened up to tourism with the construction of funicular and cog railways, and hotels were built at the edge of the Alpine glaciers, such as the Aletsch.
- Although Switzerland had been known for its spas since Roman times, substantial development of health tourism occurred in the late nineteenth and early twentieth centuries as a result of the spread of tuberculosis in the industrial cities of Europe. The pure mountain air in spas such as St Moritz Bad and Arosa was believed to provide a remedy for the disease.
- Skiing and other winter sports such as tobogganing and curling were introduced to St Moritz and the resorts of the Bernese Oberland by wealthy British tourists at the close of the nineteenth century. At first, the existing mountain railways – now operating year-round – were used to transport the skiers to the slopes, but as demand grew from the 1930s onwards, they were largely superseded by faster, more efficient aerial cableways.
- International trade had long been important to Swiss cities such as Geneva. The strict neutrality of Switzerland and its multi-lingual character encouraged the growth of all kinds of business and conference tourism. Starting with the Red Cross, Geneva became the venue for many international organisations, while Zürich and Basle are financial centres of worldwide significance. Berne and

Lausanne – the headquarters respectively of the Universal Postal Union and the Olympic Committee – also provide important conference functions.

The demand for tourism

Domestic and outbound tourism

The Swiss have one of the highest holiday propensities in the world, with around 75 per cent taking a holiday of at least 4 nights. Approximately half of all journeys with overnight stays are taken abroad. Holiday taking is at its highest among upper-income groups, the middle-aged, and those living in the larger towns or cities. Demand for domestic tourism has grown, with the high frequency of holiday-taking meaning that most domestic holidays are second or third holidays.

Domestic holidays contrast with those taken abroad as they tend to be winter sports or mountain holidays, many taken in the months of January to March. Eastern Switzerland, Schweizer Mittelland, and the Lake Geneva region are the most popular with domestic tourists. Swiss holidays abroad are concentrated into the summer months of July to September and the most popular destinations are Italy and France.

Inbound tourism

Demand from foreign visitors to Switzerland has grown in the early years of the twenty-first century to reach 8.2 million arrivals in 2009. As in Austria, Germans account for the majority of visitors. Around 40 per cent of bed nights occur in the winter season (November to April).

The supply of tourism

Transport

The private car dominates domestic travel and air transport foreign travel. As in Austria, the transport networks are tortuous and the topography often demands major engineering feats – the 18-kilometre tunnel under the St Gotthard being an outstanding example, while the roads over the Alpine passes are spectacular. Even so, roads in the High Alps are often blocked by snow from November to June. While the road network brings many remoter parts of the country within reach of day visitors, this has created congestion in holiday areas and environmental pollution from commercial vehicles on the major routes across the Alps. The opening of a second St Gotthard rail tunnel and the imposition of tolls may alleviate this congestion. The Swiss Federal Railways and the private railway companies operate 5,200 kilometres of track (1,600 kilometres are narrow-gauge) and there are many mountain railways, funiculars, and rack-and-pinion systems which are often tourist attractions in themselves. Although the cost is high, tunnels and snowploughs allow the railways to operate throughout the year.

There are international airports at Zürich, Geneva, Berne and Basle. Swissair – the former national airline – was a casualty in the wake of 9/11, and was replaced by Swiss, financed by the private sector. Other features of the Swiss transport system, which is highly integrated, include the postal coaches – which access the smallest villages – bicycle hire at many rail stations, and lake ferries.

Accommodation

The development of accommodation since the 1970s has led to an excess of supply over demand. About a third of the serviced accommodation capacity is only available in the winter season, particularly in the high ski resorts (such as St Moritz and Arosa). Most hotels are small with the few larger hotels found mainly in Zürich, Berne and Geneva. Hotels and holiday chalets (mainly catering for groups of skiers) are highly dependent on foreign labour. 'Supplementary accommodation', including holiday chalets, apartments, holiday villages and camping/caravan sites, provide a lower-cost alternative to hotels for foreign visitors, but they are also popular with domestic holidaymakers.

Organisation

In the face of declining international demand for Switzerland in the 1990s, the Swiss National Tourism Organisation was renamed 'Switzerland Tourism' in 1995 and underwent restructuring and a refocusing of priorities. It is now the Swiss National Tourism Office, responsible to the Federal Department of Public Economy for formulating and implementing national tourism policy. Switzerland's maturity as a destination is reflected in the long tradition of tourist associations and information services at local and regional levels. There are also many specialist organisations such as the Swiss Travel Bank that was founded to give less privileged workers the chance to go on holiday.

Tourism resources

The most popular area is the Alpine zone, attracting over half of all visitor arrivals. Here lie the majestic snow-capped peaks, glaciated valleys, and winter sports developments that are Switzerland's trade mark. However, tourist development has placed pressures upon the society and environment of the area and the integration of tourism into the agricultural and forest economies has needed sensitive handling. In recent seasons climate change threatens the viability of some of the lower altitude resorts as the snow has become unreliable.

Discussion point

The Austrian and Swiss Alps rank among the world's most visited destinations. Although the landforms are due to differences in geology and the effects of glaciation, much of the landscape that tourists find so appealing, comprising alpine meadows above the tree line, wooded slopes and fertile valleys, is the work of mountain farmers over the centuries. The High Alps also provide a refuge for the marmot, the chamois and the edelweiss – symbolic of the fragility of alpine ecosystems. Discuss why these landscape and wildlife resources are increasingly threatened, and suggest a number of practical solutions to the problem.

Each of the Swiss cantons has its own range of attractions, but several major tourist areas stand out, namely:

- The **Bernese Oberland.** The most spectacular Alpine scenery is found here, south of the lake resort of Interlaken. An excellent network of funicular railways and cableways provides access to the snow fields and glaciers, the most famous ascending the slopes of the Jungfrau and Eiger. At Lauterbrunnen there is a classic example of a glaciated valley with spectacular waterfalls. Long popular with British tourists, the area preserves Swiss rural traditions and at the same time has some of the most sophisticated ski resorts in Europe, notably Gstaad, Wengen and Grindelwald.
- **Valais** includes the upper Rhône valley as far as the Simplon Pass and a number of small historic towns. The most well-known resort is Zermatt, with its views of the Matterhorn, but the most popular ski area is Crans-Montana where considerable development has taken place. Crans-Montana has a number of acclaimed golf courses and is home to the Swiss Golf Open.
- **Lake Lucerne and the Forest Cantons.** The fjord-like Lake Lucerne is arguably the most beautiful body of inland water in Europe. Three cantons around the lake – Uri, Schwyz and Unterwalden – are historically important as the cradle of Swiss independence. Lucerne is a picturesque city, famous for its medieval Chapel Bridge.
- **Graubünden** (Grisons) in some respects is the most traditional part of Switzerland, due to its former remoteness. The villages of the Engadine Valley at altitudes of 1,500 metres are among the highest in Europe, where the Romansch language is still spoken and a pastoral type of rural economy persists, protected by government subsidy. This canton also contains the Swiss National Park where endangered alpine species such as the chamois are protected. In contrast are the number of spas and ski resorts catering mainly for wealthy tourists, the most famous being St Moritz, Davos, and Klosters.
- The French-speaking **Suisse Romande** on the north shore of Lake Geneva attracts a wealthy international clientele to its finishing schools, the festival resort of Montreux, and the shopping and nightlife of Geneva. This city's role as a United Nations centre is showcased by the Palais des Nations.
- The Italian-speaking **Ticino** (Tessin) enjoys the warmest climate in Switzerland due to its sheltered location and the moderating effect of Lakes Lugano and Maggiore. The landscape has Mediterranean features such as palm trees and lemon orchards, while the towns and villages are more colourful than in other regions. Travellers from northern Europe appreciate the contrast most in early spring, when they emerge from the cold and gloomy weather prevailing north of the St Gotthard into the warm sunshine of the Ticino Valley. Bellinzona preserves much of its heritage as a medieval fortress town, while Locarno, Lugano and Ascona are important holiday resorts and major conference venues.

Most of the Swiss population lives outside the Alps in the plateau region known as the **Schweizer Mittelland** to the north and west, where the major industries are located in the Basle–Winterthur–Zürich triangle. Basle, Switzerland's port on the Rhine, has a historic university and is a major cultural centre, while Zürich contains the Swiss National Museum, but Berne is probably the most interesting city from a tourist viewpoint. The picturesque old town, with its medieval shopping arcades and Clock Tower is a World Heritage Site.

The western boundary of Switzerland lies along the forested **Jura Mountains.** Less spectacular than the Alps, this region accounts for only a small percentage of tourist overnights. The small towns of the region, such as Les Chaux de Fonds, are noted for traditional Swiss crafts such as watchmaking.

Summary

- Apart from the relatively short German coastline, this part of Europe is landlocked. Physically, three regions can be identified: the northern lowlands; the central uplands; and the Alps.
- Forests, lakes and spas are important tourism resources throughout the region.
- Highly developed economies and standards of living have resulted in a considerable demand for tourism and recreation.
- Of particular note is the importance of Germany as one of the world's leading generators of international tourists.
- Austria and Switzerland are both significant destinations for tourists from the rest of Europe.
- The stagnation of international demand in the 1990s has led to the restructuring of national tourism organisations.
- Transportation in the three countries is well developed but has to overcome the harsh physical conditions and topography of the Alps.
- The federal organisation of the three countries has led to considerable devolution of tourism powers to the states in Germany, provinces in Austria, and cantons in Switzerland.
- The main tourist regions are: the coasts of northern Germany with its islands and resorts; the central uplands of Germany, including the Rhineland and the Black Forest; and the Alpine area of all three countries with its opportunities for both winter and summer tourism. The towns and cities are also important for sightseeing and as business travel centres.
- Sports facilities, museums and cultural events are an important part of the tourism appeal of the three countries.

Assignment

The response of tourism to climate change involves destination adaptation to changing circumstances. Devise a plan for the winter sports resorts in this region to adopt to unreliable snow fall and the retreat of the snowline.

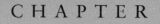

13

The tourism geography of France

Introduction

For many years, France has been the world's top tourist destination in terms of visitor arrivals, and one of the leading countries in terms of tourism receipts. This means that tourism is important in the economy, representing 6.2 per cent of GDP. France was one of the first countries to recognise the importance of the industry, setting up a national tourism office as early as 1910. It is no coincidence that much of the vocabulary used in the hotel and catering industry is of French origin.

Among the factors contributing to France's success in tourism are:

- It is the largest country in Western Europe, boasting a natural resource base which includes 5,500 kilometres of coastline, some of Europe's finest rivers, and mountain areas such as the Massif Central, the Alps, Jura and Pyrenees. The French refer to their country as 'the hexagon', with natural boundaries on five of its sides formed by the Rhine, mountain ranges and the sea.
- France is also unique among European countries in its latitudinal and altitudinal range, which gives rise to a variety of climates and landscape features. Mediterranean conditions are found in Provence, Languedoc-Roussillon and Corsica. A long dry summer with abundant sunshine, combined with mild winters, allows for a prolonged tourism season in world-famous resorts such as Nice and St Tropez. The Atlantic and Channel coasts have less sunshine and a climate favouring the more active types of recreation. Eastern France has a continental climate with cold winters, while in the mountains, snow cover is uneven and variable – especially in those ski resorts situated at low or middle altitudes.
- French culture has been widely emulated, starting in the Middle Ages with the Gothic style of architecture and the ideal of chivalry. In the seventeenth century,

Louis XIV's court and palace at Versailles was the role model for the upper classes throughout Europe, and despite subsequent wars and revolutions, France remained pre-eminent in the world of *haute-couture* and fashion. In the late nineteenth and early twentieth centuries, French artists and architects were responsible for many innovations, such as *impressionism, cubism, art nouveau* and *art deco*.

- French is one of the most widely spoken world languages. Even in the post-colonial era, France extends beyond Europe to embrace far-flung 'Overseas Départements and Territories' (DOM-TOM) in the Americas, Indian and Pacific Oceans, that we describe in later chapters. Cultural and business ties between Metropolitan France and her former colonies in Africa and elsewhere remain strong, determining the pattern of long-haul tourist flows to a large extent. Moreover a number of countries in Europe regard French as their second language rather than English or German.

- France is one of the world's leading economic powers, and has been at the forefront of technological advance. However, it was not until the 1930s that the nation reached the same level of urbanisation as England in 1851, and most of the industrial development has taken place since the Second World War. As a result, many city dwellers retain close links with the countryside. France has the largest agricultural sector in Western Europe, offering the tourist a landscape that owes much of its charm to the prevalence of small-scale mixed farming, using fairly traditional methods of production. This is particularly true of the more remote rural areas – *La France Profonde*.

- France can offer a wide variety of tourism products based on these resources. We might mention the following:
  - Special interest holidays, including wine tasting tours of Burgundy and culinary short breaks for gourmets – *foodies* – in Normandy.
  - The Club Méditerranée holiday village concept in beach and sport tourism.
  - The importance of spa tourism. Almost a hundred spa resorts are officially recognised, and most developed in the nineteenth century on the basis of mineral springs, while others on the coast offer *thalassotherapy* – seawater treatments. Although some spas have upgraded their facilities to meet changing demands for health and wellness, the sector has generally declined since the Second World War, in contrast to the situation in Germany and Italy.
  - The importance of faith tourism in a country where, although secularism has long been official policy, two-thirds of the population are, at least nominally, Catholic. Some shrines such as Mont St Michel in Normandy, Le Puy in the Auvergne, Rocamadour in Aquitaine, and Vézelay in Burgundy, were well-established in medieval times, acting as 'gathering points' on the major pilgrim routes to Santiago de Compostela in Spain. On the other hand, Lourdes and Lisieux did not become pilgrimage centres until the nineteenth century.
  - Winter sports are offered in the mountain resorts of the Alps and the Pyrenees, and for the domestic market in the Massif Central, the Jura and the Vosges. France has been an innovator in ski instruction (the short ski method), and in the development of purpose-built ski resorts above the tree line to guarantee a longer snow season. It has overtaken Austria and Switzerland as Europe's leading winter sports destination.
  - Sailing is another major activity, which has spawned a massive investment by the public and private sectors in coastal marina developments. A third of these *ports de plaisance* are located in Brittany and another 28 per cent in the Provence–Côte d'Azur region.

- Other activity and adventure-based types of tourism include:
  - boating on the superb network of rivers and canals;
  - canoeing on fast-flowing rivers, such as the Ardèche;
  - horse riding;
  - cycling – here two influences are perhaps at work – the trend toward 'green tourism' and the role of the Tour de France in raising the international profile of the sport;
  - surfing along the Atlantic coast;
  - diving along parts of the Mediterranean coast such as Corsica;
  - mountain climbing in the Alps and Pyrenees;
  - caving in the Dordogne region;
  - hiking on the very extensive network of *grandes randonées* (long-distance waymarked trails) which penetrate the scenic areas of France; and
  - golf, which is a fast growing market, with developments in the coastal resorts of northern France.

In some of these products France has few rivals. However, the country's flair for style and innovation has not always been matched by effective marketing.

The demand for tourism

The French tend to take their holidays in France, due to the country's range of tourism resources, and also the tradition of spending the summer in the south. As a consequence, the propensity of the French to travel abroad – at 10 per cent – is lower than for most other west Europeans. As recently as 1958, only 25 per cent of the French took a holiday away from home. Since the 1990s the travel propensity of the population has remained stable at 75 per cent, but this does mean that there is still a substantial minority who for various reasons do not take a holiday. There are also important regional differences in the demand for tourism.

Domestic tourism

The changing economic and social geography of France has had implications for participation in tourism. Demographic changes since the Second World War include population growth from 40 million to nearly 65 million, the correction of the previous imbalance between males and females caused by the toll of two world wars, and an increase in the numbers of young people. The birth rate is now much higher than in other west European countries such as Germany. This is due in large measure to favourable tax rates and other family-friendly policies of successive French governments, and to an influx of over 5 million immigrants from North Africa. France has also been transformed from a largely rural society into an industrial economy, with people leaving the countryside for urban manufacturing and service centres. Accompanying these changes has been a growth in the numbers employed in the service sector, increased car ownership, social tourism initiatives, and substantial rises in both disposable and discretionary incomes. This has led to an expansion of leisure spending as recreation and tourism have become a significant part of the French lifestyle.

In this respect, an important enabling factor has been the increased leisure time available to the French. Successive reductions of working hours resulted in a statutory working week of less than 40 hours. Also, the minimum school leaving age has been raised to 16 years and there is continuing pressure for early retirement. Since its introduction in 1936, annual paid holiday entitlement has grown to five weeks and many workers have six or more weeks. The fact that at least two of the weeks have to be taken between May and October has led to congestion in this peak holiday period. The downside of the social legislation affecting labour is that employers may be reluctant to recruit staff, resulting in a high rate of unemployment compared to the USA or the UK.

France has a very high proportion of domestic holiday taking, with trips demonstrating a number of characteristics:

- they are lengthy, often three or four weeks, although the traditional month away in August *en famille* is decreasing;
- they are concentrated into the peak summer months (the majority of holidays are taken in July and August) although efforts are being made to spread the load with promotional campaigns, staggering of school holidays, and the growth of winter holidays;
- in a country with such varied holiday opportunities, a wide distribution of holiday destinations is evident, though a general movement from north to south, as well as to the periphery, can be discerned, with a concentration in a number of rural areas, and at the coast – which accounts for 40 per cent of all overnight stays;
- half of all domestic trips are to destinations within, or close to, the tourist's home region;
- the car accounts for 80 per cent of domestic holiday journeys;
- self-catering, second homes and visiting friends and relatives account for the majority of holidays – simply because their cost commends them to families in peak season;
- the majority of holidays are arranged independently, but works councils and other non-profit making organisations play an important role (these range from professional organisations, who own fully-equipped holiday accommodation and rent to members at competitive rates, to those involved in social tourism); and
- short breaks have grown in popularity at the expense of the long vacation, with many people taking three or four short breaks every year. As a result, hotels and resorts have extended the tourist season, and a wide variety of products have been promoted by tourist authorities and hoteliers to meet the changing demand.

Social tourism represents a very strong movement in France and is significant for French domestic patterns of demand. There was a spectacular growth in social tourism initiatives in the 1960s, and in the late 1990s the government established a new fund to allow the unemployed and poorer citizens to take a holiday, using spare capacity in the coastal resorts. Examples of social tourism initiatives include:

- children's hostels – *colonies des vacances*;
- family holiday villages – *villages vacances familiales* (VVF); and
- government schemes such as the *cheque vacances* to boost holiday opportunities for the disadvantaged groups in society.

Second homes – *residences secondaires* – continue to play an important role in domestic travel, accounting for 15 per cent of both summer and winter overnight stays. The high incidence of second–home ownership (estimated at 3 million) and their wide distribution throughout the country are reminders that most city dwellers have rural roots. Improvements in transport have resulted in the growth of a second–home belt within a 100 to 150 kilometres radius of the major cities.

Case study 13.1

Tourism for all?

In 1999 the French government under a socialist prime minister set up a state-funded agency to act as an intermediary between charities helping poor families unable to afford a holiday and facilities in coastal holiday resorts with surplus capacity. In its first year the scheme provided holiday accommodation for up to a thousand *exclus* – people who feel excluded from society, such as single parent families, the unemployed, low paid workers and immigrants. Many of these people live in grim suburban ghettos which were the scene of rioting in the summer of 2007. Supporters of the scheme see it as a way of healing social divisions and propose that the right for all to go on holiday should be enshrined in French law. Opponents claim that the taxpayer is being asked to subsidise a project that is open to abuse. Government officials maintain that the overall cost of the scheme is minimal, as only low cost accommodation such as campsites and holiday villages would be used.

In class, debate the proposition that access to culture, sport and holidays is a fundamental human right like housing, education and medical care. What are the practical difficulties in carrying out social tourism projects in France, where individualism is a strong part of the national character?

Outbound tourism

Some 20 million trips are taken abroad, two–thirds of which are spent in other European countries, particularly Spain or Italy. This represents a growth in foreign tourism since 1945 that is rooted in the changing social and economic circumstances of France. Spending abroad by French nationals is low compared to receipts from inbound tourists and France therefore runs a surplus on its travel account. Inclusive tour holidays account for a smaller percentage of French travellers abroad than is the case in Britain or Germany, and most foreign travel is by car. However, long-haul tourism has shown consistent growth, with the USA and French-speaking destinations tending to be the most popular. The French travel trade is mainly concerned with outbound tourism, and in contrast to the UK is made up of many small and medium sized enterprises. For example, the top ten operators in France generate one-third of the total turnover in this sector, compared to Britain where the equivalent figure is well over two-thirds. The most well-known tour operators are Nouvelles Frontières for package holidays, and Club Méditerranée which pioneered the all-inclusive concept in tourism, and has over a hundred holiday villages worldwide.

Inbound tourism

France ranks as one of the world's most popular tourist destinations with around 76.8 million arrivals in 2009. The growth in inbound tourism has been helped by developments such as the Channel Tunnel and Disneyland Paris, as well as a number of sports events that attracted worldwide TV coverage. Belgium/Luxembourg, Germany and the UK are the leading generating countries, followed by the Netherlands, and Italy, although new generators, such as eastern Europe are growing in significance. The Americans account for a smaller proportion of arrivals but generate a much higher spend per capita. Most British tourists travel independently by car and tend to fall into two distinct types:

- day visitors to the Channel ports such as Calais, where shopping in the hypermarkets for wine and beer is the main objective; and
- those on a touring holiday or visiting their second homes in France. This type of visitor is attracted by the cultural differences between the two countries as expressed by the domestic architecture, the *charcuterie*, the bistros, the countryside and the French lifestyle.

The geographical position of France does mean that it attracts a very large number of day excursionists, and those passing through en route to Spain or Italy. Also, a high percentage of international tourists arrive in June, July, or August to exacerbate the already acute concentration of French domestic holidays. The growing popularity of winter holidays and the German trend to take second holidays in France in the off-peak may help to alleviate the problem.

France has always been popular for conventions and sales meetings and a government-run conference bureau co-ordinates the promotion and development of conference activities. Business travel is an important sector of French tourism, typically concentrated in major urban centres, and using higher category hotels:

- Paris has for long been the world's leading destination for international congresses, offering a range of venues, with the added incentive of a short-break holiday before or after the business trip;
- Nice now boasts Europe's largest conference venue with its 'Acropolis Centre'; and
- other important conference cities are Lyon, Marseilles, Cannes and Strasbourg.

Event attractions have also played an important role as a 'pull factor' for foreign tourists. They include:

- the 1989 celebrations for the Bicentenary of the French Revolution;
- the 1992 Winter Olympics at Albertville in the French Alps;
- the 1994 celebrations of the 50th anniversary of the D-Day landings in Normandy;
- the 1998 football World Cup; and
- the 2007 rugby World Cup.

The supply side of tourism

Tourism is a fragmented industry in France, comprising many small, often family-run, enterprises. It is therefore difficult to gauge levels of employment in the industry. Official figures estimate almost a million jobs in hotels, catering, transport and leisure, but this excludes the public sector, and clearly falls short of the real total. A further million jobs are generated as an indirect result or 'spin off' from tourism.

Transport

The private car is the transport mode used by the majority of both domestic and foreign tourists. This reflects the demand for self-catering and informal holidays, as well as the asset of a road system that ranks among the best in Europe, including 8,000 kilometres of motorway and 28,500 kilometres of *routes nationales* (first-class highways). There are few long-distance bus services in France, so the rail system handles a high proportion of inter-city travel, competing effectively with the private car and domestic air services. The state-owned railways authority (SNCF) has invested in the electrification of main line services and in high-speed trains – the famous TGV's. These run partly on dedicated track at speeds of 200 to 300 kilometres per hour, linking Paris to Lyon, Lille, Nantes, Bordeaux and Nice. The rail network continues to be focused on Paris, so that it is usually necessary to transfer between termini to make inter-regional connections. However, an overnight through-train runs between Calais and the French Riviera all year round, and between Calais and Languedoc in summer.

International air connections are comprehensive, with three airports serving Paris, while Air France is one of the world's leading airlines. Air Inter provides domestic services from Paris to over 40 destinations. Although opposed by the French, the air transport sector has undergone deregulation as part of the European Commission's liberalisation of air transport allowing new airlines to enter the market. The impact of low cost carriers has been considerable in providing business for regional airports and encouraging the foreign ownership of second homes in rural areas. The French consumer now has a wide choice of destinations for a city break, in say Marrakech or Prague, and to compete, tourism providers in France are having to be more imaginative and cost-effective.

Cross-Channel ferries are the preferred transport mode for tourists from Britain and Ireland. The former wide choice of routes has diminished as the car-carrying *Le Shuttle* train service through the Channel Tunnel becomes an established alternative, having overcome widely publicised safety and operational problems. Similarly the airlines' share of the lucrative business travel market is being reduced through competition from the *Eurostar* train service between London and Lille/Paris. Trans-Mediterranean ferry connections to Corsica, Sardinia and North Africa are provided by SNCM (*Societé Nationale Maritime Corse-Mediterranée*) from the ports of Marseilles, Toulon and Nice. The 9,000 kilometres of inland waterway are now mainly used for recreation and have become a tourist attraction in their own right, the most well-known being the Canal du Midi between Toulouse and Sète, built in the reign of Louis XIV to link the Atlantic and the Mediterranean. Converted barges – *peniches* – and hotel-boats provide an interesting way of viewing the French countryside.

Accommodation

The bedstock in France is concentrated in Paris and in the coastal resorts, and is comprehensive in terms of both self-catering and serviced accommodation. Although serviced accommodation dominates, there is an increasing trend among holidaymakers toward self-catering. In total, self-catering accounts for over 3 million bedspaces, mainly concentrated in the southern and western parts of France, and includes:

- Camping and caravanning, which are popular among both foreign and domestic tourists, and the number of sites – especially at the top end of the market – has increased. Most campsites are located on or near the coast, where demand can exceed supply at the height of the summer season – particularly on the Côte d'Azur.
- Gîtes are popular among British holidaymakers as they combine the advantages of self-catering with living in a small rural community. Typically these holiday homes are converted farm buildings which are surplus to their original purpose. In the past, *gîtes* were subsidised by the state as part of a campaign to stem rural depopulation; nowadays, they are self-financing but still subject to controls by the local authorities and the non-profit-making 'National Federation of Gîtes de France'. Some of the ferry operators and the British motoring organisations have been active in marketing this type of tourism.

- In addition, large numbers of British, Dutch and German holidaymakers own second homes, particularly in Provence, the Dordogne and the Ardèche regions.

In terms of serviced accommodation, only a small percentage of domestic nights are spent in hotels, so these increasingly rely on business travellers and foreign tourists. Despite this, hotel building, especially in the two-star and budget categories, has continued – both to attract the foreign market and also under social tourism schemes. Hotel capacity is concentrated in Paris, the Rhône-Alps region, and the Provence-Alpes-Côte d'Azur region. The hotel sector is very fragmented – less dominated by international chains than in most European countries, although the French-owned Accor is one of the world's leading hotel groups. The hotel stock includes a large number of small, budget-priced hotels (*logis de France*), inns (*auberges*) and converted chateaus (*relais-châteaux*). In addition there are a large number of *chambres d'hôte* (private houses offering bed and breakfast), most of which are unregistered. These are used mainly by French and Belgian tourists.

Organisation

The Ministry of Tourism and the state promotional and marketing agency – La Maison de la France – represent tourism in France at the national level. Since 1982 there has been some decentralisation of policy-making from Paris to the 22 regions, each of which has a CRT – *Comité du Tourisme* (Regional Tourism Council), with more scope than other public sector organisations to carry out development. Most of these regions correspond to some extent with the historic provinces of pre-Revolution France. At sub-regional level, the 95 *départements* into which France has been divided for administrative purposes since the Revolution have never achieved the same popular acceptance as the counties of the UK, and although each département has its own tourism committee (CDT), they vary considerably in resources and effectiveness. Local sentiment identifies more with the *pays*, an area with a strong geographical identity as expressed in its landscapes and food products. Le Pays d'Auge in Normandy is one of many such areas that has its own tourist association. Tourism illustrates the importance of the 'mixed economy' in France, with the public and private sectors co-operating at regional level on the regional councils and at local level in the *syndicates d'initiatives* – which in most French towns provide information for travellers (there are over 5,000 offices nationwide). Where resorts have development potential but lack private initiative, a government-run *office du tourisme* can be set up to carry out promotion and development. At national level there is some degree of co-ordination between the various government departments and agencies involved in tourism through the *Commission Interministerielle D'amenagement Du Territoire* (the Inter-ministerial Commission for Land Development).

Since the time of Louis XIV, there has been a tradition of state intervention in the economy of France, with a tendency to favour large-scale projects. The re-planning of Paris by Napoleon III in the 1850s and the public works carried out by President Mitterand in the 1980s, are the best known examples. In Languedoc-Roussillon and Aquitaine the state took direct responsibility for large-scale tourism projects. Partly as a result of public pressure, since the 1980s tourism policy has moved away from large-scale initiatives toward smaller, local projects where environmental considerations are taken into account. These initiatives are spearheaded by the regional councils with financial support from central government.

Case study 13.2

Tourism planning on a large scale: the Languedoc-Roussillon project

In 1963 the government set up an inter-ministerial commission to co-ordinate the work of various public agencies and local chambers of commerce in developing new resorts with a capacity of over 250,000 bedspaces on the Mediterranean coast west of the Rhone delta. This coastline is flat, but has the natural advantages of extensive sandy beaches backed by a series of *étangs* (lagoons). The objectives were:

- To take pressure off the congested Côte d'Azur;
- To divert holidaymakers who might otherwise go to Spain – in other words, to act as an intervening opportunity; and
- To provide greater job opportunities in a region over-dependent on agriculture, particularly the production of cheap wine for the domestic market.

The state financed the necessary land acquisition and preparation for development, including mosquito eradication from the coastal marshes. Other major works included a new motorway to improve access and an extensive programme of reforestation. Mixed economy companies – bringing together the private and public sectors – provided the infrastructure for each resort. Private developers then built the accommodation and other facilities under the direction of an architect charged with giving each resort 'unity' and 'style'. La Grande Motte is the most distinctive of these new resorts, with its pyramid-style buildings. Others have the outward appearance of a traditional Mediterranean village. All provide safe and convenient access to the beach, recreational facilities, and yacht moorings on the lagoon.

Although this is one of the world's most ambitious tourism projects, the resorts tend to be moribund outside the summer months. Many of the jobs are seasonal, and there is a danger that the region could become as over-dependent on tourism as it had previously been on agriculture.

Discussion point

Referring to what we said about tourism planning in Chapter 3, apply the flow chart (Figure 3.2) to the Languedoc-Roussillon project, and evaluate the benefits of planning for the government, the local communities, and the tourists themselves.

Tourism plays an important role in regional development, enabling the economic regeneration of stagnating rural areas such as those of the Massif Central. Government grants, loans and subsidies not only encourage the upgrading of accommodation in spas and seaside resorts throughout France, but provide much of the funding for conservation. The government showed little concern for countryside conservation until 1960, when the first national park was designated. This was due to the country's low population density, compared to England, so that the need for protection was seen as less pressing, and not least, the French passion among all classes for field sports – hunting, shooting and fishing. The majority of France's most scenic areas now have protected status as national parks or regional nature parks, under the overall control of the Ministry of the Environment.

The national parks are managed by a state agency with the primary objective of conserving the natural flora and fauna, and the impact of visitors is controlled by a system of zoning:

EUROPE

- tourism is encouraged in the outer zone with information points, accommodation and recreational facilities – for example, there are a number of ski resorts in the Vanoise National Park, which is situated in the Alps;
- a second zone supports traditional rural activities, subject to regulations on field sports and activities that might be detrimental to the natural environment; and
- the inner zone severely restricts entry to give maximum protection to individual species and eco-systems.

The regional nature parks generally consist of landscapes that have been greatly modified by human intervention and where multiple use management of resources is necessary. Unlike the national parks, the 50 regional nature parks (PNR *Parc naturel régional*) are widely distributed throughout France, and are more accessible from the major cities. Examples include St Amand Reismes near Lille, the Camargue, and the Parc d'Armorique in Brittany. The Corsican regional nature park has the triple aims of nature conservation, providing for tourism, and preserving rural life and traditions, in an attempt to stem the movement of population from the mountainous interior to the coastal resorts.

Conservation of the built heritage has a longer history in France, although there is no real equivalent to the English National Trust. The French tend to take a more robust approach to the conservation of historic buildings, with an emphasis on full-scale restoration. Notable examples include:

- the chateaus of the Loire, which were ransacked during the French Revolution;
- the medieval city of Carcassonne – which is actually a nineteenth-century reconstruction; and
- the port of St Malo, destroyed in the Second World War and subsequently rebuilt complete with the medieval fortifications.

Some 130 historic towns and districts of exceptional cultural or architectural significance are subject to strict planning controls as *villes d'art*, and as such they are often used as locations by the French film industry.

Tourism resources

The distribution of tourism in France shows important differences between the regions in the south and west, which attract a large international as well as domestic market, and the climatically less-favoured regions in the north and east (see Figure 13.1a, b). The exception is the Île de France, largely because it contains Paris. Only two regions – Alsace and the Île de France – receive more foreign than domestic tourists.

Northern France

As far as the majority of sun-seeking tourists from northern Europe are concerned, most of northern France is a zone of passage on the routes south to the Riviera, Italy and Spain. The 'cold water' resorts along the Channel coast, once fashionable with British as well as domestic tourists, have suffered a decline since the Second World War. The heritage attractions and gentle landscapes of northern France are also overshadowed by the more dramatic scenery of the south and west. The exception is of course Paris, which vies with London as the world's favourite tourist city, for the following reasons:

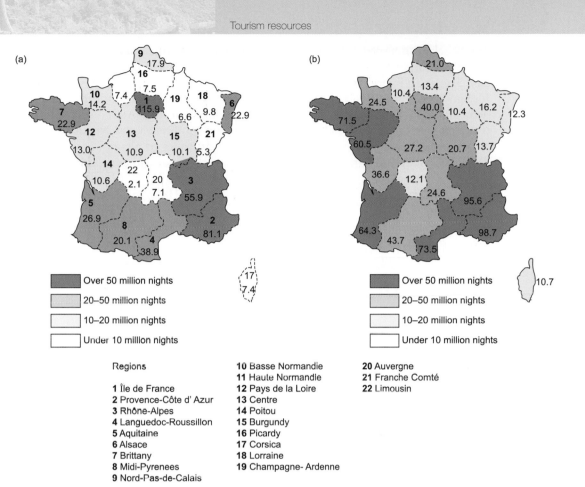

Figure 13.1 (a) Overnight stays by foreign tourists in France, 2004; (b) overnight stays by domestic tourists in France, 2004 (*Source*: Potier and Terrier (2007), 110)

- The 'city of light' offers a complete range of cultural attractions, many of which are world famous – such as the Eiffel Tower, Notre Dame, the Arc de Triomphe and the Louvre. Then there are the romantic associations evoked by the River Seine and its bridges, and the city's reputation as a centre of high fashion and stylish entertainment. Compared to most world capitals, the townscapes of central Paris within the *periphérique* (ring road) consist of low-rise buildings and broad tree-lined boulevards forming a harmonious whole. Some of the historic *quartiers* (districts) have preserved their specific character – although areas like Montmartre have become commercialised as a result of tourism. Nevertheless a considerable amount of urban renewal has taken place since the 1970s, including such exciting examples of modern architecture as the Louvre extension, the Pompidou Centre, the Bastille Opera and La Defense. The Musée d'Orsay is an example of an old building with an obsolescent function (railway station) revitalised as an impressive art gallery. For many years Paris has been the most popular city-break destination and this is likely to continue, given its improved accessibility as a result of the Channel Tunnel to the UK. However, its share of the market declined during the 1990s largely due to competition from the 'newcomers' in eastern Europe such as Prague.
- The French capital offers the opportunity of excursions to the former royal palaces at Versailles and Fontainebleau, or to the historic towns of Orleans, Chartres and Beauvais.

- The tourism industry of Paris was boosted in 1992 by the opening of the largest theme park in Europe – Disneyland Paris (operated by Eurodisney) to the east of the city. This is an interesting example of co-operation between the public sector and a foreign-owned private corporation, with the French government providing the dedicated rail link from Roissy-Charles de Gaulle Airport. After initial teething troubles, due in part to the wide cultural gap between French and North American tastes and expectations (shown for example, in attitudes to alcohol and customer service), Disneyland Paris has established itself as the leading theme park in France, with over half of its estimated 12 million visitors from abroad. Much more than a theme park, it is a resort in its own right, adding 10,000 beds to the accommodation stock in the Paris region. Faced with this competition, the Asterix Park to the south of Paris has managed to retain its share of the market, basing its appeal on traditional French themes.
- Paris is also a major destination for business travellers, and this is reflected in the availability of modern conference facilities and top quality hotels (half of the 'de-luxe' class of French hotels are located in the capital).

The North

Consisting of the Nord-Pas-de-Calais and Picardy regions, *Le Nord* has a rather negative image among the French for poor weather and a landscape blighted by nineteenth century heavy industry. In fact the scenery and the architecture of the historic towns have much in common with neighbouring Flanders, and in the past the region has been a zone of international conflict, as shown by the battlefields of the Somme, as well as commerce. Calais is the major gateway to France for British tourists travelling by car, coach or train. Dunkirk also handles a significant volume of ferry traffic, but Boulogne has lost its ferry link, and like Dover across the Channel, has had to diversify, investing heavily in the 'Nausicaa' marine-life attraction. Lille, one of a number of large manufacturing centres, has compensated for the loss of its traditional industries to become a major transport hub and business centre, thanks largely to the Channel Tunnel. Lille's cultural attractions, along with those of other historic towns such as Arras and Douai, are now more widely appreciated for short break holidays. The 'Opal Coast' south of Boulogne, particularly the attractive resort of Le Touquet, was fashionable before the Second World War. It continues to be popular with Parisians and golf is providing the impetus for rejuvenation.

Normandy

Normandy's history has been closely linked with that of England, as shown by the Bayeux tapestry commemorating the Norman conquest in 1066, and the battlefields of the Hundred Years War. In more recent times, the Normandy beaches at Arromanches were the launch-pad for the Allied campaign to liberate Europe in the Second World War. Visitors are drawn to its attractive countryside and a number of historic towns such as Caen and Rouen, but in summer the seaside resorts provide the main appeal. The Côte Fleurie between Caen and the Seine estuary remains popular with domestic holidaymakers. A creation of the late nineteenth-century *Belle Epoque*, Deauville continues to be visited by fashion-conscious Parisians, although it has invested heavily in a marina and other modern facilities. Other resorts such as Trouville are more family-oriented and suffer from competition from self-catering complexes, a surplus of hotel accommodation, and changing holiday tastes. The port of Cherbourg, usually a brief staging point for British and Irish tourists on their way south, has invested in the *Cité de la Mer* project, whereby the former ocean terminal has been transformed into a marine life exhibition. Normandy also boasts one of France's most unique and most visited heritage attractions – the medieval abbey of Mont St Michel, which is daily separated from the mainland by some of the world's strongest tides. It is now the subject of a controversial project to clear the site of car parks and other modern accretions that detract from its mystique.

Brittany

With its Celtic heritage, including the Breton language, and maritime outlook, the peninsula of Brittany, with its rugged, deeply indented coastline has long been peripheral to the mainstream of French economic and social life. Yet these characteristics have considerable tourism potential, for this region with its distinctive folk costumes and religious traditions has long attracted French artists to picturesque fishing ports such as Pont-Aven, and more recently has appealed to a growing British market. The main holiday area focuses on the part of the north coast – the Côte Emeraude – which includes the resort of Dinard and the historic seaport of St Malo. Efforts are being made to disperse tourism away from these established centres to the more rugged coastal areas of western Brittany and the neglected interior, which, unlike Normandy, is a poor area agriculturally.

Western France

Offering among its resources the heritage attractions of Anjou, La Vendée and Aquitaine, western France has a mild but sunny Atlantic climate, some of the best beaches in Europe, and is regarded by the French themselves as the land of gastronomy and the good life. On the Côte d'Argent there are old-established resorts such as Biarritz and Arcachon, which have adapted to modern trends such as surfing and camping. North of the Gironde estuary there are a number of offshore islands, such as Île du Ré, where the number of summer visitors greatly outnumbers the local inhabitants. The scenic and cultural attractions of Western France include:

- The Loire Valley, one of the best-known touring areas, where the main attractions are the chateaux and palaces associated with French royalty in Renaissance times, notably Chambord and Chenonceaux, where history is brought to life by *son et lumière* performances during the summer months.
- The caves of the Dordogne, which contain outstanding examples of Ice Age art. The most famous of these – Lascaux – was not discovered until 1940. A replica cave now diverts attention from the original paintings, which otherwise would have deteriorated from the impact of visitors.
- The wine producing area around Bordeaux, a city which is also noted for its eighteenth century Grand Theatre.
- The Aquitaine coast boasts some of the highest sand dunes in Europe and extensive lagoons backed by pine forests. In 1967 a management plan was inaugurated to make maximum use of these resources. Nevertheless, this has not achieved the success of Languedoc-Roussillon, due to insufficient public funding and opposition from environmentalists.

- Theme parks such as Futuroscope near Poitiers celebrating the film industry, and Le Puy du Fou, based on the heritage of La Vendée.
- Toulouse is the centre of the French aerospace industry, showcased by the European Space Park.

The Massif Central

This extensive area of mountain and plateau in south central France offers scope for a wide variety of recreational activities, including hang-gliding, mountain biking and white-water rafting. The landscapes include deep limestone gorges, extensive forests and the strange remnants of extinct volcanoes known as *puys*. Geothermal activity is evident today in the large number of mineral springs; as a result, the Massif Central contains more than a third of French spas. The volcanic landscapes of the Auvergne provided the inspiration for the Vulcania 'science park' near the industrial city of Clermont Ferrand. This project has attracted private sector funding from Michelin and Volvic, both major commercial enterprises based in the region. Agrotourism has been encouraged to stem depopulation from one of France's poorest farming regions, by integrating holiday villages and second homes with rural communities. There has also been some development of winter sports tourism for the domestic market.

Vichy is probably the best-known of French spas, although it now attracts fewer wealthy foreign clients than in the era prior to the Second World War. The hotels, bathing establishments, casino and opera house are grouped around the *Parc des Sources*, which is the major focus of the resort. Like other European spas, Vichy has adapted to changing demands by:

- diversification of the product into conferences, exhibitions and festivals;
- modernisation of spa treatments to appeal to today's busy executives rather than the traditional three week *cure*; and
- the provision of sports facilities to attract young tourists.

Eastern France

The swathe of France extending from the Ardennes to the Jura Mountains has been for centuries a zone of passage for trade and invading armies. It includes most of the area covered by the French Alps and the Rhône–Saône corridor. The following areas are well suited for touring by car:

- the rolling countryside of **Champagne** which includes Rheims, historically important as the religious capital of France;
- **Lorraine**, although more industrialised, boasts one of the best examples of eighteenth century town planning in the city of Nancy;
- German-speaking **Alsace** has more to offer the visitor, with its picturesque half-timbered villages and an important wine route based on Colmar, while its regional capital – Strasbourg – has acquired a major international role as a seat of the European Parliament and other EU agencies; and
- **Burgundy**, lying astride the routeways connecting the Rhine to the Rhône, and thus linking northern Europe to the Mediterranean, played a major role in European history in the Middle Ages. Its rich cultural heritage includes the Romanesque abbeys of Cîteaux and Cluny, and the historic cities of Dijon and

Beaune, although Burgundy is best known for the wines of the Côte d'Or and Beaujolais districts.

Lyon deserves special mention as the second city of France, which became of major importance through its silk weaving industry and strategic location at the junction of the rivers Rhône and Saône. It is now a major tourist and business centre, thanks to its position as an interchange on the TGV rail and motorway networks. The city is internationally recognised as a short break destination, noted for its fine architectural heritage and for its culinary attractions.

The **Franche Comté** is a forest and mountain region, deeply dissected by river valleys. It is much less developed for tourism than the Alps and attracts relatively few foreign visitors.

The French Alps

The traditional economy of this mountain region was based on pastoralism, with the livestock being moved to the high pastures above the tree line in summer and back to the villages in autumn. The economy is now dependent on tourism, including winter sports and in summer, lakes and mountains holidays. Most of the development has taken place in the north, where the mountains are higher, yet more accessible. Mountain climbing has been a major activity at Chamonix since the early nineteenth century, due to its proximity to Mont Blanc and the spectacular glacier known as the Mer de Glace. It has now become a major ski resort. Villages at lower altitudes – in the so-called Pre-Alps – are less used for skiing due to the unreliable snow cover, but are much in demand for second-home development, while Aix les Bains and Evian rank among France's most important spas.

Full-scale development for winter sports tourism began in the 1960s involving public sector investment under the *Plan Neige*. Purpose-built resorts were planned at high altitudes above the tree line, where glacial cirques provided maximum snow cover. These were to be veritable 'ski-factories' of a uniform design appealing to sports-minded tourists, with apartment blocks sited to give direct access to the lift system. Resorts such as Tignes have been criticised for their lack of human scale, severely functional design and their impact on the fragile alpine environment. Overall, the majority of the development has been in the northern Alps, where 15 major resorts account for over three quarters of the industry's turnover. Since the 1990s there has been something of a reaction favouring smaller resorts of a more traditional design.

The French Alps have become Europe's most popular winter sports destination, attracting domestic and foreign skiers alike, for the following reasons:

*   proximity to the areas generating the demand. Thanks to the Channel Tunnel, British skiers have a wide choice of routes and modes of transport to the resorts. In addition to airports at Nice (serving the southern resort of Isola 2000), Lyon, Grenoble, Chambéry and Geneva, there are Eurostar ski-trains, and 'ski-drive' arrangements are available for motorists using the excellent road network;
*   good infrastructure, including the most extensive lift system in Europe;
*   suitability for a wide range of markets, from family holidaymakers to young singles and snowboarders; and
*   an extensive range of accommodation, from first class hotels to family-run *auberges*, serviced chalets, and self-catering studio apartments.

The South of France

For the tourist travelling overland, the Rhône Valley south of Lyon provides the introduction to the region known by the French as *Le Midi*. The South of France is distinguished by its Mediterranean climate, but more tangibly by the colourful landscapes, and the quality of its light, which have attracted many world famous artists. Regional lifestyles also differ from those of northern France, while the popularity of bull fights in Nîmes, Perpignan and Arles, and the use of the Catalan language in Roussillon, reflect the influence of Spain. The South includes two major tourist regions – the Languedoc-Roussillon coast, that we mentioned earlier as an example of large-scale planning, and the French Riviera.

In **Languedoc-Roussillon** the coastal resorts have tended to draw tourists away from the interior, which includes such scenically attractive areas as the Cevennes and the Corbières. The 'Cathar Trail', following the sites associated with this mysterious medieval sect, appeals to a growing market. The historic cities of the interior include Montpellier with its university, Carcassonne, and Nîmes, which boasts a well preserved Roman arena and the Pont du Gard aqueduct.

Foreign tourists account for almost half of all visitors to the Provence–Alpes–Côte d'Azur region. In **Provence** the rural areas have been successful in attracting tourists and second-home owners. The cities of the region are also important tourist centres, with a wealth of heritage attractions dating back to Roman times, and a calendar of cultural events such as music festivals. The best known are Aix en Provence, which is a major artistic centre, Arles, and Avignon – where the Palace of the Popes is a reminder of the city's importance in the fourteenth century as a political and religious centre. However tourism is of secondary importance in Marseilles, due to the dominance of industry and commerce and its reputation for crime. Provence can also offer a number of contrasting natural attractions such as the wetlands of the Camargue and the gorges of Verdon. But it is the coast, particularly the world-famous French Riviera, that draws most tourists to this region.

The **French Riviera** is the Mediterranean coast of eastern Provence, extending almost 200 kilometres from Toulon to the Italian border, and sheltered by mountains from the blustery Mistral. The Côte d'Azur is the name usually given to the section between Cannes and Menton, where the Maritime Alps almost reach the sea. Three scenic highways – the *corniches* – hug the contours of the cliffs. Well endowed with natural attractions, the Riviera is easily accessible by road, rail and air transport and has a full range of amenities. The French Riviera has experienced several stages of development in response to changing fashions in tourism:

- **Exclusive winter health tourism**. From the mid-nineteenth century to the outbreak of the First World War in 1914, the Riviera was essentially a winter destination. Wealthy British visitors began the vogue for spending the winter on the Mediterranean coast for health reasons, which is commemorated by the *Promenade des Anglais* along the seafront at Nice. Queen Victoria made several visits, confirming the Riviera's exclusive status. Grand hotels, such as the Carlton in Cannes and the Negresco in Nice catered for a wealthy clientele from all over Europe, including the Russian aristocracy. The world famous casino in Monte Carlo opened in 1863, an initiative that almost overnight made the fortunes of the tiny principality of Monaco and its ruling family.
- **Exclusive summer beach tourism**. Until the 1920s the elite shunned the Mediterranean summer. This changed when a number of celebrities made sunbathing fashionable. Juan-les-Pins was the Riviera's first summer resort, attracting a new moneyed

Photo 13.1 Promenade des Anglais, the fashionable seafront at Nice (author's photograph)

clientele, including many Americans and the big names in literature, art and entertainment, who were quite different in their outlook from the European aristocracy, whose wealth had declined as a result of wars and revolutions. The Riviera became more accessible with the construction of a new coastal highway and the inauguration of *Le Train Bleu* (the Calais–Mediterranean express) which provided luxury travel to the resorts. The mediocre beaches of the Côte d'Azur were also improved, sometimes by importing sand from elsewhere. Market segmentation was evident as early as the 1920s, when an advertising slogan for Cannes claimed that 'Menton's dowdy, Monte's brass, Nice is rowdy, Cannes is class'. This was true to the extent that Menton had a reputation for attracting elderly invalids, whereas Monte Carlo appealed to the nouveau riches. Nice on the other hand was a bustling seaport and commercial centre as well as being a major resort.

- **Popular tourism**. From the 1950s the Riviera considerably broadened its appeal, catering for a much larger domestic market. This had been foreshadowed by the French government's decision in 1936 to introduce holidays with pay and encourage cheap rail travel to the resorts, but the Second World War was a setback to the process of democratisation. Campgrounds and a sprawl of holiday villas developed along the western Riviera, while many luxury hotels on the Côte d'Azur were converted into apartments. On the other hand, new resorts – particularly the former fishing village of Saint-Tropez – strove to retain exclusivity along with some of the established centres. Innovations in beach fashion such as the bikini ensured that the Riviera remained a focus of attention worldwide.

Today the resorts vary considerably in character, from the exclusive hideaways of the very rich – Cap Ferrat is a good example – to unpretentious places catering for the French family market such as Saint Maxime and Saint Raphael.

- Cannes and Antibes have retained their stylish image to a greater extent than the other major resorts of the Cote d'Azur. The crescent-shaped Croisette beach at Cannes is backed by a promenade lined with palms and grand hotels, and the designer boutiques of the new town contrast with the old quarter overlooking the harbour. The Cannes Film Festival and the Nice Carnival are two event attractions that are revenue earners for the Riviera.

- Nice has a range of accommodation to suit most budgets, while its airport handles not only a large volume of holiday traffic – much of it on low cost carriers – but also a substantial amount of business travel attracted by the information technology industries that have developed in this part of France. Nice is moreover a cultural centre of some significance, with a history going back to the time of Ancient Greece, and an association with some of the greatest artists of the twentieth century.
- Saint-Tropez is the leading resort of the western Riviera, offering fine beaches and a milieu that attracts a multitude of fashionistas wishing to 'see and be seen'.
- The principality of **Monaco** is much less dependent on gambling revenue than in the past, having diversified into international sport events and exhibitions as well as the business sector – many of its 27,000 residents are wealthy 'tax exiles'. With an area of less than 200 hectares space is at a premium, resulting in a 'mini-Manhattan' of high-rise buildings and land reclamation projects. Nevertheless the old town of Monaco perched above the famous yacht harbour retains some of its traditional character, in contrast to Monte Carlo. Visitor attractions include the Oceanographical Museum, associated with the undersea explorer Jacques Cousteau, and the Jardin Exotique, a unique collection of cacti, made possible by the favourable microclimate.

The rural hinterland of the Riviera offers a contrast to the sophisticated resorts, but this is changing as pressures on the coast increase. Nevertheless, the cultivation of flowers for the perfume industry at Grasse, and of fruit and vegetables for the Paris markets, are still an important part of the local economy. The numerous hilltop villages – the *villes perchés* – are a reminder of the time when the coast was menaced by Saracen pirates from North Africa rather than tourists. Some of these villages, notably Èze and Saint Paul de Vence, have become artists' colonies and specialise in a variety of craft industries aimed primarily at the tourist market.

Discussion point

The Riviera's image as a tourist destination has been associated with changes in fashion since the time of its 'discovery' by English 'milords' to the present day. What influence did these celebrities have on the development of particular resorts:

- Coco Chanel;
- Scott Fitzgerald;
- painters such as Matisse;
- Brigitte Bardot?

Can you name any other celebrities from the contemporary sport and entertainment scene who are associated with the Riviera?

What are the environmental and social problems affecting the Riviera that, if unchecked, could result in the destination becoming unfashionable?

Corsica

Known to the French as 'the island of beauty', Corsica offers some of the most spectacular scenery in the western Mediterranean. From the deeply indented western coast rise high mountains covered with forests of pine and chestnut and sweet-smelling *maquis* scrub. Tourism has underlined the differences between the coastal towns, which have always been more outward-looking, and the sparsely populated interior, where traditional lifestyles prevailed until well into the twentieth century. Tourism in Corsica is characterised by pronounced seasonality, as the majority of visitors are Parisians and Italians arriving in the months of July and August. The main resorts – Calvi, Île Rousse and Porto Vecchio lie on the west coast and offer facilities for water sports such as sailing and diving, while the island's capital – Ajaccio – has capitalised on its fame as the birthplace of Napoleon. Development plans for the island seek to redress the imbalance between the coast and the interior, although continuing to recognise the key role of tourism which provides about 25 per cent of jobs. Attention is focused on the flatter east coast, where development is taking place in a more orderly way than in the past. Improved transport links to the mainland, and the growth of inclusive tours, will ensure a greater role for tourism in Corsica. However, tourism must be seen to benefit the local population, who are keen to preserve their language and cultural identity.

The French Pyrenees

Winter sports play a less important role in the Pyrenees than in the Alps, and the region attracts fewer foreign skiers. Although the mountain peaks are not as high, remoteness from Paris and transport problems retarded the development of tourism. Nevertheless, a number of spas also function as ski centres during the winter months. In summer, visitors are attracted by the unspoiled scenery – notably the Cirque de Gavarnie, a spectacular natural amphitheatre resulting from glacial erosion – and the opportunities for eco-tourism and adventure sports. The major tourist centre of the region – **Lourdes** – is in fact one of the world's leading destinations for faith tourism and therefore deserves special consideration:

- This small town – with less than 20,000 inhabitants – annually hosts over 5 million visitors (compared to 2 million in the 1950s), and is second only to Paris in hotel capacity. With over 270 hotels and a number of campsites on the outskirts, Lourdes can accommodate more than 100,000 visitors at peak times.
- Its fame as a tourist centre is based not on a tangible physical resource, but on the visions of St Bernadette. The Grotto of Massabielle, where these occurred in 1858, very soon became the focus of pilgrimage. Miraculous cures are attributed to the spring water in the grotto and although a Medical Bureau scrutinises these claims, Lourdes is not a spa in the conventional sense (unlike nearby Cauterets).
- Lourdes was the first pilgrimage centre to be created by modern means of transport and communication, which explains its rapid growth, and it has become a role model for similar developments in other countries.
- One third of the visitors to Lourdes can be described as true pilgrims motivated by religious faith. More than 500 organised group pilgrimages take place every year, brought in by charter flights, coaches, and special trains equipped by SNCF to carry the large numbers of sick and disabled. This involves considerable organisation, in which volunteer carers play a major role.
- The distinction between the religious and secular aspects of pilgrimage is not always clear, but in Lourdes there is some geographical separation of the two. Religious activity is centred on the 'Domain of the Sanctuaries' covering an area of 20 hectares. This includes the esplanade – a vast open space for processions – and a number of large churches grouped around the entrance to the Grotto. The devotion of the pilgrims provides a stark contrast to the commercialism of the town centre, with its array of shops displaying what many would regard as tasteless souvenirs.

Summary

- Changing economic and social conditions in France since the Second World War have encouraged participation in tourism.
- The majority of French tourism is domestic, characterised by long-stay holidays concentrated in the peak summer months, although short breaks are increasing in popularity. Domestic holidays are widely distributed throughout France, and tend to be organised independently.
- Social tourism plays a more important role in France than in most other countries.
- The majority of French holidays abroad are to Spain and Italy, although long-haul destinations are becoming more popular, spearheaded to some extent by Club Méditerranée.
- Incoming tourism is more significant, and France is one of the world's most popular destinations.
- The tourism industry in France is fragmented, comprising many small businesses. A wide choice of accommodation is available, with self catering traditionally the preferred option for domestic holidaymakers, leaving the hotel sector largely dependent on the business and inbound tourism markets.
- Tourism benefits from comprehensive air, rail and road networks.
- Tourism tends to be centralised at government level, with the state also initiating major development projects, although both regional and local organisations are now playing a more important role.
- France can offer a great diversity of tourism resources and products, based on its countryside, coastal resorts and cultural heritage, and ranging from winter sports and adventure tourism in the Alps to sightseeing in Paris and the Loire Valley. Each region can offer different attractions, although tourism tends to play a more significant role in the coastal and mountain areas.

Assignments

1 The London–Paris route is one of the busiest in the world, with a wide choice of transport operators. Evaluate the various transport modes, taking into account cost, travel time between home/workplace and destination, convenience and environmental impact. Use as your examples a group of students on a European tour and a business traveller working for the government.

2 Compare the advantages of Brittany as a holiday destination with Provence, for a Swedish family with young children.

3 Explain why France has such an appeal for art lovers from all over the world.

4 Match particular types of outdoor recreation with specific areas of France, taking into account climate, topography and facilities.

CHAPTER 14

The tourism geography of Spain and Portugal

Introduction

The Iberian Peninsula, the Balearic and Canary Islands and Madeira have been favourite holiday destinations for north Europeans since the availability of inclusive tours in the 1960s. By the early years of the twenty-first century tourist arrivals in Spain and Portugal had exceeded 70 million. Spain was one of the first countries in the world to enter the mass inclusive tour market, taking advantage of its sunny climate and long Mediterranean coastline, but increasingly Spain faces competition from other destinations that can offer similar attractions to north Europeans, but at lower prices. The Spanish tourism authorities have attempted for many years to promote products other than beach tourism, but this is proving difficult for the following reasons:

- Most of the tourism development is well established on the Costas – the resort areas of the Mediterranean coast of Spain – and the Balearic and Canary Islands; and
- Spain's image of 'sun, sand and sangria', epitomised by the *chiringuito* (beach bar) is firmly engrained in the popular culture of northern Europe.

Portugal on the other hand entered the international tourism scene later than Spain. It not only made a determined effort to avoid some of its neighbour's worst excesses of tourism development, but also attempted both to control tourism's impact on the country and to attract the more affluent tourist from the outset.

In focusing too narrowly on tourism it is easy to overlook the contribution that Spain and Portugal have made to world culture. It is estimated that 500 million people speak Spanish, mainly in the Americas. Portuguese claims 170 million speakers, the majority in Brazil, but five African countries also use it as their official language.

Spain

The setting for tourism

In area, Spain is the second largest country of Western Europe after France, and occupies the greater part of the Iberian Peninsula. We should bear this in mind when planning a tour itinerary, as it is almost 1,000 kilometres by road from Bilbao or Santander on the north coast, to Málaga in the south. The dominant feature of the Iberian Peninsula is a high plateau – the Meseta – separated by rugged mountain ranges or *sierras* from the narrow coastal strips where most of the tourism development has taken place. Because of this, only the Balearic Islands and the south and east of Spain have a typically Mediterranean climate. The northern coast from Vigo to San Sebastian is not called 'Green Spain' without reason; summers are cooler and rainier and it enjoys less sunshine than the Mediterranean coast. The Meseta experiences a more extreme climate, with rather cold winters and hot summers. These physical contrasts are reflected in the country's great cultural diversity, with regional languages such as Basque, Catalan and Galician flourishing alongside Castilian Spanish.

The rugged nature of much of the Iberian Peninsula has also helped to isolate Spain from the rest of Europe. Even today, the Pyrenees are crossed by very few roads and railways. In the south, only a narrow stretch of water separates Spain from North Africa and its Islamic culture. In fact almost the whole of Spain, except for Asturias, was at one time under Arab domination. The *Reconquista* or struggle to oust the 'Moors' lasted from 718 to 1492. This forged the religious fervour and devotion to the Roman Catholic Church that still characterises much of Spain, and explains the ambivalent attitudes of Spaniards today towards their Muslim heritage and the issue of large-scale immigration from North Africa. Despite the impressive economic development and social changes (in the role of women for example) that have taken place since the 1960s, Spain differs from other West European countries in the following ways:

- the greater persistence of craft industries, notably ceramics and Toledo metalwork;
- the *fiestas*, *ferias* (fairs) and *romerías* (pilgrimages) which play such an important role in the life of many communities. These provide an opportunity to display Spain's rich heritage of regional dances and colourful costumes;
- the iconic role of the *corrida* (bullfight) in the national culture, where it is regarded as an art form and not as a sport; and
- aspects of the lifestyle, for example the traditional afternoon siesta, whereas dining out and social activity involving families and all age groups takes place very late into the night.

Spain has achieved outstanding success as one of the world's top five destinations, and can offer 1.3 million bedspaces in serviced accommodation alone. There is no doubt that tourism has contributed greatly to the transformation of the Spanish economy from that of a developing country to one of Europe's major industrial nations since the 1950s. In 2009 the tourism sector employed 10 per cent of the workforce, contributed one third of the country's export earnings and accounted for 11 per cent of GDP. However, this success has been achieved at a cost to society and the environment, for example:

- Spain's rich cultural diversity in music and dance has been set aside in favour of a commercialised version of *flamenco* for tourist consumption in the resorts;

- the demands of the tourism industry have affected family life in some areas;
- uncontrolled resort developments mar much of the Mediterranean coastline and bring pollution; and
- tourism has sharpened regional contrasts, particularly between the developed coastal areas and the interior.

Yet two-thirds of foreign tourists to Spain seek 'sun, sand and sea', and the majority of these are repeat visitors. Tourism is likely to continue as a vital sector of the economy. Spain's success in tourism is due to a variety of factors, namely:

- There was a growth in demand for holidays in the sun from countries in northern Europe once they had recovered from the effects of the Second World War;
- Spain was well placed to benefit from the development of civil aviation and changes in the structure of the travel industry, especially the introduction of low cost air inclusive tours and more recently low cost carriers;
- Spain's relatively late entry into the European tourism market allowed it to evaluate the competition and offer lower prices than those of established destinations such as Italy and the French Riviera;
- The Spanish government responded positively to the opportunities tourism offered, in the following ways:
  - abolishing visa requirements for most European tourists in the late 1950s;
  - maintaining a favourable rate of exchange for the tourist by successive devaluations of the peseta;
  - providing advantageous credit terms to developers;
  - regulating the industry to protect the consumer; and
  - creating a new Ministry of Tourism and Information in 1962 to provide more effective co-ordination and promotion.

Arguably, the tourism industry was able to benefit from the long period of political stability under the authoritarian rule of General Franco (1939–1975), as industrial unrest was outlawed. In the immediate post-war period Spain was ostracised by the international community, but the politics of the Cold War soon led the US government to reappraise the Franco regime, and in exchange for American bases in Spain, much-needed investment was made available to improve the infrastructure of the coastal areas that were the country's biggest tourism resource. The regime positively encouraged tourism as an engine of economic growth to lift Spain and her people out of poverty, while the slogan 'Spain is different' emphasised national characteristics in its appeal to foreign tourists. The government encouraged the development of large resorts where it was easier to monitor the influence of foreign tourists on local people, whose views on tourism development were also ignored in the interest of national unity and economic expediency. However, although the Franco regime tried to isolate Spain from the social changes taking place in Western Europe, tourism played a major role in bringing about the liberalisation of Spanish society through the demonstration effect.

The demand for tourism

Domestic tourism

Before the 1960s only a relatively small minority of the Spanish population could afford to take holidays away from home. The middle and upper classes escaped the summer heat of the cities by visiting spas in the mountains, the beaches of the east coast, or the northern coastal resorts such as Santander and San Sebastian. The economic progress which took place after 1960 increased personal incomes and boosted car ownership, so that tourism propensity is now around 60 per cent. Despite the social changes brought about by industrialisation, family ties remain stronger than in most other European countries, even if the present low birth rate gives cause for concern over the future. Although many Spaniards work long hours by 'moonlighting' with a second job, leisure is highly valued, and the public holidays celebrating national and religious festivals are often linked by a practice known as *puente* (literally 'bridge') to increase the number of 'long weekends' in the year. The pattern of holiday-taking by Spaniards also contrasts with that of foreign visitors, although the coastal resorts are popular with both. The large-scale emigration from the impoverished rural areas that took place as a result of industrialisation from the 1940s onwards, is a major influence; many of today's city dwellers frequently visit the villages of the interior to re-connect with their family roots. Domestic tourism in Spain also has the following characteristics:

- over 80 per cent of trips are for leisure purposes;
- only one-third of trips involve hotel accommodation, as two-thirds of domestic tourists stay with friends or relatives, or in second homes; and
- the most popular month is August, when one in four Spaniards is on holiday.

Outbound tourism

Over 90 per cent of holidays taken by Spaniards are in their own country, and it was not until the 1990s that they began to view a foreign holiday as an annual event. The most visited destinations are neighbouring France and Portugal, although touring holidays in northern Europe and Morocco are becoming more popular. The countries of Latin America are important destinations for business and leisure travel. The cruise market has grown rapidly in recent years despite recession in the economy. History, culture and education are the features sought by the Spanish abroad, with guidebooks stressing the culinary attractions of a destination. Spaniards are estimated to take a total of 25 million day trips a year to neighbouring Portugal, France and Andorra.

Inbound tourism

Although Spain is now one of the top tourism destinations in the world, it was a relative latecomer to the international tourism scene. It did not usually feature on the Grand Tour, since the generally poor state of the roads and the inns tended to deter all but the more adventurous travellers. A major improvement in the situation took place after 1928, when the government-sponsored *Patronato Nacional de Turismo* began to set up a chain of state-run *albergues* (inns) and *paradores* offering a high standard of accommodation. The small numbers of foreign visitors to Spain before the Civil War (1936–1939) were attracted by the country's picturesque traditions and not by sun, sand and sea, unlike most of today's tourists. For example, the American writer Hemingway was largely responsible for publicising bullfighting and Pamplona's Fiesta de San Fermín, which today attract a wide international following.

Tourism growth on a large scale began in the early 1950s with the influx of French and British holidaymakers to the Costa Brava, spreading to the Balearic Islands and the other Costas as soon as the introduction of jet aircraft made these areas more accessible in the 1960s. By the early 1970s Spain had become the leading holiday destination for most of the North European tourist-generating countries. However this has left Spanish tourism vulnerable to the effects of recession in these countries, with the result that demand stagnated during the 1980s and early 1990s. This prompted the search for new markets – such as the USA and Japan – and volumes recovered in the mid to late 1990s to exceed 40 million staying visitors and 20 million excursionists (the latter including cruise passengers and day visitors from France and Portugal). In 2010 there were 52.7 million tourist arrivals, but the increase in numbers since the 1990s has been largely offset by a shorter length of stay and a lower spend per capita.

The most important tourist-generating countries continue to be the UK, Germany, France, Italy, the Benelux countries and Scandinavia which together account for around 80 per cent of arrivals. The German market has declined as tourists desert Spain in favour of less expensive destinations such as Turkey, Croatia and Bulgaria. This is of particular concern for Spanish tourism as Germans tend to be higher spenders, and their visits are spread over a longer period of the year than other nationalities. Although the Spanish-speaking countries of Latin America contribute large numbers of immigrants to Spain, they account for only 1 per cent of all tourist arrivals.

Despite the efforts of both national and regional governments, tourism in Spain is highly concentrated both seasonally and geographically. Well over half of foreign visitors arrive between June and September, coinciding with domestic holiday demand, and creating congestion in the resorts. The Canary Islands do not have this problem because of their sub-tropical climate, but other areas – notably the Costa Daurada and Costa Brava – are overwhelmingly dependent on summer visitors. Seasonality creates a problem for businesses as many find it uneconomic to remain open out of season, whereas those that do reduce their staff and add to seasonal unemployment in the community. The public sector too is affected as services – such as water and power supplies – must have the extra capacity to cope with the peak demand, but are under-utilised at other times of the year. One solution to the problem is to encourage 'third age' tourism in which Spanish senior citizens stay in resort hotels at reduced rates outside the peak season.

Geographically the distribution of tourism is very uneven (see Figure 14.1). Eight provinces with a Mediterranean coastline account for two-thirds of all tourist stays in regulated accommodation, which includes campsites and holiday apartments as well as hotels. The pattern of foreign tourism shows a greater concentration than that of domestic tourism, with just four regions accounting for 84 per cent of hotel stays (compare Figure 14.2a, b). All this implies that the benefits of tourism are not spread widely throughout the country, and that tourism has contributed to the migration of labour to the coastal resorts from the interior of Spain, where for example, many mountain villages are virtually deserted. Rural tourism has grown in popularity in recent years, and may help to stem further depopulation. However, this in turn leads to another problem – loss of cultural identity – if rural communities simply become second homes for north European expatriates seeking 'the good life'.

The very nature of tourism demand to Spain has reduced the economic benefits. Spanish tourism is dominated by the demands of the major north European tour operators who provide high volumes of visitors yet demand low-priced accommodation. This encourages low-cost, high-rise hotel and apartment development in the coastal resorts and reduces the contribution of each tourist to the economy. However, the number of tourists arriving on package tours is slowly decreasing whilst those taking advantage of 'dynamic packaging', where they assemble the tours themselves and take advantage of the growth of low cost carriers, is increasing proportionately.

Although the authorities are aware that the mass market for beach tourism will continue to be important, attempts are being made to develop new holiday styles in order to reduce seasonality, spread tourism more evenly throughout Spain, and encourage higher-spending visitors. The market is becoming more sophisticated and

EUROPE

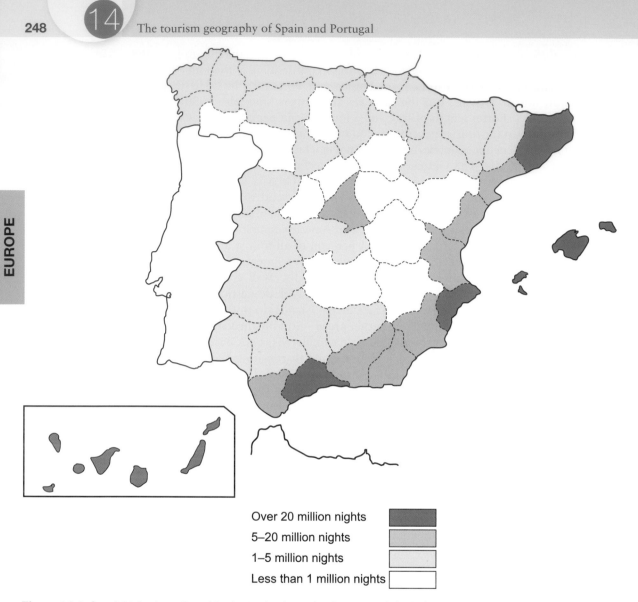

Over 20 million nights

5–20 million nights

1–5 million nights

Less than 1 million nights

Figure 14.1 Overnights by domestic and foreign tourists in regulated accommodation in Spain, 2007 (*Source*: IES, Anuario Economic de España 2009)

independent travellers from countries such as Britain now outnumber those on inclusive tours. Changes in the pattern of demand may mean that as much as 10 per cent of the accommodation stock needs to be taken off the cheaper end of the market.

In line with this approach, conferences, sport tourism, golf, and 'five star' luxury tourism are being promoted. Many Mediterranean resorts are now well equipped with marinas for the high spending yachting enthusiasts, and some have invested in aquaparks to attract the family market. Winter sports facilities have been developed in the Pyrenees, the Sierra de Guadarrama near Madrid, and the Sierra Nevada, although as yet these cater mainly for domestic demand. The Franco regime invested heavily in football stadiums, with Real Madrid gaining worldwide recognition. More recently, motor racing and other international sports events have featured in promotional campaigns.

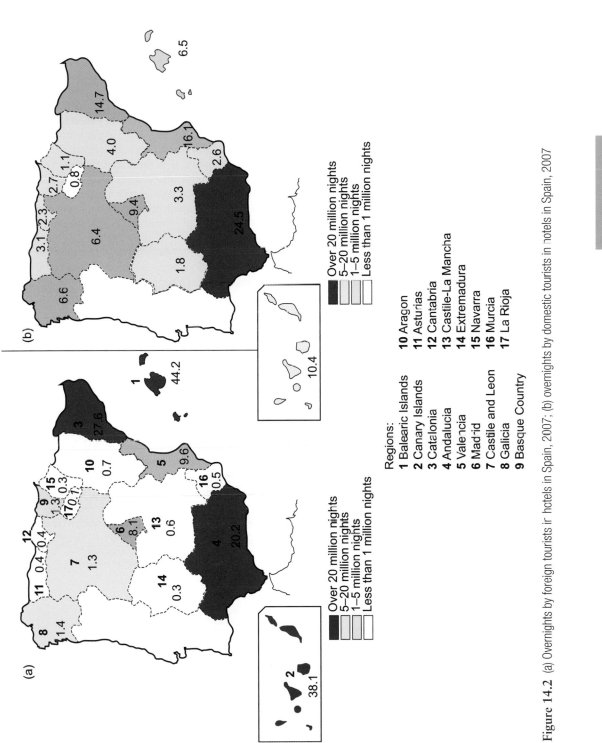

Figure 14.2 (a) Overnights by foreign tourists in hotels in Spain, 2007; (b) overnights by domestic tourists in hotels in Spain, 2007

Regions:

1 Balearic Islands
2 Canary Islands
3 Catalonia
4 Andalucia
5 Valencia
6 Madrid
7 Castile and Leon
8 Galicia
9 Basque Country

10 Aragon
11 Asturias
12 Cantabria
13 Castile-La Mancha
14 Extremadura
15 Navarra
16 Murcia
17 La Rioja

Over 20 million nights
5–20 million nights
1–5 million nights
Less than 1 million nights

EUROPE

Case study 14.1

Golf tourism in Spain

Golf tourism is encouraged by many tourism authorities because it brings in a high-spending type of visitor and results in a longer season. Madrid is particularly keen on hosting the Ryder Cup, which is a biennial competition involving American and European teams. Although golf is growing in popularity among Spaniards, the participation rate is a third of that in the UK, and it is well behind football, field sports and basketball. Most of the demand comes from foreign tourists, while the Costa del Sol accounts for the greatest concentration of golf courses in Spain. Golf tourism is controversial, since half the country suffers periodically from severe droughts. It is estimated that an 18 hole course consumes as much water as a town of 10,000 inhabitants. Proponents of golf claim that much is being done to reduce water demand and other environmental impacts. The problem mainly lies with the second home developments that have grown up around golf courses, where a typical villa with its garden and swimming pool consumes four times as much water in summer as a city apartment.

In class, debate the pros and cons of promoting golf as opposed to other types of sport tourism, in a part of Spain where the beach holiday market is declining.

The supply side of tourism

Transport

Over 75 per cent of foreign tourists arrive by air. The inclusive tour market ensures a constant supply of tourists arriving mainly on charter airlines, owned in most cases by the major north European tour operators. However, their share of the holiday market is being eroded by the low cost carriers that can offer greater flexibility in travel arrangements for the increasing numbers of visitors staying in second homes, or in rented apartments and villas. Many independent travellers touring Spain use the national carrier Iberia and its subsidiaries. Although Madrid and Barcelona are important international gateways, most north European holidaymakers fly to one of the regional airports serving a particular holiday area, namely:

- Girona for the Costa Brava;
- Reus or Barcelona for the Costa Daurada;
- Alicante or Valencia for the Costa Blanca;
- Murcia for the Costa Cálida;
- Málaga for the Costa del Sol;
- Jerez for the Costa de la Luz;
- Palma, Ibiza and Mahón for the Balearic Islands; and
- Las Palmas, Tenerife Sur, Fuerteventura, Santa Cruz de la Palma and Arrecife for the Canary Islands.

Around 20 per cent of visitors to Spain arrive by car. A growing number of British holidaymakers travelling independently use the ferry services from Plymouth and Portsmouth to Santander and Bilbao on the north coast. Touring Spain by car has been facilitated by the massive improvement of the road network that has taken place since the 1980s, including some 10,000 kilometres of motorways. The most important of these is the Autopista de Levante (east coast motorway), and the routes linking Madrid with the regional centres of Seville, Valencia and Zaragoza.

   The rail system under Spanish State Railways (RENFE) is tightly focused on Madrid and the break of gauge at the borders with France and Portugal also affects most international train services. Plans are now well advanced to integrate Spain with the rest of the European network, and rail service has improved to the extent that AVE (high-speed trains) are successfully competing with the airlines for the lucrative business market on routes linking Madrid to Barcelona and other major cities. Rail products geared specifically to the leisure market include the *Al Andalus Express*, which allows the visitor to see the countryside and cities of southern Spain in the style of the 'golden age' of rail travel in the 1920s.

Accommodation

Spain offers a variety of accommodation from luxury resort hotels to simple *hostales* (pensions). The official hotel classification scheme is based on the facilities provided rather than the quality of service. Sol-Meliá is the largest Spanish-owned hotel chain in a sector dominated by independent establishments and small groups, which have little bargaining power with foreign tour operators on pricing. In addition to the private sector, there are the state-owned *paradores*, situated away from the main tourist centres and providing accommodation in traditional Spanish style (often in converted castles, palaces or monasteries). As such, they are favoured by independent travellers touring the 'real Spain' (as distinct from the Costas) by car. Although hotels account for almost two thirds of stays by foreign tourists, their share has declined since the 1990s, and there are problems of over-supply in some areas such as the Costa del Sol. Self-catering accommodation, in the form of apartments and holiday villas is mainly found in the resort areas of eastern and southern Spain. An almost continuous series of *urbanizaciones* (second home developments), often dominated by a particular nationality, now stretches from Denia to Estepona. Financial scandals involving a number of local authorities have resulted in illegal building projects and a serious problem of over-supply, bringing Spain's construction industry to the brink of disaster. Campsites are concentrated in those locations that are most accessible from France, such as the Costa Brava and the Valencia region.

Organisation

Spain's organisation of tourism has attracted attention from countries around the world and many have adopted the Spanish model. Tourism became the responsibility of a cabinet minister in 1951 and the national tourism plans since 1953 have set the institutional and public service framework for Spain's growth and continued presence in the world tourism market. At national level, the Ministry of Industry, Tourism and Commerce is responsible for tourism policy and promotion, through its agency Turespaña (the Spanish Tourism Institute). Generally the government is anxious to provide an environment within which tourism can flourish and a variety of grants and incentives are available for developers, in addition to direct investment by the state. Spain has also developed a series of innovative national plans and strategies for tourism. There are specialist national agencies whose remit is to develop innovation in tourism and technology, promote conferences, and manage the state-owned paradores.

   Until 1978 tourism was firmly controlled by central government from Madrid, leaving the provincial authorities no scope for initiative. The Spanish Constitution of that year gave the new autonomous regions (*communidades autonomas*) wide powers as part of the post-Franco democratisation of the country. Tourism is therefore administered by 17 regional governments who have the power to approve developments and determine policy. At the local level, the *municipios* (town councils) also take on the responsibility for some aspects of tourism and can impose taxes to finance projects in their area. This may well mean that tourism receives more favourable treatment in some areas than others. In the largest resorts there are associations of business people – *centros de iniciativas* – who promote their destination and local facilities; as in other areas of Spanish politics much depends on the personality and connections of those in power.

Tourism resources

Northern Spain

Dominated by the Cantabrian Mountains and overlooking the Atlantic Ocean to the west and the Bay of Biscay to the north, the coastlands of northern Spain are characterised by a green countryside of meadows, woodlands and orchards. Appropriately enough, the attractions of coast, countryside and mountains have been promoted by the regions of Galicia, Asturias, Cantabria and the Basque Country under the banner of *España Verde* (Green Spain). For an increasing number of foreign visitors, usually travelling independently by car, the appeal lies in this 'real Spain' of unspoiled scenery, rich folk traditions and distinctive regional cuisines, in contrast to the bland international food and artificial attractions of the Mediterranean beach resorts. However parts of Asturias and the Basque Country offer a less attractive hinterland, where declining 'smokestack industries' provide the impetus to expand tourism as a means of regenerating the area.

The region of **Galicia** in the west has much in common with other areas on the 'Celtic fringe' of Europe. Although the Galicians speak a language similar to Portuguese, the folk traditions and misty landscapes are reminiscent of Ireland. This is one of the poorest areas of the Peninsula as the pocket-sized farms cannot provide a decent livelihood, so that in the past large numbers of Galicians have emigrated, particularly to South America. There is an important fishing industry based on ports such as Vigo and La Coruña, where the *rias* (submerged river valleys) provide excellent harbours. Although there are many fine beaches facing the Atlantic, few seaside resorts of significance have developed, while the region's fishing and tourism industries suffered a major setback with the *Prestige* oil spill disaster in 2003. In the interior the historic city of Santiago de Compostela has been regenerated as a result of European initiatives to promote the pilgrim route to the shrine of Saint James, and some rural communities on or near the route have also benefited.

The scenery becomes more rugged in **Asturias** and **Cantabria**, culminating in the spectacular Picos de Europa National Park. The area is ideal for activity holidays such as hiking and canoeing, and a number of spas and picturesque seaside resorts have developed along the fine beaches fronting the Bay of Biscay, including Laredo and Castro Urdiales. The largest resorts are Gijón and Santander, which is the venue for a number of international festivals. The region's heritage attractions include the medieval town of Santillana de Mar and the Altamira Caves – 'the Sistine Chapel of Stone Age art' – now protected by an award-winning replica and museum.

The **Basque Country** actually extends into the south-west corner of France. The three Spanish Basque provinces, known locally as Euskadi, lie between Bilbao and the western end of the Pyrenees. The region is marked off from the rest of Spain by its people, who speak a language unrelated to any other in Europe, and by their passion for gastronomy and unusual pastimes. The best known sport, second only to football, is *jai alai* or *pelota*, an exciting ball game which has gained an international following in the Americas. Many Basques are not content with autonomy, and have given support to the ETA separatist movement, which, despite a number of peace initiatives by Spanish governments, poses an on-going terrorism threat. There are two tourist centres of international standing, namely:

- San Sebastián (Donostia) with its wide sweep of beach between two protecting headlands, festivals and fashionable shops, is the premier resort of northern Spain. Before the introduction of air conditioning it served as the summer capital, with ministries and embassies moving from Madrid.
- Bilbao in contrast is primarily a port and a major industrial centre, which until recently had little to recommend it for tourists. This has now changed, thanks to the ultra-modern Guggenheim Museum, showcasing international art, which has transformed the waterfront area and acted as a catalyst for urban regeneration.

Eastern and Southern Spain

The majority of foreign tourists to Spain head straight for the coastal resorts where summer sunshine is guaranteed. For this reason the numerous cultural attractions of the regions of Catalonia, Valencia, Murcia and Andalucia tend to be overshadowed by the pull of the beaches. Barcelona, Seville and Granada are the most notable exceptions.

In the north-east, **Catalonia** has a strong cultural identity, expressed in the Catalan language, festivals and sport. Its people have often been at odds with the central government in Madrid, a recent example being the regional parliament's decision to ban bullfighting in Catalonia. Historically the Catalans have been more outward-looking and progressive than other Spaniards and they have made their capital, Barcelona, one of Europe's great seaports and centres of industry and commerce. **Barcelona** has long attracted avant-garde artists and architects and is pre-eminent in fashion design and haute-cuisine. The 1992 Summer Olympics focused world attention on the host city and gave the impetus for many civic improvements, notably the regeneration of the run-down waterfront area. Major sightseeing attractions in the city include:

- the street life and floral displays of the Ramblas;
- the Pueblo Español (Spanish Village) showcasing architectural styles and regional crafts from all over Spain;
- the Cathedral and its quaint medieval district – the Barrio Gótico; and
- the Basilica of the Sagrada Familia, the unfinished masterpiece of the Catalan architect Antonio Gaudi.

Barcelona is the largest cruise port in the Mediterranean. It is also a good centre for touring other places of interest in the hinterland of Catalonia, notably Montserrat – a monastery and place of pilgrimage in a spectacular setting.

Catalonia includes two major holiday areas – the Costa Brava to the north-east of Barcelona and the Costa Daurada to the south-west.

The **Costa Brava**, the rugged coastline between Blanes and Port Bou on the French border was the first area to be developed for mass tourism in the 1950s. The scenic beauty of this coast – the pine covered hills, red cliffs and sheltered coves – had earlier attracted artists and fashionable holidaymakers to picturesque Tossa and the resort of S'Agaró, purpose-built for tourism in the 1920s. Some resorts – notably Lloret de Mar – have been given over to the package holiday market and their natural assets buried under concrete. Nevertheless, some stretches of coastline – as at Begur and

Cadaqués – remain unspoiled, while the Medas Islands near the resort of Estartit have been designated as a marine reserve. Increasing numbers of independent holidaymakers are seeking out the cultural attractions of this part of Catalonia. These include the Salvador Dalí Museum at Figueres, the picturesque medieval city of Girona, and the archaeological site at Ampurias.

Discussion point

The Costa Brava no longer appeals to a mass market experiencing 'destination fatigue', and in 2004 it was dropped from the programmes of a leading British tour operator. Discuss why an area that had epitomised a Spanish holiday became unfashionable, and suggest ways in which the destination could be rejuvenated, by developing new products and targeting 'niche' markets.

The **Costa Daurada** is characterised by long beaches of golden sand and extends beyond Barcelona as far as the Ebro Delta. Its appeal is reduced by the proximity of industry in some areas. Sitges is the most attractive resort and one that is popular with Spaniards, but like others on this coast such as Cambrils, it is moribund out of season. Salou is the most popular resort with foreign holidaymakers, and has experienced a revival in its fortunes following the opening of the Port Aventura theme park in 1993.

Likewise tourism plays an important but not exclusive role in the economies of the **Valencia** and **Murcia** regions. Despite its dry climate, the narrow eastern coastal plain is one of the most productive agricultural regions of Spain, thanks to sophisticated irrigation techniques. The landscape includes citrus orchards, the villages with their blue-domed churches, the date palm plantation at Elche and the rice fields around the Albufera lagoon. These features contrast markedly with the barren mountains to the west and Europe's only desert to the south, which is a favourite location for producers of low-budget 'western' movies. The city of Valencia is primarily a seaport and industrial centre, and its tourism appeal lies not so much in historic buildings but in the culinary attraction of *paella*, ceramic products, and the spectacular *Las Fallas* festival, which culminates in the burning of elaborate paper-mache effigies. The city's go ahead outlook is shown by the impressive 'City of Arts and Sciences' – a science park commemorating the Millennium – and a model civic tourism administration. Further boosts to Valencia came in 2007, when it hosted the Americas Cup sailing event and in 2008, its first Formula One Grand Prix. The Costa Azahar to the north consists of a string of resorts, including the music festival venue of Benicassim and the historic town of Peñiscola.

The **Costa Blanca** between Denia and Alicante is one of Spain's most popular holiday areas, due in large measure to Benidorm. In 1960 this was a mere fishing village but a progressive *alcalde* (mayor) provided the impetus for its transformation into a high rise mega-resort or 'leisure factory' designed specifically for the mass market and capable of absorbing 6 million visitors a year, with as many as 350,000 arriving in the first two weeks of August. Benidorm boasts an average year-round occupancy rate of 90 per cent, thanks to a loyal domestic and international clientele, with 'third age' tourists filling the hotels during the winter months. Benidorm's success is due to its sheltered position, two fine sandy beaches, proximity to Alicante Airport, and – not least – an uninhibited entertainment industry catering for most tastes, age groups and nationalities. The area west of the old town tends to be more popular with the Spanish, whereas the Playa de Levante (east beach) caters for the foreign mass market. Benidorm has readily adapted to changes in demand, with the opening of the Terra Mítica theme park, and the state of the art Hotel Bali – one of the largest in Europe – as the flagship of a new drive to attract conference business and 'four star' tourists. Elsewhere on the Costa Blanca development tends to be low-rise, but arguably extensive villa developments have a greater social and environmental impact than 'skyscraper' hotels, as they generate large volumes of car traffic and directly compete with local agriculture for land, power and water resources. Even the coastline of the dry south-east corner of Spain has been developed for golf tourism and water sports as the 'Costa Cálida', focusing on the resort of La Manga and the Mar Menor lagoon.

The region of **Andalucia** for many people epitomises Spain, with its warm, sunny climate, easy-going lifestyle and picturesque villages. Moorish rule persisted for much longer in this part of Spain, and their heritage is particularly evident in the traditional architecture. Yet this region has had more than its fair share of social and economic problems, as much of the land is dominated by large estates given over to olive production, unemployment is high, and the gypsies, who have inspired flamenco as an art form, remain a marginalised element in society. Rural tourism is growing in importance, while horse-riding and trekking are popular holiday activities in the mountain areas. The many picturesque small towns and villages known as the *pueblos blancos* are accessible from the bustling resorts of the Costa del Sol, and yet a world apart. Nevertheless tourism is mainly focused on the major cities of the region and the coast.

- Seville is the regional capital and was historically Spain's gateway to the Americas in the colonial period. It achieved international acclaim as the host city for the 1992 World Expo, which ingeniously used water features to cope with the notoriously hot summer temperatures. Tourists arrive in great numbers each spring for the awe-inspiring spectacle of the Holy Week processions, followed a few weeks later by the colour and excitement of the April *Feria*.
- Córdoba under Muslim rule was Europe's largest city in the tenth century, and contains one of the most outstanding relics of that era – the Mezquita, now a cathedral. The new Arab-style public baths epitomise the revival of interest by Spaniards in their Moorish heritage. Córdoba is also noted for its colourful patios.
- Granada is world famous for an exquisite example of Moorish architecture – the Alhambra Palace. The adjoining gardens of the Generalife, with the snow-capped mountains of the Sierra Nevada in the background, provide an incomparable setting for festivals of music and dance. The Albaicín district nearby is also a World Heritage Site and has become an artists' quarter containing many Moroccan-style tea houses.
- Jerez is the centre for the production of one of Spain's most celebrated exports, the fortified wine known throughout the English-speaking world as sherry. The city is also renowned throughout Spain as a showcase for equestrian skills in a region devoted to horse riding and the bullfight.

The **Costa del Sol** extends for 300 kilometres from Gibraltar to Adra, and is the holiday area that has shown the most spectacular growth since the 1960s, with resorts such as Torremolinos having experienced the various stages in the tourist area life cycle from 'discovery' to 'decline'. The location of the Costa del Sol in the extreme south of Spain is advantageous for the following reasons:

- the Sierra Nevada and other mountain ranges protect this south-facing coast, guaranteeing warmer temperatures and more sunshine in winter than elsewhere in western Europe, and making it possible to cultivate sugar cane and other sub-tropical crops;

- the Costa del Sol can offer the tourist an exceptionally wide range of outdoor activities, including golf, tennis, horse-riding and sailing, while skiing can be enjoyed in the Sierra Nevada, where the snow cover lasts from December to May; and
- the coastal resorts provide easy access to the many cultural attractions of southern Spain.

This part of Andalucia has long been a winter destination for wealthy tourists, starting with Málaga in the nineteenth century, while the picturesque mountain town of Ronda served as a summer retreat for British officers stationed in Gibraltar. The development of the Costa del Sol for mass tourism did not get underway until after the opening of Málaga airport in 1962. The completion of the E340 coastal road improved access to the resorts, but it soon acquired a reputation as the 'highway of death', as high-rise ribbon development extended from Málaga to Estepona. Tourism has largely replaced fishing and farming as a source of employment for local people, and greatly improved living standards. However, in some of the villages – Mijas is a notable example – expatriates from the countries of northern Europe now make up almost half the population.

The section of the Costa del Sol to the east of Málaga contains fewer resorts and most of the development consists of holiday villas designed to blend in with the local landscape. Most of the hotel accommodation is found in the large resorts to the west of Málaga, which include:

- **Torremolinos,** which has become a byword for the ills of mass tourism and speculative development. However, this former fishing village was an upmarket, fashionable resort with a handful of luxury hotels in the early 1960s. This was followed in the 1970s by a massive expansion of accommodation in the form of high-rise hotels and apartments, using cheap mass-produced materials, to cater for an ever-growing demand from the tour operators of northern Europe. We could say that Torremolinos, along with its neighbours Benalmadena and

Photo 14.1 The bridge crossing the gorge at Ronda, one of Andalucia's most picturesque towns (©istockphoto. com/José Luis Gutiérrez)

Fuengirola, plays a vital 'honeypot' role in concentrating vast numbers of holiday-makers in a small area, providing them with familiar food and entertainment, and thereby saving the villages of Andalucia from some of the negative impacts of mass tourism.

- **Marbella** became fashionable in the 1950s, and has been more successful than the other resorts on the Costa del Sol in retaining an image of sophistication, based on a large number of five star hotels, a wealthy expatriate community, the yacht marinas of Puerto Banús – Spain's best known example of luxury tourism – golf and cultural activities. But even Marbella experienced a period of stagnation, if not decline, in the 1980s, caused by its association with sleaze and drug-related crime. Under energetic leadership, the resort has invested in improved facilities on its beach front, more efficient policing to ensure visitor security, and the diversification of its product to attract conferences and foreign business enterprise based on high-tech industries to the 'California of Europe'.
- **Málaga** differs from the other tourist centres of the Costa del Sol in being primarily a working seaport and commercial city. It has been shunned by the hordes of package holidaymakers heading straight from the airport to the beach resorts, but has the potential to attract tourists seeking a genuine Spanish ambience. Málaga has done much to renovate its waterfront and city centre, as well as restoring such important examples of Moorish heritage as the Alcazaba citadel. The city also hopes to promote its cultural appeal as the birthplace of Picasso.

Andalucia still contains extensive stretches of unspoiled coastline along both the Mediterranean and the Atlantic. These could be at risk from developers, despite controversial legislation to determine property rights and prevent any further inappropriate building on beachfront land. Plans to develop the Cabo de Gata area between Almería and Carboneras have been halted by the growing environmental movement in Spain, and it is now designated as a nature park.

The **Costa de la Luz**, Andalucia's Atlantic coastal region, has some of the best beaches in Spain. This is a popular holiday area for the Spanish but has attracted little attention so far from foreign tour operators. Some of the existing seaports are tourist centres, while the old-established resort of Isla Cristina provides a contrast to the largely unplanned development at Matalascanas. Cadiz was the leading commercial city of Spain in the eighteenth century, and is now celebrated for its carnival, while Tarifa, exposed to the easterly *Levante* winds, is ideal for windsurfing and kite-surfing. The port of Algeciras is linked by ferry services to Tangier and Ceuta, which is an alternative gateway to Morocco.

Case study 14.2

A Spanish wilderness at risk

Further development of the coast between the Guadalquivir estuary and Huelva would threaten the sustainability of one of Europe's last wilderness areas – the Marismas, part of which is designated as the Coto Doñana National Park. This contains a diversity of habitats, including coastal dunes, seasonally flooded marshlands, pine woods and cork oak scrub. About half a million birds over-winter here, and it provides a refuge for endangered species such as the Iberian lynx. For centuries much of this area was a royal hunting preserve and its ecosystems were not seriously threatened by the small-scale exploitation of its resources by local communities. This changed with the development

Case study 14.2

of mining and intensive agriculture on its northern borders, while a proposed mega-resort, Costa Doñana, was successfully opposed by environmentalists in the early 1990s. The ecosystems of the Marismas depend on the maintenance of the water table, which is being depleted to irrigate rice fields and strawberry production for the lucrative north European market.

Research and discussion

1 Although entrance to the Coto Doñana National Park is free, visitors require a permit and a professional guide. What type of visitor would be attracted to the park, given the facilities that are available?

2 Explain why the National Park's strict management policies have been unpopular with local communities and other interest groups in the area adjoining the park. Debate the issues, and assign roles to members of the class.

Spain in North Africa

The cities of Ceuta and Melilla on the North African coast have been under Spanish rule since the sixteenth century. Both enjoy free port status, and cross-border trade with Morocco is far more significant to their economy than tourism. The Spanish government has taken measures to integrate the Muslim communities who make up half the population, and to curb illegal immigration from Africa. Nevertheless these two Spanish enclaves have been a potential flashpoint for terrorism since '11-M' (the Madrid bombings of March 11, 2004).

The Spanish heartlands

The Meseta dominates central and northern Spain and presents an austere landscape, where the many historic towns, castles and monasteries provide the main attractions for the cultural tourist. The northern Meseta gave rise to the warlike kingdom of Castile, which strove for centuries to dominate the Iberian Peninsula, and whose language became modern Spanish. A number of tourist routes have been promoted to link the principal places of interest, namely:

- El Camino de Santiago (The Way of Saint James) has been followed since the early Middle Ages by pilgrims from all parts of western Europe, and experienced a major revival in the 1990s. The Spanish section of the route links the historic cities of Pamplona, Burgos and León and some of Spain's finest examples of Romanesque and Gothic architecture to the shrine of St James in Santiago de Compostela. Numerous hostels provide accommodation for pilgrims travelling on foot, horseback and bicycle.
- The 'Silver Route' links northern and southern Spain, passing through Mérida, with its Roman theatre, and Salamanca, home to Spain's most famous university. It crosses the region of Extremadura, land of the *conquistadors* – the adventurers who colonised the Americas in the sixteenth century.
- The 'Don Quixote Route' crosses the region of La Mancha, famous for its windmills and associations with the best known figure in Spanish literature.

Tourism in central Spain focuses on Madrid, and Barajas Airport, now expanded as a showpiece of modern architecture, is the gateway to Europe for many visitors from

Latin America. Madrid became the capital of Spain in 1560, and is a latecomer compared to other Spanish cities. Although the Madrid region accounts for only 6 per cent of overnight stays by foreign visitors to Spain, the capital is firmly established as a short break destination. The following features give Madrid its special appeal:

- the altitude of 700 metres makes it Europe's highest capital, with the benefits of clear skies for most of the year and invigorating mountain breezes from the Sierra de Guadarrama;
- the Prado is one of the world's finest art collections, including masterpieces by Goya and Velazquez;
- the range of restaurants offering the best of Spain's regional cuisines, speciality shopping, and first-class sports facilities;
- the vibrant nightlife, with much of the action taking place in the historic core of the city between the Plaza Mayor and the Puerta del Sol; while
- the city makes an ideal base for a touring holiday.

Cultural attractions recognised by UNESCO as World Heritage Sites within easy reach of Madrid include:

- the university town of Alcalá de Henares;
- Toledo, the religious capital of Spain, which has preserved its medieval character;
- Ávila, famous as the birthplace of the great visionary St Teresa. The town still retains its medieval walls, making it a favourite location for film-makers;
- El Escorial is the austere monastery-palace built by Philip II as the nerve-centre of the Spanish empire, contrasting with the gardens of Aranjuez, the former summer palace of the Bourbon kings of Spain;
- Segovia boasts a well-preserved Roman aqueduct and the romantic castle known as the Alcazar; and
- Cuenca is noted for the picturesque 'hanging houses' overlooking the River Júcar, and its reputation as an artists' resort.

The region of **Aragón** includes most of the basin of the River Ebro. This former kingdom played a major role in Spanish history, where for centuries Moors and Christians co-existed to create the *Mudejar* style of architecture typical of towns such as Teruel. The capital, Zaragoza is one of the great cathedral cities of Spain, whose importance as a business centre is set to grow due to its position on the AVE rail link between Madrid and Barcelona, and as the venue for the 2008 World Expo.

The Spanish Pyrenees

The mountains along the French border include the Aigüestortes and Ordesa National Parks, spas and winter sports developments, notably in the Aran Valley. Wildlife and traditional lifestyles, for long protected by isolation, are threatened by improvements in the transport infrastructure such as the Somport Tunnel, hydro-electric power projects and the growth of summer recreation.

Andorra

Andorra is a small, formerly remote principality in the eastern Pyrenees, where improved communications with France and Spain has led to the growth of summer and winter tourism, and economic development as one of Europe's tax havens. Duty-free shopping is the main attraction for large numbers of tourists and day visitors from

France and Spain, but the great majority of these are concentrated in the capital, Andorra la Vella. Nearby is one of Europe's largest centres of spa tourism. Andorra is attempting to improve its image as a low-cost skiing destination by attracting more upmarket tourists, but this could be a high-risk strategy.

The Spanish islands

The two groups of Spanish islands – the Balearics in the western Mediterranean and the Canaries in the Atlantic – are different in many respects from Peninsular Spain, and are therefore usually regarded as separate holiday destinations. These islands contain only 2 per cent of the national territory and 7 per cent of the population of Spain. Yet together they account for more than half of hotel overnights by foreign tourists in Spain.

The Balearic Islands

The Balearic Islands, consisting of Mallorca (Majorca), Menorca, Ibiza and Formentera, account for a quarter of all tourism to Spain (Mallorca alone has more hotel beds than Portugal), and tourism is estimated to account for almost 50 per cent of the regional domestic product. In a few decades the Balearic Islands have been transformed from one of the poorest regions of Spain, with a high rate of emigration, to one of the wealthiest. However, two countries dominate the market – Germany and Britain – with domestic tourists accounting for only 10 per cent of arrivals. The negative effects of tourism on the islands include:

- A coastline damaged by badly-planned development.
- Pollution resulting from emissions of carbon dioxide from tourist coaches and hired cars, inadequate waste disposal systems, and litter.
- Problems of water supply. The islands are limestone in their geology and agriculture largely depends on ground water resources. Excessive demands have caused a lowering of the water table and penetration of the aquifer by sea water. Tourists during the peak summer season consume the equivalent of 440 litres of water daily, reaching 800 litres for those staying in luxury hotels.
- The outnumbering of the population by tourists. In mass market resorts such as Magalluf and Arenal in Mallorca, fast food outlets, tawdry souvenir shops, pubs and *bierkellers* provide a 'home from home' for British and German holidaymakers. This, and the growth of second home ownership by affluent foreigners has led to the feeling among many islanders that they have lost their cultural identity.

Each of the Balearic Islands has distinctive landscapes, folklore and dialects.

Mallorca is by far the largest island, with a coastline 550 kilometres in length and mountains rising to over 1,000 metres in the northwest. Between these and a lower range in the east lies a fertile plain meeting the sea in a number of fine bays. Unlike the other islands it seemingly has the physical capacity to absorb the 12 million tourists who arrive in the Balearics each year. Mass tourism – the 'Majorca' of popular repute – is largely confined to a few mega-resorts around the Bay of Palma, within easy reach of Palma airport, which in summer is one of Europe's busiest. The 'other Mallorca' promoted by the more upmarket tour operators continues to attract wealthy celebrities and the discerning tourist.

In fact tourism in Mallorca is not a new phenomenon, and Fomento, the island's tourist board was established in Palma in 1905. In the years prior to the Spanish Civil War the island attracted artists such as Joan Miró, and foreign celebrities were accommodated in the luxury hotel at Formentor. The British poet Robert Graves did much to publicise the island's attractions from his home in the mountain village of Deià, when it took the best part of three days' travel to reach the island from Britain. In the period immediately following the Second World War there were few foreign visitors to fill the hotels, so Mallorca was promoted by the government as 'the isle of love' for Spanish honeymooners, an image also guaranteed to appeal to north Europeans. By 1960, 80 per cent of tourists were foreigners. Foreign tour operators financed the building of hotels in exchange for a guaranteed number of rooms on preferential terms. To induce holidaymakers on package tours to spend money in the island, hoteliers made sure they were provided with appropriate entertainment.

The worst excesses of sun, sea and sand tourism are confined to Magalluf–Palma Nova. The rugged west coast was saved from development, because it was not easily accessible, although communications have now improved, with a direct highway link through the mountains from Palma to Soller. The east coast, indented with numerous small coves, is given over mainly to self-catering villa developments. Away from the beaches, some aspects of the island's heritage have been promoted to appeal to the average tourist. These include:

- the Caves of Drach, an outstanding example of a geological feature imaginatively developed as a showpiece attraction;
- the former monastery at Valldemossa, now a museum devoted to Chopin, where the composer was inspired to write his *Preludes*; and
- the island's industries, notably the manufacture of artificial pearls.

Palma, the regional capital, is one of the leading seaports of the Mediterranean, with ferry services to the mainland and the other islands. It boasts an imposing cathedral and castle among its heritage attractions, and except for one small district, has been relatively unaffected by mass tourism.

Since the early 1990s the Balearic regional government has followed a policy of sustainable tourism; a third of the island's area has been designated for conservation, while steps have been taken to improve the environment of the most overcrowded resorts. However, it is debateable whether the further development of golf courses is truly 'green' tourism, while the buying up of rural properties, mainly by Germans, has implications for the social balance of the Mallorcan countryside.

Ibiza is relatively small in terms of area and population, and it is here that the impact of tourism has perhaps been greatest, to the extent that it accounts for 80 per cent of jobs. The island was much poorer economically in the pre-tourism era than Mallorca or Menorca, and was less able to cope with the influx. Ibiza has passed through the following stages of tourism development:

- The initial period of 'discovery' by hippy-style travellers in the early 1960s, who were attracted by the island lifestyle that was perceived to be more tolerant than the rest of Spain at that time. Some of these visitors later became permanent residents, to the extent that 30 per cent of the population are expatriates, and Ibiza remains something of an artists' community.
- The introduction of direct charter flights to Ibiza airport shortly after led to the growth of the inclusive tour market, mainly from Britain, catering for family beach holidays. The resorts of Santa Eulalia and San Carlos continue to serve this market.

- Since the 1980s there has been a growing emphasis on the international youth market and the all-night clubbing culture, which now accounts for 12 per cent of all tourists. The binge drinking and 'hooliganism' of some north European tourists has attracted unfavourable publicity in the media, which in turn has deterred holidaymakers from the older age groups from visiting Ibiza.

The major impacts of mass tourism are mainly confined to San Antonio, which is a noisy, high-rise 'tourist ghetto' catering for the lower end of the market. The island's capital Eivissa (Ibiza Town) has managed to retain some of its character as an historic Mediterranean seaport and offers nightlife that is more reputable and expensive. There is concern that the traditional way of life based on agriculture has all but disappeared, while the island is reaching saturation point as far as tourism is concerned due to problems of water supply. A major highway project has met with opposition from the island's fledgling environmental movement.

Formentera is the smallest of the Balearics. It is comparatively barren, sparsely populated, and scenically low-key. It does however have some good beaches, and because it is featured by few tour operators, and can only be reached by ferry from Ibiza, attracts holidaymakers seeking relative seclusion.

Menorca is scenically and culturally much more diverse, and its economy is less dependent on tourism. The Franco regime was reluctant to invest in the island, which, unlike Mallorca, had supported the losing side in the Spanish Civil War. On the other hand, the island authorities have managed to secure greater control over tourism development than was the case in Ibiza, with well-planned holiday villages at Binibeca and Fornells catering for upmarket tourists. The island's main tourism resource are its fine harbours which provide an ideal environment for yachting. The largest of these – Mahón – was an important base for the British navy in the eighteenth century, when it replaced the old city of Ciudadela as the island's capital.

Case study 14.3

Payback time for tourists in the Balearics?

The idea of an 'eco-tax', imposed on the tourism sector specifically for environmental projects, came about as a result of pressure from local communities in the Balearic Islands affected by mass tourism. In 1999 it was adopted by an alliance of the socialist and 'green' political parties in the regional parliament. The tax was opposed by most of the islands' hoteliers and the conservative Popular Party who were then in power in Madrid. Outside Spain, opposition came from British and German tour operators, and the Association of British Travel Agents (ABTA) threatened to cease holding its annual convention in Palma. The eco-tax did not come into force until May 2002, and was a watered-down version of the original proposal. The tax was applied principally to hoteliers, who then had to collect it from their guests, instead of the regional government directly taxing all foreign tourists, using all types of accommodation, on their arrival in their islands. The proceeds of the eco-tax, until its abolition in October 2003, were used to fund a large number of small-scale projects to conserve the heritage of the islands.

In class, debate the proposition that the eco-tax was a good example of the 'polluter pays' principle as applied to tourism, but one that was flawed in its application. Can you suggest any alternatives whereby the tourist would pay voluntarily toward the funding of conservation projects?

The Canary Islands

While the Balearics are essentially summer sun destinations, the Canaries have the advantage of a sub-tropical climate, which favours beach tourism throughout the year. Winters are pleasantly warm, while the cool ocean current moderates summer temperatures; but this also means that sea temperatures are rather too cold for bathing for much of the year. The islands are of volcanic origin and contain some magnificent scenery, but on the other hand there are relatively few fine beaches. Situated some 1,000 kilometres to the south-west of Cadiz, they are much closer geographically to Morocco and the Western Sahara than to mainland Spain. The location of the islands, on important shipping routes, resulted in the 'discovery' of Tenerife and Gran Canaria as winter destinations by wealthy British travellers and returning colonial officials in the nineteenth century. Large numbers of cruise ships still call at the ports of Santa Cruz and Las Palmas, which offer duty-free shopping as their main attractions. Since the 1960s the great majority of visitors have arrived on charter flights and are drawn from a wider range of countries and socio-economic groups. Most north European tourists still arrive during the winter months, whereas Spanish holidaymakers from the Peninsula are more evident in summer.

Tenerife is the largest of the islands and offers the greatest variety of scenery and climate, due to the effect of the spectacular peak of Teide on the prevailing trade winds. The strange volcanic landscapes of Las Cañadas National Park in the centre of the island offer a marked contrast to the desert-like south, the forested mountain slopes, and the fertile valley of Orotava, with its banana plantations to the north. In this part of the island, Puerto de la Cruz is a well-established resort catering primarily for the older age groups. This is because its position on the windward slopes of Teide means that sunshine cannot be guaranteed, and its lack of beaches is only partly compensated by a magnificent lido. The south coast has the climatic advantage, where hotels and time-share apartments line beaches within easy reach of the international airport. Playa de Las Americas – a creation of the tourist boom of the 1970s – is now the most popular resort on the island. The capital, Santa Cruz, is enhancing its cultural attractions with a carnival to rival that of Rio de Janeiro and a magnificent new auditorium. Nevertheless, both Tenerife and Gran Canaria have tended to develop artificial attractions with an international appeal, rather than promote the islands' folklore, traditional crafts and architecture, or the heritage of the Guanches, the mysterious indigenous people who inhabited the islands at the time of their conquest by the Spanish in the fifteenth century.

Gran Canaria has on balance more to offer mass tourism than Tenerife, particularly in the fine sandy beaches of its southern coast. This supports a tourist concentration second in size only to Benidorm, consisting of the resorts of Playa del Inglés, San Agustín and Maspalomas, attracting mainly German and lesser contingents of British, Scandinavian and Spanish holidaymakers. Away from the resorts, the interior of Gran Canaria has been described as 'a continent in miniature' offering spectacular contrasts in scenery.

Lanzarote is still volcanically active, and the craters of Monte del Fuego in the Timanfaya National Park are a major attraction. This is one instance where tourism can be said to have improved a rather barren landscape of lava spreads dotted with white villages. This is largely due to the inspiration of the architect César Manrique, who ensured that most development was planned with imagination and care for the local environment. Upmarket tourists are catered for at Costa de Teguise and sports enthusiasts at La Santa, while Puerto del Carmen is the most popular resort.

Fuerteventura is the driest of the Canary Islands, due to its closeness to the Western Sahara, and is the most sparsely populated. Persistent trade winds provide ideal conditions for windsurfing, while the vast beaches attract jeep safaris and are popular mainly with German tourists.

Gomera, La Palma and **Hierro** the three western islands, have remained relatively untouched by mass tourism due to their relative isolation, lack of good beaches, and the rugged topography. The prospects for tourism are most promising in La Palma, which can be reached by direct air services from northern Europe, and where the main attraction is the beautiful mountain scenery, culminating in one of the world's largest volcanic craters – the Caldera de Taburiente. There is also the appeal of a more traditional lifestyle, based on agriculture and handicrafts such as cigar-making, rather than tourism.

Gibraltar

Although Gibraltar is one of Britain's few remaining colonies, it is physically attached to Spain, while the people are a mixture of Mediterranean cultures and equally fluent in English and Spanish. Britain's interest in Gibraltar was primarily due to its strategic location guarding the entrance to the Mediterranean. Nowadays its military role is less significant and the Royal Navy dockyard has closed, forcing the colony to develop other roles as an offshore financial centre and tourist destination.

Gibraltar is a small territory, only 6 square kilometres in area, dominated by the great limestone mass of the Rock, which towers 400 metres above the densely packed town and busy harbour on its western flank. Since 1985, when the frontier with Spain was re-opened, Gibraltar has attracted millions of Spanish excursionists, as well as cruise passengers and much smaller numbers of staying tourists, mostly from Britain. The Spanish are motivated by curiosity and the lure of shopping bargains, while the British, many of whom are first time visitors overseas, are reassured by the familiar language, food, currency, British-style 'bobbies' and pubs, combined with Mediterranean sunshine. Apart from these, the colony's main attractions include:

- The world famous Rock, which is honeycombed with caves and 'galleries' constructed for military purposes. It also provides a habitat for Europe's only ape colony.
- The duty free shopping in Main Street.
- The historical associations with the British army and navy.
- The relics of the Moorish and Spanish occupations.
- The facilities for water sports, including a yacht marina. On the other hand there are only a few small beaches in the shadow of the Rock.
- Its proximity to Morocco, using the hydrofoil and ferry service to Tangier.
- Its proximity to the holiday resorts of the Costa del Sol. Prior to the 1960s, Gibraltar was the gateway to this part of Spain, and since 1985, growing numbers of British visitors have again been using it as a base for touring Andalucia.

However, the expansion of tourism in Gibraltar faces a number of problems, namely:

- The shortage of land, necessitating development on sites reclaimed from the harbour.

- The threat posed by the erosion of the Rock, caused by massive tunnelling in the past.
- The accommodation stock consists of a small number of hotels, guesthouses and self-catering complexes that need to be upgraded and extended.
- The restricted site of the airport that lies on 'neutral territory' with its runway on land reclaimed from the Bay of Gibraltar. To the south the airport is hemmed in by the sheer face of the Rock, while the Spanish frontier lies immediately to the north; which brings us to the most deep-seated problem –
- The long-standing political difficulties with Spain. Although Gibraltar has been British since 1703, Spain has never relinquished its claim to sovereignty. During the last major dispute, which lasted from 1969 to 1985, telecommunications were cut, the land border was closed, and the ferry service to Algeciras was severed by the Spanish government. Cut off from its natural hinterland, Gibraltar was forced to develop its own tourist attractions and recruit labour from Morocco. Another bone of contention is Gibraltar's alleged role as a tax haven in smuggling contraband from North Africa to Spain. The response of the Spanish authorities has been to subject motorists crossing the border at La Linea to lengthy delays. Spain's willingness to consider 'joint sovereignty' with Britain is rejected by the great majority of Gibraltarians. Nevertheless, the 2007 agreement between London and Madrid does allow for freedom of air travel to and from Gibraltar.

Portugal

Portugal is a much smaller country than Spain, both in population and land area. Due to its long Atlantic coastline, Portugal's climate tends to be milder and more humid, and the landscape generally greener, than is the case in most of Spain. Portugal has been a united nation for much longer than Spain, and the Moorish heritage is much less evident. In culture and temperament, the Portuguese differ from the Spanish in a number of ways; for example, the music form – *fado* – is full of the melancholy or *saudade* which is part of the national character and the Portuguese bullfight is an altogether gentler affair than the Spanish *corrida*. Portugal's contacts with its former colonies, particularly in Asia are reflected in its cuisine and the ornate decoration of its churches and country houses. In recent years Portugal has co-operated with Spain in a number of projects, such as an AVE high-speed rail link between Madrid and Lisbon and motorway connections between the two countries. Historically relations between the two countries have not been so close, and sometimes marked by hostility, as shown by the number of castles and fortified towns in eastern Portugal near the Spanish border.

Agriculture, fishing and textiles still play a major role in the Portuguese economy, but tourism has made a major contribution, supporting 6 per cent of jobs and 10 per cent of GDP. Although the country has made impressive economic progress since the 1990s, Portugal has one of the lowest standards of living in the European Union, and this is reflected in the continuing high rate of emigration.

The demand for tourism

Domestic and outbound tourism

Portuguese holiday propensities at around 50 per cent are lower than those of Spain, fewer trips are taken abroad, and budget accommodation is generally sought at the destination.

Inbound tourism

Inbound tourism on the other hand has grown steadily since the 1960s, with the exception of a downturn following the 1974 'Carnation Revolution', which introduced democracy and industrial unrest after a long period of authoritarian rule. This affected the hotel industry that also had to cope with a massive influx of refugees from the former Portuguese colonies of Angola and Mozambique. The early 1990s were a second period when international arrivals were depressed, partly as a result of over-pricing. This prompted a fierce debate as to a future strategy for Portugal and resulted in major changes in the organisation and approach to tourism, as outlined later in this chapter. This new strategy was successful and in 2009 arrivals of foreign tourists reached 6.4 million. Most visits are for holiday purposes; however, day visitors are around 16 million – Spaniards crossing into Portugal for shopping, or cruise passengers visiting Funchal and Lisbon on shore excursions. Portugal's hosting of the European football championship in 2004 boosted arrivals, not just to Lisbon, but to lesser known venues throughout the country, providing a legacy of stadiums that are unlikely to be profitable in the long term. Spain is by far Portugal's largest market; accounting for most of the visitors arriving by road, but these are usually short stay. Portugal's other main markets of Britain, Germany and France have different characteristics:

- air inclusive tours are the norm;
- there is a marked summer peak in demand;
- visitors stay longer; and
- spending per capita is higher than is the case with Spanish visitors.

The supply side of tourism

Transport

Portugal's location in the south-west corner of Europe necessitates a long journey if road or rail are used as travel modes. This has prompted a major road upgrading programme, including the construction of 2,000 kilometres of motorways. Nevertheless air transport is the dominant mode for tourists arriving from northern Europe, and the importance of fly-drive arrangements for those staying in self-catering accommodation in the Algarve. The national airline, TAP, underwent a programme of privatisation to take it into the millennium and the low cost carriers operate flights into Lisbon, Faro (for the Algarve), Oporto and the island of Madeira.

Accommodation

As in Spain, villas used as second homes or retirement properties have created a long-stay market, particularly in the Algarve and Madeira. Around two-thirds of visitors to Portugal use hotel accommodation, although an increased preference for cheaper forms of accommodation has become evident as more Spaniards visit Portugal and use campsites or stay with friends. Nonetheless, Portugal's accommodation stock is well developed, with a concentration of larger hotels in the Algarve, at Estoril, and on Madeira (both catering for inclusive-tour clients), and in Lisbon, where business travel is important. The government owns a chain of hotels – *pousadas* – similar in concept to the Spanish paradores. Likewise the *estelagems* operated by the private sector often use converted country houses or *quintas*. Camping and caravanning is important on the Algarve, especially around Faro, and attracts German, French, and Spanish visitors, while the many sites around Lisbon are a popular and cheaper alternative to the capital's hotels. The British and Dutch prefer to stay in apartments, again mainly in the Algarve.

Organisation

The importance of tourism as a 'safety net' against a decline in demand for Portugal's traditional products in agriculture, fishing and textiles was reflected in the government's response to depressed arrivals figures in the 1990s. The organisation of tourism was changed by merging government departments to create *Investimentos Comercio e Turismo de Portugal* (ICEP) in 1992. This new body has put into a place a successful new tourism strategy to:

- diversify source markets;
- introduce quality controls;
- reduce bureaucracy;
- establish a new image for Portugal stressing historic and cultural resources; and
- use the *fundo de turismo* (tourism fund) to create new products and upgrade existing ones.

In addition, Portugal is anxious to control the impacts of tourism on both the environment and Portuguese society. There are a number of national nature reserves and management plans exist for national parks, as well as the estuaries and coasts in the more popular recreational and tourist areas. Impacts are also reduced by Portugal's emphasis on the upper and middle sectors of the tourism market, in contrast to Spain's domination by mass market tourism, and this is reflected in the generally higher quality of the Portuguese tourism product compared to Spain. Portugal is also attempting to spread the load of tourism more evenly, both seasonally and geographically (well over a half of foreign arrivals are between June and September). The Algarve is already nearing saturation in terms of tourist development, and contrasts with the more remote interior provinces – such as Tras-os-Montes – which see few foreign tourists. Counter-attractions are being developed in the Oporto–Espinho area in the north and at Setúbal, south of Lisbon. Finally, Portugal is diversifying its tourist product by encouraging activity holidays, conference tourism, and sport tourism.

Tourism resources

Southern Portugal

The **Algarve** is Portugal's most popular holiday region, thanks to an exceptionally sunny climate, fine sandy beaches, rocky coves, and picturesque fishing villages. Tourism did not develop until the mid-1960s when Faro Airport was opened and the April 25 Bridge across the Tagus from Lisbon greatly reduced travel times by road to what had been a remote region. In the late 1990s, a second bridge – the Vasco da Gama – opened, giving a further boost to coastal tourism south of Lisbon. Many of the resort developments (for example, near Lagos, Albufeira, and Portimão) are in the form of self-contained holiday villages. Sports facilities (above all, golf courses) have been important in attracting investment from northern Europe. However, not all the development has been of a high standard – the haphazard growth of Quarteira compares unfavourably with nearby Vilamoura, planned around its yacht marina. Tourist development is extending westwards towards Cape St Vincent, following the upgrading of the coastal road, whereas the low-lying coast east of Faro remains largely undeveloped with the exception of the resort of Monte Gordo. The cultural heritage of the Algarve is relatively neglected; this includes the medieval walled town of Silves of Moorish origin, traditional handicrafts and markets, and Sagres, with its associations with Prince Henry the Navigator and the great age of Portuguese exploration in the fifteenth century.

In contrast to the Algarve, the **Alentejo** region and the interior of southern Portugal has been neglected for tourism. This region is characterised by wide plains, large country estates and extensive forests of cork oak trees – a resource threatened by changes in the international wine trade. The only tourist centre of significance is Évora with its important Roman heritage, but it is likely that a major power project on the River Guadiana will be the catalyst for large-scale development near the Spanish border. The coast of Alentejo, promoted as the Costa de Ouro, is attracting development on a small scale, with large stretches protected as nature reserves.

Central Portugal and Lisbon

Tourism in central Portugal around Lisbon has been established for much longer, and there is a wealth of attractions available for the cultural tourist as well as the sun-seeker. **Lisbon**, on the wide Tagus estuary, is one of Europe's major seaports, while Portela Airport is a hub for international flights to Europe, South America, and Africa. The capital is rich in reminders of Portugal's maritime history, notably the Tower of Belem and the Jéronimos Monastery, which contains the tomb of the great explorer Vasco da Gama. Tourism received a boost with the 1998 World Expo focusing on the oceans. Planning for this international exhibition involved the regeneration of the waterfront area. Lisbon is becoming a popular short break destination, with its mix of old fashioned trams, quality shopping and exuberant nightlife. Tourism resources close to Lisbon include:

- The strip of coast to the west of Lisbon – known as the Costa de Lisboa – has good beaches, hotels and facilities for sport and entertainment, especially at Cascais. The casino at Estoril, the premier resort, was a major attraction for Spaniards, as this type of gambling was prohibited by Franco's regime.
- South of the Tagus, the coastline around Setúbal underwent considerable development during the 1980s with much self-catering accommodation.
- North of Lisbon, and extending from Peniche almost to Oporto, the **Costa de Prata** is mainly popular with Portuguese holidaymakers. Its long sandy beaches are, for the most part, exposed to the Atlantic surf. The most important resorts are Nazaré (famous for its traditional fishing industry) and Figueira da Foz.
- Away from the coast, this part of Portugal boasts many places of interest, readily accessible from Lisbon. They include:
  - Sintra, in a scenically beautiful location overlooking the capital, was once favoured as a health resort by Portuguese royalty and wealthy foreigners;
  - Caldas da Rainha – a spa town noted for its ceramics;
  - Obidos – a picturesque medieval town;
  - Fátima is a world-famous shrine rivalling Lourdes in significance (in May each year vast numbers of pilgrims are attracted to the Basilica for candle-lit processions); and
  - Coimbra is an attractive university town noted for its contribution to fado music.

The North

Tourism development is being encouraged in northern Portugal, assisted by regional development schemes and upgraded road transport. Resources include:

- Aveiro, known as the 'Venice of Portugal' with its large sheltered lagoons, ideal for water sports.
- Oporto (Porto) at the mouth of the river Douro is Portugal's second city, its major commercial centre and the gateway to the northern region. Oporto's main claim to fame is its association with the port wine industry, although the actual vineyards are located 150 kilometres upstream, and the picturesque sailing barges seen on the waterfront are no longer used to transport the wine. Oporto's status as a World Heritage Site and nomination as European capital of culture in 2001 has helped to boost its tourism industry.
- Stretching from Oporto north to the Spanish border lies the **Costa Verde**, which is attracting increasing numbers of foreign visitors, travelling independently by car rather than using inclusive tours. Espinho, Povoa de Varzim, and Viana do Castelo are the chief resorts in this area.
- The Peneda Gerês National Park on the Spanish border offers wild granite mountain scenery. The small historic towns of the Minho region are interesting places to visit, notably Braga, the religious centre of Portugal with its spectacular Bom Jesus shrine, and Guimarães, celebrated as the cradle of Portuguese independence.

The Portuguese Islands

In addition to mainland Portugal, there are two groups of islands of volcanic origin in the Atlantic that we can treat as separate destinations – Madeira and the Azores. Unlike the Canary Islands, they were uninhabited at the time of their discovery in the fifteenth century, but there are similarities in the native vegetation. Since 1975 the islands have enjoyed a degree of autonomy from Lisbon. In view of the limited resource base of the islands, and with fewer opportunities than in the past for the islanders to emigrate to the Americas or South Africa, tourism should play an important role in the economy. However, tourism has been much more successful in Madeira than in the Azores, and this is largely due to differences in accessibility.

Madeira

Madeira is situated 800 kilometres south-west of Lisbon and slightly nearer to Casablanca. Of greater significance is the position of the harbour of Funchal on the main shipping routes from Europe to South America and South Africa. It was largely for this reason that Madeira became a fashionable winter destination for well-to-do British travellers in Victorian times. The island was able to broaden its appeal after 1964 when the international airport was opened east of Funchal, and the number of visitors increased fivefold between 1970 and 1990. However, mass tourism in the way it has occurred in the Canary Islands is ruled out by:

- the impossibility of extending the airport, which is not capable of handling wide-bodied jets;
- the shortage of land for development generally, on this mountainous but densely populated island; and

- the absence of beaches, except on the small and otherwise barren island of Porto Santo some 50 kilometres away from Funchal.

The regional government of Madeira has therefore aimed at promoting quality tourism. Foreign visitors are attracted by the beautiful scenery of mountains, coastal cliffs, and sub-tropical vegetation and the almost ideal climate – winter is still the peak season for the British, Germans, and Scandinavians. Hiking trails follow the intricate network of *levadas* (irrigation channels) which carry water from the mountains to the pocket-sized farms. The road network is being improved to make the interior more accessible, sports facilities are being developed to attract a younger market, and traditional craft industries such as embroidery are encouraged.

The Azores

The Azores are situated 1,500 kilometres west of Lisbon and 3,500 kilometres east of New York. Their mid-Atlantic location was important in the early years of trans-Atlantic flight when Faial and Santa Maria acted as staging points, but with the introduction of longer-range aircraft the islands have been by-passed. Although the Azores have three international airports – Santa Maria, Lajes (on the island of Terceira), and Ponta Delgada (on São Miguel) – few foreign airlines as yet operate scheduled services, and charter flights from Europe are discouraged by the Portuguese government. The islands are dispersed over 800 kilometres of ocean, making it difficult to organise multi-centre holidays. Unlike Madeira, the Azores are not regarded as a winter sun destination because, although the climate allows the cultivation of sub-tropical produce such as tea and pineapples, sunshine hours compare unfavourably with Mediterranean resorts. There are few beaches and the islands' main appeal is the spectacular volcanic scenery, the best-known examples being the crater lakes, hot springs, and geysers on São Miguel. Yachting, whale-watching (replacing the traditional whaling industry), sea angling, and horse riding in the countryside offer prospects for the growth of tourism.

Summary

- The Iberian Peninsula and the holiday islands of Spain and Portugal are among the world's major tourist destination areas. This is partly due to Spain's early entry into mass tourism in the 1960s based upon its holiday resources of an extensive Mediterranean coastline and accessibility to northern Europe. Portugal was a later entrant into the tourism market and is attempting to avoid mass tourism, focusing instead on more affluent markets.
- Tourist accommodation is concentrated at the coast, on the islands, and in the major cities. The principal resort areas are served by a well-developed transport infrastructure.
- In Spain uncontrolled resort development has caused environmental damage, deepened regional contrasts, and affected Spanish lifestyles to such an extent that many other countries – including Portugal – have been anxious to avoid these negative effects of tourism.
- The attractions of both countries are mainly based on the coastline and there are major resort concentrations on the islands, the Spanish Mediterranean Costas, and the Algarve.

- Sport tourism, particularly golf, is a major growth sector in both countries.
- Cultural tourism is reviving with the growing interest in the art treasures and historic buildings of the cities of Spain and Portugal.
- Rural tourism is becoming an important sector of the market. The landscapes of the Iberian Peninsula and the islands have great natural appeal, but the level of environmental protection is variable.

Assignments

1 Explain why Benidorm continues to be successful as a holiday resort, despite changes in fashion.
2 Describe the social impact of mass tourism on Spanish communities, particularly those on or near the Costa del Sol.
3 Identify those aspects of Spanish and Portuguese culture most likely to appeal to north European, Japanese or North American visitors.
4 Set out the advantages of Spain and Portugal as venues for international sports events.

The tourism geography of Italy and Malta

Introduction

Italy is one of the largest countries of western Europe, while the island-nation of Malta, lying 90 kilometres to the south of Sicily is tiny by comparison. Geographically the two countries occupy a strategic position in the centre of the Mediterranean Basin, while historically the Roman Catholic Church has played a major role in both countries, politically and culturally.

Italy

As a tourist destination Italy for many people means sunshine, good food, music and romance. Others are attracted by the style and quality of Italian fashion and engineering products.

Tourism in Italy has a long pedigree. Domestic tourism was certainly flourishing in ancient times, when the wealthier citizens of Rome visited their summer villas in resorts such as Baia on the Gulf of Naples. After the fall of the Roman Empire the pre-conditions for tourism – security and economic prosperity – were to cease for many centuries. Nevertheless, Rome continued to be the destination for Christian pilgrims from all over Europe. The Middle Ages were marked by the rise of the Italian city states, whose merchants grew rich as international bankers and as intermediaries in the trade in luxury goods from the Middle East. Venice, Pisa and Genoa also made vast profits from shipping pilgrims and Crusaders to the Holy Land. Following the Renaissance, what we would now call cultural tourists were attracted to Florence and Venice, then at their zenith as the cutting edge of European civilisation. Shakespeare was strongly influenced by Italian literature, and a host of writers and artists from northern Europe, including Milton, Goethe and Shelley, visited Italy for inspiration. In the eighteenth century it was the custom for wealthy young aristocrats to go on the Grand Tour, accompanied by a tutor and an entourage of servants, which involved a stay of at least a few months in Italy. Here they completed their education (in more ways than one), buying classical sculptures (not all genuine), and paintings as souvenirs of their travels, while on their return they renovated their country houses in the style of Palladio and other Italian architects. In a sense, the expansion of the railways in the nineteenth century allowed entrepreneurs such as Thomas Cook to popularise the idea of a European tour, bringing Italy within the reach of the expanding middle class of Victorian Britain.

Even today, most tourists to Italy have a cultural motivation, and the country's art and architectural heritage is the main reason it ranks among the world's top five destinations. Tourism products of a cultural nature include:

- short city breaks and longer touring holidays, appealing mainly to art lovers;
- music festivals, usually associated with a composer's home town, such as Pesaro (Rossini) and Lucca (Puccini) (Italy originated opera as an art form and there it enjoys widespread popular support);
- courses in Italian art and literature for foreign students in university towns such as Perugia; and
- faith tourism, with Rome, Assisi, Loreto and Padua as the most visited destinations in Italy for Catholic pilgrims.

With some notable exceptions, such as the Gran Paradiso National Park in the western Alps, Italy's environmental record has been relatively poor compared to the countries of northern and central Europe, and ecotourism is less developed. Conservation of the nation's cultural heritage is also a major problem, given the vast number of art treasures and the limited public funding that is available.

The setting for tourism

Physical features

Italy is separated from northern Europe by the high mountain barrier of the Alps and has a coastline 7,000 kilometres in length, facing the Adriatic and the western Mediterranean. The Apennines form the rugged spine of the Italian Peninsula, presenting a formidable obstacle to east–west communications. Between these mountains and the Alps lies the North Italian Plain, which contains most of the country's productive farmland and some of Europe's largest and most prosperous industrial cities. Much of Italy is geologically unstable, as shown by the earthquakes in Udine (1976), Assisi (1997) and L'Aquila (2007), the frequent landslides in the Apennines, and the volcanic activity in the Naples area and Sicily. Nevertheless, Italy's abundant geothermal resources have given rise to a flourishing spa tourism industry, with resorts such as Abano, Montecatini Terme and Ischia having an excellent international reputation.

Social and cultural features

The Italian lifestyle has always been an attraction for visitors from the more reserved countries of northern Europe, as shown by the elegance on display in the evening *passegiata* or parade in every town. Although Italy now has one of the lowest birth-rates in Europe as a result of the economic and social changes since the Second World War, family ties remain very strong. The Roman Catholic Church continues to play an important role, and religious festivals remain popular. Italian culture is characterised by great regional variety, expressed in food specialities, handicrafts and dialects. This is due largely to the fact that the Risorgimento, the reunification of Italy, was only partially achieved in 1861. Italians continue to have stronger loyalties to their city or region than to the state as a whole, and one of the biggest obstacles to national unity is the long-standing negative attitudes of north Italians toward the south, known as the Mezzogiorno, which they regard as socially backward and a burden on the economy.

Demand for tourism

Domestic tourism

Despite Italy's appeal to the foreign visitor, it is the large domestic market that dominates and sustains the tourism industry, accounting for 80 per cent of all overnight stays. Italians have a legal entitlement to at least four weeks annual leave, and well over half the population take at least one holiday away from home. The domestic market is largely seasonal with nearly 75 per cent of trips taking place in July and August, while average lengths of stay are falling as the three or four week vacation becomes less popular. Seasonality is a problem, since although participation in winter sports and activity holidays is growing, summer beach holidays remain the most popular type of domestic tourism. Whereas some of the resorts of the Adriatic coast and Liguria are also very much part of the international tourism scene, many of the small seaside resorts of Tuscany, Lazio and the south see few foreign holidaymakers.

Outbound tourism

An increasing number of Italians are travelling abroad, especially to long-haul destinations, and Italy ranks among the world's leading tourist-generating countries. However, it is only relatively recently that the country has become sufficiently affluent to generate a massive demand for foreign travel, and there is a wealth of attractions nearer home. In consequence Italy has a substantial surplus on its travel account.

Inbound tourism

Tourism accounts for 6.5 per cent of Italy's GDP. During the late 1980s and much of the 1990s the industry stagnated due to unfavourable publicity. This related to:

- overcrowding and unsatisfactory environmental conditions in the main resorts;
- obsolescent hotel stock, where facilities compared unfavourably with other Mediterranean countries such as Spain;
- high prices; and
- high crime rates, terrorist incidents and Mafia trials.

In the late 1990s tourism recovered, only to be checked by the impact of 9/11. In 2009 Italy received 41 million tourist arrivals. There is a considerable volume of business travel to Italy, which is one of Europe's leading countries for trade fairs and exhibitions. The most important venues, with the exception of Bari and Naples, are in the north, and include Milan, Turin, Genoa and Bologna. International sports events are also important, particularly motor racing, with world famous circuits at Monza and Imola. For most foreign visitors, however, holidays are the main reason for visiting Italy. In contrast to the pattern of domestic tourism, foreign visitors tend to be concentrated in a few regions that are well known for their art cities or resort attractions (compare Figure 15.1 a and b).

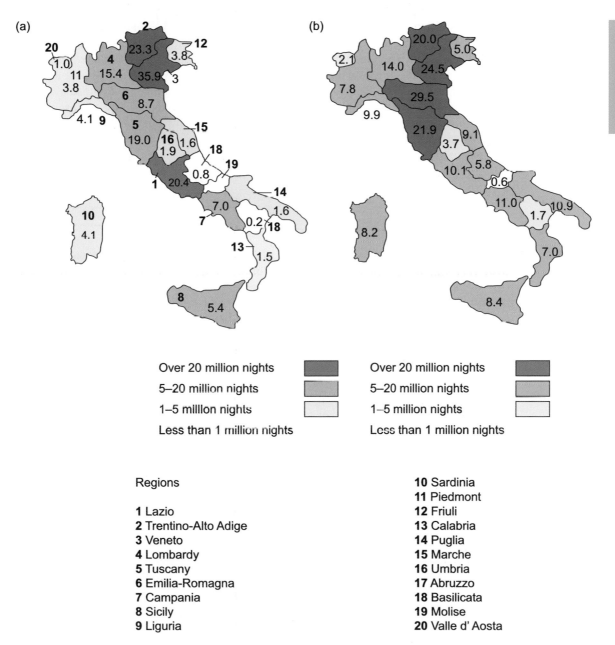

Figure 15.1 (a) Overnights by foreign tourists in Italy, 2009; (b) overnights by domestic tourists in Italy, 2009 (*Source*: ENIT, 2011)

Germany is by far the most important market in terms of arrivals and overnight stays, on account of the good road access. The most popular destinations for German tourists are:

* Lake Garda and the Veneto region;
* the South Tyrol (Alto Adige) region for winter sports;
* Campania for camping holidays;
* the Adriatic coast; and
* Sicily.

Other important markets are the USA, France, the UK, Japan and Austria. The French and Austrians typically arrive by car and visit the beach resorts and historic cities. British tourists have been less inclined to be independent travellers, with over half arriving by air; here low cost carriers are taking market share from charter airlines. For the British, Venice, Rome, Lombardy, Tuscany and the Sorrento Peninsula are the most popular destinations. Visitors from the USA typically spend only a short time in Italy, which is just one of the countries visited on a European tour, where the main attractions are the major art cities. Not surprisingly, most of Italy's luxury hotels are concentrated in Rome, Florence and Venice.

Supply of tourism

Transport

Domestic and international tourist travel is mainly by surface modes of transport. Italy has an excellent road network, including approximately 6,500 kilometres of *autostrada* (motorways). This is effectively linked to the wider European system, despite the bottlenecks, caused mainly by excessive numbers of trucks, which do occur on the approaches to the Brenner Pass and other routes through the Alps. This problem should be eased, together with the associated pollution, by the completion of a number of rail tunnel projects. The engineering problems involved in building the autostrada in mountainous terrain are shown, for example, in Liguria, where there are more than 100 tunnels and almost as many viaducts in a distance of less than 100 kilometres. The Autostrada di Sole from Milan to Reggio di Calabria is used by hordes of sun-seeking tourists from Germany and other countries of northern Europe, since it is possible to travel by car at high average speeds from Flensburg on the German–Danish border to the southern tip of the Italian Peninsula. However, accident rates in Italy are high by British or North American standards.

The rail network is also extensive, and generally offers travellers an efficient service with some of the lowest fares in Europe, although overcrowding is a problem in summer. Italian State Railways (FS) own most of the network, apart from a few narrow gauge lines. A number of high-speed trains operate between the major cities, including the *Direttissima* linking Florence and Rome; most of the funding for these high speed rail projects comes from the private sector rather than the government.

Italy's long coastline and location in the mid-Mediterranean has encouraged a history of seafaring; for example Genoa, the birthplace of Columbus, is one of the leading ports of Europe. Although few tourists arrive by sea, cruise ships operating in the Mediterranean usually call at Italian ports such as Venice and Naples. A number of ports, namely Livorno, Civitavecchia (serving Rome), Ancona and Brindisi are essential nodes in a network of coastal shipping services and international ferries linking various parts of the Mediterranean, not just neighbouring Corsica, Tunisia, Croatia and Greece, but also Turkey, Israel and Egypt. High speed hydrofoils operate on the short sea crossings between the mainland and the smaller islands such as Capri. They are also used for sightseeing excursions on the lakes of northern Italy.

Italy is well served by air transport. The most important airports are Fiumicino (Rome) and Linate (Milan) which rank among Europe's busiest. Alitalia, the national airline, is active in tourism promotion, working closely with the national tourism organisation. Alitalia and its subsidiary ATI provide a network of domestic services, while a number of charter airlines link the islands and resort areas to the tourist-generating areas in northern Europe. Low cost carriers also link Italian cities to regional airports across Europe.

Case study 15.1

Pilgrimages in the modern world

Faith tourism, according to the UNWTO was worth an estimated 13 billion euros in 2006. The Vatican has a specialist agency for pilgrimages, the ORP. It is very aware of the need to facilitate the movement of pilgrims, now the demand for this type of tourism is becoming ever greater, and yet fewer people have the time or inclination to travel in the traditional way. In 2006 the ORP organised transport for more than 50,000 pilgrims, working with scheduled airlines. However, the airports used by these airlines are at some distance from the sacred sites that pilgrims wish to visit. The Vatican's solution to the problem was to organise its own charter flights together with Mistral Air, a company owned by the Italian Post Office. As a result the cost of the journey for pilgrims was reduced by 10 per cent in the first year of operation. This airline now links a number of Italian airports with the pilgrimage centres of Lourdes, Fátima, Czestochowa in Poland, Guadalupe in Mexico, and the Holy Land. Some see this as a commercial venture, which the ORP denies.

Accommodation

Italy has almost 4.5 million beds distributed among hotels, campsites, pensions and *locande* (inns) which are favoured by domestic tourists. Hotels are most numerous in the north-east of the country, and are generally small family concerns, while large hotel chains are less dominant in the resort scene than elsewhere in Europe. The government agency Agriturist has done much to promote rural tourism, and a variety of accommodation is available, particularly in Tuscany, ranging from converted farm buildings to luxury villas. There is a trend toward greater use of self-catering accommodation, and campsites are numerous, especially along the Adriatic coast. A number of holiday villages are also available, run on similar lines to Club Méditerranée by the Italian tour operator Valtur.

Organisation

There is a clear demarcation between public sector tourism support at the national and the regional level.

National level

Italian governments since the Second World War have usually been weak coalitions lasting on average less than a year, making it difficult to implement clear policy objectives on tourism promotion and development. In contrast to a flourishing business sector, much of the public sector is characterised by inefficiency and widespread political corruption. This has resulted in one of the largest unregulated 'black economies' in Europe. The Italian State Tourist Office (ENIT) which was set up as long ago as 1919, has tried to remedy this situation. In 1993 the Ministry of Tourism and Performing Arts was disbanded and replaced by a small department of tourism reporting to the prime minister. ENIT's main purpose is promotion and research, and one of its aims is to diversify Italy's tourism product away from beach holidays and the 'big three' historic cities – Rome, Florence and Venice – to other forms of tourism. At the same time ENIT is hoping to achieve a more balanced spread of visitors by including less well known cities in the classical tours, by promoting the ski resorts in the eastern Alps, and by developing tourism in the Mezzogiorno, aided by INSUD, the public sector agency promoting tourism to the south. With reduced public sector commitment to tourism ENIT is involved in co-operative marketing with the private sector and the airlines. ENIT is also looking to promote Italy as a destination to emerging markets such as Brazil, China, South Korea, India and the countries of eastern Europe.

Regional level

Each of Italy's 21 regional governments has responsibility for tourism, although some – notably the autonomous regions of Sicily, Sardinia, Valle d'Aosta and South Tyrol – have been more active than others in planning, development and promotion.

Nonetheless it is at regional level that most activity is occurring, with funding based on the number of inhabitants of the region, rather than the number of tourists visiting.

At local level voluntary associations known as 'Pro Loco' draw on the civic pride of people living in the historic towns of central and southern Italy. They work closely with tourist offices to organise festivals, revitalise traditional craft industries and enhance the appeal of their communities.

Tourism resources

Northern Italy

The Italian Alps

The Italian Alps have a generally sunnier climate than the mountains of Austria and Switzerland, but this does mean that the skiing season tends to be shorter. We can divide the Alps for convenience into central, western and eastern sections.

The central Alps are dissected by long transverse valleys that end in a number of lakes of glacial origin. Because of their long-established importance as a holiday destination we need to treat the Italian Lakes as a separate entity. The central Alps include a number of ski resorts, such as Bormio, Livigno and Madessimo that are popular with price-sensitive foreign skiers, and accessible from airports at Milan and Bergamo.

The western Alps include the highest mountain peaks in the system. The most important resorts are located within easy reach of Turin, for example Sauze d'Oulx and Sestrière, which was developed by the Fiat corporation. The regional government of Valle d'Aosta has done much to promote tourism in an effort to stem rural depopulation. Cervinia on the slopes of Monte Cervino (better known as the Matterhorn) is a major resort in this area along with Courmayeur near Mont Blanc. Both resorts form part of cross-border ski circuits, with Cervinia linked with Zermatt, and Courmayeur with Mégève in the French Alps. This French-speaking region is also rich in heritage attractions due to its location on the approach to the Great St Bernard Pass, historically one of the most important routes across the Alps. It also includes one of Italy's finest wilderness areas, the Gran Paradiso National Park.

The eastern Alps offer different scenic attractions and cultural features, with many communities speaking German or Ladin as their first language. Although the Dolomites are by no means the highest part of the Alps, these mountains present a spectacular array of landforms resulting from erosion of the limestone rock. They present a challenge to mountain climbers, and the more adventurous breed of hikers using the *via ferrata* system of trails. The area boasts one of Europe's longest ski circuits – the Val Gardena – and one of its most stylish resorts – Cortina d'Ampezzo. Merano in the South Tyrol is one of Italy's most important spa towns. Until it became part of Italy in 1918, this region had been ruled by the Austrian Habsburgs for more than six centuries. The prevalence of the German language, styles of village architecture, and the traditional handicrafts are reminders of this heritage.

The Italian Lakes owe their elongated shape and their great depth, to glaciation of the mountain valleys during the most recent Ice Age (Lake Como for example, is over 400 metres deep, which means the lake bed is 300 metres below sea level). The southern ends of the lakes open out into relatively flat countryside, while their northern sections are hemmed in by mountains. The vast quantities of water stored in the lakes, and a location sheltered from northerly winds, results in a milder, sunnier climate than the Lombardy Plain to the south. The most important lakes for tourism are from east to west, Garda, Como, Lugano and Maggiore, each having specific attractions:

*   Lake Garda is the largest, with a western shoreline – the 'Garda Riviera' offering high class accommodation. The best beaches are however on the south shore where the picturesque spa town of Sirmione is situated.
*   Lake Como is only 60 kilometres from Milan and is therefore popular with day visitors, while its southern fringes have been affected by industrial development. In contrast, Bellagio, at a scenic location between two arms of the lake, is the most stylish of the resorts. Most tours of the lake feature a visit to the villas built by wealthy landowners in the eighteenth century, which are admired by garden-lovers worldwide.
*   Most of Lake Lugano falls within Switzerland. The resorts on the Italian side are little more than villages, with the exceptions of Porlezza and the gambling centre of Campione.
*   Lake Maggiore's northern tip is also Swiss territory. Much of the development is on the western shore, where Stresa is the most popular resort. Growth was rapid after the opening of the Simplon Tunnel in 1906 greatly improved access to the area.

The Italian Lakes appeal to a wide variety of visitors, including water sports enthusiasts, families travelling independently, and older holidaymakers on 'lakes and mountains' inclusive tours. The larger resorts such as Riva del Garda and Stresa offer conference facilities of international standard, and feature music festivals among their attractions.

The North Italian Plain

In contrast to the Alps, the lowlands extending from Turin to the Adriatic coast are rather featureless, except where hills of volcanic origin rise above the plains, as in the Veneto region. This part of Italy has a continental rather than a Mediterranean climate, with cold, often foggy winters and hot rainy summers. Its main river, the Po, has changed course many times over the centuries, and is held in check by an extensive system of artificial embankments. Rice fields are a feature of the landscape in some areas, and this is Italy's main food producing region. Apart from the culinary attractions, the appeal to tourists lies in the many historic towns, where, despite industrialisation, the art treasures and buildings of medieval and Renaissance times have been preserved. The most important of these are:

- **Venice**, a city which is truly unique, car-free, where all transport is on foot or by water, due to its island setting in the middle of an extensive shallow lagoon. It is not individual attractions that define this city's appeal, but the townscape and canal network that have changed remarkably little over the centuries. The Republic of Venice was once a great power in the eastern Mediterranean, using the profits from the trade in silks and spices from Asia to embellish merchant's palaces, churches and other public buildings. Tourism mainly focuses on St Mark's Square and the remarkable group of buildings around it. Event attractions such as the Venice Carnival and the *Regatta Storica* on the Grand Canal are an important part of the city's traditional image, while its contemporary role is exemplified by the film festival held in Lido di Venezia, the city's beach resort on the Adriatic. By focusing on Venice it is easy to overlook the other art cities of the Veneto region, notably Vicenza, Padua and Treviso.

- **Milan** is Italy's second largest city and main business centre, world famous for its fashion industry. More important in terms of employment are the car industry and engineering, and apart from the magnificent multi-spired Gothic cathedral, the skyline is dominated by office buildings. Nevertheless, this brash, bustling city has much to attract cultural tourists, as the home of La Scala, the world's greatest opera company, and Leonardo da Vinci's masterpiece, *The Last Supper*.

- **Turin**, as the capital of the kingdom of Piedmont-Savoy, played a leading role in the struggle to re-unite Italy, which is commemorated in the Museum of the Risorgimento. The city is better known as the centre of the Fiat corporation. Turin Cathedral is a focus of pilgrimage, as it contains among its treasures the shroud which is venerated as a relic of the Crucifixion.

- **Verona** has one of the world's best-preserved Roman arenas. Capable of seating 20,000 spectators, this forms an atmospheric setting in summer for one of Europe's most popular music festivals. However, tourists are more likely to visit this beautiful city because of its associations with the legendary Romeo and Juliet.

- **Bologna**, along with the other cities of the Emilia-Romagna region, has been overshadowed as a cultural centre by Venice and Florence, despite having one of Europe's oldest universities. It is better known as a focus for Italy's railway network and for its food industries, but the city has much to offer the tourist, including medieval shopping arcades and 'leaning towers' to rival those of Pisa.

- **Ravenna** is famous for its Byzantine art treasures, a reminder that this city was the capital of the Roman Empire at the time of its demise, vividly depicted in *The Last Legion*.

- **Trieste** is set to grow as a short break destination. During the Cold War this city's peripheral location on the border with the Eastern Bloc was a disadvantage, but this has changed with the accession of Slovenia to the EU. Trieste was historically important as the main seaport of the Austro-Hungarian Empire.

The extensive sandy beaches of the northern Adriatic coast offer safe bathing and a wide range of facilities, appealing to families as well as young tourists. Scenically, most of the coastline is flat, and the type of development is not particularly attractive, consisting of high-rise apartments and hotels, separated by extensive camping areas. Rimini, with more hotel beds than any other Italian tourist centre, is the gateway and chief resort of the **Adriatic Riviera,** and along with Cattolica caters for mass tourism from the industrial cities of Lombardy, particularly Milan. In the 1950s and 1960s, before Spain became the most favoured destination, Rimini and Cattolica were more popular with British holidaymakers than they are today. As elsewhere in Italy, most beaches are privately owned and well maintained, with catering concessions in the hands of family businesses.

The Italian Riviera

The coast of **Liguria,** also known as the 'Italian Riviera' is very different in character from the Adriatic coast. Mountains to the north offer protection from cold weather, and it was the mild climate that initially attracted foreign as well as domestic tourists in the nineteenth century. It is divided into two sections:

* the Riviera di Poniente, the western section between the French border and Genoa, which has the better beaches; and
* the Riviera di Levante, lying to the south east of Genoa, which is for the most part rocky.

Of the many resorts along this coast, San Remo is probably the best known and remains highly fashionable, with a yacht marina among its amenities. Portofino, once a small picturesque fishing village, has become an exclusive yachting centre on the most attractive stretch of the Riviera di Levante. Most of the other resorts such as Alassio have seen better days and are suffering from over-development and overcrowding, now that much of the coast is accessible by motorway as well as by rail from the industrial cities of Piedmont and Lombardy. Genoa itself has raised its international profile through designation as European Capital of Culture in 2004 and acting as host city for the G8 summit conference in 2001.

Central Italy

South of the Apennines the landscape changes and is scenically much more attractive than the plains of Lombardy and Emilia-Romagna. It is characterised by small farms, vineyards, olive groves and rolling hills crowned by a small town or village, which on first impressions appears to have changed little since medieval times. This picturesque countryside largely explains the appeal of Tuscany, and to a lesser extent Umbria and Marche, for rural tourism. In fact the area of Tuscany near Siena has attracted so many British second home owners that it has been nicknamed 'Chiantishire' after the well known local wines. The rather flat coastline gets less attention from foreign tourists despite the fine beaches, with the exceptions of the lively resort of Viareggio, and the island of Elba, famous for its associations with Napoleon. However, it is the many historic towns and cities, rather than the coast or the countryside which have made Tuscany one of Europe's most popular destinations. The tourist centres that have received wide international recognition for their cultural attractions include:

* **Florence,** situated on the River Arno, is the capital city of Tuscany and since the fourteenth century has been a leading cultural centre in literature (Dante and Bocaccio) and the visual arts. Thanks to the wealth and power of its ruling dynasty – the Medicis – during the Renaissance, Florence was able to attract the

best artists of the day, including Leonardo da Vinci, Michelangelo and Botticelli. As a result, the city can boast three of Europe's finest art collections. The skyline is still dominated by the Duomo (dome) of the cathedral, a major achievement of fifteenth century technology. Other attractions include the covered bridge known as the Ponte Vecchio and the Palazzo Pitti. The city is also famous for its luxury trades, including leather and jewellery. Unfortunately Florence has suffered from pollution and overcrowding due to its popularity as a tourist destination.

- **Pisa** is included on the international tourist circuit very largely because of the world famous 'Leaning Tower' – actually one of a group of medieval buildings around the cathedral square. Pisa's international airport is the gateway to Tuscany.
- **Siena** is a fascinating medieval city, with narrow streets opening onto the Piazza del Campo, where the Palio horse race is held twice every year in July and August. Facing this square are the cathedral, beautifully decorated in black and white marble, and the spectacular city hall.
- **San Gimignano** is a small hilltop town famous for its towers built by rival families in the Middle Ages, and a reminder of the strife that characterised Tuscany in that era. It is a favourite location for film-makers and music festivals.

Umbria and Marche are much less visited by foreign tourists than Tuscany, despite their heritage attractions. Assisi's fame as a place of pilgrimage is due to its association with two great spiritual leaders – St Francis (nowadays widely regarded as the patron of ecology) and St Clare. Urbino was a major cultural centre during the Renaissance and is famous as the birthplace of the artist Raphael. One of the many picturesque towns in the Apennines, **San Marino** is the most visited, mainly because of its curiosity value as the capital of a small independent republic surviving from medieval times. The Adriatic coast of Marche is scenically attractive, with a number of important resorts such as Pesaro and Gabicce Mare.

Rome is a bustling modern capital, with acute traffic problems and a heritage that presents many problems for developers. It is known as the 'Eternal City' as it has been a centre of civilisation, despite many vicissitudes, for the best part of 3,000 years. The Pope is not only the spiritual head of more than one billion Catholics worldwide, but is also the temporal ruler of Vatican City, all that remains of the formerly extensive Papal territories in Italy. The main gathering place for pilgrims is St Peter's Square, which provides a magnificent setting for the world's largest church, St Peter's Cathedral. The Sistine Chapel, part of the Vatican Palace, is famous for its paintings by Michelangelo. Rome was given a makeover in the seventeenth century by Bernini, the architect and sculptor, and many of the city's monuments, fountains, public squares and historic buildings date from this period. Nevertheless, traces of the ancient city can still be seen as reminders of the grandeur of the Roman Empire. They include:

- the Colosseum, where the populace spent much of their leisure time watching 'the Games' – subsidised entertainment that included gladiators and other displays of violence;
- the Forum which was the 'nerve centre' of ancient Rome;
- the Baths of Caracalla which are a reminder of the importance of public bathing as a recreation activity in Roman times;
- the Pantheon which is the best preserved Roman temple, largely because it was converted into a Christian place of worship; and
- the Via Appia, the route taken by the Roman legions to the port of Brindisi. Although this ancient highway is protected within a regional park by the authorities and UNESCO, it is under threat from property speculators and illegal development.

Other attractions in the Lazio region include:

- lakes of volcanic origin;
- the summer palace of the Emperor Hadrian at Tivoli;
- the seaside resorts of Ostia, Sperlonga and Terracina; and
- the monastery at Monte Cassino, founded by St Benedict as a role model of order and learning in the sixth century, destroyed because of its strategic importance in the Second World War, and subsequently rebuilt.

Southern Italy

The Mezzogiorno or 'land of the noonday sun' tends to be more traditional than northern Italy in its outlook and lifestyle, with a much larger proportion of its population dependent on agriculture. Due to widespread poverty and a lack of resources the region has experienced two great waves of emigration:

- to the New World, mainly the USA and Argentina in the early 1900s; and
- mainly to northern Italy during the economic boom of the 1950s and 1960s.

The Italian government after 1950 made great efforts to redress the economic disparities between north and south through the Cassa de Mezzogiorno, which initiated development projects and improved transport infrastructure. Funding was made available for hotel building and upgrading along with other tourism facilities. In 1984 the role of the Cassa was largely taken over by the eight regional governments. Southern Italy is now largely dependent on financial assistance from EU regional funding, INSUD and private investors. Yet, despite the efforts of the agencies concerned, the south has not attracted international tourism on a large scale, with the exception of well-established areas such as the Neapolitan Riviera. Also the stranglehold of secret societies, namely the Camorra and the Mafia on local business and politicians, particularly in Naples and western Sicily, has tended to discourage long term investment in tourism as well as other industries.

Campania is a popular destination, as it includes the Neapolitan Riviera, the name given to the resorts and islands of the Bay of Naples. The region is subject to earthquakes and volcanic activity, and near Pozzuoli numerous hot springs, steam jets and emissions of sulphurous gases characterise the landscape of the area known as the Phlegrean Fields. In AD 79 the towns of Herculaneum and Pompeii were destroyed by an eruption of Vesuvius. The excavated streets and buildings of Pompeii, that had been smothered under a thick layer of ash for many centuries, now provide a fascinating glimpse of many aspects of life in Roman times. The ruined city is a must-see attraction on the tourist circuit, while other classical sites such as Paestum and Cumae are relatively neglected.

Most of the holiday resorts are located on the Sorrento Peninsula on the south side of the Bay of Naples. Beaches are in short supply and the main attractions, especially for the older foreign visitor, are:

- the superb scenery of the coastal road from Sorrento to Amalfi;
- the picturesque resorts of Positano and Ravello, and the historic city of Amalfi; and
- the easy-going lifestyle and the sentimental popular music of the Neapolitans, which for many tourists epitomises Italy.

Excursions are available from Sorrento to the island of Capri, world famous for its Blue Grotto, and to Ischia, which is renowned for the therapeutic qualities of its radioactive springs. Both Capri and Ischia attract fashion-conscious Italians as well as large numbers of foreign visitors.

Although Sorrento is the largest holiday resort of Campania, Naples is the gateway to the region. Unfortunately, as Italy's third largest city and busiest seaport, Naples has a reputation that tends to deter, rather than attract tourists. Before the reunification of Italy it was the proud capital of an independent kingdom and featured prominently on the Grand Tour. Since that time the city has had more than its fair share of problems, including chronic unemployment and political corruption. Naples deserves to be better known for its cultural attractions, which include:

* the Teatro San Carlo, the nation's oldest opera house;
* numerous Baroque churches; and
* the National Archaeological Museum which has a collection of artefacts recovered from Herculaneum and Pompeii.

Case study 15.2

Pompeii is one of the world's most remarkable archaeological sites, visited by more than 3 million tourists a year. It is also one of the largest; since its discovery in the eighteenth century more than 40 hectares of the Roman town have been uncovered while another 22 hectares remain to be excavated. The vast majority of foreign visitors arrive by tour bus from Rome and Salerno, allowing only two hours for sightseeing. Some allege that bureaucratic inertia on the part of the authorities is responsible for a situation where the tourism experience is diminished by poor site management, poor signage and damage due to visitor pressure and inadequate supervision. Although Pompeii receives large foreign donations, there is never enough money for maintenance, restoration and further excavations – in fact far fewer excavated buildings can be visited now than was the case in the 1950s. As a solution the tourism councillor for the regional government has proposed there should be a limit on the number of visitors, to improve the tourism experience, and to increase revenue from the site by leasing the ruins as a location for film-makers or as a setting for corporate business events. Debate the pros and cons of this proposal and suggest alternative ways of protecting this fragile and unique attraction.

Tourists are now 'discovering' the unspoiled beaches of Calabria, backed by spectacular mountain scenery, and the range of heritage attractions that other parts of the south can offer. These include medieval castles, curiosities such as the *trulli* of Puglia – the traditional beehive-shaped village architecture – and the cave dwellings of the town of Matera, excavated from the soft volcanic tufa. Matera was notorious for its poverty until the 1950s but is now a World Heritage Site. The Abruzzo region has a number of ski resorts catering for domestic demand and some of the finest scenery in the Apennines, which is designated as a National Park.

The Italian islands

Italy's islands, because they are widely scattered, are less important in the international tourism scene than the islands of Greece, Croatia and Spain. With the exceptions of Capri, Ischia and Elba, most of the smaller islands see few foreign tourists. The two largest islands – Sicily and Sardinia – are each almost the size of Belgium and are holiday destinations in their own right. Nevertheless, together they account for only 6 per cent of overnight stays by foreign visitors in Italy.

Sicily

Only the narrow Straits of Messina separate Sicily from the Italian mainland, but it is very much a region apart from the rest of the nation. This is due to the island's closeness to North Africa and its extraordinary history under the domination of a series of foreign invaders, notably the Arabs and the Spanish. Although Sicily's former overlords left a rich architectural heritage, the natural environment has suffered from centuries of exploitation and widespread deforestation. Many of the tightly packed hill towns rise out of a parched landscape and are over-dependent on agriculture. They have a neglected, somewhat forbidding appearance; Corleone (of *Godfather* fame) is a typical example. Tourism has made more headway on the coast, where a number of fishing villages have become beach resorts.

Sicily has much to offer the tourist. The weather is generally warm and dry, although the heat of summer is oppressive when the Sirocco wind blows from North Africa. The rich cultural mix is evident in the Sicilian dialect, food specialities, handicrafts and folklore, and the religious intensity of Holy Week. The two major cities – Palermo in the west and Catania in the east – are ports of call on Mediterranean cruises. Ferries serve the island from Genoa, Livorno and Naples, as an alternative to the Reggio-Messina crossing and the long journey by road down the Italian Peninsula. Sicily will become even more accessible once the controversial project for a fixed link between Messina and the mainland goes ahead.

Sicily's natural attractions include Mount Etna, one of the world's largest active volcanoes, where the crater can be approached by road or by cableway. The region also includes many smaller islands. Outlying Lampedusa has become a staging point for illegal immigration from North Africa. The Lipari Islands off the north coast are volcanic and offer the spectacular scenery of Stromboli as well as opportunities for scuba diving. Sicily's heritage attractions include:

- Archaeological sites, including an array of temples and theatres built by the ancient Greeks that rival anything to be found in Greece itself. The most outstanding example is the Valley of Temples at Agrigento. Other important sites from the period (c. 300 BC) can be seen at Syracuse, Segesta and Selinunte.

Photo 15.1 Mount Etna in Sicily is one of the world's largest active volcanoes (©istockphoto.com/Robert Gennaro)

- The cathedral at Monreale, which is a blend of Norman-French and Arabic styles.
- Taormina is Sicily's most sophisticated and fashionable resort. With Etna as a backdrop, this is a spectacular setting for the cultural events that are staged in the beautiful Greco-Roman theatre overlooking the Mediterranean.
- Cefalú caters more for families and is favoured by foreign tour operators, as it has an asset that Taormina lacks – a fine beach. It is also a picturesque fishing port with an impressive cathedral.

Sardinia

Tourism is an important part of Sardinia's economy. Because of its relative isolation, tour operators feature the island as a separate destination, particularly for beach tourism. Until the 1960s Sardinia was a remote backwater, outside the mainstream of Italian culture, while the sparsely populated interior had a reputation for lawlessness. Tourism products include four-wheel drive expeditions and rural tourism involving the participation of local farmers, but most of the tourism development is based on the island's white sandy beaches. One of the first areas to be developed was the Costa Smeralda, north of Olbia, which includes some of the most expensive hotels and holiday homes to be found anywhere in the Mediterranean, blending perfectly with the natural scenery. Most of Sardinia is not exclusive, and Alghero in particular caters for package holidays. Sardinia is well connected by charter flights to the cities of northern Europe and by ferry services to the Italian mainland, Corsica and mainland France.

Malta

Despite its geographical closeness to Italy, in language and culture Malta has closer links to Britain and North Africa. Although the Maltese islands are poor in natural resources, they are strategically important due to their location in the mid-Mediterranean between the Straits of Gibraltar and the Suez Canal. Malta's fine natural harbours also made it a valuable prize for foreign invaders over the centuries. The most important of these, prior to the British takeover, were the international Crusading order known as the Knights of St John who made Malta their base in the sixteenth century. As a result the islands were in the front line of the military struggle between Christian Europe and the Ottoman Empire. In the nineteenth century and for most of the twentieth, Britain used the Grand Harbour at Valletta as a base for the Royal Navy. The smaller island of Gozo was neglected, and remains something of a backwater compared to the main island of Malta, although it is greener and scenically more attractive. The first impression of Malta is an apparently barren landscape of small terraced fields, separated by drystone walls and dotted with villages built from the honey-coloured rock. Due to the limestone geology of the islands and the rather dry climate, water supply is problematic, and tourism has to compete with other demands for this resource.

Demand for tourism

Before independence from Britain in 1964, Malta was not a major destination. The departure of the British armed forces meant that the government had to transform the country's economic base, by concentrating on the service sector, including tourism.

Tourism to Malta rapidly expanded during the 1970s, reaching 700,000 by 1980. Most visitors were from Britain, as Malta (along with Cyprus and Gibraltar) was part of the sterling area and therefore exempt from the currency controls imposed by the British government. In the first half of the 1980s visitor numbers declined, but have since grown steadily to reach just over 1.2 million arrivals in 2009. Malta's membership of the EU should boost tourism in the long term. The tourism authorities are concerned at Malta's dependence on a few markets, with the UK accounting for just under half of all arrivals followed by Germany, Italy and France. The national carrier Air Malta also operates services to Libya and Egypt, demonstrating the importance of the Arab market in business travel. Valletta has been successfully promoted as an international conference venue and financial centre, yet despite this the majority of arrivals to Malta are holidaymakers attracted by sun, sand and sea. About a quarter of Malta's visitors are cruise passengers, with much smaller numbers, mainly Italians, arriving on ferries from Sicily and Naples. Most visitors arriving by air are on inclusive tours, but an increasing number are using low cost carriers to visit their second or retirement homes on the islands.

Supply of tourism

Accommodation

Malta has a large stock of hotel and self-catering accommodation, amounting to over 39,000 bedspaces. The lower end of the package holiday market is concentrated in Sliema, while there are a number of new resort developments by international companies responding to the government's strategy to upgrade facilities. In contrast, Gozo's tourism industry is much less developed as it is highly dependent on day visitors from the main island.

Organisation

Government commitment to tourism is demonstrated by the Malta Tourism Authority (MTA) which was created in 1999 with the mission of marketing and planning Maltese tourism and upgrading the product. The MTA is anxious to maintain Malta as a competitively priced destination, but is faced by a number of problems. These include:

* water supplies, with the islands depending largely on desalinisation;
* development pressures on the main island, which already has one of the world's highest population densities; and
* poor standards of accommodation in some areas.

These problems have led to restrictions on further development in St Paul's Bay, Sliema and the south-east of the island. There is also the realisation that, if Malta has reached saturation point in terms of tourism development, then the only way the industry can expand is to use the spare capacity in the off-peak months and to attract a higher spending type of tourist. For this reason the MTA is determined to re-brand Malta as a selective destination, with a product offer that concentrates on the islands' heritage and culture, event attractions, niche markets and luxury accommodation. Gozo is positioned to attract upmarket tourists and scuba divers with its tranquillity, and can also take advantage of EU regional funding to improve its transport infrastructure, particularly the ferry services to the main island. This should redress the social and economic imbalance between Malta and Gozo and improve employment prospects for its young people.

Tourism resources

Malta's main appeal for holidaymakers is the warm sunny climate, with sheltered, unpolluted bays and harbours providing ideal conditions for sailing, windsurfing and diving. Sandy beaches are largely restricted to the north-west of the main island, whereas most of the resort development has taken place along the east coast. Although the Maltese people are service-oriented and used to dealing with foreigners, they have retained their traditional culture that has some Middle Eastern influences as well as being characterised by a strong devotion to Catholicism. Each village has its *festa* (religious festival) and elaborately decorated church. For its size Malta has a remarkable variety of cultural attractions that include:

* The heritage of the Knights of St John in Valletta and 'The Three Cities', as expressed in fortifications, Renaissance palaces, the Manoel Theatre, and many churches. Some of the palaces and *auberges* that housed the knights have found a new role as conference centres or luxury hotels. St John's Co-Cathedral is outstanding for its works of art.
* The archaeological sites, many of which date back to 2000 BC or earlier. The most significant of these is the Hypogeum, apparently a temple linked to a fertility cult.
* The medieval walled town of Mdina, the former capital known as the 'Silent City', in contrast to the bustle of Valletta.
* The traditional *dghaisas* which ferry tourists across the Grand Harbour.
* Handicrafts such as pottery and lace-making.

Discussion point

As a tourist destination Malta faces problems common to many small islands that relate to its carrying capacity, and planners have to balance development needs against conservation issues. In class discuss whether the MTA's strategy of re-branding can address issues such as water supply, traffic problems, population pressures and heritage conservation to benefit all the stakeholders in the tourism sector.

Summary

* Italy has a long pedigree as a tourist destination, whereas in Malta tourism is a relative newcomer.
* In Italy tourism is mainly cultural in nature, whereas Malta is known primarily as a beach destination despite a wealth of cultural resources.
* Italy is a major generator of international tourism but domestic tourism is of even greater significance.
* Road and rail is the transport mode used by most tourists both to and within Italy, whereas Malta is dependent on air transport for international tourism.
* Due to its size and historical background Italy is divided into a number of culturally distinct regions, and the contrast between the north and the south of the country is

particularly significant. Even in Malta there are contrasts between the main island and Gozo, which qualifies for EU regional funding.

- In Italy the mountainous character of much of the country is an obstacle to surface transport, but one that has been largely overcome through superb engineering. In Malta, the small size of the islands and their limited natural resources impose a capacity ceiling for tourism development.

Assignments

1 Assess the importance of religion, including religious festivals, art and music, in attracting tourists to Italy and Malta.
2 Identify the physical, social and cultural features that distinguish the south of Italy from the north as tourist destinations.
3 Compare the advantages and disadvantages of different modes of transport for an elderly American couple planning a tour of Italy.
4 Discuss whether Italy is a suitable destination for a young model seeking a 'health and wellness' holiday.

The tourism geography of South-Eastern Europe

Introduction

Apart from their location in the eastern half of the Mediterranean, we think there is justification for including Greece, the countries of the Balkan Peninsula, Turkey and Cyprus in the same chapter. Most of these countries have developed tourism industries based on beach holidays, serving the North European market. Cultural tourism is also important, and part of their attraction for visitors is a heritage that is a blend of Western and Middle Eastern influences. During the period of Turkish expansion in the sixteenth century almost the whole region became part of the Ottoman Empire, and some of the Greek islands and Cyprus formed the front line in the struggle waged by the Republic of Venice and the Knights of St John in the defence of Christian Europe. The heritage of the Ottoman Empire can be seen in the architecture, cuisine and handicrafts of south-eastern Europe, and most of these countries have large Muslim communities.

Greece (Hellas)

The setting for tourism

The location of Greece on the periphery of the European Union, and its relatively weak economy, have tended to obscure the unique contribution that this small country has made to European culture:

- Greece is regarded as the birthplace of European civilisation. The Minoan culture of Crete flourished at the same time as ancient Egypt (circa 2000 BC) and was in some respects more advanced. It was followed by the more warlike Mycenean culture on the mainland, which formed the basis of legends such as the Iliad, the Odyssey, and Jason's Argonauts. Greece as 'the land of gods and heroes' has inspired a good deal of European art and literature.

- Later (after 500 BC), Classical Greece under the leadership of Athens developed many of the ideas and institutions which became central to the Western heritage, such as democracy and the Olympic Games. Architectural achievements such as the Parthenon, continue to provide inspiration, and the dramas of Sophocles are still performed for modern audiences in the original open-air theatres as at Epidauros. Hellenic culture was spread far beyond Greece, particularly by Alexander the Great, and strongly influenced the Romans.
- After the fall of the Roman Empire in the West, the torch of civilisation was carried on by the Greek-speaking Byzantine Empire, based in Constantinople (now Istanbul). The Greek Orthodox Church spread to much of eastern Europe and Russia, strongly influencing religious art (for example, the use of ikons) and architecture.

Geographically, Greece forms part of the Balkan Peninsula, and has a cultural outlook different from Western Europe. It shares with other countries in the region:

- Orthodox Christianity, rather than Roman Catholicism;
- the Cyrillic rather than the Roman alphabet; and
- a history of centuries of domination by the Ottoman Empire.

Greece is also situated at the threshold of the Middle East, and Greek communities have long been a feature of the Levant – the eastern shore of the Mediterranean – from Alexandria to Asia Minor. Middle Eastern influences are evident in many aspects of modern Greek culture, including food and music. However, relations with Turkey have often been strained, with emotional responses based on historical grievances getting in the way of international co-operation that would benefit tourism in both countries as well as in Cyprus. The entry of Turkey into the European Union should reduce these tensions. The geographical proximity of Greece to some of the world's 'trouble spots' in the Balkans and the Middle East has also had a negative impact on the country's tourism industry. For example, the Western media have alleged lack of security at Athens Airport on several occasions.

The country's geography also explains why Greece has a maritime outlook extending well beyond the Mediterranean. The 16,000 kilometre-long coastline is deeply indented and has many islands, while the interior is, for the most part, mountainous – in Greece the sea and the mountains are never far away. The landscape has been devastated by soil erosion (largely due to deforestation) and good agricultural land is scarce. Not surprisingly, Greeks have been seafarers throughout their history, while Greece today has one of the world's largest shipping fleets and is active in cruise tourism. Due to the lack of economic opportunity there has been a great deal of emigration, particularly from the Aegean islands, to countries such as Australia or the USA. In fact, the Greeks of this overseas diaspora far outnumber the population of Greece itself. As far as tourism is concerned, the multiplicity of islands and harbours provides an ideal environment for sailing holidays and cruising, while the clear water of the Aegean favours diving.

Tourism is vital to the Greek economy, since it accounts for about 15 per cent of GDP and is a significant source of foreign exchange, compensating for nearly half the country's international trade deficit. Around 18 per cent of the workforce are employed in the tourism industry during the peak summer months, according to official figures. However, the contribution of tourism to job creation is even higher if we consider the 'black economy' of unregistered businesses, which is a fact of life in Greece as in other south European countries. Tourism is also responsible for facilitating economic and social development in areas where other opportunities for wealth creation are lacking. Tourism has stemmed the tide of emigration from the Aegean islands, and there is now a reverse flow, including entrepreneurs from the mainland (which is not always to the advantage of the island economy).

The demand for tourism

Domestic and outbound tourism

Although nearly half the population engage in tourism, only a small percentage of trips are to foreign countries, mainly due to the economic problems in Greece in the new millennium and also concerns for safety. In some of the Greek islands, notably Rhodes, domestic tourists are far fewer than foreign holidaymakers, and their length of stay tends to be much shorter. Domestic tourism includes summer excursions to the coastal resorts and islands, winter skiing in the mountains, and pilgrimages to Orthodox shrines, such as Tinos in the Aegean.

Inbound tourism

Cultural tourism has a long history in Greece, and although the country was not included in the Grand Tour, it was visited by the more adventurous travellers, notably Lord Byron, who did much to promote the cause of Greek independence in the early nineteenth century. However, organised tourism did not take place on any scale until the 1950s. Along with other Mediterranean destinations, Greece developed rapidly during the 1970s largely on the basis of price and the attractions of the Greek islands. The hosting of the 2004 Olympics in Athens provided the impetus for major improvements in infrastructure, although the economic benefits were less evident. However, arrivals increased by 14 per cent the following year, and exceeded 17 million in 2006. There has been a decline since then, with less than 16 million arrivals in 2008. The majority of tourists to Greece are visiting for recreational rather than cultural reasons – in search of sun, sand, sea, the nightlife, and for a substantial number of visitors, the so-called 'Shirley Valentines' – romance. The Greek tradition of hospitality known as *philoxenia* (literally love of strangers) has probably been an asset in developing a vast service sector dominated by small family-run enterprises. Britain and Germany supply about 30 per cent of the total number of visitors, most of whom arrive on inclusive tours. Italy, the Netherlands, Austria, Albania and the Scandinavian countries are also major generators of tourism to Greece. Large numbers of tourists also come from the USA, attracted mainly by the heritage of Classical Greece.

The success of the Athens Olympics has boosted national pride and self-confidence. Greece is determined to downplay its image as a beach destination for north Europeans, and develop ecotourism, which is in its infancy. This will require greater investment in infrastructure.

The supply side of tourism

Transport

More than three-quarters of visitors to Greece arrive by air, encouraged by the growth of budget airline services across Europe. The most important gateways are Athens, serving southern and central Greece, and Thessaloniki for the north. The national carrier Olympic Airways and its associate Olympic Aviation operate a network of domestic air services based on Athens throughout this fragmented country, although it no longer holds the monopoly. Some Greek islands can be reached by direct charter flights from the cities of northern Europe, the most significant being Corfu (Kerkira), Cephalonia, Zante (Zakinthos), Crete (Iraklion and Chania), Mykonos, Rhodes and Kos. Greece receives around 6 per cent of its visitors from cruise ships plying the eastern Mediterranean. Overland travel by road or rail is also an option, but it is time-consuming as it involves:

- ferry crossings from Ancona or Brindisi to Patras if the visitor is arriving via Italy; or
- the possibility of lengthy delays at border crossings if the visitor is travelling through the republics of the former Yugoslavia. Before the break-up of that country and the subsequent wars in Croatia, Bosnia and Serbia (1991–1999) this was the preferred route, but it remains potentially unsafe, given the likelihood of another crisis in the Balkans.

The rail network within Greece, operated by Hellenic Railways (OSL) has suffered from chronic under-funding and many of the lines are single-track, reducing capacity and speed. However, fast inter-city services do link Athens to Thessaloniki and Patras. Much of the road system is also poor by European Union standards, especially on the islands where the accident rate among tourists hiring mopeds for example, is unacceptably high. On the other hand, Greece has one of the world's most extensive networks of coastal shipping services. The system is not ideal from a tourist's viewpoint, as most ferries operate from the hub of Piraeus, the port of Athens, inter island connections can be infrequent, and shipping companies are reluctant to provide an integrated service. 'Island-hopping' is part of the attraction of Greece for many tourists, but it requires patience and an element of planning. Ferries are subject to delays and even cancellations, especially in the Aegean, when the *meltemi* wind blows during the summer months. In good weather, the more remote islands can be reached by *caiques* (converted fishing boats).

Accommodation

The accommodation and catering sectors are well represented in Greece, and consist mainly of small and medium sized enterprises (SMTEs). The official stock of hotels and self-catering villas, apartments and studios is considerable (over 300,000 beds in serviced accommodation alone), but it is exceeded by unregistered accommodation known collectively as *parahoteleria*, amounting to perhaps one million bed spaces. Most of the establishments offering rooms to let to visitors arriving in the Greek islands fall into this category. A large number of campsites are also available.

Organisation

The importance of tourism is recognised by the government. The Ministry of Tourism shares responsibilities with the Greek National Tourism Organisation (GNTO) for promotion, planning, the implementation of policies at both national and regional levels and co-ordination of the public and private sectors in tourism development. Government involvement currently is less than in the 1970s when it took a direct role in encouraging tourism, itself building facilities on a considerable scale, and offering a wide range of incentives to private developers. Tourism is included in the

Five Year plans for economic and social development, supplemented by European Union funding.

The GNTO faces a number of problems brought about by both the nature of tourism to Greece and the vulnerability of many of the country's resources. They include:

- **Seasonality.** The emphasis on 'summer sun' tourism does mean that there is a major problem, as 75 per cent of tourist arrivals are concentrated in the months May to September. This forces those employed in the tourism sector to work excessively long hours, to the detriment of the traditional family values characteristic of the Greek way of life.
- **Geographical concentration.** Tourism development is mainly restricted to Athens, the coastal resorts and some of the islands. This makes it difficult to spread the benefits of tourism more evenly throughout the country, and to provide adequate accommodation and other facilities to cope with demand.
- **The negative social impact of mass tourism.** During the off-season, the Greek islands are almost crime-free, but health and police services are stretched to the limit in some popular resorts during the peak summer months – to cope with the effects of alcohol and drug abuse by some north European holidaymakers. This type of behaviour is offensive to the host community but is tolerated because tourism brings in much needed income.
- **Over-dependence on foreign tour operators.** Attempts by hoteliers to introduce higher standards and prices mean that the mass market no longer sees Greece as an inexpensive destination, while high-spending tourists are deterred from visiting the popular resorts and the country faces competition from cheaper destinations in the region.
- Substantial leakages in tourism earnings, due to the islands in particular having to import many of the goods needed to supply tourists.
- **Environmental degradation.** The development of tourism has often been characterised by unplanned, haphazard building that has blighted the landscape. The rapid development of tourism, and its concentration in the dry summer season has placed severe pressure on water supply systems. Marine pollution has been caused by inadequate sewage treatment and waste disposal. Noise pollution is a feature of the popular resorts, and has contributed, for example, to the decline of an endangered species of turtle on the island of Zakinthos. It is estimated that two thirds of the forest fires that afflict Greece each summer are deliberately carried out to clear land for development.
- The lack of a co-ordinated strategy for tourism development.

These issues do mean that, while Greece is endowed with superb tourism resources, the country's tourism industry does not always fulfil its potential.

Tourism resources

We should divide Greece for tourism purposes into:

- the Greek mainland, which consists of a number of regions, namely the Peloponnese in the south, Sterea Hellas (central Greece, including Athens), Epirus in the west, and Thessaly and Macedonia in the northern part of the country; and
- the Greek islands, which include Crete and a number of separate groups or archipelagos. The most popular of these are the Ionian Islands lying to the west of the mainland, the Cyclades in the central Aegean, and the Dodecanese to the south-east.

Mainland Greece

The mainland of Greece is divided into two by the Corinth Canal, itself a major engineering achievement. To the south is the Peloponnese, where mass tourism has as yet made little impact, largely due to the absence of good beaches. Tolon and Naplion are significant holiday resorts, within easy reach of Athens. The government has encouraged the revitalisation of traditional communities such as the Mani in the extreme south, famous for its fortified villages. This formerly remote area has been opened up for walking and special interest holidays, which include Mystra, an important city in the Byzantine era. The Peloponnese contains some of Greece's most important archaeological sites. Some of these are included in classical tours based on Athens, namely:

- Olympia – site of the original Olympic Games, celebrated from 776 BC to 390 AD;
- Mycenae – associated with the legends of the Trojan War; and
- the well-preserved theatre at Epidauros, dating from the fourth century BC, that is still used for cultural events.

Tourism in Athens has declined significantly since the 1970s, when it was still the centre *par excellence* for sightseers. This has come about partly as a result of the growth in popularity of the Greek islands, at the expense of cultural tourism. Ugly urban sprawl and severe air pollution resulting from motor vehicles and factory emissions have also diminished the sightseeing experience. As a solution, the civic authorities have regularly banned private vehicles from the city centre, usually on a rota basis, in an attempt to reduce the *nefos* (smog) which endangers both health and historic monuments. The 2004 Olympics was the catalyst for urban regeneration, with infrastructure improvements such as a new airport and metro system. Two and three star hotels were upgraded, while manufacturing industries were given incentives to move out of the city.

The capital's main attractions include:

- The Acropolis, the fortified hill which was the core of ancient Athens, containing a number of important temples such as the Parthenon, are reminders of the glory of Ancient Greece. The site is now interpreted by a fine new museum.
- The Agora, once the market place of Athens in Classical and Roman times, which has only partly been excavated. There are plans to unite all these sites as one archaeological park.
- To the east of the city lie a number of beach resorts – the so called 'Apollo Coast' which are mainly visited by domestic tourists and day trippers.
- To the south of Piraeus are the Argo-Saronic Islands, the most popular being Aegina, while Spetses is perhaps the most attractive, providing a welcome relief from the extreme summer heat and congestion of Athens.
- To the north-west is the classical site of Delphi in its beautiful mountain setting. This was an important place of pilgrimage in ancient times.

In northern Greece, the well-wooded Halkidiki Peninsula with its fine beaches has been developed for recreational tourism, with yacht marinas, golf courses and holiday villages. The area is close to Thessaloniki, which is second in importance only to Athens as a business centre. This city tends to be overlooked by tour operators, although it is a significant cultural destination with a legacy of Classical and Byzantine architecture. On the other hand, the more recent Ottoman heritage of mosques and bath-houses is neglected, largely because Thessaloniki (formerly Salonica) was under Turkish rule until 1912. Elsewhere, the emphasis has been on selective tourism to:

- stem rural depopulation;
- revive traditional village industries; and
- conserve the region's natural and cultural heritage.

Attempts to develop winter sports tourism in the Pindus Mountains as a means of reducing seasonality have not been particularly successful, and northern Greece is mainly visited for its national parks – the Vikos gorge is outstanding – and its cultural attractions, such as the monasteries of Meteora in their spectacular setting.

The Greek islands

Of the hundreds of Greek islands, relatively few are served by regular ferry or hydrofoil services, and an even smaller number have been developed for international tourism. Each of these islands offers a unique product on the basis of its scenery and cultural heritage, rather than the quality of its beaches.

Crete is the largest by far of the islands, with a coastline almost 1,000 kilometres in length, and a mountainous interior where the traditional lifestyle has persisted to a greater extent than elsewhere in Greece, contrasting with the well-developed international tourism scene along the north coast. Mallia has borne the brunt of mass tourism, while Aghios Nikalaos, with its attractive harbour has remained more up-market. Crete can offer those tourists looking for more than beaches and nightlife:

- the heritage of Venetian rule in towns such as Chania;
- the Samaria Gorge, one of the most impressive examples of its kind in Europe (unfortunately, its very popularity with hikers has caused ecological damage to this national park and disruption to its wildlife); and
- the impressive remains of the Minoan civilisation at Knossos, the source of the Minotaur myth. This too is popular with tourists on day excursions from the nearby resorts. Phaestos on the less visited south coast is an uncrowded alternative.

The **Cyclades** are generally rather barren in appearance, and the small island communities are characterised by their white cube-shaped buildings, interspersed with tiny blue and white chapels. On these and other Aegean islands, we can usually identify two types of tourist centre, which are complementary in terms of the facilities they provide – the port, and the *chora*, the traditional focus of island life – often situated some distance inland. The most popular islands in the group are:

- Mykonos perhaps most closely resembles the tourist stereotype of a Greek island, but it is in fact a sophisticated resort, with expensive bars and boutiques, and a large gay clientele;
- Paros as a hub of the Aegean ferry network is ideal for the independent traveller;
- Ios likewise attracts swarms of young backpackers during July and August, on account of its fine beaches and non-stop nightlife;
- Naxos contains more scenic variety and is the most fertile of the islands (until the completion of a new airport with European Union funding in 1990, tourism took second place to agriculture and is still relatively low-impact in nature); and
- Santorini (Thira) is undoubtedly the most spectacular of the Greek islands. It features prominently on cruise itineraries, thanks to its unique volcanic scenery – the harbour is the centre of a huge caldera – and the remains of the Minoan city of Akrotiri, buried by a volcanic eruption circa 1500 BC.

Skiathos is the most popular island in the group known as the **Sporades** in the north-west Aegean, thanks to a combination of pine-covered landscapes and fine beaches;

Skyros, in contrast, has developed a niche market in 'holistic community' holidays as a solution to the stress of modern life.

The islands of the **north-east Aegean** include Lesbos, Samos and Chios. Here agriculture and shipping continue to be the mainstays of the local economy, rather than tourism, which is dominated by the domestic market.

The **Dodecanese** are a group of twelve islands situated far from the Greek mainland and close to the coast of south-west Turkey. Their cultural heritage is different from other Greek islands as they were ruled successively by the Knights of St John, the Ottoman Empire from the sixteenth century until 1912, and then by Italy until the Second World War. For the most part they are relatively undeveloped for tourism, with the exceptions of Kos and Rhodes where mass tourism has made a major impact. By the late 1990s Rhodes had a capacity of 50,000 registered bed spaces or 10 per cent of the stock for Greece as a whole. This large island offers natural attractions such as the 'Valley of the Butterflies' at Petaloudes, and many heritage sites, as well as a number of cultural events, festivals and *son et lumière* shows bringing history to life. The old town of Rhodes retains its medieval walls, castle and hospital built by the Knights of St John. The main touring circuit is along the east coast to the picturesque town of Lindos which has been carefully preserved, and where almost all the accommodation consists of rented rooms with local families. In contrast, Faliraki is characterised by unplanned hotel and self-catering development, and has acquired notoriety as a resort catering primarily for the British youth market. Rhodes needs to diversify its markets to reduce its dependence on package tours and overcome the problem of seasonality.

The **Ionian Islands** include three popular destinations – Corfu (Kerkira), Cephalonia and Zante (Zakinthos). They are mountainous but fertile, with a softer climate than the Aegean islands and a greener landscape. Their cultural heritage reflects a long period of rule by the Republic of Venice, and also British occupation (from 1815 until 1864).

Corfu has for long been a favourite with British holidaymakers, and a large number of resorts have developed, particularly along the east coast, although the west coast has the best beaches. Mass tourism has had an adverse effect on Corfu, particularly in Ipsos and Benitses that have become mass-market resorts, while Kavos is very much an enclave for the youth market, attracted by its throbbing nightlife. In contrast, the town of Corfu has a number of cultural attractions.

Cephalonia and Zante have less to offer in this respect, as they were badly affected by an earthquake in 1956 and underwent subsequent rebuilding. Zante is the more popular of the two and much of the development for the package holiday market has been insensitive, especially in the resort of Laganas. The island is a good example of the struggle between environmentalists, who want part of the coast to be designated as a marine national park, and local hotel developers and boat operators eager to increase their profits. Tourism to Cephalonia has been boosted by the popular film *Captain Corelli's Mandolin*.

Discussion point

The study of Greek classical literature and ancient history declined in British and American schools and colleges in the course of the twentieth century, and as a result few tourists today have more than a superficial knowledge of the heritage of Ancient Greece. Discuss whether the tourist authorities in Greece could do more to interpret and 'bring to life' this heritage for the foreign visitor. Can movies such as *Troy, 300* (the battle of Thermopylae in 490 BC between Spartans and Persians), and *Alexander the Great* have a role in stimulating interest in Ancient Greece among the general public?

EUROPE

The Balkan countries

Between 1945 and 1989 most of the countries of the Balkan Peninsula, with the important exceptions of Greece and Turkey, formed part of the Communist Eastern Bloc, sharply differentiated in their political and economic make-up from the countries to the west of the 'Iron Curtain'. However, this impression of unity was to a large extent imposed by the Soviet Union following its victory in the Second World War, and concealed the deep-seated differences between the many and varied ethnic groups which make up the population of the region. Most countries had substantial ethnic minorities at variance with the majority culture, and all had experienced long periods of foreign rule. Most of the region formed part of the Ottoman Empire, but Croatia, Dalmatia, Slovenia and Transylvania were ruled until 1918 by the Habsburg Empire based in Vienna and Budapest, and as such, tended to be more advanced in their social and economic development than their neighbours to the east of the Dinaric Alps and south of the Carpathians. The period between the First and Second World Wars was marked by the political instability caused by these tensions in the new independent nations, particularly Yugoslavia. During the era of Soviet domination, the Black Sea beaches of Bulgaria and Romania were, in some respects, the East European equivalent of the Spanish costas, attracting sun-seeking tourists from the more developed socialist countries of Poland, East Germany and Czechoslovakia. Since the collapse of Communism, the Balkan countries have made progress in varying degrees toward democracy and closer association with Western Europe. In 2004 Slovenia was among the 'accession states' to join the EU, followed two years later by Bulgaria and Romania. Croatia is next in line, while Montenegro has already adopted the euro as its currency. Membership of the European Union should encourage investment in tourism, and boost demand in countries where travel propensities are relatively low.

Albania

The change from Communism to a free market economy has perhaps been most traumatic in Albania, which is also the poorest and least developed of the former Eastern Bloc states. Although only a narrow stretch of water separates it from Corfu, the country was virtually unknown, let alone frequented by tourists until the 1990s. A small mountainous nation, known to its people as Shqipri (land of the eagles), Albania is different in language and culture from its Greek and Slav neighbours. In 1991, following the fall of Communism, the government envisaged ambitious plans for tourism development, under a new Ministry of Construction and Tourism. There is little doubt that the country has considerable potential, including an extensive and as yet unspoiled Mediterranean coastline where ramshackle developments are now being cleared away, spectacular lake and mountain scenery, and potential ecotourism based on the great biodiversity of the country with its bears, lynx and golden eagles. However, Western-style tourism has been held back for the following reasons:

- The historical legacy of the hard-line Communist regime established by Enver Hoxha between 1945 and 1989, which imposed a policy of economic self-sufficiency, closed mosques and churches, and isolated the Albanian people from contacts with foreigners. Some 700,000 concrete bunkers survive as reminders of that time.
- Inadequate infrastructure. The road network is poorly developed, with horse-drawn vehicles impeding the traffic flow. Many mountain villages remain inaccessible by

road. External transport links by road, air and ferry are limited, there are constant power cuts, and water supplies are of poor quality.

- Lack of investment due to the poor state of the economy. It could be said that 40 years of collectivisation and a closed economy were followed by rampant individualism and unregulated capitalism. The collapse of get-rich-quick 'pyramid' investment schemes in the 1990s discredited government attempts to introduce a free market economy. Since 2000 the construction industry (much of it illegal) and remittances from Albanian emigrants have sustained the economy.
- Political instability. In the northern part of Albania there has been a resurgence of the traditional blood feuds between clans that characterised much of the country's pre-1945 history, and visitor safety cannot be guaranteed.

By 2005 inbound arrivals exceeded 700,000 a year, and domestic tourism was a significant growth sector. To provide for this market, the European Bank for Reconstruction and Development (EBRD) is closely involved with the funding of facilities suitable for Western tourists, such as hotels, holiday villages and campgrounds with a total capacity of around 8,000 beds. Most of the development will be on the coast, particularly south of Vlore. The EBRD would like developers to concentrate on a relatively few upmarket projects. However, the Albanian government desperately needs the foreign exchange earnings from tourism to modernise the country's infrastructure, and some observers fear that this will put pressure on Albania's unique ecological and cultural resources. These include:

- The archaeological sites at Apolonia and Butrint – the 'lost city' of the ancient Illyrian civilisation, and one of the best-preserved classical sites in the Mediterranean. Because of its accessibility from the beach resort of Ksamil and Corfu, Butrint may have to cope with visitor numbers well beyond its present capacity.
- The mountains of the interior. These contain a number of medieval fortress-towns which played a major role in the Albanian struggle for freedom against the Ottoman Empire; of these Berat, Gijrokastro and Kruje are the most important.
- The lakes on the borders with Macedonia and Montenegro.

The changes that have taken place in Albania since the fall of Communism are mainly evident in the capital, Tirana, which has tripled in population since 1990. Under Hoxha the city was effectively a car-free zone, but it now has severe traffic problems, exacerbated by the lack of planning and infrastructure. The private sector, often with Italian financial backing, is providing hotels and restaurants in competition with Albturist, the state travel organisation.

The republics of the former Yugoslavia

The pre-1991 Yugoslavia has been described as an experiment to unite many peoples of widely differing languages (including two alphabets), religions and historical backgrounds. It was a federation of six republics – Serbia, Croatia, Slovenia, Bosnia-Herzegovina, Macedonia and Montenegro – and two autonomous regions – Kosovo and Vojvodina. This complex arrangement was made to work largely through the authority of Marshal Tito, who ruled the country from 1945 to 1979. Furthermore, as a non-aligned country following Tito's break with Stalin, Yugoslavia set out earlier to attract foreign investment, and was far more successful than Bulgaria or Romania in attracting package holidaymakers from Western Europe. In 1960 Yugotours was set up to market the country and in 1965 restrictions on the movement of foreign visitors were removed. In the same year the Adriatic Highway was completed with Western aid, permitting the development of resort facilities along the coast from Istria to Montenegro. By 1988 Yugoslavia was attracting 9 million foreign visitors annually, but these were highly concentrated geographically on the Adriatic coast, while the former West Germany accounted for a third of the total. Although domestic tourism was mainly accommodated in low-cost holiday villages away from the main Adriatic resorts, Yugoslavs were not discouraged from contact with Western tourists at home and had greater freedom than other East Europeans to travel to Western countries.

However, the communist system of 'worker's control' caused problems in hotel administration and marketing, and did little to encourage private enterprise. The ending of the Cold War also brought about the revival of nationalism and ethnic rivalries, initiated by Serbia. This caused the break-up of the Federation, swiftly followed by a series of wars that lasted throughout most of the 1990s. Needless to say, this was disastrous for the tourism industries of the former Yugoslavia, although the republics of Croatia and Slovenia have now recovered most of their former popularity.

Croatia

Croatia has both Mediterranean and central European characteristics in its national make-up. The country can offer the visitor a great diversity of landscapes and cultural attractions and a well-established tourism industry. The coastline is deeply indented, extending to 5,800 kilometres if we include the thousand or so islands in the Adriatic. The coastal regions of Istria and Dalmatia are protected by the parallel ranges of the Dinaric Alps from the cold winters experienced in the interior. However, where there are gaps in the mountains, the blustery *Bora* wind can be disruptive in spring and autumn. The eastern part of Croatia, known as Slavonia, is plains country similar to neighbouring Hungary. The west on the other hand is mountainous, and here we can find some of the best examples of karst limestone scenery in Europe, culminating in the lakes and waterfalls of the Plitvice National Park.

Croatia accounted for over 80 per cent of tourist nights in registered accommodation in the former Yugoslavia during the late 1980s, but received a much smaller proportion of the revenue from tourism, which was shared out among the other republics in the federation. Nevertheless, tourism did much to benefit the economy of the Dalmatian islands and stemmed out-migration, which was a problem in the early part of the twentieth century. With the apparent resolution of the ethnic strife in Bosnia and Kosovo, the country has regained its position as a major holiday destination, but this time as an independent nation. The revival, spearheaded by the Ministry of Tourism through a privatisation policy, has attracted a flow of investment into the tourism sector since 2000. The Croatian National Tourist Board promotes the country as 'The Mediterranean as it used to be' with an emphasis on culture and unspoiled nature. In 2007 Croatia attracted 10.8 million arrivals, The great majority of foreign tourists come from neighbouring countries and central Europe. Germany is in the lead with over 20 per cent of overnight stays, followed by Italy, Slovenia, Austria, the Czech Republic and Hungary. Croatia has been slower to regain its pre-1990 popularity with British tourists, who account for only 3 per cent of arrivals, mainly on inclusive tour holidays. The domestic market is relatively small, accounting for only 10 per cent of overnight stays.

Croatia has a good transport infrastructure, with international airports at Zagreb and Dubrovnik, and Croatian Airways as its national carrier. Ferries operate from the ports of Rijeka and Split to Italy and Greece, and a network of hydrofoil services links the Dalmatian islands to the mainland.

Much of the tourism development since the 1960s has been in the form of self-contained hotel and apartment complexes, such as the Babin Kuk peninsula near the historic city of Dubrovnik and the 'Makarska Riviera'. However, 'hotels and resorts' accounted for less than 20 per cent of the available bedspaces in 2006. Private houses make up the largest category of accommodation, followed by campgrounds, which are mainly used by tourists from central Europe. Marinas also provide a significant supply of accommodation.

Tourism in Croatia is largely based on the coastal resources of Istria and Dalmatia, and has a long history. For example, Opatija, which has good road and rail links to Central Europe, was a fashionable resort for the Austrian and Hungarian elites before the First World War, when it was known by its Italian name, Abbazia. The Istrian Peninsula has good beaches, easy access to Italy, and the major resorts of Porec and Rovinj. Dalmatia offers more spectacular scenery, but its disadvantage for family holidays is the lack of sandy beaches. The numerous sheltered deep-water harbours have encouraged cruising and sailing, while the clear unpolluted sea is ideal for diving and bathing. Some of the Dalmatian islands – such as Brioni and the Kornati group – are protected as national parks, while others – notably Hvar, Korcula and Rab – have been developed as holiday resorts.

The coast can also offer a rich cultural heritage, including:

* important Roman remains, such as the arena at Pula, and the impressive remains of the palace of the Emperor Diocletian, which now form part of the old quarter of Split;
* the architecture of the coastal towns and islands, showing the influence of Venice, which was the major power in the region in medieval times; and
* Dubrovnik, an almost perfect example of a medieval seaport, complete with city walls and pedestrianised streets and squares. The buildings damaged by the Serbian bombardment of 1991/92 have been meticulously restored, while the international summer festival continues to be a major attraction.

Away from the coast, tourism in Croatia mainly gravitates to the capital, Zagreb. This is an attractive historic city as well as being an important business centre, hosting conferences, international trade fairs, and sports events.

Slovenia

With a small area of 20,000 square kilometres and a population of only 2 million, Slovenia has nevertheless a broad tourism appeal and the government has implemented an ambitious tourism marketing and development strategy, boosting international arrivals to nearly 3 million by 2010. The country was economically advanced compared to most of the former Yugoslavia, and its state carrier, Adria Airways, has energetically promoted business travel from Western Europe to replace the loss of Yugoslav markets for its products.

Although Slovenia has only a short stretch of Adriatic coastline, this includes the popular resort of Portoroz and the seaports of Piran and Koper with their Venetian-style architecture. Other attractions include the spectacular and much-visited network of caves at Postojna, the equestrian centre at Lipica, and a number of themed touring routes. Austrian influence is particularly evident in the attractive capital, Ljubljana, and in the mountain villages of the Julian Alps, which resemble those of the Tyrol.

Winter sports facilities have long been established at Kranjska Gora, Bovec and Rogla, while the lake resorts of Bled and Bohinj provide a range of summer activities.

Montenegro

Montenegro's biggest asset is its section of the Adriatic Coast, which includes some good beaches and the magnificent Gulf of Kotor (which contrary to most travel guides, is a tectonic feature, not a fjord). International-style resorts were developed in the 1960s at Budva and Sveti Stefan – which is unique in being a one-time fishing village converted to a luxury hotel complex. The interior of Montenegro, with its stony mountains, deep gorges, and 'eagles nest' villages, is very different from the lush greenery of the coast, and is much less developed for tourism. The former capital, Cetinje, is a reminder that Montenegro was an independent kingdom before the First World War, and this small city, approached by a spectacular road, is one of the curiosities of the Balkans. Inbound tourism has suffered from the effects of the sanctions directed at the Serbian regime in Belgrade and the Kosovo refugee crisis in 1999, and for a time the industry was dependent on holidaymakers from Serbia. Since regaining independence from Serbia in 2006, Montenegro's Ministry of Tourism and the Environment has focused on Western markets and tried to develop products other than beach tourism. The coast accounts for 95 per cent of all overnight stays, which are moreover concentrated in July and August. The former Yugoslav/Soviet naval base at Tivat has been transformed into an upmarket resort with marina facilities for wealthy tourists, while prime seafront sites are being bought for second homes by Russians and other foreign developers taking advantage of weak planning controls. Some see it as ironic that Montenegrins, who fought so hard to maintain their independence from the Ottoman Empire, risk losing their birthright to international tourism.

Serbia

Serbia's tourism industry has been handicapped by its landlocked situation, and throughout the 1990s by economic sanctions, culminating in the NATO bombing raids of 1999. Prior to the break-up of Yugoslavia, Belgrade, as the capital of the federation, was a major business and conference centre, and Serbia received a large volume of transit traffic en route to Greece or Turkey. Winter sports facilities were developed at Kopaonik and Zlatibor, but these attracted little attention from foreign tour operators. In 2008 Serbia attracted little more than half a million predominantly short-stay foreign visitors.

The Vojvodina region of Serbia north of the Danube is characterised by fertile lowland landscapes similar to those of Hungary, and quite different to the rest of the country, which is hilly or mountainous. Serbia's cultural heritage includes a number of medieval Orthodox monasteries – Studenica and Sopocani are World Heritage Sites – but these are little appreciated in the West compared to the art treasures of Croatia. The cities of Belgrade and Novi Sad have promoted festival tourism to attract visitors, and this may explain why Serbia took the hosting of the 2008 Eurovision Song Contest so seriously, as it marked the return to international acceptance after years of ostracism. The future of international tourism will depend to an extent on political stability, the curbing of extreme nationalist movements, and not least, whether Serbia can come to terms with the independence of Kosovo. This is problematic, as the 'Field of Blackbirds', where the Serbs suffered a catastrophic defeat by the Turks in 1389, is situated in the breakaway republic.

Kosovo

This part of the former Yugoslavia, smaller than Yorkshire in area, is predominantly Albanian in language and culture. Its independence in 2008 was recognised by the USA and most EU countries, but not by China and Russia, and it is probable that a NATO military presence will continue to be necessary to protect the Serb community and other ethnic minorities. Tourism resources are limited to the capital, Pristina, a number of Orthodox monasteries and a small ski resort.

Macedonia

Provisionally known as FYRM – the former Yugoslav Republic of Macedonia – in deference to Greece, this small country was the poorest region of Yugoslavia before independence. The re-opening of the Greek border has allowed Macedonia to develop its trade and fledgling tourism industry. This is based not so much on Skopje the capital, which was rebuilt after a major earthquake in 1963, but on Ohrid, which is scenically located on the deepest lake in Europe.

Bosnia-Herzegovina

Bosnia's war-ravaged economy and refugee crises have allowed even less scope for tourism than the other republics and considerable reconstruction is needed. The 1995 Dayton Agreement secured an uneasy peace after three years of civil war on the basis of power-sharing between the three principal ethnic groups – the Muslims, the Croats and the Serbs. In the former Yugoslavia, Bosnia's diversity of cultures and religions was no small part of its appeal for foreign visitors, most of whom were based in Dubrovnik and other holiday resorts on the Adriatic coast. Tourists were particularly attracted to the old Turkish quarter of Sarajevo, and the picturesque Turkish bridge over the River Neretva at Mostar, a casualty of the civil war which was restored in 2005. The Yugoslav federal government also invested heavily in Sarajevo as the venue for the 1984 Winter Olympics, as part of its policy to spread the benefits of tourism from the coast to the mountainous interior. Since 2008 Sarajevo has experienced a tourism revival, with visitors from many countries viewing the relics of the epic siege from 1991 to 1993. The city also hosts a major film festival as a mark of its resurgence. Pilgrimages to Medjugorje continue to flourish, despite a lack of government encouragement or, for that matter, approval by the Vatican. Since 1981 this formerly obscure Croat village in Herzegovina has attracted well over 30 million Roman Catholics, making it a shrine of worldwide significance.

Bulgaria

Bulgaria is a small country in the heart of the Balkan Peninsula, which is best known in Western Europe for budget-priced beach and skiing holidays. It does, however, offer a great variety of scenery and is rich in the remains of many civilisations. The country is traversed from east to west by several thickly forested mountain ranges, rising to over 2,000 metres, which attract heavy snowfalls in winter. Between the mountains lie fertile valleys enjoying a warm sunny climate which have given Bulgaria its reputation as 'the market garden of Eastern Europe', producing fine tobacco and the famous perfume known as 'attar of roses'. Before the violent break-up of Yugoslavia, the country received a good deal of transit tourism due to its location on the E5 route from

Belgrade to Istanbul. Proximity to Turkey in the past was a disadvantage, resulting in Bulgaria being submerged in the Ottoman Empire for several centuries. It regained its independence, with Russian help, in 1878 – a fact commemorated by the elaborate Alexander Nevsky Cathedral in Sofia. Despite the presence of Turkish and Pomak (native Muslim) minorities, the Islamic contribution to the cultural heritage has been neglected. Restoration projects have focused instead on the 'museum towns' such as Veliki Turnovo, which played a major role in the medieval period or in the National Revival leading to independence.

The country was one of Europe's poorest and most underdeveloped before the Second World War, with over 80 per cent of the population employed in agriculture. The development of an industrial economy since the 1950s has greatly improved living standards, while the introduction of the two-day weekend encouraged the ownership of second homes, which are situated mainly around the capital Sofia and on the Black Sea coast. As in other East European countries, spas play an important role, the most popular being Sandanski, Kustendil, Hissarya, and Velingrad. However, throughout the 1990s the country suffered a severe economic crisis, which has depressed the demand for domestic as well as outbound tourism, although inbound tourism has grown steadily to around 4 million international trips annually.

Bulgaria recognised the importance of tourism as a source of hard currency in the 1960s and concluded agreements with a number of Western tour operators. Balkantourist was the state agency responsible for international tourism, owning most of the large stock of hotel accommodation, particularly on the Black Sea coast. As a result, most Western visitors are on low-budget inclusive packages and the rate of return per individual tourist is small. Since the collapse of the Communist regime Bulgaria has moved towards a free market economy, encouraging joint ventures with Western hotel and banking enterprises and encouraging investment in transport and tourism infrastructure. The Ministry of Economy implements tourism policy, working with the Bulgarian national tourist board and various industry organisations. They are supported by a regional and local network of tourist organisations.

We can identify three key resources that Bulgaria can offer the visitor:

1 the beaches of the Black Sea coast;
2 skiing in the mountains; and
3 culture and ecology for special interest tourism.

The **Black Sea coast** of Bulgaria receives the majority of tourists in the country and is the location of almost two–thirds of the bedspaces. It is scenically more varied than that of Romania with fine beaches that are ideal for family holidays. Resort development has centred around Varna in the north – where Zlatni Pyasatsi (Golden Sands), Albena, and Drouzhba are the main resorts – and Bourgas in the south – where Slunchev Bryag (Sunny Beach) is the most popular centre. Most of these resorts offer international entertainments and are rather characterless; however, the holiday village of Dyuni has been developed in a more traditional style. Since the 1990s some of the accommodation has been upgraded to meet international quality standards by Spanish and other Western hotel chains.

Bulgaria is also a **winter sports** destination with major resorts at Borovets and Bansko in the Pirin Mountains; Aleko on Mount Vitosha which caters for large numbers of weekend skiers from nearby Sofia; and Pamporovo in the Rhodope Massif. However, facilities, although improving, are not as sophisticated as those of the Alps, and the Balkan ranges cannot offer the high-altitude skiing favoured by Western tour operators.

There is more scope for future development in promoting **special interest holidays.** These include 'eco-paths', spas, wine tours, musical folklore (the country is noted for its fine choirs), archaeology (the Thracian civilisation was probably the earliest in Europe), and caving. Bulgaria is also noted for its monasteries, often situated in remote mountain settings where the Orthodox Church preserved the national identity during the centuries of Ottoman rule. The most famous of these are those of Rila to the south of Sofia and Boyana on the outskirts of the capital. For such cultural tourism to be successful, more attention needs to be paid to improving accessibility and visitor management facilities to a standard appropriate for Western tourists.

Romania

Romania is the largest country in the Balkan region, with a population of 21.5 million. The Romanian people regard themselves as different – Latins surrounded by Slavs – but although in language and temperament they are akin to Italians, their religion is Orthodox, and the climate is definitely continental, with severely cold winters, rather than Mediterranean. The forested Carpathian Mountains divide the country in a great horseshoe-shaped arc, separating picturesque Transylvania from the broad plains of Wallachia to the south and the rolling plateau of Moldavia to the east. Whereas Wallachia and Moldavia were separate principalities on the fringes of the Ottoman Empire until 1858, Transylvania was part of Hungary until 1918. As a result, Transylvania has substantial Magyar and German minorities who differ in religion as well as language from the Romanians. There are also perhaps 2 million Roma or gypsies who form a marginalised group in society (as elsewhere in Eastern Europe) but who play an important role in Romanian folklore.

During the 1960s the Romanian government embarked on a major investment programme for the Black Sea coast, creating a number of new holiday resorts. In 1971 a Ministry of Tourism and Sport was established, and the state tourism organisation ONT and its subsidiary Carpati set out to increase numbers of visitors from the West as well as from other socialist countries. During the 1970s they were successful in attracting Western tour operators. However, after 1979 the economic situation in Romania deteriorated and the Ceauçescu regime became increasingly repressive with its 'social engineering' policies. As a result, tourism receipts fell by 40 per cent between 1981 and 1986. The violent overthrow of Ceauçescu in December 1989 was followed by a slow progress toward economic reform. In a bid to upgrade standards and facilities by attracting investment, the Romanian Ministry of Transport, Construction and Tourism implemented a 'master plan for tourism' covering key elements of the industry. These mainly focus on two contrasting areas – the Black Sea coast, and the Carpathian Mountains in the north west of the country.

The flat **Black Sea coast** forms part of the Dobruja region and is scenically the least interesting part of Romania, but offering broad, gently shelving beaches and a holiday season lasting from mid-May to September, it has become the main destination for foreign holidaymakers, and accounts for the majority of all bedspaces. Mamaia is the largest resort, situated on a sandspit between the sea and an extensive lagoon. Like the tourist complexes of Aurora, Jupiter, Neptune, Venus, and Saturn, it offers a variety of accommodation and sports facilities. The older resort of Eforie with its mud-bathing establishments is well known for health tourism. Further north, the Danube Delta is a wetland environment over 4,000 square kilometres in extent, teeming with wildlife and now protected as a nature reserve and a UNESCO biosphere reserve.

The spas and resorts of the **Carpathian Mountains** have not received as much investment as those of the Black Sea. Neither as high nor as rugged as the Alps, the Carpathians form a number of separate massifs, of which the most impressive are the Bucegi and Retezat Mountains, noted for their lakes and glaciated landforms. Exploitation of the region's forest resources has gone hand-in-hand with tourism and there are a large number of dispersed mountain chalets to supplement hotels and campsite accommodation in the resorts. Before the Second World War Sinaia attracted the Romanian aristocracy, but nowadays the main resort is Poiana Brasov, purpose-built for winter sports, but also a centre for hiking and adventure holidays. Between the mountain ranges lies the fertile Transylvanian Plateau, where the rural communities preserve much of their traditional culture. The historic towns have a strong German influence in their architecture, so that the 'Gothic' ambience of Sibiu and the castle of Bran, in its picturesque mountain setting, are inevitably associated with the Dracula legend.

The tourist attractions of **Moldavia** include the capital, Jassy, and the unique painted monasteries of the Bucovina region; amazingly the exterior frescoes have survived since the fifteenth century.

Bucharest, Romania's capital lies in the rather less appealing plains of Wallachia bordering the Danube. The city, with its spacious boulevards, took much of its culture from France and was known before the Second World War as 'the Paris of the East', but it has less to offer the tourist nowadays. This is due to the destruction of many churches during the Ceauçescu era to make way for the dictator's grandiose projects such as the 'House of the Republic'. The Herastrau Village Museum, however, is one of the best of its kind.

Discussion point

The Tara Canyon is situated in the interior of Montenegro, offering scope for white-water rafting and adventure. Like many other natural attractions in the Balkans it is as yet barely exploited for tourism. Discuss the possibilities that different countries in the region have for the following types of sport and recreation:

- Tennis
- Caving and potholing
- Skiing and other winter sports
- Sailing and windsurfing.

What do you think are the factors holding back the development of tourism products based on sport and adventure in the Balkan countries?

Turkey

Although only 3 per cent of its territory – the region known as eastern Thrace – is geographically part of Europe, Turkey belongs to that continent rather than to the Middle East. The country is in many ways distinct from its Arab neighbours to the south, and throughout history has acted as a cultural 'bridge' between East and West. It controls the Dardanelles and the Bosphorus, the strategic waterways linking the

Mediterranean to the Black Sea. Turkey's European credentials are underlined by its participation in a number of sport and cultural events, and the selection of Istanbul as European capital of culture for 2010.

Turkey under the Ottoman Sultans dominated not only much of Europe between the fifteenth and nineteenth centuries but also the Middle East and most of North Africa. However this was a multi-cultural empire quite different in character from the national state of today. The heritage of the Ottoman Empire is a major part of the fascination the country holds for Western visitors. Turkish traditional culture, including one of the world's finest cuisines, craft industries such as carpet weaving, and the performing arts, help to give the country a clearly defined tourist image. Yet for many centuries prior to the arrival of the Turks from Central Asia, the region then known as Asia Minor was occupied by many earlier civilisations, including the Hittites, Ancient Greece, and the Roman and Byzantine empires. Turkey is extraordinarily rich in antiquities as a result, but not all of these are given adequate protection.

Turkey is a large country by European standards, with the natural advantage of having an extensive, and for the most part, picturesque coastline along four seas. The heartland of Turkey is less attractive, largely consisting of the semi-arid steppes of the Anatolian Plateau. This is separated from the fertile coastlands by a ring of mountain ranges. The climate is generally favourable for tourism, except in the mountainous north-east, which suffers from winters of almost Siberian intensity. The Black Sea coast receives a good deal of rain throughout the year, in contrast to the rest of the country, and is noted for its forests and tea plantations.

Compared to most of its neighbours Turkey is politically stable, with an economy that is strong enough for its application for European Union membership to be taken seriously. This is due in no small measure to the reforms carried out by Kamal Atatürk after the abolition of the sultanate in 1923. He imposed Western institutions, the Roman alphabet, and Western dress, and removed organised religion from politics. As a result, the influence of Islam is much less evident than in neighbouring Iran and the Arab countries of the Middle East. Nevertheless, there are contrasts in lifestyles between the cities with a large Westernised middle class and the rural communities of the Anatolian Plateau. Since 2003 the moderate Islamist Justice and Development Party (AKP) has been in power, and many see its success as a challenge to the secular state. As in other developing countries, the population is growing faster than job creation and the provision of public services. This explains the continuing high rate of emigration and the growth of shanty towns (known as *gekekondu*) around Istanbul and Ankara. Another ongoing problem is the unrest among the Kurdish minority in the south-east of the country, with the separatist PKK movement instigating a number of terrorist incidents.

The demand for tourism

With a population of approximately 75 million, there is a large domestic market for tourism, but travel propensities are low by west European standards. Domestic tourists are more evenly spread throughout the country, and are not only attracted to resorts such as Fethiye and Marmaris on the Aegean coast, but also those on the Black Sea, which see few foreign visitors other than backpackers. A number of ski resorts in the northern mountains mainly serve internal demand from Ankara and Istanbul. Domestic tourists and returning Turkish expatriates tend to stay with relatives rather than use hotel accommodation.

Inbound tourism

Despite having much to offer the tourist, Turkey did not participate in the boom in Mediterranean beach tourism that characterised the 1970s because:

* it was expensive to reach;
* the country was poorly promoted; and
* Turkey did not seek to enter the inclusive tour market.

This situation changed when tourism was included in the government's Five Year Plans, charter flights were permitted, and the country was 'discovered' by the major European tour operators. As a result, the numbers of visitors trebled during the 1980s but growth subsequently slowed as a result both of the 1991 Gulf War and also the adverse publicity about the poor standard of some accommodation in the Aegean holiday resorts of Bodrum and Kusadasi. In 2010 Turkey attracted 28.6 million international visitors.

Germany is by far the most important generator of tourism, followed by Russia and the Central Asian republics, which have cultural and business ties with Turkey. The UK was a latecomer on the scene, but despite predictions to the contrary, Turkey's popularity with the British market as a value-for-money destination shows no sign of waning. Business and conference tourism is being encouraged by new convention centres in both Istanbul and Ankara.

The supply side of tourism

Transport

In the early stages of tourism development most visitors arrived by surface transport, but since the 1990s the majority of visitors arrive by air. Istanbul's Atatürk Airport is the busiest gateway, serving the country's leading cultural and business centre, while Ankara, despite being the capital since 1923, ranks far behind in terms of international traffic. A number of regional airports have been developed to serve the west European holiday market in south-west Turkey, namely Izmir, Bodrum-Milas, Dalaman and Antalya. The national carrier Turkish Airlines provides a network of international and domestic services. Travel by road and rail from the main generating countries to Turkey is at a disadvantage, not only because of the distances involved, but also through the delays at border crossings caused by political turmoil in neighbouring countries. Turkish State Railways operates over a limited network, but most internal travel is by road, using inter-city bus services, and over shorter distances by the *dolmus*, a type of collective taxi. Other than cruise passengers and day excursionists from Rhodes, relatively few visitors arrive by sea, although Turkish Maritime Services operate ferries from Izmir to Italy and Greece, and from Mersin to Turkish North Cyprus.

Accommodation

Turkey can offer a considerable stock of both hotel and self-catering accommodation which is mainly used by foreign visitors.

Organisation

Tourism is the responsibility of a minister at cabinet level, and tourism development is included in the government's Five Year Plans for the economy. Holiday tourism is both highly seasonal and concentrated in a small part of the country, namely the south-west coastal strip. This is largely the result of short-sighted planning in the 1980s when the Ministry of Tourism envisaged coastal development on a massive scale to create jobs and maximise foreign exchange earnings.

Tourism resources

South-west Turkey

West European tourists are mainly attracted to the beaches of the southern Aegean coast and the Gulf of Antalya. Club Méditerranée pioneered beach tourism in the 1970s with their holiday villages at Foça, Kusadasi and Kemer. Since that time a number of resorts have experienced most stages in the tourist area life cycle, namely:

- discovery by wealthy Turkish families, yachtsmen and a few backpackers;
- development by small specialist tour operators; and
- consolidation by large companies serving the mass market.

In some resorts the environmental and cultural impact of tourism has been considerable, notably at Marmaris and Gumbet on the Bodrum Peninsula. Bodrum itself, although a lively resort, has preserved much of its Turkish ambience, due largely to its setting on a beautiful bay dominated by a Crusader castle. Elsewhere, as at Olü Deniz, famed for its beautiful beach and lagoon, development has been carefully controlled. In a rare instance, that of the Dalyan delta, development was halted altogether following protests by environmentalists.

The **Turquoise Coast** or 'Turkish Riviera' around the Gulf of Antalya is backed by the pine-covered Lycian and Taurus mountain ranges. The resorts of Antalya, Alanya and Side contain many large up-market hotels, but other resorts, such as Kalkan, lack suitable beaches and are small and less sophisticated. The purpose-built resort of Belek caters mainly for golf tourism.

Case study 16.1

Sailing Turkish-style: a sustainable alternative

The coast of south-west Turkey has the following features that make it ideal for a sailing holiday:

- a shoreline extending for over 1,000 kilometres with many suitable harbours and a scenic hinterland;
- sheltered coves that are inaccessible by road, giving privacy for swimming, sunbathing and beach barbecues;
- a warm, sunny climate with reliable afternoon breezes from May through October.

Bareboat yacht charter is available, but most holidaymakers prefer to relax cruising on a gület, a motor yacht distinguished from other vessels by traditional features in its craftsmanship and design. A number of companies offer cruises lasting from 4 to 14 nights with full board and a Turkish skipper and crew. There is sometimes the option of staying in a hotel at the start or the end of a cruise.

In class, discuss the 'green' credentials of a gület cruise.

The mountains of Lycia provide opportunities for trekking, jeep 'safaris' and white-water rafting. Excursions can also be made from the coastal resorts to the calcified springs at Pammukale, and a number of cultural attractions that include:

- Efes (Ephesus), in ancient times one of the greatest cities of the Roman Empire, and of particular religious significance; with its well-preserved theatre and library it is a 'must see' attraction;
- Bergama (Pergamum) is less well known and as a result, much less crowded;
- the site of the legendary city of Troy, strategically located near the entrance to the Dardanelles; and
- the modern town of Gelibolu (Gallipoli), further north along this vital waterway, was the scene of a major military campaign in the First World War, which attracts large numbers of Australians and New Zealanders for patriotic reasons.

South-east Turkey

The eastern Mediterranean coast extending to the border with Syria has not been developed for beach tourism. The area has potential for cultural tourism, such as the heritage of the ancient cities of Tarsus and Antioch with their biblical associations. To the north, the Anatolian Plateau also has much to offer, although the sites are widely dispersed. They include:

- the strange lunar landscapes of Cappadocia where the soft volcanic rock provided a refuge for early Christian communities, complete with underground churches and cave dwellings;
- the city of Konya, famed for its 'whirling dervishes' – a feature of the mystical Sufi version of Islam; and
- the ancient monuments at Nemrut Dagh, a World Heritage Site. Even in this remote area, visitor management and conservation are major issues.

Istanbul

Istanbul is the major cultural destination for most visitors to Turkey, as the former capital of the Byzantine and Ottoman Empires. This city of 15 million people has become a popular short-break destination for the following reasons:

- it is a major meeting point of East and West, with two bridges across the Bosphorus literally linking Asia to Europe;
- it contains the finest achievement of Byzantine architecture – Aya Sofya (Holy Wisdom), built in the sixth century by the Emperor Justinian as the largest church in Christendom, converted into a mosque by Sultan Mohammed II in 1453, and secularised as a museum by Atatürk;
- the Blue Mosque, with its six minarets, is one of the most outstanding examples of Islamic architecture;
- the Grand Bazaar is a 'must-see' for bargain-hunters, with over 4,000 shops under one roof;
- the Topkapi Palace evokes the splendour, intrigue and mystery of the Ottoman empire, particularly the *harem* or women's quarters; and
- The Cagaloglü Hamman provides the experience of a Turkish bath, another traditional institution of the Muslim world, with separate sections for men and women.

The recreation hinterland of Istanbul includes a number of islands in the Sea of Marmara which attract large numbers of day visitors from the city during the hot summer months.

Cyprus

Cyprus is the third largest of the Mediterranean islands, offering a great variety of coastal and mountain scenery and the heritage of many civilisations. The cultural ties between Greece and Cyprus go back thousands of years, far longer than the periods of Turkish and British rule. This may explain why it is a divided island, occupied by two different ethnic groups – the Greeks and the Turks – separated by language, religion, history and since 1974 by a military/political frontier – the Green Line – which also divides the capital, Nicosia. The Greek-speaking Republic of Cyprus occupies two-thirds of the island, contains 75 per cent of its population, and accounts for perhaps 95 per cent of its tourism industry. The Turkish Republic of North Cyprus (TRNC) on the other hand is not recognised by the international community. The location of Cyprus, only 200 kilometres from Beirut, has meant that tourism is affected not only by the long-running dispute between Greece and Turkey over the island itself, but also by the uncertain political situation in the Middle East. In the 1990–1991 Gulf War, for example, tourism suffered badly.

The demand for tourism

Inbound tourism

Before Cyprus gained independence from Britain in 1960 few tourists visited the island. In the late 1960s it was 'discovered' by British tour operators, since Cyprus (along with Gibraltar and Malta) was part of the 'sterling area' and not subject to the strict currency exchange controls imposed by the British government at that time. After the invasion and occupation of the northern part of the island by the Turkish army in 1974, there was a drastic decline in tourist numbers, as most of the hotel stock was destroyed in the conflict. However, a major investment in tourism facilities in southern Cyprus followed, including the opening of a new airport at Larnaca to replace Nicosia, and the rapid development of Ayia Napa as a resort for the mass market. By 2010 international tourist arrivals had grown to 2.1 million. The British inclusive tour market remains important to the island's tourist industry, using charter flights to the airports at Larnaca and Paphos. There are also substantial numbers of independent British visitors travelling to their holiday villas and retirement homes on the island. As is the case in Greece, the Cyprus government discourages seat-only charters.

Domestic tourism

There is a considerable internal demand for the island's recreational resources, generated not just by the Cypriots themselves, but also by the United Nations peacekeeping force in Nicosia, and the British armed forces stationed at the Sovereign Base of Akrotiri.

The supply side of tourism

The Republic of Cyprus has a more varied resource base for tourism than the TRNC, supported by a good infrastructure and a considerable stock of accommodation of international standard, although there are relatively few first class hotels to attract the top end of the market. Before the 1974 invasion, Famagusta (Magusa) and Kyrenia (Girne), now in the TRNC, were the major resorts of the island. They are much less popular nowadays, as few Western tour operators are prepared to risk retaliation by the Greek or Greek Cypriot authorities by including the TRNC in their programmes. Nevertheless, the best beaches of Cyprus are in the Turkish-occupied zone, and there is also scope for cultural tourism, as the mountains near Kyrenia contain a number of monasteries and castles dating from the time of the Crusades. Apart from Turkish visitors from the mainland, a small but growing number of British and other West European tourists are attracted to the TRNC, arriving on Turkish Airlines flights at Erkan Airport via Istanbul or Izmir. Many of the British visitors have purchased second homes in this part of Cyprus; Greek Cypriots maintain their title to the land is dubious, given the circumstances of the Turkish takeover.

Organisation of tourism in the Republic of Cyprus

Tourism in the Republic of Cyprus is represented at ministerial level as it is so important to the economy (accounting for over 20 per cent of GDP). This over-dependence upon tourism also causes concern regarding the industry's use of scarce resources and its social and environmental impacts. The Cyprus Tourism Organisation (CTO) has promotion, development and licensing responsibilities. In this respect, the CTO is very concerned about the risks of over-development of the coastline – already evident in resorts such as Limassol and Ayia Napa – and is aiming for high quality, high-spending tourism by upgrading the tourism product. It has successfully promoted the island as an all-year round destination, and as a result the Scandinavian countries and Germany have become important generators of tourism to Cyprus. The CTO is also actively seeking new markets, notably Russia, Israel and the Arab states of the Middle East.

Tourism resources of the Republic of Cyprus

We can summarise the main tourism products of the Republic of Cyprus as follows:

- Beach tourism, based on major resort developments at Paphos, Limassol, Larnaca and Ayia Napa. The trend is to go up-market with the provision of golf courses and yacht marinas, although Ayia Napa is likely to appeal mainly to the mass market, particularly young tourists interested in the vibrant club scene.
- Conferences and incentive travel are catered for by the larger resort hotels and a conference centre in Nicosia.
- Agro-tourism in the rural villages which are being carefully restored to attract visitors to the 'traditional Cyprus'.
- Ecotourism, specifically birdwatching in the Akamas National Park, the one remaining undeveloped stretch of coastline in the south-west of Cyprus.
- Skiing during the winter months in the pine-covered Troodos Mountains. During the summer, mountain resorts such as Platres continue to be visited by Cypriots escaping the intense summer heat of the plains around Nicosia. There are a number of small country hotels.
- Business tourism in Limassol and Larnaca (which is being positioned as a hub for air services to the Middle East). Tourism in Nicosia is discouraged by the political situation, but the city has nevertheless become an important communications and financial centre for a large part of the Middle East.
- Cultural tourism based on the heritage of Cyprus includes Ancient Greek theatres at Kourion (now used for music festivals) and Amathus; Byzantine monasteries; Crusader castles; and Islamic monuments from the Ottoman Empire.
- Cruises to the Greek islands, Israel and Egypt from the port of Limassol.

The Republic of Cyprus was admitted to the European Union in 2004, but the future growth of tourism will depend to a large extent on the reunification of the island under a federal system of government with the agreement of Turkey. In the meantime, a limited amount of cross-border traffic is taking place.

Summary

- With the exception of Greece, which has a long tradition of cultural tourism, most countries in the region are comparative latecomers to the industry.
- The heritage of the Ottoman empire is evident in the culinary and architectural resources of most countries in the region.
- Political instability and ethnic strife has been a feature of most countries in the region, partly as a legacy of Ottoman rule.
- Most of these countries have benefited from their accessibility to the tourist-generating countries of central and northern Europe and the demand for 'sun, sand and sea' holidays.
- Travel propensities throughout the region are low, and outbound and domestic tourism are much less significant than incoming tourism.
- The primary resources are the attractive coastal and mountain environments, while the Mediterranean climate of the islands is ideal for recreational tourism. The islands of Greece, Croatia and Cyprus also have a rich cultural heritage, blending south European and Middle Eastern influences; however, cultural tourism tends to take second place to beach holidays.
- Cultural attractions include well-preserved archaeological sites, Orthodox monasteries, Crusader castles and music festivals.
- One of the main problems facing tourism is a pronounced summer peak in demand, especially in Greece. Attempts to develop winter tourism have met with little success, with the notable exception of Cyprus.
- The domination of the industry by foreign tour operators makes it difficult for local entrepreneurs to respond with new quality products as the markets are price-sensitive.
- After a long period of neglect, there is a growing awareness by the authorities in each country of the need to protect the coastal and mountain environments, as well as the archaeological heritage, from the impacts of mass tourism.

Assignments

1 Compare the Greek Islands, Croatia, Montenegro, and Turkey as destinations for sailing holidays.
2 Explain why the heritage of ancient Greece is important for the tourism industry of modern Greece.
3 Describe the cultural features, including food specialities, traditional crafts etc. that are shared by most of the countries in the region.
4 Explain why most north European tourists visit Turkey and Cyprus for recreation rather than for cultural reasons.
5 Identify the factors that are holding back the development of tourism in the Balkan countries.

CHAPTER

The tourism geography of Eastern Europe, Russia and the CIS

Introduction

Eastern Europe is the name given to the great tract of land, over a million square kilometres in area, extending from the Baltic to the Black Sea. It has acquired a special identity mainly for political reasons since 1945, but its historical background puts it definitely in the mainstream of European culture. This is particularly true of the Czech Republic, Slovakia and Hungary which can be considered as part of Central Europe, because of their geographical location and a cultural heritage that these countries share with Austria and Germany. Russia, on the other hand, includes vast Asian territories extending to the Pacific Ocean, and most of the former USSR lies outside Europe. Except in a few favoured coastal areas, the climate is definitely continental, with much colder winters than are experienced in the same latitudes in Western Europe.

Between 1945 and 1989 the countries of Eastern Europe could be said to form a political and economic region sharply differentiated from those on the western side of the 'Iron Curtain'. Together with Bulgaria and Romania, these countries were closely associated with the Soviet Union (USSR) as the Eastern Bloc. However, the imposition of unity under Communism concealed the deep-seated differences between the many ethnic groups that make up the population of the region. A case can be made for dividing 'Eastern Europe' and the former Soviet Union into three groups of countries:

- The first group of countries – the Czech Republic, Slovakia, Hungary, Poland, and the Baltic States – are the most advanced economically and have a strong cultural orientation towards the West, and as we saw in the last chapter, the same is true of Slovenia and Croatia in the former Yugoslavia.
- The second group includes Russia, Belarus and Ukraine, which share similar east Slavic languages, history and culture. These countries were the founder members of

the Commonwealth of Independent States (CIS), following the break-up of the USSR in 1991.

- The third group includes the countries south of the Caucasus and those of Central Asia, which culturally have more in common with Turkey and the Middle East than with Russia.

The historical setting for tourism demand

Nevertheless, the adoption of Communism as the political and economic model, first by Russia after 1917 and then by the countries of Eastern Europe after 1945, has had a profound effect on tourism in the region. Communism, which entails the state ownership of the means of production and distribution, influenced both the nature of the demand for tourism and recreation and the type of facilities that were on offer. Governments in the so-called 'socialist' or 'peoples' republics' had virtual monopoly control over all aspects of tourism from strategic planning to owning and managing accommodation. Public institutions were closely involved in 'social tourism' or 'trade union tourism' by subsidising workers' holidays and providing tourist facilities. The type of holidays on offer differed fundamentally from commercial mass tourism as it developed in the West.

Some East European countries had well-developed tourism industries before 1939, but, with the notable exception of Czechoslovakia, the majority of the population were too poor to afford holidays. Following the Communist take-over, the luxury hotels in spas, seaside resorts, and cities were nationalised and put to other uses. Concern for leisure and tourism revived in the 1960s when the economic restructuring was well under way, and considerations of housing, education, and health care were less pressing. The rights of all citizens to recreational opportunities had been recognised in the constitutions drawn up by the new republics. Pressure for longer holidays and two-day weekends coincided with the growing movement from the rural areas to the industrial cities. Demand also grew for the introduction of leisure goods, including cars, although choice was greatly restricted and ownership levels remained at only a fraction of those in the West. Domestic holidays were customarily spent at the seaside or in spas, where rather spartan accommodation was provided, often in the form of holiday villages or workers' sanatoria, provided by the government-controlled trade unions. However, the *nomenklatura* – the Communist Party elite and other favoured groups – had access to more luxurious facilities, including, in some cases, private beaches and hunting reserves. In the cities, the government provided generous subsidies to the arts and cultural attractions that to some extent compensated for the restrictions and consumer shortages that made everyday life drab for most citizens. The rich folklore of the various ethnic groups was also encouraged as a tourist attraction.

Demand for outbound international tourism grew slowly due to currency and visa restrictions. Inevitably, most outbound travel was to other socialist countries and its volume was regulated by bilateral agreements between the governments of the region. Inbound tourism from the West was initially viewed with suspicion, but in most countries was actively sought from the 1960s, as it earned hard currency to purchase much-needed imports from outside the COMECON trading bloc. Indeed, Western visitors had privileges denied to most of the population, as they could buy goods from so-called 'dollar shops', which accepted only hard currencies. Giving preference to group travel, which could be carefully supervised, was one way of ensuring favourable publicity for 'socialist achievements'. However, low standards of service, outdated infrastructure, and bureaucratic controls inhibited the growth of international tourism, while the simple lack of bedspaces held back domestic tourism.

The dramatic political changes which have taken place in Eastern Europe and the former Soviet Union since 1989 have had a profound effect on the pattern of tourism development. The state tourism organisations, which were, in effect, tour operators and travel agencies like the USSR's Intourist, lost their monopoly position. A range of new organisations have since emerged, including private companies, co-operatives and state-run concerns, all placing a greater emphasis on marketing. The prospect of local community involvement in decision-making, instead of the 'top-down' approach to planning by central government, has required a radical shift in attitudes. Changes have been most rapid in those countries such as the Czech Republic, Poland and Hungary which had a flourishing tourism industry before 1939, and where there is a strong entrepreneurial tradition. A flurry of tourism plans and significant investment in tourist infrastructure and accommodation has been evident as the countries of the region bring their tourism sector up to international standards. Accommodation is in short supply in some categories, so joint ventures in partnership with Western companies have often been necessary to obtain the necessary capital and expertise, and act as a catalyst for other businesses to adapt their practices to a competitive market environment.

On the other hand, the switch to a market economy has had a damaging effect on social tourism. In some countries domestic tourists were priced out of international hotels, where previously they had been charged very preferential rates. The introduction of democracy has given the peoples of Eastern Europe and the former Soviet Union much greater freedom to travel to the West, and this flow will increase as the economic outlook of the countries in the region continues to improve. The admission to the European Union of most countries in the former Eastern Bloc will also accelerate this trend. Increasing levels of Internet use, which in some countries match those in the West, is another factor favouring the growth of tourism demand.

Since the mid-1990s a growing number of East Europeans and Russians have been visiting the Mediterranean coastal resorts and the ski slopes of the French Alps. The majority of Poles and Czechs, for example, arrive by car, coach or charter flights and use budget self-catering accommodation. Many so-called tourists from the poorer countries of Eastern Europe, such as Moldova, are in fact would-be immigrants in search of a better life in the West. The unacceptable face of this new mobility is the trafficking in women and girls to supply the sex industry.

The surge in car ownership in Eastern Europe, and the growth in demand for touring holidays in the region has necessitated massive investment in road improvement schemes to meet West European standards, while public transport has been relatively neglected. Continuing economic difficulties make it difficult for governments to deal effectively with the region's already numerous environmental problems. In the long term, the demand for travel to these countries by the 'new tourists' will decline if these issues are not addressed.

An overview of tourism resources in Eastern Europe

Eastern Europe is rich in tourism resources, although these are of a kind more likely to attract visitors with cultural or special interests than the mass market. Beach tourism is well established on the Baltic and Black Sea coasts. The mountain ranges, notably the

Carpathians, provide opportunities for winter sports, although facilities rarely attain the standard of the ski resorts of the Alps. Spa tourism is another growth sector, based on the abundance of mineral-rich springs, and exploiting the vogue for healthier lifestyles in the West. Generally facilities need to be upgraded considerably if they are to meet upmarket Western standards. Domestic demand for these resources is also likely to increase as people adopt more sedentary lifestyles as a result of the decline of heavy industry, growing affluence, and a traditional diet that is rich in fats, preserved meats and carbohydrates.

All the countries of the region have designated national parks or reserves, but considerable land use conflicts need to be resolved if the wildlife resources are to be adequately protected. The region's great rivers and lakes offer scope for recreational tourism. The main attraction of most countries is likely to be the heritage of past cultures, exemplified in historic cities such as Tallinn and Krakow, and the colourful peasant folklore of the rural areas. Cities and countryside alike reflect the strong national differences to be found within Eastern Europe.

In detailing the resources and the type of development that has taken place in each of the countries of the region, we start with the Czech Republic, Slovakia and Hungary – countries that consider themselves to be part of Central Europe, rather than Eastern Europe, and where German is the second language. The Carpathian mountain ranges are a dominant feature of all three countries, along with Poland, Romania and the Ukraine. In 2011 these countries agreed on a policy of sustainable tourism development to protect the environment of the Carpathians, which provides a refuge for Europe's largest populations of brown bears, wolves, lynx and eagles.

The Czech Republic

In January 1993 the Federal Republic of Czechoslovakia was dissolved with the Czech Republic and Slovakia henceforth following separate paths. The Czechs of Bohemia and Moravia differ from the Slovaks not only in language but also in cultural traditions. When Czechoslovakia was established in 1918 the Czech lands had been part of the Austrian Empire for four centuries, whereas Slovakia had been ruled by Hungary for much longer. The Czech Republic is not only much larger than Slovakia, with twice the population, but is also disproportionately wealthier. Since the 'Velvet Revolution' of 1989 it has attracted considerable foreign investment as a result of its drive to a free market economy. Although the Czech Ministry of Economics does not have a strong tourism policy, the Czech Republic has a well-established tourism industry which contributed 2.9 per cent of GDP in 2009.

Tourism demand and supply

The Czech Republic has long been famous for its therapeutic springs and spas. Karlovy Vary (formerly Carlsbad) and Marianske Lazne (Marienbad) in Bohemia were the favourite meeting places for the statesmen and the wealthy of Europe in the early 1900s. Under Communism the luxury hotels were taken over by labour unions and fell into neglect, but since 1990 there has been a strong revival as a result of the growing demand for health and wellness tourism. With developments spearheaded by the Czech Tourist Authority (CTA) and Cedok, the former state tourism organisation and now the largest hotel and travel company, a wide range of products are available to today's foreign visitor, including city breaks, spa treatments, sporting holidays, stays in lake and mountain resorts, and touring holidays.

After the 1989 revolution, tourist numbers more than doubled to exceed 20 million arrivals in the early years of the twenty-first century, while Prague has become one of the world's most visited cities. However, the great majority of these are day excursionists, mainly from neighbouring Germany and Austria and the number of staying visitors is around 5 million.

The country's new-found popularity highlighted the shortage of accommodation, especially the three- and four-star hotels favoured by Western tour groups, and the need to upgrade standards is one of the most pressing needs of the tourism sector. Until recently, most of the demand has come from other East European countries where expectations are lower, and this has resulted in a proliferation of low-cost camping sites. The situation is improving as a result of joint ventures by Cedok with Western corporations for the larger hotels and privatisation of the smaller hotels and pensions, with new hotels opening in Prague and a programme of renovation of older properties.

Domestic tourism is important as an advanced industrial economy has given most Czechs comparative affluence by East European standards. Sport and an interest in physical fitness and the outdoor life had been fostered by the *Sokol* movement even before 1918. This has resulted in a growing demand for a wide range of outdoor recreation activities and for second homes in the countryside.

Tourism resources

The Czech Republic offers scenic variety and a physical environment that is generally favourable for tourism. The large number of rivers and small lakes make up to some extent for the lack of a coastline. Forests cover 20 per cent of the country and are particularly extensive in the mountain ranges along the national borders. These forests are managed as a recreational resource, with nature reserves, waymarked trails and areas set aside for hunting – an important earner of foreign currency. Skiing is popular during the winter months in the resorts of Harrachov in the Giant Mountains and Spicak in the Sumava Mountains. Southern Bohemia and Moravia also boast spectacular limestone caves among their natural attractions.

A rich natural and cultural heritage is given a considerable degree of environmental protection, with the establishment of a 400 kilometre-long 'green corridor' linking Prague to Vienna, designed for hiking, riding and cycling holidays, or leisurely touring by car. This tourist route includes some of the historic towns of southern Bohemia – notably Cesky Krumlov, with its unique Baroque theatre – and a number of castles. Cedok has converted some of these to luxury hotels, while others are being restored to their former aristocratic owners after a long period of neglect under Communism. Interpretation of the heritage is achieved through open air museums. Despite these initiatives, the Czech Republic has its share of conservation problems. These include:

- serious pollution from smokestack industries using lignite, in north Bohemia and north Moravia – Silesia; and
- as a result of a lack of government funding historic buildings have fallen into disrepair, while art treasures illegally acquired from the country's churches have found their way to the international art market.

Case study 17.1

Prague

The towns and cities of the Czech Republic contain many heritage attractions, but only Prague has achieved worldwide recognition as a top-ranking tourist centre. This city's cultural appeal is due to:

- A strong musical heritage, including associations with Mozart and the Czech composers Smetana and Dvorak;
- A unique architectural heritage with outstanding examples of buildings in the Gothic, Baroque and Art Nouveau styles. In contrast to other European cities, Prague escaped destruction in the Second World War and subsequent redevelopment of its historic centre;
- A vibrant contemporary arts scene that has attracted a large expatriate community from other countries, particularly the USA.

As Prague has more than one historic centre, tourist attractions tend to be clustered in three distinct areas, namely:

- Hradcany – the original fortress-capital on a hill overlooking the River Vltava. This contains Prague Castle – seat of Bohemian kings, Holy Roman emperors and Czech presidents, St Vitus Cathedral, and the picturesque street known as Golden Lane;
- The Old Town on the east bank of the river, which is linked to Hradcany by the highly decorative Charles Bridge. Two of the finest masterpieces of Gothic architecture in the Old Town are Tyn Church and the clock tower in Old Town Square;
- The New Town – which was actually planned as early as the fourteenth century but rebuilt in the nineteenth century. It focuses on Wenceslas Square, the setting for some of the key events in Czech history, nowadays lined with hotels, apartment buildings, restaurants and shops. Many of these are decorated in the Art Nouveau style associated with the great Czech artist Alfons Mucha.

Tourism has brought economic benefits to Prague, including international funding of much-needed restoration work. However, the enormous influx of visitors, especially tour groups and young backpackers from all over the world, is threatening to turn the city into another Florence. This has had the following effects:

- The commercialisation of the historic city. As a result of the upsurge in land prices, neighbourhood shops have been replaced by those catering for tourists. Historic buildings have been altered in inappropriate ways and defaced with advertisements. Local residents can no longer afford the high rents for their apartments, or the prices in bars and restaurants, and have been forced to move to the suburbs;
- Wear and tear on the most popular attractions, such as Charles Bridge, which is constantly thronged with buskers, street traders and crowds of tourists;
- A predatory attitude by many of the city's taxi operators toward Western tourists.

It remains to be seen whether the civic authorities can achieve a balance between the encouragement of business enterprise and the need to preserve Prague's historic townscape. This is threatened by the growth of car ownership and the commercial pressures brought about by the free market economy and the international leisure industry.

EUROPE

Other cities are mainly important as centres for business travel, namely:

- Plzen (Pilsen) and Ceske Budejovice (Budweis) are famous for their brewing industries; and
- Brno, the capital of Moravia is noted for its engineering industries, and as an important venue for trade fairs.

Slovakia (the Slovak Republic)

Slovakia made slower progress with free market reforms than the Czech Republic and consequently tourism is not as developed. Before the Second World War, it had a predominantly agrarian economy, and more recently the country became over-dependent on the heavy industries introduced under Communism. Slovakia is a country with great tourism potential, and whilst it has benefited from the share-out of federal assets following its 'divorce settlement' with the Czech Republic, significant investment in tourist infrastructure is needed. The situation has improved since 2004, now that both countries are EU members. Slovakia has both its own national airline SkyEurope and national tourist organisation – the Slovak Tourist Board with marketing and development powers.

The main appeal of Slovakia for foreign visitors lies in its beautiful mountain scenery rather than the attractions of the capital, Bratislava. Unlike the Czech Republic this is a wine rather than beer drinking nation, with some cultural similarities to neighbouring Hungary; for example, gypsy folk music is an important part of the entertainment on offer to foreign tourists in both countries. Slovaks take great pride in their rural peasant traditions, and a considerable variety of village architecture has been preserved. Other heritage attractions include medieval mining towns, the castles of the former Hungarian nobility, and in eastern Slovakia, Orthodox churches are a reminder of the region's proximity to Romania and the Ukraine.

Tourism is mainly focused on the following areas:

- The High Tatras on the border with Poland, which contain the highest peaks of the Carpathians. Apart from the superb lake and mountain scenery, the area can provide some of the best skiing to be found in Eastern Europe.
- The karst limestone region of eastern Slovakia, which boasts the spectacular UNESCO-listed Dobsina ice cave as well as waterfalls and rock formations.
- The spas of western Slovakia, the most important being Piestany, which attracts large numbers of wealthy Arab and German tourists.
- Bratislava and southern Slovakia, which forms part of the Danube Plain. Bratislava is known primarily as a modern industrial city and its cultural attractions have been overshadowed by those of Prague. It is now a major port, thanks to the controversial power project on the Danube at Gabcikovo which, in taming the river, also threatens to damage the wetland environment of the area.

Hungary

Hungary is famous for its spicy cuisine and a language – Magyar – which is markedly different from those of its neighbours. The country is only a third of its size prior to 1918, when it was a partner in the Habsburg empire. Although most of Hungary, including Budapest, was under Ottoman rule for almost two centuries, their legacy here is much less apparent than in the Balkan countries to the south. The major physical feature is a great plain in the middle of the Carpathian Basin, crossed by the rivers Danube and Tisza. In the north there are the foothills of the Carpathians and in the south-west around Pécs uplands rising to over 800 metres. Winters are cold and cloudy, but summers approach Mediterranean conditions in heat and sunshine.

Tourism demand and supply

Tourism has become an important part of the economy, accounting for 5 per cent of GDP and over 6 per cent of employment. This is due partly to the successful marketing of Hungary's two main attractions, namely the capital Budapest and Lake Balaton, which together account for the majority of foreign visitors. The tourism strategy is now to focus on quality and high yield tourism rather than mass tourism, which requires improvements in the infrastructure.

Domestic and outbound tourism

As visa and currency restrictions have been relaxed, and the economic position has improved, increasing numbers of Hungarians are travelling abroad, with Croatia, Spain and Greece as popular destinations and a small, but growing long-haul market. Although annual holiday entitlement averages 20 days, effective demand for domestic tourism is reduced by the widespread practice of 'moonlighting' at several jobs to make ends meet so that holiday propensities languish at around 33 per cent. The majority of domestic tourists stay with friends or relatives, or in cottages in the countryside.

Inbound tourism

Even under Communism, Western tourists were encouraged by the removal of restrictions, and a limited amount of foreign investment in hotels was permitted. During the 1980s the number of visitors from the West almost trebled, whereas those from other socialist countries actually declined. This was largely due to the low value of the Hungarian *forint* relative to Western currencies, whereas it was overvalued compared to the non-convertible currencies of the Soviet Bloc. Hungary's success in attracting international tourists has continued, with around 42 million arrivals in 2007.

Transport and accommodation

The majority of tourists arrive by car and are short-stay, particularly the Austrians, who cross the border on shopping forays to towns such as Sopron and Szombathely. The gateway for air travellers is Budapest's Terihegy Airport, while large numbers of excursionists use the hydrofoil service on the Danube from Vienna. A high proportion of the accommodation stock is in campsites or private homes. There has been significant investment in hotels, both within and outside of Budapest, with the major chains represented.

Organisation

Before 1989 the state-owned Ibusz company handled both inbound and outbound tourism, but it has since been reorganised as part of the new government's policy of economic liberalisation, and faces competition from a multiplicity of independent travel agencies. The industry is managed by the Tourism State Secretariat of the Ministry of Economy and Transport, supported by the Hungarian National Tourist Office and tourist boards responsible for marketing at regional level.

Tourism resources

Hungary's tourism resources include:

- Numerous spas based on the thermal springs that underlie the Carpathian Basin. Hungary has gained an international reputation for high standards of medical treatment and therapy, and the facilities for health and wellness tourism attract a growing conference market.
- Excellent facilities for activity holidays, such as horscriding, cycling and watersports.
- Cultural attractions appealing more to the older tourist. These include the traditional peasant dances and crafts – notably embroidery – of the villages of the Great Hungarian Plain where rural tourism is growing. Pécs, which was designated as European capital of culture for 2010 on the basis of its craft industries and architectural heritage, is one of a number of historic towns that attract growing numbers of visitors.

Budapest is one of Europe's most attractive capitals. Formed from what were two separate cities – Buda, picturesquely situated on the hills above the Danube, and Pest, the commercial centre on the river's left bank – it contains many reminders of its pre-1918 role as the joint capital of the Austro-Hungarian Empire. These include:

- the magnificent neo-Gothic Parliament Building in Pest and the Fisherman's Bastion in Buda, the city's two major landmarks;
- the Hungarian State Opera which is a reminder that Budapest vies with Vienna as a centre of art and music;
- the shopping boulevards, café society and vibrant nightlife;
- spa establishments such as the Hotel Gellert, and the Szechenyi Baths, with year-round open-air bathing; and
- business opportunities in the new climate of economic liberalism. Since 1990, Budapest has attracted an international business community and the city is growing in importance as a conference venue.

Budapest is close to the other main tourist areas of Hungary, namely:

- The Danube Bend, where the great river changes its course between mountain ranges, is a popular excursion zone. It contains some of Hungary's most historic towns including Szentendre, with its *skansen* or museum of Hungarian rural life.
- Lake Balaton is one of Europe's largest at 77 kilometres in length, but averaging only 3 metres in depth. Its shores are fringed by beaches, modern hotels, and campsites, while a number of areas have been designated as nature reserves. Demand for accommodation in summer frequently exceeds supply and the threat of pollution from intensive agriculture has to be constantly monitored. Heviz is the most well known of a number of spas in the vicinity of Lake Balaton, due to its unique thermal lake.
- The Great Hungarian Plain, where the *pusztas* or vast, treeless pasturelands east of the Danube provide Hungary with many of its characteristic landscapes and traditions, such as the *csikos* (cattle herders), whose displays of horsemanship are a

tourist attraction. Many of the *csardas* (country inns) feature the traditional folk music and dances that inspired Liszt and other Hungarian composers. Ecotourism is being promoted in areas such as the Hortobagy National Park near Debrecen, where aspects of the traditional culture and the steppe ecosystem have been carefully preserved.

Discussion point

Health and wellness is one of the fastest growing sectors of leisure and tourism, and Hungary in particular has pioneered low-cost medical treatments and therapies. Investigate the reasons for the growth in demand for spa tourism in the West and carry out a SWOT analysis of a selection of spa resorts in the former Eastern Bloc countries. How well can they compete with health tourism destinations in other parts of the world?

Poland

Poland is one of the largest countries of Europe, with a population of almost 40 million. Its exposed situation on the North European Plain between Germany and Russia has resulted in a history of invasion, fluctuating boundaries, and a long period of foreign rule when the country was partitioned between the Russian Empire, Austria and Prussia. Over 90 per cent of the population adhere to the Roman Catholic Church, which has long been identified with Polish nationhood and resistance. Largely as a result, less than 20 per cent of Poland's farms were collectivised by the Communist regime after 1945. At the same time, massive industrialisation brought about the Solidarity free trade union movement that did so much to inspire opposition to Communism during the 1980s. In some respects, Poland was better placed than most East European countries to make the transition to a market economy after 1989.

The demand for tourism

Until the early 1990s, tourism played only a minor role in the Polish economy. The majority of visitors originated from the former socialist countries and tended to be short-stay. This market has declined in importance now that more appealing destinations are available to the Russians, Czechs and East Germans and Poland's inbound tourism has suffered as a result. However, to a greater extent than other East European countries, Poland can attract a large ethnic market in North America, the UK and other countries of Western Europe. Most of the tourism from these countries has been for VFR or business purposes, but increasing numbers are visiting Poland on inclusive tours or on tailor-made holiday arrangements, primarily for cultural reasons. The recovery of Poland from the economic crisis of the early part of the 1990s has also led to considerable growth in domestic and outbound tourism.

The supply side of tourism

A much greater choice of accommodation is now available to Polish holidaymakers than was the case in the past. Tourism's higher profile has led to a change in government policy, with the Polish Tourist Organisation, which is responsible to the Ministry of Sport and Tourism, now promoting the country. It aims to stimulate further investment and growth in the sector, in line with the government's National Development Strategy, and is involved in tourism training initiatives with West European countries. Orbis, the national tourism organisation, has been privatised, although it remains one of Poland's major tour operators and hotel companies.

Tourism resources

The main tourist areas of Poland are situated near its southern and northern borders, and a fair distance from Warsaw, the capital and gateway for air travellers.

The **Baltic Coast** has been renowned since ancient times as a source of amber, hence the designation of the section along the Gulf of Gdansk as the 'Amber Coast'. The coast is by far the most popular destination, accounting for a third of all holiday overnights. On offer are 500 kilometres of sandy beaches and coastal lagoons, backed by pine forests, but the climate is often cloudy and windy. Extending east from Miedzyzdroje at the mouth of the Oder a string of resorts attract Swedish as well as domestic holidaymakers. Sopot is a popular and long-established resort adjoining the historic seaport of Gdansk. Two of Poland's most important recreational resources lie a short distance inland from the Baltic coast, namely:

* the lake country of Pomorze (eastern Pomerania) which includes the medieval fortress of Malbork (formerly Marienburg) built by the Teutonic Knights, a reminder of the former German domination of this region; and
* the Mazurian Lake District, an area of forests, lakes and low hills of glacial drift, which is popular for sailing, canoeing and camping.

The border country of **southern Poland** offers more interesting scenery and facilities for winter sports. To the west lie the Sudeten Mountains, adjoining Bohemia, where a number of spas have long been established. Further east, the Carpathian Mountains, culminating in the Tatry and Beskid ranges adjoining Slovakia, rise to over 2,000 metres, and account for a fifth of all holiday overnights in Poland. Zakopane in the Tatry Mountains is a well-developed resort with a year-round season. In addition to skiing, organised walking tours and white water rafting through the gorge of the Dunajec River are available. Tourism has greatly benefited the economy of this formerly remote and poverty-stricken mountain region.

The flatlands of **Central and Western Poland** are scenically less attractive, but the countryside does provide opportunities for fishing and riding holidays, often based on the manor houses of the former Polish aristocracy. On the eastern border with Belarus the Bialowieza National Park provides a refuge for rare animals such as the European bison.

Poland's cultural attractions are mainly to be found in the cities, although most of these suffered wholesale destruction in the Second World War. The historic cores have generally been meticulously restored, and provide a welcome contrast to the bleak industrial suburbs. The most important cities from the viewpoint of international tourism are Warsaw and Krakow, whereas others such as Poznan, Lodz and Wroclaw are primarily business centres.

Warsaw is one of the world's most impressive examples of urban reconstruction. The old city was painstakingly rebuilt 'as it was' in Baroque style, on the basis of old paintings, photographs and plans, as hardly a building was left standing at the close of the Second World War. As a short break destination, the Polish capital is popular with art and music lovers – especially Chopin enthusiasts. One of Warsaw's most impressive – if not best loved – landmarks is the Palace of Culture and Science built during the Stalinist era.

Krakow is important for tourism as Poland's former royal capital and religious centre, which has been designated as a World Heritage Site and European City of Culture. The city, which largely escaped wartime destruction, has retained its medieval atmosphere, and has attracted world-wide interest due to its association with Pope John Paul II. The major attractions include the impressive Market Square, the Cloth Hall and Wawel Castle. Unfortunately, the restoration programme has had difficulty in keeping pace with the ravages of pollution from the steelworks at Nowa Huta nearby. Krakow is conveniently near the ski resorts and scenic attractions of the Carpathian Mountains. In addition, a tour based on the city might include:

- the salt mines of Wielisza, which are famous for the art works made from this resource;
- the shrine of the Black Madonna at Czestochowa, which is Poland's most important pilgrimage centre; and
- The former concentration camp at Oswiecim (better known by its German name of Auschwitz) – one of many established in Poland during the Nazi occupation. It is regarded by the international Jewish community as the main site of the Holocaust and as a place of national martyrdom by the Poles.

The Baltic States

Like most of Poland, the three small countries of Estonia, Latvia, and Lithuania on the eastern shore of the Baltic Sea formed part of the Russian Empire from the eighteenth century to 1918. Between the two world wars they enjoyed a brief period of independence before being annexed by the Soviet Union in 1940. The Baltic States have much closer cultural ties with the Scandinavian countries and Germany than with Russia (although there are large ethnic Russian minorities), and since regaining their independence in 1991 they have sought economic association with those countries and see tourism as an important source of foreign currency. In 1993, all three states agreed to co-operate in the sphere of tourism policy and promotion.

The scenery is low key, the highest point reaching only 300 metres above sea level, but is made attractive by the combination of pastureland, forest and a myriad of lakes, a landscape which offers opportunities for a range of outdoor activities. Much of this is given a large measure of protection as national or regional parks. During the period of Soviet rule the coastal resorts were popular with Russian tourists, and Intourist developed some of its best hotels in the region. The beaches have been adversely affected by the pollution of the Baltic Sea, into which flow the industrial wastes of east Germany, Poland and Russia, but this problem is now being addressed.

Since the 1990s the accommodation sector, comprising hotels, guesthouses and holiday villages, has been upgraded with the improvement in the economy. Low cost carriers link the capitals Vilnius, Riga, and Tallinn with cities in Western Europe, so that these cities are successfully competing for the short break West European market. Outbound tourism has also increased dramatically and Estonia has benefited from improved ferry services to Finland. All three countries are noted for their music festivals and folklore, in which national identity was nurtured during the long period of foreign domination.

Estonia

Estonia has close affinities with Finland, but would prefer to reduce its dependence on the Finnish day visitor market – mainly attracted by cheap alcohol – by promoting itself as a cultural destination for British and other West European tourists. It has been successful to the extent that arrivals have increased from 400,000 in 1995 to over 1.9 million in 2007.

The German heritage of Estonia and Latvia is apparent in the castles built by the Teutonic Knights in medieval times, the ports which belonged to the powerful Hanseatic League, and the country houses, now mostly converted into hotels and spas, which belonged to the Baltic German landowning class. There are also many reminders of Swedish and Danish rule. International tourism mainly focuses on Tallinn, which is one of the best-preserved medieval cities of northern Europe. It is also a major yachting centre, and was chosen as the venue for the sailing events in the 1980 Olympics. The university town of Tartu, the port of Pärnu, and the fortress town of Narva, which is close to St Petersburg, are significant tourist centres.

Estonia's coastal resources include a number of offshore islands. The largest of these, Saaremaa, has only recently been developed for tourism; under Soviet rule it was off-limits as a military zone. The Lahemaa National Park to the east of Tallinn is noted for its lakes and waterfalls.

Latvia

Latvia's capital, Riga is the industrial hub of the Baltic States, while the national carrier Air Baltic operates an extensive network of international services. The city's elegant art nouveau architecture is a reminder of the period before 1914 when Riga was the leading port of the Russian Empire. Jurmala on the Gulf of Riga was then fashionable as the 'Baltic Riviera', and is now investing to improve its beachfront facilities. The western part of Latvia was known historically as the Grand Duchy of Courland, and offers a number of heritage attractions in and around the city of Liepaja.

Lithuania

Lithuania was united with Poland for much of its history and is likewise staunchly Roman Catholic. The impressive 'Hill of Crosses' on the outskirts of Siauliai is the country's most visited religious site, which serves as a reminder of the country's resistance to Soviet rule. The capital Vilnius (Vilna) is a major cultural centre with many fine Renaissance buildings, and is famous for its university. Trakai has an impressive lakeside fortress dating from the fourteenth century, when Lithuania was a major power.

Although Lithuania has a much shorter coastline than its neighbours, this does include the remarkable Curonian Spit, a sand feature 100 kilometres in length which separates an extensive lagoon from the Baltic Sea. Klaipeda, which is the country's only seaport, and Palanga are popular beach resorts on the mainland.

Photo 17.1 The Hill of Crosses is a reminder of Lithuania's resistance to Soviet rule (©istockphoto.com/ Simon Podgorek)

Discussion point: 'Dark tourism'

A number of visitor attractions in Eastern Europe draw upon the experiences of living under totalitarian rule and the near-annihilation of the region's formerly large Jewish population during the Second World War. These attractions include the 'House of Terror' and Holocaust Museum in Budapest, the Genocide Museum in Vilnius, and the Museum of the Occupation in Tallinn. Likewise a number of sites, of which Auschwitz is the best-known, commemorate the experience of Nazi occupation in Poland, along with Terezin and Lidice in the Czech Republic. In the former Soviet Union there has been a greater reluctance to acknowledge the atrocities committed by the Stalinist regime. Few of the sites of the former *gulags*, the notorious labour camps, where millions of political prisoners died as a result of the appalling conditions, can be visited. In part this is due to the inaccessibility of many locations, particularly those in north-east Siberia.

Discuss how these 'dark tourism attractions' can handle the issues of death and suffering with sensitivity, without sensationalism and a 'theme park' approach to interpretation. Should visits to such places be part of the school curriculum?

The Commonwealth of Independent States (CIS)

Russia was very clearly the dominant country in the former Soviet Union. Its role is much less evident in the loose grouping of republics known as the Commonwealth of Independent States (CIS) that replaced the USSR in 1991, but which the Baltic States refused to join. Russia's economic power is challenged by the West in Transcaucasia and Central Asia. Nevertheless, Russia's vast resources of oil and natural gas provide a means of exercising control over the countries in what Russians call their 'near abroad', such as Georgia, Ukraine and Belarus.

Russia (the Russian Federation)

Physical features

Although much smaller than the USSR, the Russian Federation is still almost twice the size of the USA and spans eleven time zones. In other words, a difference of half a day separates Kaliningrad on the Baltic coast, from Petropavlovsk on the Bering Sea, 12,000 kilometres (7,500 miles) to the east. As you might expect, there is a great range of climatic conditions in a landmass that also extends across nearly 40° of latitude, and we can broadly distinguish the following life zones, starting in the north:

- Treeless boggy tundra bordering the Arctic Ocean from the Kola Peninsula in the west to the Bering Straits in the east, very sparsely occupied by groups of reindeer herders.
- The wide zone of the *taiga* – the world's largest forest – covering 8 million square kilometres of northern Russia, including the greater part of Siberia. Due to the harsh sub-arctic climate and poor soils this is almost entirely dominated by a few tree species such as birch, firs and larch.
- A belt of mixed forest, typifying the more varied landscapes of central Russia.
- A zone of treeless grassland or steppe in the south, although most of this now lies in an independent Ukraine and Kazakhstan. This zone has very fertile 'black earth' soils and was the 'bread-basket' of the USSR, but it is often prone to devastating droughts.
- The high mountains along part of the southern border, namely the Caucasus and Altai ranges.
- Landscapes and climates comparable to those of the Mediterranean are found only in sheltered pockets along Russia's short Black Sea coastline.

The continental climate that characterises almost the whole of Russia is a major constraint on tourism development. Winters are severe – for example, snow lies on average for 150 days in Moscow and 160 days in St Petersburg. The *rasputitsa* (spring thaw) causes widespread disruption to communications for a period of about two weeks. Some 7 million square kilometres of northern Russia are affected by permafrost, which in parts of Arctic Siberia reaches a depth of 1,000 metres or more.

Cultural features

The world's greatest land empire had modest beginnings as a collection of principalities in central European Russia, and it was a long time before the rulers of Moscow were able to establish their supremacy. With no secure natural borders, Russia was vulnerable to invasion, culminating in two centuries of domination by Mongols from the steppes of central Asia. This traumatic experience had a lasting impact on the Russian psyche, as a yearning for strong, centralised government under the autocratic rule of the tsars. Ivan the Terrible, Peter the Great and Catherine the Great made Russia a great power, bringing many non-Slav peoples under their dominion.

As a result of this history of expansion and conquest, the Russian Federation is a mosaic of over 300 ethnic groups, although Russian Slavs account for perhaps 80 per cent of the population of around 140 million. There are 21 autonomous republics and eleven autonomous regions that represent the principal non-Russian minorities. As a result of *glasnost* (the policy of open government), religion and nationalist feeling, previously suppressed under Soviet Communism, revived in the late 1980s. The Russian Orthodox Church has regained some of the prestige it enjoyed under the Tsars before the 1917 Revolution. There is also a large Muslim minority, particularly in Tatarstan, and the area to the north-east of the Caucasus, including Dagestan, Ingusettia and Chechnya. Here the Chechens have a history of resistance to Russian rule and pose an on-going terrorist threat.

The demand for tourism

Domestic tourism

Domestic tourism under the Soviet system was mainly the responsibility of the state-controlled trade unions. Health care and rest from labour was provided in a network of sanatoria and purpose-built holiday centres which provided groups of workers with a subsidised, if somewhat regimented, two week vacation. Only a small proportion of this accommodation was allocated to families, while children were catered for by the Young Pioneer camps. The transition to a market economy after 1990 dealt this system of subsidised domestic tourism a severe blow. *Perestroika* (the restructuring of the economy) was accompanied by rampant inflation and the devaluation of the rouble. The consequent rise in the prices of food and other essentials drastically reduced the amount of discretionary income available to the average citizen. The Ukraine and Georgia, which contained most of the Black Sea resorts, were now independent countries. The funding for subsidised holidays from public sector organisations was drastically reduced. As a result tourism propensities are low compared to the European average. Although outbound travel has grown considerably since 1990, domestic tourism has declined. On the other hand, *glasnost* encouraged rising expectations, fuelling a demand for independent holidays on the Western model.

The amount of leisure time available to Russians has, at least in theory, increased since 1990 and about half the workforce are entitled to 24 days of holiday with pay. With the demise of Communism, the public holiday that celebrated the October Revolution was replaced by The Day of National Unity, which has its roots deep in Russian history. Until 2004 Russians enjoyed nine consecutive days off in May, beginning with International Labour Day and ending on Victory in Europe Day on May 9. Now they have ten days off in January, including the Russian Orthodox Christmas. Many in the business sector are convinced that this is costly to the economy, but any changes in the situation would be highly unpopular. Nevertheless, the demands of the market economy have forced many Russians to work harder than before.

Activity holidays have grown in popularity, especially canoeing, camping and cross-country skiing. Russians on a touring holiday prefer to use *tubaza* (tourist bungalows) which provide cheap but basic accommodation, as they are paid for in roubles rather than US dollars, unlike Western-style hotels. The trend for independent holidays will increase as car ownership levels rise – at present these are low by Western standards. Most Russian city dwellers have to be content with a stay nearer home, in a *dacha* (country cottage) in one of the villages on the outskirts, which they may own themselves, part-own through a garden co-operative, or rent.

Outbound tourism

Under Soviet Communism few Russians, with the exception of favoured groups, had the opportunity to travel abroad, and continuing economic problems during the 1990s ensured that foreign travel was largely restricted to the *nouveau riches* 'New Russians' who had benefited most from the transition to a market economy. The economic recovery that has taken place largely as a result of the rise in oil prices in the new millennium, the relaxation of visa restrictions, and the granting of traffic rights to foreign airlines has enabled much greater numbers to travel, to a wider range of destinations than hitherto. In 2007 Russia joined the top ten tourist-generating countries with a spend of US$ 22 billion.

Inbound tourism

Since the late 1980s the appeal of Russia has broadened, tourist volumes and receipts have increased (particularly from other former Soviet republics) and a diversity of products are available for foreign visitors. In 2009 international arrivals exceeded 19 million, more than double those recorded in 1990 for the whole of the Soviet Union. In addition to sightseeing tours, hunting expeditions, river cruises, conference tourism, adventure holidays, and homestays with Russian families are available.

The supply side of tourism

The growth of Western-style tourism faces a number of problems, namely:

* the language barrier;
* visa restrictions – large areas are still closed to visitors, ostensibly for military reasons;
* the lack of nightlife – although casinos are springing up in many cities throughout Russia, they are not always reputable;
* a continuing shortage of accommodation, particularly in the major centres, where hotels are pre-booked by the travel companies;
* tour itineraries still need to be pre-booked and paid for in hard currency, leaving the independent traveller at a disadvantage;
* foreign investment in the tourism industry, as in the economy generally, is deterred by the absence of a reliable banking system, bureaucratic inertia and corruption, and uncertainty over the laws relating to private property;
* the lack of small and medium sized business enterprises; and
* the prevalent low standards of service in hotels and restaurants.

On the other hand, the younger generation in the workforce is well-educated and eager to adopt Western-style methods.

Transport

The sheer size of Russia, the difficult climate and terrain of most of the country, and the undeveloped nature of surface transport means that aviation has long played a major role. Many communities in Siberia are only really accessible by air, since they lie more than 1,600 kilometres from the nearest railhead, the earth roads are impassable during the spring thaw and the autumn rains, while the rivers are ice-free only in the brief summer.

In the former USSR the state-owned Aeroflot had a monopoly of domestic air services, making it the world's biggest airline. With the break-up of the Soviet Union it was likewise divided up between the various republics and separate national airlines emerged. Aeroflot-Russian International Airlines, reorganised as a joint-stock company in 1992, still provides a world-wide network like its Soviet predecessor. However, its former domestic network, which provided service to 3,600 destinations in the USSR, was divided among a large number of regional carriers. One World S7 has now emerged as Russia's leading domestic carrier, and with its subsidiary Globus provides services to a large number of destinations, mainly in the CIS and Eastern Europe. Air fares remain relatively low, even for foreign tourists paying in US dollars. On the other hand, flights can be irregular due to recurrent fuel shortages, staff morale is affected by low pay, and aviation experts have alleged that safety standards are below those considered acceptable in the West, a situation that should change with the revival of Russia's aerospace industry.

We mentioned in Chapter 5 that Russia has the world's longest railway – the Trans-Siberian – that provides the major west to east transport link. Although the journey from Moscow to Vladivostok – a distance of almost 10,000 kilometres – takes over a week, and the trains make few concessions to tourism, the Trans-Siberian has become one of Russia's most sought-after travel experiences. Most rail services are cheap by Western standards but also slow, and security on the trains is a problem. Although it is now possible to drive from St Petersburg to Vladivostok on all-weather highways, road transport is deficient in many areas, and the standard of road maintenance, even between major cities in European Russia, is well below Western standards. On the other hand, Russia has a very extensive network of inland waterways. These link the great rivers Dnieper, Don and Volga, which have played a major role in Russian history, to the Baltic, White and Black Seas. In the summer months, fleets of hydrofoils ply the waterways with large numbers of domestic passengers, and Russian expertise in the field of hydrofoil design may yet see a new role for this type of vessel elsewhere. River cruises on more conventional ships are becoming increasingly popular with Western tourists, especially those linking St Petersburg to Moscow via Lakes Ladoga and Onega, which provide a leisurely way of absorbing the timeless quality of Russia's countryside.

Organisation

Inbound tourism contributed only a small proportion of the Soviet Union's foreign exchange earnings, and attitudes towards foreign visitors have been ambivalent since the times of the Tsars. Bureaucracy, an obsession with state security, and travel restrictions characterised Russia even before the 1917 Revolution, and seem likely to persist long after the demise of Communism. Large areas were officially closed to foreign visitors, tourists had to follow approved itineraries and stay only in officially designated accommodation. The Soviet authorities saw tourism as a means of promoting the achievements of the world's first socialist state, and in 1929 Intourist was founded as an all-purpose agency to serve foreign visitors. Although most tourists were travelling for cultural rather than ideological reasons, official itineraries included visits to factories and collective farms. In 1957 international youth travel to the USSR became the responsibility of the Sputnik organisation, part of the Komsomol (League of Young Communists), with a network of camps and low-budget hotels. From 1966 onwards investment in tourism infrastructure and training became part of the government's Five Year Plans. Additional impetus was given by the choice of Moscow as the host city for the 1980 Olympic Games.

With the demise of the Soviet Union Intourist lost its state monopoly and was privatised, along with Sputnik. As a commercial organisation it has advantages over its competitors, with offices in a number of Western and Asian countries, as well as an established network of agencies in all the countries of the former Soviet Union. It still owns and manages hotels and restaurants, arranges surface transportation for clients, organises excursions and tickets for cultural events, and supplies guides and interpreters. In the public sector tourism is closely linked to physical culture and sports, and is regulated by the 1996 Tourism Law. There is a strong organisation at city level that recognises the fact that most Western tourists to Russia spend at least part of their stay in the cities of St Petersburg and Moscow. Indeed the lack of tourism infrastructure elsewhere is a major constraint on visitation.

Tourism resources

Russia's tourism resources are primarily cultural, with a major concentration in the cities of Moscow and St Petersburg.

St Petersburg is probably the most beautiful city in Russia, and occupies a special place in the country's history for these reasons:

* It was founded as the capital of the Russian Empire in 1703 by the modernising Tsar Peter the Great as Russia's 'window on the west'. No expense was spared to import the best European architects of the time to design a city on classical lines, with broad streets, canals and impressive public buildings.
* The Bolshevik attack on the Winter Palace in October 1917 brought Lenin and the Communist Party to power in Russia (for this reason the city was renamed Leningrad during the Soviet era).
* The city endured an epic siege from 1941 to 1943, epitomising the almost unimaginable sacrifices made by the Russian people in the Second World War.

Because of its northerly latitude St Petersburg is best visited during the season of the 'white nights' (from May to July). Among its many cultural attractions, the following are of special significance:

* the Hermitage is one of the world's largest art collections, occupying the former Winter Palace of the Tsars;
* the Maryinsky Theatre, home of the renowned Kirov Ballet;
* the Church on the Spilled Blood, built in traditional Russian style, which commemorates Tsar Alexander II, who liberated the serfs but was assassinated by revolutionary extremists; and
* the former palaces of the Tsars on the outskirts of the city, which were restored by the Soviet government at enormous cost after the Second World War as part of the national heritage.

St Petersburg is also convenient for excursions to the well-preserved medieval city of Novgorod and the island-monasteries of Lakes Ladoga and Onega.

Moscow is a much older city than St Petersburg, and is now a sprawling metropolis of 10 million people. The historic nucleus is the Kremlin – the walled inner city of the Tsars, and later the seat of power of the rulers of the USSR and the Russian Federation. It is adjoined by Red Square and Russia's most well-known building – St Basil's Cathedral with its distinctive onion domes. Under Stalin, the city acquired its Metro system – with ornately decorated stations – and 'wedding-cake' skyscrapers, one of which accommodates the University of Moscow. After the fall of Communism, a dynamic mayor embellished the capital with some impressive new projects, including the reconstructed Cathedral of Christ the Saviour – symbolic of the revival of the Russian Orthodox Church after 70 years of official atheism. Other attractions include:

- the Bolshoi Theatre, world famous for its touring ballet company;
- the Moscow State Circus with some 16,000 performers;
- the Pushkin and Tretyakov art collections;
- the Exhibition of Economic Achievements, showcasing technology; and
- the Izmaylovo market where the tourist can buy antique samovars, icons and Soviet memorabilia.

Moscow also has one of the world's largest conference centres – the Palace of Congresses in the Kremlin. The international airport at Sheremetyevo was expanded for the 1980 Olympics but has since acquired an unenviable reputation among foreign business travellers for bureaucratic delays and indifferent service, problems to be addressed by a redevelopment programme.

Moscow is a good base for excursions to the following places of interest in central Russia:

- The **Golden Ring** of historic towns to the north-east of the capital, including Rostov the Great, Vladimir, Sergiev Posad and Suzdal. These have preserved much of the Old Russia of wooden 'onion-domed' churches, fortified *kremlins*, colourful Byzantine-style monasteries, traditional craft industries and *troika* rides during the winter months.
- The country houses of Tchaikovsky at Klin, and of Tolstoy at Yasnaya Polyana attract lovers of Russian music and literature.
- Star City, the centre of Russia's space programme.

The River Volga provides a major tourist route linking a number of important centres, including:

- Kazan – which is not only the capital of the largely Muslim Tatar republic, but also one of the holy cities of the Russian Orthodox Church;
- Ulyanovsk – famous as the birthplace of Lenin; and
- Volgograd (formerly Stalingrad), scene of one of the epic battles of the Second World War.

The Ural Mountains to the east are important primarily for their mineral resources rather than their scenic attractions. One of the cities in this region, Yekaterinburg, is a place of pilgrimage, as it was here that Tsar Nicholas II and his family were murdered by the Bolsheviks in 1918.

In north-western Russia, the port of Archangel is the base for visiting the island monasteries of Solovetsky in the White Sea, which acquired a sinister reputation soon after the Bolshevik Revolution as a prison for dissidents. Murmansk, despite its location well to the north of the Arctic Circle, is one of Russia's few ice-free ports and a 'boom town', thanks to the natural gas fields of the Barents Sea. Environmentalists are concerned at the threat to the marine life and the international fishing industry.

In the extreme west the Russian enclave of Kaliningrad, faced with the decline of its military importance, hopes to become a trading gateway to the EU, once the problem of transit through Lithuania has been resolved. It is also exploiting its German heritage for tourism (until 1945 the city, then known as Königsberg, was the capital of East Prussia).

The Black Sea and Caucasus

Russia's Black Sea coast has long been a major holiday destination thanks to its agreeable climate. In the Soviet era this formed part of a much more extensive 'Russian

Riviera' that included the Crimea and part of Georgia. In the 1980s Sochi alone attracted 6 million tourists from all over the USSR to its beaches. Russia's principal Black Sea resort is now repositioning itself as a destination for Western holidaymakers. It is also close to the ski slopes of the northern Caucasus favoured by the Russian elite, and for this reason has invested heavily in infrastructure and facilities for the 2014 Winter Olympics. Apart from a number of spas dating from the late nineteenth century and mountain climbing centres, the number of tourists to the northern Caucasus was restricted until recently, and the natural mountain habitats were largely undisturbed. Although part of the area is designated as a national park, state-controlled corporations have been given the go-ahead for large-scale development. From the viewpoint of international tourism the northern Caucasus will be at a disadvantage until the problems in nearby Chechnya have been resolved.

Siberia comprises the vast expanse of the Russian Federation lying to the east of the Urals. Since the seventeenth century Russians have regarded the territory with its wealth of furs and minerals as a land of opportunity, but this has been overshadowed by a fearsome reputation as a place of exile and forced labour for dissidents. The large-scale eastward migration of peasants from European Russia did not take place until the late nineteenth century (at much the same time as the USA was experiencing its great wave of westward expansion).

The western half of Siberia is predominantly lowland, with large expanses of peat bog covered with forest. It also contains some of the world's largest reserves of natural gas. Eastern Siberia is physically more varied and includes a number of mountain ranges.

Since the early 1990s Siberia has to some extent been open to Western business enterprise and tourism, although for reasons of climate and accessibility most of the development has taken place in the south, based on the cities linked by the Trans-Siberian Railway and its extension, the Baikal–Amur line. There are now opportunities for special interest tourism undreamed of in the old Soviet Union, including:

* white water rafting and ecotourism in the Altai Mountains, an area of unspoiled wilderness bordering Kazakhstan and Mongolia;
* summer cruises on the great rivers – the Ob, Yenisei and Lena – that flow northwards for 4,000 kilometres to the Arctic Ocean; and
* ecotourism and adventure holidays based at the spa resort of Listvyanka on the shores of Lake Baikal, one of the world's greatest natural attractions.

Even Siberia's climate can be viewed by some as a pull factor; for example the remote community of Oymyakon is exploiting its reputation as 'the coldest place on Earth', where winter temperatures regularly fall below –60°C.

The cities of Siberia are of less interest to tourists, except for those that have preserved the traditional wooden buildings of the pre-Soviet era, such as Tobolsk and Irkutsk. Novosibirsk with its modern industries and universities is the business capital of Siberia, while the scientific community of Academgorok nearby is a centre for space research.

In Soviet times the mining communities of northern Siberia were heavily subsidised by the government in Moscow, but now face an uncertain future. On the other hand the age-old way of life of the non-Russian indigenous peoples, including their religious practices, is no longer suppressed by the authorities. Some, like the Yakuts and the Buryats, are enjoying a cultural renaissance as a result of tourism.

With the Cold War a distant memory, Russia's sector of the Arctic Ocean is slowly opening up to the Western market for ecotourism, and most of the island of Novaya

Zemlya has been designated as a national park. As yet only a small number of locations feature on Arctic cruise itineraries, such as the bird colonies of Franz Josef Land, and access to these is highly dependent on the extent of pack ice and fog. However, Russia's actions in the North polar region have spurred other nations with Arctic territories – Canada, the USA, Denmark and Norway – to also assert their sovereignty and stake their claims to the potential mineral wealth. At the present time Russia's strategic Northern Sea Route from Murmansk to the Bering Sea is navigable only with a fleet of icebreakers during the brief summer season. Global warming would bring the dream of a commercially viable 'North-east Passage' to reality, shortening the sailing time from Europe to the Far East by a week, but also posing a serious threat to Arctic ecosystems.

The Russian Far East

The Pacific coastal region includes the important naval city of Vladivostok, and the ferry terminal at Nakhodka which provides ferry services to Japan. Russia's Far East is influenced by the monsoon, and the forests include species that are typical of the warmer climates of east Asia. These resources, which include the rare Amur tiger, are under threat from illegal hunting and the logging industry.

Kamchatka, despite its raw, foggy climate and remote location, has considerable potential for ecotourism with the ending of Cold War travel prohibitions, as it is geographically close to Alaska on the other side of the Bering Sea. Helicopter tours provide access to the peninsula's resources, which include glaciers, no less than 33 active volcanoes, a large number of geysers and hot springs, salmon fisheries and abundant wildlife.

Case study 17.2

Lake Baikal, 'the pearl of Siberia'

Ecotourism in Russia is not yet as developed as in the West, and the fledgling environmental movement faces many obstacles from industry and government. The controversy over development around Lake Baikal is a good example.

Lake Baikal is a major tectonic feature, over 1,600 metres in depth, which is estimated to contain a fifth of the world's fresh water. The lake supports a variety of unique species, including seals, making it a natural laboratory for scientific research. Such an extensive body of water has a moderating effect on the local climate, giving it maritime features, but even so by late February the lake is covered by ice 70–110 cm thick, which melts in early May.

As early as 1916 Russia's first nature reserve was established here, but it was not until 1987 that the entire lake shore was protected from logging and other development by designation as a national park. This was partly in response to many years of campaigning by local communities, who had opposed the building of a cellulose plant at the mouth of the Selenga River. Even though the water is remarkably pure by European standards, Baikal's ecology continues to be threatened by effluent from pulp mills, fertilisers, and air pollution originating in the nearby cities of Irkutsk and Ulan Ude.

Discuss the political and economic circumstances that make the environmentalist's task more difficult in Russia than in the West. What further measures could be taken to protect this unique resource?

The East European nations of the CIS

Ukraine

Since the 'Orange Revolution' of 2003, the Ukrainian government has loosened its economic ties with Russia, and made progress towards democracy and a market economy. Nevertheless this remains a country divided between the Russian-speaking east and the Ukrainian-speaking centre and west. The western part of the Ukraine was ruled by the Austro-Hungarian Empire until 1918, and subsequently became part of Poland. Eastern and central Ukraine bore the brunt of Stalin's forced collectivisation of agriculture in the 1930s, and the resulting famine is commemorated by the Holodonur monument in Kiev. Earlier in the twentieth century there was large-scale emigration to North America, and the descendants of those emigrants are now an important market for incoming tourism.

The Ukraine is better known for its agricultural and industrial resources rather than for its tourist attractions. Yet the country's landscapes are much more diverse than the image of fields of sunflowers and wheat stretching to the horizon. Winters are less severe than in Russia, with snow lying an average of 80 days in Kiev. The State Service for Tourism and Resorts is responsible for promotion, but development is hindered by deficient infrastructure and sub-standard accommodation. The Ukraine's attractions include:

- Kiev, the capital attractively sited on the River Dnieper, historically the nucleus of the first Russian state before its destruction by the Mongol invasions in the thirteenth century. The surviving medieval heritage includes the Caves Monastery and the Cathedral of Saint Vladimir.
- L'viv is the principal city of western Ukraine and boasts many Baroque buildings as reminders of its Austrian heritage.
- The forested Carpathians offer a number of ski resorts catering mainly for domestic demand.
- Odessa was founded by Catherine the Great and her favourite Potemkin as the Russian Empire's major port on the Black Sea, and is renowned for its theatres and elegant architecture.
- The southern part of the Crimea Peninsula, where the warm climate and beautiful coastal scenery – in contrast to the uniformity of the Ukrainian steppes – attracted the Russian nobility before the 1917 Revolution. Under Communism resorts such as Yalta were made available to all Soviet citizens, and following the collapse of the Soviet Union, to foreign tourists with hard currency to spend. The battlefields of the Crimean War (1854–1856) near the fortress of Sevastopol provide a secondary attraction for British and French visitors.

Belarus

Belarus has been slow to change from a centrally planned economy, and exemplifies the problems faced by the former Soviet republics in promoting a tourist image and identifying a unique selling proposition (USP). At first sight the resource base is not particularly promising; the country has been overshadowed by Poland and Russia and repeatedly invaded throughout its history. It was also more badly affected than the Ukraine by the 1986 Chernobyl disaster. On the other hand Belarus can offer the largest remaining area of the unmodified mixed forest that once covered most of Europe, interspersed with extensive marshes and peat bogs. There is potential here for ecotourism, as well as hunting and fishing trips, as currency earners. The forest also produces the raw materials for the traditional craft industries that have largely disappeared elsewhere. As for the cities, Brest and Minsk lie on the main route from the West to Moscow, and although transit tourism is important, there is as yet little to persuade visitors to stay for longer periods.

Moldova

Between 1918 and 1945 Romania ruled over what is now Moldova west of the River Dniester, and the two countries share a similar language and culture. However, there is a large Russian minority with separatist ambitions who have created a de facto state within Moldova – Transdniestria – which is recognised by Russia, but not the rest of the international community. Moldova has the advantage of a relatively warm, sunny climate that favours large-scale wine production, so not surprisingly wine tours feature prominently among the country's tourist attractions. The government also plans to develop cultural tourism based on the capital, Chisinau, rural tourism and 'health and beauty' tourism – which is problematic, given the country's poor infrastructure.

Transcaucasia

The three countries to the south of the natural barrier formed by the Caucasus Mountains have more in common with the Mediterranean region or the Middle East than with Russia. However, while Orthodox Christianity is central to the national identity of Armenia and Georgia, Azerbaijan is predominantly Muslim and has fostered close trade links with the Central Asian republics east of the Caspian Sea. All three countries have great tourism potential – a favourable climate, spectacular scenery, a rich cultural heritage going back to ancient times, and populations with a tradition of hospitality and business enterprise. Yet the prospects for tourism and economic development have been blighted since the late 1980s by inter-communal violence, for example the war between Armenia and Azerbaijan over the enclave of Nagorno-Karabagh, and the separatist movements in Georgia. The failure to resolve these disputes by peaceful means is an obstacle not only to regional co-operation in tourism promotion, but also to the exploitation of the oil resources of the Caspian Basin and the development of trade links with the West. Armenia has for example, opposed the BTK (Baku–Tiflis–Kars) railway project linking Azerbaijan to Turkey.

Georgia

Georgia has a well-established reputation throughout Russia for its wines and reputation for the good life, in contrast to the mediocre catering which is characteristic of most of the former USSR, while its national dance troupe has achieved international fame. Since the 2003 'Rose Revolution' Georgia has been ruled by a government with strong pro-Western sympathies. However, the country's economic development has been hampered by the difficulties with Russia over the separatist movement in South Ossetia, that culminated in a brief war beteeen the two countries in 2008.

The Department of Tourism and Resorts is responsible for promoting Georgia abroad. The capital, Tblisi, and the second city, Kutaisi, contain most of the country's cultural attractions, while Gaudari in the Caucasus Mountains is a centre for winter sports and trekking. Georgia also includes two autonomous republics:

- Abkhazia in the north-west in Soviet times attracted millions of Russians to the Black Sea resorts of Sukhumi, Gagra and Pitsunda. In 1991–1992 the tourism industry here was devastated by the civil war between the central government in Tblisi and Abkhazian separatists. This breakaway state is not recognised by the international community and tourism has not recovered.
- Adzharia in the south-west has fewer beaches but offers lush subtropical landscapes featuring tea plantations and lemon orchards. Batumi, the capital of the autonomous republic is a port of call for cruise ships and a base for excursions to other parts of Georgia.

Armenia

Tourism in Armenia has been overshadowed by the effects of the 1988 earthquake, the country's landlocked situation with two hostile neighbours, and historical memories of the 1915 genocide of a million Armenians. The snow-capped peak of Ararat is a holy mountain and national symbol for Armenians, dominating the horizon in the capital, Erevan, yet it is virtually inaccessible as it lies across the border in Turkey. The economy is dependent on remittances from the millions of ethnic Armenians living in the USA, Canada, France and Russia, who also account for the majority of the half million international tourist arrivals. Armenia can claim to be the world's oldest Christian nation, and hoped to boost tourism by staging celebrations for the 1,700th anniversary in 2003. In fact the country's main attractions are the ancient churches and monasteries in a spectacular lake and mountain setting. Armenia's physical isolation as a high plateau separated by mountain barriers from its neighbours is reinforced by border tensions and the lack of rail, road and even air links with Azerbaijan and Turkey.

Azerbaijan

Azerbaijan has immense oil resources and for this reason it has attracted a much greater amount of foreign investment than Armenia and Georgia combined. The Ministry of Culture and Tourism has ensured that a good deal of this money has gone into hotel building in the capital, Baku, for a new wave of business tourists. Some of the oil wealth is being used to conserve the rich cultural heritage that has affinities with Iran and Turkey, and create a system of national parks that will eventually cover 10 per cent of the national territory. Although Baku has been an oil boom town before – in the early years of the twentieth century – much remains from earlier periods, and the well-preserved historic quarter has a strong Middle Eastern ambience with its minarets and bazaars. Azerbaijan has considerable biodiversity, from mountain and desert landscapes in the west to the subtropical coastlands along the Caspian Sea in the east, while ecotourism has an important role to play in stemming the depopulation of small rural communities.

The Central Asian Republics

Throughout recorded history the steppes of Central Asia have been the breeding ground of nomadic warrior tribes who periodically threatened the security of the civilisations to the west, east and south. In contrast, oasis cities such as Samarkand were important in ancient times as trading centres. Russian rule, particularly during the Soviet era, introduced modern industries, secular education, and a number of new cities, notably Tashkent and Almaty. Nevertheless the Muslim religion and heritage remain dominant throughout the region. The Soviet authorities were also responsible for most of the environmental problems in the region. The best known example is the shrinkage of the Aral Sea, which was brought about by vast irrigation projects for cotton cultivation. This has resulted in a deterioration of the local climate, with salt and sand-laden winds blowing in from the dried-up lake bed. The effect of 9/11 and the ongoing conflict in Afghanistan since 2001 has been to align the Central Asian republics with the USA, to counter the threat of Islamic fundamentalism to their secular, authoritarian regimes.

Approaches to tourism vary, but generally tour operators in the new private sector are more efficient than the state-run organisations. A variety of accommodation is now available, including international hotel chains, small hotels and apartments in the major cities, and even stays in a yurt, the traditional dwelling of the nomads.

Uzbekistan offers the richest heritage in the region, and has a well-developed tourism industry, but one that still discourages independent travel. Its capital, Tashkent, is the major air hub of Central Asia and an important conference venue. The Fergana Valley in which it is situated is a fertile agricultural region, but prone to earthquakes. However, tourism is mainly concentrated in the historic oasis cities of Khiva, Samarkand and Bokhara:

* Samarkand is the best known as it boasts one of the world's most striking Islamic monuments – the Registan, resplendently decorated in blue tiles and gold leaf;
* Khiva is a perfectly preserved 'museum-city'; whereas
* Bokhara is a hive of activity, with bazaars similar to those of the Middle East.

Kazakhstan is the world's largest land-locked country and can offer steppe, desert and spectacular mountain landscapes. It is also culturally diverse; while Kazakhs make up half the population, there are considerable numbers of Russians, ethnic Germans, and other minorities from all over the former Soviet Union who were deported here en masse during the Stalin era. The republic's vast empty spaces also made it an ideal testing ground for military hardware. One legacy of this is the Baikonur space centre.

Tourism promotion is the responsibility of the Kazakhstan Tourist Association which is a co-operative non-profit organisation. Tourism activities include white-water rafting on the River Ili, skiing and ice skating in the resort of Medeo, and trekking in the Altai and Tien Shan Mountains. The former capital, Almaty has direct air links to a number of West European countries. Astana, the new capital, was built in the middle of the steppe with the revenue from Kazakhstan's immense oil and natural gas reserves. It is a showpiece of modern architecture, and has been called the 'Brasilia of Central Asia'.

Kyrgystan is dominated by the glaciated Tian Shan mountains, and offers considerable scope for adventure tourism and equestrian activities. The main attraction is Issik Kul, the world's second largest alpine lake. This has long been a destination for health tourism and now also offers kayaking and other water sports.

EUROPE

Tajikstan is a small country with few natural resources dominated by the Pamirs, one of the world's most rugged mountain ranges. Throughout the 1990s it was the most politically unstable of the Central Asian republics, and this has held back the development of its tourism industry. The country was the least affected by a century of Russian rule, and traditional lifestyles still prevail. The Wakhan region on the border with Afghanistan offers scope for escorted trekking.

Turkmenistan consists essentially of a ring of populated areas surrounding the empty Kara Kum desert. The country is noted for the traditional carpet weaving industry based in Ashqabad and Merv. In ancient times, Nissa was the power base of the Parthians, who competed with the Roman Empire for control of the Middle East. With vast reserves of natural gas at its disposal, the government has seen little need to encourage leisure tourism, with the exception of a large luxury resort development on the coast of the Caspian Sea.

Case study 17.3

The Silk Road

Until the sixth century AD China was the world's only source of silk, and its manufacture was a closely guarded secret. Silk was in great demand by the ancient Mediterranean civilisations as a luxury product, to the extent that the cost of importing it may well have contributed to the decline of the Roman Empire. The 'Silk Road' linking Xian in China to the Mediterranean was in fact a series of overland trade routes, and in rugged mountain regions such as the Pamirs the trails could only be negotiated by camel caravans proceeding in single file. Because of the great distances and the physical dangers of desert and mountain travel, very few ever undertook the complete journey. For the most part silk and other commodities such as satin, musk and precious stones, some originating in the Indian sub-continent, were traded at a number of staging points along the route through intermediaries. Oasis towns such as Samarkand grew rich and culturally cosmopolitan as a result of the interchange, not only in goods, but religious ideas and technological innovations (for example, paper manufacture, gunpowder).

In 1993 the World Tourism Organisation began a long-term project to promote the Silk Road as a tourist route. This was given additional impetus with the 2002 Bukhara Declaration that such development should be sustainable. The project has done much to relax irksome border restrictions for foreign travellers and improve professionalism among those working in the tourism sector in the participating countries. Tourists can now follow in the footsteps of Marco Polo, the thirteenth century Venetian merchant-adventurer, but travelling in relative comfort and staying in international standard hotels. However, much needs to be done to improve the road networks in central Asia and transportation links between Europe and Asia generally. This problem is being addressed by international co-operation through the United Nations Economic and Social Commission for Asia and the Pacific (UNESCAP), with funding from the Asia Development Bank.

Summary

- A long period of state control over tourism, amounting to over 40 years in Eastern Europe and 70 years in the former Soviet Union, have left a legacy which differentiates these countries strongly from those of Western Europe.
- Since 1989 this has been followed by a strong liberalising trend, characterised by economic restructuring, foreign investment, privatisation, and the encouragement

of local initiative. Western involvement in the development of tourism has greatly increased.

- Entry, exit, and currency restrictions were severe under the Communist regimes but have eased with their demise.

- The former regimes encouraged social tourism linked to health and education, but as incomes rise with the successful transition to a market economy, Western-style domestic tourism will increase in significance.

- Outbound tourism is showing more rapid growth as the region's economy improves. Entry to the European Union by a number of countries in the region has encouraged investment in tourism and boosted demand.

- The removal of Communism has improved the image of the region in Western eyes. This needs to be reinforced by each country emphasising its individual attractions; the differences between countries were previously concealed by the grey uniformity of Communism and are now much more evident.

- There is increasing scope for innovation in tourism products and niche marketing. Some countries, notably the Czech Republic, have made much more progress than others.

- External air links to Eastern Europe have improved, but there is a danger that the encouragement of mass tourism in the form of short city breaks might well result in the region's cities becoming a cheap playground for West Europeans.

- Environmental problems are already widespread, and ecotourism is in its infancy in most of these countries.

- Internal transport systems need to be improved, to cope with rising car ownership levels and the expectations of Western tourists.

- Future growth in tourism could also be severely constrained by the negative factors of political instability, ethnic strife, and rising crime levels, as economic growth fails to meet people's expectations.

- Poor standards of service, and mediocre products may also deter tourists, once the novelty of visiting a previously 'forbidden' destination has faded.

Assignments

1 Identify the most significant changes that have taken place since 1990 in (a) the structure of tourism and (b) tourist flows in Eastern Europe and the CIS.

2 Describe some of the environmental problems impacting on tourism in Eastern Europe and Russia, and explain why these are difficult to resolve.

3 Explain the importance of infrastructure for the development of business tourism and Western-style leisure tourism in Eastern Europe and the CIS.

4 Explain the significance of cultural attractions for inbound tourism in Russia and specific countries in Eastern Europe.

5 Analyse the factors influencing the demand for domestic and outbound tourism in Russia and specific countries in Eastern Europe.

6 **The Danube: Story of a River.** Draft a commentary for a cruise on the River Danube from Passau to the Delta, pointing out the places of interest in their historical context, including the engineering projects that have 'tamed' the river in more recent times. The commentary should be accompanied by an annotated map (not necessarily to scale) indicating the countries through which the Danube flows by their national flags, and the places of interest to be visited or sighted in the course of the cruise.

The Middle East and Africa

CHAPTER 18

The tourism geography of the Middle East

Introduction

Our definition of the Middle East differs from that of the UN World Tourism Organisation by including Iran, and excluding Libya. The UNWTO also regards Israel as part of Europe, but not Palestine, which makes little sense geographically. We include the countries of south west Asia and the Levant – the eastern seaboard of the Mediterranean (with the exceptions of Turkey and Cyprus). Vast petroleum resources and the Arab-Israeli conflict have brought the Middle East under the international spotlight since the Second World War, culminating in the Gulf War of 1990–1991 and its sequel the Iraq War in 2003. However, these are but recent episodes in a history of trade, migration and conquest which goes back at least to the third millennium BC. The Middle East is strategically located at the crossroads of trade routes linking the Mediterranean to the Indian Ocean and the Far East – and at the interface of three continents – Europe, Asia and Africa. The component countries are similar in much of their physical geography and similarities in religion, language, architecture, food specialities and other aspects of lifestyle, plus a shared historical experience link almost all of the countries in the region, together with those of North Africa.

Cultural features

As far as the cultural similarities are concerned, you should be aware that:

- All but two of the countries in the region (Israel and Iran) are Arabic-speaking.
- All of these countries (except for Iran), at one time formed part of the Ottoman Empire based in Constantinople (now Istanbul). During much of the twentieth century, Britain exercised various forms of control over most of the countries in the

region while France was active in Syria and Lebanon. Events in the new millennium have confirmed the USA as the dominant power in the Middle East.

- The Middle East is predominantly Muslim in religion, except for Israel and Lebanon. However the Muslim world is as divided on sectarian lines as Christendom, with the Sunni branch of Islam dominant in most Arab countries while the adherents of Shia are more numerous in Iraq and Iran.
- There are substantial ethnic as well as religious minorities in most countries of the region (Syria is a classic example), while the Kurds, 'a nation without a state' are divided between Turkey, Iraq, Iran and Syria.

Western perceptions of Islam have been strongly influenced on the one hand by historical memories of the Crusades and the threat posed to Europe by the Ottoman Empire, and on the other by highly romanticised images of the region created by European writers and artists in the nineteenth century. More recently, unfavourable publicity in the Western media has been a reaction to the growth of Islamic fundamentalism. Although it is true to say that, in this secular age, religion plays a greater role in everyday life in Muslim countries than in most other parts of the world, the influence of Islam does in fact vary greatly in strength from country to country. Only a few governments, for example, impose *sharia law* based on the Koran, rather than on the Western legal systems. Attitudes towards the status of women and towards foreign tourists also range from the strict (for example, Saudi Arabia) to the relatively liberal (Jordan, Lebanon and the United Arab Emirates). We should take into account the following aspects of Islam as they influence the tourist experience and business practice:

- The obligation of Muslims to pray five times a day with special emphasis on Friday (the Muslim Sabbath). The mosque with its distinctive minaret forms a dominant feature in the skyline, but as figurative art is discouraged by the Koran, the decorative features of traditional architecture tend to be limited to abstract patterns or inscriptions in Arabic.
- The requirement to fast between sunrise and sunset during the month of Ramadan, the fifth month of the Muslim year. As this is based on a lunar calendar the timing of Ramadan varies from year to year.
- At least once in a lifetime, Muslims should make the pilgrimage or *haj* to the holy city of Mecca, the birthplace of Mohammed. The haj takes place during the twelfth month of the Muslim year, resulting in a mass movement of people that is concentrated both in time and space. There are also secondary pilgrimages known as *umrah* that can be undertaken throughout the year. The pilgrim routes extending to all parts of the Muslim world became important for trade, and were therefore well supplied with inns (known as *khans*, *fonduks* or *caravanserais*). Some of these traditional types of accommodation still survive (although the camel caravan has long since been replaced by motorised transport).

Another important cultural feature of the region is the contrast between the cities and the countryside, where settled and nomadic lifestyles appear to have changed little since biblical times. Even in the cities, the older districts have a seemingly chaotic street pattern while the colourful *souks* and bazaars retain many traditional features. These are essentially covered markets with whole sections devoted exclusively to a particular trade or type of merchandise. Traditional domestic architecture is characterised by rooms opening off an enclosed courtyard, allowing privacy for the extended family and protection from the sun. The major cities have well laid-out, modern districts similar to those of Europe – Tel Aviv is a good example here – very different in character from the adjoining Arab town of Jaffa with its maze of twisting, narrow streets.

Physical features

There is no clear physical break (the Suez Canal and Red Sea hardly count) and as we have seen, no distinct cultural boundary between North Africa and Asia. Most of the Middle East region forms part of the arid climate zone, and irrigation is essential. Agriculturally, productive land is restricted to a few areas that in turn have attracted the great majority of the population, which is concentrated in these areas at densities similar to or exceeding those of Western Europe. They comprise:

* the coastal plains adjoining the Mediterranean and Caspian Seas which enjoy relatively good rainfall;
* a narrow strip along the river Nile in Egypt; and
* the alluvial plains of the rivers Tigris and Euphrates, which link up with the Mediterranean coastal plain in Syria to form the so-called 'Fertile Crescent'.

To the east of the coastal strip, mountain ranges and high plateaux prevent rain-bearing winds from penetrating further into the interior. Often the dividing line between the desert 'wilderness' and the cultivated area is very distinct. Not surprisingly, water supply and distribution is a major problem in the Middle East, and this precious resource is the subject of local and even international disputes.

Most of the region is characterised by extremes of heat in summer, and even the Mediterranean coast can be oppressive. In winter, the weather is usually mild or pleasantly warm, with the important exception of some mountain areas that experience heavy snowfalls. Conditions are particularly severe in Kurdistan, where temperatures are comparable to those of Russia. Cold, overcast weather is not uncommon – even as far south as Amman and Jerusalem which are situated at quite high altitudes – in contrast to the sub-tropical warmth and sunshine of the Red Sea coast.

Tourism demand and supply

Considering its location and resources, the Middle East region accounts for a relatively small share of world tourism – almost 6 per cent of arrivals. The countries of the Middle East are close enough to the inclusive tour markets of northwest Europe to have developed a tourism industry based on sun, sea and sand. This is a logical extension of the coastal resort developments of Mediterranean Europe, facilitated by improvements in air transport. However, the response to this opportunity has been uneven, with some countries – such as Dubai – investing heavily in tourism in an attempt to diversify the economy. Most countries with the potential to enter the market have only done so since the 1980s. Long before the expansion of mass tourism, Israel and Egypt had based their tourism industries on the attractions of the Holy Land and the relics of ancient civilisations. More recently, the oil-based prosperity of Saudi Arabia and the Gulf States has attracted a large business travel market. There is also a considerable volume of travel between countries in the region, involving business tourism, returning migrant workers visiting relatives, pilgrimages and health tourism.

Contrary to popular belief in the West, only some of the countries in the Middle East have become affluent on oil resources, so that foreign exchange earnings from tourism are needed to even out regional imbalances. The population, as in most developing countries, contains a high percentage of young people and tourism is seen as a means of providing much-needed employment. In fact since the 1980s economic development has not kept pace with population growth, with a consequent decline in living standards. With only modest progress in education, telecommunications and access to information technology, most countries in the region are ill-equipped to meet the challenge of globalisation. Nevertheless foreign investors as well as national governments have provided much of the infrastructure needed for international tourism, including good roads, a large number of airports of international standard, and hotel development in the major cities and coastal resorts. You would expect external transport links to be efficient as the region is a crossroads between Europe, Africa and Asia and its airports are important as staging points for business on the long-haul routes between Western Europe and the East Asia–Pacific region. Although most tourists visiting the Middle East arrive by air, movements within the region are predominantly by road. The main exception is the Arabian Peninsula, due to the vast distances and difficult terrain. Throughout the Middle East, rail networks are poorly developed, and there are few international services. Given the abundance of cheap oil, an ever-growing demand for car ownership, even in the poorer countries, and a lack of environmental awareness, this situation is not likely to change.

Tourism resources

The Middle East has many strengths as a destination region, with opportunities for further development, but these are constrained by a number of serious problems. We can summarise the tourist resources of the region as:

- A wealth of cultural attractions, due to the fact that this region gave rise to the world's earliest civilisations and three major world religions – Judaism, Christianity, and Islam. Successive invaders, including the Greeks and Romans in ancient times, followed by Crusaders from western Europe defending the pilgrim routes to the Holy Land, have all left their mark. Some of the best known of these sites can be visited on a Mediterranean cruise. However, overland cultural tours, taking in several countries, have not developed to the same extent as in Europe, due to the political situation in the region.
- A generally favourable climate for beach tourism, although in some countries this is restricted by cultural and religious attitudes. A growing number of tourists now visit the region purely for the sake of recreation and relaxation. Resorts have developed to meet their needs, but with the exceptions of Israel and Dubai, facilities are generally not to the same standard as those of the western Mediterranean.
- Mountain ranges provide relief from the summer heat in the cities, and here a number of health resorts meet the domestic demand, such as Kasab in Syria and Taa'iz in Saudi Arabia.
- The mountains in the north of the region also provide opportunities for winter sports. At present, ski resorts have developed to meet the needs of the small domestic market and are generally not well-equipped by international standards.
- There is also scope for adventure holidays in the more accessible mountain and desert areas.
- Although some countries pay lip service to ecotourism, in practice it has made little progress, except in Israel and Jordan.

The main threats to tourism are twofold. First, the political situation has been a major factor in preventing the region realising its tourism potential. Since the Oslo initiatives in 1994, tourism has ebbed and flowed to the region depending upon the prospects for peace. The region is still torn by internal unrest – often provoked by religious fundamentalism – and since 2001, by the war on terrorism, culminating in the Iraq War in 2003. Terrorism by groups such as Hezbollah and Hamas in Lebanon, Israel and the Palestinian territories has resulted in much negative publicity. Most governments in the region have a poor or indifferent record on human rights. The popular uprisings in Egypt, Syria and Bahrain – the so-called 'Arab Spring' of 2011, demanding political and economic reforms, have added a new ingredient to the turmoil. In consequence, tourism has suffered, despite the region's accessibility and its wealth of natural and man-made attractions. The Gulf War of 1990–1991 for example, not only disrupted tourism throughout the Middle East, but disturbed world tourism flows, although the actual hostilities were highly localised.

Secondly, the unique appeal of the region lies in its antiquities and cultural sites. These need careful management and have a limited capacity to receive visitors. This implies that there is a limit to the numbers of tourists that the region can absorb if these attractions are to remain available for future generations. The heritage is also under threat from the widespread trafficking in artefacts from archaeological sites, and from industrialisation, where dam-building by Turkey on the upper Euphrates threatens sites downstream in Syria.

Egypt

In many ways, Egypt typifies the contrasts found in the Middle East. It is a meeting place of East and West; it is mysterious and yet highly accessible. Cairo is the hub of the air routes between Europe, Asia and Africa, while the Suez Canal is one of the world's most important shipping routes. With around 85 million inhabitants Egypt is the most populous of the Arab countries and a cultural centre for the Arabic-speaking world. Its people are the inheritors of an ancient civilisation that flourished many centuries before the rise of Islam, and in many respects, the way of life of the *fellahin* (peasant farmers) along the Nile has changed little since the time of the Pharaohs. The Nile is also a reminder that Egypt has strong connections with sub-Saharan Africa to the south.

The bulk of Egypt's territory is desert, but we should make a distinction between the dune-covered expanses of the Western Desert extending into Libya, and the rugged scenery of the Eastern Desert and Sinai Peninsula. In between lies the narrow green ribbon of cultivated land along the Nile, widening in the north as the Nile Delta. Just as in ancient times, Egypt is 'the gift of the Nile', highly dependent on the river's vagaries. Although it is the most highly industrialised of the Arab countries, Egypt is not self-sufficient in petroleum and its economy cannot provide enough jobs for its population. In this context, the contribution made by tourism is crucial as it filters down to the lowest levels of society and employs 14 per cent of the workforce. The government recognises this and has had a long involvement in tourism.

Tourism demand

Inbound tourism

Travellers from the West have visited the Pyramids at least since Roman times, although modern tourism did not begin until the late nineteenth century. To a large extent, this was due to the British travel company – Thomas Cook – who inaugurated steamship services on the Nile, luxury river cruises and the development of Luxor as a winter resort. Since the 1960s tourists from other Arab countries, visiting primarily for recreational rather than cultural reasons, have formed a growing share of the Egyptian market. Arab visitors tend to stay during the summer months, when the Mediterranean coast around Alexandria is cool by comparison with the stifling heat of the Arabian Peninsula. Most Western sightseers arrive during the winter season, which is pleasantly warm and much drier than other Mediterranean destinations.

Egypt is the dominant destination for international tourists in the Middle East. In the 1950s there were fewer visitors but they stayed for an average of one month, and even in the 1980s, the main reason for visiting was to view the cultural sites. However, recreational tourism has become increasingly important and international arrivals rose steadily in the 1990s, despite the setbacks of terrorist attacks and the Gulf War, and exceeded 14 million by 2010, comprising both Western and Arab markets. Although there are few charter services, most tourists arrive by air in Cairo. Domestic tourism is also significant and this includes social tourism as well as travel by a relatively affluent middle class.

Tourism supply

Egypt has more than 5,000 hotel rooms. Most of this capacity is in the capital, followed by Alexandria and Luxor, but there is also significant growth in Sinai. The government encourages investment in the accommodation stock by both Egyptian and foreign companies, and tourism is given priority at the highest levels of government.

Tourism organisation

The first formal tourist authority was established in 1935, and the present Ministry of Tourism dates from 1967. In addition the Supreme Council for Tourism, chaired by the Prime Minister acts to co-ordinate public sector actions in this important part of the economy. The aim of the Ministry is to upgrade infrastructure, improve the image of Egypt and diversify to include new products such as golf tourism. The Tourism Development Authority was set up to identify potential areas for growth; Egypt is therefore attempting to widen its resource base by encouraging conferences and special interest tourism. The objective is to tempt tourists away from the Nile Valley, where the tourism industry is competing with other economic sectors for scarce water, power and land resources. This is problematic as Ancient Egypt – notably the Pyramids and the Valley of the Kings – is the subject of worldwide interest, probably to a greater extent than any other bygone civilisation.

Tourism resources

To develop its full potential, tourism has to overcome a number of problems, not the least of which is Egypt's infrastructure, particularly overloaded water and power supplies and an inadequate road system. Environmental considerations are also important, especially along the Red Sea coast where there is concern for the ecology of the coral reefs. But perhaps the main problem is the uncertain political climate of the region, which causes severe fluctuations in tourist arrivals, especially from the USA. Although the government is pro-Western and Egypt was the first Arab state to normalise relations with Israel, the country suffers from acute social and economic tensions. This has contributed to the rise of Islamic fundamentalism among the poorer classes in society, fuelling hostility to the Coptic Christian minority. All of which is causing concern for the future stability of the country and the future of its tourism industry.

Most Western tourists stay firmly on the cultural circuit, the highlights of which are:

- The Pyramids of Giza just outside Cairo. These are the only survivors of the 'seven wonders' of the ancient world.
- The temples and other antiquities near Luxor, which is the main centre for touring Upper Egypt. These include the world famous Valley of the Kings.
- The temple at Abu Simbel near Aswan, which UNESCO campaigns saved from inundation by the Aswan High Dam project.

Although the very dry climate of the Nile Valley has ensured the survival of artefacts for over four thousand years, safeguarding the monuments from pollution for future generations is a matter of concern. Tourist pressure on the Pyramids has led the government to implement drastic conservation measures, including attempts to curb the activities of unauthorised guides and entrepreneurs. A popular way of visiting the sites in Upper Egypt is by a river cruise on the Nile, as an alternative to road transport or domestic air services from Cairo. In fact Nile cruises have long been Egypt's best known tourism product.

The emphasis on the relics of the Pharaohs has obscured the fact that Egypt has a more recent heritage and many other attractions. This is particularly true of Cairo, although the congestion in this city of over 15 million people can be a traumatic experience. In addition to early Islamic buildings such as the Citadel of Saladin, there are Coptic churches, a reminder that this early form of Christianity was flourishing in Egypt centuries before Islam. But for most tourists, the main attraction is shopping in the bazaars for an assortment of souvenirs.

Other tourist resources include:

- The Fayyûm oasis, 100 kilometres to the west of the Nile Valley, culturally interesting and a good deal less hectic than Cairo. A number of hotels have been built in this area.
- Sailing in a traditional *felucca* on the Nile offers a more authentic experience of rural Egypt than a luxury cruise in a 'floating hotel'.
- Trekking in the Sinai Desert, including a visit to St Catherine's Monastery with its biblical associations.

The greatest potential for attracting a wider market lies in the development of Egypt's coastal resorts where a year-round season is possible, and there are good facilities for water sports.

The Mediterranean coast west of Alexandria has long attracted well-off domestic tourists, with beach resorts such as Mersah Matruh. This area also appeals to military history buffs as the theatre for the Western Desert campaign, culminating in the battle of El Alamein (1942) in the Second World War. Alexandria is a cosmopolitan seaport with Greek and French cultural influences, but much of its former elegance faded after the 1952 revolution which overthrew the monarchy and brought Nasser to power. Almost nothing remains of the ancient city of Roman times, famed for its library and the long-lost palace of Cleopatra.

The Red Sea coast, promoted by the Ministry of Tourism as the 'Red Sea Riviera' has clear water and coral reefs that are a major attraction for divers. Tourism on a small scale took place during the Israeli occupation of the Sinai Peninsula between 1967 and 1982, but the impetus for growth came when the Egyptian government provided generous loans for hotel development. The resorts of Hurghada, Nuweiba and Sharm al Sheikh are now established holiday destinations for Western tourists, and include luxury hotels with conference facilities among their amenities.

THE MIDDLE EAST AND AFRICA

Israel

Within an area not much larger than that of New Jersey, two nations – Israel and the Palestine NAR (National Autonomous Region) – have so far failed to find a formula for peaceful co-existence.

With a population of little more than 7 million, Israel has a significance out of all proportion to its size. The country is poor in natural resources, but has the asset of a workforce that is enterprising and highly skilled in the latest technology. Few other countries can offer such a great variety of scenery and climate, including the snows of Mount Hermon in the north, the sub-tropical fertility of Galilee, and the heat and aridity of the Dead Sea, which lies more than 400 metres below sea level. People's perceptions of Israel are largely coloured by their political or religious background, for example:

- To Jews, a nation dispersed in exile since Roman times, Israel is their homeland. Jewish religious observance plays an important role in this otherwise secular state.
- To Christians the world over Israel is largely synonymous with the Holy Land, containing most of the places associated with the Bible. Christian Arabs historically formed a significant minority of the population, which is decreasing, in both Israel and the Palestinian territories.
- To Muslims a number of these sites are also of great religious significance. Many regard Israel as an intruder and are sympathetic to the cause of the Palestinian Arabs. Moreover, Muslim Arabs form a substantial minority in Israel itself as well as the majority in the Palestine NAR.

Since the founding of Israel in 1948, the Jewish state has been under siege from its Arab neighbours. Internal security is also threatened by the Palestinians in the occupied territories of the Gaza Strip and the West Bank which Israel acquired after the 'Six Day War' in 1967. The Oslo agreement in 1994 laid the foundations of a Palestinian state by giving autonomy to Gaza and most of the West Bank. However the Palestinian *Intifada* (uprising) since 2001 has been a major setback to the peace process and tourism development, and the situation deteriorated further when the hard-line Hamas party gained power in Gaza. The Palestinian Authority was unable to restrain terrorist activity, while the Israeli government, faced with the problem of absorbing large numbers of immigrants from the former USSR, had permitted the growth of Jewish settlements in the occupied territories. In response to the threat from Palestinian *shaheeds* (suicide bombers), Israel has implemented a security barrier around the West Bank. This, together with the existing military checkpoints, has effectively fragmented the territory of the Palestine NAR and disrupted the tourism-based economy of Bethlehem and other Palestinian communities. Security is a major consideration for travel in Israel itself, and El Al, the national carrier, routinely carried armed air marshals on its flights long before 9/11 made it a global issue.

The demand for tourism

Domestic and outbound tourism

With a GDP per capita that is higher than many European countries and a good transport infrastructure, the propensity for tourism is high. Most Israelis have a southern European lifestyle, and trips to the beaches of the Mediterranean resorts and

Eilat are a major feature of domestic tourism. Israelis took over 3 million trips abroad in the early years of the twenty–first century, leaving a deficit on the international tourism account. However, they are prevented from visiting most countries in the Middle East, with the exceptions of Egypt, Jordan and Turkey. Security problems at home have favoured the growth of outbound travel at the expense of domestic trips. Given its small population, Israel is well represented in the tourist arrivals for many long-haul destinations.

Inbound tourism

Despite its security problems, Israel attracted over two million international tourists in the Millennium, although numbers decreased significantly due to subsequent events and the industry is currently in crisis. The USA, which has a special relationship with Israel, is a major generator of demand. European countries, including Britain, have become important markets since the liberalisation of charter flights in 1976. The Israeli Ministry of Tourism endeavours to develop new markets, such as Japan, in close co-operation with the national carrier – indeed the majority of arrivals are by air. There is also a health spa authority to co–ordinate this important sector of tourism, particularly foreign visitors seeking treatment for psoriasis.

Tourism resources

Israel can offer a great variety of tourist products including:

* Summer holiday resorts along the Mediterranean coast at Herzliya and Netanya north of Tel Aviv, and at Ashkelon to the south.
* Eilat, Israel's outlet to the Red Sea, separated by 200 kilometres of desert from Jerusalem, has become a popular winter sun destination, with facilities for underwater photography, diving and water skiing.
* Spa tourism has been developed around picturesque Lake Kinneret (better known as the Sea of Galilee), and in a more spectacular setting on the shores of the Dead Sea, utilising the unique resource provided by the mineral-rich lake and its microclimate.
* Working holidays on a kibbutz, the uniquely Israeli experiment in communal living. The kibbutz lifestyle is nowadays much less popular among Israelis than it was in the early years of the Jewish state, as a result of the decline of the agricultural sector and the move from socialism to a market economy. Indeed, many *kibbutzim* have departed from their socialist ideals by providing guest house accommodation to paying tourists.
* The attraction of seeing a nation in the making, composed of Jewish immigrants from all over the world. Israel's achievements in making the Negev Desert productive are particularly interesting.
* Adventure holidays, including trekking in the Negev Desert.
* Cultural tourism based on the large number of archaeological sites, many of which are mentioned in the Bible. Herod the Great's hilltop fortress at Masada is a shrine to the Jewish struggle for freedom against Rome and subsequent oppressors. In medieval times the historic port of Acre (Akko) played a major role in the Crusades.
* Christian pilgrimages to Galilee and Jerusalem, with a peak in demand during the Easter holidays.

Photo 18.1   The Dome of the Rock in the Old City of Jerusalem, with new buildings under construction (©istockphoto.com/ Irena Kofman)

Business travel gravitates to the three major cities of Tel Aviv, Haifa and Jerusalem.

Tel Aviv is the business and financial centre of the country. The city is very much a creation of the twentieth century, with a good deal of nightlife and a Southern European beach culture.

Haifa is Israel's largest seaport, catering for tourists arriving by ferry from Greece, Cyprus and Turkey as well as cruise passengers. It is also a place of pilgrimage for followers of the Bahai religion.

Jerusalem, the capital of ancient Judea and since 1967, of the modern state of Israel, is an important venue for conferences. It is a world class tourist destination as the meeting place for three major religions, and also a potential flashpoint for disputes involving Christian, Jewish and Muslim fundamentalists. Some allege that the Israeli authorities have insensitively handled hotel expansion in the old Arab quarter of East Jerusalem. Major points of interest for the visitor include:

- Yad Vashem – Israel's major memorial to the Jewish Holocaust of the Second World War;
- The sites associated with Christ's Passion, including the Mount of Olives, the pilgrim route known as the Via Dolorosa, and the Church of the Holy Sepulchre;
- The Temple Mount, an area sacred to Christians, Jews and Muslims alike. The Al Aqsa Mosque is the holiest site in Islam after Mecca and Medina. The Western Wall is all that remains of the Jewish Temple after its destruction by the Romans in 70AD, and is a place of lamentation for Orthodox Jews; and
- The nearby Arab town of Bethlehem in the Palestine NAR is a major centre for Christian pilgrims, attracted to the Church of the Nativity.

Jordan

Without significant oil resources and consisting largely of semi-arid plateaux and desert, Jordan is a small and relatively poor Arab country. The population includes two very different communities – the Palestinian refugees, mainly concentrated in the capital Amman – and the Bedouin tribes of the desert. Despite these tensions, the country has remained politically stable, thanks to the statesmanship of King Hussein who ruled from 1953 to 1999.

Tourism plays an important role in the economy, accounting for 13 per cent of GDP and second only to remittances from the large numbers of Jordanians working abroad. Over three million international arrivals are recorded annually. However, over-reliance on the attractions of East Jerusalem, Bethlehem and Jericho meant that most of Jordan's appeal, as well as its hotel stock, were lost when Israel occupied those territories (the West Bank) in 1967. Jordan had then to redevelop tourism east of the river Jordan, on a less promising resource base. The major attractions now include:

* Petra – the ancient city of the Nabatean civilisation – in a unique setting concealed in a deep valley, which accounts for a substantial part of Jordan's tourism revenue, and has encouraged hotel development in the area;
* the desert scenery of Wadi Rum, where ecotourism is being developed, and which is associated with the exploits of Lawrence of Arabia during the First World War;
* the eastern shores of the Dead Sea where spa tourism is being developed;
* the Crusader castle at Kerak;
* the well-preserved Roman city of Jerash with its annual festival;
* the pilgrim sites on the east bank of the river Jordan; and
* the beaches and water sports of Aqaba on the Red Sea coast, which has been developed as a rival to Eilat.

Tourism has been restricted by the lack of infrastructure and good hotels, although the Middle East peace initiatives have encouraged hotel investment, particularly in Amman, Aqaba and by the Dead Sea. Most hotels are located in Amman although a network of formerly government-run 'rest houses' (now privatised) provides accommodation in the areas likely to be visited by tourists. The normalisation of relations with Israel after 1994 enabled Jordan to benefit from the Millennium tourist boom with the easing of restrictions on travel between the two countries. The Ministry of Tourism and Antiquities has encouraged sustainable tourism. This includes community tourism projects such as the award-winning Taybeh-Zaman tourist village close to Petra, where visitors can see local craft skills in action and stay in traditional rural houses.

Jordan also undertakes joint marketing campaigns with Syria and Lebanon under the banner of 'three countries, one destination' to raise international awareness of their attractions and boost hotel occupancy rates.

Syria

Unlike Jordan, the regime that has ruled Syria since 1971 has done little to encourage foreign investment or Western tourism, although since the Iraq War the country is no longer shunned by the international community as a 'pariah state'. Relations with the USA have improved, but not with Israel, due to the continuing border dispute over the Golan Heights. Roughly the size of England and Wales, Syria comprises a large section of the Fertile Crescent, contrasting with the stony Syrian Desert in the south-east. Poor infrastructure, such as unreliable power supplies, is a major constraint on tourism development. Nevertheless the country has major tourism potential with international arrivals in the middle of the first decade of the new millennium exceeding four million (although most of these are from Lebanon and Jordan). The economic potential of tourism is taken seriously by the government with a Ministry of Tourism and a 'Supreme Council of Tourism' that has a co–ordinating role under the prime minister. Most of the limited development has taken place in the western part of the country, focusing on the historic cities of Aleppo and Damascus. There are beach resorts on the Mediterranean coast north of Lattakia as well as mountain resorts taking advantage of the cooler climate of the Anti-Lebanon, but these are visited almost exclusively by domestic tourists. Of greater appeal to Western sightseers is Syria's cultural heritage, represented by:

- the capital Damascus, reputedly the world's oldest city – it is famed for its association with St Paul and contains the Ommayad Mosque and numerous bazaars;
- the ruins of the ancient trading city of Palmyra in the Syrian Desert; and
- the Krak des Chevaliers, the most spectacular of the castles built by the Crusaders.

Most of Syria's 15,000 hotel beds are geared to the business market, being concentrated in the major cities of Damascus, Aleppo and Lattakia. As yet, few tour groups from European countries visit Syria. Although Damascus airport is an important regional gateway, most visitors arrive overland from neighbouring Arab countries and their length of stay tends to be short. There seems little scope for expanding holiday tourism until the international situation in the Middle East improves.

Lebanon

Although Lebanon is a small, mountainous country its people have been involved in overseas trade since at least the first millennium BC, when the Phoenicians from Tyre and Sidon dominated the Mediterranean sea routes, and Lebanese communities and cuisine are now found all over the world. Lebanon is a classic example of a multi-cultural society peopled to a large extent by successive waves of refugees from other parts of the Middle East. Until 1975, when civil war broke out between the two main communities – the ruling Maronite Christians and the various Muslim groups, including Palestinian refugees – Beirut was not only the financial capital of a large part of the Arab world but also its main entertainment centre. Arab tourists came to Lebanon not only for relief from the intense summer heat of their own countries, but also to escape the prohibitions on gambling and nightclubs imposed by a strict interpretation of Islam. Since the end of the conflict in 1991 the economy has made a slow recovery and Beirut is no longer a divided city. European tour operators have added Lebanon to their stock of destinations, and MEA, the national airline, has staged a comeback, with a new airport to the south of the capital, all contributing to around one million international arrivals annually. Aside from a revitalised Beirut, the country's tourist attractions include:

- Mount Lebanon, where a number of ski centres have developed only a short drive from the beach resorts of the coast. Both are mainly frequented by domestic tourists and visitors from other Arab countries such as Jordan and Saudi Arabia. Unfortunately the cedar forests which covered the mountains in biblical times have largely disappeared.
- The fertile Bekaa Valley to the east. This includes the ancient temples of Baalbek which provide a romantic setting for cultural events.

Accommodation in the Lebanon tends to be expensive, and tourism has been given little encouragement by the government, which is based on a complicated power-sharing agreement between the religious communities. Nevertheless there are a number of rural tourism initiatives by the private sector, including the development of a hiking trail linking the coast to the mountains.

> ### Discussion point
>
> A mixed group of English college students aged between 18 and 30 wish to visit a number of archaeological sites in Syria, Jordan, the Palestinian territories and Israel. Discuss the factors that need to be considered in planning an itinerary for such a tour, including information on transport and accommodation, security and border crossings, food and drink, clothing, and shopping for handicrafts. What advice on cultural attitudes would you give the students? Why are some of these archaeological sites under pressure, and how should the group explain the issues of tourism and conservation to other students on their return?

The Arabian Peninsula

Extending between the Red Sea and the Gulf, the Arabian Peninsula offers some of the most extreme contrasts to be found in the Middle East. It mostly consists of desert landscapes, culminating in the notorious Rub-al-Khali (Empty Quarter) which remained unexplored until the 1930s. There are mountain ranges along its western and south-eastern edges that attract some rainfall, and support a greater variety of vegetation. Saudi Arabia dominates the interior and contains most of the region's population, while the Gulf States – Kuwait, Qatar, Bahrain, the United Arab Emirates and Oman – are maritime in their location and outlook. To the south Yemen remains more traditional in its outlook and is largely undeveloped for tourism.

The rapid development of the vast oil reserves of the countries around the Gulf has led to a tremendous growth in demand for all kinds of goods and services from a population which, a generation ago, were largely nomads, fishing communities and peasant farmers. It has also attracted many temporary immigrants, comprising skilled professionals from Western countries, Palestinians, and a large number of labourers and domestic servants from Third World countries such as Pakistan and the Philippines, as well as from the poorer Arab countries such as Jordan and Yemen. In some of the Gulf States, expatriate workers form the majority of the population. The whole region has become an important generator of international travel, led by Saudi Arabia, and per capita expenditure on foreign travel is among the highest in the world. In the 1990s the major outbound flows were to the UK and France, but since 9/11 demand for travel to the USA and Europe has fallen, and Egypt, Lebanon and Cyprus are more significant destinations. Outbound travel is concentrated between June and September when the summer heat is intense.

In the early 1990s spending abroad by residents of the region was estimated to be almost twice that of inbound foreign visitors, who came mainly for business reasons. This is changing with the development of the winter sun holiday market in the United Arab Emirates and Oman. Tourists have benefited from fluctuations in the business travel market after the oil boom in the 1980s, as the region's airlines – notably Gulf Air and Emirates – are anxious to fill aircraft seats, while the luxury hotels of the Gulf states also need to increase their occupancy rates. The airport infrastructure is impressive, with terminal buildings that combine traditional design with ultramodern facilities. Bahrain and Dubai are major staging points on the intercontinental routes between Europe and the Far East, and have largely replaced Beirut as banking centres for the Middle East. Surprisingly the impact of 9/11 was less damaging for the region's airlines than for world aviation as a whole, and carriers such as Emirates, Etihad Airways and Gulf Air have prospered in the new millennium.

The Gulf States are well aware that oil resources will soon be exhausted and are using their wealth to diversify their economies, including investment in tourism-related projects. These countries are experiencing a tourism boom that is unprecedented in other parts of the world. Each capital now boasts a seafront *corniche* highway, marinas, luxury hotels, shopping malls, and other state of the art amenities. The natural assets for tourism include a number of fine beaches along the Gulf coast – although oil spills in this shallow, enclosed sea are a potential problem – and the mountains and deserts of the interior.

The United Arab Emirates

The United Arab Emirates (UAE) is now a major player in international tourism, although the states of Ajman, Fujairah, Ras Al Khaimah, and Umm-al-Quwain have remained relatively inconspicuous compared to Sharjah, Abu Dhabi and Dubai. These three cities are for the most part thoroughly modern in appearance, and most of the traditional architecture, including the picturesque wind towers (a device for cooling buildings through evaporation) has been swept away.

Dubai has done most to attract Western tour operators, and is an example of economic diversification – less than 10 per cent of its revenue now comes from oil. 'Dubai Incorporated' is a partnership between the ruling family of the emirate and the private sector through the Dubai World holding company. Dubai offers free port status, an open skies policy to foreign airlines, and not least, a tolerance of other cultures. The city has retained its historic port, but has invested massively in showpiece facilities and man-made attractions for the recreational tourist, led by the Dubai Commerce and Tourism Promotion Board. These include:

* a cruise terminal;
* a number of world-class golf courses in the desert (each course uses around three million litres of desalinated water a day);
* yacht marinas;
* ultramodern shopping malls and traditional markets, such as the gold souk, appealing to bargain-hunters stopping over on intercontinental flights;
* nightlife that has made Dubai 'the playground of the Middle East', although gambling is not permitted, and the penalties for drug and alcohol abuse can be severe; and
* sport tourism, including the Dubai World Cup – which showcases the Arab love of horse-racing – and the ATP tennis tournament.

More ambitious projects include the creation of a number of artificial resort islands – notably the Palm Jumeirah – a major theme park, and an indoor winter sports centre. In contrast to these futuristic developments, four-wheel drive expeditions into the desert, including 'wadi-bashing', appeal to Western expatriates and adventure-seekers.

Abu Dhabi is aiming to be a centre of cultural excellence, rather than simply emulating Dubai. Operas and other musical events are held in the government-owned

Emirates Palace Hotel, itself a showpiece attraction. The emirate is creating a Cultural District on Saadiyat Island that will include a maritime museum, a centre of the performing arts, a new Guggenheim to rival that of Bilbao, and a new Louvre (with the agreement of the French government). Another offshore island, Yas, is the venue for Formula One Grand Prix motor racing. The Abu Dhabi Tourism Authority hopes to appeal not only to high-spending tourists, but also the family market, with eco-friendly attractions based on the natural world.

Qatar

The Qatar Tourism Authority has used its wealth, based on vast reserves of natural gas, to become a 'sustainable niche market destination'. Doha's international airport, built on land reclaimed from the Gulf, is designed specifically to handle the new generation of Airbus 'superjumbos'. The emirate has hosted international conferences, a number of sports events, including the 2006 Asian Games, and cultural projects include a museum of Islamic arts.

Oman

In contrast to Dubai, Oman can offer the tourist a more genuine experience of traditional Arab culture. The country has a long history of seafaring and traders from the port of Muscat sailed widely across the Indian Ocean many centuries before Europeans ventured into the Atlantic. In this they were aided by the regular seasonal shift in wind direction known as the monsoon. Winds blow directly from the north east during one part of the year, and from the south west during the rest of the year, so early voyagers to India, East Africa and South east Asia could be sure of returning to their home port.

The Batinah coast to the north-east is being developed as a winter sun destination for Europeans. In contrast, the Dhofar region in the south appeals to Arabian families, who tend to avoid instead of seeking out sunshine, as a summer destination. The Indian monsoon has an important influence on the climate of this part of the Arabian Peninsula. As a consequence demand is concentrated in the rainy season from June to September, when temperatures are a 'cool' 30°C compared to a stifling 50°C in the interior. At the same time the monsoon brings dramatic changes to the normally parched landscape.

Saudi Arabia

Saudi Arabia has the largest GDP in the Middle East, largely because it has one quarter of the world's oil reserves. The country's rulers have found it necessary to respect the puritanical views of the powerful Wahabi sect of Islam in their drive for modernisation.

The demand for tourism

As far as the West is concerned, Saudi Arabia is primarily a destination for business travellers, focusing on Riyadh and Jeddah, as visas for other purposes are difficult to obtain. This may change, as the Supreme Commission for Tourism re-evaluates the role that tourism can play in providing jobs for a rapidly growing population, expected to reach 40 million by 2020.

Outbound and domestic tourism

Saudis take well over 4 million trips abroad each year, of which two thirds are for leisure purposes and the rest equally divided between business and VFR travel. The average length of stay is relatively high at just over two weeks. Saudis tend to travel in large family groups, and shopping is the preferred activity. The most popular destinations are the UAE, Egypt and Syria, whereas the UK has declined to only one per cent of the market. The General Commission for Tourism and Antiquities is promoting domestic tourism, and many Saudis escape Riyadh and other cities at weekends to camp out in the desert or the mountains.

Inbound tourism

A third of the over 11 million arrivals in Saudi Arabia – including some 100,000 British Muslims – are visiting for religious reasons, to perform the *haj* to the holy cities of Mecca and Medina, or the lesser pilgrimage known as *umrah*. The haj is concentrated in a five day period in Mecca during the last month of the Muslim calendar, and involves a major effort in logistics and organisation on the part of the Saudi authorities. The Ministry of Haji Affairs co-ordinates the accommodation, catering and transport arrangements for the pilgrimage. Nevertheless, security and crowd control are major problems, such that fatal accidents often occur during the climax of the rituals around the Kaaba, Islam's holiest shrine. As in other aspects of life in this deeply traditionalist country, the *mutawwain* (religious police) play an important role. For many Muslims the cost of travelling to Mecca is prohibitive, but the number of pilgrims has nevertheless quadrupled since the 1960s. The Saudi government has spent a substantial part of its oil revenues on highway construction, and the expansion of terminal facilities at Jeddah Airport, as the majority of pilgrims nowadays arrive on chartered flights rather than use the slow and perhaps dangerous land and sea routes. The *umrah* pilgrimages have the advantage of being spread over 11 months of the year, and a relaxation of visa restrictions now allows Muslim pilgrims to travel throughout the country for up to 30 days, giving much more scope for leisure tourism.

The number of non-Muslim tourists from Europe and North America is small, and is largely restricted to group travel. Niche markets include diving in the Red Sea, trekking in the deserts and mountains, and visits to a number of archaeological sites, such as the Nabatean city of Madain Salah. However, some allege that the government, influenced by fundamentalist hardliners, has neglected Saudi Arabia's cultural heritage, even those sites associated with the early history of Islam.

Yemen

Yemen is much poorer than the other countries of the Arabian Peninsula and tribal traditions persist to a much greater extent. The central government in Sana'a has been ineffective in maintaining law and order in the more remote areas; in fact the negative publicity following the kidnappings of some Western tourists by dissident tribesmen seriously damaged the country's fledgling tourism industry in the late 1990s. Yet this mysterious country has much to offer the more adventurous tourist, namely:

- a unique architectural heritage of mud-brick tower houses and palaces, particularly in Old Sana'a, Zabid and Shibam which have been designated World Heritage Sites; and
- the remains of the ancient Sabaean civilisation, probably the biblical Sheba (although this is disputed by Ethiopians).

The capital, situated at an altitude of 2,200 metres in the northern highlands has an attractive climate and setting. This is less true of Aden in the sweltering coastal plains of the south, which is the country's business centre.

Case study 18.1

Socotra

The remote island of Socotra in the Indian Ocean belongs to Yemen but is geographically closer to Africa. During the Cold War it served as a military base for the Soviet-backed regime of South Yemen. Socotra has been described, somewhat misleadingly, as the 'Galapagos of the Indian Ocean', as many of the plant species – such as the 'dragon trees' – are unique to the island. Like other isolated tropical islands, Socotra is highly vulnerable to the environmental impact of tourism, which needs to be carefully controlled. At present access is limited, as the scheduled services from Aden and Sana'a provided by Yemenia, the national airline, are infrequent, and there is a lack of hotel accommodation.

Research and discussion

Investigate the potential of Socotra as a tourism destination, by looking at a number of niche markets, such as diving. What are the threats to the island's natural and cultural heritage, and what are the opportunities for tourism development? How will the political crisis of 2011 in mainland Yemen affect tourism to the island?

Iraq

Two of the most important countries in the Middle East – Iran and Iraq – have strongly influenced the development of tourism elsewhere in the region, while tourists have been deterred from visiting by unfavourable publicity in the Western media. The war between the two countries during the 1980s interrupted the flow of Iranian pilgrims to the Shia shrines of Karbala and Najaf, and confirmed Qom as the religious capital of Iran. The 2003 war and the subsequent strife between Sunni and Shia meant that Iraq became virtually a 'no go area' for tourism, but since 2009 a few tour operators have negotiated access to certain areas. The mountainous region in the north of the country, which was declared a 'safe haven' for Kurds after the 1991 Gulf War, is autonomous and relatively stable, but has done little to encourage tourism.

The major part of Iraq is made up of the fertile plains of the Tigris and Euphrates, historically known as Mesopotamia, which gave rise to one of the world's earliest civilisations – that of Sumeria, based on complex irrigation systems, in the fourth millennium BC, and the country is rich in archaeological resources.

Until the 1970s Iraq was one of the most prosperous countries of the Middle East. Tourism development was encouraged by a secular government, and projects such as the Habbaniya Tourist Village near Baghdad catered for wealthy foreign visitors as well as Iraqis. Prior to the Gulf War a number of archaeological sites were restored, such as Nineveh, capital of ancient Assyria, and more controversially, Babylon, as a showpiece for the Saddam regime. The long period of sanctions that followed the Gulf War halted any further growth, although Baghdad's hotels continued to attract business travellers from Russia and other countries circumventing the economic blockade.

Baghdad is predominantly a modern capital and little remains of the city of the Abbasid Caliphs that inspired the *Arabian Nights* in the ninth century. The major attraction for Western tourists is the National Museum, which contains the art treasures of Ur and other ancient cities of Mesopotamia. The threat to this heritage was highlighted by the Iraq War, but in fact the pillaging of archaeological sites is a long-standing problem.

Iran

Known as Persia until 1935, Iran is different in language, ethnicity and culture from its Arab neighbours, with a history of powerful dynasties pre-dating the introduction of Islam by many centuries. Before the 1979 revolution, which overthrew the pro-Western Shah and installed a fundamentalist Islamic regime under Ayatollah Khomeini, Iran attracted, and also generated, a significant volume of international tourism. After the revolution, Western hotel chains were expelled and tourism is now under the authority of the Ministry of Culture and Islamic Guidance – which implies the primacy of the Muslim heritage in the tourism product, and the prescription of acceptable forms of entertainment and recreation for both Iranians and foreign visitors. Despite these restrictions international tourist arrivals exceeded one million in the early years of the twenty first century, but these were mainly from neighbouring countries, with relatively small numbers from Western Europe and even fewer from the USA. Tourism received a further setback in 2003 as a result of the earthquake which destroyed the historic citadel of Bam in the south-east of the country.

Iran is the second largest country in the Middle East after Saudi Arabia, consisting mainly of an arid central plateau surrounded by high mountain ranges, so domestic air services are an important part of the transport system. The prevalence of desert landscapes explains the Iranian reverence for irrigated gardens. Traditionally these were supplied by an intricate system of *qanats* – underground channels conveying water from the mountains to the plains.

Tehran is the modern capital and gateway to the country. Since 1979 it has experienced massive growth, partly through rural out-migration. This congested, polluted city of around 12 million inhabitants is the main generator of domestic tourism and a force for social change, with a predominantly young population wishing to express a long-suppressed demand for Western-style leisure activities.

Iran's tourism resources include:

- Some of the world's finest examples of Islamic architecture, particularly in Isfahan 'the city of mosques', and Shiraz, 'the city of roses' which is also celebrated for its associations with Omar Khayyam and other poets.
- The remains of the pre-Islamic Persian civilisations. The most impressive of these is Persepolis, capital of the empire of Darius and Xerxes. This was the setting for the

spectacular celebrations of 2,500 years of Persian monarchy staged by the last Shah in 1971.

- The ski centres of the Alborz Mountains north of Tehran; these were developed prior to the 1979 revolution and cater for a growing domestic demand.
- The summer resorts along the Caspian Sea, particularly Ramsar. These have a favourable climate, attractive scenery and are within easy reach of the capital.
- The island of Kish in the Gulf, which has been developed as a more upmarket winter destination, but as elsewhere in Iran, with strict segregation of male and female bathers.

The position of tourism in Iran mirrors the situation in the Middle East generally. Further growth will depend upon the extent to which modernisers can prevail over hard-line fundamentalists in their efforts to revive the economy, effect social reforms, and improve relations with the USA.

Summary

- The countries of the Middle East are close enough to the tourist generating markets of northern Europe to have developed a sizeable tourism industry. Yet only Israel, and more recently Dubai, have developed beach tourism on a scale comparable to other Mediterranean destinations.
- Cultural tourism is more significant in the region, but only Israel and Egypt have attracted cultural tourists in large numbers.
- Saudi Arabia and the Gulf States receive a considerable volume of business tourists, and this part of the Middle East is also a major generator of outbound international tourism.
- Domestic tourism is significant in most countries of the region, but is mainly VFR, rather than hotel-based.
- The region's tourism products are varied, including summer and winter sun beach holidays, spas and ski resorts in the mountains, adventure holidays in the desert, religious pilgrimages, and cultural tours.
- The Middle East can offer many natural and man-made attractions, some of which are unique. The region's history as the setting for many civilisations over thousands of years is important, while religion continues to play an important role in everyday life.
- Historically, the Middle East lies at a crossroads in world communications, where Europe, Africa and Asia meet. Transport to and within most of the region is good, and highways and airports have been provided to meet the increased demand for international travel.
- There are many problems affecting the further growth of tourism. The prevailing warm, dry climate, allied to demographic and economic pressures has put a severe strain on the region's scarce water supplies.
- Governments need to pay more attention to the conservation of the cultural as well as the natural resources on which tourism depends.
- The greatest threat is the political instability of most countries in the region, fuelled by religious fundamentalism, social and ethnic tensions, sectarianism, the unresolved conflict between Palestinians and Jews, the legacy of the Gulf War, and the on-going war against terrorism.

Assignments

1   Identify the constraints on Western-style beach tourism in most countries of the Middle East. How should tourists respond?

2   Discuss the importance of religion in the Middle East and the extent to which sectarianism affects the stability of countries in the region.

3   Explain the success of the UAE and Israel as tourist destinations. How much of this is due to:
   • each country's natural resources
   • cultural attractions
   • improved accessibility
   • other factors (which you should specify).

CHAPTER 19

The tourism geography of Africa

Introduction

We mentioned in Chapter 18 that the countries of North Africa share many characteristics with those of the Middle East region. There are indeed major cultural and physical differences between North Africa and the rest of the continent. Physically, Morocco, Algeria and Tunisia consist largely of fold mountains that are geologically similar to those of southern Europe. Much of the scenery, with the exception of the desert zone, resembles that of Greece, Spain or southern Italy and the people are predominantly Arabs or Berbers. In contrast, most of Africa south of the Sahara consists of plateaux and block mountains, with only a narrow coastal plain separated from the interior by high escarpments. In terms of their ethnicity and culture, the emerging nations of sub-Saharan Africa are different from the Arab states of the north. For most of the twentieth century all of these countries, with the exceptions of Ethiopia and Liberia, were under colonial rule. However, this was also the experience of the countries of North Africa, which play an important role in the African Union (AU). Although the Sahara Desert acted as a formidable physical barrier between the countries of North Africa and those to the south, it was frequently crossed by camel caravans, allowing an exchange of merchandise and ideas.

The setting for tourism

The sheer size of Africa is at once an asset and a hindrance to developing a tourism industry. On the one hand, most of the continent is sparsely populated, offering wide-open spaces, an almost unique wealth of wildlife, spectacular scenery, and tribal cultures (around 2,000 languages are spoken in Africa). Yet apart from North Africa, which has taken advantage of its proximity to Europe, and South Africa, with its well-developed infrastructure, the continent's tourism potential is largely untapped. This is due to the following factors.

Accessibility. Before the advent of air travel, much of the interior of Africa was virtually inaccessible. Although air transport has shown substantial growth, air traffic control and airport infrastructure are deficient by Western standards, and many experts consider this is holding back the development of tourism. The same is true of surface transport. There are very few natural harbours along the coast, and even penetration up the largest rivers – the Congo or Zambezi for example – is blocked by rapids and waterfalls. Road and rail infrastructure is generally inadequate in most African countries, so that touring holidays can be a major undertaking. In the absence of adequate public transport, improvised alternatives, such as the 'bush taxis' of the Gambia and the *matatu*s of Kenya can be used by the more adventurous independent travellers.

A low level of economic development. Most African countries fall in the 'least developed' category with only a few having reached the intermediate level of development. They tend to be rural in character, although the populations of the national capitals are expanding faster than the provision of jobs or public services. Levels of poverty and illiteracy generally mean that outbound travel is restricted to an elite, while the volume of domestic tourism is insignificant compared to Western countries. Although some countries do see tourism as an important source of foreign currency and a stimulus to the economy, many governments give tourism a low priority for investment compared to other economic sectors.

Poor organisation. There is a generally poor level of organisation, particularly at the regional level. Governments also place bureaucratic obstacles in the way of tourists, making travel between countries difficult. Education and training for the tourism sector is of a poor standard, and marketing budgets are inadequate.

Political instability. Some of the world's 'trouble spots' are located in Africa, fuelled by tribal unrest, ethnic rivalries, or border disputes, as the political boundaries drawn up in the colonial era rarely correspond to natural features or tribal territories. Few African countries are therefore nation-states in the European sense. This instability has led to concern in the Western media over the physical security of tourists, and has also discouraged Western investment in the tourism industry.

Perceived health and safety risks. The high incidence of AIDS, as well as insect-borne diseases such as malaria and yellow fever, is due in large measure to the inadequate infrastructure of public health services in most of Africa.

Sceptical investment environment. Investors are often reluctant to invest in tourism in countries where the political climate is changeable, where a return on their investment is not guaranteed, and price inflation is not under control. This is however changing, with the arrival of China on the world stage. In its demand for Africa's wealth of raw materials, China has to a large extent replaced the USA and the ex-colonial powers as a major source of investment, but this may have costs as well as benefits for the recipient countries.

All these constraints and structural weaknesses have frustrated Africa's ability to capitalise on the growing long-haul market, and it is clear that tourism is still a fledgling industry. This is borne out by the statistics – for the whole of sub-Saharan Africa there were around 30 million international tourist arrivals in 2010 – less than for some individual countries in Europe in an average year, while North Africa attracted a further 18 million. Indeed, for a continent that contains 15 per cent of the world's population and a third of the land area, it receives a small share of the tourist market, amounting to only 4 per cent. Out of more than 50 countries considered in the region, less than half have developed significant tourism industries. In the remaining countries, hotel accommodation is rarely found outside the national capital. However, there are a number of positive factors that are boosting Africa's tourism in the new millennium:

- interest in African peoples and cultures;
- the increasing pace and variety of tourism development;
- Africa will be attractive to segments of the population in the generating markets who have both the time and the income to travel;
- the growing importance of ethnic ties between Africa and Europe – there has, for example, been a considerable emigration since the 1990s from North and West Africa to Europe, and also a two-way flow of migrants between Britain and South Africa;
- the growth of sport tourism, bringing together participants from many countries in the region, as shown by the Africa Cup of Nations football event and the All–Africa Games;
- the pursuit of free market economic policies in many African countries; and
- improved air access.

North Africa

In contrast to most of sub-Saharan Africa, the North African countries, with the significant exception of Libya, have developed a sizeable tourism industry, based on beach holidays and inclusive tours for the north European market. This is an extension of the resort developments around the Mediterranean coast of Europe, although the cultural setting is quite different. This region accounts for over a third of foreign tourist arrivals to the African continent, with more than half arriving from countries across the Mediterranean, namely France, Spain and Italy. Morocco was the first country to enter the market in the 1950s and both Tunisia and Algeria soon followed.

We can divide North Africa into three main zones based on its physical geography:

- The fertile coastal plains, which have a Mediterranean climate.
- The Atlas Mountains, which reach their greatest extent in Morocco. In relation to their limited natural resources, these highlands are quite densely populated. There are frequent snowfalls during the winter months.
- The deserts of the south where productive land is restricted to the oases. The Sahara provides the region with its best known tourist image, but in reality, vast expanses of sand dunes are not the only landscape feature. Moreover, nomadic tribes now make up only a small minority of the population, while the camel caravan has been superseded by motorised transport.

Morocco, Algeria, Tunisia and Libya have formed an important part of the Muslim world since their conquest by Arabs from the Middle East in the eighth century AD. Arabic is the official language of all four countries, and Arabs form the majority of the population, especially in the cities. However, the earlier inhabitants – the Berbers – still carry on their traditional way of life in the Atlas Mountains and the fringes of the Sahara. To some extent they have been marginalised economically, and the Berber languages receive little official encouragement. During the first half of the twentieth century, France ruled Algeria, Tunisia and the greater part of Morocco. As a result, French is the second language and some French cultural characteristics have been adopted by the educated classes of the cities. The French were also responsible for constructing a good highway system, and well-planned European-style cities. To a lesser extent, the Spanish in their zone of Morocco, and the Italians in Libya, left a similar legacy. However, the influence of the Middle East remains predominant, as evidenced by the mosques and the souks, along with the crowded *medinas* and *kasbahs* (the old Arab districts) of the cities. Traditional handicrafts – notably leather, metalwork and pottery – are important in the local economy and have been stimulated by the growth of tourism – often with government encouragement.

The main problem facing the Maghreb countries (Morocco, Algeria and Tunisia) is the 'demographic timebomb', causing acute pressure on land and water resources – half the population of about 80 million is under 21 years of age. Poverty, illiteracy and unemployment are widespread, both in the cities – which are surrounded by *bidonvilles* (shanty towns) – and in the countryside. The national economies cannot produce enough jobs to meet expectations, even for those with a Western-style education. This situation has contributed to the rise of Islamic fundamentalism in Algeria and the largely secular 'Jasmine Revolution' in Tunisia that initiated the 'Arab Spring' democratic movement. Popular unrest has so far been checked in Morocco. Not surprisingly, Western tourists with their relative wealth are also seen as an obvious target for exploitation by unlicensed guides, vendors and touts of every description – Tangier in Morocco is a notorious example.

Morocco

The timeless, almost biblical scenes that can be found in Morocco, both in the Arab *medinas* and the Berber communities of the Atlas, have a particular appeal. This has made the country a favourite location for film-makers and for the adventurous tourist travelling overland from western Europe, it is the gateway to Africa. The markets assault the senses with a medley of sights and pungent aromas, and the widespread poverty can add to the 'culture shock' for Western visitors. Yet the cities also contain some of the most exquisite examples of Islamic architecture. This most 'oriental' of North African countries extends further west geographically than any part of the European continent, and can be reached by a three-hour flight from the cities of western Europe. Morocco is also unique among North African countries in having been an independent kingdom for many centuries, whose power at one time extended over most of Spain and the western Sahara. It experienced only one period of foreign domination (from 1912 to 1956) when it was divided into French and Spanish protectorates. Under the rule of a monarch who has both near-autocratic powers and is revered as a religious leader, it has remained politically stable, with the government steering a course between traditional Islam and modernisation.

The demand for tourism

Morocco received over 9 million annual international tourist arrivals in 2010, of which a third are Europeans, mainly from France and Spain, which dominate the market, followed by Britain and Germany. This is not surprising given the development of air-inclusive tours to Morocco, the convenient ferry links from Spain and Gibraltar, and the opening up of low cost air routes. Algeria used to supply large numbers of tourists, but this market has largely disappeared as a result of the dispute over the Western Sahara. Moroccan expatriates working in western Europe and returning for their annual holiday form a large proportion of the remaining arrivals, along with tourists from other Arab states. However, this is not reciprocated, as those Moroccans who can afford foreign travel prefer to visit Europe. Domestic tourism is less significant, with middle class families visiting the beach resorts near Casablanca and resorts such as Ifrane in the Middle Atlas Mountains which have both a summer season for health tourism and a winter skiing season.

The supply side of tourism

Transport

Morocco has one of the best transport systems in Africa, with tarmac highways penetrating mountains and desert, and a network of inter-city bus services, supplemented by *grands-taxis*. The national carrier, Royal Air Maroc, operates an efficient domestic air network. On the other hand rail transport is poorly developed, and overland travel from Algeria has been disrupted by the closure of the 1,500 kilometre long border between the two countries since 1990.

Accommodation

Two thirds of Morocco's accommodation is in hotels and the rest in self-catering. The French tour operator Club Mediterranée pioneered all-inclusive holiday villages on the Mediterranean coast and at Ouarzazate in the Sahara. As part of its conservation strategy, the government has encouraged the use of heritage buildings as hotels, while stays in *riads* – courtyard houses once belonging to wealthy merchants in the medinas of cities such as Fez and Marrakech – are increasingly popular with Western tourists.

Organisation

The Ministry of Tourism has the overall responsibility for the financing and development of tourism projects as well as promotion. Following a reduction in arrivals in the first half of the 1990s, the government revised its approach to tourism.

Case study 19.1

Vision 2010: an example of state involvement in tourism planning and development

In 2001 a new strategy for tourism – Vision 2010 – was launched on the personal initiative of King Mohammed VI, as part of a programme of social and economic reforms. It is a partnership between the government and the General Confederation of Moroccan Enterprises (CGEM). Vision 2010 put tourism centre-stage to attract foreign investment, as a means of spreading economic growth from the Rabat–Casablanca region to the less developed parts of the country, with the following objectives:

- to create 60,000 new jobs in tourism;
- to increase tourist arrivals from 2.3 million in 2001 to a target of 10 million a year by 2010;
- to increase the number of bedspaces by 150,000 between 2001 and 2010.

Case study 19.1

The *Plan Azur*, a blueprint for coastal tourism, envisaged the creation of six new resorts, emphasising quality development and 'beach plus' tourism. Under the plan each resort offers a different product; for example, Plage Blanche in the remote deep south of Morocco specialises in ecotourism; Taghazout and Port Lixus are very sport-oriented; while Mogador attracts cultural tourists with its proximity to the historic seaport and World Heritage Site of Essaouira.

Nevertheless critics of the strategy cite insufficient government funding, bureaucratic obstacles, and a lack of infrastructure in rural areas, including inadequate water supplies, for tourism development on the scale required. There is also a need to develop local programmes of tourism training in rural communities, if the social objectives of Vision 2010 are to be fully realised.

Discussion point

Are these criticisms justified? Is a target of 10 million tourist arrivals, facilitated by an open skies policy encouraging low cost carriers, compatible with the government's objective of attracting the affluent, culturally aware type of tourist?

Tourism resources

The heartland of Morocco is a fertile plateau separated by rugged mountain ranges from the Sahara Desert to the south and east, and the Mediterranean coast to the north. The High Atlas, rising to 4,000 metres near Marrakech, is the most spectacular of these mountain ramparts. Morocco is fortunate in having an extensive coastline on both the Atlantic and the Mediterranean. The climate of the Atlantic coast is particularly favourable for tourism, due to the influence of the cool Canaries Current, which ensures that the summers are usually free of the excessive heat and dust-laden winds found elsewhere in North Africa. Winters are much warmer, drier and sunnier in southern Morocco than in the north, which explains why Agadir is promoted as a winter-sun destination whereas Tangier and the resorts along the Mediterranean coast cater for summer holidays. A regional survey of Morocco shows the diversity of its natural and cultural resources, offering the tourist a variety of opportunities for recreation and sightseeing.

The Moroccan heartland

Cultural tourism to Morocco focuses on the 'Imperial Cities' circuit that combines Fez, Meknes, Rabat and Marrakech – all of which at different times have served as the capital of Morocco:

- Marrakech has been fashionable as a winter sun destination since the 1930s but is now mainly visited for its *souks* and the colourful market square known as the Djemaa el Fna, which is ideal for people-watching. Here crowds gather around entertainers such as storytellers, snake charmers, acrobats and musicians. Berber folklore features in the event attractions known as *fantasias*, which feature impressive displays of horsemanship by local tribesmen. The most attractive features of Marrakech are the gardens which provide a refuge from the extreme summer heat; those of the Mamounia Hotel are world-famous.

- Although its extensive medina is a World Heritage Site, **Fez** is not as well known as Marrakech and has been less affected by tourism. Its main attractions are the Attarine Medrassa (one of a number of Muslim colleges), the Karaouine Mosque and the spice market. Those interested in Moroccan leather can visit the dyeworks and tanneries where medieval industrial methods are still carried on. Fez is also an important festival venue.
- Business tourism gravitates to the modern city of Casablanca which is Morocco's financial and commercial centre, complementing the capital Rabat. Both cities have conference facilities of international standard.

The North

This part of Morocco is dominated by the rugged terrain of the Rif Mountains, and following independence was neglected by the government for decades. The major tourist centres include:

- **Tangier**, which is a popular beach resort as well as being a major seaport, now undergoing revitalisation as a result of Vision 2010. For many visitors arriving by ferry or cruise ship, the medina of Tangier is their first impression of Morocco and a stressful one – due to the hordes of hustlers. From 1912 to 1956 the city had special status as an International Zone open to free trade and tolerant of alternative lifestyles, hence its enduring reputation as a centre for gay tourism.
- **Tetouan** was the capital of Spanish Morocco during the protectorate, and the cultural influence of Spain is still evident here and in the picturesque towns of Asilah, Chefchaouen and Larache. Beach tourism has developed along the Mediterranean coast near Tetouan and further east at Al Hoceima, which was badly damaged by an earthquake in 2004. These coastal resorts suffer from the problems of seasonality and under-investment, but this may change with the development, as part of the *Plan Azur*, of the Saadia project, which has received considerable attention from foreign investors.

The High Atlas

This is mainly a destination for trekking, where the attractions include spectacular mountain scenery and Berber villages that have remained apparently unchanged over the centuries. A number of tourism projects ensure that the benefits reach local people, by providing jobs, purchasing supplies and funding community services, such as education in areas where 80 per cent of Berber women are illiterate.

Southern Morocco

South of the Atlas Mountains the landscape becomes progressively more arid, until the true desert is reached. Major attractions include the oasis towns of Zagora and Ouarzazate, the gorges of the Todra and the Dadès, and the distinctive fortress-villages, built of red sun-dried clay by the local Berbers. The coast is still largely undeveloped, with the significant exception of Agadir, which is Morocco's most popular international beach resort. The old town was destroyed by an earthquake in 1960, and a modern resort of high-rise hotels and apartment blocks soon took its place to meet the demand for accommodation. Later expansion has been more sensitively designed, in the form of low-rise developments in the traditional Moorish style.

Since 1975 Morocco has occupied the **Western Sahara**, a former Spanish colony. However, this is disputed by the Polisario independence movement, whose claims are supported by some African countries. These include Algeria, which provides a refuge for the many Saharauis opposed to Moroccan rule. Although the conflict is as yet unresolved, the situation has normalised to the extent that a limited amount of tourist activity is taking place in the coastal desert zone, particularly near Aaiun, the regional capital and at Dakhla, where conditions are favourable for surfing.

Tunisia

With a long history of contact with other parts of the Mediterranean, Tunisia is one of the most tolerant of the Arab states. This has been a factor in the development of the country as a holiday playground for Europeans seeking sun, sea and sand. Tunisia not only has the advantages of superb beaches and especially in the south, a favourable winter climate, but tourism development has been encouraged and carefully managed. Until the 2010 revolution Tunisia had a reputation for stability, where the government consistently applied liberal social and economic policies. Tourism is an important sector of the economy and government involvement has been extensive. In 2010 tourism accounted for 6 per cent of GDP and provided employment for a fifth of the workforce.

Tourism demand and supply

Tourism caters mainly for the mass market, and this is shown by the fact that about half of the 7 million annual arrivals are mostly package holidaymakers from France, Germany and Britain, concentrated during the summer months. Nevertheless, Tunisia has been successfully promoted as a winter-sun destination and this has boosted arrivals between October and March. The country's dependence on the inclusive tour European market leaves it vulnerable to recession in the generating countries and also to the international political situation.

As you would expect in a country dependent on the mass market, the majority of visitors arrive by air. Tunis airport mainly handles scheduled services, but most holidaymakers on inclusive tours arrive at Monastir, which was specially built to handle charter flights. La Goulette and Bizerta are the ports of arrival for cruise passengers. Tunisia's professional approach to tourism includes upgrading the welcome facilities for travellers at the major gateways.

Hotel accommodation on the coast is mostly in low-rise developments, physically separate from the local communities, designed in the traditional style, and blending with the local environment. Other forms of accommodation include youth hostels and campsites. The French tour operator Club Mediterranée chose Tunisia as the location for several of its all-inclusive holiday villages.

The National Ministry of the Economy formulates the policy and context of tourism but its day-to-day implementation is carried out by the Tunisian National Tourism Office (ONTT). Since the 1980s Tunisia has diversified the tourism product away from the sea, sun and sand image, by promoting:

- an upmarket marina and sports complex at Port El Kantaoui adjoining the city of Sousse;
- a number of golf courses of world-class standard;
- the Tabarka area in the north-west – the 'Coral Coast' – as a scuba-diving destination;
- 'soft adventure' tourism in the desert south, where a number of luxury hotels are available in oasis towns such as Tozeur; and not least
- the rich cultural heritage of the country.

Tourism resources

Most tourists prefer to spend their time on the beaches and holiday complexes of the coast, the most important being Hammanet, Monastir and Sousse. In the south, the island of Djerba with its myriad palm trees is an important winter-sun destination, while the Kerkenneh islands offer a less sophisticated holiday product.

Tunisia is a relatively compact country, giving the holidaymaker based on the coast a wide choice of excursions, including:

- The capital, Tunis where the spacious boulevards of the modern city provide a contrast with the medieval Arab medina. The Bardo Museum has a world-renowned collection of finds from the site of Carthage, the great trading centre of ancient times, which under Hannibal challenged Rome for domination of the Mediterranean. After completely destroying Carthage in the last of the Punic Wars, Rome built a new city on the site.
- The remains of the Roman cities of Dougga and El Djem – where the amphitheatre is almost as large as the Colosseum in Rome. This part of Africa was not only the granary of ancient Rome, but also the supplier of many of the wild beasts that were slaughtered for public entertainment in the arenas throughout the empire.
- The holy city of Kairouan, famous for its Great Mosque and traditional crafts, such as saddle-making and carpet-weaving.
- The troglodite community of Matmata and the oases of southern Tunisia. Although very few Tunisians are Saharan nomads, tour operators have exploited Western visitors' perceptions of the country by staging 'Bedouin feasts' that are really pseudo-events. Excursions by jeep or camel, from oasis towns such as Douz, provide a more genuine desert experience.

Algeria

In some respects Algeria is the most Westernised of the North African countries. It experienced a much longer period of French rule, and was in fact treated as part of metropolitan France. After the war of independence that ended in 1962, the FLN government established a secular, socialist-leaning state, using Algeria's considerable oil revenues to industrialise the country, expand education and redistribute wealth. Tourism was not given a high priority, and the number of arrivals was much smaller than in neighbouring Morocco and Tunisia. The situation worsened after 1991, as a result of the vicious struggle between Islamic fundamentalists and the Algerian army. In these circumstances, it has been impossible to guarantee visitor security in much of the country, including the capital.

Tourism demand and supply

Algeria received almost two million inbound arrivals in 2009; most of these are VFR tourists, as large numbers of Algerians work abroad, particularly in France, and return home for their annual summer holidays. French tourists visiting Algeria – and even more so Algerians visiting France – have been subjected to visa restrictions as a result of the controversy over Algerian immigration. The majority of international tourists arrive by air, with the exception of Tunisians who use road or rail transport. Algeria has five international airports and scheduled flights are operated by the major European airlines as well as Air Algerie – which also serves the extensive domestic network. Air transport is important in a country more than four times the size of France, and allows access to remote desert and mountain areas. The country has good ferry links to Marseilles in France operated by the French Societé Nationale Maritime Mediterranée (SCNM) and the Algerian state-owned shipping line. There is a very extensive road network and excellent bus services allow visitors in less troubled times to travel throughout the country and into Tunisia. Rail transport is less efficient and surface transport links with Morocco have been disrupted by the dispute over the Western Sahara.

Even in good times, Algeria's tourism industry has suffered from an acute shortage of accommodation. This has been made worse by the need of many foreign companies to accommodate their employees in hotels, owing to the shortage of housing. At the same time, service standards are poor. The difficulty is at its worst in Algiers, where accommodating delegates attending conferences is a continual problem. Most hotel beds are located in the purpose-built tourist centres on the coast and in some of the Saharan oases. Like other sectors of the economy, tourism is closely controlled by the state. Policy is decided by the Ministry of Tourism and Handicraft, which has established a tourism development agency and is embarking on a policy of sustainable development to upgrade Algeria's product.

Tourism resources

Algeria offers a diversity of natural and cultural resources to the tourist. In the extreme north, the Mediterranean coast is largely undeveloped for mass tourism, consisting of 1,200 kilometres of small bays backed by cliffs, and scenically not very different from the Côte d'Azur. During the 1970s a number of beach resorts (Tipasa, Zeralda and Sidi Ferruch) were developed on the coast to cater for European tour operators. These were planned as self-contained towns in Arabic style, complete with well-designed souks, entertainment and sports facilities. However, the coastal lowlands – the Tell – contain 84 per cent of Algeria's population and the bulk of its industry, so marine pollution is a serious problem.

Algiers itself – a metropolis of over 3 million people – is famous for its Kasbah, the fortified old town built under Ottoman rule. Despite having been declared a World Heritage Site, conservation has been neglected and its buildings are grossly overcrowded.

A series of mountain ramparts separate the coast from the Sahara. However, much of this mountain region, particularly the Aures Massif and Kabylie, is off-limits to tourists. The semi-arid area between the two main Atlas ranges, the Plateau of the Shotts, contains a large number of salt lakes. The true desert – and the date palms for which Algeria is famous – are reached at Laghouat, some 400 kilometres south from Algiers. From here, the Trans-Saharan Highway, the most important of the desert routes, runs a further 2,400 kilometres to Kano in northern Nigeria. Apart from the expanses of sand dunes known as *erg*, the Algerian Sahara is scenically quite varied, including the volcanic rock formations of the Hoggar rising to 3,000 metres, and eroded badlands, criss-crossed by a network of wadis. Each oasis town has a distinct character, the most interesting being those of the M'zab region, while Tamanrasset is the main centre of the 'people of the veil' - the Tuareg nomads. Prehistoric rock paintings at Ain Sefra and in the Tassili Mountains show that the Sahara once enjoyed a much wetter climate. Although UNESCO has declared these a World Heritage Site, entire frescos have faded as a result of exposure to tourists or even been removed as part of the illicit trade in artefacts.

Libya

As a major oil producer, the government of Libya saw little need to encourage tourism until recently, while the UN trade embargo, imposed in retaliation for the Islamic socialist regime's support of terrorist movements throughout the Middle East, effectively restricted demand to a trickle of business travellers. After the Iraq War the political climate changed and scheduled air services linked Tripoli and Benghazi to a growing number of cities in Europe. However, the outbreak of civil war in 2011 exposed the long-standing cultural differences between Tripolitania in the west of the country and Cyrenaica in the east, not to mention the Fezzan region in the south.

Although 95 per cent of Libya is desert, vast reserves of ground water are believed to exist. There is a shortage of hotel accommodation and other facilities for Western holidaymakers, but the country has the following resources for tourism;

- the longest stretch of pristine Mediterranean coastline;
- important Roman remains at Leptis Magna and Sabratha (near Tripoli) and Cyrene (near Benghazi) that were systematically excavated in the 1930s by Mussolini's Fascist regime to remind the world of an Italy recalled to imperial greatness; and
- the oases of Ghadames and Ghat on the former caravan routes across the Sahara.

East Africa

Tour operators regard the countries of Kenya, Tanzania, and Uganda as constituting East Africa. Their tourism resources are similar, and before independence they had a measure of unity under British rule. The wider geographical region also includes the Sudan, and the countries of 'The Horn of Africa' – Ethiopia, Somalia, Eritrea and Djibouti – where tourism is still in its infancy, and where the economy has been disrupted for many years by drought and political strife. The Swahili language is widely understood throughout East Africa, while the heritage of Islam and Arab traders is evident throughout the coastal belt.

The setting for tourism

Contrasts of scenery, climate and culture are particularly evident in East Africa. Most of the region consists of an undulating plateau over 1,000 metres in altitude, but it also contains the most spectacular scenery to be found anywhere on the continent. Part of the Rift Valley – a deep gash in the earth's surface extending from the Dead Sea to Lake Malawi – cuts through the region as two branches. The western branch contains Lakes Albert, Edward, and Tanganyika, while the eastern branch is bounded by a high escarpment in western Kenya. The earth movements which formed the rift also raised the high mountains of volcanic origin on either side, notably Mounts Elgon, Kenya, and Kilimanjaro. The valley floor is littered with a number of craters (the most famous being Ngorongoro, which is a spectacular wildlife sanctuary), and there are numerous lakes. Some of these, for example Naivasha, contain fresh water and are rich in fish, whereas others – Nakuru, Magadi, and Natron – have deposits of salt and soda which have attracted the attention of mineral developers, as well as of conservationists who wish to protect the millions of flamingos which breed there.

Most of East Africa has a tropical wet-dry climate but, because of its position astride the Equator, the region has two dry seasons and two rainy seasons. The coast is also influenced by the seasonal shift in wind direction known as the monsoon over the Indian Ocean. Altitude too has an important effect. Conditions in Nairobi at 1,800 metres are ideal for Europeans with daytime temperatures between 20°C and 25°C all year round. The main tourist seasons for East Africa's big-game areas are December to early March and July to early October as these correspond to the dry seasons when the animals are concentrated around the water-holes and the grass is short, aiding visibility. Travel is also easier at this time, whereas the earth roads are often impassable at the height of the rains.

East Africa contains a large variety of habitats for wildlife, ranging from the semi-deserts of northern Kenya and Somalia which support herds of antelope and gazelle, to the dense rain forests of the Ruwenzori on the Uganda–Congo border which shelter the chimpanzee and gorilla. The dominant type of vegetation is thorny scrub in the drier areas, alternating with open plains or savanna where the tall grasses, dotted with umbrella-shaped acacia trees support large herds of grazing animals and the great predators such as the lion.

Safari tourism in East Africa

Wildlife is the basis of East Africa's tourism industry. The organisation of big-game hunting safaris began at the end of the nineteenth century, although the first national parks were not designated until the 1940s. Since independence, Kenya, Tanzania and Uganda have devoted large areas to wildlife conservation, either by designation as national parks, which conform to the high standards of protection laid down by the IUCN, or as game reserves. This has entailed a social cost as local communities have lost their traditional rights to these lands. For example, the semi-nomadic Masai on the Kenya–Tanzania border, who have a symbiotic relationship with the wildlife, were prohibited from grazing their cattle in the Masai Mara Wildlife Reserve. Wildlife resources are under threat, for the following reasons:

* poaching for skins, ivory, and rhinoceros horn – (greatly valued in both Yemen and the Far East, but for different motives); and
* the encroachment of the human population (growing at the rate of 3 per cent annually) on wildlife habitats; this is a more serious long-term problem, although it is poaching that receives wide publicity in the Western media. Most of the best land has already been given over to the production of cash crops for export rather than to food staples, while African farmers see wildlife as a threat to their crops, not as a resource.

The term 'safari' has come to include the following types of products;

- Budget-priced mini-bus tours of the most accessible national parks such as Amboseli and Masai-Mara, based on Nairobi or one of the coastal resorts. Drivers often approach the game too closely so that tourists can get a better view. Tourists also spend most of their time looking for the 'big five' – lion, leopard, elephant, rhino and buffalo, causing bottlenecks in the process.
- In the higher price bracket, tour operators include stays in one of the government-run game lodges in the national parks. These are designed to blend in with the local environment, the most famous being 'Treetops' in the Aberdare Mountains, and Seronera in the Serengeti National Park. They offer five star service and to an extent tourists are cut off from the realities of life in the African bush.
- Camping safaris, for example in the Tsavo National Park, are a much more authentic and sustainable alternative.
- Balloon safaris provide an ideal way to view game, but it is said that the noise from the burners frightens away the animals, while the back-up vehicles damage the terrain in the wet season.
- Other options include camel safaris in the remoter parts of northern Kenya; fishing expeditions to Lake Turkana; trekking and mountain climbing on Mount Kenya or Kilimanjaro; and escorted expeditions to privately-owned game reserves and game ranches.

The negative impacts of safari tourism can be minimised by:

- visitor management, ensuring that tourist numbers do not exceed the carrying capacity of the area; in other words, low volume, high spending, low impact 'ecotourism' rather than mass tourism; and
- involvement of the local community, so that they derive tangible benefits from tourism. For example the Masai have set up 'cultural *bomas*' – villages where they can sell their traditional crafts directly to tourists.

Discussion point

The international trade in ivory is one of the biggest threats to Africa's wildlife resources. In 1989 the Convention on International Trade in Endangered Species (CITES) imposed an outright ban, which succeeded in halting the decline in elephant numbers, particularly in Kenya. Subsequently four Southern African countries – South Africa, Botswana, Namibia and Zimbabwe – were allowed to stockpile ivory for export, provided it came from 'rogue' elephants or those that had died from natural causes. Japan, which had a good track record in preventing illegal trading, became the sole legal importing country. However, most of the demand for ivory originates in China, which has largely replaced Europe and the USA as the main trading partner for many African countries. In 2008 China successfully bid to become the legal importer. It is estimated that 23,000 elephants are killed illegally each year to satisfy the demand for ivory, with countries such as the Democratic Republic of Congo and Sudan acting as transit points for the trade.

In class, discuss the following issues:

- The reasons for the demand for ivory, particularly in the Far East.
- The effectiveness of CITES and other organisations in controlling the supply and shipment of ivory.
- The need to get local communities in the bush on-side in the fight against poaching. Local people may have more immediate concerns than ecology and the contribution that wildlife makes in foreign exchange earnings to the national economy.
- The case for restricting the size of elephant herds.

Kenya

Kenya is the most developed of the East African countries, and until the eruption of inter-tribal violence following the elections in 2007, appeared to be far more stable than its neighbours. Prior to independence it had a large number of white European settlers and an Asian middle class, which generated a sizeable demand for domestic tourism. Following independence in 1963 political stability and government support encouraged foreign investment in Kenya's tourism industry. The Kenyan Ministry of Tourism reflects the importance placed on tourism as the major source of foreign exchange, and it enjoys private sector support from the Kenya Tourist Board which has responsibility for promotion. Although it has pursued a policy of 'Kenyanisation' replacing foreign nationals by Africans, the government in other respects has had a 'laissez-faire' attitude toward the private sector and foreign tour operators. This is changing in response to the impact of mass tourism in the more accessible national parks and on the coast. The tourism authorities are also faced with a decline in arrivals as fears about crime in Nairobi, international terrorism and political unrest have grown. Such is the problem that neighbouring countries are set to challenge Kenya's crown as the leading tourism destination in the region. This is a serious issue as tourism represents over 10 per cent of Kenya's economy. Since the early 1990s ecotourism has been encouraged by the government's Kenya Wildlife Service (KWS), while the government's development plan aims to diversify the tourism product and to attract high income, low volume tourism. Here, privately owned game ranches play an important role, as they integrate tourism, wildlife and cattle farming. Tourists can participate in activities on the ranch, while local communities benefit, with the enterprise providing jobs and funding for schools.

Tourism resources

Kenya became one of Africa's most popular destinations (approaching 1.5 million arrivals in 2009), because it has a wealth of tourism resources, including some of the best-known game reserves, such as the Masai-Mara, Amboseli and Tsavo, and an attractive coastline along the Indian Ocean. The capital Nairobi is a modern city, with facilities for shopping and entertainment, and good communications by air, road and rail to most of the region, making it the recognised gateway to East Africa. Most foreign tourists spend one or two nights in Nairobi, and the Kenyatta Conference Centre is a major venue for business travellers.

The old city of Mombasa, with its modern port facilities at Kilindini, and extended international airport, is the gateway to the Kenya coast. In the old port, Arab *dhows* can still be seen and the markets sell tourist curios such as Masai beadwork, wood and soapstone carvings and animal trophies. The modern resort developments near Mombasa and at Malindi attract large numbers of winter-sun package holidaymakers, mainly from Germany, Britain, Switzerland or Italy, while beaches and hotels tend to be dominated by a particular nationality. Tourism suffered a major setback in 2002 with the bombing of a hotel which was owned and mainly frequented by Israelis. Until then beach tourism had been expanding in Kenya, while visits to game reserves (except by Americans) were declining. The long white sandy beaches, and lagoons protected by an offshore coral reef, provide safe conditions for diving and other water sports. Although the underwater wildlife is protected by marine national parks at Malindi and Watamu, excessive numbers of glass bottom boats, and illegal shell collecting for the lucrative souvenir trade, have caused extensive damage to the reef. Western visitors have also caused offence to a traditional Muslim society by their dress and behaviour, and social mores are changing to the extent that sex tourism is a problem. The island of Lamu has minimised these environmental and social impacts by carefully controlling tourism. The income is used for conservation projects, so that the Swahili-Arabic heritage of this attractive resort has been retained.

Tanzania

Tanzania has a less-developed tourism industry than Kenya. In part, this is due to history – until 1989 government policy encouraged African-style socialism with the state taking a major shareholding in tourism enterprises. Western-style tourism did not fit easily into this scheme and foreign companies were reluctant to invest. Since 1990 the government has adopted a more pragmatic approach, liberalising the tourism sector, and is ambitious to become a leader in this field. This has been aided by the decline in tourism in neighbouring Kenya. The Tanzania Tourist Board, created in 1992, has revitalised the sector so that it supports 27,000 jobs and generates a quarter of the country's foreign exchange. By 2009 international arrivals were just over 700,000.

Tourism resources

Tanzania's most well-known attractions lie close to the Kenyan border and this has made the task of promotion more difficult. They include:

- Africa's highest mountain – Mount Kilimanjaro;
- the world famous Serengeti National Park, with its spectacular seasonal migrations of animals in search of water and grazing; and
- the Ngorongoro Reserve, an extinct volcanic caldera, with excellent game viewing from the crater rim.

Photo 19.1 Kilimanjaro, Africa's highest mountain (©istockphoto.com/ Graeme Shannon)

Ironically, it is easier to reach these attractions from Nairobi than from Tanzania's former capital, Dar-es-Salaam, on the coast. This induced the government to build an airport near Arusha (Kilimanjaro International) and invest heavily in hotel complexes in that city. The enormous game reserves of southern Tanzania are under-utilised as they lie off the tourism circuit and are usually reached by fly-in safaris.

Lake Tanganyika is another major attraction, as yet barely developed. It is 1,500 metres in depth and is estimated to contain 18 per cent of the world's fresh water. In contrast to Lake Victoria, there are few large towns or industries to cause pollution. A small number of lakeside sites offer opportunities for diving or a beach holiday combined with a safari, usually focusing on chimpanzees in the forested mountains nearby.

Tanzania's primary focus of tourist attention is the coast, particularly the islands of Zanzibar, Pemba and Mafia, where game fishing and diving are the main attractions. Zanzibar, particularly 'Stone Town' (the old trading city) also offers major cultural attractions from the times of the Arab sultans, but development projects for Western-style beach tourism have aroused controversy because of their social and environmental impact.

Uganda

Uganda, in contrast to Tanzania, had a flourishing tourism industry before the Amin regime brought disorder and maladministration to the country in the 1970s. Relative stability since the 1990s has led to the growth of ecotourism, based on the country's rain forest resources, which have the highest biodiversity in East Africa. Another major attraction is Murchison (Kabegera) Falls near the headwaters of the River Nile. However, the main areas of tourist interest – the Queen Elizabeth National Park and the Ruwenzori Mountains – lie close to the Congolese border, and are threatened by the turmoil prevalent in Central Africa. Entebbe is the gateway for Uganda, with ferry services across Lake Victoria linking it to Kenya and Tanzania. By 2009 international arrivals reached 800,000 annually.

The other countries of East Africa

The Sudan

In 2011 after many years of conflict The Sudan was divided along religious and cultural lines between the Arab-speaking, Islamic north and the newly-independent South Sudan which is mainly black African and Christian or animist in religion. The northern Sudan has close cultural links with Egypt and the Middle East. The capital, Khartoum is situated at the confluence of the White Nile and the Blue Nile, which has its source in the highlands of Ethiopia, but neither river is used to any extent as a tourist route. There are opportunities for diving along the Red Sea coast, near the old trading port of Suakin. Other attractions include the Dinder National Park, a major wildlife reserve near the Ethiopian border, and the volcanic highlands of Jebel Marra in the western Sudan, which provide a refuge from the extreme heat of summer, but where tourism is in abeyance, due to the conflict in the Darfur region.

Tourism in South Sudan is less developed due to lack of infrastructure, where even Juba, the capital of the new state lacks modern amenities. The vast areas of wetlands known as the Sudd provide a contrast to the desert landscapes of the north.

Ethiopia

Formerly also known as Abyssinia, Ethiopia has huge tourism potential and is of particular interest to cultural tourists. The Amharic-speaking heartland of this country is a high plateau where an ancient Christian civilisation has survived, isolated for many centuries by mountains, deserts and often hostile Muslim neighbours. Coffee originated here, and its cultivation remains an important part of the economy. However, it was not until the end of the nineteenth century that Ethiopia was effectively united, with a new capital at Addis Ababa. Most of the population of around 80 million is concentrated in the *voina dega* ('wine highland') climate zone at altitudes of between 1,800 and 2,500 metres. The main tourist circuit links Addis Ababa to the art treasures of the historic towns of Axoum, Gondar and Lalibela. There are few hotels outside the capital, which was developed as a conference venue for Africa by the last Emperor, Haile Selassie. To the east of Addis Ababa lie the game reserves of the Rift Valley and the walled Muslim city of Harar. Tourism is co-ordinated by the Ethiopian Tourism Commission and arrivals approached 150,000 in the early years of the twenty-first century.

Eritrea

Eritrea's national identity derives from half a century of Italian rule and the long struggle for independence from Ethiopia which ended in 1993, although border disputes between the two countries continue. The country offers two contrasting environments – the arid but sweltering Red Sea coast, and the cool, fertile highlands around Asmara. The government recognises the importance of tourism, and plans include the restoration of the spectacular railway linking the capital to the port of Massawa, which is also the point of access for the diving sites in the Dahlak Archipelago.

Somalia

Most of Somalia was also an Italian colony, except for the north-west which was under British control. These former divisions and bitter clan rivalries re-surfaced in the 1990s, leading to the breakdown of government authority outside Mogadishu. Two separatist states – Somaliland and Puntland – were set up in the north, where despite the lack of recognition by the international community, some of the infrastructure for tourism remains in place. The situation has become even more complex with the rise of Islamic fundamentalism and intervention by Ethiopia. Somalia's long coastline has tourism potential, but its beaches are unlikely to be developed while piracy continues in this part of the Indian Ocean.

Djibouti

With few other resources, the small ex-French colony of Djibouti has exploited its deepwater harbour at the entrance to the Red Sea with the view to becoming a major trading centre between Africa and the Middle East.

Southern Africa

The countries of Southern Africa recognise the importance of wildlife conservation as a major part of their tourism appeal. To counter the threats of drought, poaching and development pressures to wildlife, a number of cross-border parks have been proposed, which would allow the animals to migrate freely within their natural ecosystems. These international 'peace parks' now include the Kgadaladi Transfrontier Park in the Kalahari, involving South Africa and Botswana, and the Great Limpopo Transfrontier Park, with an area of 35,000 square kilometres, involving South Africa, Mozambique and Zimbabwe.

Most countries in the region have strong economic and cultural ties with Britain, and have succeeded in attracting visitors from the main generating markets. International air services to Southern Africa improved considerably during the 1990s. There is scope for more regional co-operation under the Southern Africa Development Community (SADC) in reducing border formalities to encourage travel between the various countries, and in overseas promotion, by expanding membership of the Southern Africa Regional Tourism Council (SARTOC). However the future growth of tourism will depend to a great extent on the continuance of political and economic stability in South Africa, which is by far the leading country in the region, accounting for 85 per cent of its GDP.

South Africa

South Africa differs from the rest of the continent in having a large number of people of European origin – over 5 million or 13 per cent of the population – while Asians and those of mixed race account for another 11 per cent. Under white rule, South Africa – particularly the Cape area with its Mediterranean climate – was often perceived as an outpost of Europe. Since the coming to power of the ANC government in 1994 attitudes have changed; the country is no longer isolated by world opinion as it was in the era of *apartheid* (the policy of racial segregation), and it is now taking a larger share in the development of the African continent. We can regard South Africa as a developed country rather than part of the Third World for the following reasons:

- It has an advanced economy based on vast mineral resources, with only 14 per cent of the workforce employed in agriculture (compared to 80 per cent in Kenya for example). South Africa also accounts for over half the electricity generated in the continent. The 'powerhouse of Africa' has attracted some 5 million immigrants from countries as distant as the Congo, but mainly from Zimbabwe and Mozambique.
- Literacy levels are generally quite high.
- It has a well-developed infrastructure, with good air, road and rail systems.
- There are fewer health risks than in other parts of Africa (AIDS excepted), and malaria is confined to the Lowveld region on the eastern border.

The setting for tourism

South Africa has a warm temperate climate which is almost ideal for outdoor recreation, particularly beach tourism and water sports, as sunshine hours exceed those of most Mediterranean resorts. With the exception of the Western Cape, most of the rainfall occurs in the summer months (October to April). There are important differences in climate and landscapes between the coastal areas and the high interior plateaux – the Karoo and the Highveld, where night-time temperatures frequently fall below 0°C during the winter months. The Drakensberg Mountains to the east form a high escarpment rising to 3,000 metres, offering some of South Africa's most spectacular scenery, including the Blyde River Canyon. The Atlantic Coast north of Table Bay is less suitable for sea bathing than the Indian Ocean, as it is cooled by the cold Benguela Current, but conditions are generally favourable for surfing.

The demand for tourism

Tourism is a major industry in South Africa, accounting for over 7 per cent of GDP and supporting one million jobs. Demand is influenced by the vast disparities in wealth, to the extent that most of the black majority continue to live in conditions of Third World poverty, without basic services in the tribal homelands or in the 'townships' – the urban agglomerations adjoining Cape Town and Johannesburg. Although there has been social mobility since the ending of apartheid, with the rise of a black middle class, wealth and the ownership of land is still concentrated in the hands of the white minority. Most black South Africans are too poor to generate an effective demand for tourism.

Domestic and outbound tourism

Domestic demand accounts for two-thirds of all tourism in South Africa – some 37 million trips in 2007. White South Africans travel widely throughout their country, and the great majority of trips are made by car, using the excellent road network. Self-catering accommodation is often used in preference to hotels. Sports events, and to a lesser extent cultural festivals, are an important motivation for travel. Although the climate is suitable for tourism for most of the year, the timing of school holidays in the Christmas and Easter periods results in a seasonal peaking of demand, which places pressures on accommodation, particularly in Durban and other resorts of the Natal coast. This is the main holiday area for South Africans, especially those from the interior provinces of Gauteng (which includes Johannesburg), and the largely Afrikaans-speaking Free State. The Drakensberg Mountains are visited by large numbers of people from the coast during the hot, humid summers, and the towns of Pietermaritzburg, Estcourt and Ladysmith have a long-established tourism industry to meet their needs. Although the mountains are sufficiently high for snow during the winter months, there is only a modest winter sports industry, based in Tiffindell near the border with Lesotho, which caters for domestic demand.

As regards outbound tourism, while the depreciation of the rand since the 1990s has made South Africa a competitively priced destination for international tourism, it has also made foreign travel much more expensive for South Africans. Considering their geographical isolation, they are well represented in the tourist arrivals for a large number of long-haul destinations, including Britain and the USA, as well as neighbouring African countries.

Inbound tourism

In the apartheid era much of the inbound tourism from Britain and other European countries had been for VFR or business purposes. Since the 1990s there has been a substantial growth of interest in South Africa as a holiday destination by tour operators. Sport tourism has also played a significant role, including the Rugby World Cup in 1995, and this should increase as a result of the hosting of the FIFA World Cup in 2010. In 2010 around 8 million arrivals were recorded, many from other African countries. The biggest overseas markets are the UK, Germany and the USA. The Netherlands accounts for only a small percentage of overseas visitors, despite the strong historical links with the first white settlers – the Afrikaaners, whose language derives from Dutch. South Africa attracts visitors with a wide range of special interests, including botanical tours and wine-tasting in the Western Cape, industrial and transport heritage – such as steam locomotives and the gold and diamond mines – and for history buffs, the battlefields of the Zulu and Anglo-Boer wars in KwaZulu-Natal. The ending of apartheid has also strongly influenced patterns of tourism demand. Contemporary South African culture, heritage sites commemorating the struggle for Black African freedom, and township tours are now part of the tourism product. Another niche market is health tourism, particularly cosmetic surgery, in which South Africa has the following advantages:

- a good health infrastructure, with excellent medical services and clinics;
- from the viewpoint of British visitors, an English-speaking population, and a journey necessitating only a minor time-change;
- a weak currency, so that five star hotels are affordable, and
- a range of post-treatment sightseeing opportunities.

The supply side of tourism

Transport

The great majority of overseas visitors arrive by air and with deregulation of South African airspace arrivals have increased. Johannesburg, at the hub of a network of intercontinental and regional services, is the major gateway to South Africa, followed by Cape Town. South African Airways operate most of the scheduled domestic services, with several flights a day linking the main cities. Another convenient way of seeing the country is by South African Railways. The luxury 'Blue Train' is one of the country's most famous tourist products, linking Pretoria and Cape Town and passing through some magnificent scenery on its descent from the Karoo Plateau to the coast. A large number of tours by coach or mini-bus are also available.

Accommodation

A wide range of accommodation is available, from luxury hotels to ecolodges and *rondavels* (African-style huts, with modern facilities) in the game reserves.

Organisation

South Africa's tourism industry is effectively organised and marketed, within the legal framework of the 1993 Tourism Act and subsequent amendments. The continuing legacy of apartheid is reflected in the politics of tourism in South Africa with different political parties and ethnic groups (there are ten official Bantu languages for example), each having their own agendas for the sector. Policy-making is largely the responsibility of the Environmental Affairs and Tourism Ministry, which has a mission to promote sustainable development, and South African Tourism which is charged with maintaining standards of accommodation and services, with promotion, and also the development of new products.

Tourism resources

Although the early white settlers wiped out much of the game they encountered, the remaining wildlife habitats have long been given a high degree of protection by the South African government. There are eleven national parks and many game reserves, most of which are small in area compared to other countries in southern Africa. The exception – and the most popular – is the Kruger National Park located in the Lowveld along the Mozambique border, which is served by an extensive all-weather road network and well supplied with self-catering accommodation. Prior reservation is necessary for foreign visitors, due to the heavy domestic demand. Other notable reserves - Hluhluwe and Umfolozi – are situated in KwaZulu-Natal. There are also a large number of private game reserves – such as the Sabi-Sabi adjoining the Kruger National Park – which permit hunting and the viewing of wildlife on foot as well as in open vehicles. They provide luxury chalet accommodation and most have their own airstrips, while Americans generate much of the demand.

Areas increasingly sought out by tourists from Europe include the following.

The **Cape Peninsula**, where cold and warm ocean currents meet, and the hinterland of Cape Town, often considered to be the most beautiful part of South Africa. Contrasts of climate have created an extraordinary range of habitats for wildlife, and the coasts are ideal for whale-watching. Cape Town, situated on one of Africa's few good natural harbours, is the country's oldest European settlement, the second largest city, and its legislative capital. This cosmopolitan city is home to many ethnic groups and cultures, and has a tolerant attitude to alternative lifestyles. The historic waterfront has been redeveloped as an international focus for retailing, restaurants and entertainment. Cape Town is dominated by the world famous landmark of Table Mountain, and there are many fine beaches, such as Camps Bay. Attractions in the hinterland include the vineyards of the Hex River Valley and farmhouses in the distinctive 'Cape Dutch' style of architecture. Offshore lies Robben Island, the former prison of Nelson Mandela and now a museum commemorating the struggle against apartheid.

The **Garden Route** – the stretch of coast between Port Elizabeth and East London – offers rugged, attractive scenery, in which forest covered mountains alternate with fertile valleys and small sandy bays. Plettenberg Bay is the best-known of the many beach resorts.

Natal and Transkei also offer resources for beach tourism. Durban is a cosmopolitan seaport as well as being a major resort, while a string of small seaside towns to the south are known as the 'Hibiscus Coast'. In contrast, the 'Wild Coast' of the Transkei is less developed. To the north of the Tugela River the principal attractions are the game reserves, and Zulu communities that have retained the traditions of a warrior nation.

On the central plateau the main tourist centres are the cities of Johannesburg, Pretoria and Bloemfontein. Johannesburg is South Africa's largest and most prosperous city, largely due to the gold mines of the Witwatersrand. Not surprisingly, one of its major attractions is the Gold Reef City theme park which interprets this mining heritage. Johannesburg has become a regional centre for financial services, comparable with the great cities of Europe and North America. The township of Soweto nearby is actually a city of three million people. It is closely identified with the apartheid struggle, and attracts the more adventurous and socially-aware tourists for this reason. Some

THE MIDDLE EAST AND AFRICA

tour operators encourage visitors to interact with the local community in restaurants and *shebeens* (bars).

Pretoria, the administrative capital of South Africa, and Bloemfontein, its judicial capital, are centres of Afrikaaner culture, and as such form a contrast to the cosmopolitan brashness and bustle of Johannesburg. Sun City was developed in the apartheid era as a gambling centre to rival Las Vegas, in what was then the quasi-independent state of Bophutatswana, as casinos and multi-racial entertainment were illegal in the Republic itself. In the new South Africa it continues to be a major resort, offering cabarets that attract international stars, world-class golf courses and other sports facilities, and the 'Lost City' theme park developed by a South African entrepreneur.

One of the great challenges facing the government is to balance the economic aspirations of black Africans with the need to retain white expertise and attract foreign investment, and here tourism is playing an important role. The future growth of tourism in South Africa will depend on the maintenance of political and economic stability, and the extent to which the new multi-racial 'Rainbow Nation' can offer opportunity to all ethnic groups, including the thorny issue of land reform. Since the 1990s levels of crime have increased to become among the world's highest, particularly in Johannesburg, and the resulting insecurity is one of the biggest problems facing the country and its tourism industry.

Discussion point

To what extent can tourism satisfy black South African aspirations for a better life? For example, game reserves with luxury accommodation are located close to some of the most impoverished villages in KwaZulu. This has led to demands that local communities should benefit more from tourism, along with the townships near the big cities, which are visited by an increasing number of foreign tourists, but very few white South Africans.

The other countries of Southern Africa

Most of the other countries in Southern Africa are landlocked, so that their external surface transport links (and to an extent their economic fortunes) are vulnerable to the political situation in South Africa and Mozambique. The small kingdoms of Lesotho and Swaziland are particularly dependent on South Africa. Most of their visitors are South Africans, who tend to be short-stay and interested primarily in gambling in the hotel casinos of Maseru and Mbabane. But these countries have more to offer.

Lesotho (known as 'the Roof of Africa' or 'The Kingdom in the Sky') is situated high in the Drakensberg Mountains. Apart from the impressive scenery, there are facilities for pony-trekking, and even skiing (although the season is restricted to July and August). Four wheel drive vehicles are necessary for travel because of the rugged terrain.

Swaziland (or Ngwane) is not quite as mountainous, and includes a section of the game-rich Lowveld along its boundary with Mozambique. The country's tribal traditions are among the best-preserved in Africa.

Namibia and Botswana likewise have strong economic ties with South Africa, but with the advantage of direct air services from Europe to the capitals of Windhoek and Gaborone, they have been more successful in attracting overseas visitors. They are mostly made up of desert landscapes, but the Kalahari is not as arid as the Sahara and supports a surprising variety of game. Because of the vast distances and sparse population, fly-in safaris are a major element in their tourism industries.

Botswana is one of the more stable countries in Africa, with an economy based on diamond exports. The government has sought to avoid the negative impacts of tourism by emphasising conservation and limiting the supply of accommodation. National parks and game reserves make up 17 per cent of the national territory.

Case study 19.2

The Okovango Delta; a lesson in ecotourism

This vast inland delta is formed by the Okovango River where it drains into the Kalahari Desert on the site of an ancient lake. It is one of Africa's largest and most ecologically productive wetland areas, a web of slow-flowing waterways, islands and lagoons, many of which change shape and even disappear in response to an annual flood cycle. At the peak of the flood season the delta can extend over an area of 16,000 square kilometres, shrinking to less than 9,000 square kilometres in the dry season. The delta supports a wide variety of wildlife that congregates on the edge of the newly flooded areas between May and October, which is the best time for game viewing. Part of the delta is designated as the Moremi Game Reserve, with the Chobe National Park in the north-east. The speciality of the Okovango – its USP – is safari tours by water transport, using traditional dugout canoes and motor launches, which are restricted to the main waterways.

The policy of the Botswana government is to restrict tourism in the Okovango Delta to ensure the conservation of its fragile ecosystems. This is achieved by:

- Limiting accessibility. The Okovango is difficult to reach, as Maun, the village which is the recognised gateway to the delta, is served exclusively by Air Botswana, the state carrier, and fares are kept high.
- Restricting access by price. Visitors must pay a park entrance fee of around US $30 a day.
- Keeping the cost of accommodation high. The operators of the 40 or so camps and ecolodges have to pay substantial concession fees, resource royalties and community charges to the government.

Nevertheless tourism has not really benefited the tribal communities living in or near the delta as most supplies are not purchased locally, but flown in from outside. The government has also been criticised for forcing the nomadic San (widely known as the Bushmen) to relocate and adopt a settled way of life.

Namibia differs from its neighbour in having a long Atlantic coastline, and a large white minority of mainly German or Afrikaaner origin. The country was ruled by South Africa prior to 1990 and was a latecomer to international tourism. On offer are a large number of game reserves and some of Africa's most interesting attractions, including:

- the Etosha Pan, which attracts great concentrations of wildlife during the dry season;
- the Fish River Canyon, a spectacular geological feature;
- the Waterberg Plateau, famous for its rock paintings – created by the San hunter-gatherers who were the original inhabitants of Southern Africa; and
- the 'Skeleton Coast' – where the Namib Desert meets the Atlantic Ocean. Fogs from the cold Benguela Current offshore sustain some unique plants and animals although

the climate is virtually rainless. This coastal area also boasts some of the world's highest sand dunes.

In contrast to Namibia, the countries of Zimbabwe, Zambia and Malawi usually receive an adequate rainfall, and since they mainly consist of highlands and plateaux rising over 1,000 metres above sea level, they have a climate which is cooler than is usual for the tropics. Under British rule the three countries were briefly united as the 'Central African Federation of Rhodesia and Nyasaland', but after 1962 they followed different paths.

Zimbabwe

Between 1964 and 1980 Zimbabwe (then known as Rhodesia) had a tourism industry serving a sizeable domestic market – essentially the dominant white community – and South Africans. There were few overseas visitors due to the economic sanctions imposed by Britain and the country's political isolation. With the coming to power of the ZANU government in 1980 Zimbabwe's independence was formally recognised by the international community. As a result, overseas visitor numbers grew rapidly, aided by political stability and the good infrastructure laid down under British rule. The Zimbabwe Tourist Authority was formed in 1996 with responsibility for promotion and development reporting to the Ministry of Environment and Tourism. However, the Land Distribution Act in 2000 was followed by the collapse of the economy, and unfavourable publicity in the Western media regarding the seizure of white-owned farms and the abuse of human rights. With the fragile political situation, Zimbabwe's tourism industry is in crisis, and this has put the country's wildlife resources increasingly at risk.

Hotel accommodation is concentrated in the cities of Harare and Bulawayo – which have hosted international conferences, trade fairs and the All-Africa Games – and near the country's principal attraction, Victoria Falls on the border with Zambia. Zimbabwe can offer a variety of other tourism resources, including a system of national parks which make up 12 per cent of its territory. These are administered by the Zimbabwe Parks Department which operates a three-tier entrance fee policy. As elsewhere in Africa, the designation of the Hwange and Gonerezhou National Parks in the 1950s and 1960s involved the eviction of thousands of tribespeople from their lands, but since the 1980s government policy has changed, with local communities regaining hunting rights and becoming directly involved in ecotourism. One of the main problems facing the tourism sector is the over-commercialisation of Victoria Falls compared to the under-exploitation of some of the game reserves and the scenic attractions of the Eastern Highlands. Below the waterfall the River Zambezi attracts large numbers of canoeists and white-water rafting adventure-seekers. In comparison Lake Kariba – a vast inland sea created by the Kariba Dam in 1959 – offers few facilities.

The country's cultural heritage is also viewed differently by the white and African communities. For example, the Matapo Hills south of Bulawayo – an area of dramatic granite scenery – has been promoted to Western tourists as the burial place of Cecil Rhodes, the founder of the British colony, whose place in history is controversial. The Chinhoyi Caves, which played an important role in the independence struggle, are as yet barely exploited as a heritage attraction. On the other hand, the mysterious ruins of Great Zimbabwe are now seen as a reminder of African achievement centuries before the colonial era.

Zambia

Zambia's economy is precariously dependent on the export of copper and other minerals, and tourism is increasingly seen as a more reliable way of earning foreign exchange. The government has put a high priority on conservation – almost a third of its area is devoted to national parks and game reserves, although facilities are generally not as well developed as in Zimbabwe. In the most popular national parks – Kafue and the South Luangwa – accommodation is in thatched lodges blending in with the local habitats. The main tourist centres are Livingstone – situated close to Victoria Falls, which has benefited from the deterioration of the economic situation in Zimbabwe, and the capital Lusaka which has good conference facilities.

Malawi

Malawi's main attraction is the lake of the same name, the third largest in Africa, with some of the world's best fishing, and attractive beaches along its 600 kilometre shoreline. There are good facilities for water-skiing, sailing and windsurfing at the resorts of Salima and Monkey Bay. Compared to some other countries in southern Africa, it is not rich in big game. However its undulating green plateaux and mountains are ideal for riding and trekking holidays. Since the mid-1990s a new government has liberalised the tourism sector, created a Ministry of Tourism and there has been healthy growth in international arrivals.

Angola and Mozambique

Angola and Mozambique retain some of the heritage of centuries of rule by Portugal. Independence in 1975 was soon followed by many years of civil war and the exodus of well over a million Portuguese settlers. Since the early 1990s the socialist governments of both countries have adopted a more pragmatic approach to economic development.

Mozambique had a small tourism industry before 1975, catering mainly for white South Africans and Rhodesians. This was concentrated in the capital Maputo (then called Lourenço Marques), and to a lesser extent in Beira. The beaches along over 2,000 kilometres of coastline facing the Indian Ocean are the country's principal tourist asset. Since the ending of the civil war there has been some development of inclusive tours, especially to the Bazaruto Islands that offer resort facilities, scuba diving and sport fishing. Ecotourism is being encouraged by the government in the northern part of the country, and the Gorongosa National Park, devastated during the civil war, is in the process of being re-stocked. Cultural attractions include Mozambique Island, founded by the Portuguese as a trading post in the early sixteenth century, but as yet undeveloped for tourism.

Angola consists largely of a plateau averaging 1,200 metres in altitude, and has a long Atlantic coastline, resulting in a cooler climate than is generally true of Mozambique. The country has great mineral wealth but the benefits have yet to filter down to the mass of the population. The hotels of the capital, Luanda cater almost exclusively to business travellers, but there is tourism potential in Angola's historic ties with Brazil, its wildlife resources, and the waterfalls of the interior. Sport tourism is another possibility, with Luanda hosting the 2010 African Cup of Nations football tournament. Angola has become one of the main beneficiaries of Chinese investment, particularly in road building, but the former rail links have yet to be restored.

The islands of the western Indian Ocean

To the east of the African continent lie several island groups, which are very different from the mainland in geology, flora and fauna, and where the cultures have been strongly influenced by France and Asia. All island ecosystems are vulnerable to the impact of climate change, tourism and other types of development, and the wildlife resources of the Indian Ocean islands are particularly at risk:

* pressures are most severe in Madagascar, habitat of the lemur and other unique animals;
* in Mauritius only one per cent of the original forest still survives and up to 50 per cent of the fringing coral is dead or dying; and
* in the Seychelles much of the coral reef around the island of Mahe was destroyed to make way for the international airport.

Madagascar, the Comores and Réunion were formerly French colonies, whereas Mauritius and the Seychelles, although originally colonised by the French, later experienced a long period of British rule.

Madagascar

Officially known as the Malagasy Republic, Madagascar stands in a class of its own as the world's fourth largest island, with an area greater than France and a coastline 5,000 kilometres in length. The country combines the red soil of Africa and the rice fields of South-east Asia, but also has landscapes that are unique, with the 'traveller's tree' as an emblematic feature. A central spine of mountains dominates the country, separating the dry savannas of the west from the lush vegetation of the east coast. Population growth and inefficient agricultural methods have caused extensive deforestation, threatening destruction of the wildlife that is Madagascar's most important tourism resource. The island is also culturally interesting with its mix of Indonesian, African and Arab ethnic groups. Other distinctive features are the elaborate tombs and funeral ceremonies based on ancestor worship.

The capital Antananarivo, located high on the central plateau offers picturesque markets and the palaces of the Merina monarchs who ruled the country before it came under French control. However this diversity of resources has not been paralleled by a thriving tourism industry. The island is expensive to reach, and once there, surface transport is poor. The principal beach resorts, situated on the offshore islands of Nosy Bé and Nosy Boraha (Ile Ste Marie), can only be reached by domestic air services. Since independence the government has given tourism a low priority, but this is changing now that relations with France and South Africa – Madagascar's largest potential markets – have improved.

The Comores

The Comores comprise four volcanic islands lying between Madagascar and Mozambique. The people are Muslims and Arabic influences are dominant in the culture. While the other islands have opted for independence, Mayotte has retained its links with France and is the most prosperous of the group. Anjouan is the most picturesque island, but Grand Comore contains the international airport and most of the few hotels. Diving and sport fishing provide the main appeal for foreign tourists, mainly wealthy Americans and Europeans, although South Africa has provided much of the investment in hotels.

Réunion

Réunion is another volcanic island, situated to the east of Madagascar. It has perhaps the most impressive scenery of any tropical island, with high mountains rising to 3,000 metres within a short distance of the coast, and boasting spectacular calderas, an active volcano – the Piton de la Fournaise, and sheer lava cliffs enclosing deep canyons. There are hiking trails between the craters and good surfing off the west coast. The island's close relationship to France (it is an overseas département) has benefited the infrastructure and allows French tourists to take advantage of cheaper flights from Paris to the capital, St. Denis. International tourism is handicapped by the proximity of Mauritius, which has much better beaches. Réunion has potential as a stopover on flights between Europe and Australia on the island's carrier, Air Austral.

Mauritius

Mauritius has the advantage of direct flights from Britain and South Africa, whereas the smaller dependent island of Rodriguez is remote and much less developed. Mauritius is encircled, except to the south, by a coral reef that is responsible for the island's greatest assets – 150 kilometres of attractive coastline with calm seas ideal for water sports and white sand beaches. Mauritius is a good example of how tourism, properly handled, can benefit a small developing country. In the 1960s the island was faced with a decline for sugar, its principal export, and a seemingly inexorable pressure on resources from a rapidly growing population. Tourism (along with light industry) was seen as a solution to the grave economic situation, but the government was determined from the outset that Mauritius should be an up-market destination. This has been achieved by:

- a ban on charter flights, while the national carrier, Air Mauritius is noted for its professionalism;
- the resort hotels are built to high standards of design and landscaping, taking maximum advantage of the beach and lagoon setting;
- hotels use local resources, so that profits have stayed within Mauritius;
- a professional Ministry of Tourism, Leisure and External Communications, aided by the Mauritius Tourism Promotion Authority (MTPA) created in 1996; and
- standards of service and cuisine that bear comparison with the best in Europe, North America and Asia.

By 2010 Mauritius was attracting 900,000 international visitors, of whom approximately half came from Europe. Mauritius has the advantage of a highly skilled workforce (15,000 are employed in tourism), where the different ethnic communities – Hindus, Muslims, Chinese, Creoles (of African origin) and Europeans – live in apparent harmony. Beach resorts such as Grand Baie are the main attraction, but with the achievement of economic success, the government is giving conservation a higher priority, in a bid to attract eco-tourists.

Compared to other Indian Ocean islands, the scenery of the interior is unspectacular, although there are numerous waterfalls where the central plateau of Mauritius meets the coastal plains. Away from the beaches, the main tourist centres are the multi-cultural capital St Louis – with its markets and festivals around the calendar – Curepipe with its casino and textile shops, and the Royal Botanical Gardens at Pamplemousses. The possible disadvantages of Mauritius as a winter sun destination for North Europeans are distance; there is high humidity and occasional cyclones from December to April; and there is little nightlife compared to more accessible destinations such as the Caribbean islands.

The Seychelles

The Seychelles are strategically located on the major shipping routes for oil tankers from the Gulf, midway between East Africa, India and Madagascar. The country has a small population and land area compared to Mauritius, but lays claim to over one million square kilometres of Indian Ocean. The islands are ecologically interesting because they contain many species of birds and plants which are unique to the Seychelles. The islands fall into two main groups:

• The main islands of Mahe, Praslin, La Digue, and Silhouette are of granite formation, the possible remnants of a 'lost continent'. The combination of picturesque coves, rock formations, palm-fringed beaches and rugged mountains gives these islands a rare beauty.
• The outer islands are low-lying coral atolls. Fresh water is scarce and the islands are mostly uninhabited. The largest, Aldabra is also the most remote and is world famous for its giant turtles.

The construction of the international airport at Mahe brought an isolated destination within reach of the main tourist generating markets of Western Europe and South Africa, with the result that tourist arrivals increased from less than a thousand in 1970 to 175,000 in 2010. Tourism now accounts for 70 per cent of foreign exchange earnings and 30 per cent of jobs and is the focus of a new integrated plan for sustainable development – Vision 21. As a result, while foreign investment in tourism is encouraged, the government has given conservation a high priority, so that only a few localities – mainly on Mahe – have been developed with low-rise hotels. However, tourism has not made the islands less vulnerable to recession in Europe than their previous dependence on agricultural exports such as cinnamon. Standards of service and facilities in the Seychelles have in the past been compared unfavourably with those of Mauritius, as tourism was grafted on to a less developed economy and social system. As in other small developing countries, tourism has caused or aggravated a number of problems, namely:

• the industry is dominated by foreign tour operators and foreign-owned hotels, so that the bulk of tourist spend does not benefit the country;

- the tourism sector has attracted workers away from agriculture, to the extent that the islands are now dependent on food imports from Europe and South Africa to meet local as well as tourist demands; and
- the need to train Seychellois workers in the skills and attitudes necessary to serve affluent foreign visitors, has undermined the government's policy of socialism and nation-building based on the Creole language and lifestyle. Those involved with tourism tend to be upwardly mobile, imitating Western lifestyles – the so-called 'demonstration effect'.

West Africa

We can think of West Africa as being two distinct regions. A southern tier of states occupying the forested coastal belt from the Gambia to Gabon and a northern tier – the Sahel states – extending from Mauritania to Chad along the southern edge of the Sahara Desert. This region is characterised by extreme summer heat and recurrent droughts, the dry season getting progressively longer as we travel further from the Equator, so that savanna grassland gradually merges into semi-desert.

The setting for tourism

Tourism and business travel in West Africa gravitate to the coast where commercial export-based agriculture is well developed. The climate here is characterised by sultry heat, except during the dry season – usually from December to March – when the 'Harmattan' wind blows from the Sahara, drastically lowering the humidity but also bringing dust clouds that can disrupt air transport. In Victorian times, the unhealthy reputation of the region earned it the name 'White Man's Grave'. However, conditions are by no means uniform – the coasts of Ghana and Togo, for example, are much less humid than Liberia or Equatorial Guinea.

Most of West Africa has failed to develop significant tourism industries, due to the chronic political instability affecting most countries in the region and inadequate infrastructure. Yet these countries are just within reach of the markets of Western Europe for winter-sun beach holidays. The Gambia is only six hours flying time from London, and unlike the Caribbean, it has the advantage of being in the same time zone. The Gambia's dry and sunny winter climate allows it to compete with the Canary Islands as a beach destination for the British and Scandinavians – with an extra ingredient – the chance to experience African markets and village life. Similarly, French tourists are attracted to their former colonies, especially to the beaches of Senegal, the Ivory Coast and Togo.

Apart from beach tourism West Africa can offer:

- **Cultural/special interest tourism.** The contribution of West African woodcarving, textile design, and dance rhythms to Western art and music is increasingly recognised. The more adventurous tourists seek out countries like Ghana, Mali and Senegal for this reason.
- **Ecotourism.** West Africa offers a considerable diversity of wildlife habitats. Gambia attracts birdwatchers to its Abuko reserve, while a rainforest project in Ghana's Kakum National Park has won acclaim from environmentalists. Game parks exist in several countries but safari tourism has not developed on any scale, because the attractions are not as well publicised as those of East and Southern Africa, the 'big

five' game animals are much less numerous, and the parks are less accessible.

- **Adventure tourism,** based on four-wheel-drive expeditions.
- **Ethnic tourism,** from the populations of West African origin in Europe and the Americas.

Case study 19.3

Tourism as a search for identity

The 'African diaspora', made up of the descendants of West Africans forcibly transported to the Americas as slaves, is potentially a huge market for tourism in Brazil, the Caribbean islands and the USA. The publication of Alex Haley's novel *Roots*, set in his ancestor's homeland in Gambia, stimulated interest in West Africa generally in the 1980s. It is anticipated that the visit of President Obama to Ghana in 2009 will have a much greater impact on the growth of demand for 'ethnic tourism' among black Americans. Inclusive tours, styled 'roots packages' are now available for those wishing to connect with their origins, and a visit to the heritage sites of the slave trade is regarded as a kind of pilgrimage to be undertaken during one's lifetime.

The trans-Atlantic slave trade was at its peak in the eighteenth century, when as many as 70,000 men, women and children a year were transported on the infamous 'middle passage' to the plantations of the New World, to satisfy the European demand for sugar, rum, tobacco and cotton. This was part of the 'triangle of trade', in which ports such as Bristol, Liverpool and Nantes were engaged. Armaments, alcohol and manufactured goods were traded with African chiefs for slaves obtained in inter-tribal wars. A chain of forts along the west African coast, extending from St Louis at the mouth of the River Senegal to Benguela in Angola, acted as holding points for the slave trade. On arrival in the Americas slaves were stripped of their tribal identities and took the name and religion of their white masters. For this reason their descendents, unlike European emigrants to the New World, are unable to identify their homelands with any precision. Although Britain took the lead in bringing an end to the slave trade, it continued until late in the nineteenth century when slavery was abolished in Brazil and Cuba.

The tangible heritage of the slave trade is found in a number of West African countries, the Congo region and Angola. In Senegal, the island of Gorée near Dakar is one of the major attractions of that country, where the picturesque buildings belie its grim history as one of the main centres of the French slave trade. In Benin there are reminders that some of the more warlike African kingdoms such as Dahomey took an active part in procuring slaves, particularly those destined for the sugar plantations of north-east Brazil. However, Ghana is the country that is best placed to develop this type of ethnic tourism, and Black Americans are an important market, accounting for around 10,000 visitors a year. The Ghana Tourist Board has therefore focused attention on the 'castles' – fortified trading posts – that were built on the Gold Coast to hold slaves. Elmina was founded by the Portuguese in 1482, but most date from the seventeenth century, when Denmark, Sweden and Holland were among those who jostled with Britain for control over the lucrative trade. Most of these heritage attractions are managed by the Ghana Museums and Monuments Board and guided tours are available.

The majority of the visitors to these heritage attractions are Ghanaians, who have different perceptions to those held by Africans of the diaspora. Black Americans tend to regard their visit (with mixed feelings of pride, sorrow and anger), as a return to the motherland. Ghanaians, however tend to regard them not as guests and fellow-Africans but as *obrumi*, foreigners like white tourists, marked out by their affluence, lifestyle and behaviour from the host community, and the tourists often complain of hassle and exploitation. Whereas Afro-Americans regard the castles as places of death and suffering, to Ghanaians they are simply part of their national heritage, to be regarded as showpieces, to be restored and provided with modern lighting and tourist facilities. To many black Americans this is 'whitewashing' history; for example, they successfully objected to a proposed restaurant above the dungeon for male slaves in Cape Coast Castle (Bruner: 1996). There are also differences of opinion regarding the way the heritage of the slave trade should be interpreted. Elmina Castle, for example, has changed hands and been used for different purposes in the course of its long history. When the Dutch took over from the Portuguese in 1637 they converted the Catholic chapel into a slave auction market. This raises the question of which aspects of the heritage should be preserved or reconstructed. Stakeholders with a view on this include the international aid agencies who provide most of the funding, but organisations representing the African diaspora also have a great deal of influence. This is less true of people in the local communities, who may be denied access to these heritage attractions for the convenience of foreign tourists.

Case study 19.3

Supply of tourism

There has been some degree of co-operation among West African countries to promote tourism to the region. In 1976 the Economic Community of West African States (ECOWAS) was formed to bring together French- and English-speaking countries. The Francophone states constitute the majority and, with few exceptions, chose to retain close links with France after independence. Several countries (Côte d'Ivoire, Burkina Faso, Niger, Togo, and Benin) are also united by the Conseil de l'Entente whose tourism committee aims for the harmonisation of entry requirements and greater uniformity in the standard of hotels. A number of West African countries have state-run hotel corporations. However, their main purpose is to attract business travellers rather than tourists, and hotel rooms are often unavailable in the major cities such as Accra due to block-booking for regional conferences.

Lagos, Abidjan, and Dakar are the focus of air routes into West Africa. The winter-sun destinations of the Gambia, Sierra Leone, and Côte d'Ivoire are encouraging charter flights to counter the high fares of scheduled airlines. Road and rail transport is geared to the commercial objectives laid down in colonial times, so that routes lead from the interior to the seaports. This inhibits travel between the countries of West Africa, but does, to some extent, allow excursions from the coastal resorts to the hinterland.

Gambia

Of the five English-speaking states, only Gambia has attracted much attention from British as well as Scandinavian tour operators. No larger than Yorkshire or Connecticut in area, the country consists of little more than a narrow strip of territory along the River Gambia, and a short stretch of Atlantic coastline where the resort facilities are concentrated. Tourism is encouraged by the government to reduce the country's dependence on groundnut exports. With the help of the World Bank, Yundum Airport has been extended, the infrastructure improved, and a hotel training school established. Yet relatively few tourists venture far beyond the beaches on excursions up the River Gambia, one of the finest waterways in West Africa. Almost all the hotels are foreign-owned and many of the economic benefits of tourism are not retained, while there is concern in this traditional Muslim society about some of its social manifestations such as sex tourism and beach hustling by *bumsters*. The military coup in 1994 severely affected tourism to Gambia with an estimated 40 per cent reduction in the number of foreign tourists. However, by 2009 there were around 120,000 arrivals.

Senegal

Senegal is the oldest of France's former colonies, and is a mixture of French sophistication and African traditions, best exemplified in the capital Dakar. In Senegal we can observe two contrasting approaches to tourism:

- French expatriates staff the Club Méditerranée village at Cap Skirring, and there is little contact with the local population; whereas
- in the *campements rurales integrales* near Ziguinchor, the tourist shares the life of an African village, the accommodation being provided by a co-operative of the villagers with government support.

Côte d'Ivoire (Ivory Coast)

Until the outbreak of tribal unrest in 2004, the Ivory Coast had been more successful than most West African countries in developing its tourism industry and its economy in general, due in part to a long period of stability following independence and very substantial foreign (primarily French) investment. State-owned hotels and travel companies are involved in the provision of tourist facilities, mainly along the coast east of Abidjan, where the beaches are protected by a series of lagoons from the heavy surf of the Atlantic. However, the resorts of the 'African Riviera' are expensive and beyond the reach of all but a privileged minority of the Ivorians themselves. In the interior there are a number of game parks, and the new administrative capital of Yamassoukro which boasts a cathedral second in size only to St Peter's in Rome. Abidjan remains the commercial centre of the country with good conference facilities.

Togo

Togo's capital, Lomé, has also become a leading conference destination as well as attracting tourists (many of them from other West African countries) to its beaches and entertainment facilities.

Nigeria

Nigeria is essentially a business travel destination. It is the most populous nation in Africa, with around 160 million inhabitants, and as the world's fifth largest oil producer, it should be one of the wealthiest. Income from petroleum has fuelled an enormous demand for Western consumer goods and costly development projects. It has also generated a demand for foreign travel, to the extent that Nigeria has a substantial deficit on its international tourism account. However, the collapse in oil prices during the 1990s and mismanagement of the country's resources have led to a situation in which shortages of basic commodities and power failures are a fact of everyday life. There is also a shortage of hotels, especially in Lagos, which remains Nigeria's main commercial centre, although the federal capital was moved to Abuja nearer the geographical centre of the country. This was done to satisfy the four main ethnic groups – the Fulani and Hausa – who are Muslims – in the less developed north, and the mainly Christian and more business-minded Yoruba and Ibo in the south-west and south.

Responsibility for tourism development is centred in the Ministry of Culture, Tourism and National Orientation. For the independent traveller, the main interest of the country lies in the traditional lifestyle of Kano and other cities of northern Nigeria, while the Yoruba city of Benin is noted for the skills of its people in metalworking.

The other countries of West Africa

Nigeria's eastern neighbour **Cameroon** offers even more scenic variety and has been described as 'Africa in miniature'. In the Korup National Park part of the equatorial rain forest has been protected, in contrast to the unrestricted commercial logging prevalent in the Ivory Coast. Volcanic Mount Cameroon nearby is the highest mountain in West Africa. The drier northern part of the country includes extensive savannas where a number of game reserves have been designated, the most important being the Waza National Park. Yaoundé, the administrative capital, and Douala, the country's commercial centre, attract a substantial volume of business travel, while the beaches of Kribi on the Gulf of Guinea are increasingly popular with tourists. More than most African countries, it is made up of a bewildering variety of tribal groups, but has the advantage that both French and English are the official languages.

Elsewhere in West Africa tourism is in its infancy, or has even declined since the 1980s. In French-speaking **Guinea** and **Benin**, along with **Guinea-Bissau** (an ex-Portuguese colony) tourism was for many years after independence given a low priority by their governments – apparently for ideological reasons – and these countries have only recently encouraged private enterprise;

French-speaking **Gabon** with its great mineral wealth has seen little need to attract tourists, other than business travellers to the capital, Libreville. This thinly populated country has great potential for ecotourism, thanks to the biodiversity of its rainforests, and in 2002 this was recognised with the designation of 13 national parks. Similar conservation initiatives, funded mainly by the USA, are proposed for neighbouring countries in West and Central Africa.

The former Spanish colony of **Equatorial Guinea** lacks the basic infrastructure for tourism. However the beautiful volcanic island of Bioko (formerly Fernando Po) has potential for beach tourism, and business travel should increase with the exploitation of the country's oil resources in the Gulf of Guinea.

Both **Liberia** and **Sierra Leone** had tourism industries on a small scale before the outbreak of civil war in the 1990s. Liberia had strong cultural and economic ties with the USA, and its capital Monrovia was one of West Africa's leading conference venues. The former British colony of Sierra Leone, whose capital Freetown has one of Africa's finest harbours, attracted tour operators to the fine white sand beaches of the Freetown Peninsula. The unrest in both countries is partly due to the historic tensions between the Westernised elites of the coast and the strongly tribal societies of the interior.

Ghana on the other hand made an economic recovery during the 1990s. Tourism is important to the economy, accounting for 10 per cent of foreign exchange earnings, with the USA, Britain and Germany as the main markets. Attractions for the independent traveller include the rainforests of the south, the markets of Accra and the heritage of the once powerful Ashanti kingdom in the interior.

In the **Sahel** states, tourism is handicapped for the following reasons:

* their landlocked situation (with the exception of Mauritania);
* the low level of economic development and poor infrastructure;
* there are few hotels outside the national capitals; and
* political instability and ethnic strife.

In most of these countries there is a north–south divide between the Saharan nomads of the north (Moors, Tuaregs and Arabs) and the black African farming communities of the south. This is particularly evident in Chad, whereas in Mauritania the Moors are clearly the dominant group, and the country has close ties to Morocco.

Yet this region has seen the rise of great African civilisations in the past. **Mali** can boast the legendary trading centre of Timbuktu, which now hosts a desert music festival, and the great mosque at Djenné, which is a superb example of Sudanese mud-brick architecture.

Similarly, in the **Niger Republic** the ancient Tuareg city of Agadès attracts many tourists due to its location on the main trans-Saharan Route. Compared to the Nile, the great River Niger is under-utilised as a commercial waterway and tourist route, as it is only navigable for part of the year.

Mauritania has a variety of spectacular desert landscapes, and also the historic towns of Chinguetti (where the heritage is threatened by the encroaching dunes), Atar and Wadan for the adventurous tourist.

There has been some development of safari tourism in **Burkina Faso**, focusing on the 'W' National Park where the country borders on Benin and Niger.

Central Africa

This region is essentially landlocked with only a short section of coastline near the mouth of the River Congo. It includes Africa's most extensive river system and its largest area of tropical rainforest. Most of this region is virtually inaccessible, especially during the rainy season, which prevails for most of the year near the Equator. Hotels of international standard are few, and those in the major cities – Kinshasa, Kisangani, Bangui, and Brazzaville – cater for business travellers attracted by the region's vast mineral resources.

The prospects for tourism in the **Democratic Republic of the Congo** (DRC) have been jeopardised by mismanagement and civil war. In the colonial era this vast country, then known as the Belgian Congo, had been a pioneer in wildlife conservation, and as a legacy 12 per cent of its territory is, in theory at least, designated as protected areas. The most important resources are:

* the Virunga National Park which shares with neighbouring Uganda the spectacular Ruwenzori Mountains with their strange high altitude vegetation;
* the Ituri Forest – home of the Pygmies; and
* two of Africa's largest lakes.

Transport on the River Congo and its tributaries is confined to small-scale local commerce, and many improvements will need to be made, to both vessels and port facilities, before this network of inland waterways is viable for international tourism. In the absence of a viable road or railway system, a large number of airlines provide domestic services, but few, if any, meet international safety standards.

Rwanda on the other hand, a small, densely populated, mountainous country with few natural resources, has achieved political stability and attracted considerable foreign investment. Long-standing ethnic strife between the Hutu and the Tutsi, the former ruling class, culminated in the 1994 genocide, now commemorated by the Memorial Centre in the capital, Kigali. Tourists are mainly attracted to the Volcanoes National Park, famous for the mountain gorilla sanctuary associated with Dian Fossey, and the Nyungwe National Park with its monkeys and abundant bird life. Even so, many of Rwanda's 20,000 annual visitors are part of the safari circuit in Kenya and Tanzania and stay on average only three days.

The Atlantic islands

To the west of the African continent lie several groups of volcanic islands in the Atlantic Ocean. They are isolated from the mainstream of international trade, and tourism is handicapped by the difficulty and expense of reaching them. They include three British territories:

- **St Helena** does not yet have an airport, and is served only by infrequent shipping services linking Europe to South Africa. Known mainly for its associations with Napoleon, the island has potential for tourists interested in dolphin-watching, game-fishing and the colonial heritage;
- **Ascension** has a military airport, acting as a staging point between Britain and the Falkland Islands, but this barren island has little to attract visitors; and
- **Tristan da Cunha** is stormswept, rugged and harbourless, and must rank as one of the world's most remote communities.

The prospects for tourism are brighter in the former Portuguese colonies of São Tomé and the Cape Verde Islands, which are linked by scheduled air services to Lisbon.

São Tomé and its smaller neighbour Principe are situated on the Equator. Their main assets are the fine beaches backed by a lush setting of forests and cacao plantations. The islands' economy is likely to be transformed with the exploitation of the oilfields in the Gulf of Guinea.

The Cape Verde Islands lie to the west of Senegal, and are climatically not very different from the Canaries. There are nine islands in the group, which vary considerably in their landscapes and tourism potential. Sal's international airport was originally built to serve South African Airways in the apartheid era, when the airline was prohibited for political reasons from over-flying the African continent. Although popular with windsurfers, Sal is rather barren, and the other islands offer more attractive scenery. Santiago, the largest and most fertile, contains the new international airport at Praia and this is where most of the resort and second home projects are taking place. The location of Cape Verde Islands within five hours flying time of Britain, and the availability of direct charter flights from London to Santiago has dramatically improved the prospects for holiday tourism. The country has few natural resources and water supply is a major problem, but the government has received substantial investment from the World Bank to improve the infrastructure. Mindelo on the island of São Vicente is the most cosmopolitan centre, with a cultural scene, expressed in music, that resembles Brazil rather than West Africa. Tourism should revive the economy which is largely dependent on remittances from the large numbers of Cape Verdeans working overseas. Tourist activities on offer include windsurfing, sailing, diving, and trekking in the mountains.

Summary

- Africa is the second largest of the continents and is rich in both natural and cultural tourism resources.
- Although there is a large North African tourism industry serving the mass inclusive-tour markets of Europe, sub-Saharan Africa's tourism potential is largely unfulfilled.
- This can be attributed to a rudimentary transport network, the generally poor organisational framework, and the low level of industrial development of most African countries.
- Yet in such a vast continent generalisations are inappropriate; South Africa, for example, has an advanced economy, a high standard of tourism organisation and infrastructure, and it also generates international tourists.
- Some African countries have identified tourism as an area for expansion to attract foreign currency and enhance their economic position. This has been most evident in Southern Africa and some of the islands of the Indian Ocean, but most of the countries of West and Central Africa have been less successful.
- The tourism resources of North Africa are based on both winter and summer beach resorts with the added ingredient of a taste of Arab and Berber culture and excursions to the Sahara.
- East Africa's tourist resources primarily comprise the national parks and game reserves, but developments at the coast allow combined beach and safari tourism.
- South Africa's attractions include beaches and wildlife, as well as spectacular scenery and a warm temperate climate.
- In West Africa, beach tourism is important, but here, as in the rest of the continent, holidaymakers can sample the colourful everyday life of African communities.

Assignments

1 Analyse the strengths and weaknesses of South Africa as a destination for business and leisure tourism.
2 Compare Mozambique and Gambia as destinations for beach tourism.
3 Identify the constraints that prevent specified African countries from realising their full potential as tourist destinations.
4 Explain why some of the countries of East Africa and southern Africa are the world's most important destinations for safari tourism. Discuss how this type of tourism could be made more sustainable and bring greater benefits to local communities.
5 Explain the appeal of Morocco and Tunisia as holiday destinations, and why Libya has failed to attract this type of tourism.

Asia and the Pacific

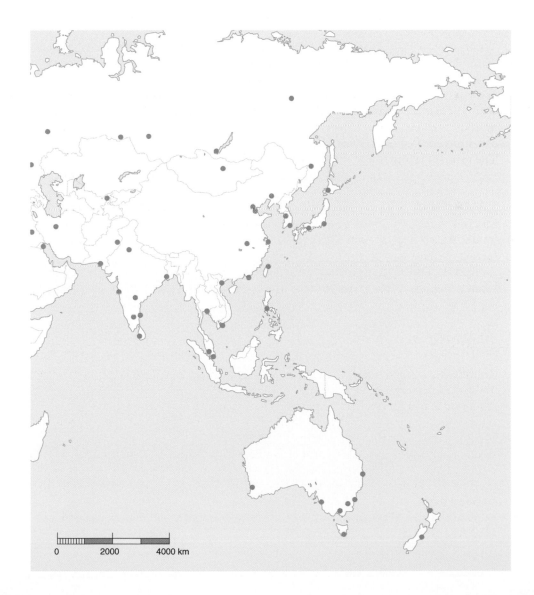

CHAPTER 20

The tourism geography of South Asia

Introduction

Asia is the world's largest continent, accounting for 60 per cent of the world's population. In recent decades most Asian economies have been growing rapidly, largely as a result of globalisation. Nevertheless, around 900 million people are living in absolute poverty on an income of less than US$1.25 a day, which means that Asia, for all its economic success, still accounts for two-thirds of the world's poor.

First we need to divide Asia into regions of more manageable size, made up of countries which are broadly similar in cultural terms. Three regions which are geographically part of Asia – the Central Asian republics and Siberia, and the Middle East – we described in Chapters 17 and 18. This leaves South Asia, better known as the Indian sub-continent, which the World Tourism Organisation (UNWTO) regards as a separate world region, and South-east Asia and the Far East, which UNWTO includes as part of the East Asia-Pacific region.

The governments of most Asian countries realise the importance of tourism, and many have joined organisations such as the Pacific Asia Travel Association (PATA) to promote travel to the region more effectively. From the viewpoint of the Western tourist, these countries offer interesting contrasts in landscapes and cultures, living costs are generally low, and hotel service is more personalised than in the West. On the other hand, the provision of infrastructure outside the main tourist areas is often poor. Until recently the Asian countries themselves generated few tourists, and those that did travel abroad tended to do so within the region. As the economies of Asian countries develop, so does demand for tourism, particularly in the business sector.

Physical features of South Asia

The seasonal changes in the landscape brought about by the monsoon, and the importance of the bamboo plant in the material culture, are the defining features not only of the Indian sub-continent, but also of South-east Asia and the Far East. In summer warm, humid air from the Indian Ocean and the south west Pacific Ocean moves into southern and eastern Asia bringing heavy rainfall – the 'summer monsoon'. In winter the continental heartland of Asia is dominated by a strong centre of high pressure from which there is a flow of air to the south and south-east. This 'winter monsoon' brings several months of clear, dry weather.

The Indian sub-continent consists of three major physical divisions:

1 **The northern mountain rampart**, which separates the sub-continent from the bulk of the Asian landmass. This includes the Himalayas to the east, and the Pamirs, Hindu Kush and Karakoram mountain ranges to the west. These rise to over 6,000 metres and boast the world's highest summits. They also have the following important characteristics:

   - They act as a barrier to the movement of the very cold air masses building up over Central Asia in winter, so that the lowlands to the south enjoy a warm climate throughout the year.
   - They also act as a barrier to north-south communications. Few roads cross the high mountain passes, and unlike the Alps, no railways penetrate the ranges. Even the pattern of air routes is affected to some extent.
   - Because of their altitude, the mountains themselves have a much cooler climate than the lowlands, and support a number of contrasting *life zones* based on differences in rainfall as well as temperature. The western Himalayas for example are much drier than those to the east – where Cherrapunji in the Assam foothills has the unenviable distinction of being one of the world's wettest places.
   - In relation to their resources the mountain valleys are often densely populated. The growth of tourism poses a threat to local communities already under pressure, as well as providing economic opportunity.
   - In the past the mountains contained a number of independent kingdoms, which were protected from outside influences by their remoteness and rugged terrain. At the present time only Bhutan, and to a lesser extent Nepal, have managed to preserve their cultural as well as political integrity. Sikkim and Ladakh have been absorbed by India, while Tibet has been forcibly integrated into China. On the other hand, some of the ethnic groups remain essentially nomadic, ignoring the modern frontiers.

2 **The Northern Plains**, through which flow the great rivers Indus, Ganges and Brahmaputra. These lowlands contain most of the historic cities and business centres of South Asia. The western part of the region has an arid climate, as shown by the Thar Desert on the India–Pakistan border. Elsewhere winter tends to be the dry season, with a large daily range of temperature. Stifling heat (with temperatures frequently exceeding 40°C) can be expected from April to June before the onset of the summer monsoon. This provides over 90 per cent of India's water supply, so not surprisingly it has a vital influence on the landscape and the lifestyle. The arrival of the rains is one of the world's most dramatic weather events and is also remarkably predictable, starting in Kerala at the end of May, and sweeping north to reach Mumbai (Bombay) by June 5 and Delhi by June 29. The monsoon provides some initial relief from the excessive heat, but is soon followed by months of

sweltering weather, as the high humidity negates any cooling effect the slightly lower temperatures might have. Each summer torrential monsoon rains disrupt communications and leave a trail of devastation in much of the sub-continent.

3 **Peninsular India and the islands.** This part of South Asia is dominated by the great plateau of volcanic rocks known as the Deccan and the coastal mountain ranges known as the Western and Eastern Ghats. The region has a more moderate tropical climate than the northern plains, making it a suitable winter-sun destination for tourists from Europe. Coastal locations such as Goa and Kerala, as well as the island states of Sri Lanka and the Maldives in the Indian Ocean have developed tourism industries based primarily on their beach resources.

Cultural features of South Asia

Despite the attractions of beaches and spectacular mountain scenery, the tourist appeal of South Asia is to a large extent cultural. The street life, bustling markets, colourful festivals and distinctive foods are fascinating for Western tourists, who also experience a degree of 'culture shock' on arrival. Religion has a major impact on everyday life, and the best of the cultural heritage is to be found in temples and shrines rather than secular buildings. The perceived 'other-worldliness' of countries like India and Nepal attracts many Western tourists alienated by materialism, some of whom seek spiritual guidance in religious communities or *ashrams*. Auroville near the former French colony of Pondicherry is a much-visited example of a planned community based on religion and 'New Age' beliefs.

At this point we feel some explanation of the major religions is necessary:

• Hinduism, with over 700 million believers is the majority religion in India, and its rituals have profoundly influenced Indian civilisation for at least three thousand years – far longer than Christianity in the West or Islam in the Middle East. The Hindu belief in *karma* and reincarnation often results in a fatalistic attitude to life that most Westerners find difficult to accept. Hindu temples are dedicated to a particular god or goddess (Brahma, Vishnu and Shiva are the most important), and are sumptuously decorated with polychrome sculptures.

• Buddhism also originated in northern India, but is now much more widespread in Sri Lanka, the Himalayan kingdoms, South-east Asia and the Far East. Common to all Buddhists is a belief in the importance of meditation as the path to *Nirvana* (enlightenment). Buddhist temples usually contain stylised images of the religion's founder – Gautama Siddhartha who is venerated as the Buddha (enlightened one). However styles of architecture vary widely – temples in Sri Lanka and Burma are quite different from those in Bhutan for example.

• Islam is the predominant religion in Afghanistan, Pakistan, Bangladesh and the Maldives. The Mogul Emperors imposed Islam on northern India in the sixteenth century, and were responsible for some of the world's finest Islamic architecture, including the Taj Mahal.

• Sikhism originally arose as a resistance to the Islamic domination of northern India. Sikhs differ from Hindus in being montheistic, placing much less emphasis on ritual, and rejecting the rigid social distinctions or castes that have characterised traditional Indian culture. Although they account for only 2 per cent of the population of India and are based mainly in the Punjab, they play an important role in commerce and the professions.

Religious tensions also threaten the political stability of most countries in the region, and thus reduce their appeal to tourists. Differences between Muslims and Hindus in British India led to its partition into two separate countries on independence in 1947. However, this left unresolved the status of Kashmir, causing a long-running dispute between the Republic of India and Pakistan and disrupting communications between the two countries. In the late 1990s the rise of Hindu fundamentalism in the Republic of India posed a threat to the government's policy of secularism and religious toleration, culminating in the inter-communal massacres that occurred in Gujarat in 2002. Muslim fundamentalism influences social attitudes to women and minority groups in Afghanistan and Pakistan, where religion and politics are less clearly separated than they are in India. Nevertheless, discrimination against the *dalits* or low caste Hindus, although strictly illegal, persists in some parts of India, and is a barrier to their participation in many social activities, including tourism.

Western cultural influence was largely due to the British, although the Portuguese arrived in the region much earlier. In fact, almost the whole of the Indian sub-continent was under British rule or protection during the nineteenth and early twentieth centuries, with the exception of a few small Portuguese and French enclaves, namely Goa, Diu, Daman, Chandernagore and Pondicherry. The legacy of the British *Raj* remains after independence in the widespread use of the English language and administrative framework, sporting and military traditions, an extensive railway network, and a supply of mountain resorts known as hill-stations. These had provided British officials and their families, in the days before air-conditioning, with a refuge from the summer heat of the plains. These places still retain much of their colonial architecture, although they are now resorts for middle-class domestic tourists. They include:

- Murree in Pakistan;
- Simla in the Himalayas (the summer capital of British India);
- Ootacamund in the Nilgiri Highlands of southern India; and
- Nuwara Eliya in Sri Lanka.

Approaches to tourism

South Asia as a whole accounts for around 1 per cent of international world tourism arrivals. Over half of all tourist arrivals, and over three quarters of receipts are accounted for by the largest of the nine component countries of South Asia – the Republic of India. Elsewhere in much of the region tourism is of little significance, notably for Afghanistan due to political unrest rendering the country unsafe for travellers, and for Bangladesh, where more pressing economic concerns overshadow tourism development. The majority of countries have encouraged inbound tourism, and most have a positive balance on their tourism account, with the notable exception of Pakistan, where outbound travel is much greater in terms of expenditure.

We can see a variety of approaches to tourism within the region including:

- stringent restriction on visitor numbers in the case of Bhutan – in contrast to neighbouring Nepal;
- a policy of tourist segregation from the local communities in the Lakshadweep and the Maldive islands; to
- promotion of Western-style beach holidays in Goa.

India

India demands our attention for a number of reasons. In extent and cultural variety it is the equivalent of Europe, but with a much older civilisation. There are at least 15 major languages, although Hindi is the most widely spoken. The country is a mosaic of different religions, ethnic groups and castes.

With a population now well over a billion, India will surpass China as the world's most populous country by 2030. It has almost 20 per cent of the world's population on just 3 per cent of the world's land area, so that demographic pressures on the resource base are severe. Over half of India's population is under 25 years of age, 40 per cent of adults are illiterate, and a third struggle to live below the official poverty line (two US dollars a day). Although India is a predominantly rural country, it also contains three major world cities – Delhi, Mumbai and Kolkata (Calcutta), each with 20 million inhabitants.

Despite these pressures and many other socio-economic problems, India has retained a democratic form of government since independence, although the Congress Party has been dominant in politics for most of that time. The cultural diversity of the country is recognised in the federal system of government, in which each of the 29 states and six autonomous territories has a large degree of control over its internal affairs, including tourism development.

For many years following Independence, India was to a large extent a centrally planned economy. After 1991 the government embarked on a policy of liberalisation, removing many restrictions on business enterprise, and the country was opened up to foreign investment. India is set to become one of the world's leading industrial nations, with technological expertise as part of its vast human resources. Bangalore and Hyderabad for example are among the world's leading centres of information technology. On the other hand great improvements need to be made in basic infrastructure, which is inadequate by Western standards, while bureaucratic controls and inertia continue to inhibit progress.

Demand for tourism

Domestic and outbound tourism

A substantial middle class, estimated to be between 15 to 20 per cent of the population – or over 150 million people – has the means to participate in domestic tourism in India and the volumes are impressive, exceeding 740 million trips a year. Traditionally a good deal of domestic travel has been undertaken for religious reasons, as all the major faiths encourage pilgrimages to shrines or holy places. The best known of these is the Hindu centre of Varanasi (Benares) on the River Ganges, where the *ghats* – the steps leading down to the water's edge are the focus for ritual bathing, readings from the sacred texts by gurus, and cremations. There are many other shrines, some in remote locations in the Himalayas and Kashmir. Often these pilgrimages entail an arduous journey, partly on foot, and embrace all classes of society, including large numbers of wandering *sadhus* (holy men). Bodhgaya is the main pilgrimage centre for Buddhists, while the Golden Temple at Amritsar is the holy place of the Sikhs. Visits to family entertainment centres and amusement parks – reflecting India's fascination with high technology – as well as stays in beach and mountain resorts, are expected to increase as incomes rise among a middle class with a Western style education and aspirations.

Outbound tourism is much smaller in volume, but nevertheless accounted for 12 million departures in 2010, including nearly 3 million to neighbouring countries such as Nepal. Business travel accounts for 25 per cent of these journeys. Leisure travel to countries outside South Asia should grow with the relaxation of strict foreign exchange controls imposed by the Indian government. For many years Britain has been the most popular European destination, reflecting the cultural and family ties between the two countries. Future travel patterns may well be influenced by the fact that the United States is now India's main trading partner, and there are four times more Indian students in American universities than in British universities.

Inbound tourism

Despite having vast tourism potential, India receives only a small share of world tourism, amounting to 5.6 million arrivals in 2010. Even so, tourism has shown impressive growth since 1970, when 290,000 visitors were recorded. Tourism is now India's third largest earner of foreign exchange, and provides employment directly and indirectly to around 24 million people. The impact is even greater if we consider the informal sector of the economy, and the very large numbers engaged in the handicraft industries. A number of factors are holding back the expansion of tourism in India:

- inadequate infrastructure, especially water and power supplies;
- negative publicity in the Western media – for example, outbreaks of disease and inter-communal strife, in reality confined to specific areas, are seen as affecting the whole country;
- promotion of this enormous and complex country as one destination, whereas India consists of many quite different destinations and tourism products – there is a need to market specific destinations and target specific types of tourist;
- the seasonal concentration of visits in the final quarter of the year, creating occupancy problems for India's hotels;
- a shortage of medium-priced accommodation, particularly in Delhi; and
- other negative factors include air pollution in the cities during the dry season, noise, poor hygiene, and harassment by beggars and street vendors.

The main generating markets for India include Britain, Germany, France, the USA, the Middle East and Japan. Many arrivals from the Middle East and Britain are in fact returning expatriates, who tend to stay with friends or relatives and make little use of tourist facilities. The most popular time to visit India is from October to December when the weather is at its best, but there is a steady flow of business travellers throughout the year. The average length of stay of tourists to India – at 28 days – is among the world's highest – backpackers for example, from Europe, Australia and North America, who are including India as part of an Asian tour, spend at least three weeks in the country. These young budget travellers have played an important role in opening up new destinations to conventional tourism. However the typical backpackers of the new millennium are different from their predecessors of the 1970s in at least two respects:

- they are usually following an established route pattern, staying at hostels and cheap hotels patronised by other Western budget travellers; and
- they are less concerned with a search for 'spiritual values' – nowadays, an extended visit to India is seen more as an interesting way of filling the 'gap year' between college and a career.

ASIA AND THE PACIFIC

Discussion point

In class, discuss the proposition that the average Western backpacker is ill-informed about the realities of life in India, is overly concerned with travelling as cheaply as possible, and often behaves in ways that cause offence to local communities. Would a code of conduct be the best solution to the problem?

The supply of tourism

Transport

The vast majority of foreign visitors to India (other than those from neighbouring Bangladesh and Pakistan) arrive by air. Delhi and Mumbai (Bombay) are the most important gateways, and have invested heavily in improving facilities for air travellers. Kolkata (Calcutta) and Chennai (Madras) serve the eastern and southern parts of the country. The Indian government has responded to the growth in air travel by adopting a liberal open skies policy, which allows foreign charter airlines to fly direct from Europe to resort areas such as Goa. Moreover the national carrier Air India has a code-sharing agreement with the American airline Continental Airways. Only a small minority of Western tourists travel overland to India, due to the political situation in Afghanistan which has closed the historic route through the Khyber Pass, while the long-standing dispute between India and Pakistan over Kashmir places another obstacle in the way of travellers.

Internal transport is less fraught with difficulties. Indian Airlines operate domestic services to over 70 destinations within the country as well as neighbouring states. With deregulation in the late 1990s, a number of low-cost carriers such as Air Deccan, Jet Airways and Air Sahara have entered the market, and there has been a spectacular growth in the number of passengers, most of whom are first-time fliers. Kingfisher, operated by a brewing entrepreneur, caters for a more upmarket traveller with Western tastes and aspirations. The airlines are now competing with Indian Railways for a share of the domestic market, offering cheap fares and comfortable travel as well as greatly reduced journey times. India inherited from Britain the most extensive railway network in Asia, amounting to over 70,000 kilometres of track, and this is used by some 11 million passengers a day. From the viewpoint of the foreign tourist, the train provides a cheaper and more interesting way of touring than by air, with express services linking all the main cities. As the system is heavily used, foreign tourists need to purchase *Indrail* passes or make prior reservations to ensure travelling in comfort and without hassle. In some areas steam locomotives are still used, as for example on the narrow-gauge Darjeeling–Himalaya railway, which is a major tourist attraction in its own right. Luxury rail products such as the 'Palace on Wheels' and the 'Royal Orient' are promoted by the India Tourism Office as a way of touring the classical sites in the north west of the country.

In contrast, India's one million kilometre road network is inadequate to cope with the great increase in traffic resulting from rapid economic growth, as there are few four-lane highways. Livestock on the road add to the chaos, and accident levels are very high by Western standards. The introduction of the Nano, a low cost 'people's car' in 2007, while reducing the number of over-laden motor cycle combinations, could exacerbate traffic and pollution problems. For the foreign visitor, long-distance road travel, even by express bus, can be a noisy and exhausting experience. This situation should improve with the development of a national 'superhighway' network almost 6,000 kilometres in length, based on the 'Golden Quadrilateral' linking India's four major cities. It is hoped this will boost the country's economy and reduce the huge disparities of wealth that exist between cities such as Bangalore and the impoverished rural areas of states such as Bihar, Orissa and Madhya Pradesh.

Accommodation

India's accommodation stock is extensive, ranging from luxury hotels to basic hostels used by young tourists on a tight budget, who are more concerned about price than fire safety standards. Modern Western-style hotels catering for both business and leisure tourists are found in all large cities and the popular tourist centres. Indian-owned chains, namely Taj, Oberoi and the state owned India Tourism Development Corporation (ITDC), dominate this sector. More unusual types of accommodation include:

- the luxury houseboats moored on Lake Dal at Srinagar, a heritage of British and Mogul rule in Kashmir;
- the former palaces of the Indian princes or maharajas who were semi-independent under the British Raj – these have now been converted into 'heritage hotels', the most famous being the Lake Palace Hotel at Udaipur in Rajahstan, in a highly romantic setting;
- *dak* bungalows, used primarily by government officials as rest houses, are sometimes available for overnight stays by tourists in remote areas;
- hostels provided by religious organisations; and
- tourist bungalows providing self-catering facilities and private guesthouses are available in resort areas. Campgrounds have also been developed along the main overland routes and forest lodges are available in wildlife reserves such as the Kanha National Park.

Tourism organisation

In the 1960s tourism development began to form part of the government's Five Year Plans (whose primary objective is to raise living standards) and more recently tourism has been the subject of specific 'action plans'. The Ministry of Tourism and Culture is responsible for formulating policy at cabinet level. The Ministry is supported by a number of other agencies including:

- The India Tourism Development Corporation Ltd (ITDC) was set up by the government in 1965 to develop infrastructure in those areas where the private sector was reluctant to invest. Apart from hotels the ITDC also owned resorts, restaurants and transport operations, some of which have since been privatised.
- The Tourism Finance Corporation of India established to assist with tourism financing.
- The Indian Institute of Travel and Tourism Management (IITTM) established to set up high quality training and education in tourism.

As well as supporting many projects through the ITDC, the government also provides financial incentives to domestic and foreign companies in the private sector. At the regional and local levels the various state and city authorities have a regulatory role, and some have set up development corporations to carry out tourism projects. In recent years however, the public sector has not been particularly active in encouraging tourism. It is perhaps not surprising that in a country with so many pressing social and economic problems, the development of tourist facilities, which the majority of the Indian population cannot afford, is seen as a low priority.

Tourism resources

On offer is a unique blend of ancient civilisations, religious monuments, spectacular scenery, beaches, mountain resorts and wildlife reserves, that has been promoted in the West as 'Incredible India'. We can summarise the main tourism products as:

- **Cultural tourism** – usually focusing on a particular region, and taking the form of a tour circuit linking a number of sites to a gateway city.
- **Beach tourism**. At present this is mainly found in the states of Goa, Kerala and Tamil Nadu, and little of India's 7,500 kilometre-long coastline has been developed for tourism.
- **Adventure tourism,** including trekking, mountain climbing and river-running, which is mainly focused on the more accessible parts of the Himalaya region.
- **Ecotourism.** India is second only to Africa in the variety of its wildlife resources. This is perhaps surprising given the demographic pressures and the threats of increasing pollution and deforestation (only 13 per cent of the country has any type of forest cover). The first national park – Jim Corbett to the north of Delhi – was established under British rule in 1911 due to the efforts of a hunter turned conservationist. There are now over 500 areas protected as national parks or wildlife sanctuaries, although most are much smaller than those of Africa. The federal government has effected a number of conservation measures; the most widely publicised is 'Project Tiger' which seeks to protect India's best known national icon. Kanha National Park in Madhya Pradesh, the setting for Kipling's *Jungle Book*, is the best known of these game reserves. Much of the responsibility for wildlife management has devolved to the individual states. Limited funding is a problem, and issues of economic development often conflict with conservation.
- **Spa tourism** is characterised by yoga techniques based on *ayurveda*, an holistic medical system that has been practised in India for at least two millennia.
- **Sport tourism.** The hosting of the 2010 Commonwealth Games in Delhi, and India's sponsorship of cricket are examples of the country's significance as a venue for sports events.

Due to its extent India is usually treated as four regions, based on the gateways of Delhi, Mumbai, Chennai and Kolkata.

Northern India

This region has played a major role in the history of India, and contains the best-known cultural attractions. The so-called 'Classic Triangle', a tour circuit linking the cities of Delhi, Agra and Jaipur, is the most popular route for foreign visitors.

Delhi actually consists of two cities – the old and the new. Old Delhi was the capital of the Mogul Empire, and is a maze of narrow streets, chaotic traffic and bustling bazaars. Among its Islamic monuments are the Jama Masjid Mosque and the Red Fort, once a royal palace. The British planned New Delhi as the capital of India in the closing decades of the Raj. The most important of its broad ceremonial avenues is the Rajpath linking India Gate to the President's Palace.

Agra is mainly visited for the Taj Mahal, the white marble mausoleum commemorating Shah Jehan's love for his favourite wife Mumtaz. This beautiful building is under threat from tourist pressure, leaving in its wake litter in the gardens and even graffiti on the monument itself; and pollution. Although tourism provides a livelihood for many thousands employed in the craft and service sectors, Agra is also a major industrial city – sulphur dioxide emissions have caused a massive deterioration in the stonework.

Within easy reach of Agra are other relics of historic India:

- Fatehpur Sikri, the remains of a short lived capital of the Mogul Empire;
- Orchha, which has undergone less restoration and is not as commercialised; and
- the temples at Khajuraho, with their erotic sculptures, are also a well-established stop on the tour circuit.

Jaipur is the gateway to **Rajahstan**, a state which to many epitomises India, with its colourful costumes, ethnic crafts, and the palaces of the former maharajas. It also exemplifies the problems brought about by tourism in an arid region where there are few other sources of income. Some allege that conventional organised tourism does not benefit local communities as profits mainly go to the owners of 'heritage hotels', who furthermore prefer to employ immigrant Nepalis, who are prepared to accept even lower wages than the locals. On the other hand, backpackers have also been criticised for showing little respect for Hindu traditions, while the Pushkar camel market has become a commercialised tourist event. Of the tourist centres, Jaipur itself is famous for its markets and the 'Palace of the Winds', but suffers from chronic pollution and lack of investment. Other attractions in the region include:

- Jodhpur, which gave polo to the British, is noted for its *son et lumiere* performances recreating the warrior traditions of the Rajput princes.
- Udaipur, the best preserved of the Rajput cities, with a beautiful setting on Lake Pichola.
- Jaisalmer, was once a major trading centre for camel caravans crossing the Thar Desert, but is now a picturesque stop on the tourist itinerary. Income from tourism enabled the authorities to provide a piped water supply, but this, together with vastly increased water consumption, has caused widespread subsidence as the town's open drains cannot cope. As a result, many of the *havelis* (merchant houses) are in urgent need of repair.

The **Valley of Kashmir** offers among its attractions beautiful mountain scenery and a cool climate, in contrast to the heat and dust of the plains of northern India. This made it the favourite resort area for the Mogul rulers, who designed the famous Shalimar Gardens in Srinagar. It has become popular with domestic tourists, despite the heavy security presence of the Indian military authorities. This was imposed as a response to a number of terrorist incidents in the late 1980s and early 1990s. However, checkpoints and curfews have made everyday life irksome for Kashmiris, many of whom depend on tourism for a livelihood. Although Gulmarg was developed in the 1970s as the premier golf and skiing resort of India, since the troubles there has been little outside investment in the region. Moreover, foreign tourists have been deterred by the chronic dispute with Pakistan. On the other hand, **Ladakh**, although part of the state of Kashmir, is not a disputed area and has become a trekking destination. This region offers spectacular, if rather barren, high mountain landscapes and a Tibetan culture which is still largely intact.

Eastern India

The eastern India region is centred on Kolkata, the capital of West Bengal, which as Calcutta was the former capital of British India. In the West, the city is better known for its overcrowding and Mother Teresa's work among the destitute than for its cultural attractions, which outshine those of Delhi. Although rickshaws still feature in the traffic, Kolkata boasts India's only metro system, and its technological achievements are showcased in 'Science City'. Within easy reach are the beach resorts of the Bay of Bengal, including Puri, which is also a major religious centre for Hindus. It is one of a number of temple-cities in the state of Orissa, the others being Konarak and Bhubaneswar. Kolkata is also the gateway to the eastern Himalayas, particularly the mountain resorts of Darjeeling and Shillong, which are noted for their tea plantations. Large areas of this sensitive frontier region are tribal territories under military control, and access is restricted for security reasons.

Southern India

The Dravidian peoples of southern India are culturally distinct, and overseas trade has played an important role in the history of the region. The port of Cochin for example was noted for its trade in pepper and other spices in ancient times, and in the picturesque fishing villages Hinduism has co-existed peacefully with Christianity and other religions.

With its favourable climate, lush scenery and fine beaches, the state of Kerala is set to rival Goa as a holiday destination. A unique asset is provided by the 'backwaters', a system of canals adapted from transporting agricultural produce to recreational use. With the introduction of charter flights in 1995, Kovalam has become a major beach resort, particularly for British holidaymakers. However, this has failed to benefit the local community to the same extent as the small-scale informal tourism of earlier years, and stands in apparent contradiction to the socialist leanings of the state government. Most of the Coromandel Coast is less attractive for tourism development, due to the heavy surf, and was the area of India most affected by the 2004 tsunami. Nevertheless, Chennai has fine beaches as well as being a major cultural centre, offering the classical *kathakali* dance-dramas, adapted for a Western tourist audience. It is a good base for exploring the temples of Madurai and Kanchipuram, which are spectacular examples of Hindu architecture.

Western India

Beach tourism has developed to a greater extent in western India along the Malabar Coast. The region is dominated by Mumbai, India's major port and business centre, while Goa is the leading holiday destination.

Mumbai is a new city by Indian standards, with many reminders of the British Raj when Bombay was the 'gateway to India'. It is seen as a city of opportunity by rural immigrants, who pour in at the rate of a thousand a day. With little room for expansion on a narrow peninsula, the city's congestion is acute, and the contrasts between skyscrapers and grand hotels on the one hand, and the *bustees* (slums) on the other, are extreme. This may explain the dominant role of 'Bollywood' – Mumbai's booming film industry – in popular culture. Apart from shopping, the city's attractions include Chowpatty Beach, with its snake charmers and other performers, the 'hanging gardens' of exclusive Malabar Hill, the Gandhi Memorial and the art collections of the Prince of Wales Museum. The ancient history of India is brought to life at the Elephanta Caves, while Mumbai is a good base for visiting the Buddhist and Hindu temples of Ajanta and Ellora.

Discussion point

Poverty as a tourist spectacle

It is now possible for Western tourists to visit the slums of Mumbai on a guided tour. Here people live in grossly overcrowded conditions, at densities of over 2,000 per hectare, without basic services. The sensory experience is unpleasant, with the stench of open sewers clogged with garbage, incessant noise, the acrid smoke from pottery kilns, not to mention the health and safety hazard posed by tangles of improvised electricity cables. On the positive side, these slums provide an opportunity for thousands of small enterprises, many of them engaged in recycling useful articles out of the waste materials discarded by more affluent city-dwellers.

Debate whether these tours can be regarded as pro-poor tourism, helping to alleviate poverty. Are the organisers motivated by profit, or do they donate some of the proceeds from tourists to charitable work, such as providing street children with a basic education?

Are the tourists voyeurs motivated simply by curiosity, or are they on a guilt trip? Does visiting poverty-stricken areas and meeting some of their inhabitants provide valuable insights into the 'real India' that most tourists never experience, or does it merely exploit the slum-dwellers?

Photo 20.1 One of Goa's tropical beaches (©istockphoto.com/ Tobias Helbig)

Case study 20.1

Goa

Goa's small area offers scenic variety, over 100 kilometres of fine beaches, and a relaxed lifestyle. Culturally it is unique – a blend of Indian and 'Latin' influences. Both Catholic carnival and Hindu festivals are celebrated here, while alcohol is freely available, unlike the situation elsewhere in India. Portugal ruled Goa for four and a half centuries until ousted by the Indian Army in 1961, and the Portuguese influence is evident in the architecture, music and the cuisine. The immense Baroque church of Bom Jesu in Old Goa – the former capital – contains the tomb of St Francis Xavier, the greatest of Jesuit missionaries to the East.

Western tourists are not attracted to Goa primarily for cultural or religious reasons, for since the arrival of the 'hippies' in the 1960s the focus has been on beach tourism. Nevertheless we can distinguish between different categories of visitor, and a range of accommodation and services has developed to meet their needs. These include:

- Low budget backpackers, mainly from Europe and Australia, who are stopping off in Goa as part of an extended Asian tour. They stay in cheap guesthouses in the Anjuna area, 'discovered' by the hippies of a previous generation.
- Indian domestic tourists taking seaside holidays, cultural tours and business trips, who stay at hotels in Panaji, the state capital, or other towns.
- Package holidaymakers from the UK, Germany and other West European countries arriving during the winter season on direct charter flights to Goa's Dabolim Airport. They stay in three star hotels contracted to particular tour operators. Due to the rapid growth of charters since 1987, fishing villages such as Calangute have become commercialised resorts.
- Middle-class West European holidaymakers who take advantage of the cheap air fares but who prefer to use locally-owned small hotels and guesthouses.

Tourism has arguably brought economic benefits to Goa, but the state government's policy of encouraging upmarket tourism has been opposed by local non-governmental organisations (NGOs) concerned with the social and environmental issues associated with tourism development. These include:

- the diversion of scarce resources, such as water and power from agriculture to the hotel sector – some claim that one five star hotel consumes as much water as five villages;
- violations by the hotel sector of state laws that prevent building within 200 metres of the shoreline;
- unlike the locally owned small hotels and guesthouses, the luxury hotels are linked with international chains or owned by Indians from outside Goa – the state government's attempts to control the beach shacks selling food etc. is seen as favouring the hotels at the expense of local people's livelihood;
- the expansion of tourism has resulted in the decline of traditional occupations such as fishing and cashew nut cultivation;
- Goa is a religious, conservative society and local people are often deeply offended by the attitude of many Western holidaymakers, expressed in drug-taking, uninhibited sexuality and immodest dress and behaviour; and
- Carnival has been exploited to promote tourist activities, rather than being primarily a religious festival for the benefit of the local community.

ASIA AND THE PACIFIC

Discussion point

Goa has reached the stage in the tourist area life cycle where it is facing growing competition as tour operators discover more unspoiled beach locations. How should the state government and tourism sector respond?

The islands of India

India's island territories as yet remain largely untouched by Western-style tourism, although they attract a growing number of domestic visitors. They include:

- the Lakshadweep (Laccadives) archipelago in the Indian Ocean, composed of small coral atolls similar to the Maldives further south – Bangaram is the only island open to Western tourists for diving holidays; and
- the Andaman and Nicobar Islands in the Bay of Bengal, which are rugged and largely forest covered – there is potential for eco-tourism and diving, but development is restricted by lack of infrastructure and the sensitive nature of relationships between mainstream India and the indigenous tribes, an example of a 'Fourth World' culture which is increasingly under threat.

Sri Lanka

Formerly known as Ceylon, Sri Lanka is a large island rich in tourism resources. Its capital Colombo is well placed in relation to the air and shipping routes crossing the Indian Ocean. In the past, the island's closeness to India and fabled wealth attracted Arab traders who were followed by the Portuguese, Dutch and British. This resulted in a mix of cultures and one of the country's highest mountains – Sri Padu (Adam's Peak) is sacred to all four major religions. Until the 1970s Sri Lanka had been one of the more stable countries in South Asia and the prospects for tourism seemed bright. The Ceylon Tourist Board (now the Sri Lanka Tourist Board) was established in 1966, when 19,000 visitors were received. By 1982 this had grown to over 400,000, most of whom were on air inclusive holidays, organised by West European tour operators (the entrepreneur Freddie Laker was largely responsible for introducing Sri Lanka as a long-haul beach destination to the British market). However, there had long been tensions between the Sinhalese and the Tamil minority, who were originally brought in by the British from southern India to work in the tea plantations. During the 1980s these erupted into civil war, which rendered much of the north and east of the country off-limits to tourists, and as a result, Sri Lanka lost favour with Western tour operators and visitor numbers fell dramatically. With the defeat of the Tamil separatists, international tourism has now largely recovered, with arrivals approaching 350,000 in 2009.

The Ministry of Tourism has overall responsibility for the sector, while the Sri Lanka Tourist Board is responsible for promotion and market research. Although Sri Lanka has suffered from the lack of a clear tourism policy, a master plan commissioned in the 1990s provides the necessary framework for growth. The government, while encouraging foreign investment, has responded by steering development to the coastal areas close to Colombo in the west, and the port of Trincomalee in the east, in this way protecting the country's cultural and wildlife resources from the impact of tourism. The plan also stimulated a change in emphasis of tourism development to 'beach plus' products, in contrast to the sun, sand and sea formula of earlier years.

Tourism resources

Sri Lanka's tourist attractions include:

- Extensive sandy beaches along the south and west coast, although sea conditions can be rough during the period of the south west monsoon from May to July. Here the Sri Lanka Tourist Board has developed resort hotels of an international standard, particularly at Bentota. The beaches on the east coast are less developed, although they are more sheltered and enjoy a drier climate.
- The 'cultural triangle' of the interior, based on the historic cities of Kandy, Anuradhapura and Polonnaruwa, each of which served at one time as capital of a powerful kingdom. The Rock Fortress at Sigiriya, rising above the northern plain is particularly impressive, as are the remains of ancient temples, palaces and complex irrigation systems. Traditional crafts and dances continue to flourish in Kandy, which contains the 'Temple of the Tooth', a world famous Buddhist shrine.
- The wildlife resources, including the elephant orphanage at Pinnawela, and a number of national parks, such as Yala and Gal Oya, which offer bungalow accommodation.
- Colombo is a major business and conference centre, as well as providing shopping opportunities for jewellery, batik and wood-carving.

Discussion point

Although Thailand received the most media coverage, three countries of the Indian sub-continent were badly affected by the tsunami of December 26, 2004. Sri Lanka alone suffered the loss of 38,000 lives and damage to its tourism sector amounting to 250 million dollars. The state government of Tamil Nadu in southern India, and the government of Sri Lanka, responded by designating a coastal regulation zone, where any new development or rebuilding was prohibited within 200 metres of the sea. This was ostensibly to prevent any future disasters, but it has adversely affected the fishing communities that have been re-located, while in effect prime coastal sites have been requisitioned by the authorities to favour future luxury hotel projects rather than small tourism enterprises. In class, debate the issues involved in the reconstruction after the tsunami, from the viewpoint of the various stakeholders, including NGOs, representatives of local communities, government officials, hoteliers, guesthouse owners, and tour operators.

The Maldives

The Maldives is an independent republic, very small in land area but occupying a large expanse of the Indian Ocean south-west of the Indian sub-continent. Geographically, the Maldives is a unique collection of 26 coral atolls, containing almost 1,200 coral islands, of which only a small number are permanently inhabited. The government has done much to encourage Western tourism, but on its own terms. For example, the islanders are Muslims, and no alcohol is allowed except in those islands that have been designated for tourists as self-contained resorts. Tourists are only allowed to visit the inhabited islands on escorted tours, and are expected to respect the traditions of Islam in terms of modest dress when visiting the capital, Male. This is a small town with little to attract the visitor, although it contains two thirds of the Maldivian population, and is the gateway to the islands through Hulhule International Airport.

The prime tourism resource of the islands is the pristine marine environment where the quality of the coral reefs and marine life is unrivalled anywhere in the world. The majority of visitors arrive in the Maldives to experience this marine environment and also for water sports. Each of the resort islands has a diving base and the resort *house reef* is commonly within wading or swimming distance from the accommodation.

The Ministry of Tourism oversees tourism development and regulates the resorts. In the late 1990s the Maldives Tourism Promotion Board was created to market the islands internationally. The Maldives aims to become the world's premium eco-tourism destination, and to diversify its markets. The authorities are acutely aware of the threat of rising sea levels resulting from climate change, as no point on the islands rises above 3 metres. The atoll of Baa, for example, has been particularly active in environmental and social programmes. These include the conservation of the mangroves, which are very effective in absorbing carbon emissions and protecting the islands from frequent cyclones; the use of renewable sources of energy in the resorts; recycling; and a ban on shark fishing.

Pakistan

Despite having a varied resource base and a fairly extensive coastline, Pakistan has been less successful than India in attracting Western tourists and the sector accounts for 3 per cent of GDP. In part, this is due to the strength of Islamic tradition, security concerns, poor infrastructure and the restrictions on cross-border travel. Most of the country consists of mountain and desert landscapes, and some of the world's most difficult terrain separates Pakistan from its neighbours to the west and north. In 2009 around 270,000 arrivals were recorded, the most important generating countries being the UK and the USA. In addition, domestic tourism is significant, and set to grow, with an estimated 40 million trips a year.

An agency of the Ministry of Tourism, the Pakistan Tourist Development Corporation, offers a wide selection of hotels, motels, and rest houses (known as *musafir khanas*) and tours operated by its subsidiary, Pakistan Tours Ltd. The national airline Pakistan International Airlines (PIA) provides a network of international and domestic services. Transport by road and rail is less efficient, and compares unfavourably with the situation in India.

Although Urdu is the official language, Pakistan is made up of a number of ethnic groups and the country has been less politically stable than India. In the north-west of the country, government control is only loosely exercised over the Pathans and other tribes. In the time of the Raj, this was the North-West Frontier of British India, immortalised by Rudyard Kipling; nowadays it is an area rife with guns and refugees as a result of the continuing crisis in neighbouring Afghanistan. For this reason, the Khyber Pass has ceased to function as an overland tourist route, although the regional capital – Peshawar – is visited by the more adventurous travellers. The majority of Pakistan's population live in the irrigated valley of the River Indus, which also contains the major tourist centres:

- Lahore is the religious and cultural centre of the country, conserving much of the architectural heritage and pleasure gardens of the Mogul emperors of India.
- Multan is another historic walled city which is the focus of Muslim pilgrimages. It is situated close to the remains of the much older Indus civilisation which flourished at Mohenjo–Daro and Harappa in the third millennium BC.
- Karachi is Pakistan's largest city and major international gateway by air and sea.
- Islamabad, which was deliberately planned as the capital of the new Muslim state, and the old city of Rawalpindi nearby, are mainly centres for business travel.
- In the north of Pakistan, Gilgit provides facilities for skiing, trekking and mountain climbing, while adventure-seekers can follow the Karakoram Highway. This spectacular feat of engineering threads its way between some of the world's highest mountains and glaciers into China.

Bangladesh

From 1947 to 1971 Bangladesh, formerly east Bengal, was a detached part of Pakistan, but strong cultural differences led to a war of independence. The new nation had to face severe economic and environmental problems, namely:

- It is densely populated even by Asian standards, relying on an economy dominated by agriculture, and with few industries other than textiles. In the capital, Dhaka, people still rely to a large extent on rickshaws for transport.
- Most of the country is low-lying and is effectively a 'waterland' after the monsoon rains. Unusually devastating floods occur when tropical cyclones from the Indian Ocean coincide with heavy monsoon rains in the eastern Himalayas.
- The country's many rivers are an obstacle to an effective road and rail network, while ferry links are below Western standards.

Nevertheless, Bangladesh is no longer regarded as an economic 'basket case' by some Western experts, and business travel to Dhaka is growing in importance. Small enterprises are expected to play a major role in any expansion of tourism. Aside from the capital, the main areas of interest for tourists are:

- the hill country of Sylhet in the north;
- the vast wetland environment of the Sundarbans, formed by the deltas of the Ganges and Brahmaputra, which provides a refuge for wildlife; and
- Cox's Bazaar, which boasts one of the most extensive beaches in Asia, as yet little developed.

Afghanistan

Afghanistan is located where the Indian sub-continent borders on Central Asia and the Middle East, and historically it has been both the meeting place of civilisations and a refuge for different ethnic groups. In the 1970s Afghanistan was a transit area and Kabul a welcome staging point for Western tourists on the overland route to India. Since then the country's economy and infrastructure have been devastated as a result of the Soviet invasion in 1979 and civil war arising out of long-standing tribal feuds. The fundamentalist Taliban regime from 1996 to 2001 actively discouraged tourism and even destroyed much of the country's pre-Islamic heritage, such as the Buddhist monuments at Bamian. The pre-conditions for tourism development, namely security and an adequate road network, have yet to be realised, as most of the country remains outside the control of the government in Kabul. Although much of Afghanistan consists of arid, rugged mountains, these are punctuated by fertile valleys and historic cities such as Kandahar and Herat – celebrated in *The Kite Runner*.

Nepal

Although the Gurkhas had long played an important role in the British Army, their homeland, the Hindu Kingdom of Nepal was closed to the outside world until the 1950s. After its discovery by 'hippies' and overland travellers in the 1960s there was a rapid growth of tourism. However events such as 9/11, the massacre of Nepal's royal family, and an on-going Maoist rebellion in the west of the country have had a severe impact, such that arrivals fell from 460,000 in 2000 to only 200,000 in 2002. Numbers have since recovered to 370,000 in 2009.

Within an area only half that of Great Britain, Nepal can offer a great variety of climates and scenery. There are three main physical divisions running east to west, namely:

- The Himalayas, which contain eight of the world's highest mountain peaks, including Everest and Annapurna, attracting trekkers, mountain climbers and adventure-seekers from many different countries. The foothills, including the valleys of Kathmandu and Pokhara, contain the majority of the population. Cultural attractions abound in the form of Buddhist temples, as at Bhadgaon and Patan.
- The sub-tropical lowlands, known as the Terai, which still contain areas of jungle, including the Royal Chitwan National Park and its famous 'Tiger Tops' game lodge.
- Buddhists from all over the world are attracted to Lumbini, the birthplace of Buddha.

The Ministry of Tourism and Civil Aviation, along with the Department of National Parks and Wildlife is responsible for tourism organisation, and the Nepal Tourism Board is a public/private sector partnership body. In practice, Nepal relies very much on foreign aid for tourism development, and on Indian tour operators to bring in the visitors. In the 1990s, air policy underwent a degree of liberalisation allowing in other carriers to supplement Royal Nepal Airlines.

Poor access, pollution, inadequate infrastructure and frequent shortages of power and water supplies are major constraints on the growth of the tourism sector. In addition, criticism from environmentalists about the pollution found on the mountains, and the lack of robust environmental policies (for example, on timber cutting to maintain tourist lodges) may also constrain tourism growth.

Adventure tourism is the mainstay of tourism in Nepal with activities including mountain climbing, river-running and mountain biking. Trekking, where tourists on foot are escorted and supplied by local porters and guides, is the most popular activity in the Himalayan zone of Nepal, accounting for over a quarter of all visitors. Nepal offers a great variety of trekking opportunities including some of the world's most spectacular scenery; the trails are well-maintained, and trekkers are rarely far from a village. Although remote areas such as Mustang are being opened up to meet the demand, trekking also shows a high degree of concentration in particular areas of central and eastern Nepal, including:

ASIA AND THE PACIFIC

- the Annapurna region west of Pokhara: and
- the Everest route, from Lukha to the base camp at the foot of Mount Everest.

Bhutan

This Buddhist kingdom is much smaller than Nepal in area and population as well as being more remote. Culturally it is similar to Tibet as it was prior to the Chinese takeover, with prayer flags much in evidence and numerous fortified monasteries known as *dzongs* dominating the countryside. The government has promoted a 'Gross National Happiness Index' rather than GNP as a measure of the country's well-being – a concept now being looked at by a number of Western countries. It is determined to preserve traditional lifestyles from the impact of tourism, which is therefore strictly controlled, and certain activities such as mountain climbing are prohibited, to protect the country's forest and wildlife resources. Until 2001 access was restricted to a few accredited tour operators offering special interest holidays to small groups of visitors, in contrast to trekking on the Nepalese model. The government now allows some development of upmarket resort hotels, where access is controlled by price. With the king introducing democracy in 2008, pressures to improve the GNP through economic development, rather than preserving 'gross national happiness' are likely to increase.

Summary

- South Asia contains some of the world's most densely populated countries, at various stages of economic development but nevertheless poor by Western standards.
- Most countries in the region are developing an inbound tourism industry to earn much-needed foreign exchange and provide jobs for rapidly growing populations.
- The generally low level of incomes means that domestic tourism is less significant while volumes of outbound tourism are small; however both are set to increase due to the growth of a middle class, especially in India.
- Despite a wealth of resources, South Asia accounts for only a small percentage of world tourism.
- The attractions of the region are based on the exotic cultures and landscapes, and a lifestyle in which religion plays a major role. Of particular note are the classic tour circuits in India, the beaches and gentle way of life of the Indian Ocean islands, and the spectacular scenery of the Himalayas.

Assignments

1 Investigate the strengths and weaknesses of India as a destination for business and leisure tourism.
2 Identify the natural disasters and political crises that have made an impact on tourism in South Asia, and describe how different countries in the region have dealt with these problems.

ASIA AND THE
PACIFIC

3 Discuss whether deficiencies in transport and infrastructure generally are holding back the development of tourism in the Indian sub-continent.

4 Explain the appeal of religion, cultural heritage and lifestyle in attracting Western tourists to a number of South Asian destinations.

5 Discuss the role of the film industry, music and dance, television documentaries, and literature in publicising particular South Asian countries. Compare the images portrayed with those presented by the official national tourism organisations.

CHAPTER 21

The tourism geography of East Asia

Introduction

East Asia consists of two distinct regions – South-east Asia – lying within the tropics, and the countries to the north, which Europeans refer to as the 'Far East' – although to an Australian or a Californian this would seem geographically inappropriate. Most countries in East Asia have experienced rapid growth since the 1970s and have adopted Western technology without sacrificing their cultural identity, which is based on older civilisations and religions than those of the West. Economic growth has fuelled the demand for business travel, and also encouraged a significant volume of outbound leisure tourism, and now China is well on the way to becoming a dominant force in outbound tourism to the rest of the world. Demand for tourism in the region has been affected by a number of events, which we can categorise as:

1 Man-made events, which include the financial crisis of 1997–1998; the rise of Jihadist (Muslim extremist) terrorism in southern Thailand, the Philippines and Indonesia, culminating in the Bali bombings in 2002; and the SARS (severe acute respiratory syndrome) outbreak of 2003.
2 A series of natural disasters, including earthquakes in China, Japan and Indonesia, the 2004 tsunami, and the 2008 cyclone which devastated much of Myanmar.

Domestic tourism has become increasingly significant as living standards have risen, expressed in car ownership and the purchase of leisure equipment. The more traditional patterns of travel to religious shrines and mountain resorts are changing as a growing middle class emulates Western fashions. As a result, beach resorts and theme parks, combining American and Asian motifs are growing in popularity. Nevertheless, the family unit remains much stronger than in Western societies and individual freedom is less highly regarded, due to the influence of Confucian and Buddhist teachings. As far as incoming tourism to the region is concerned, cultural attitudes may mean that those employed in the service sector try to comply with unrealistic demands by Western tourists rather than lose face, leaving considerable scope for misunderstanding.

East Asia offers a wide variety of landscapes and attractions, although in most countries business and cultural tourism are more important than beach tourism. In 2010 international tourist arrivals exceeded 180 million for East Asia as a whole. This is reflected in the impressive growth of air traffic in the region with the emergence of budget carriers and new airlines. Demographic trends – the region already contains well over a third of the world's population – the global economy, and the rise of China as an economic superpower, are responsible for a rate of passenger growth which is among the world's highest. Aircraft movements suffered a temporary setback after 9/11 on the routes linking Europe and North America to the main East Asia hubs – Singapore, Tokyo, Osaka, Hong Kong, Seoul, Taipei and Bangkok. Many Asian airports are reaching the limits of their capacity and there is a flurry of airport expansion schemes and new airport plans. Only a few – notably Hong Kong's Chep Lap Kok, Singapore's Changi, and Kuala Lumpur's Sepang – are equipped to handle the new breed of aircraft, seating up to 800 passengers, envisaged by the region's airlines. The airspace over the South China Sea is already one of the most congested in the world. In most countries – except for Japan, China and Vietnam – road transport plays a more important role in domestic tourism than the railway systems. However the Eastern Orient Express, linking Bangkok, Kuala Lumpur and Singapore has shown there is a market among Western tourists for luxury train services.

South-east Asia

The part of Asia extending from the Andaman Sea to the Philippines was culturally influenced many centuries ago by India to the west, and China to the north. Ethnic Chinese communities play a significant role in the economic life of most countries in the region and indeed throughout the Pacific. In the nineteenth century, the economic and political influence of Western Europe and the USA became increasingly important. During the first half of the twentieth century the whole of South-east Asia – with the exception of Thailand – was under the colonial rule of the following countries:

- Britain ruled Burma (now officially re-named Myanmar), Malaya, Sarawak and North Borneo (now united as Malaysia), Singapore, Brunei and Hong Kong;
- France ruled Indo-China; this consisted of Cochin-China, Annam and Tonkin (now united as Vietnam), Laos and Cambodia;
- The Netherlands ruled the Dutch East Indies and western New Guinea (now Indonesia);
- Portugal ruled East Timor and Macau; while
- The United States administered the Philippines, which it had acquired from Spain after the war of 1898.

The Western powers were soon challenged by Japan, which although defeated militarily in the Second World War, has subsequently become the major economic influence in the region. After the Second World War most countries in South-east Asia suffered a good deal of political upheaval that was part of the wider struggle between the West and the Communist powers. This adversely affected the growth of tourism, which was also restricted or given a low priority by those countries with a socialist regime.

Ten countries in the region have joined together to form ASEAN (Association of South-east Asia Nations), which promotes economic integration across the region. This is an important objective, given that ASEAN has a combined population of around 500 million, but produces only 10 per cent of the economic output of the USA, despite its wealth of natural resources. Although member countries compete for visitors, they each see the advantages of joint promotion aimed at the main tourist-generating markets. On the other hand, ASEAN has been less effective at coping with environmental issues, notably the severe pollution in the region.

There are wide disparities in wealth between the different countries of South-east Asia, with some reaching the emerging market stage of development. The per capita incomes of Singapore and Brunei approach those of Western Europe, while Myanmar, Laos and Cambodia rank among the world's least developed nations. There are also great contrasts in economic and social development within many countries, particularly between the major cities on the one hand, and the impoverished rural communities on the other. The countries of South East Asia also contain tribal societies, often regarded as primitive by the mainstream culture. These include:

- the hill tribes on the Thailand-Myanmar border;
- the Montagnards (mountain tribes) of Vietnam;
- the forest-dwellers of Malaysia; and
- the indigenous peoples of Western Papua (formerly known as Irian Jaya) in Indonesia.

Traditional cultures such as these fascinate Western tourists, but they are highly vulnerable to the negative impacts of tourism, as well as the exploitation of their environment by commercial logging and plantation agriculture.

Almost the whole of South-east Asia lies within the tropics, and experiences warm to hot weather throughout the year, with frequent but brief torrential downpours. The northern parts of the region do have a clearly defined cool dry season, while the timing and duration of the rainy season in the coastal areas of West Malaysia, southern Thailand and Indonesia depends on their exposure to the monsoon winds; this has important consequences for beach tourism. During the colonial era, mountain resorts, similar to the hill stations of British India, were established to provide relief from the heat and humidity for the expatriate community. These are now important for domestic tourism, although their development is often hampered by poor road access. Examples include:

- Maimyo in Myanmar (Burma);
- Cameron Highlands in West Malaysia;
- Dalat and Sapa in Vietnam;
- Bogor in Indonesia; and
- Baguio in the Philippines.

More important in vying for the international tourist market are the beach resort developments on the palm-fringed coasts of the region. These are either based on established seaports (as at Penang) or have been planned on a comprehensive scale (as in the Langkawi Islands), using two examples from West Malaysia. Often such development has aroused criticism not on visual grounds (they are usually low-rise and well-designed) but on account of their impact on local communities. This is particularly the case where golf courses have been included in the resort as they make excessive demands on land and water supplies. Nonetheless they play an important role in generating much-needed foreign exchange, the main sources of demand being Japan, Australia, Western Europe and the USA. Tourism within the region is being encouraged by new low cost airlines such as AirAsia, CebuPacific and Tiger Airways.

ASIA AND THE PACIFIC

Singapore

Singapore is one of the most prosperous and stable countries in Asia, despite being a group of small islands lacking natural resources. It owes its importance to its strategic location on the shipping routes linking the Indian and Pacific oceans, which have made the city one of the world's largest seaports as well as the gateway to South-east Asia. The people are culturally diverse, with a Chinese majority, but united by the English language and a firm belief in the value of education, advanced technology and enterprise. Since independence, the government of the small island republic has encouraged foreign investment in a free market economy, but has also imposed a degree of social discipline that many Westerners would find draconian. As a result, Singapore is less plagued by squalor, car-dominated traffic, and crime than most other urban societies throughout the world, and can offer Western tourists a sanitised glimpse of 'Instant Asia'. The country's high-profile national carrier – Singapore Airlines – is the largest in the region in terms of passenger-kilometres, and it works closely with the Singapore Tourism Board. Singapore's Stock Exchange and World Trade Centre rank among the world's most important financial institutions – not surprisingly, it has become a major conference venue and business tourism destination.

Singapore attracts a large volume of inbound tourists – around 9 million arrivals in 2010 – but with a short length of stay. The majority are from other east Asian countries, with China in second place after Indonesia. Many Chinese tourists are attracted to the casinos of Singapore, as gambling is not permitted in China. Duty-free shopping accounts for a large part of the tourist spend, particularly by Western visitors, who see the city primarily as a stopover rather than as a sole destination. In an attempt to attract longer stay visitors, the government has developed a new tourism strategy by promoting niche markets such as education and health tourism, as well as considerable investment in four large integrated resorts. It is also emphasising Singapore's cultural diversity, and safeguarding what remains of the old-style colonial heritage, once threatened with obliteration as a result of the drive to modernisation. A number of former 'shophouses' for example, have been converted into stylish boutique hotels. The refurbished Raffles Hotel with its historical associations, the markets and outdoor food stalls, contrast markedly with the ultra-modern shopping malls and high-rise office buildings. Singapore's attractions are primarily man-made and include:

- a number of zoos and wildlife parks;
- the waterfront area of Clarke Quay, with its leisure, theatre and shopping developments;
- the Suntec conference and exhibition centre;
- the beach resort of Sentosa Island, which includes a number of Asian-style theme parks; and
- the Esplanade Centre for the performing arts, epitomising Singapore's drive to become a cultural destination.

Singapore is compact, densely populated and low-lying, and the lack of scenic variety, together with urban pressures, generate a large volume of outbound tourism. Most of this is to neighbouring Malaysia – easily reached by the causeway to Johor, or to the beach resorts of Bintam and Batan in Indonesia's Riau archipelago which are only a short distance away by hydrofoil. There is a significant volume of long-haul travel, especially to the USA.

Malaysia

Like Singapore, Malaysia is a multi-cultural nation, but here the Muslim Malays are the dominant ethnic group politically. The country is a federation of 13 states but one party has dominated politics since independence and the nine hereditary sultans have little effective power. Malaysia also consists of two culturally distinct areas, separated by the South China Sea, namely:

• Peninsular or West Malaysia, known under British rule as Malaya, which is the southernmost peninsula of mainland Asia, and
• East Malaysia, consisting of the states of Sabah and Sarawak, which form part of the island of Borneo.

Unlike Singapore, Malaysia is rich in natural resources such as rubber, tin, petroleum and tropical hardwoods. These provided the basis for rapid industrialisation after 1980, and a number of large-scale development projects, while rising incomes led to a considerable demand for outbound tourism. The 'Petronas Towers' dominating the skyline of Kuala Lumpur and the ultra-modern shopping malls in the capital were the products of an economic prosperity that was badly affected by the 1997–1998 financial crisis. Nevertheless, the choice of Kuala Lumpur as the venue for the 1998 Commonwealth Games, the introduction of Formula One motor racing and the opening of a new international airport at Sepang, underline the importance of tourism as an earner of foreign exchange. The government has encouraged tourism through the Ministry of Culture, Arts and Tourism (MOCAT), with the Malaysia Tourism Promotion Board responsible for promotion.

The infrastructure for tourism is efficient, including a good highway network in Peninsular Malaysia and air services operated by both the Malaysian Airline System (MAS) and a new low fare airline 'AirAsia' which also flies internationally. The great majority of the 24 million international arrivals in 2010 came from other Asian countries, with Singapore accounting for more than half. There has been considerable investment, particularly by the Japanese, in resort hotels and golf courses. However, in response to tourism growth, accommodation supply has been overestimated and occupancy rates are low.

Malaysia can offer the following resources for tourism:

• The beaches of West Malaysia.
• A variety of cultural attractions.
• Facilities for conferences and meetings including the Putra World Trade Centre and the Malaysian International Exhibition Centre in Kuala Lumpur. In 2007 the Malaysian government inaugurated a new administrative capital at Putrajaya, 20 kilometres to the south, that will provide more facilities in a spacious setting.
• The wildlife resources of the interior mountains and rainforests.

Most of the tourism development has taken place in **West Malaysia**. Seasonality is not a major problem, thanks to the pattern of the monsoons, which bring heavy rain to the west coast of Peninsular Malaysia between June and September, and to the east coast from November to February. Much of the west coast is low-lying, with extensive areas of mangrove swamp along the estuaries. The best beaches are found on the off-shore islands that include:

• Penang, which has retained its commercial importance as well as being a major destination for West European holidaymakers on inclusive air tours. Most of the resort development has taken place around Batu Feringhi on the island's north coast.

- The Langkawi Islands, that provide an ideal environment for scuba diving, but which offer much less in the way of nightlife, shopping and cultural attractions than Penang.
- Pangkor and its small neighbour, Pangkor Laut that has developed a niche market in spa tourism.

Although boasting finer beaches and attractive scenery, the east coast is less developed, and the traditional Malay lifestyle is much more evident in the villages. Tioman Island and Cherating are the main resort areas.

West Malaysia's attractions also include:

- The Taman Negara National Park, covering much of the forest covered highlands of the interior. With a huge biodiversity of species, it attracts growing numbers of ecotourists.
- The Batu Caves, a major religious shrine for Hindus.
- The old Portuguese trading centre of Melaka (Malacca), with its colonial heritage providing a contrast to the modern architecture of Kuala Lumpur.
- The mountain resort of Genting Highlands, with its 'City of Entertainment', casino, golf course and funicular railway.
- Agro-tourism on some of the rubber plantations.

East Malaysia is much less developed, with a very limited road network, and caters mainly for adventure tourism, based on Kuching (Sarawak) and Kota Kinabalu (Sabah). From Kuching, tourists travel upriver to visit the villages of the Dyak tribes and perhaps stay in one of the traditional longhouses. The state of Sabah boasts some of the world's largest limestone caves and Kinabalu, the highest mountain in South-east Asia, which attracts climbing and trekking expeditions.

Brunei, which is located in the same region, derives most of its considerable wealth from petroleum, and tourism development is not a priority. Royal Brunei Airlines and the capital, Bandar Sara Begawan, cater mainly for business travellers.

Indonesia

In contrast to tiny Brunei, Indonesia is one of the world's largest nations, extending 4,000 kilometres from west to east, spanning three time zones, and with a population approaching 250 million, of which 90 per cent are Muslims. There are also substantial Buddhist, Hindu, Christian and animist communities. This cultural diversity is both a strength from the viewpoint of tourism and a challenge to the process of nation building. The country is also physically very diverse, consisting of a multitude of islands, of which 6,000 are inhabited, some 400 volcanoes, and landscapes that include the rice paddies of Java, the rainforests of Kilimantan (Borneo) and the snow-capped mountains of New Guinea. The possibilities for ecotourism are indicated by the 'Wallace Line', east of Bali, which separates islands with an Asian flora and fauna from those having species typical of Australasia.

Although Indonesia has shown significant economic growth in the new millennium, it faces a number of socio-economic problems that affect not just the growth of international tourism but also the domestic demand for tourism:

- The Asian financial crisis of 1997–1998 affected Indonesia more severely than others in the region.
- The fall of the authoritarian Suharto regime destabilised the country, bringing to the surface ethnic and religious tensions, with attacks on the ethnic Chinese, who dominate the commercial sector, and on the Christian community in Maluku (the Moluccas).
- The political and economic dominance of Java, which contains almost two thirds of the population and most of the country's industrial development. The Suharto regime attempted to relieve the acute pressures of over-population and rural poverty in Java by a policy of 'transmigration', settling farmers in the more sparsely populated islands among people of a very different cultural background, such as the Dyaks of Kilimantan and the Papuans of western New Guinea.
- A number of terrorist incidents by Jihadists in Java, and 'Black October' – the Bali bombings.

In addition to these problems, Indonesia has been affected by both earthquakes and the 2004 tsunami, both of which impacted on tourist arrivals. Nevertheless, tourism continues to be a priority for the new democratic government, with the restructured Directorate General of Tourism developing the market for conferences, exhibitions and incentive travel. Despite a government policy of spreading tourism throughout the islands, most of the growth in hotel capacity has taken place in Bintam Batan and Bali (for leisure tourism) and in Java (mainly for business tourism, particularly in the major cities of Jakarta, Surabaya and Yogyakarta). International hotel chains dominate the accommodation sector, particularly in the mid-range and luxury categories. Although the government has moved toward a more liberal civil aviation policy, the national carrier Garuda and its subsidiaries dominate air transport. There is a substantial demand for domestic tourism, particularly from the growing middle class in the cities of Java.

Tourism resources

Relatively few of Indonesia's many islands have developed significant tourism industries. Travelling from west to east, these include Sumatra, Java, Bali, Lombok, Sulawesi and some of the Lesser Sunda Islands.

Sumatra has an important oil industry and tourism is less developed than we might expect from an island with such a diversity of resources. Tourism in the northern part of the island has been held back by the separatist uprising in Acheh province and the damage to infrastructure caused by the 2004 tsunami. Large areas of rainforest still remain, providing a refuge for the orang-utan and other threatened wildlife species. Lake Toba is a major natural attraction, set amid one of the world's largest craters and ringed by volcanic mountains. Sumatra also has many cultural attractions that include the distinctive folklore of the Menankabau people.

Java remains the economic and political heartland of Indonesia, and receives the majority of business and leisure tourist arrivals. It is dominated by a chain of high volcanic mountains, some of which – notably Mount Bromo in the east of the island – are still active. Over many centuries land has been brought under cultivation by an elaborate system of terracing and the island's fertility has supported a number of advanced civilisations. The most spectacular examples of this heritage are the temple at Borobodur, which is the world's largest Buddhist edifice, and the lesser-known Hindu temple at Prambunan nearby. The palaces of former sultans at Solo and Yogyakarta also attract growing numbers of cultural tourists. The legacy of colonial rule is still evident in the historic port area of Jakarta, formerly known as Batavia, that was the hub of the Dutch trading empire in Asia.

Bali is the best-known of the islands of Indonesia, and the jewel in its tourism crown. Bali's appeal is based on the photogenic qualities of its landscapes and people, with resources that include:

- A tropical climate favouring beach tourism, with a dry season lasting from May to October. This coincides with the winter months in Australia to the south, which provides much of the tourism demand.
- A spectacular landscape featuring emerald-green rice terraces carved out of the hills, mountains clothed in lush vegetation, and crater lakes.
- Recreational resources include the surfing beaches, offshore reefs for diving, mineral springs for spa tourism, and a range of activities that have been introduced as a result of demand from affluent foreign tourists and the international youth market.

The great majority of foreign visitors to Bali, and a high proportion of domestic tourists, arrive by air. Indeed, the opening of the airport at Denpasar in 1968 was the catalyst for the expansion of tourism on a large scale. Internal transport is by road, using a variety of vehicles such as *bemos* (mini-buses), trucks, cars, coaches and taxis.

Bali offers a range of accommodation from luxury five star hotels to simple beach bungalows. Small hotels and guesthouses, known as *losmen* or 'homestays' provide inexpensive, informal accommodation, giving visitors the opportunity to sample the islanders' way of life. As they are usually run by local families, a much higher proportion of the visitor spend is retained within the local community than is the case with the larger hotels owned by companies based in Java or outside Indonesia. The former fishing village and artists' colony of Sanur was the first resort to be developed with a mix of large hotels and bungalows, and now attracts tourists from Europe, Japan and Australia. Kuta Beach first attracted Australian surfers in the 1970s, and now offers a third of Bali's bedspaces, mostly in small hotels and guest houses. Luxury hotels are

Photo 21.1 Bali's tropical climate and landscapes make it a favourite long-haul destination (©istockphoto. com/ Terraxplorer)

mainly concentrated in the planned resort of Nusa Dua, which is a good example of 'enclave tourism'.

Lombok has been the main beneficiary of government policy to spread tourism away from Bali. The two islands are roughly the same size and are superficially similar – indeed Lombok is often regarded as a less developed version of Bali, but it has a drier climate and a Muslim culture. Development is focused on the resort of Senggigi, while the offshore Gili Islands are popular with scuba divers. The authorities have set out to attract upmarket tourists with luxury hotels and the associated infrastructure including a new international airport, and improvements to ferry services, port facilities and the road network.

The **Lesser Sunda Islands** to the east of Lombok remain largely undeveloped, but Flores is among those which are increasingly sought out by divers and surfers. The climate is characterised by a long dry season influenced by monsoon winds from Australia, which lies not far to the south. Ecotourism has potential for growth in some of the islands, for example Komodo which is famous for its 'dragons' (actually giant lizards).

Sulawesi offers world class diving, particularly in the north near Manado where the Benaken National Park is an outstanding example of marine conservation in a region notorious for overfishing and damage to coral reefs. Under the new government's decentralising policies the park authorities set their own entrance fees, with the proceeds benefiting the local communities. In the mountainous interior the Toraja villages with their unique architecture and ceremonies based on ancestor worship provide the main attraction for tourists.

Case study 21.1

The impact of tourism on the culture of Bali

Can cultural tourism create what is in effect a tourist culture? The perception of Bali is one of a gentle, artistic people living in harmony with their environment, and the graceful *legong* dancer is its best known tourist icon. Throughout their history the Balinese have adopted cultural traits from other peoples – the Hindu dance dramas from India for example – and made them part of their own distinctive lifestyle. Art and religious ritual are part of everyday life in this 'island of the gods', with processions of women carrying fruit, rice cakes and other colourful offerings to the temples that are a feature of every village. Balinese festivals integrate the visual arts, *gamelan* music, drama and dance. The Balinese apparently do not mind the presence of outsiders at their religious ceremonies, and even the elaborate cremations have become a must-see tourist attraction.

Balinese painting and sculpture first became a commercial activity in the 1930s when the island was 'discovered' as an exotic destination for elite Western tourists. European expatriate painters encouraged local artists to experiment with new techniques and develop a much greater range of styles. As a result, Ubud with its long-established artist colony is widely regarded as the cultural centre of the island. A number of villages specialise in a particular handicraft, such as silverware, woodcarving and stone-carving.

Although the Balinese had little say in determining the overall development of their island, they have benefited economically from tourism, which provides jobs for 20 per cent of the adult population, a source of income for local farmers who can let rooms to backpackers, and a ready market for handicrafts, as well as a textile industry specialising in beachwear. The Balinese have been able to market their culture, which has, apparently, been remarkably resilient to the negative impacts of mass tourism compared to other tropical island destinations.

However the rapid growth of tourism has put a heavy strain on limited land and water resources, with negative impacts that include:

- damage to coral reefs and coastal erosion;
- problems of water supply, with priority given to luxury hotels and golf course projects rather than local communities;
- the 'packaging' of traditional culture, where the dance performances have been adapted for the short attention span of the average Western tourist; and
- prostitution and drug-taking.

The social impacts are most evident in Kuta Beach, where a host of traders compete to offer scantily-dressed tourists goods and services including 'beach massage'. In some respects, Kuta is to Australians what some Mediterranean resorts are to young British holidaymakers – a tourist experience based on 'sun and fun', nightclubs, bars and discos, rather than any respect for the local culture. Young Balinese have adopted the surfing lifestyle, and the surfboard has become another opportunity for artistic self-expression. In Nusi Dua on the other hand, the cultural impact of tourism is minimised by physical separation. Here the only Balinese allowed entry are hotel employees or invited dance troupes.

East Timor (Democratic Republic of Timor-Leste)

East Timor gained independence from Indonesia after a long and bitter struggle in 2002, followed – as is often the case – by political in-fighting, which has not improved its tourism prospects. This small country includes an enclave in Indonesian territory to the west, and the island of Atauro to the north. Tourism is seen by the government in Dili as playing an important role in the process of rebuilding the economy, with technical assistance from China, Singapore, Brazil and Portugal. Potential resources include:

- the annual Darwin – Dili yacht rally, providing a sporting link with Australia;
- the heritage of Portuguese colonial rule, including the revival of Carnival as an event attraction; and
- diving sites, particularly off Atauro.

Development of these resources is hampered by poor infrastructure, while the high cost of air travel from Darwin, Singapore and Bali to Dili is a deterrent to the backpackers who often pioneer new destinations.

The Philippines

Like Indonesia, the Philippines is a populous island-nation containing many ethnic groups and a landscape dominated by volcanic mountains. Culturally however, it is quite different from the other countries of South-east Asia. There are few impressive monuments from pre-colonial times, and the islands have been greatly influenced by their experience of three centuries of Spanish rule, followed by half a century of administration by the USA. The Spanish legacy of devout Roman Catholicism is evident in the churches and religious festivals culminating in Holy Week, whereas the Americans introduced the English language and sports such as baseball; the result is a culture in which Western influences and attitudes are stronger than elsewhere in Asia.

Tourism received a major boost under the Marcos regime in the 1970s, which hosted international events such as the Miss Universe beauty pageant, leaving Manila with a glut of luxury hotels. Since that time the emphasis by the Department of Tourism has been on planning resort clusters of international standard on a number of islands, which are linked to an international airport by boat and domestic air services. The Department's mission is to develop tourism for the economic benefit of the country and a convention and visitors bureau has been established to encourage business tourism. The main tourist markets are Japan, the USA, Taiwan, South Korea, and the millions of overseas Filipinos working in many countries around the world. However, natural disasters and terrorist incidents, including the kidnapping of tourists in Mindanao (where there is a large Muslim minority and separatist movement), have had a negative impact on arrivals and perceptions of the country, and compared to the rest of the region international arrivals are modest – at around three million a year. Damage to coral reefs is a cause for concern. Also problematic is the prevalence of sex tourism, particularly in Manila and Olongapo. In many areas the transport infrastructure, including roads and domestic air services, falls short of Western standards of efficiency, although ferry links between the islands have greatly improved.

Tourism is concentrated mainly in the following areas:

- South Luzon, particularly in and around Manila. The capital's attractions include:
  - the Malacanang Palace, former residence of the Marcos family;
  - the Nayong Pilipino – an exhibition village showcasing the country's regional cultures;
  - the historic district of Intramuros; and
  - the highly decorated *jeepneys*, which play a vital role in the city's transport system.
- A number of beach resorts, Lake Taal and the volcano of that name, and the Pagsanjan waterfalls are located within easy reach of Manila. However, one of the country's major attractions and a World Heritage Site – the rice terraces at Banaue – can only be reached by a long road journey and are much less accessible.
- The Visayas, a group of islands in the central Philippines are served by the international airport at Cebu, which has direct flights to Hong Kong, Seoul, Taipei, Singapore and Tokyo. The island of Boracay is the best known, having evolved from 'discovery' by backpackers in the 1970s to become an upmarket destination.
- Palawan, until recently one of the more remote islands, offers world-class diving facilities and a number of small upmarket resorts that have escaped the pollution problems experienced by Boracay.
- Mindanao, much of which is still forest covered, is developing ecotourism and has an 'ecotourism village'. Beach tourism is being developed around the cities of Davao and Zamboanga.

The countries of the Mekong Basin

The Mekong, rising in the Himalayas and reaching the South China Sea near Saigon, is one of the great rivers of Asia and is a feature that can be used for joint promotion by the countries through which it flows, including the south-west of China. During the Cold War era most of this region, with the exception of Thailand, was an area where tourism was not encouraged. These countries are now co-operating to make international tourism easier, by improving air links, opening more border crossings and relaxing visa regulations.

Thailand

Thailand (formerly known as Siam) is the only country in South-east Asia not to have experienced Western colonial rule and its monarch still exercises real power and is revered by the Thai people. On the other hand, Thailand has been the country most affected by Western-style tourism. Growth has been phenomenal, from less than 500,000 international arrivals in 1970, to almost 16 million in 2010, with a corresponding increase in hotel capacity. Tourism has become the country's biggest earner of foreign exchange and a major employer, but it has also exacerbated Thailand's socio-economic problems, notably the disparities in wealth between Bangkok and the rural areas of the north and east. These problems in turn have contributed to the growth of a flourishing sex tourism industry in Bangkok and the resort of Pattaya, with damaging consequences to the country's image as a destination.

Tourism demand and supply

The reorganised Tourist Authority of Thailand (TAT) is the national body for tourism and one of the oldest in the region having been established in 1960; like other NTOs, it has responsibility for promotion, development and training. It has strategies in place to develop human resources, 'electronic tourism', events and festivals, and niche markets such as medical tourism. Thailand is one of the 'tiger economies' of Asia and economic development has seen the growth of a substantial middle class, who have the means not only to engage in domestic tourism but also to travel abroad for leisure purposes as well as for business and study.

Although there is considerable cross-border traffic between Thailand and Malaysia, the majority of international tourists arrive by air on inclusive tours and around 10 per cent are business travellers. Leisure tourists come from a wide range of generating countries, including Western Europe, North America, Japan and Australia. Bangkok's Don Muang airport is the main gateway which is served by over 40 scheduled airlines, while the north and south of the country are visited from Chiangmai and Phuket respectively. Thai International and its domestic arm, Thai Airways, operate an extensive network of air routes, while express bus and overnight rail services also link Bangkok to the major regional centres of the country.

Tourism resources

Thailand is a multi-destination country, with different areas offering sightseeing tours (there has been a substantial growth in visits to historic sites), beach tourism and adventure holidays.

Bangkok is the primary destination. Despite acute traffic congestion – partly relieved by a 'skytrain' monorail system – this sprawling city has a wide range of attractions, and its Western-style hotels enjoy high occupancy rates throughout the year. Highways have replaced many of the city's canals, but the Chao Praya River, with its long-tail boats and floating markets, remains a major artery. As you might expect from a country devoted to Buddhist rituals and traditions, Bangkok is noted for its *wats* – temple-monasteries of a highly distinctive appearance, along with a multitude of lesser shrines.

Shopping for Thai silk and other handicrafts is an important part of the city's appeal to Western tourists. Specific tourist attractions in Bangkok and the surrounding area include:

- the spectacular Grand Palace, which contains the Temple of the Emerald Buddha, the most important place of pilgrimage for Thais;
- the Rose Garden Country Resort, 33 kilometres west of the capital, features cultural shows for visitors, including traditional dances, ceremonies and the distinctive Thai style of boxing;
- the nearby beach resort of Pattaya, which began as a 'rest and recreation' centre for American servicemen during the Vietnam War in the 1960s. It is noisy and over-commercialised, despite attempts by the government to clean up the environment, curb the jet skiers, and tone down the exuberant nightlife offered by the bars, discotheques and massage-parlours, whereas
- Hua Hin is a long-established, upmarket resort.

Chiangmai has been developed as a counter-attraction to Bangkok in the northern part of the country, with the advantage of a cooler, less humid climate. Although the city is a major centre of Thai culture, most backpackers and Western tourists regard it as a convenient base for trekking tours among the hill tribes of the mountainous country bordering Myanmar and Laos, which forms part of the notorious 'Golden Triangle' of opium production. Concerted efforts by the government to crack down on the trade in narcotics carry the risk of fuelling border tensions and alienating ethnic minorities. It is also alleged that tourism does not benefit these communities but merely exploits them as a curiosity.

Peninsular Thailand and the offshore islands in the Andaman Sea, together with those in the Gulf of Thailand to the east, cater in varying degrees for beach tourism, in response to the quest, first by backpackers, and later by tour operators, for 'unspoiled' holiday destinations. This region was affected by the 2004 tsunami but the tourism sector recovered rapidly from this setback with government support, which was not always the case with the local communities.

- Phuket was the first island to be developed, to the extent that mass tourism has now displaced its traditional mining and fishing industries. Phang Nga Bay is famous for its spectacular karst limestone rock formations; and
- Koh Samui is less developed and more upmarket.

Eastern Thailand is an economically poor region, but offers wildlife for eco-tourists and the remains of the ancient Khmer civilisation for cultural tourists. The Tourism Authority of Thailand hopes that visitors will be attracted to a number of parks focusing on this heritage.

ASIA AND THE PACIFIC

Discussion point

The Phi-Phi Islands in the Gulf of Thailand are said to be a classic example of a 'tropical island paradise'. As a designated marine reserve they have been given a measure of protection by the government of Thailand, but many environmentalists fear that development is inevitable. Ironically the movie *The Beach* has been blamed, because of the worldwide interest in the islands which followed the filming. In class, debate whether this is justified, or are other factors just as important?

Indo-China

Until the 1990s the countries of Indo-China remained on the margins of international tourism as a consequence of half a century of conflict that culminated in the Vietnam War. The socialist governments of the region gave tourism a low priority, restricting the numbers of foreign visitors (by closing the border between Thailand and Laos, for example), and discouraging Western investment. These countries are now in the 'involvement' stage of *the tourist area life cycle* with Vietnam clearly in the lead.

Cambodia

The kingdom of Cambodia is renowned for its majestic tiered temples, flanked by moats and reflecting pools that were built by the Khmer civilisation between the ninth and thirteenth centuries. The temple-cities and the complex irrigation systems that supported them were subsequently abandoned and taken over by the jungle until they were revealed by French archaeologists during the colonial period. By the late 1960s Angkor, the best-known and most accessible of these temple-cities, was attracting 45,000 visitors a year and the nearby town of Siem Reap had a flourishing hotel and restaurant trade. Tourism development was halted by Cambodia's unwilling involvement in the Vietnam War and the isolation imposed by the fanatical Khmer Rouge regime, but revived in the 1990s after decades of conflict and neglect.

In the 1990s Cambodia's fledgling tourism industry was dominated by cultural tourists from Western Europe and the USA, whose attention was focused on Angkor. A range of handicrafts had developed to meet this demand, taking their inspiration from the art and sculpture of the Khmer civilisation. By 2003, 70 per cent of tourists were coming from other Asian countries, particularly Japan, South Korea, Taiwan and China. East Asian expatriates provide much of the investment in hotels, casinos, golf courses and other facilities, particularly in Siem Reap, and the tourism products on offer now increasingly meet the demand from the middle-range inclusive tour Asian market. Most of these tourists are less concerned with 'authenticity' than their Western counterparts, and a range of mass-produced items, usually imported, are available to meet the demand.

The Museum of Genocide in Pnom Penh is an example of 'dark tourism', commemorating the 'killing fields' where the Khmer Rouge regime carried out its atrocities in the late 1970s. Tourism in the capital has another dark side with the growth of the sex industry, which exploits a desperately poor, traumatised people. Cambodia is viewed as an alternative to Thailand, where the government has imposed stricter controls in response to Ecpat's campaigning. Much of this so-called sex tourism is in fact a modern version of the slave trade in which people-traffickers supply child prostitutes to visiting paedophiles from Western Europe, Japan and the USA.

Cambodia offers other tourism resources such as the following:

- a coastline along the Gulf of Thailand, including the port of Sihanoukville, and offshore islands, some of which are designated for development as luxury resorts;
- the wetland ecosystem of Tonle Sap, a lake which varies greatly in size according to the seasons; and

- areas of karst limestone scenery and temples to rival those of Angkor in the north-west of the country, which at present are only accessible by helicopter tours. For the benefits of tourism to be spread more widely, the road network needs to be greatly improved, training provided for those working in the sector, and small-scale community-based tourism ventures should be encouraged.

Laos (Lao People's Democratic Republic)

In contrast to much of Thailand, the Laotian lifestyle is still pre-industrial in its pace, and this is an important part of the country's appeal for Western tourists. With a much lower population density than Thailand or Vietnam, there is less pressure on natural resources. Laos can therefore offer great biodiversity, almost 20 per cent of its territory is protected, and ecotourism is encouraged by the Lao National Tourism Administration. On the other hand these resources are at risk from logging, wasteful 'slash and burn' farming methods, and the illegal trade in wild animals and birds. Environmentalists are also concerned about dam-building on the River Mekong, which is not only the main artery of Laos, but also crucial to the economies of neighbouring countries.

The transport infrastructure is a major constraint on tourism development in Laos. Nevertheless, Laos received over one million arrivals in 2009, the majority coming from Thailand. The Friendship Bridge over the Mekong near the capital, Vientiane, is the most frequently used border crossing. Domestic demand for tourism is facilitated by the extended family networks that provide for mutual hospitality. Western culture-seekers focus mainly on Luang Prabang, the former royal capital and religious centre, which is a World Heritage Site due to its wealth of Buddhist temples.

Vietnam

From 1986 onwards the Vietnamese government opened the country to foreign investment and allowed a significant amount of private enterprise to develop. As a result, Vietnam is one of the fastest growing economies of Asia. In the cities motor cycles have largely replaced bicycles, *cyclos* (pedicabs) and rickshaws, but the graceful white *ao dai* costume remains part of the street scene.

The demand for tourism

Inbound tourism

Tourism is a fast growing sector. The Western media have ensured that interest in the Vietnam War will continue long after its ending in 1975, and it was not until 1994 that the USA lifted the trade embargo imposed after the Communist victory. The locations of that bitter conflict, including the Ho Chi Minh Trail, China Beach near Danang, and the Cu-Chi tunnels near Saigon that sheltered the Vietcong guerrillas from American firepower, are now the basis of a lucrative niche tourism market. The Vietnam National Administration of Tourism (VNAT) has implemented a national action plan for tourism and attracting foreign investment as part of a policy of gradual economic liberalisation. In 2010 Vietnam attracted over five million international arrivals. China, Japan and

Taiwan are the most important markets, but Vietnam is also visited by some 350,000 Americans. These include many Vietnam War veterans, Vietnamese emigrants and the children of refugees who now live in the USA. The VNAT also aims to attract tourists from other Western countries who are interested in trekking, and canoeing on the country's many rivers.

Domestic tourism

Free market reforms have created a new entrepreneurial middle class which has the discretionary income to visit the tourist sites in their own country, resulting in a considerable volume of domestic tourism. However, tour guides and others working in the tourism sector, accustomed to dealing with affluent Western visitors with cultural motivations, find it difficult to adjust to the demands of Vietnamese tourists with very different expectations.

Tourism supply

Accommodation capacity has increased substantially with the major hotel chains taking advantage of the growth in tourism in Vietnam. Nevertheless tourism development is hampered by an inadequate road system, unreliable power supplies, and a bureaucracy resistant to change.

Vietnam can offer an impressive range of tourism resources. These include a 3,400 kilometre-long coastline, forested mountains, waterfalls, the Mekong and Red River deltas, and a rich cultural heritage. The western highlands and the mountains of northern Tonkin have potential for ecotourism, and national parks have been designated in these areas. Trekking has already become an important source of income for many mountain tribal communities. Coastal resources include Ha Long Bay which is a superb example of tropical karst topography, but designation as a World Heritage Site is no guarantee of protection from excessive development. This unique natural attraction, made up of a great number of picturesque islands and caves, attracts three million visitors a year, and is exposed to pollution from tourist boats as well as industrial effluent. Cultural tourism is mainly focused on the cities of Hanoi, Hue and Saigon:

- Hanoi was the power base of the Communist North during the Vietnam War, and with re-unification it became the national capital, offering a number of showpiece attractions celebrating the country's heritage.
- Hue is located in the centre of the country and was the scene of bitter conflict during the Vietnam War. Despite this many Buddhist pagodas remain as reminders of the city's historic importance as the capital of the former kingdom of Annam.
- Saigon (now officially renamed Ho Chi Minh City) was the capital of South Vietnam and following re-unification remains the nation's main commercial centre with a population of around 8 million. Here business enterprise is flourishing to a much greater extent than in Hanoi, and the vibrant entertainment scene has revived as a result of international tourism. The French colonial influence is still evident in the architecture and restaurants. A number of beach resorts have developed near Saigon and these are attracting Western investment.

Case study 21.2

Medical tourism in South-east Asia

It can be difficult to distinguish between 'health tourism' or 'spa tourism' – travel for reasons of health and well-being – and 'medical tourism', usually defined as travel to a hospital or clinic for a specific course of treatment paid for by the patient. Medical tourism has become an important niche market for a growing number of Asian countries. The Thai Authority for Tourism (TAT) among others, prefers to promote its facilities as 'wellness tourism', emphasising relaxation therapies and cosmetic surgery rather than the treatment of disease.

The demand for medical tourism has grown in Western Europe, particularly Britain, as a result of dissatisfaction with the long waiting lists for operations in the national health services of those countries. In the case of the USA, where many Americans lack medical insurance, it is fuelled by concern at the high cost of treatments. Even allowing for the air fare, American patients travelling overseas for treatment are making a considerable saving, with the cost of an operation in Thailand being less than half the outlay in the USA. Since 9/11 and the subsequent security measures, much of the demand in the Arab countries of the Middle East for the medical services traditionally provided by the USA and Britain has been diverted to Asian countries.

On the supply side, the 1997 financial crisis in Asia had a serious impact on disposable incomes, resulting in surplus bed capacity in private hospitals. Thailand can be regarded as the pioneer of medical tourism in the region, which featured in the 'Amazing Thailand' campaign of the 1990s, building on a centuries-old tradition of spa and massage therapies. It continues to be the leading destination in this field, with well over a million tourists arriving for medical treatment in 2007. Foreign visitors and expatriates now account for over 40 per cent of the patients in the two leading private hospitals in Bangkok. Japan is the largest generator of demand, followed by the USA, Britain, Taiwan, ASEAN countries, and the Middle East. Other important destinations for 'medical tourists' include Malaysia, South Korea, and Singapore – which attracted 0.5 million arrivals in 2004, despite costs that are significantly higher than in Thailand – while the Philippines is hoping to increase its share of the market.

Information technology is a key factor in Thailand's success as a destination for medical tourism, with hospitals providing foreign patients with ready access to the treatments available, and often arranging for flight tickets, the stay in hospital, and post-operation convalescence in a holiday resort to be sold as an inclusive package. To assure foreign patients of a quality experience, the hospital has become more like a luxury hotel. This entails a makeover in design and service standards, with a central lobby, hostess service, and sometimes a food court, similar to those found in American shopping malls, becoming standard features. However, this might mean that local health care needs are not being met. People from the poorer Asian countries are spending up to a year's wages on their medical treatment and also have to bring in their own food, while Western visitors are staying in the equivalent of luxury hotels, and combining a holiday with 'bargain-basement' surgery.

Discussion point

Discuss whether medical tourism is a contradiction, since it is associated with sickness, suffering and loss of personal freedom, and would appear to be incompatible with tourism as a leisure activity.

Myanmar (Burma)

Before achieving independence, Burma was ruled as part of British India, and the government's renaming of the country, its cities and major physical features is part of a campaign of nation-building, with the Burmese as the dominant national culture over more than a hundred other ethnic groups. In 2005 this was reinforced with the designation of a new capital at Naypyidaw, located deep in the interior of the country. For decades after independence, the country was isolated from the West by the government's policy of socialist self-sufficiency; visas were difficult to obtain and tourists were not permitted to stay for more than a few days. Security continues to be a major problem, with uprisings by dissident ethnic groups, such as the Shans and the Karens, in the mountainous border areas. Myanmar is also physically isolated by high mountains to the north and east, and an inhospitable coastline of mangrove swamps and dense forests to the west.

Since the early 1990s the military regime has encouraged foreign investment in the fledgling tourism industry, primarily from Japan. Nevertheless visitor numbers remain small compared to Thailand, with less than a quarter of a million arrivals at Yangon Airport in 2010. Tourism development has been carried out by the government using unpaid 'volunteers' (in effect, forced labour) to build the necessary infrastructure, namely much-needed roads and railway improvements, and the new airport at Bassein. In some areas villagers have been relocated to make way for tourist facilities.

Although its transport infrastructure is poorly developed, Myanmar has much to offer both the ecotourist and the cultural tourist, including for example:

- A number of wildlife parks and sanctuaries.
- The Irrawaddy River runs through the country's heartland, providing a major transport artery, as in Kipling's time, from Yangon (formerly Rangoon) to Mandalay. River transport is now being revitalised after decades of neglect, including luxury cruises by Eastern and Orient Express.
- Yangon, the nation's largest city and former capital boasts one of the world's most impressive Buddhist temples – the Shwe Dagon Pagoda, which is covered in gold and precious stones.
- Bagan is renowned for the 3,000 or so Buddhist monuments set in a vast archaeological zone, a reminder of Burma's 'golden age' during the thirteenth century.
- Mandalay was the royal capital prior to British rule, and remains the religious centre of the country. The palace has been restored as a tourist attraction, using forced labour.
- Inle Lake – a major scenic and cultural attraction, with its unique fishing communities.
- Some of the country's tribal minorities – notably the Padaung (famed for their long-necked women) – have become the focus of tourism, but some claim that this is exploitation that fails to benefit these communities.

The Mergui Islands are the only part of Myanmar's long coastline that has much potential for beach tourism and diving holidays.

Discussion point: 'Ethical tourism'

The government's apparent disregard for human rights, shown by the violent repression of the 'Saffron Revolution' led by Buddhist monks, and the manner in which tourism development has been carried out, has aroused much controversy. Opponents of the military regime, such as the democrat leader Aung San Kyi, claim that tourism revenue simply enriches those in government circles who have invested in the new hotels, and urge a boycott of the country. This is supported by pressure groups in the West, notably Tourism Concern. On the other hand Lonely Planet and some tour operators take the view that tourism can be a powerful force for liberalisation and social change that will ultimately benefit the Burmese people. Also tourism's contribution to the country's foreign exchange earnings is small, compared to the exports of teak, precious stones and natural gas to China and India.

In class debate these issues.

The Far East/North-east Asia

The lands around the East China Sea and the Sea of Japan include some of the world's largest modern cities, as well as some of its oldest civilisations. In contrast to the tropical conditions prevalent in South-east Asia, the climate is characterised by four well-defined seasons, not unlike those of Europe and North America. Spring and autumn are the best times for visiting, as winters can be bitterly cold and summers oppressively hot and humid. Japan and South Korea have long been important destinations for the business traveller and the cultural tourist, but since the 1990s, China has emerged as a formidable competitor for the world travel market.

Japan

The setting for tourism

Japan is the leading industrial nation of Asia with an economy based on overseas trade. Despite experiencing a long period of economic stagnation since the 1990s, it boasts a GDP second only to the USA, and four times greater than that of the UK. In response to the economic situation there has been a certain amount of industrial restructuring and deregulation, outbound tourism has suffered and the country has become more open to foreign investment. Nevertheless, Japan is the largest generator of tourists in the East Asia-Pacific Region in terms of spend, with a very large deficit on its international tourism account.

Japan consists of four main islands located off the eastern fringe of the continent – Honshu, Hokkaido, Kyushu and Shikoku – and groups of much smaller islands, such as the Ryukyus and Iwo Jima, lying to the south. The total area of the Japanese islands is only slightly greater than the British Isles, but with more than twice the population. The pressure on land resources is even more acute when we consider that over 80 per cent of the country is mountainous. Geological instability has produced the beautiful mountain landscapes of Japan – Mount Fuji is the best known example – and the numerous hot springs, but it is also responsible for natural disasters such as the earthquakes which devastated Kobe in 1995 and the Tohoku region of northern

Honshu in 2011. Japan has to import nearly all the petroleum it needs, mainly from the Middle East, which explains the strategic importance of the Straits of Malacca to the Japanese. The development of nuclear power as an alternative source of energy received a major setback with the Fukoshima incident.

The climate is influenced by the warm Kurosiwo Current in the Pacific Ocean and the cold Oyashio Current in the Sea of Japan, and there are considerable differences between the south-east of the country and the northern island of Hokkaido. For example, the arrival of cherry blossom, celebrated in Japan as a symbol of life and re-birth, usually takes place in mid-March in Kyushu, but does not reach Hokkaido until mid-May.

As a nation Japan has the following characteristics:

* it is remarkably homogenous, with one language, few social divisions and ethnic minorities account for only 1.5 per cent of the population;
* it has enjoyed political stability since 1945;
* respect for tradition co-exists with admiration for the new;
* there is a readiness to adopt the latest technological innovations; and
* society is bound by discipline and respect for authority, which keeps crime levels low by Western standards.

During its long history Japan has absorbed some cultural influences, notably from China, but has otherwise been self-contained, with an ambivalent attitude toward the West. Following a century of encounters with European traders and Catholic missionaries, in 1640 the Tokugawa shogun isolated the country and its people from almost all contact with the West, with the exception of the Dutch, whose trading activities were confined to the small island of Deshima in Nagasaki harbour. This self-imposed isolation continued until 1853, when Japan was compelled by the US Navy to open its ports to international trade. This was followed by the coup in 1868 which abolished the shogunate, restoring the Emperor Meiji to effective power, and greatly limiting the role of the samurai, the feudal warrior class. The new regime quickly saw the advantages of adopting Western technology, but Western-style freedoms and democracy were not introduced until after the defeat of Imperial Japan in 1945.

The demand for tourism

Due to a low birth rate and high life expectancy, the Japanese population is ageing, with a higher proportion of people aged over 65 years than the USA and Western Europe; and the 'grey market' is well catered for. Rather than encouraging immigration as a response to future manpower shortages, there has been considerable investment in robotics for personal services as well as in manufacturing. There are social trends toward a more relaxed and individualistic lifestyle, a greater emphasis on leisure and sport, particularly among young people, and a greater readiness to adopt Western fashions. Even so, the concept of an annual holiday has only slowly been accepted in Japan, which is still largely a work-oriented society. Working hours are longer than in Europe or the USA and paid annual leave amounts to 15 days; however, Japanese workers often take only 9 days out of their full holiday entitlement out of loyalty to colleagues or to cover for illness. Holidays and leisure activities generally are frequently sponsored by large industrial corporations for their employees; however, this paternalism is not resented by most Japanese, who are prepared to accept a degree of regimentation that Westerners would find irksome. After-work drinking parties are seen by 'salarymen' (white collar workers) as an opportunity to bond with their employers, when the strict formality that usually prevails is relaxed.

Domestic tourism

Domestic tourism is more significant in volume and spend than international tourism for the Japanese travel market. Holidays account for the majority of trips, with business and VFR accounting for the remainder. Pilgrimages to Shinto and Buddhist shrines continue to be popular with family groups, while *onsen* (hot spring resorts) appeal more to the stressed executive at weekends. The Western influence is evident in the rapid growth of skiing, golf, baseball, water sports, and visits to theme parks such as Tokyo Disneyland. The scarcity of land for recreation particularly affects demand for skiing and golf:

* Skiing is practised by some 15 million Japanese. The mountains of Northern Honshu and Hokkaido receive abundant snowfalls during the winter months, and this has encouraged the development of a large number of ski resorts. However, apart from Nagano in the Japanese Alps and Sapporo in Hokkaido which have both hosted the Winter Olympics, few resorts approach Western standards, and overcrowding on the slopes is a major problem.
* Golf courses are few and far between and green fees are prohibitively expensive. Most would-be players are confined to multi-storey driving ranges, and real golf can only be played on overseas trips. This goes far to explaining why the Japanese are active in purchasing tourism developments overseas, and in providing Third World governments with aid for projects where golf is a major component.

Outbound tourism

During the long period of Japan's self-imposed isolation from the West under the rule of the Tokugawa shoguns, foreign travel was strictly forbidden. After 1868 a limited amount of tourism was sponsored by the government for the purpose of business or study. Tourism for leisure received no such encouragement, and it was not until 1964 that restrictions on foreign travel were lifted. In the late 1980s the government made a positive effort to encourage overseas travel through the 'Ten Million Programme', as a way of restructuring Japan's trade balance with the rest of the world and promoting mutual understanding. Even so, partly due to recent economic problems and world events, participation in outbound travel is small by European standards, accounting for only 13 per cent of the population. The number of trips has actually decreased since 2001, and with limited holiday time available the length of stay is short, averaging 8 days. Yet in 2010, 16.6 million overseas trips were taken. In many countries the Japanese are the largest source of tourists, and they tend to be the biggest spenders. Over half visit destinations in Asia – mainly Taiwan, South Korea and Hong Kong; around a third go to the USA – particularly to honeymoon in Hawaii and Guam; and the remainder travel to Europe or Australasia. Group travel is important, and so is *omiyake*, the customary purchase of gifts for friends, relatives and employers. Young unmarried women – the so-called 'office ladies' – constitute a major market, particularly for travel to the countries of Western Europe.

Case study 21.3

Foreign themes in Japanese domestic tourism

It could be argued that much of the domestic tourism in Japan is a substitute for foreign travel. A large number of visitor attractions provide the Japanese with a simulated holiday experience in a foreign country without the trouble and expense of the real thing. The Japanese are fascinated by Western technology and popular culture, and they are also interested in other Asian cultures, particularly those of China and Korea. This interest in 'foreignness' is often expressed by visiting the 'Chinatowns' that exist in Kobe and other cities and by contacts with expatriate communities. Out of a total of 1.8 million foreigners there are some 0.2 million *gaijin* (Westerners) living in Japan, not just in the big cities, but also in small towns as a result of the exchange teachers' programme. Nevertheless the Japanese continue to be curious about many aspects of Westerners' lifestyles and even their physical appearance. Japanese youth are attracted to *gaijin* communities and the United States military bases, particularly in Okinawa, where they can practice their English language skills without embarrassment. This island provides numerous examples of museums, theme parks, restaurants, nightclubs and festivals which celebrate American popular culture.

There are many purpose-built visitor attractions based on international themes. Tokyo Disneyland, which attracts around 16 million visitors a year, is the most popular of a number of theme parks that appeal mainly to the family market and which showcase Western culture. Whereas Tokyo Disneyland offers a fantasy version of the USA, Universal Studios near Osaka aims to give the Japanese visitor a 'genuine American experience'. The *gaikoku mora* ('foreign country villages') focus to an even greater extent on international themes. The oldest of these, 'Little World' near Nagoya opened in 1983, and is a collection of such attractions, each offering the regional cuisines, products, music and the performing arts of a particular country. The aim throughout is for authenticity; nearly all the villages employ foreigners as interpreters or performers, and feature buildings that are replicas of foreign originals, where great attention is paid to detail. For example, Huit den Bosch near Nagasaki celebrates Japan's special relationship with Holland with replicas of famous Dutch landmarks such as the Royal Palace in Amsterdam. Other foreign country villages include 'British Hills' near Tokyo with its English pubs; 'Lucky Kingdom' with its Bavarian architecture and fairy tale characters; Parque España (Spain); 'Russian Village'; and the 'Turkish Culture Village'. Nearly all the European villages have churches or chapels which are rented by couples for a Western-style wedding, which are viewed by the Japanese as a modern fashion statement, allowing for many photo-opportunities, rather than as a Christian ceremony. At least this avoids the expense of travelling to Hawaii with the same objective.

Visiting attractions that celebrate foreignness allows the Japanese to play at being foreign as well as the opportunity of learning about other cultures. Each country is seen in terms of its unique products, images and attractions – the *meibetsu* ('famous things') that must be visited on a foreign tour. Knowledge of these has been previously obtained from the media, *manga* (adult comic books) and from the travel experiences of others. Most of these visitor attractions feature famous writers or fictional characters among other tourist icons, and these have become well-known brand names in Japan. Shopping for merchandise in a foreign country village is a preparation for a future trip overseas, teaching Japanese tourists not only what they should see, but also what they should bring back as gifts for friends, relatives and work colleagues.

Inbound tourism

Inbound tourism stood at over 8 million visits in 2010 – and the difference with outbound tourism is even greater in terms of spend. These relative low volumes are due to Japan's distance from the traditional generating markets of Western Europe and the USA, and the country's reputation for being expensive. This is despite the country jointly hosting the FIFA World Cup with South Korea in 2002. Business travellers account for about a quarter of incoming tourists, with the cities of Tokyo, Osaka and Nagoya as the major destinations. South Korea is the largest source of tourists, due to cultural and business ties with Japan. South-east Asian countries account for half of all visitors, with a further 10 per cent coming from the USA.

The supply side of tourism

Transport

For domestic travel, road and rail is most commonly used. The northern island of Hokkaido is linked to Honshu by the world's longest rail tunnel, and bridges similarly integrate Kyushu and Shikoku with the main transport network, supplementing the ferry services. There is an extensive network of railways (20,000 kilometres), including the famous *Shinkansen* (bullet trains), linking Tokyo to Osaka and Fukuoka to the west, and Niigata and Morioka to the north. For foreign visitors, train travel is preferable to driving due to the problems of road congestion and inadequate signage. Most foreign visitors arrive by air, the majority through Tokyo's Narita Airport. However, other airports are growing in importance, particularly Osaka's Kansai Airport (built on an artificial island), which has the advantage of being much closer to downtown than Narita, which is 60 kilometres from central Tokyo. Tokyo's other airport, Haneda, handles domestic flights to a large number of destinations. The busiest air routes are to South-east Asia, Hawaii and the USA. The aviation sector is dominated by two airlines – Japan Airlines and ANA – but with deregulation since 1996 they face a growing challenge from newcomers.

Accommodation

The hotel industry is driven by domestic demand, but occupancy rates for other than budget and medium-priced hotels has declined as a result of the economic problems and the resulting cutbacks in corporate entertaining by Japanese business executives. Tourists can stay in Western-style hotels, or in *ryokan* – Japanese inns where the food service, bathing facilities and furnishings of *tatami* matting follow native traditions, and these are increasingly sought out by Western visitors. Tokyo and Osaka are the main locations for major hotel projects, some of which are financed by international chains. These tend to be very expensive, but an alternative is available for the budget traveller in the so-called 'capsule hotels' – stacks of cubicles, each consisting of little more than bed-space. Subsidised family 'travel villages' and lodges are also available for the domestic market.

Organisation

Responsibility for the industry lies with the Ministry of Land, Infrastructure, Transport and Tourism, which supervises the Japan National Tourist Organisation (JNTO) whose role is to promote 'a fair and realistic image of Japan' to increase understanding of the country, particularly among the international business community. The Japan Convention Bureau (JCB) plays a leading role in developing facilities for the important conference market.

ASIA AND THE PACIFIC

Tourism resources

Japan's traditions are a major part of its appeal to Western tourists. These include:

- the cuisine, where the presentation of food is treated as an art form;
- the tea ceremony;
- the delicacy and artistry evident in handicrafts, such as engraving on wood or silk;
- Kabuki theatre
- Sumo wrestling; and
- the distinctive architecture and miniaturised landscape gardening characteristic of Shinto and Buddhist temples and shrines.

Japan has a unique human resource in the skills of the *geiko* hostesses and entertainers (better known as geishas in the West), but there is evidence that this is a declining tradition, with fewer girls willing to undertake the long training as *maikos* (apprentice geishas). The corporate business market for this type of entertainment was reduced considerably by the economic crisis of the 1990s and many *okiya* (geisha houses) closed as a result.

Innovation as opposed to tradition is evident in contemporary Japanese art forms such as *anime* (the animated cartoon film), the fashion scene among young people in Tokyo and other cities, and in pachinko parlours, karaoke bars, 'host bars' (exclusively for women), and other forms of entertainment. Sony is one example of a Japanese corporation that has been in the forefront of developing visitor attractions employing the latest technology.

Although the drive for industrialisation has caused severe pollution problems, the Shinto religion inspires reverence for the natural world, and much has been done to preserve the country's coasts, mountains and forests, including the designation of 28 national parks in the most scenic areas. Unlike their counterparts in North America, these are not for the most part wilderness areas, but contain hundreds of rural communities, such is the pressure on land and water resources.

Western visitors are mainly drawn to southern **Honshu** and to its cities which include:

- Tokyo, which is above all a business centre, but also a city of over 12 million people containing many temples and museums. The Ginza district includes the Stock Exchange, while leisure activities are concentrated in the Shinjuku district.
- Kyoto, as the former Imperial capital is Japan's main cultural centre, which preserves the country's traditions, including hundreds of Shinto shrines and temples, the Gion district with its geisha houses, and gardens inspired by Zen Buddhism. However, this city of one and a half million people is no museum-piece, but one that is increasingly under threat from the pressures of modernisation, despite strict planning regulations against high buildings and neon advertisements.
- Nikko, Nara and Ise are also religious centres, preserving much of the feudal past of Japan.
- The Inland Sea between western Honshu and Shikoku is probably the most scenic region of Japan, studded with picturesque islands and numerous Buddhist temples.

Kyushu has a long history of contact with other cultures, and this is an important part of its appeal, particularly to the Japanese. The island offers a wide variety of attractions, including:

- Space World near Fukuoka;
- Nagasaki, the first port to be opened to trade with the West and the setting for Puccini's opera '*Madam Butterfly*', which (along with Hiroshima) has been in the forefront of efforts to promote international understanding, stemming from its experience of nuclear warfare in 1945; and
- Beppu, the most important of a number of spa resorts based on the island's abundant geothermal resources.

In contrast to the rest of Japan, **Hokkaido** is not densely populated, and has landscapes which are different, with forests, cereal farming and pasture replacing rice-fields. The climate is similar to that of eastern Canada, with abundant snowfalls during the long, bitterly cold winters. Moreover, the island was not settled by the Japanese until late in the nineteenth century. The native Ainu people have largely been assimilated, and what remains of their culture is preserved in a few tourist villages. Hokkaido offers the tourist scenic attractions that include:

- Lake Toya, a volcanic caldera surrounded by geothermal springs, a favourite summer destination for vacationers, and also for conferences; and
- the Daisetsuzan National Park, which includes the volcanic peak of Asahi and forests that provide a refuge for the brown bear and other wildlife.

Sapporo is the main commercial centre of Hokkaido and is noted for its annual snow festival.

The **Ryukyu Islands** enjoy a sub-tropical climate. The people have a culture and outlook that is sufficiently different from the rest of the country for the islands to be regarded almost as a foreign destination by the Japanese. Okinawa is the main island of the group, and is visited by large numbers of Taiwanese tourists. It is best known in the West as the scene of some of the bloodiest fighting in the Second World War, and the economy is largely dependent on the US bases that were set up after 1945. In 1975 Okinawa attracted worldwide attention as the venue for the International Ocean Exposition, and the islands offer many facilities for diving.

China (The People's Republic of China)

The setting for tourism

With 1.3 billion inhabitants, China accounts for over a fifth of the world's population. Since 1979 the government has responded to a looming demographic crisis with the one child per family policy. The result is an uneven gender ratio of 1.2 males per female with the social problems this presents, and the prospect of an ageing population. There are great disparities in wealth between the coastal 'eastern crescent' extending from Beijing to Guangzhou (Canton), which has benefited most from the market economy, and the largely rural interior provinces which remain under-developed.

Throughout the long history of the 'Middle Kingdom' under various dynasties, China's rulers had a world view that regarded all other nations as barbarians, an attitude not unlike that of the Roman Empire. This made China resistant to change at the time of European expansion in the nineteenth century. The Chinese Empire under the Qing (Manchu) dynasty was forced into humiliating trade and territorial concessions by the Western powers – Britain, France and Germany – as a result of the so-called 'Opium Wars', which resulted in the loss of Hong Kong and the 'Treaty ports' of

Qingdao and Wei-hai-weh. In 1911 the last emperor was replaced by a secular republic, but this did not bring stability, and for most of the twentieth century China experienced immense social and economic upheaval, culminating in the Communist revolution led by Mao Zedong who established a totalitarian state. Following the chaos of the Cultural Revolution and Mao's demise, the government from 1978 onwards gradually moved toward a free market economy, although the Communist Party, backed up by the People's Liberation Army (PLA) remains firmly in control. Since the 1990s the rate of economic growth has been among the highest in the world, attracting foreign investment on an unprecedented scale. Some commentators believe that China is on course to become the major power of the twenty-first century and certainly it is set to dominate outbound tourism in both the East Asia region and the world in decades to come. China is now the world's second importer of oil along with many other raw materials to fuel its industries, with huge implications for the global economy.

The landmass of China is equivalent in size to the USA. It contains a great range of climates from the extreme winter cold of northern Manchuria to the tropical warmth of the island of Hainan in the south. It boasts some of the world's highest mountains and plateaux, one of the most inhospitable deserts – the Takla Makan – and the world's fourth longest river – the Yangtse. Throughout history China has been prone to natural disasters on an epic scale in the form of earthquakes, floods and famines, and its rulers have been faced with the need to control the erratic flow of the rivers Yangtse and the Hwang-Ho. One major constraint on development is water supply, as China, with 20 per cent of the world's population, has only 7 per cent of its freshwater resources. The problem is particularly acute in the north, necessitating a diversion of water from other areas to Beijing.

China has one of the world's oldest civilisations, characterised by an alphabet, a code of ethics based on the teachings of Confucius and Lao Tse, and art and medical traditions that were already well established at the time of the Han dynasty in the second century BC, which gave its name to the dominant culture of the country.

The demand for tourism

Domestic tourism

Travel for pleasure is a recent phenomenon in China, and domestic tourism was discouraged by many restrictions under Mao's totalitarian regime. Deng Xiaoping's economic reforms in the 1980s encouraged mobility as part of the process of modernisation, and returning rural migrants from the cities were regarded as a 'civilising influence' on the countryside. Since the mid-1990s domestic tourism has increased rapidly, encouraged by the rise in living standards, and not least, by an increase in leisure time, including the introduction of the five day working week in 1995. In 1999 the government introduced three weeks of public holidays, known collectively as the 'golden weeks'. These celebrate Chinese New Year (January/February), Labour Day (the first week in May) and National Day (the first week in October). A growing urban middle class has the means and the desire to participate in leisure tourism, as part of a trend away from a 'savings culture' to one of conspicuous consumption.

Family visits to Buddhist and Daoist shrines, such as the sacred mountain of Tai-Shan in Shandong province are popular, providing a link with Chinese tradition. Western-style beach tourism has been slow to develop, as the Chinese prefer landscapes modified by human action rather than the sea, which is often viewed as a source of danger rather than a recreational opportunity. The contrast with Western attitudes extends to sunbathing, as importance is still placed on modesty and a fair complexion. However, beach resorts within reach of the major cities attract growing numbers of middle class families. The citizens of Beijing visit Beidahe, Wei-hai and Qingdao. These resorts were initially developed by European expatriates in the 1920s, and after the Communist revolution the hotels were taken over for the use of the Party elite and favoured groups of industrial workers. Xiamen in the south-east of the country is visited by holidaymakers from Shanghai.

The demand for outdoor recreation is growing, but many projects have failed because developers overestimated the spending power of China's middle class. There is now an effective demand for golf and skiing where none existed before 1990. The most developed ski resort is near Beijing at Nanshan, where snow-making machines compensate for the lack of snowfall in North China's cold but very dry winter climate.

Cultural visits are a much more significant part of domestic tourism. These are seen by the authorities as a force for education in citizenship. Groups of workers from the same companies or work units are encouraged to visit 'patriotic education sites' and other places associated with the nation's history and Mao's revolution in particular. The emphasis on education and indoctrination combined with entertainment extends to the theme parks that have been developed on the periphery of major cities, such as 'Splendid China' and 'Windows of the World', which replicates famous buildings from many different countries. Heritage plays an important role in tourism based on China's 'old towns' and 'ethnic villages', but the manner in which it is conserved and interpreted differs from the approach in Europe and North America. These are standardised attractions selected by the tourist authorities at the highest level, rather than as a result of local initiatives. In 'old towns' the historic core is marked off from the rest of the urban area by a ticketing gate and a reconstructed town wall, and various improvements are carried out, such as re-paving and street widening. Other typical features include a shopping street selling souvenirs and an accommodation area allocated to tour groups. Cultural performances are another element of the tourist experience, taking the form of re-enactments of ceremonies in a real or imagined past. In the ethnic villages the minority groups are encouraged to put on dance performances and wear their traditional costume when tourists visit. Chinese tourists realise they are being offered staged performances, but unlike Western cultural tourists who value 'authenticity', they expect, and indeed appreciate such experiences as an escape from the realities of everyday life.

Since the millennium there has been a huge increase in the use of the Internet, and this has encouraged the growth of independent travel, particularly among young people. Like their Western counterparts, Chinese backpackers value the freedom of travel, and seek adventure and cultural experiences in relatively remote areas. They are city-based and well educated. Participants are brought together for a specified trip by the voluntary efforts of like-minded individuals using independent web sites. Nevertheless, these travellers are highly organised, with an ethos that emphasises the welfare of the group, rather than encouraging the hedonistic attitudes characteristic of youth tourism in the West.

Outbound tourism

The demand for foreign travel in China has been shaped by government policy, which generally discouraged such trips until quite recently. In 1983 package tours for 'family reasons' were permitted to Hong Kong and Macau. In 1990 Thailand, Singapore and Malaysia became the first countries to receive Approved Destination Status (ADS) by bilateral agreement with the Chinese government. In the new Millennium this pro-gramme has been extended to include the European Union, Australia, and the USA. The relaxation of visa restrictions, the emergence of the low-cost carrier AirAsia, and the strength of the Chinese currency against the US dollar, have encouraged the growth of foreign travel. At present only 5 per cent of the population has the means to travel abroad, but growth is such that China has already overtaken Japan as the leading generator of international tourism in Asia, in terms of the number of departures. Most of the demand comes from the three major urban belts of Beijing/Tianjin, Shanghai and the Yangtse Delta, and Guangzhou/Shenzhen in south China. In 2010 the Chinese took 50 million trips abroad, and they now form the largest market in most countries of South-east Asia, where there are large ethnic Chinese populations. Tourism to Europe is constrained by cost, language and cultural barriers, and the unfamiliarity of Chinese travel agents with long-haul destinations. The great majority of Chinese tourists travel in organised groups due to visa regulations and for cultural reasons, the exception being Hong Kong where independent travel has been permitted since 2003.

As was the case in the 1950s with the 'ugly American' stereotype in Western Europe, Chinese tourists are not always viewed favourably by the host communities in the countries they visit. In Vietnam, which has a history of strained relations with its northern neighbour, they are perceived to have an attitude of superiority. In Singapore and Hong Kong on the other hand they are regarded as lacking in sophistication. The Chinese government views tourists as their country's representatives, and has issued tour operators and travel agencies with directives warning against anti-social behaviour (such as spitting in public spaces and queue-jumping) that would reflect badly on its image abroad. There is also the risk that Chinese tourists might be exposed to subversive foreign ideas.

Inbound tourism

Inbound tourism has been encouraged by the government since 1978 as part of the campaign to make the Chinese more receptive to Western ideas and technology, and also to generate the foreign exchange needed to modernise the economy. Growth has generally been rapid, although the adverse publicity following the suppression of the pro-democracy movement in Beijing's Tiananmen Square, brought about a downturn in Western visitors in the early 1990s, and the SARS outbreak of 2003 significantly impacted upon both inbound and outbound tourism. Nevertheless, the 1997 PATA Conference was held in Beijing, highlighting the fact that China had become one of the world's leading tourist destinations. The hosting of the 2008 Olympics in Beijing further boosted international arrivals and in 2010 over 55 million tourist arrivals were recorded. The most important markets are Japan, Russia, the countries of South-east Asia, and the USA, while Britain, France and Germany account for 5 per cent of arrivals. This success in tourism has not been achieved without growing pains. Pricing, poor service standards, and a shortage of trained personnel remain problems, as does the adjustment of a centrally-planned economy to one trying to accommodate enterprise and market forces. Positive changes have taken place in the following areas:

- improvements in the transport infrastructure;
- a greater choice of destinations, with more than 500 cities or areas open to visitors compared to 30 in 1982;
- a greater choice of attractions within established destinations such as Beijing and Shanghai;

- more competition between tour operators and travel agencies, (in the past, group travel had been monopolised by the state-controlled China International Travel Service (CITS) which has had to improve its performance for Western tourists), and
- an increase in hotel capacity and a much-needed improvement in standards.

Business travel accounts for a third of inbound tourism and gravitates to the major cities of Beijing, Shanghai and Guangzhou. China plans to have 150 world-class conference centres in place by 2020, catering particularly to the demand for trade exhibitions and corporate meetings. On the other hand, the market for associate meetings, which might be concerned with controversial issues, has been slow to develop in China, due to the lack of government support.

The supply side of tourism

Transport

Most travel in China is by rail or air, as the road network over most of this vast country is deficient by Western standards. Some improvements had been made in preparation for the Beijing Olympics, but these have failed to keep pace with the rapid growth in car ownership, resulting in acute traffic congestion in the major cities.

Until recently rail travel was arduous and time-consuming, but the government has made a massive investment in magnetic levitation technology, so that by 2015 China will have the world's most comprehensive high-speed rail network. Fast trains already link Wuhan in central China to Guangzhou, and Beijing to Shanghai. The rail journey between the capital and the nation's economic hub, a distance of over 1,300 kilometres, now takes less than 5 hours, giving the domestic airlines serious competition. There are also ambitious plans to extend the network to the countries of south-east Asia. Nevertheless there are concerns about safety issues, given the pressure on officials to meet central government targets. The Lhasa – Qinghai Railway linking Beijing to Tibet ranks as another major engineering achievement. Pressurised carriages are necessary for passengers as the track at one point reaches the breathtaking altitude of 5,200 metres (16,600 feet). The project also took account of the need to protect the fragile grassland ecology of the Tibetan Plateau.

China has an extensive system of domestic air services, but only a few airports are, as yet, capable of handling large volumes of international traffic. Air China and a number of regional airlines compete for the growing market for air travel, while the Civil Aviation Administration of China (CAAC), which in the 1980s exercised a state monopoly of air transport, now focuses solely on its regulatory role. The CAAC has given foreign airlines more rights to use the gateway airports at Beijing, Shanghai and Guangzhou.

Accommodation

Most Western-style accommodation is concentrated in the major cities, notably Beijing, Guangzhou, Shanghai and the Shenzhen Special Enterprise Zone adjoining Hong Kong. Thanks to the 2008 Olympics there is probably an over-supply of five-star hotels in Beijing for the international tourist market. The shortage of more budget-priced hotels and motels for Chinese business and leisure tourists is being addressed by the private sector, notably by chains such as Home Inns. These tend to offer a much higher standard of facilities than the 'economy-type' hotels run by local authorities or state-owned companies.

Organisation

Since 1984 the China National Tourism Administration (CNTA) has been responsible for defining overall tourism policy and overseeing its implementation, and tourism development is firmly integrated with the Five Year Plans for the national economy. The governments of the 23 provinces and five autonomous regions are now allowed considerable initiative, resulting in a flurry of master plans and investment schemes for tourism across China. Nevertheless, most tour operators and travel agencies are closely associated with government departments, which restricts the independence of the private sector. The industry is represented by the China Tourism Association and the National Travel Trade Association, and is becoming more organised and professional.

Tourism resources

China is mainly famous for its age-old craft industries, traditional styles of architecture, and distinctive landscapes. Since the 1980s Western fashions and styles of advertising have largely replaced the drab uniformity normally associated with Communist regimes, and traffic jams are now commonplace in cities where bicycles and pedicabs used to be the only forms of transport. On the other hand, in the headlong rush to industrialise, air and water pollution have become major health problems in the cities, and great damage has been inflicted on the forest and wildlife resources of the mountain areas. Nevertheless, a reverence for nature is part of Chinese tradition, and the government has made great efforts to protect the habitat of the giant panda, China's most iconic animal, in the forests of the south-west. The country's cultural heritage is also at risk due to the under-funding of conservation, inappropriate restoration methods, and the urge to replace the old by the modern.

In such a vast country there are considerable regional differences, in climate, landscapes, dialects and lifestyles – including cuisine. Although the Han Chinese are the dominant group, there are 55 ethnic minorities who together make up about 10 per cent of the population, living mainly in the west and south-west of the country. For convenience we have grouped China's provinces and autonomous regions according to their geographical location.

The North-east

Known historically as Manchuria, this was the homeland of the last imperial dynasty, but nowadays the Manchus are an ethnic minority in their own country. During the twentieth century the region experienced Russian and Japanese occupation along with large-scale industrial development. The main centres are Shenyang (formerly Mukden) and Harbin, which is noted for its annual snow festival. The border town of Heihe on the River Amur illustrates the changing nature of relations with Russia; past tensions between the two countries have been replaced by a thriving trade in consumer goods, supplied by Chinese entrepreneurs to Russian visitors from nearby Blagoveshchensk.

North China

North China, centering on the Hwang Ho river basin was the historic cradle of Chinese civilisation and the power base of the Chin and Han dynasties that were the first to unite the country. The region has a continental climate with severe winters and hot, humid summers. The region is characterised by treeless landscapes of wind-blown loess, but it has much to attract the cultural tourist, including:

- the burial place of the First Emperor at Xian, which yielded the famous terra-cotta warriors;
- the Great Wall of China – over 3,000 kilometres in length – built as a defence against the Mongol nomads to the north (the section most visited by tourists, and subject to considerable pressure, is at Badaling, reached by a 50 kilometre rail link from Beijing), and
- the summer resort of the Qing dynasty at Chengde, with its gardens, palaces and pagodas.

Beijing (formerly Peking) was the creation of the Ming dynasty in the fourteenth century, and contains many reminders of its imperial past, including the Forbidden City (the former palace compound of the emperors), the Temple of Heaven, and the Ming Tombs. In contrast, the Great Hall of the People, occupying one side of the vast public space known as Tiananmen Square, symbolises post-revolution China. The 2008 Olympic Games have provided the impetus for improvements to Beijing's transport infrastructure. Apart from the sports facilities, the capital now boasts an array of new museums, art galleries and theatres. However in the rush to modernise, most of the picturesque *hutongs* (densely packed courtyard dwellings) have been demolished to make way for faceless apartment buildings and shopping malls.

East Central China and Szechwan

This part of China centres on the River Yangtse.

Shanghai is China's largest city and owes its rise as one of the world's great seaports to trade with the West. In the 1920s when the city was dominated by foreign concessions, Shanghai was renowned for its wealth and uninhibited nightlife. The impressive skyline of the new Pudong special enterprise zone underlines the city's revival as an international business centre, while the historic waterfront area known as the Bund has been restored.

To the west of Shanghai lie a group of historic cities that have played a major role in Chinese history as capitals or cultural centres. These include Nanjing, Hwangzhou, Wuxi (famous for its silk industry), and Suzhou, noted for its traditional Chinese gardens.

The Yangtse provides a popular tourist route to the fertile but mountainous province of Szechwan, deep in the interior of China. The modern cruise ships and the landing stages thronged with porters typify the contrasts between the old China and the new. The highlight of the cruise is the impressive Three Gorges between Wuhan and Chongqing. This is the location for the world's largest flood control project, involving the displacement of 1.5 million people. Taming the Yangtze will prevent a repetition of the 1998 floods that claimed 4,000 lives and provide 10 per cent of China's power requirements, but critics fear that the project will cause long-term environmental damage.

Western China

The city of Lanzhou is often regarded as the gateway to the arid and mountainous west. This includes the autonomous regions of Inner Mongolia, Ningxia, Xinjiang and Tibet, and the province of Qinghai, which is mainly Tibetan in its traditional culture. The West is mainly inhabited by ethnic groups who are culturally distinct from the Han

Chinese. For example, the Uighur speak a Turkic language, are predominantly Muslim, and have a way of life based on pastoralism. The central government in Beijing has made great efforts to improve the communications infrastructure as part of a policy of integration. Tourist interest in the region focuses on the Silk Road (which we described in Chapter 17) and the historic towns along its route, such as Kashgar and Khotan. Domestic tourism from the cities of eastern China is encouraged by the government to boost the economy of the region, and provide the funds to combat desertification.

The Mogao Caves near Dunhuang are the major attraction on the Silk Road, and it was hereabouts that Chinese traders made contact with those from Persia and central Asia. Dating from the time of the Tang dynasty, this former Buddhist sanctuary is decorated with a vast collection of wall paintings and sculptures which was 'discovered' by a European explorer in 1907. Although the art treasures have been rescued from centuries of neglect and the encroaching desert sands, this World Heritage Site now faces a more insidious threat from mass tourism.

South China

South China is Cantonese, rather than Mandarin-speaking, with a climate and topography offering considerable potential for ecotourism, adventure holidays and beach tourism. The major tourist centres include the following:

- Guilin is famous for the spectacular karst mountain scenery along the River Li that has inspired a Chinese art tradition.
- Kunming is the centre for trekking tours into the rugged, densely forested, and formerly inaccessible 'hill country' of the provinces of Yunnan, Guangzhi and Guizhou, where many tribal minorities preserve much of their original culture. The transformation of 'ethnic villages' into tourist destinations has encouraged the revival of cultural practices as a matter of local pride as well as a source of income.
- Guangzhou is the major business centre of the region, hosting two annual trade fairs in the Palace of Exhibitions which provide a showcase for the Chinese economy. In contrast, the city's markets display exotic foods and health remedies that recall an older China.

The tropical island of **Hainan** until well into the twentieth century was neglected by the Chinese government, which regarded it as a place of exile, inhabited by uncivilised tribes. Since the 1990s it has been promoted as the holiday destination of choice for China's growing middle class, particularly the resort of Sanya. Hainan now has its own regional airline, has hosted the Miss World beauty pageant, and is being promoted as a winter sun destination for the West European market.

Discussion point

The Beijing Olympics have given China the best opportunity to showcase its achievements, regain its place in the sun after centuries of being sidelined by the West, and demonstrate its green credentials. Discuss whether criticism of China's environmental record is justified, given the efforts the government is making to reduce dependence on coal and oil by harnessing renewable sources of energy. Also discuss whether there is a case for the Chinese government's attitude to ethnic minorities and human rights activists, particularly in Tibet, bearing in mind China's turbulent history and recent events in the former USSR.

Hong Kong and Macau

Hong Kong and Macau deserve to be treated as separate destinations in their own right because of their special status within China and their former status as European colonies – Hong Kong was British from 1841 to 1997, while Macau was ruled by Portugal from the mid-sixteenth century to 1999. They include parts of the mainland of South China and a number of offshore islands. Hong Kong and Macau have a large measure of autonomy as special administrative regions (SARs) under the Chinese government's 'one country, two systems' policy, which in effect means a 'hands-off' approach to their free enterprise economies.

Hong Kong

Densely built up around its magnificent harbour, with The Peak in the background, the city of Hong Kong has one of the world's most famous skylines. As an SAR, Hong Kong retains some of the features of British rule, including:

- free port status and a free-wheeling private enterprise economy;
- border controls with the rest of China, although visa controls have been relaxed to allow individual as well as group travel;
- the Hong Kong dollar as its official currency;
- the use of English and Cantonese as official languages shows the region's separate cultural identity from the rest of China, where Mandarin is the language of administration; and
- its own tourist authority for promotion and development – the Hong Kong Tourism Board (HKTB).

Most of Hong Kong's commercial growth has taken place since 1950, as the result of a massive influx of refugees from the PRC, liberal tax laws, and its geographical location at the focus of air and shipping routes. The SAR consists of a dozen islands at the mouth of the Pearl River, the peninsula of Kowloon, and the New Territories on the mainland. These are linked by an efficient transport system, including the famous Star Ferry, road tunnels, and the MRT, Hong Kong's underground railway network, which carries more passengers (more efficiently) than its London counterpart. The high levels of air pollution at street level, and the humidity that prevails for most of the year, explains the widespread use of travelators and elevated walkways in this high-rise city.

Hong Kong is one of Asia's major destinations, and is a base as well as a port of call for ocean cruises. The availability of charter flights, and a well developed business travel market have encouraged inbound tourism. This provides most of the revenue for Cathay Pacific, one of the leading airlines in the East Asia-Pacific region. The new international airport at Chep Lap Kok has enhanced the importance of Hong Kong, as a very restricted site had handicapped its predecessor – Kai Tak.

In 2010 Hong Kong attracted 36 million visitors, of whom almost two-thirds are from mainland China, with the USA and Europe between them accounting for only 8 per cent of the market. Tourism is the second largest earner of foreign exchange, but it faces increasing competition from Macau and Shenzhen. Rising educational and living standards, combined with urban pressures, also make Hong Kong an important generator of tourism to the rest of the East Asia-Pacific region and to the USA. The challenge for the HKTB is to entice foreign tourists to stay longer and spend more, and to persuade residents to take more weekend breaks and day trips within the SAR. These include visits to rural communities in the New Territories and the promotion of

ASIA AND THE PACIFIC

nature-based excursions. The government is committed to sustainable tourism, with some 40 per cent of the SAR designated as country parks, providing a much-needed recreation resource. However, most of the beaches, such as Repulse Bay are overcrowded on summer weekends and both airline and hotel capacities are reaching ceilings of development. Air and marine pollution continue to be serious problems, and Hong Kong is some way from meriting its name, which means 'Fragrant Harbour'.

For the foreign visitor, Hong Kong is a unique blend of Western business culture and Eastern traditions, such as *feng shui* in hotel and office developments, and *tai chi* as a popular form of recreation. There is a great variety of attractions, which include:

* shopping for consumer goods and Chinese items such as jade;
* the *sampans* and floating restaurants of Aberdeen;
* themed attractions such as the Sung Dynasty Village and the Middle Kingdom (showcasing China's history), Ocean Park, and the Space Museum; and
* the outlying islands with their temples and peaceful countryside, providing a relief from the hectic pace of urban Hong Kong.

Macau

This Special Administrative Region lies 120 kilometres to the west of Hong Kong, consisting of the city of Macau and the tiny islands of Taipa and Coloane. These are now linked by the Cotai Strip with major new casinos and resort hotels opening to rival Las Vegas. Some 85 per cent of Macau's visitors are from mainland China (where there is a huge suppressed demand for gambling) and Hong Kong. Western tourists are more likely to be attracted to old Macau, which has preserved much of its colonial heritage and a blend of Chinese and Mediterranean culture. Event attractions include the Grand Prix motor race (modelled on that of Monaco). Although Macao now has its own international airport, the majority of visitors are short-stay, arriving by fast ferry from Hong Kong.

Case study 21.4

Tibet: the cultural impact of Chinese tourism

In 2007 anti-Chinese riots in Lhasa brought Tibet and its spiritual leader in exile, the Dalai Lama, under the international spotlight. As a destination Tibet is unique for the following reasons.

* It is the highest and most extensive plateau on Earth, for the most part above 5,000 metres altitude, at the upper limits of human habitation. Lhasa, situated in a deep valley at the relatively modest altitude of 3,700 metres, is one of the world's highest cities.
* The region is hemmed in by even higher mountains which in the past made it virtually inaccessible. This physical seclusion produced a civilisation based on a distinctive form of Buddhism. Until the Chinese government asserted control in 1951, Tibet was a closed society ruled by a theocracy of monks, with its people living in medieval conditions. The importance of religion in everyday life, as shown by prayer flags and red-robed monks, is an important part of the country's appeal to Western visitors who often perceive it to be the mystical 'Shangri-La' of legend.

In view of the widespread concern about the impact of Western tourism on local cultures, it is worth pointing out that only 6 per cent of the 2.3 million visitors to the

Tibetan Autonomous Region in 2006 were foreign tourists. The Chinese government has only recently promoted tourism in Tibetan areas after decades of restricting access by both Han Chinese and foreign visitors alike. Chinese tourists are attracted in increasing numbers, despite the negative way that Tibetans as a people have long been regarded by the Han Chinese.

Improved air transport and the railway linking Lhasa to Beijing are part of the Chinese government's strategy to bind Tibet more closely to the national economy. However, there are few urban centres and the country has only a rudimentary road network. As a result tourism is focused on Lhasa, which has as its showpiece attraction the Potala Palace, the former residence of the Dalai Lama. In its application to UNESCO for the Potala to be given World Heritage status, the Chinese government declared the monument to be an achievement of 'the peoples of China', downplaying its significance as a symbol of Tibetan cultural identity. In contravention of international guidelines for the conservation of historic areas, the authorities have redeveloped an adjoining district, replacing many small Tibetan-owned shops by a museum and public square. A number of monasteries have indeed been restored by the Chinese government, out of many that were closed and pillaged by Chinese Red Guards during Mao's Cultural Revolution. These include the Jokhang Temple, one of the holiest places of Tibetan Buddhism, where devout pilgrims intermingle with Chinese package tourists seeking a photo-opportunity, who are seemingly unaware of the significance of the religious ceremonies. A growing number of young independent Chinese tourists now use the small hotels and cafes that originally catered for Western backpackers. Many of these, like their Western peers, perceive the traditional culture of Tibet to be exotic and having spiritual qualities, rather than regarding it as 'primitive' or 'superstitious'.

The economic development of Tibet has been accompanied by a massive influx of Han Chinese immigrants who increasingly dominate business opportunities, including the tourism sector, and thus accelerate the process of cultural change.

Case study 21.4

ASIA AND THE PACIFIC

Taiwan

In 1949, following the Communist victory on the mainland, the supporters of the Nationalist government of Chiang Kai Shek retreated to the island of Taiwan (then known in the West as Formosa). Here they established the regime which regards itself as the legitimate Republic of China in opposition to the PRC in Beijing. The islands of Quemoy (Kinmen) and Matsu close to the Chinese mainland subsequently became potential flashpoints during the Cold War. Since the 1990s there have been moves toward eventual reunification, including the restoration of air and sea links and the relaxation of visa controls. In 2008 direct flights between Taipei and Beijing were inaugurated, resulting in an influx of tourists from the PRC.

In 1987 the previous restrictions on travel were lifted as part of the government's transition towards democracy. Taiwan is one of the most successful Asian economies, with a well-educated population that has the means and motivation to visit a wide range of overseas destinations. The country's diplomatic isolation has had little effect on the volume of outbound travel, which exceeds 7 million trips annually. As there were only 5.5 million international arrivals in 2010, Taiwan has a substantial deficit on its tourism account. Taiwan's main tourist markets are Japan (for golfing holidays) and the United States, due to the special relationship that exists between the two countries.

The capital Taipei is a major business destination, but has less appeal to the leisure tourist apart from shopping opportunities and a number of museums displaying Chinese art treasures from the former imperial capital. Taiwan has a lifestyle where

Buddhism and ancient Chinese tradition co-exist with modernity, and which is arguably less materialistic than the PRC. Visitors are attracted by the island's sub-tropical climate, and its mountain and coastal scenery, much of which is protected in a number of national parks. The resources for tourism include:

* the Taroko Gorge, on the East–West Highway crossing the island;
* Sun Moon Lake, a favourite resort for Taiwanese holidaymakers;
* the beaches of the east coast and offshore islands;
* the numerous hot springs that are a feature of the island's geology and which were developed as resorts by the Japanese during their occupation of Taiwan (1895–1945); and
* the island's indigenous tribes, now greatly outnumbered by Han Chinese from the mainland, are increasingly valued as a cultural resource.

South Korea

The setting for tourism

Korea occupies a mountainous peninsula lying between China and Japan. After centuries as an independent kingdom under the Chosun dynasty, which tried to isolate the country from foreign influences, in 1910 it became a colony of Japan, a situation which lasted until Japan's defeat in 1945. Since the Second World War the country has been divided between the Communist North, and South Korea, which has become a major industrial power under a free market economy. Since the end of the Korean War (1950–1953) an uneasy stand-off persists between North and South, long after the ending of the Cold War elsewhere. In fact Seoul, the capital of South Korea, lies only 60 kilometres from the demilitarised zone that separates the two regimes. Since 2000 the two Koreas began a process of rapprochement, although re-unification is still a long way off. For example, teams from both countries participated in the 2002 Asian Games held in Pusan.

The demand for tourism

Domestic and outbound tourism

Since emerging from the devastation of the Korean War, South Korea has experienced an 'economic miracle' that has been even more spectacular than that of Japan. The 1997 financial crisis badly affected the banking sector, but the government responded swiftly by reforming the economy to concentrate on advanced technology, harnessing the skills and strong work ethic of a highly educated population. At the same time it allowed more democratic freedoms, which had been severely restricted by decades of military rule. This resulted in a release of creative energy in the arts, to the extent that Korea, historically a recipient of culture from China, Japan and the USA, is now a trendsetter in the fields of fashion and the media for East Asia, as well as exporting high quality manufactured goods to the rest of the world. In 2004 the five day working week was introduced, and the travel propensity of the population now exceeds 70 per cent. As you might expect from the world's most 'wired-up' society, cyber-competitions attract as much national attention as baseball and other sport events in the country's stadiums. A high proportion of domestic trips are family visits to coastal resorts,

Buddhist shrines, heritage attractions, and theme parks such as Everlands Festival World. The government has taken an active part in tourism development, creating a number of 'leisure cities' to relieve the pressure on the Seoul–Pusan region.

The demand for outbound tourism was suppressed for decades after the Korean War in the interests of building up the national economy. In the late 1980s restrictions on foreign travel, which had previously been limited to those on government or company business, were removed, and the country soon became one of the major generators of tourism in the East Asia-Pacific region, with over 7 million departures annually.

Inbound tourism

Responsibility for tourism falls to the state-run Korea Tourism Organisation (KTO) under the Ministry of Culture and Tourism. The main impetus was initially business tourism, but the 1988 Seoul Olympics, the Asian Games, and the 2002 FIFA World Cup have provided the country with the opportunity to showcase its achievements and leisure tourism has followed. In 2010 almost 8.7 million international arrivals were recorded. The majority of foreign visitors are from other East Asian countries, including Japan, Taiwan and Hong Kong, who are mainly attracted by the entertainment scene and cultural attractions of Seoul, while 'film tourism' also plays an important role. The popularity of *hallya* ('Korea Wave') culture in these countries has led the authorities to preserve specific movie locations as visitor attractions. The USA is less important as a market, despite the millions of Korean expatriates living there, and the large numbers of American ex-servicemen who have been stationed in South Korea. It would appear that Seoul ranks behind Tokyo and Beijing as a destination for Americans, although it is not as expensive as Japan and provides less of a culture shock than China.

Tourism supply

South Korea has an efficient transport infrastructure, which includes two national airlines – KAL and Asiana – while Inchon Airport is growing in importance as an international gateway. The accommodation stock is also impressive, with most hotels providing the latest facilities in information technology.

Seoul is a modern capital of over 10 million people which has preserved some of its heritage, such as the palaces which belonged to the last ruling dynasty of old Korea. Other cultural attractions include the Leeum Museum of Art, sponsored by the Samsung corporation, and the Hyundai Gallery. Western tourists looking for ancient temples and traditional ambience may find that Kyongyu, the former royal capital of the Silla dynasty, has more to offer. South Korea can also offer the following tourist destinations:

* the port city of Pusan, which is also a major holiday resort;
* the beaches of Cheju Island in the extreme south; and
* the mountainous interior, which contains Sorak and other national parks, hot spring resorts, and ski centres that cater mainly for domestic demand.

North Korea (DPRK)

The distance between Seoul and and Pyongyang, the capital of North Korea, is only 250 kilometres, but the two cities are a world apart in terms of traffic, animation and the amenities of the twenty-first century. North Korea has discouraged international tourism, and only a small number of tour groups from the West are allowed entry. Although it has a short border with the Russian Federation, visitors from that country have greatly decreased since the break-up of the USSR. Business travellers from China, North Korea's main trading partner, provide the bulk of the demand for the country's hotels and limited facilities. Like all totalitarian states, tour sites extol the 'achievements' of the regime. The social controls operating under a hardline command economy minimise contact between North Koreans and tourists, and also severely restrict domestic tourism, while the government effectively prevents outbound travel by withholding exit visas and access to the internet. The country's chronic economic difficulties, pressure from China, and dialogue with the USA over its nuclear programme may yet reduce its self-imposed isolation.

Mongolia

Mongolia has more in common with Central Asia and Siberia than the Far East. The former 'Outer Mongolia' emerged from obscurity and moved from Communism to a free market economy during the 1990s, following the collapse of the Soviet Union. The country's national hero is Genghis Khan, who in the thirteenth century conquered a vast swathe of Asia from the South China Sea to the Russian steppes. In more recent times this vast, sparsely populated and landlocked country has been overshadowed by its neighbours Russia and China, but its people still retain much of the nomadic way of life and warrior traditions, such as displays of horsemanship, archery and wrestling. The climate is extreme, with temperatures ranging from –40°C in winter to +40°C in summer. Although the Gobi Desert and steppe landscapes are the dominant features, the Altai Mountains border the country to the north and there are extensive forests around Lake Hovsgol, where the reindeer, rather than the horse or the camel, has defined the traditional lifestyle.

In the absence of hotels outside the capital Ulan Bator, tourists are accommodated in *gers*, the portable structures of felted material traditionally used by the Mongol nomads. Private tour companies compete with the state agency for the growing numbers of Western ecotourists.

Summary

- East Asia contains some of the world's most populous countries, as well as countries at varying stages of development.
- The region is remote from the major tourist-generating countries of Europe and North America, but improved air transport is overcoming the friction of distance.
- Many countries are developing an inbound tourism industry as a source of foreign exchange and to provide jobs.
- Domestic tourism in many countries of the region is now as significant as international tourism, and arguably has as great a cultural impact on local host communities.
- Outbound tourism is also growing, particularly from the established market of Japan and the new market of China. Business travel is important throughout the region.
- Away from the more established tourist destinations, the infrastructure for tourism

is of a comparatively low standard, though many countries are remedying the situation, mainly by improvements in airport facilities.

- Cultural tourism is of primary importance in the countries of the Far East, which have much to offer in the way of historic cities, temples and landscapes.
- Cultural tourism is less significant in the countries of South-east Asia where the climate favours winter sun beach tourism, and where adventure travel and eco-tourism increasingly play a major role.
- Asian tourists view cultural attractions in a different way from Westerners, and there is less concern about 'authenticity' and staged performances.
- Although most countries in the region have national parks, more needs to be done to protect natural resources and wildlife from the pollution and excessive development that has occurred in China and some of the countries of South-East Asia.
- Shopping is a major motivation for travel to, and within the region, particularly for Singapore and Hong Kong.
- China, once the 'sleeping giant' of the region, has become a major economic player on the world stage and a significant force in global tourism.

Assignments

1 Evaluate the strengths and weaknesses of Japan as a destination for business and leisure tourism.
2 Discuss whether tourism can be regarded as a force for economic and social change in China and the countries of South-east Asia.
3 Identify a USP and a potential niche market for tourism in the following destinations:
   - East Timor
   - Tibet
   - Mongolia
   - North Korea.
4 Explain the importance of transport in the development of tourism in the island-nations of East Asia.
5 Describe some of the natural disasters that have occurred recently in Japan and the countries of South-east Asia, the response by the authorities, and the impact on tourism.

ASIA AND THE PACIFIC

The tourism geography of Australasia

Introduction

Australia, New Zealand, and the islands of the Pacific east of Indonesia and the Philippines form a separate geographical entity called Australasia. An alternative name – Oceania – is also appropriate as most of the constituent islands are insignificant in comparison with the vastness of the Pacific Ocean, which covers a quarter of the earth's surface and spans a distance of more than 12,000 kilometres from east to west at its widest extent. The only large land masses are:

- Australia – often called the 'island-continent';
- the eastern half of New Guinea; and
- the two main islands of New Zealand.

The total population is small compared to that of neighbouring South-east Asia – about 36 million – and there is generally less pressure on resources. Australia and New Zealand are economically, culturally and politically part of the developed Western world, but both countries play an important developmental role with regard to the other countries in the South Pacific region. In the northern Pacific, the islands of Hawaii are geographically part of Polynesia, but they became the 50th state of the USA in 1959 and are therefore included in Chapter 23. Likewise in the southern Pacific, Easter Island is administratively part of Chile and is included in Chapter 25. The rest of Australasia is economically part of the developing world, consisting mainly of island mini-states with small populations and limited land resources. Most have become politically independent only since the 1960s, while some of the smaller islands are still governed by countries lying outside the region, notably France and the USA. Yet, despite their 'paradise' image, there has been civil unrest in the islands, particularly Fiji and the Solomons. With the ending of the Cold War, the islands are no longer supported by the defence industries of the Western powers and must become economically more self-sufficient. For this reason, tourism and the exploitation of the islands' potentially vast marine resources increasingly play a vital role.

The Pacific Asia Travel Association (PATA) represents all the countries in the region. There are prospects for considerable growth in tourism, as the region can offer generally favourable climates, unspoiled coastal and mountain scenery, and in the main, political stability. The market potential is certainly present with the Pacific Rim of Asia and North America an area of impressive economic growth. Since 1970, Australia and New Zealand have loosened their ties to Britain and forged closer trade links with the USA and the other countries of the East Asia-Pacific region, notably Japan. This pattern of trade has resulted in a growing volume of air traffic across the Pacific, facilitated by long-range wide-bodied jets. Air transport now plays a vital role in the economy of all the countries in the region, and the peoples of Australasia are very aviation-minded. However, these Pacific destinations are still a long way from the major tourist-generating countries – particularly those of Europe – and are therefore vulnerable to downturns in travel caused by terrorism and international crises, as well as competition from more accessible parts of the world that can offer similar attractions.

The native peoples of Australasia suffered severely as a result of Western colonisation in the nineteenth century, losing most of their tribal lands and much of their culture in the process. This was particularly true of the Australian aborigines, who became a small, marginalised minority. Since the 1970s there has been a growing recognition of the value of indigenous arts, crafts and folklore as cultural resources, and native peoples not only take greater pride in their heritage, but also increasingly take an active role in the tourism industry.

Australia

Until the 1980s Australia was not important as a holiday destination, the great majority of visitors being business or VFR travellers. In the 1980s and 1990s growth rates for inbound tourism accelerated, delivering arrivals approaching 6 million a year by 2010. This has in part been due to the promotional efforts of both the Australian Tourist Commission (ATC or Tourism Australia) and the Australian state governments, the showcasing of Australia for the 2000 Olympics, and competitive air fares. Tourism is now one of Australia's leading sources of foreign exchange, supporting well over half a million jobs.

Australia is the only nation occupying a whole continent, with an area of 7.6 million square kilometres – comparable in size to the USA, but with only 7 per cent of its population. Since 1901, when the six former colonies united as the Commonwealth of Australia, the country has functioned under a federal system of government, similar to that of Canada, in which the states and the two territories – Northern Territory and Australian Capital Territory – enjoy much freedom to manage their own affairs, including the development and regulation of domestic tourism.

The setting for tourism

Physical features

Australia has great tourism potential, thanks to its warm sunny climates, unique wildlife and natural features, as well as a coastline – over 36,000 kilometres in length – which includes some of the world's finest beaches and the largest coral reef.

However, many of Australia's natural attractions are separated by vast distances, making tourism development in much of the continent problematic. Most of the Australian landmass has been worn down by eons of erosion and as a result, is relatively low-lying compared to other continents, with only a few mountain ranges and inselbergs – isolated rocky outcrops rising abruptly from the surrounding plains. More varied landscapes are to be found in the mountain system – known as the Great Dividing Range – which runs for 3,600 kilometres along the eastern margin of the continent, reaching its highest point – 2,200 metres – at Mount Kosciuszko. These mountain ranges separate the fertile coastal belt – where most of the cities and tourist facilities are located – from the interior. Australia can also claim to be the world's driest continent. Most of the outback – the vast, thinly populated bush country extending west of the River Darling – is desert or semi-desert, where the lakes shown on the map are usually expanses of salt and the rivers merely a succession of pools or *billabongs*.

The most interesting natural resources of Australia are the plants – mainly drought-resistant gums and wattles (eucalypts and acacias), resulting in very distinctive landscapes – and the marsupial animals which are only native to the island-continent. Much of this natural heritage was devastated by the plants and animals introduced by nineteenth century British settlers. In response, Australia now has more than 2,000 protected natural areas, including national parks, testament to the unique flora and fauna of the continent. The World Heritage Sites designated by UNESCO are listed in Box 22.1.

These landscapes provide great opportunities for tourism. Tourists can go 'bush walking' (hiking with a difference!), prospect for gold or gemstones, go on whale or dolphin-watching trips, take part in four-wheel-drive vehicle safaris that allow the more adventurous to visit remoter areas away from the all-weather roads, or try adventure sports such as abseiling and white-water rafting. The Australians are leaders in minimising the environmental impact of these recreational activities, and there are a number of state and federal ecotourism strategies and awards for sustainable tourism practices.

The size of Australia and its geographical location in the Southern Hemisphere means that it experiences a wide range of climatic conditions, without the prolonged

Box 22.1

- Kakadu National Park in Northern Territory, an area of tropical wetland and savanna;
- Uluru (Ayers Rock) in Northern Territory;
- the Wet Tropics of north Queensland, an area of virgin rainforest;
- the Great Barrier Reef off the Queensland coast;
- Fraser Island – the world's largest sand island – also off the coast of Queensland;
- the Gondwana Rainforests (formerly the Central Eastern Rainforest Reserves) in Queensland;
- Willandra Lakes in New South Wales, actually dry claypans that hold evidence of early aboriginal cultures;
- the Blue Mountains in New South Wales, much of which is true wilderness despite its proximity to Sydney;
- Lord Howe Island, situated 700 kilometres north-east of Sydney in the Tasman Sea, is a semi-tropical paradise for nature-lovers;
- Tasmanian wilderness, much of which is almost impenetrable temperate rainforest;
- Shark Bay in Western Australia, noted for its marine life; and
- the Riversleigh and Naracoorte fossil mammal sites, situated in Queensland and South Australia respectively.

winter cold typical of northern lands. Most of Australia, with the exception of Tasmania, lies within tropical or subtropical latitudes. The desert interior has a more extreme climate; in winter pleasantly warm days are followed by nights with temperatures dropping below 0°C. The northernmost region of Australia around Darwin experiences a tropical monsoon type of climate with a rainy season known as 'the wet' between December and May, accompanied by high temperatures and humidity. The great majority of Australians live in the south-eastern part of the country and enjoy a warm temperate climate, which in general is ideal for outdoor recreation. Even so, summer temperatures often exceed 35°C due to winds from the desert interior, which bring the risk of bush fires to the suburbs. Snow is almost unknown, except in Tasmania and the southern sections of the Great Dividing Range, and even here it cannot always be guaranteed to provide good skiing conditions during the Southern Hemisphere winter, which lasts from June to September. Perhaps the best climate is around Perth in Western Australia where summers are dry but not excessively warm due to a constant sea breeze.

Cultural features

The population of Australia is 21.5 million, of which only 2 per cent are Aborigines. The boomerang-shaped coastal belt extending from Brisbane to Adelaide, while only accounting for 5 per cent of the area of the country, contains 80 per cent of its inhabitants. Until the 1980s the great majority of Australians were the descendants of British and Irish settlers, but the composition of the population has changed with the influx in the latter half of the twentieth century of immigrants from southern and eastern Europe, and more recently from Asian countries. In contrast to its outdoor image, the nation is highly urbanised, with almost 40 per cent of the population living in Sydney and Melbourne. The urban character of Australia's population has an important influence on the patterns of tourism which have developed. A developed and diversified economy means that Australians enjoy a high standard of living. Car ownership, for example, approaches North American levels, and the effects are seen in suburban sprawl around the major cities. Participation in outdoor activities is high by European standards. The most popular participant sports are tennis, swimming, sailing, and surfing. Sports facilities are excellent, boosted by the Sydney Olympics in 2000, and spectator sports include football, cricket, and horseracing – epitomised by the Melbourne Cup. Gambling is also popular, with casinos and clubs producing considerable revenue and attracting foreign visitors, particularly from Asia.

Case study 22.1

The Aboriginal heritage: a neglected resource?

Only recently have white Australians recognised that the history of their country did not begin with Captain Cook, and the arrival of the First Fleet at Port Jackson in 1788. Aboriginal tribes had been living there for many thousands of years. The archaeological evidence suggests that their occupation even pre-dates the arrival in Europe of the Cro Magnon people during the last Ice Age. As hunter-gatherers they successfully adapted to a range of challenging environments, including tropical northern Queensland, the arid 'red centre' of Australia, and the dank rainforests of Tasmania. However, their long isolation from other cultures ensured that their level of technological development remained in the Stone Age, to be dismissed as primitive by the European settlers. The petroglyphs or rock art of the native Australians is not only comparable to the cave paintings of Ice Age Europe, but is a tradition preserved and added to by many generations until recent times. These paintings provide an invaluable record of how the Aborigines observed the natural world, including animals that have long been extinct. There are an estimated 100,000 rock shelters containing aboriginal art, although a systematic inventory has yet to be made. Some of the most significant of these sites are in the Arnhem Land region of Northern Territory and the Pilbarra region of Western Australia. Unlike European cave paintings, most sites are exposed to erosion, to which must be added damage through vandalism, urban development and mining activity. Many aboriginal communities have also lost their connection with this aspect of their heritage, as a result of the demoralising impact of contact with Europeans.

Nevertheless, aboriginal arts and crafts are now increasingly appreciated as part of the Australian heritage, and a number of communities are participating in tourism in the following ways:

- as guides and trackers on eco-tours;
- by selling artwork based on traditional themes directly to tourists or through art dealers;
- by hosting cultural tours, which may include traditional dances; or
- by owning and operating heritage sites or tourism ventures.

Demand for tourism

Domestic tourism

Each year Australians take, on average, at least two pleasure trips involving a stay away from home, and travel has become an important element of discretionary spending. The domestic market is significant simply because of the wide range of experiences on offer in the continent, and it is the mainstay of the tourism economy. Although only a small proportion of trips cross state boundaries, partly because of the distances involved, in the early years of this century domestic travel has increased as international travel has been depressed by world events. Deregulation of domestic airlines in the early 1990s led to a lowering of air fares and boosted the domestic industry. The majority of holidays are taken in December and January, mostly to the beach resorts between Sydney and north Queensland. During the winter months there is a smaller but much more concentrated migration to the semi-tropical beaches of Queensland and large numbers also head for the ski slopes of the Australian Alps, while others seek the unspoiled desert scenery around Alice Springs.

Outbound tourism

Australia is the largest generator of international tourism in the Southern Hemisphere, with 7.1 million trips taken in 2009. Despite their distance from other destinations, Australians feel a strong need to explore other parts of the world. The majority of Australian tourists who travel abroad are residents of the two most prosperous states, New South Wales and Victoria, which between them contain almost two-thirds of the population. Despite the high costs involved, large numbers of Australians visit Europe on holidays extending over a few weeks, during which several countries may be visited. They include a high proportion of young people combining a European tour with work experience, some travelling overland from Singapore via India and the Middle East. Other popular destinations are the USA, including Hawaii, New Zealand and the

Pacific islands such as Fiji, Vanuatu and New Caledonia. A glance at the map will show that Australia is in fact much closer to South-east Asia than it is to Europe or North America, with Indonesia being less than 1,000 kilometres from Darwin. This accounts for the popularity of the beach resorts of Bali, Thailand and Malaysia, although the Bali bombings in 2002 depressed travel to Indonesia.

Inbound tourism

Only a small percentage of foreign visitors to Australia come on inclusive tours, and VFR tourism is decreasing in importance from Britain and Ireland as holiday tourism becomes more important. The main inbound markets for Australia are New Zealand, North America, the UK and Asia – particularly Japan. The Japanese and North American markets were affected by 9/11 and also by the collapse of Ansett, Australia's second airline. The Japanese are predominantly in the younger age groups and are mainly attracted to the resorts of the Queensland coast. The Americans, on the other hand, are generally older with a high propensity to travel; they feel an affinity with the pioneering spirit of Australia and are most likely to take a touring holiday. A growing number of tourists come from China, Singapore, Hong Kong, and other Asian countries, and many of these are in the student category. Such has been the turnaround in the demand for tourism that Australia now runs a surplus on its travel account, and tropical destinations such as Cairns and the Whitsunday Islands are taking market share from places such as Fiji.

Supply of tourism

The tourism industry in Australia caters in the main for the large domestic demand, and until the 1980s little attention was paid to the needs of foreign visitors. Choice was limited and service standards were indifferent, partly because of the egalitarian attitudes prevalent in the country. Change has come about largely as a result of the influx of large numbers of immigrants from southern Europe and Asia. These *New Australians* have expanded the range of entertainments and restaurants on offer in their adopted cities and greatly improved standards in Australia's hotels, of which there are more than 4,000 in total.

Transport

The great majority of foreign visitors to Australia arrive in the international airports serving Sydney and Melbourne and relatively few travel beyond New South Wales or Victoria to take advantage of lower domestic fares. This is despite attempts to spread arrivals to other gateways such as Cairns – where Qantas' new holiday airline is based. Deregulation of the domestic airlines in 1991 attracted new airlines to Australia, but none succeeded until the arrival of Virgin Blue and Jetstar in 2001. In that year more services were developed and airfares fell – such that domestic air movements stood at 57 million in 2001. Airports across Australia are also being privatised and upgraded. In contrast, surface transport in such a vast, sparsely populated country can be problematic; for example, travel across the continent from Perth to Sydney (3,300 kilometres) involves a two hour time change and a journey by train or bus lasting three days. Despite its length (40,000 kilometres) the Australian rail system is not a viable alternative to flying as the network is incomplete and interrupted by changes of gauge at state boundaries. An exception is the *Indian Pacific Express* which allows direct travel from Sydney to Perth. Dedicated tourism rail services are also being developed and include the *Great South Pacific Express* between Sydney and Cairns, and *The Ghan* between Adelaide and Darwin.

Tourism organisation

Each state has a tourism marketing agency and most also have a government tourism department. At federal level, tourism began to be taken seriously in the early 1990s with a number of strategy initiatives and the appointment of a tourism minister to the cabinet. The federal Department of Industry, Tourism and Resources co-ordinates policy and action plans whilst the ATC is responsible for tourism marketing, and is funded by the federal government with contributions from the tourism industry. Despite a very well organised tourism sector at both regional and federal level, apart from some significant destinations – Sydney, Melbourne and the Gold Coast – the organisation of tourism is weak at the local level.

Tourism resources

New South Wales

Australia's most populous state accounts for over a third of overnights spent by foreign visitors. Tourism in New South Wales is dominated by its capital, Sydney. The city has developed around one of the world's finest harbours and the beaches of the Pacific are within easy reach by hydrofoil or ferry. Sydney's attractions include:

- the famous suspension bridge across the harbour, which visitors can now ascend;
- harbour-side attractions such as the Sydney Opera House, the ferry terminal at Circular Quay, shopping, restaurants and hotels on the waterfront and revitalised areas such as 'The Rocks', with art galleries and specialist shopping;
- Darling Harbour has been revitalised with the Sydney Aquarium and Wildlife World, the Maritime and Powerhouse Museums, and an IMAX Cinema;
- around the harbour are heritage sites and buildings such as Fort Dennison and the Quarantine Station where emigrants first landed, now converted into a hotel;
- the city has many cultural attractions such as the Art Gallery of New South Wales and a range of museums; and
- districts such as Paddington and Kings Cross with their distinctive lifestyles.

The best known of Sydney's beaches is Bondi, with its superb conditions for surfing; but since the strong tidal surges can be dangerous, many families prefer the more sheltered beaches of Port Jackson or the small seaside resort of Manly with its Oceanworld attraction. Sydney's hosting of the 2000 Olympics gave tourism a major boost and involved the building of 14 new hotels, improving the transport infrastructure and the provision of new sports facilities.

Recreational areas within easy reach of the city include:

- the Snowy Mountains with ski resorts such as Thredbo and Perisher;
- the gorges of the Hawkesbury River;
- the Hunter Valley vineyards,
- the Blue Mountains, a scenic area of forested ridges, deep valleys, caves, and waterfalls. Cable-cars and a funicular railway provide access from the resort of Katoomba to a variety of viewpoints.

From Sydney a scenic coastal route passes north through resorts such as Coffs Harbour, Port Stephens, Port Macquarie, Byron Bay (a famous surfing beach) and the rainforest in the Dorrigo National Park.

Queensland

This largely tropical state is predominantly a destination for beach tourism, accounting for a quarter of overnight stays by foreign visitors. The area 50 kilometres south of Brisbane, known as the **Gold Coast**, is one of the most popular holiday regions for Australians, but also caters for international visitors, particularly the Japanese. The coast is a highly developed strip of resorts, 70 kilometres in length, with Surfer's Paradise at its heart. Much of the development is badly planned and commercialised with many high-rise hotels, and the area is in need of revitalisation. The Gold Coast is the setting for both sporting events and a number of major theme parks, reminiscent of Florida, namely:

* Seaworld;
* Warner Brothers Movie World;
* Wet'n Wild waterpark; and
* Dreamworld (a Disney-type park).

Lamington National Park in the hinterland of the Gold Coast is well known for its birdlife.

Brisbane, the state capital, received a boost to tourism in 1988 by hosting Expo, and the site has been redeveloped as the Southbank Parklands – a cultural and park area on the south bank of the Brisbane River. The city has a spectacular setting on the river where *CityCat* catamarans ferry visitors and commuters, and offers a range of cultural venues, museums and galleries.

Close to the coast near Brisbane is Fraser Island, which is the world's largest barrier island composed of sand deposits. Other offshore islands are both recreational areas for Queenslanders and also good locations for dolphin and whale watching. To the north of Brisbane, the **Sunshine Coast** has excellent beaches stretching from Caloundra to Rainbow Beach. One resort – Noosa Heads – has specialised in fine dining. In the hinterland are the Noosa and Cooloola national parks.

Case study 22.2

The Great Barrier Reef

One of Australia's unique tourist attractions, visited by over 4 million people annually, the Great Barrier Reef begins 350 kilometres north of Brisbane and extends northwards for 2,000 kilometres to Cape York. It actually consists of about 2,000 individual reefs, which provide a habitat for 350 species of hard corals, 1,500 fish species, and 240 bird species. It is designated as a marine park, and is managed by the Great Barrier Reef Marine Park Authority (GBRMPA) which shares responsibility with the state government of Queensland. The reef provides opportunities for scuba diving that are unequalled elsewhere, but there are fears that global warming and the 'crown of thorns' starfish are damaging the coral. Between the reef and the coast lies an enormous sheltered lagoon dotted with hundreds of islands. Some of these have been developed as exclusive holiday resorts with marinas, golf courses, and other sports facilities, while others cater more for campers. Examples include:

Case study 22.2

- Hamilton Island in the Whitsunday group has its own jetport with flights from Brisbane;
- Green Island specialises in eco-friendly tourism;
- Great Keppel Island is for young travellers; and
- Bedarra specialises in honeymooners.

Pollution and over-fishing are problems on the more popular islands with consequent danger to the reef ecosystem; to remedy this some areas have been designated as nature reserves. The ports of the Queensland coast, notably Cairns, Townsville and Port Douglas are the starting point of excursions to the Reef and offshore islands by boat and helicopter.

Discuss the effectiveness of the various measures, including zoning, the issue of permits, and management plans, that have been taken to control fishing and pollution, cope with the tourist influx, avoid conflicts between a diverse range of recreational activities, and not least, educate the public on conservation and sustainability issues.

In northern Queensland, Cairns is now an important international gateway, particularly for Asian visitors, and is a booming resort city offering a range of hotels and a casino. Inland, sugar plantations, the rainforests of the Daintree National Park and the Atherton Tableland provide the main interest away from the coastal resorts. The Kurunda Skyrail provides a 7.5 kilometre ride over the rainforest canopy, with the Tjapukai Aboriginal Cultural Park at its foot. From Cairns northwards to Cape York lie the excellent and largely deserted white beaches of the *Marlin Coast*, However, transport can be problematic in much of northern Queensland during the cyclone season, due to widespread flooding.

Victoria

Victoria experiences more variable weather conditions than other states of mainland Australia, with rural tourism playing a more important role. The capital of Victoria – Melbourne – rivals Sydney as the commercial capital of the country, but with a more conservative, less flamboyant lifestyle. The city has as wide a range of retailing, restaurants, cultural and sporting attractions and is almost as cosmopolitan as Sydney, with large Italian and Greek communities. Melbourne offers major sporting venues such as the Melbourne Cricket Ground (MCG) and Albert Park, where the Australian Formula One Grand Prix is held; however it is the Melbourne Cup – not only a sporting event but a fashion show – that attracts most interest. The city has its own beach resort at St Kilda and is conveniently placed for touring the vineyards of the Yarra River. Other tourist resources accessible from Melbourne include:

- the Victorian Alps – a popular region for walking, skiing (in resorts such as Mount Buller) and white water rafting;
- the Great Ocean Road drive along the picturesque Victoria coast with rock features such as the *Twelve Apostles*;
- Phillip Island with its burrowing penguins;
- the Gippsland Lake District;
- reminders of Victoria's nineteenth century mining heritage with 'living museums' at Ballarat and Bendigo recreating the 1850s Gold Rush, and Beechworth, which is associated with Ned Kelly, Australia's most famous outlaw; and

- old-style steamboat trips on the Murray River, an important commercial waterway before the coming of the railways.

Australian Capital Territory

Canberra is the capital of Australia and is spaciously planned in a beautiful lakeland setting near the Snowy Mountains. It is a relatively small city and cannot compare in vitality to Sydney or Melbourne, but boasts major cultural attractions, including the National Gallery and Museum, as well as national institutions such as the Australian Institute of Sport and Parliament House.

Tasmania

The small island-state of Tasmania is separated from the mainland by the Bass Strait, and accounts for only 2 per cent of overnight stays by foreign visitors in Australia. It can be reached by ferry or fast catamaran from Melbourne or by air to Launceston or Hobart. With its mild oceanic climate and perpetually green countryside, Tasmania contrasts with the rest of Australia and has its own flora and fauna – such as the Tasmanian Devil. The small resorts along the north coast (such as Stanley) are not unlike those of England's West Country, and are particularly attractive for senior citizens escaping the summer heat and more hurried lifestyle on the mainland. Inland there is mountain and lake scenery in the Cradle Mountain – Lake St Clair National Park and the Cataract Gorge, a spectacular ravine popular for adventure sports. Ben Lomond is an important ski resort, with a season lasting from July to late September. The south-west of the island receives the heaviest rainfall in Australia and is covered by barely explored rainforest. The Tasmanian Wilderness Railway – once used for transporting minerals – has been restored as a 30 kilometre journey through virgin wilderness. The island has a range of heritage attractions such as the Port Arthur historic site, a reminder of Australia's most notorious penal settlement.

Western Australia

The largest and most thinly populated of the states, Western Australia suffers as a destination due to its great distance from the more popular tourist regions of the east coast and as a result, accounts for only 10 per cent of overnights by foreign visitors. It is nevertheless developing markets based on ecotourism, adventure tourism and its mining heritage. Perth is a green spacious city close to good surfing beaches (such as Scarborough and Margaret River) fronting the Indian Ocean, while Fremantle gained wide publicity by hosting the America's Cup yacht race and now has a maritime museum. The city has a variety of attractions including the Perth Mint, Cultural Centre and gemstone shopping in the suburbs. Perth is also a good base for exploring the Outback, including:

- the Punululu/Bungle Bungle National Park with its multi-coloured rock formations;
- the even more remote Kimberley region, over 2,000 kilometres north of Perth, a wilderness of sandstone gorges, transformed during the rainy season into a riot of vegetation and cascading waterfalls (the El Questro wilderness park provides a variety of accommodation for tourists); and
- Kalgoorlie and Coolgardie with their gold-mining heritage.

ASIA AND THE PACIFIC

Attractions along the coast include:

- Shark Bay which is renowned for its marine wildlife, including the dolphins of Monkey Mia that interact freely with visitors, but this situation could change if tourist numbers become excessive;
- Exmouth on the **Coral Coast** is the base for exploring the Ningaloo Reef; and
- Broome, famous for its former pearl diving industry, and now an upmarket beach resort.

South Australia

Most of South Australia is desert country, but in contrast the spaciously planned and landscaped capital, Adelaide, has promoted itself as the 'Festival City' with a range of event attractions. Adelaide is close to the coastal resort of Glenelg and the vineyards of the Clare and Barossa Valleys. To the north lie the scenic Flinders Mountains National Park. To the south, Kangaroo Island can be reached by ferry services, and is noted for its coastal scenery and remarkable variety of wildlife. These resources are protected by the Flinders Chase National Park and a comprehensive plan for sustainable tourism. The opal mining town of Coober Pedy is located deep in the interior, where visitors can stay in the Desert Caves Hotel, built underground like most dwellings in this community to avoid the extreme summer heat.

Northern Territory

The Stuart Highway links Australia's southern city of Adelaide with the northern city of Darwin. The only city of any size in the 'Top End', Darwin itself has a limited range of attractions, but is used as a base for exploring the region's tourism resources. These include Australia's tropical northlands with their game-rich grasslands and reserves on which the Australian aborigines continue their traditional lifestyle. In the Tiwi Islands it is possible for visitors to interact with the aborigines. A number of areas significant for tourism are accessible from Darwin:

- the Kakadu National Park is probably the most popular attraction in this region – it was the setting for the movie *Crocodile Dundee*, and is rich in the wildlife of tropical wetland;
- Litchfield National Park is closer to Darwin, famous for wildlife, aborigine rock art and the Gagudju Crocodile Hotel – so called because of its design; and
- Arnhem Land is a large unspoilt wetland area under aborigine management where visitor numbers are strictly controlled by a permit system.

Further south lies the 'red heart' of Australia, an area of spinifex desert, salt lakes and strange rock formations such as the Olgas (known as Kata Tjuta in the local aboriginal language) and the more famous Uluru, better known as Ayers Rock. The only town in the region, Alice Springs, offers a range of attractions such as:

- the Telegraph Station, a reminder of the city's pioneering role in communications;
- the Alice Springs Cultural Precinct showcasing the history of central Australia;
- the School of the Air Outback Radio Service; and
- the base of the Flying Doctor Service.

Case study 22.3

Uluru: an Australian national icon

Alice Springs owes its importance as a tourist centre more to its function as the gateway to the Uluru National Park and its prime attraction – the Rock – despite an intervening distance of 300 kilometres. The Rock has achieved internal recognition as an icon of Australia, due to its unique character as the world's largest monolith – it measures nine kilometres in circumference and 300 metres in height – and the way the rock changes colour at sunrise and sunset. The Rock became much more accessible with the opening of an airport and purpose-built resort at Yulara in the 1980s. This provides a range of accommodation from budget camping to the five star Ayers Rock Resort Hotel. Guided tours of the Rock and the surrounding area interpret aborigine culture and legends of the *Dreamtime*, and visitors can sample *bush tucker* – the natural foods of the outback. Nevertheless, the ever-growing number of visitors raises a number of issues regarding the future of tourism in the area, namely:

- **Sustainability** Burgeoning demand may exhaust ground water supplies, already under pressure from the cattle industry. Although the Yulara resort is built to an aesthetically high standard, it is difficult to justify air conditioning and swimming pools as being compatible with ecotourism.
- **The potential for conflict between tourists and the host community** Uluru is a sacred site for the aboriginal people, but to most tourists, it is a photo-opportunity and an objective to be climbed. Many aborigines regard this as an act of desecration.

New Zealand

Although New Zealand shares cultural similarities with Australia, including a love of sport and the outdoor life, and a certain informality of outlook, it is different in many other respects, both in terms of its physical geography and culture.

The setting for tourism

New Zealand is separated from Australia by the Tasman Sea, which is 1,900 kilometres wide and often stormy. New Zealand is scenically very different from its big neighbour, boasting volcanoes, glaciers and fjords among its natural attractions – the backdrop for the filming of the *Lord of the Rings* trilogy. The native flora and fauna is quite unlike that of Australia. Much of this, including the unique flightless birds, was threatened with extinction as a result of the introduction of new species by Europeans in the process of clearing 'the bush' for farmland. New Zealand was among the first countries to establish national parks on the American model, to conserve what remained of the natural heritage. There is a widespread interest in environmental issues, exemplified by the opposition to the French nuclear testing in the Tuamotu Islands. New Zealand has also been active in protecting its extensive coastline and offshore waters with a system of marine reserves.

Physical features

Most of New Zealand is hilly or mountainous and the country's greatest tourist asset is the beauty and variety of its scenery. The two large islands that make up the bulk of

Photo 22.1 Lyttelton harbour, the port for Christchurch, New Zealand (©istockphoto.com/ Daniel Thomson)

New Zealand offer quite different environments. Much of the North Island consists of a volcanic plateau, while the South Island is dominated by a range of high fold mountains, the Southern Alps, which contain glaciers, snowfields, and a rugged, deeply indented fjord coastline.

The climate of New Zealand favours the more active types of outdoor recreation, with its equable temperatures and pollution-free atmosphere. Although the islands enjoy more sunshine than the British Isles, sunshine is not guaranteed, and the range of latitude occupied by the islands means that while Auckland has a sub-tropical climate, at Invercargill 1,600 kilometres further south the temperatures more closely resemble those experienced in the western islands of Scotland. This puts domestic tourism at a disadvantage compared to foreign destinations such as Australia's Gold Coast, Bali, and the islands of the Pacific. The mountains in both the North and South Islands are high enough to receive heavy snowfalls, with the skiing season lasting from July through October.

Cultural features

New Zealand's cultural heritage includes an export-oriented pastoral economy, and a nineteenth century gold rush in Westland and Otago reminiscent of the Australian experience. However, New Zealand was colonised by the British from the outset with free settlers, in contrast to the convict origins of Australia's first British and Irish colonists. The indigenous Maori people had a highly developed, if warlike, culture derived from their homeland in Polynesia. They now account for some 12 per cent of the population and their cultural heritage, expressed in crafts and dances, forms an important ingredient in New Zealand's tourist appeal. The Maori have become more fully integrated into the mainstream national culture than the native peoples of Australia, although the incidence of unemployment and other social problems in Maori communities is higher than the national average.

Tourism demand

Inbound tourism

The New Zealand government was one of the first to recognise the importance of tourism, setting up an official tourist organisation as far back as 1901. Tourism now is a significant export earner and foreign visitor arrivals in 2010 exceeded 2.5 million a year, compared to only 100,000 in 1970. This growth has been achieved in spite of the remoteness of this small island nation from the world's major trade routes and centres of population, by successful promotion and development of the country's resources, and clever use of the islands as the setting for the *Lord of The Rings* films. Tourism New Zealand works closely with the private sector to attract the more adventurous type of tourist who is interested in scenery, meeting people and the outdoor life. New Zealand can offer the unique resource of uncrowded countryside, with a population of only 4.3 million occupying an area comparable in size to the British Isles.

Australia provides around one third of incoming tourists, followed by North Americans, many of whom are interested in hunting and fishing holidays. East Asian countries such as Japan and South Korea are also significant source markets. The Japanese are interested in New Zealand not only as a destination for skiing holidays, when the Northern Hemisphere season has ended, but also for other types of outdoor activities. The UK market has stayed fairly constant at around 10 per cent of arrivals since the 1950s. but its composition has changed, with fewer British visitors falling into the VFR category, and an increasing number opting to purchase tailor-made holidays rather than inclusive tours. The choice of New Zealand as the host nation for the 2011 Rugby World Cup underlines the country's appeal to sport-lovers.

Domestic and outbound tourism

Three quarters of New Zealand's population live in North Island, and of these, 40 per cent are concentrated in the country's largest city, Auckland. The standard of living is high, with motor vehicle ownership approaching Australian levels, although cars have to be imported. The economy is still dependent on the export of primary products such as meat and wool, but the service sector, including tourism, is becoming increasingly important. Nevertheless, despite the distances that must be covered, and the high cost of air fares, New Zealanders have a high propensity to travel abroad, and with much the same preferences regarding destinations as the Australians. About half of all overseas visits are to Australia, with the encouragement of cheap air fares.

A much greater number of New Zealanders take annual summer holidays in their own country, mostly during the six weeks from mid-December to the end of January. Since this coincides with the peak period of arrival for foreign visitors, there is considerable pressure on hotel rooms in most resort areas. Motels are the type of accommodation most favoured by domestic holidaymakers, although caravanning, camping and youth hostelling are also popular. Many families also own, or share, a second home, a holiday cottage known as a 'bach' or 'crib', at the coast. In the past, most of these were basic, albeit brightly painted, structures of corrugated iron, but nowadays thousands of 'designer' baches have proliferated, and 'bach-hopping' using the Internet has become a popular activity.

Supply of tourism

Transport

New Zealand's transport system is well developed. The mountainous topography has encouraged the widespread use of domestic air services connecting the main cities – Auckland, Wellington, Christchurch and Dunedin – and the resort areas. Specially equipped light aircraft bring the Southern Alps within easy reach of tourists, while hiking trails and scenic mountain highways are used by the more adventurous. Rail transport has declined, except on a few scenic routes. A network of bus services provides access to most parts of the country, while the Wellington–Picton ferry service across Cook Strait acts as a vital link between the North and South Islands.

Auckland and Wellington serve as important gateways to the South Pacific region and are major centres for business travel.

Accommodation

Most tourism enterprises in New Zealand are small businesses catering mainly for domestic demand. However, foreign visitors are often attracted to remote and sparsely populated rural areas, where it has been uneconomic for the private sector to develop resort facilities of international standard. In the past, the government intervened by financing the Tourist Hotel Corporation to operate quality hotels in scenic locations. Since the 1980s the international hotel chains have developed large hotels in the main resorts, catering mainly for the inclusive tour market, whilst luxurious lodges cater for the top end of the independent traveller market. Farm-stays are also available throughout New Zealand, providing welcome income to the agricultural sector which no longer receives any government subsidy.

Tourism resources

New Zealand has an extensive resource base for sightseeing, ecotourism and adventure tourism, which includes some unusual, if not risky, pastimes such as jet-boating, parapenting, zorbing and bungee-jumping, as well as sea kayaking and white-water rafting. Beach tourism, catering mainly for domestic demand, is well developed on the east coast of North Island, with resorts such as Hastings and Napier, and surfing is a popular activity. Auckland, Rotorua and Wellington are the major tourist centres in **North Island**, catering for the bulk of the international demand.

- **Auckland**, sited between two fine harbours, is known as 'The City of Sails', and attracted the world's attention in the summer of 1999–2000 when it was the venue for the Americas Cup yacht race. New Zealand's largest city has a population of over one million, which includes a large number of Polynesian immigrants from the islands of the South Pacific. Auckland is the centre for touring the sub-tropical north of the country with its kauri forests, surfing beaches and opportunities for game-fishing.
- **Rotorua** is situated in the volcanic plateau in the centre of North Island, which contains some of the world's most unusual scenery, including the Pohutu geyser, and Mount Tongariro – which is still active. Rotorua became a resort in the late nineteenth century when it was fashionable to bathe in the hot springs. It is also the centre of traditional Maori culture as interpreted for tourists. Although tourism provides employment for Maori entertainers and craftsmen, most of the business enterprises are owned by *pakehas* (white New Zealanders), resulting in fewer economic benefits to local communities.
- **Wellington**, the capital of New Zealand, has a harbour setting reminiscent of San Francisco and a range of cultural attractions. The city is convenient for visiting the vineyards of the Marlborough Sounds area of South Island, New Plymouth with its rugby football museum, and the beaches of Hawkes Bay, where Napier is noted for its Art Deco architecture – the legacy of reconstruction following the 1931 earthquake.

South Island was the setting for much of the filming of *Lord of the Rings*. The Mount Cook National Park boasts New Zealand's highest mountain and the Tasman Glacier, one of the largest in the Southern Hemisphere outside Antarctica. In the Westland National Park, glaciers flow almost to the sea amid dense evergreen forests. Ecotourists are particularly attracted to Fiordland, a barely explored wilderness which is New Zealand's largest national park. One of its most spectacular features is Milford Sound that can be reached by boat, or overland on a popular hiking trail. Another important centre for ecotourism is Kaikoura, a Maori community not far from Christchurch, which has become world famous for whale watching. In contrast to Rotorua, tourism enterprises are operated by local people, who claim exclusive use of marine resources in a bid to discourage competition by white New Zealanders. Other important tourist centres include:

- **Christchurch** is the international gateway to South Island and a garden city with a reputation as the most English city in New Zealand. It is now attempting to diversify this image by promoting the scenic attractions and ski resorts of the Southern Alps, which are within easy reach. The city's Canterbury Museum focuses on Antarctica, a reminder that Christchurch has been the point of departure for many expeditions to the 'white continent'. In 2011 the city suffered a devastating earthquake which severely affected its tourism sector and infrastructure.
- **Queenstown** on Lake Wakatipu has two tourist seasons, as a ski resort in winter, and as a centre for mountain climbing, hiking and a whole range of activity holidays in summer, including 'extreme sports' for adrenalin addicts. Queenstown also has a vibrant entertainment scene, attracting young people from all over New Zealand.

The Pacific Islands

The 'South Sea Islands' image of blue lagoons, palm-fringed coral beaches, lush scenery and hospitable islanders has a powerful appeal to would-be escapists from the industrialised societies of the West. So far, the great distances separating the Pacific islands from the tourist-generating countries has prevented the development of mass tourism, based on sun, sand and sea, so collectively they only account for 0.15 per cent of world arrivals. The exceptions are Hawaii and, to a lesser extent, Fiji. There is little demand for domestic or outbound tourism, and most of the arrivals at airports in many of the islands are returning emigrants visiting their families.

Most of the Pacific islands have a tropical humid climate, characterised by abundant rainfall and strong solar radiation, with air and sea temperatures averaging well above 20°C, throughout the year. Sea breezes mitigate the heat and humidity, especially in Polynesia, but tropical storms are frequent during the rainy season and can cause widespread damage. The larger islands are generally of volcanic origin, mountainous, and covered with luxuriant vegetation, with fringing coral reefs along the coast. The smaller islands are mostly coral atolls, low-lying and consisting of little more than a narrow strip of sand, almost enclosing what may be an extensive lagoon.

Inter-island distances are great compared to the Caribbean, making it difficult to visit more than a few countries in one itinerary, while the lack of inter-line agreements between the various national airlines adds to the cost of travel. In the past, shipping services connected the islands, but these have long been in decline. However, most governments in the region recognise that, given their limited financial resources, some degree of international co-operation is necessary. The South Pacific Tourism

Organisation (SPTO) plays an important role in promoting most countries in the region. Investment for the development of facilities has to come mainly from external sources of capital, not only in the West but also increasingly in Asian countries such as Japan and South Korea. Hotel accommodation is generally of a high standard, designed in sympathy with the environment and local building traditions. The main problems are a lack of infrastructure, especially poor roads, and an insufficiently skilled local workforce.

Tourism, along with other aspects of Western consumer society, has been a mixed blessing to the Pacific Islands. Most islanders have lost their skills for self-sufficiency in agriculture and fishing and have come to rely heavily on imported foods, with a negative effect on dietary standards. The native culture had in any case been under severe pressure for two centuries from Western missionaries, traders and administrators imposing their own value systems. Governments in the region see tourism as almost their only chance of raising living standards and reducing the dependence of the islands on world markets for their exports of copra and other products. Tourism has helped to revive the folklore of the islanders and provide new markets for their traditional handicrafts. However, much of the spending by tourists fails to benefit the local economy as it does not stay in the islands. Most of the hotels are owned by foreign companies, and considerable imports of food and drink have to be made to meet tourist requirements. Unless the development of tourism is carefully planned with regard to carrying capacity, further damage is likely to be inflicted on the traditional culture of the islands and the fragile marine environment that is their primary resource. The latter is already under threat from the effects of climate change, with higher sea temperatures resulting in a massive die-off of corals throughout large areas of the Pacific, while low-lying atolls are exposed to rising sea levels and more frequent storm surges.

As with the Caribbean, it is a mistake to stereotype the Pacific islands as offering similar tourism products. In fact, we need to distinguish three culturally distinct regions, namely:

- **Micronesia** in the western Pacific, lying to the east of the Philippines:
- **Melanesia,** with its darker skinned peoples, in the south-west Pacific, and
- **Polynesia,** roughly forming a triangle drawn between Hawaii, Fiji and Easter Island, and covering a vast expanse in the centre of the Pacific Ocean.

Micronesia

The thousands of small islands that make up Micronesia total less than 3,000 square kilometres in area, scattered over 8 million square kilometres of ocean. With the exception of the Marianas, which are volcanic and mountainous, most of the islands are coral atolls, with Kiribati claiming the world's largest atoll – Christmas Island. Following Japan's defeat in the Second World War, most of the region, except for the former British colonies of Kiribati and Tuvalu, was administered by the USA, until the islands gained independence in the early 1990s as four separate republics, namely:

- The Northern Marianas, including Saipan;
- Palau;
- The Federal Republic of Micronesia (formerly the Caroline Islands); and
- The Marshall Islands, including Majuro.

Micronesia's main tourism resources are the beaches and lagoons that are ideal for sailing and diving. Palau boasts some of the world's best dive sites, including the Truk Lagoon, scene of a major naval battle in the Second World War. Here the wrecks of numerous Japanese ships and aircraft have been transmuted with the passage of time into colourful artificial reefs.

Guam is the most developed tourism destination in Micronesia. It was acquired by the USA from Spain in 1898, continues to be administered as a United States territory and, offering more attractions and facilities than the other islands, receives a large number of tourists. There are important American military bases on some of the other islands, and United States aid is crucial in the development of infrastructure projects such as airports and harbours. As a result, tourism has grown rapidly, although as yet it has made little impact on the more remote islands. The USA, Japan and South Korea provide the majority of tourists to Micronesia, some of whom are ex-servicemen and their families revisiting the battlefields of the Second World War.

Melanesia

Melanesia mainly consists of fairly large, mountainous and densely forested islands. In fact, commercial logging has become a major earner of foreign exchange, but the rapid depletion of the forest cover could have a serious effect on the islands' wildlife, water supplies and offshore coral reefs. Melanesia includes the following destinations.

- **Papua-New Guinea** is the second largest country of Australasia, boasting its highest mountains, its largest area of rain forest and a great variety of wildlife, including the bird of paradise. Until the 1930s thousands of native communities in the interior were completely isolated from contact with the outside world. Pidgin-English, as elsewhere in the western Pacific, became the means of communication in a country where there are no less than 400 different tribal languages. With surface transport poor or non-existent, domestic air services play an essential role, and most tribes, especially those in the central highlands, have moved from the Stone Age to the Jet Age within a generation. There are few tourist facilities, but a number of tour circuits have been established based in the capital, Port Moresby, or at Mount Hagen in the central highlands.
- **New Caledonia** offers more sophisticated facilities and an attractive coastline, protected by a barrier reef. The capital of this French territory, Nouméa, has been styled with some exaggeration, as 'the Paris of the Pacific'. The island attracts substantial numbers of tourists from Australia and Japan.
- **Vanuatu** comprises the volcanic islands known prior to independence as the New Hebrides, when they were ruled jointly by Britain and France. This unique arrangement did little to encourage the development of the country, although the legacy of bilingualism has probably been an advantage for tourism. Vanuatu also earns considerable revenue from its status as a tax haven and flag of convenience. Tourist facilities have developed based on water sports and 'safaris' to native villages. Pentecost Island is celebrated for the ritual in which young tribesmen leap from towers with a jungle vine securing their ankles. It may be that bungee-jumping, developed as a commercial activity in New Zealand, originated in Vanuatu.
- The **Solomon Islands** receive relatively few tourists, in part due to political instability, and there is a lack of facilities outside Guadalcanal and the capital Honiara; however the islands do offer some of the world's best dive sites.

Polynesia

Polynesia arguably contains the most attractive islands of the Pacific, offering a climate in which malaria and other tropical diseases are largely absent, lush scenery, and a culture in which music, dance and seafaring play major roles. The various island groups are separated by vast expanses of ocean, but the Moahi (Polynesians) developed the double-hulled outrigger canoe and the navigation skills to make long voyages.

Tourism has developed most on those islands acting as staging points on the trans-Pacific air and shipping routes. This is particularly true of Hawaii and Fiji and to a lesser extent, of Tahiti and Samoa. At the other extreme the most remote islands – such as Pitcairn (of *Mutiny on the Bounty* fame) lack airports and, moreover, are served by very infrequent shipping services. Cruise ships call at an increasing number of Pacific islands, but this can be a mixed blessing. As in the Caribbean, the economic benefits of cruising compared to long-stay hotel tourism have been questioned, while the arrival of a thousand Western visitors at a time can cause considerable disruption to a small, unsophisticated island community. We will now look at some of the destinations of Polynesia in more detail.

French Polynesia

This overseas territory of France is usually promoted as 'Tahiti and her islands'. There are actually five separate archipelagos, spread out over 4 million square kilometres of ocean, but Tahiti is the largest and best known island, containing the capital, Papeete, and along with neighbouring Mooréa, the bulk of the tourist accommodation. In contrast, the outlying Marquesas and Austral Islands are much less developed. Tahiti has its own airline – Air Tahiti Nui – linking it to Los Angeles, Honolulu and Auckland. Since their discovery by Europeans in the eighteenth century, the islands and the seemingly free-spirited islanders have captured the Western imagination, inspiring artists such as Gauguin, writers and film-makers. Islands such as Mooréa and Bora Bora are exceptionally beautiful, and essentially unspoiled, offering a landscape of mountain peaks, waterfalls, forests and sheltered lagoons. Much of the development is in the form of *fare*, Polynesian-style bungalows built on stilts over the waters of a lagoon. The promotion board – Tahiti Tourisme – has been successful in attracting American, Japanese and Australian visitors, which now outnumber those from France, while Club Méditerranée operates holiday villages on Mooréa and Bora Bora. Although the beach and water sports are the main attraction, horse-riding and mountain trekking are also encouraged. Tourism has helped to revive the traditional dances and handicrafts such as pareo-weaving. Although French Polynesia is a very expensive destination to visit, few hotels are profitable due to high labour costs. Most supplies are imported, and the economy is heavily dependent on huge subsidies from France.

Fiji

As an ex-British colony, where rugby and cricket are the national sports, Fiji has a different appeal. The country consists of two large volcanic islands – Viti Levu and Vanua Levu – which contain most of the population, and hundreds of small coral islands. As a nation Fiji faces the problem of reconciling the aspirations of two distinct ethnic groups – the native Fijians, and the descendants of Hindu immigrants from

India, brought in under British rule to work the sugar plantations, who now dominate the commercial sector of the economy. Although ethnic tensions have contributed to civil unrest, resulting in temporary downturns in tourist arrivals, multi-culturalism is also one of Fiji's assets as a destination.

Viti Levu contains the capital, Suva – which is a major port of call for cruise ships and the hub for domestic air services to outlying islands. Nadi is one of the most important airports in the south Pacific, with the national airline, Air Pacific providing direct flights to Los Angeles, Tokyo, and a number of cities in Australia and New Zealand. Tourism development is well established along the drier west coast of Viti Levu and the 'Coral Coast' to the south, which offers fine beaches and water sports facilities. Australians and New Zealanders have for long been the most important tourist markets, but visitors from the USA, Japan, Britain and other EU countries are now growing in number. Many tourists, especially honeymooners, are seeking out the outlying islands, such as Wakaya, which offer tranquillity. Resort hotels vary from the luxurious, with spa and golf facilities, to those with impeccable 'green' credentials. All boast beaches of fine white sand and unpolluted seas offering ideal conditions for diving. Fiji also offers a number of cultural attractions, which include fire-walking and traditional war dances, but these tend to be of secondary importance compared to the beaches and duty-free shopping.

Samoa

The islands of **Samoa** are divided between the USA and an ex-British colony, now independent. American Samoa centres on the important harbour of Pago-Pago. Western Samoa offers a more traditional lifestyle, where much of the tourist accommodation is in the form of beach *fales* with an open verandah and thatched roof, operated by local families and located in village communities. Most of the tourist attractions, including waterfalls and the former home of the great writer Robert Louis Stevenson, are located on the island of Upolu.

Tonga

Tonga is unique as the only south Pacific country that has never been colonised by Europeans, and has retained among other traditions a native monarchy which exercises considerable authority. Most visitors arrive by cruise ship at Nuku'alofa, but since the expansion of the airport in the early 1990s, the numbers of long-stay tourists have been steadily increasing. Tonga provides opportunities for surfing and other water sports, and a mix of accommodation that includes resort villages and guest houses.

The Cook Islands and Niue

While these islands are self-governing, New Zealand is responsible for their defence and external affairs. The Cook Islands have encouraged tourism to the extent that it now dominates the economy and the native culture, particularly on the main island – Rarotonga – which is often visited by cruise ships. Niue on the other hand is much less visited and has retained its traditions without the commercialisation that characterises Tahiti and other islands.

The islands of the Southern Ocean

The expanses of stormy ocean lying to the south of Australia and New Zealand are much less favourable for tourism. The Southern Ocean is the realm of the albatross, containing only a few small, uninhabited islands. Most of these lie close to the Antarctic Convergence, where the cold surface water spreading outwards from Antarctica meets warmer water from the north. The climate is characterised by poor weather and overcast skies year-round. In the nineteenth century the marine resources of the islands were exploited by sealers, whalers, and even would-be colonisers, who introduced species that devastated the native plants and birds. Some of the islands, such as Macquarie Island (which is an Australian World Heritage Site), and the Auckland and Campbell Islands (which belong to New Zealand) feature on cruise itineraries to Antarctica, but shore visits are restricted to protect the remaining wildlife. The French Southern and Antarctic Territories (TAAF), which include Kerguelen Island with its spectacular fjords and mountains, receive even fewer visitors. We will investigate Antarctica itself in Chapter 25.

Summary

- Australasia is located mainly in the Southern Hemisphere, and consists of Australia, New Zealand and a large number of relatively small islands separated by wide expanses of ocean.
- The 'tyranny of distance' from the rest of the world is now being overcome by the development of air transport, but the distance from the major tourist-generating countries of the Northern Hemisphere has prevented the region from becoming a major holiday destination.
- Australia and New Zealand clearly belong to the affluent West, while most of the Pacific islands have more in common with the developing countries of the Third World.
- The tourism industries of Australia and New Zealand have primarily developed to satisfy demand from their own populations, and incoming tourism is not nearly as significant or as vital to the economy as it is to the smaller, poorer islands of the Pacific.
- Australasia is primarily a destination area for those travelling for recreational rather than cultural reasons, although ecotourism is of growing importance in most of these countries.
- The climates of Australasia are generally favourable for tourism, and there is less population pressure on available resources than is the case elsewhere. Environments such as the Australian outback, the Great Barrier Reef, the Southern Alps of New Zealand, and the atolls of the South Pacific, offer a range of opportunities for adventure holidays.
- Another factor favouring the development of tourism is the political stability prevailing in most of the region, creating good conditions for investment.

Assignments

1 Compare a specific area of the Australian outback with the Fiordland National Park in New Zealand as destinations for adventure tourism and ecotourism. You

should take into account such factors as accessibility, climate, the physical resources for different types of activity, and the available support facilities.

2   Compare the role of indigenous communities in tourism development in Australia, New Zealand, and French Polynesia. To what extent have they benefited from tourism?

3   The Sydney Opera House and Ayers Rock are widely recognised 'tourist icons' for Australia. Identify features that could similarly be used to promote the following destinations, giving reasons for your choice of icon:
   *   French Polynesia
   *   Fiji
   *   Papua-New Guinea.

4   Explain why zoning and visitor management are necessary to protect vulnerable tourism resources, giving examples from Australia, New Zealand and the smaller oceanic islands.

The Americas

CHAPTER 23

The tourism geography of North America

Introduction

Although the World Tourism Organisation treats the Americas – North and South – as one region, the two continents need to be investigated separately in view of their extent and the striking differences between North and South America, particularly in terms of ecology and culture. In our definition North America excludes Mexico, which we treat as part of Central America in Chapter 25, but includes Hawaii, which is one of the constituent states of the USA.

Both the United States and Canada boast a wealth of natural resources in a vast physical setting. Although the contribution of the native peoples is increasingly recognised, both countries are predominantly 'nations of immigrants', who have blended to produce a distinct North American culture. The English language is dominant, despite being challenged by Spanish in Florida and the south-western USA, and by French in parts of Canada, notably Québec. Both countries have developed democratic federal structures of government and legal systems largely inherited from Britain. They are informal and competitive in their outlook, and share similar attitudes to business enterprise and the freedom of the individual. This has favoured an innovatory approach to leisure activities and tourism, especially in visitor management, marketing and merchandising.

In 2009 North America received more than 10 per cent of the world's international tourist arrivals and accounted for almost a quarter of the world's hotel capacity. From a visitor's point of view the size of the continent is important – extending over eight time zones and including most of the world's climates – but equally important is the rich variety of landforms and ecosystems. The western part of North America is dominated by high mountain chains, including the spectacular scenery of the Rockies and the Sierra Nevada. Near the eastern seaboard rise the forested Appalachians, much lower in altitude than the Rockies. Between these two mountain systems lie vast interior plains, drained by great rivers such as the Mississippi and its tributaries in the south, and by the St Lawrence, Athabasca and Mackenzie in the north.

The climate of North America is largely determined by relief and tends to be more extreme than similar latitudes in Western Europe, with warmer summers and colder winters. In winter Arctic winds penetrate far to the south, and occasionally bring freezing temperatures to the Gulf coast and northern Florida. Yet in summer most of the continent is open to tropical airstreams originating in the Gulf of Mexico, so that humidity tends to be high in the eastern half of the United States. Along the western seaboard high mountain ranges intercept moisture-bearing winds from the Pacific Ocean, bringing heavy rainfall to coastal areas, which also experience much milder temperatures than the interior and eastern seaboard. Most of the western USA, however, has a dry climate, due to its situation in the 'rain shadow' of the mountain barriers. The most important climatic divide is between the *Frostbelt*, consisting of Canada and the northern states of the USA, and the *Sunbelt* stretching from California to the Carolinas. This has far-reaching social and economic implications in that industry and population as well as tourism increasingly gravitates from the northern states, with their declining industries and cold winters, to more attractive environments in the south and west.

Compared to the rest of the world North Americans have been profligate in their use of natural resources, favoured by relatively low energy costs. This has not encouraged sustainable forms of development, as shown by the dominance of the motor car and the prevalence of urban sprawl. Nevertheless the USA and Canada are very much involved with issues of environmental protection. Despite the fact that the great majority of the population live in cities, the unsettled wilderness is very much part of the national heritage in both countries, and determined efforts have been made to save areas of unique scenery from development. The United States was the first country in the world to designate a system of national parks, starting with Yellowstone in 1872; Banff in the Canadian Rockies followed in 1885. Such areas are owned and managed by the federal government with the objectives of conservation and providing access for outdoor recreation. Most of the services required by tourists are however operated by the private sector on a concession basis. The national parks are widely regarded as a major North American contribution to world tourism, and a role model for good practice in both landscape and wildlife conservation and interpretation. However, national parks tend to be resource-oriented and they are mostly located in areas distant from the major centres of population. Closer to urban areas, this has led to the development of recreation areas that are more user-orientated, providing a range of facilities, such as the state parks in the USA and some of the provincial parks in Canada.

North America also offers a host of man-made attractions celebrating its achievements in science, technology and the arts. Canada and the United States are 'young nations' compared to those of Europe, while their cities are undergoing a continual process of renewal and reinvention, so that historical buildings are few. Those that have survived tend to be associated with celebrities or important events in the process of nation-building. They have been carefully restored, or in some cases reconstructed, as heritage attractions, with costumed guides and craft workers interpreting the lifestyle of the past – Colonial Williamsburg in Virginia is an outstanding example. This, like many others, operates as a non-profit making trust. Theme parks on the other hand, along with a great number of smaller visitor attractions, are part of the much larger private sector of the tourism industry.

Big cities play a major role in the cultural life of the USA and Canada, with significant museums, theatres and art galleries. There are 35 such 'metropolitan areas' with populations exceeding one million in the USA, and another three in Canada. As population centres, they generate most of the demand for holiday travel, and as commercial centres, they attract a considerable amount of business travel. The *convention* (conference) industry plays an important role, with city governments competing to increase market share with ever-more impressive facilities. Sports events are of major significance, although soccer has only a limited following in the USA and Canada, compared to the huge interest in the Super Bowl and the World Series, not to mention basketball and ice hockey. The USA is the world's largest sport market and boasts many of the world's largest sporting venues.

However, from the viewpoint of tourists from Europe relatively few North American cities are attractive in themselves. This is particularly the case in the USA, where 'the flight to the suburbs' by the middle class has left areas of dereliction and deprivation around the downtown area. The pattern of high-rise central business districts, commercial strip development along the highways, and low-density suburbs is repeated throughout the continent. A number of cities have attempted to regenerate their run-down inner city areas, with projects aimed at attracting the leisure shopper and tourist. Many visitors from Europe and Asia find the out of town shopping malls more appealing, although they are no longer as unique to North America as they were in the 1980s.

The United States

The period since 1918 has been called the 'American Century', during which the United States has consistently been one of the world's leading generators in international tourism, especially long-haul travel. With a wealth of natural resources and technical know-how, the USA boasts the world's largest economy, and since the collapse of the Soviet Union it has become the only superpower. Although there is a tendency toward cultural homogeneity, regional differences persist. Each of the 50 constituent states is self-governing to a large extent, and Americans retain a strong attachment to their home state. United States territory also extends beyond the North American continent to the islands of the Caribbean – specifically Puerto Rico and the US Virgin Islands – (see Chapter 24), and to the Pacific – Guam and American Samoa (which we described in Chapter 22).

The USA is also one of the world's leading destinations, with tourism accounting for 8.8 per cent of the gross domestic product, and employing 7.9 million people. In contrast to some other sectors of the economy, the tourism industry is made up largely of small- and medium-sized enterprises, and these have contributed substantially to the high rate of economic growth and job creation that the country has enjoyed since its recovery from the 1980s recession.

The demand for tourism

Domestic tourism

The USA can offer an unrivalled range of natural attractions and opportunities for outdoor recreation, so it is not surprising that domestic tourism is many times larger than outbound tourism. Also, in the event of a recession, Americans are much more likely to forego a holiday trip than is the case in Europe. Some 30 per cent of American households do not take a holiday away from home, a 'staycation' in the true sense.

An important constraint on the demand for tourism is the limited leisure time available to most Americans of working age. The USA is an affluent but 'leisure poor' society compared to most European countries, and predictions made in the 1970s of a 'leisure boom' have not materialised. Since that decade productivity has trebled but the amount of leisure time has been reduced substantially over the same period, despite the introduction of flexible working hours. Thanks to 'downsizing' and the resulting job insecurity Americans are working harder than before. For example:

• The average working week in the USA is 43 hours, compared to 38 hours in the UK.
• Workers in the USA on average have 18 days of paid annual leave (including public holidays) compared to 37 days for workers in France.
• In the USA the amount of leave is usually tied to length of service with a particular company. Moreover the corporate culture at the workplace tends to discourage employees from taking two weeks off at a time.
• Almost two thirds of American workers take substantially less than their full leave entitlement.

This means that holidays for middle-income families tend increasingly to be in the form of short weekend breaks rather than a long summer vacation. There continues to be peak in demand for domestic holidays in the months of July and August, so that beaches are generally deserted before Memorial Day in late May and after Labor Day in early September. Thanksgiving in late November is the time when family reunions, often necessitating long journeys by car or by air, are almost obligatory.

Outbound tourism

Only a small percentage of trips are to overseas destinations. In 2006 it was estimated that 85 per cent of Americans had never travelled outside their own continent and only 27 per cent owned passports (compared to 80 per cent in the UK). The situation is changing as a result of 9/11 and the war on international terrorism. Until the Department of Homeland Security insisted on their use as identification documents to re-enter the USA, Americans did not need passports to visit Canada, Mexico, and most of the Caribbean region. There is seemingly a huge untapped market for overseas travel. However national tourism organisations in Europe and elsewhere are aware that the US market is lucrative but volatile, notoriously sensitive to any hint of unrest in a particular region.

Travel abroad by Americans has grown steadily since the 1990s, despite a downturn in the aftermath of 9/11, to reach 61 million trips in 2009. Nevertheless over half of all outbound tourism is to Canada and Mexico. Much of this is business travel, stimulated by the success of the North American Free Trade Agreement (NAFTA) to which the three countries belong. Trips to Canada tend to be short-stay and undertaken mainly by car, whereas visits to Mexico tend to be of longer duration and involve air travel to the destination. The major overseas destinations for American tourists are the UK, Italy and Japan. The Caribbean attracts a large number of leisure tourists, including a major share of the growing cruise market.

Inbound tourism

Inbound tourism continued to grow steadily over the last two decades of the twentieth century, to exceed 50 million arrivals a year by 2000, but then falling back to 41 million as a result of 9/11. Tourism has since made a healthy recovery, to reach

60 million arrivals in 2010. The growth is even more impressive in visitor spend, due largely to the weakness of the US dollar against other currencies.

Canadians make up almost one third of the total, in addition to many more day-visitors. Mexico generated over 13 million arrivals in 2010, but this tends to be a low spend market, with a high volume of trips in the VFR category, due to the close family ties with Mexican-Americans. Other important markets are Japan, South Korea, Brazil, and increasingly China. Among European countries the UK is by far the most important generator of demand, followed by Germany, France and Italy. The most popular destinations for foreign tourists are New York, California and Florida, which together account for almost 75 per cent of arrivals.

The supply side of tourism

The resource base for tourism

In the public sector a number of organisations are involved with the supply of recreational resources at the federal level of government. These include:

- the National Park Service, the Fish & Wildlife Service, and the Bureau of Land Management, which come under the jurisdiction of the Department of the Interior; and
- the Forest Service, which is part of the Department of Agriculture.

The National Park Service (NPS) was set up in 1916, taking responsibility for a range of protected areas, variously designated as National Parks, National Recreation Areas, and National Monuments (which are usually specific sites rather than large areas). Most of the national parks are located in the western states, and can be visited in practice only by private transport, making them inaccessible to the inner city populations of the north-east. Nevertheless the number of visitors to the national parks trebled between 1960 and 1994 and by 2010 exceeded 275 million. This has caused the following problems:

- popular attractions and campgrounds in the most visited parks regularly reach their capacity at peak holiday times;
- traffic on access routes and on roads within the parks has also risen considerably; and
- footpath erosion is severe in the most visited areas, while vegetation and wildlife have been disturbed by trail bikes, hiking off the designated trails and careless behaviour by campers.

Measures to curb car use in a few of the most popular parks, namely Yosemite, the Grand Canyon and Zion, have met with some success, but the size and physical configuration of most national parks makes it difficult to implement 'park and ride' schemes and circular bus tours. Under-funding of the national park system is a matter for concern, given the mandate of the NPS that it should both promote outdoor recreation and protect nature.

The Forest Service is responsible for the National Forest system, where the emphasis is on multiple-use management, including grazing, watershed control and wildlife conservation as well as forestry and recreation. Some 17 per cent of National Forest land is classified as *wilderness areas* under a 1964 Act of Congress prohibiting road building and other development for the benefit of backpackers and canoeists seeking unspoiled nature and physical challenge.

The coastline of the United States provides a more accessible and popular resource, particularly the beaches of Southern California, the Gulf of Mexico, and the Eastern seaboard from Cape Cod to Florida. Off the Atlantic coast is the world's longest series of *barrier islands*, acting as natural sand breakwaters that form parallel to a low-lying coastal plain. Miami Beach and Atlantic City are the best-known examples of resort development on such offshore islands. Unfortunately these resources are threatened by massive population growth in coastal communities, over-development, pollution from effluents, and by rising sea levels, not to mention the occasional hurricane sweeping up from the Caribbean. Many coastal communities have built sea walls as protection from destructive waves, but these merely accelerate erosion elsewhere. Others like Miami Beach have called upon the United States Army Corps of Engineers to carry out beach re-nourishment, using sand dredged from other locations. However the best long-term solution is for the state governments to introduce land use management regulations in the coastal zone.

Theme parks and similar visitor attractions now account for over 330 million visitors annually and provide half a million jobs. Although its antecedents can be found in the amusement parks, seaside piers and fairgrounds of nineteenth century Europe, the theme park is an American invention and has reached its fullest expression in the USA. Old-style amusement parks such as New York's Coney Island found it difficult to compete with other forms of entertainment, and are mainly places for young people to meet, rather than being regarded as suitable destinations for family outings. Theme parks fulfil this function, and differ from the old-style amusement parks in the following ways:

- Development is planned around a single theme, with the rides, shows, shopping and catering facilities promoted as a co-ordinated set of attractions.
- Location is all-important – they are market-oriented attractions. Theme parks are built between major cities and near motorway interchanges so that as large a population as possible lives within a 160 kilometre radius.
- There is an all-inclusive admission charge.
- Theme parks are imaginatively landscaped. Millions of dollars are spent on maintenance, upgrading facilities, and on new rides and shows using the latest technology.
- Theme parks are staffed by young people who are well-motivated and trained to provide a high standard of service.

Theme parks require massive capital investment and are therefore owned by large corporations with interests in television, the film industry, or – in the case of Busch Gardens, Florida – a major brewing company. The Disney theme parks are world-class destinations in their own right, and Walt Disney must certainly be regarded as one of the greatest innovators in leisure and tourism. In 1955 he opened his first theme park – Disneyland – at Anaheim, near Los Angeles on a 60 hectare site developed around five themed areas. Disneyland's success encouraged a sprawl of development in its vicinity. To avoid a repetition, the second theme park – Walt Disney World (WDW) – was constructed on 1,000 hectares of swampland in central Florida, over which Disney had complete planning control. It is a self-contained destination with its own transport system, hotels, and facilities for a wide range of outdoor activities. Disney theme parks aim to insulate the visitor from the world of reality by means of:

- the Disney corporate ethos; staff are known as 'cast members';
- the concepts of 'imagineering' and 'animatronics', using the cutting edge of technology; and

- a sophisticated infrastructure, that is concealed from the visitor, and the use of non-polluting transport modes within the park.

The Disney theme parks provide a clean, safe and wholesome environment for families, but some would argue that the experience is too sanitised and that too much control is exercised over visitors and staff.

In contrast to the large theme parks such as Six Flags and Disneyland, there are a vast number of small-town attractions, each striving to boost the local economy. Some showcase aspects of the American heritage, notably achievements in sport, industry and entertainment, while others attempt to replicate the cultures of Europe and Asia in the New World. Many of these attractions lack authenticity or an appropriate setting. A number of communities have also re-invented themselves to attract heritage tourism. These include the 'Danish village' of Solvang in California, Nauvoo in Illinois with its Mormon associations, and the Alpine theme town of Helen in Georgia. By the 1960s this former gold mining and lumber town in the Appalachians was in poor shape economically, but thanks to local business initiative, the buildings were remodelled and painted in Bavarian style, while event attractions such as 'Octoberfest' were introduced. As a result, Helen is now the most popular destination in Georgia after Atlanta and Savannah.

Transport

Transport in the USA is highly developed, as you might expect from a nation constantly on the move. The following characteristics are worth emphasising:

- the private car is the dominant transport mode for all types of journeys;
- domestic air services are widely used; and
- public transport, except in some major cities, is poorly developed.

The United States has the highest car ownership in the world, with the number of motor vehicles in some states exceeding the resident population. Well over 80 per cent of holiday trips are taken by car. Although the internal combustion engine was not an American invention, the first car show was held in New York in 1900, and it was largely due to Henry Ford that ownership of an automobile was brought within reach of people on modest incomes. As a result, by 1930 there were 23 million cars registered in the USA, whereas in Europe similar levels were not reached until the late 1950s. Demand from vehicle manufacturers and motorists led to much-needed road improvements, such as the legendary Route 66 from Chicago to Los Angeles. Scenic routes or *parkways*, such as the Skyline Drive in the Blue Ridge Mountains of Virginia, were designed in the 1930s to encourage sightseeing by car. From the late 1950s onwards some of the older highways – including Route 66 – were superseded by the Interstate Highway system, financed very largely by the federal government. This provided a nationwide motorway network – 69,000 kilometres in length – linking most of the major cities, and resulted in a threefold increase in the number of kilometres travelled by car between 1950 and 1980. Motoring in the USA is subject to fewer inconveniences than elsewhere in the world and fuel costs are relatively low. However the American love affair with the car has had an adverse environmental impact, including:

- Pollution – despite strict regulations on motor vehicle emissions. These measures have been rendered less effective by the growth in four-wheel drive sports utility vehicles (SUVs) since the 1990s.

- Visual blight – with large areas given over to parking lots.
- Urban sprawl – which in turn necessitates ever-lengthening journeys to work, shopping and recreational facilities.

Since the early 1990s even cities as wedded to the car as Los Angeles and Miami have realised that road-building alone cannot solve traffic congestion, and they have invested heavily in rapid transit schemes.

Air transport accounts for some 8 per cent of domestic holiday trips, and most medium-sized towns in the USA have an airport within easy reach by car. A growing number of the larger airports serve as international gateways. Airfares are relatively cheap, largely due to competition between the airlines. After 1978, when the civil aviation industry was deregulated, routes were organised on a 'hub and spoke' system, with a few major airports handling the bulk of the traffic. As a result of deregulation many small airlines came into service, but some old-established carriers failed to adjust to the new conditions. The largest casualty was undoubtedly Pan-Am, which had largely pioneered intercontinental air services before the Second World War. The airlines that have clearly emerged as front-runners include *United*, *American*, *Delta*, *and Continental* – while Denver, Chicago, Atlanta and Dallas have developed as major hubs. A large number of regional carriers, often code-sharing with one of the major airlines, provide feeder services.

The Federal Aviation Administration (FAA), the agency responsible for the safety of air travel, came under scrutiny as a result of 9/11. A new agency, the Transport Security Administration (TSA), now oversees airport security. Stricter controls are problematic given the vast scale of air travel in the USA. For example, at noon on a typical day over 6,000 commercial and general aviation aircraft are flying in US airspace. There are also some 8,000 small airports and airfields that are used by charter airlines catering mainly for business executives.

Public transport by road and rail compares unfavourably with the situation in most other developed countries. The major bus company – *Greyhound* – does provide an extensive network of intercity services, as well as inclusive tours and bargain fares for foreign tourists. Nevertheless coach travel (in its British rather than American meaning) accounts for less than 3 per cent of the domestic market and is widely regarded as downmarket. The train provides a more stylish alternative. To a large extent the railways 'made America', but in the 1950s passenger services declined as a result of competition from the airlines and the private car. They might have disappeared altogether from the long distance routes had not the federal government intervened in 1970 with the introduction of Amtrak, a semi-public corporation that operates passenger trains over the network of a dozen private railroad companies. Amtrak has upgraded rolling stock, in some cases introducing double-decker 'superliners' for scenic viewing. Historic routes have been revived, such as the 'Empire Builder' which takes 46 hours to cover the 3,500 kilometres from Chicago to Seattle. The introduction of high-speed trains is inhibited by the cost of upgrading track, some of which dates from the nineteenth century; also much of the network is single-track, with precedence given to freight trains. Amtrak has achieved most success in the densely populated 'north-east corridor' linking Washington with Boston via Baltimore, Philadelphia and New York City. This is by far the most important route, accounting for 50 per cent of Amtrak's revenue, and where *Acela Express* trains compete effectively with the airlines for the lucrative business market. Elsewhere in the USA, train services, where they exist, tend to be infrequent. This situation may change as Americans feel the impact of higher fuel costs, and become more aware of the safety and environmental issues posed by growing congestion on the highways, at airport terminals, and in the airways. For

THE AMERICAS

this reason plans for a second high-speed corridor in California, linking San Diego with San Francisco, are under consideration. Congress has been reluctant to further subsidise Amtrak's investment programme, as politicians are inclined to take the short-term view of reducing public spending.

Accommodation

Americans have long demanded high standards of convenience in their accommodation, resulting in the concept of the hotel in holiday destinations as a 'resort', a self-contained leisure complex. Across North America, the supply of accommodation is closely linked to patterns of transport. In the largest cities hotels are most numerous in the *downtown* areas or CBDs. Elsewhere the distribution tends to be peripheral, with hotels clustering around an airport or located in the commercial strip developments fanning out along the main highways, alongside restaurants and other businesses. The first motels developed in the 1930s as family enterprises offering fairly basic accommodation. From the 1950s, following the example of the *Holiday Inns* chain, the trend was to go more upmarket with facilities such as swimming pools, and toward standardisation of the product in terms of service and décor. Hotels themselves have become increasingly innovative, with such features as the atrium lobby pioneered by Regency Hyatt, and the concept of theming, which is best seen in Las Vegas, to appeal to niche markets. Bed and breakfast in private homes is a growing sector, although it has a more upmarket image than its British counterpart, particularly in New England where much of the accommodation is in restored colonial buildings. Apartments in condominiums, campsites and trailer parks for recreational vehicles are a major part of the accommodation sector.

Organisation

The promotion and development of tourism has generally been weak at the national level of government. This is primarily due to two factors:

- the belief in free enterprise with the minimum of government interference; and
- the division of responsibilities between the federal government in Washington and the state governments.

It was not until 1981 that the United States Travel and Tourism Administration (USTTA) was set up to co-ordinate federal government policies regarding tourism and to promote the country more effectively abroad. The demise of the USTTA meant that the USA entered the new millennium without an overall tourism strategy or tourist information service for the whole country. Following 9/11 the federal government has reappraised the role of tourism. The Office of Travel and Tourism Industries (OTTI) within the Department of Commerce now plays an active role in marketing and formulating policy relating to the sector, while the Tourism Policy Council (TPC) co-ordinates the policies and programmes of a range of federal agencies as far as these affect tourism. The OTTI is assisted in promotion and research by the Travel Industry Association (TIA) representing those involved in the industry.

The states on the other hand do have some kind of official tourism organisation. For the most part these are concerned with marketing, and few have policies on sustainable tourism development. At local level most cities and some counties have a convention and visitors bureau, although these vary considerably in their effectiveness. This situation has led a number of state governments to combine their resources to promote a particular region on the international stage.

The regional distribution of tourism resources

The North-east

The North-eastern states constitute the most densely populated and one of the most visited parts of the country, including the four major gateway cities of Boston, New York, Philadelphia and Washington. The urbanised belt – 'Megalopolis' – extending from Boston to Washington contains over 45 million inhabitants and has excellent transport facilities in the form of road, rail and shuttle air services. In contrast, there are large areas of forested wilderness in the mountains of the northern Appalachians.

New England is probably the most interesting region in the USA from an historical standpoint. In the seventeenth century it was occupied by English settlers who were Puritans seeking freedom to practice their religious beliefs. What came to be known as the 'Yankee' traits of hard work, thrift and ingenuity, and the American belief in their country's 'exceptionalism', were forged in the struggle to wrest a livelihood from a harsh environment of cold winters and infertile soils. This explains the importance in the region's history of fishing, whaling, overseas trade and manufacturing industry. New England played a crucial role in the struggle for independence from British rule in the 1770s, notably the 'Boston Tea Party' and the battle of Lexington. The region has a strong cultural tradition, as shown by the international reputation of its universities – particularly Yale, Harvard and the Massachusetts Institute of Technology – and it has produced many famous writers. Since the mid-nineteenth century New England has become a multi-cultural society as a result of further immigration, particularly from Ireland and Italy.

The rural interior is noted for its forested mountains and picturesque villages of clapboard houses grouped around a wooden church; two of the most visited examples are Sturbridge and Pittsfield in western Massachusetts. Many of the farms have long been abandoned and are now used as weekend or summer retreats by city dwellers. In the fall (autumn) the brilliant foliage displays attract crowds of weekend visitors, particularly to the state of Vermont. During the snowy winters skiing is a major activity, particularly at Bretton Woods and Mount Washington Valley in New Hampshire, and at Stowe in Vermont.

The coast is equally appealing. In the state of Maine it is rugged, deeply indented, and backed by a sparsely populated hinterland of rivers and forests; sailing, fishing and canoeing are popular activities. Further south there are many fine beaches and a number of historic seaports. Tourists are particularly attracted to the following areas:

- The Cape Cod peninsula, with its extensive sand dunes. Summer resorts such as Hyannisport cater for wealthy second-home owners, while ferries connect to the islands of Nantucket and Martha's Vineyard. At Plymouth there is a 'living museum' commemorating the original settlement of the Pilgrim Fathers in 1620.
- Newport, Rhode Island was once the exclusive summer resort for America's millionaires. It is now a major yachting centre and a popular venue for music festivals.
- Salem is mainly visited because of its association with the witch trials of 1692, an example of Puritan intolerance.
- New Bedford and Mystic are historic seaports associated with the nineteenth-century whaling industry.
- Boston is a major North American city that has retained its compact character and mellow brick buildings, although these are often overshadowed by examples of

modern architecture such as Government Center. The 'Freedom Trail' commemorates Boston's role in the American struggle for independence.

The **Middle Atlantic Region** is less easily defined. Even in colonial times it was settled by immigrants from a variety of origins, including English Quakers, Irish Catholics, Dutch, Germans and Scandinavians. The mountainous interior, which forms part of the Appalachians, the beach resorts of Long Island, New Jersey, and the Delmarva Peninsula (Delaware, Maryland and Virginia east of Chesapeake Bay), are mainly visited by domestic tourists. The attractions of most interest to foreign tourists are to be found in the big cities, for example:

- **New York** owes a great deal to its historic role as the major port of entry to the USA, with the advantages of a deepwater harbour and access via the Hudson River to the interior of North America. Until the 1960s the Statue of Liberty was, for most immigrants and visitors, their first sight of the New World. It is the largest city of North America, with over 15 million people living in the metropolitan area. The terrorist attacks of 9/11 on the World Trade Center have highlighted its importance as one of the world's top ten destinations. Tourism is of major importance to the city's economy, generating about 31 billion dollars in revenue and supporting 300,000 jobs. Although it is not an administrative capital, New York is the nation's primary city in almost every other respect. It is for example, the USA's leading financial centre and conference venue, and also a major centre for fashion and the arts. New York City boasts world-class cultural attractions such as the Metropolitan Opera House and Carnegie Hall, while the Madison Square Garden, Shea Stadium and Flushing Meadows are among the country's top sport venues. New York has an international role as the seat of the United Nations Assembly, but transactions in Wall Street have an even greater impact on the global economy.

- **Philadelphia,** the fourth largest city in the United States, is regarded as the birthplace of the nation, witnessing the Declaration of Independence (1776) and the ratification of the US Constitution (1788). Independence Hall, The Liberty Bell and Congress Hall are reminders of the early history of America. It is a major sports venue and cultural centre, while Penn's Landing is a maritime heritage attraction.

- **Washington DC** has a unique appeal, as the capital of the United States. It was planned as such at the beginning of the nineteenth century, with wide avenues lined with neo-classical buildings and attractive parks, and a skyline protected by a limit on the height of buildings. The most important feature is the Mall, extending from the Lincoln Memorial to the Capitol housing the American Congress; grouped nearby are other important public buildings such as the White House, the Smithsonian museums, and the National Gallery of Art. The federal government and various international agencies such as the World Bank generate a considerable volume of business travel. The capital is served by three international airports – Reagan National, Dulles International and Washington-Baltimore.

The Northern Appalachians constitute the rural hinterland of the cities of the Eastern Seaboard. They are made up of forested mountain ridges, narrow river valleys and rolling hill country. In parts of West Virginia and Pennsylvania the landscape has been blighted by coal mining and heavy industry, leaving behind polluted rivers. However there are widespread opportunities for field sports, white-water rafting (mainly in West Virginia) and skiing during the winter months.

'Upstate' New York boasts a variety of scenic attractions, providing a contrast to the bustle of New York City. These include the Finger Lakes, and the Adirondack Mountains, which contain extensive wilderness areas as well as Lake Placid, venue for

Photo 23.1 A view from the Appalachian Trail (©istockphoto.com/ Richard Mirro)

the 1980 Winter Olympics. The Catskills have long been popular as a resort area for New Yorkers. The Hudson Valley, with its vineyards, historic mansions and wooded scenery, has been called 'the Rhineland of North America'. Two tourist centres in New York State deserve special mention – Cooperstown, 'the home of baseball' – and Rochester, where George Eastman made photography accessible to a mass market. The state's most famous attraction – although half of it lies in Canada – is Niagara Falls. Since the nineteenth century a variety of facilities has been provided for viewing the spectacle, but some of the development, particularly on the American side, is excessively commercialised and inappropriate for the setting.

Pennsylvania offers the Pocono and Allegheny Mountains, the Civil War battle-field of Gettysburg, and Lancaster County, famous for its Amish communities of German origin who have rejected technological progress. The Amish have accepted tourism on their own terms, but it nevertheless poses a threat to their traditional way of life.

The coastal resorts. These include the Hamptons on Long Island, Atlantic City and Cape May in New Jersey, and Ocean City in Maryland. Although some resorts aimed for exclusivity, Atlantic City in particular was the creation of the railroad and developed to meet the needs of the growing numbers of industrial workers, the main focus being the elevated *boardwalk* (promenade) along the beach. In the 1920s the resort achieved fame for its event attractions, such as the Miss America beauty pageant. After the Second World War fashions changed as alternative destinations such as Florida became more accessible, and Atlantic City entered a long period of stagnation. The resort's fortunes revived in the late 1970s, following the decision of the state government to legalise gambling. Its casinos now attract more visitors than those of Las Vegas, although their length of stay tends to be much shorter.

The South

The South is the most distinctive region of the USA, although its boundaries are difficult to define. Many regard the Ohio River and the Mason-Dixon Line separating Virginia from Pennsylvania as the northern limit. We can regard the South as having these features:

- a climate characterised by long sultry summers, short mild winters and abundant rainfall;
- the importance given by Southerners to the American Civil War (1861–1865), in which the Confederacy, made up of eleven slave-holding states was defeated in its attempts to secede from the USA;
- the presence of a large Black minority, who for a century after the Civil War continued to suffer from many forms of discrimination;
- a lifestyle which is more traditional, family-orientated, and religion-based than other regions of the USA (the strength of fundamentalist Christianity explains the use of the term 'Bible Belt' for much of the region) and
- An economy in which areas of dynamic growth and prosperity – the so-called 'New South' – contrast with pockets of rural poverty.

The heritage of the period before the Civil War, often highly romanticised, is an important part of the South's appeal for tourists, usually focusing on the plantation houses of the former slave-owners. Of wider significance is the contribution the region has made to literature and popular music, including jazz, country and western, rhythm and blues, gospel etc. The South is also well endowed with recreational resources which include:

- Large areas of forest, particularly in the Southern Appalachians.
- The wetlands of the coastal plains, such as the Okefonokee Swamp in southern Georgia, and the *bayous* of the Mississippi Delta, that provide a unique refuge for wildlife.
- A number of large man-made lakes providing facilities for water sports. These are a legacy of the hydro-electric power projects of the Tennessee Valley Authority (TVA). This was a federal government agency set up to boost the region's economy, as part of President Franklin D. Roosevelt's New Deal in the 1930s.
- The abundance of golf courses, particularly in the hilly, well-wooded Piedmont zone between the Appalachians and the coastal plains. Pinehurst in North Carolina and Augusta in Georgia are the most popular golfing resorts.
- The barrier islands of the Atlantic and Gulf coasts provide many fine beaches. Some have been developed as resorts – Hilton Head Island is one example – while others such as Cape Hatteras and Cumberland Island are preserved from development by federal and state governments.

We can divide the South for tourism purposes into a number of sub-regions, starting with Virginia.

Virginia was the first English colony in the New World. It played a major role in the struggle for independence – George Washington and Thomas Jefferson were both Virginians. During the American Civil War, Richmond, less than 200 kilometres from Washington DC, was the capital of the Confederacy. Not surprisingly, heritage attractions play an important role. They include:

- George Washington's home at Mount Vernon.
- The Civil War battlefield site at Fredericksburg.
- 'The Historic Triangle', consisting of Jamestown – site of the first English settlement; Yorktown and Williamsburg, the capital of Virginia in colonial times. Of these Williamsburg is the most popular, and it has become a role model for similar attractions in other countries, due to its meticulous attention to detail.

- The western part of the state includes the scenic Blue Ridge Mountains and the Shenandoah Valley National Park. All these attractions are within easy reach of Washington.

The South-east consists of Georgia and the Carolinas, states which have shown remarkable economic growth since the 1950s.

Atlanta is the main conference venue of the South-east with its modern hotels and excellent communications. As a major hub its airport has overtaken Chicago in terms of domestic traffic and is growing in importance as an international gateway – one of the main reasons it was chosen as the venue for the 1996 Olympics. As a major centre for finance and broadcasting, Atlanta is a symbol of the 'New South'. The city also has important associations with Martin Luther King and the Civil Rights movement of the 1960s. Other attractions include 'Underground Atlanta' – a project to revive the decaying inner city; the 'World of Coca Cola' museum celebrating the city's best-known product; and Stone Mountain – reputedly the world's largest granite monolith.

The seaports of Savannah and Charleston have based their tourism industries on the heritage of the Old South. Charleston attracts a large number of foreign as well as domestic tourists to its well-preserved *'ante-bellum'* (pre-Civil War) mansions, with garden tours being especially popular. Strict zoning regulations ensure that the tourist facilities are kept separate from the historic district of Old Charleston.

The Southern Appalachians, a series of forest covered ranges separated by deep valleys, rise to the north of Georgia and to the west of North Carolina, accounting for most of Tennessee and Kentucky. In the more remote mountain valleys the persistence of craft industries is a legacy of the old pioneering days. Gatlinburg and Cherokee, on the fringes of the much-visited Smoky Mountains National Park, are examples of rural communities that have exploited this heritage. To the west of the mountains lie the fertile Nashville Basin and the 'Bluegrass Country' of Kentucky – an area noted for its bourbon distilleries and equestrian sports. Kentucky also boasts the world's most extensive cave system in the Mammoth Cave National Park. In Tennessee, Nashville and Memphis rank among the most important tourist centres in the South:

- Nashville is widely regarded as the 'capital' of the country and western music industry. This is showcased in the Grand Ole Opry auditorium and a number of theme parks in the area, but many find that the clubs and bars in 'Music Row' provide a more authentic experience.
- Memphis is particularly rich in musical traditions, focusing on the historic district of Beale Street, known as the 'birthplace of the blues'. However the most popular attraction is undoubtedly Graceland, visited by Elvis Presley fans from all over the world.

The Deep South usually refers to the states of Alabama, Mississippi and Louisiana, where Southern traditions are strongest. Tourism is of particular importance to Louisiana, where the economy has been affected by the fall in oil prices. This state is renowned for the spicy cuisine associated with its Creole and Cajun communities, and the cultural heritage of French and Spanish rule.

New Orleans is a major port on the Mississippi River, and prior to the *Hurricane Katrina* disaster in 2005, ranked among the five most popular cities visited by foreign and well as American tourists. Much of the city lies below river level, and is protected by high artificial banks or *levees*. Tourists are mainly attracted to the historic core of the city, known as the Vieux Carré or the French Quarter, focused on Bourbon Street and St Louis Cathedral. New Orleans has a long-established reputation for entertainment and gambling, but its tourism industry is also firmly based on conventions and sporting events. The city's fame as the birthplace of jazz appeals to many tourists, and the annual Mardi Gras carnival is one of the USA's most popular event attractions. The Mississippi's historical role as a major transport artery is recalled in the sternwheeler steamboats that are now used for short river cruises.

Other tourist centres include Lafayette for visiting 'Cajun country', Natchez, famed for its pre-Civil War plantation houses, and the beach resorts of Gulfport and Biloxi, which were severely damaged by the *Katrina* disaster. In 2010 the BP oil spill in the Gulf of Mexico had a serious impact on the shrimp fishing industry and marine wildlife generally.

The **Ozarks** in Arkansas and southern Missouri are similar in many respects to the Appalachians. Tourism centres on the spa resort of Hot Springs and the small town of Branson, which boasts no less than 40 theatres featuring big-name performers in the music industry. This success is difficult to explain in resource terms, but it is clearly demand-led, with most of the 7 million annual visitors arriving from other parts of the South and the Mid-West.

Florida

Although the northern part of the state – particularly the 'Panhandle' west of Tallahassee – is typically 'Southern', most of Florida is quite different from the rest of the South, in the following ways:

* its tourism industry is on a larger scale, with a constant flow of visitors all year round;
* retired people from the northern states make up a high percentage of its population; and
* the influx of Cuban immigrants to southern Florida since 1960 has made Miami a largely Spanish speaking city and effectively the financial centre of Latin America.

Florida is among the world's leading holiday destinations, with an annual income from tourism exceeding Spain's receipts from its foreign visitors. Orlando alone receives over 50 million visitors a year as the world's 'theme park capital'. At the beginning of the twentieth century Florida was largely wilderness, one of the least developed and most sparsely populated regions of the USA. Tourism was to change all that, along with the development of large-scale agriculture, and the aerospace industry after the Second World War. The population grew from 2.7 million in 1950 to over 18 million in 2010. This growth has put enormous pressure on the water resources and fragile ecosystems of the Florida Peninsula, which is low-lying and of limestone formation.

The great majority of Florida's visitors are Americans, mainly from the states east of the Mississippi, and Canadians. Overseas tourists come mainly from Latin American countries and from Western Europe, where the UK is the leading market for air-inclusive holidays. Florida's success can be attributed to its subtropical climate, a coastline of white sandy beaches, and not least, to a major investment by the private sector in sports facilities, theme parks and other man-made attractions. Florida is readily accessible, with domestic air services to all parts of the USA and three international airports – Miami, Orlando and Tampa. The main east coast highway (US 1) brings the Atlantic coast resorts within the reach of the family motorist living in the cities of the Eastern Seaboard.

Florida originated as a winter destination for wealthy Americans in the 1890s, with the opening of hotels in the old Spanish town of St Augustine. By the 1920s, with the extension of the railroad, Palm Beach (catering exclusively for the wealthy) and Miami Beach (for those a little less affluent) had been established on barrier islands off the Atlantic Coast. Since the 1950s, with the vast improvement in road and air transport, Florida has broadened its appeal to become a summer destination within reach of the majority of Americans. However the southern third of the state has retained its image as a winter haven for Northerners and Canadians, and this is reflected in lower hotel prices during the summer months. Large numbers of foreign visitors have invested in holiday and retirement homes.

The city of Miami – as distinct from Miami Beach – is primarily a business centre with a population of over 3 million. Miami Airport is the major gateway to the Caribbean islands and the countries of Central and South America, while the port of Miami is the base for most Caribbean cruises.

In the south-east of Florida a string of resorts have developed, including:

- Fort Lauderdale, known as the 'Venice of Florida', with its extensive marina facilities. During the spring vacation the resort has long hosted an influx of fun-seeking college students, but fashions change, and this market is now more widely dispersed.
- Miami Beach with its concentration of high-rise accommodation suffered from a period of stagnation in the 1960s and 1970s with an ageing clientele and falling property values. It has since restored its Art Deco hotels, reclaimed its beachfront and re-invented its image as a centre of fashion.
- The Florida Keys – a chain of coral islands to the south of Miami – provide ideal opportunities for scuba diving. Key West, with its Hemingway associations, is the most developed tourist centre.

The development of tourism on such a large scale has created problems. Many hotels and condominiums have been built so close to the sea that the beaches have been badly eroded, while a great deal of the best recreational land has been bought up as sites for private homes. The demand for water by large-scale agriculture and the residents of Greater Miami has endangered the unique wetland ecosystem of the Everglades.

The south-west of Florida along the Gulf coast is much less developed, with the exception of the Tampa Bay area. The most important resorts are St Petersburg – one of America's largest retirement centres – Sarasota, and Clearwater, each catering for different markets. Further south, Naples and Fort Myers provide less expensive self-catering accommodation.

The beaches of the northern Gulf coast cater for summer visitors from Alabama and Georgia rather than foreign tourists, with Panama City Beach being the clear favourite. Another important recreational resource in this part of Florida is the hundreds of crystal-clear freshwater springs underlying the surface. Some of these have been developed as secondary attractions, a notable example being Weeki Wachee Springs with its 'mermaid show'.

Central Florida is the fastest growing tourism area, thanks largely to the success of Disneyworld since its opening in 1971. In 2007 this theme park complex was estimated to receive over 45 million visitors – a world record for any attraction. The success of Disneyworld has encouraged other leisure projects. The main impact has been on Orlando – a medium-sized town noted only for its citrus industry prior to 1971, but now an international gateway. The other major attraction in Central Florida is the NASA space research centre at Cape Canaveral.

The Mid-West

In marked contrast to Florida, this region, with its cold winters and hot humid summers is a tourist-generating area and a zone of passage rather than a destination. Lying to the west of the Appalachians and south of the Great Lakes, the Mid-West is one of the world's most productive agricultural areas. From the air, the landscape from Iowa to Ohio appears like a huge chessboard, with fields, roads and settlements laid out on a regular grid pattern. Further north in Wisconsin, Minnesota and Michigan, the scenery is much more diverse with innumerable lakes and landforms resulting from past glaciation, and large areas of forest. The Great Lakes themselves are a major attraction; there are fine beaches along the southern shores of Lakes Michigan and Huron, while Lake Superior, the largest and deepest, has a shoreline of spectacular cliffs. Nevertheless, the lakes, which contain 20 per cent of the world's freshwater, have been damaged by pollution, and this is being addressed by a water quality agreement between the US and Canadian governments. The state of Michigan has a well-established tourism industry based on its lake and forest resources. The resorts cater mainly for the demand from the region's cities, notable examples being Lake Geneva 30 kilometres from Chicago and Kensington, which serves Detroit. In winter large areas of northern Minnesota and northern Wisconsin are set aside for snowmobile trails, while Upper Michigan provides facilities for skiing.

Some of the cities of the Mid-West are important cultural as well as business centres:

- Detroit in the 1950s was the world's leading city for motor vehicle manufacturing, but it suffered severely from the recession in the 1980s and 'white flight' to the suburbs. This city is now a byword for urban decline, with large areas of dereliction and a population that has halved since its boom years. At nearby Dearborn, Henry Ford revolutionised transport and tourism with the Model T, and later founded Greenfield Village as an open-air museum of small-town America prior to the advent of the automobile.
- Cleveland offers the Rock and Roll Hall of Fame, mainly because this industrial city provides some of the largest audiences for this type of music; an example of an attraction based on demand.
- Chicago can claim to be the transportation centre of the USA and is its second largest city. O'Hare Airport is one of the world's busiest, the city is a major rail terminal, and despite its distance from the sea it is also a port – thanks to the St Lawrence Seaway. Chicago is renowned for its architectural achievements, particularly those associated with Frank Lloyd Wright and Mies Van de Rohe. Its many cultural attractions include the Museum of Science and Industry and the Art Institute. As a commercial centre it has excellent facilities for conventions and trade fairs. The city is also a major sports venue and its recreational facilities include 24 kilometres of public beaches, yacht marinas and parks along the shores of Lake Michigan. The popular perception of Chicago however owes more to its reputation for gangsterism in the Prohibition era of the 1920s and early 1930s, an image which the city has tended to downplay although it appeals to many visitors.
- Indianapolis boasts the Motor Speedway stadium, where the world's oldest and largest motor racing event takes place.
- Dayton, Ohio is famous in aviation history as the home town of the Wright brothers.
- St Louis historically played a major role in the nation's westward expansion, which is commemorated by the iconic Gateway Arch monument, and has an interesting musical heritage.

The West

The West is defined by American geographers as the part of the USA lying beyond the 100th meridian, where the climate becomes too dry in most years to support arable farming and ranching is more significant. Most of this vast region is sparsely populated and its appeal for tourism is based on the 'great outdoors', and the heritage of the frontier. This has been evoked in countless 'western' movies, which have also made the extraordinary landscapes of the region familiar to millions. The West also contains the great majority of the Indian reservations – tribal lands set aside by treaty with the federal government – where the Native American way of life continues to flourish. Indian handicrafts are much in demand, and Indian traditions have influenced white Americans seeking alternative, more holistic lifestyles. Tourist accommodation is available on some reservations, while a few Indian nations have taken advantage of their special status in relation to federal and state law to open gambling casinos. On the other hand tourism may prove to be a threat as well as an opportunity to communities already under pressure, with levels of unemployment and alcohol abuse well above the national average.

Tourism ranks as the most important employer in four western states – Colorado, Nevada, New Mexico and Wyoming – and is in second place in five others. Because of its extent we need to divide the West into a number of sub-regions as follows.

The **High Plains** stretching from Oklahoma to North Dakota. This was the setting of the 'dustbowl' of the 1930's and is often afflicted by extreme weather events such as tornadoes. It is for the most part relatively featureless. One major exception is the granite Black Hills of South Dakota that rise abruptly from the surrounding prairies. The famous sculptures of Mount Rushmore are located in this area, along with the Crazy Horse Memorial commemorating the Indian resistance led by the Sioux chief of that name. Another tourist attraction is the former mining town of Deadwood – notorious in 'Wild West' mythology. Further south in Nebraska the Scotts Bluff National Monument was one of the landmarks on the trail of the covered wagons that carried millions of pioneers westward during the nineteenth century.

The **Rocky Mountains** form a barrier 2,000 kilometres in length, 500 kilometres wide, and reach a height of 4,000 metres. They are in fact a series of ranges separated by a number of enclosed basins. Winters provide dry 'powder' snow for skiing in the mountains of Idaho – where Sun Valley was developed in the 1930s – and in Colorado, where Aspen, Vail and other resorts became established in the 1950s. These are easily reached from the gateway city of Denver. Aspen in particular has a fashionable reputation and hosts an all-year programme of cultural events. Wyoming boasts two world-class national parks – the Tetons with their glaciated landscapes, and the better-known Yellowstone which contains many remarkable geothermal features. A touring circuit 237 kilometres in length provides access to the popular sites – the Yellowstone Falls, Mammoth Hot Springs, and Old Faithful – the most famous of the 200 or so geysers. These parks also provide a refuge for wildlife, notably bears, buffalo, antelope, elk and beaver. The National Parks Service has aroused controversy by introducing wolves to Yellowstone, and using controlled forest fires to create a more balanced ecosystem. Further to the north, Montana is less visited. It contains a number of old mining towns, forests and ranchlands, and the lake and mountain scenery of the Glacier National Park.

The **South-west** is distinguished by its cultural heritage as well as its climates and scenery. The whole of this region, along with Texas and California was once part of the Spanish Empire and later Mexico, before its acquisition by the United States in 1848. Most of the South-west is desert 'basin and range' country with a sparse cover of sage brush and mesquite vegetation, or consists of high plateaus dissected by deep gorges or canyons. The tourist appeal of the region is based on these features:

- The warm, dry, sunny climate that has long attracted winter visitors and a growing number of retired people to cities such as Phoenix and Tucson. Health tourism is particularly important in Arizona with its many spa facilities.
- The facilities for water-based recreation, unusual in a desert region, in Lakes Powell, Mead and Havasu. These lakes were created by the damming of the Colorado River in the 1930s for power generation and irrigation projects.
- *Dude ranches* providing the tourist with accommodation, riding expeditions, and the opportunity to sample the cowboy lifestyle. Many communities also hold rodeos, where professionals display the horsemanship and other traditional skills associated with cattle ranching.
- A wealth of scenic attractions, including the Grand Canyon, Monument Valley – a much photographed group of *mesas* (flat topped landforms formed by erosion) and the lesser-known Bryce and Zion Canyons in Utah.
- The Native American heritage. Archaeological excavations at Canyon de Chelly and the Mesa Verde National Park provide evidence of an advanced Indian culture centuries before the arrival of the Spanish missionaries and colonizers. The contrasts between the Hopi and Navajo illustrate the diversity of Native American culture today. The Navajo's lifestyle is semi-nomadic, based on stock-raising, and their reservation occupies an area the size of Belgium. The Hopi live in *pueblos*, permanent farming communities where religious ceremonial continues to play an essential role. To respect these traditions, tourism needs to be carefully managed.
- The heritage of the 'Wild West'. In the late nineteenth century the region's rich mineral resources supported thriving mining communities, which have now become 'ghost towns'. Some of these have been restored, notably Tombstone in Arizona, scene of the shoot-out at the OK Corral.

Case study 23.1

The Grand Canyon

Over millions of years the Colorado River has carved its way through many layers of sedimentary rocks to create one of the world's most spectacular features – the Grand Canyon. It is almost 2,000 metres deep, 300 kilometres in length and on average 25 kilometres wide, and is distinguished from the surrounding plateaus by the colour of its redwall limestone cliffs. The North Rim of the canyon at an altitude of 2,700 metres has a climate not unlike that of Scandinavia, with forests of pine, spruce and aspen covering this part of the Colorado Plateau. In contrast the canyon floor is characterised by extreme summer heat and an annual rainfall of less than 20 centimetres, which can support only sparse desert scrub.

Although the Canyon had been 'discovered' by the Spanish over three centuries earlier, it was not systematically explored until 1869. Recognition of its unique character led to its designation as a National Monument by President Theodore Roosevelt in 1902, followed by national park status in 1919. In the meantime the Topeka & Santa Fe Railroad had made the area more accessible, opening a spur line from the town of Flagstaff to the South Rim of the canyon, where several resort hotels were built for wealthy tourists. The 1950s saw a massive increase in the numbers of tourists arriving by car, which resulted in the closure of the Grand Canyon Railway in 1968. It has since been revived, this time as a tourist attraction in its own right.

The vast majority of the Canyon's 4.5 million annual visitors are based in Las Vegas and Phoenix and spend only a few hours at vantage points on the South Rim. Flight-seeing tours give some idea of the immensity of the Canyon, but for a true appreciation it needs to be explored on foot or by mule, camping overnight. Another alternative is to follow the example of the explorer John Wesley Powell, by participating in one of the white-water rafting expeditions on the River Colorado that are organised by tour operators.

Substantial areas of the Grand Canyon lie outside the boundaries of the National Park, and belong to the reservations of the Havasupai and Haalapai. As full owners of the land, these Native American tribes are not subject to the same regulations as the National Park Service as regards 'flightseeing' tours and the operation of boats and rafts on the Colorado River. For this reason the Haalapai were able to go ahead with the controversial 'Skywalk' project that allows sightseers an uninterrupted view of the canyon floor 1,200 metres below. The Haalapai see this as an economic opportunity for their isolated community, but the skywalk has been strongly criticised, not only by conservationists, but also by other Native American groups.

In class, debate the issues involved in the Skywalk project. What activities and facilities, in your view, are appropriate to the Grand Canyon, given its unique character?

Tourism in **Nevada** is a special case, thanks to this state's liberal attitudes to marriage and divorce and above all to gambling, which elsewhere in the USA was illegal for most of the twentieth century. The sex industry also flourishes, legally in most of the state, where it is tightly regulated, and illegally in Las Vegas; as a result most of the proceeds go to organised crime rather than generating revenue for the city government. However the legalisation of prostitution is opposed by religious groups and the convention industry, which accounts for a quarter of the city's income.

Despite its desert location, Las Vegas has developed rapidly since the 1940s, sustained by power generated from the Hoover Dam on the Colorado River. Its airport – McCarran International – is linked to all major cities in the USA and a growing number of foreign countries. It is now a city with over half a million inhabitants and one of the world's top tourist destinations, attracting around 35 million visitors a year, of whom 15 per cent are foreign tourists. It can offer 140,000 hotel rooms, almost twice the capacity of New York City. Activity is centred on the Strip, a 6 kilometre-long boulevard flanked by casinos and large hotels. The enormous revenues from the casinos have made Las Vegas the 'world's entertainment capital', offering 'the total leisure experience'. Since the 1990s Americans have been able to gamble in many places outside Nevada. In response, the city has invested on a major scale in theme parks, shopping malls and museums, while also going upmarket with luxury hotels and golf courses.

Arguably, Las Vegas represents the tourism of the future, in which themed attractions provide a simulated, risk-free substitute for a real destination or an imagined past. The first themed hotel was Caesar's Palace in the 1960s, based on Ancient Rome (as interpreted by Hollywood). Since then, advances in technology have made it possible to replicate a volcanic eruption (The Mirage); a naval battle (Treasure Island); Arthurian legend (Excalibur); and a foreign destination (such as Venice).

Two other tourist centres in the South-west deserve specific mention, both very different in character from Las Vegas:

* Santa Fe is the historic capital of New Mexico, with a well-preserved Spanish-Indian heritage of adobe buildings and traditional handicrafts. Large numbers of artists have been attracted to the city and nearby Indian communities such as Taos.
* Salt Lake City is both a business and religious centre, where the Church of Latter Day Saints (Mormon Church) plays a dominant role. As a consequence, in most of Utah alcohol is prohibited. Visitors are attracted to the Mormon Tabernacle and the Family History Library, which contains the world's largest collection of genealogical records. The Wasatch Mountains provide first class ski facilities, largely explaining why Salt Lake City was chosen as the venue for the 2002 Winter Olympics. The Great Salt Lake has been used for attempts on the world land speed record.

Texas

For historical reasons, the 'Lone Star State' is as much part of the South as it is of the West, while its closeness to Mexico is reflected in its food, architecture and music. Texas has a booming economy that has generated a considerable volume of business travel to its major cities. Dallas is a major financial and distribution centre, while the neighbouring city of Fort Worth takes pride in its cattle industry heritage. Houston is noted for its oil and aerospace industries, where the major attractions are the Space Center, the Astrodome – the world's largest covered sports facility – and the Astroworld theme park. The fine beaches of the Gulf coast are within easy reach, notably those of Galveston and Padre Island. Other tourist centres include Austin, the state capital with an important music-recording industry, and San Antonio which celebrates its 'Latin' traditions. This city's best known tourist attraction is the Alamo, the old Spanish mission that played a major role in the Texan struggle for independence from Mexico, and which is presented as a site of 'Anglo' rather than Latino heritage. The Paseo del Rio (Riverwalk) is a fine example of a major event attraction – the 1968 Hemisfair Spanish American Exposition – providing the impetus for inner city regeneration.

California and the Far West

The West Coast, particularly California, is much more populated, cosmopolitan and dynamic in its outlook than the interior. It faces the other countries of the Pacific Rim and is at the cutting edge of the new technology – 'Silicon Valley' around San Jose and the Boeing plant outside Seattle are just two examples. Since 1849, when gold was discovered near Sacramento, Americans have regarded California as the land of opportunity. It has long been the richest state, with a population that is extraordinarily mobile even by American standards. The 'Golden State' is renowned for its warm, sunny climate and the remarkable variety of its scenery. This includes lush farmlands, forests of giant redwood and sequoia, strange volcanic landforms, and the high peaks of the Sierra Nevada – contrasting dramatically with Death Valley, one of the lowest, driest and hottest locations on Earth. All these, and a wealth of man-made attractions, explain why California is the primary holiday destination for Americans, and one of the most popular states for foreign tourists. However, tourism is less important to the Californian economy than the engineering industries and agriculture, unlike the situation in Florida, where tourism is the main source of income.

There are important differences in climate between the Pacific coast, which is cooled by the California Current, and the Central Valley east of the Coast Ranges where summer temperatures frequently exceed 40°C. Northern California also has a generally cooler and wetter climate than the south, where conditions are ideal for outdoor

THE AMERICAS

recreation. Nevertheless California has its share of environmental problems. These include:

- the earthquakes associated with the San Andreas Fault and other lines of weakness in the Earth's crust – these destroyed San Francisco in 1906 and threatened Los Angeles in 1998;
- the devastating fires that occur in summer in the dry *chaparral* scrub, and the equally destructive floods and landslides affecting slopes cleared for development;
- the severe air pollution in Los Angeles which occupies a valley hemmed in by mountains; and
- the demands for water that may not be sustainable in the long term.

Tourism in California is mainly concentrated in the following areas.

- **Los Angeles**. 'LA' is not so much a city as a sprawling conurbation covering an area of 2,000 square kilometres and consisting of no less that 82 separate local authorities and many ethnic communities. It is held together by the most extensive freeway network in the USA, and the automobile is the only practical way of visiting the dispersed attractions. Los Angeles has grown to prominence on the basis successively of the citrus industry, oil, motion pictures, aerospace and music recording. The city's tourism industry was given a major boost by the 1984 Olympic Games. With the San Bernardino Mountains and the Mojave Desert at its backdoor, and with an extensive shoreline along the Pacific, Los Angeles offers a wide range of recreational opportunities. The beach resorts of Santa Monica and Venice Beach have been trend-setters in leisure fashions, epitomising the Californian obsession with youth and physical fitness. Southern California can claim to be the birthplace of the American theme park, the best known being Disneyland, but in this respect it now suffers by comparison with Florida. The glamorous image of Hollywood is a major draw for visitors, and some of the film studios have been transformed into tourist attractions. Even the desert interior has been affected by tourism by its closeness to Los Angeles, and in some areas trail bikes and 'dune buggies' have had a severe environmental impact. One of the most important resorts of Southern California is Palm Springs, an oasis of golf courses in the midst of the Mojave Desert.
- **San Francisco**. The 'City on the Bay' is very different from Los Angeles. It is relatively compact, with a good public transport system, and is widely regarded as the most scenic and 'European' of all North American cities. San Francisco has also acquired a reputation for tolerance of lifestyles that do not conform to the mainstream culture; it played a prominent role in the 'hippy' movement of the 1960s, centred on the district of Haight-Ashbury, and it has attracted a large gay community. The city developed after the 1849 Gold Rush as a major seaport on one of the world's finest natural harbours. Much of the waterfront is now devoted to tourism, restaurants and entertainment, notably at Fisherman's Wharf. Other major attractions include the largest Chinese community in North America, the famous 'cable cars' (actually nineteenth century trams), a flourishing theatre and arts scene, and the Golden Gate Bridge spanning the entrance to the harbour. The cold current offshore deterred would-be escapers from the former prison on Alcatraz Island, and results in San Francisco having the lowest summer temperatures of any major city in the USA, often accompanied by coastal fog.

Within easy reach of San Francisco are:

- the exclusive beach resorts of Carmel and Monterey;
- the wine producing area of the Napa Valley, including the spa town of Calistoga;

- the ski resorts around Lake Tahoe and the Sierra Nevada mountains;
- the Yosemite National Park with its spectacular waterfalls and sheer granite cliffs (Yosemite Valley is crammed to capacity at summer weekends), and
- the redwood forests to the north of San Francisco, reached by a scenic coastal highway.
- **San Diego** is the third gateway city to California, lying close to the Mexican border. The city is primarily a naval port, but visitors are attracted by an ideal climate and the excellent beaches such as those of La Jolla, with facilities for sailing and sport fishing.
- **Santa Barbara** deserves special mention, out of the many beach resorts of Southern California, for its attractive Spanish-style architecture. The city originated – like so many others in California – as a Spanish mission. However its buildings are not relics from colonial times but the result of a deliberate planning initiative following an earthquake in 1925.

The North-west

The other states of the Far West – Oregon and Washington – have been less affected by tourism. In fact the environmentally-conscious state government of Oregon has severely limited development along its coastline. The unspoiled national scenery provides the main appeal for tourists. Outstanding attractions include:

- Crater Lake, a perfect example of a volcanic caldera;
- the Olympic National Park, an area of heavy rainfall that supports dense temperate rain forests; and
- the Mount Rainier National Park, which boasts large numbers of glaciers, lakes and waterfalls. This forms part of the Cascades Range, which includes a number of active volcanoes such as Mount St Helens.

Portland and Seattle are the gateway cities to the North-west. Seattle has the advantage of an attractive coastal setting. One of its main landmarks is the Space Needle, erected for the 1962 World Fair. Seattle is also the main gateway to Alaska for visitors by sea.

Alaska

As much of Alaska lies within the Arctic Circle, it is climatically distinct from the rest of the USA and is isolated from the 'lower 48' states by some of Canada's most difficult mountain terrain. Only the narrow Bering Strait – ice covered in winter – separates it from Siberia on the other side of the International Date Line. In fact Alaska was purchased from the Tsar of Russia in 1867, and the Orthodox cathedral in Sitka is one of a number of sites that evoke the Russian heritage. To most Americans, Alaska is the 'last frontier' – a wilderness image that has persisted since the 1898 Gold Rush. The gruelling Iditarod dog sled rally from Anchorage to Nome is an annual reminder of those pioneering days. Nowadays air transport is crucial to this sparsely settled state, and Alaska's main external links are also by air. Its major city, Anchorage, lies on the trans-polar route from Europe to Japan. However there are alternative ways of reaching Alaska, namely:

- the Alcan Highway, over 2,000 kilometres in length, was constructed during the Second World War from Edmonton to Fairbanks, and remains the only practical overland route from Canada; and
- the Alaska Marine Highway System operates ferry services linking Prince Rupert in British Columbia to the coastal communities of southern Alaska, including Juneau, the state capital, which is not accessible by road or rail.

THE AMERICAS

In most of Alaska the climate is a major constraint on tourism development. The south-east of Alaska has the greatest tourism potential, offering spectacular fjords, rugged mountain scenery, and some of the largest glaciers in the Northern Hemisphere. The climate here is relatively mild but excessively rainy. A sheltered coastal waterway – the Inside Passage – provides a route for summer cruises operating out of Long Beach, San Francisco and Seattle. However the rapid expansion of cruise tourism, now over one million arrivals a year, has brought problems to the small coastal communities in the form of overcrowding, intrusive sightseeing by passengers and marine pollution – a sensitive issue since the 1989 *Exxon Valdez* oil spill disaster. Ports that respond by levying higher passenger taxes risk alienating the powerful cruise operators based in Miami.

Elsewhere in Alaska ecotourism and adventure tourism are growing in popularity, bringing some economic benefit to the native Indian, Aleut and Inupiat (Eskimo) communities. On the other hand the growing energy crisis has led to renewed demands to exploit wilderness areas for their mineral resources. One high-profile example is the Arctic National Wildlife Refuge, a tundra wilderness which is under threat from proposals to expand the oil industry already well established at Prudhoe Bay. These are supported by the Inupiat, but not by the neighbouring Indian community whose traditional way of life is based on the caribou. With less than a million people inhabiting an area the size of western Europe, the majority of Alaskans are not opposed to development, and some resent what they see as interference by environmentalists from the 'lower 48'.

The Denali National Park – boasting Mount McKinley, North America's highest summit – is already experiencing visitor pressure despite its rigorous sub-arctic climate and lack of tourist facilities. Denali can be accessed by road and rail from Anchorage, whereas other natural attractions, such as the volcanic landscapes of Katmai National Park, are even more remote, and as a result, much less visited.

Hawaii

The location of the Hawaiian Islands in mid-Pacific, 4,000 kilometres south-west of California, sets them apart from the rest of the USA as a destination. Hawaii received nearly 6.5 million visitors in 2009, of whom two-thirds are Americans from the mainland. The Japanese market is much smaller in volume but highly significant in terms of visitor spend. Hawaii has become one of the world's best known holiday destinations on the basis of the climate, superb volcanic scenery and surfing beaches of the islands, and their Polynesian heritage, romanticised by the Hollywood film industry. These resources have become accessible to the North American mass market through cheap domestic air fares and competitive tour pricing.

Oahu is the most visited of the islands, and most of the tourism development has been concentrated there. It contains 75 per cent of the population, the naval base of Pearl Harbor and the state capital, Honolulu, which is the gateway to the islands. It is also a major city which has become increasingly important as a business centre for trade between North America and the East Asia-Pacific region. The 'North Shore' (the north-west coast of Oahu) offers some of the best conditions for surfing, a sport that was invented by the native Hawaiians.

Since the 1960s the state government, increasingly concerned about the undesirable impacts of mass tourism on Oahu, has encouraged quality development projects on the other major islands. Maui contains the Haleakala National Park with its impressive volcanic scenery, and the former whaling port of Lahaina. Kauai is particularly renowned for its lush landscapes, exemplified by the Fern Grotto at Wailua, the Waimea

Case study 23.2

Waikiki: Playground of East and West

The lighting of tiki torches at sunset, Hawaiian dance performances, the *wahine* carrying her surfboard to the beach, and the streets thronged day and night with people of all ages and ethnic origins – all these features give Waikiki an ambiance that is different from any other American resort.

Waikiki is the recreational business district (RBD) of Honolulu, located a few kilometres to the east of downtown. This compact and densely built up area, consisting mainly of high rise hotels, is marked off from the sprawl that characterises most of the city, by the Ala Wai Canal and yacht harbour to the north and west. To the east is the green expanse of Kapolani Park and the cliffs of Diamond Head, an extinct volcanic crater, which forms an impressive backdrop to the world famous beach.

Waikiki provides a range of accommodation for the 80,000 to 90,000 visitors who arrive each week. The most expensive hotels occupy prime sites near the beachfront, while lower value properties, including time-share apartments, are located further back, between the commercial artery of Kuhio Avenue and the Ala Wai Canal. Two of the flagship hotels – the elegant Moana Surfrider with its carriage entrance (1901) and the art deco Royal Hawaiian (1927) – were built long before the age of mass tourism and still retain something of their former exclusivity. Their individuality in design and décor contrasts with the standardised 'leisure factories' that have been developed since the 1950s.

The beach itself is not particularly wide and is slowly eroding. In the central section, public access to the foreshore is restricted to narrow passageways between the hotels and areas of beach have been roped off for the private use of their clients. The eastern shore towards Diamond Head has been designated as a marine conservation area.

Although the restaurants and entertainments on offer cater mainly for the middle-income North American family market, Waikiki is also a Japanese resort. It particularly attracts groups of young people who during their brief stay can experiment with a more relaxed 'western' lifestyle than is available back in Japan. Users of the trolley service to the Ala Moana shopping centre and downtown Honolulu are predominantly middle-aged Japanese tourists. Many businesses are Japanese-owned, while others, such as the indoor shooting ranges, are geared to the Japanese market. One emporium selling duty-free merchandise has signs and literature exclusively in the Japanese alphabet. Some of Waikiki's hotels are popular wedding locations for Japanese couples, who insist on a formal western-style ceremony.

Tourists looking for authentic Hawaiian arts and crafts in Waikiki, however, will probably be disappointed. The numerous ABC convenience stores supply an almost identical range of leisurewear and souvenirs, as is the case with the International Marketplace, where the stalls display an array of kitsch merchandise, much of it imported from Taiwan.

Canyon and the beaches at Hanalei, (the location for 'Bali Hai' in the film *South Pacific*). The 'Big Island' of Hawaii (from which the state takes its name) offers great climatic and scenic variety, due to the effect of the high volcanic peaks of Mauna Loa and Mauna Kea on the prevailing trade winds. Hilo on the windward side of the island receives heavy rainfall, whereas Kona on the west coast is much drier. Frequent volcanic eruptions have created a lunar landscape of craters and lava caves in the south-eastern part of the island, in contrast to the rainforests, coffee plantations and cattle ranches elsewhere. Molokai and Lanai are islands as yet little influenced by tourism and sparsely populated Niihau has rejected it altogether. The remote and uninhabited north-western

Photo 23.2 Boogie board hire at Waikiki, a favourite destination for young Japanese tourists (author's photograph)

islands have been designated a National Monument – in effect, the world's largest marine reserve – after the US government was alerted to the environmental disaster unfolding in the north Pacific.

Canada

Canada is second only to the Russian Federation in area, and is larger than the United States, but has only a tenth of its population. Climatic factors, such as the chilling effect of Hudson Bay and the Labrador Current, largely explain why the great majority of Canadians occupy a narrow belt of territory lying within 200 kilometres of the United States border. Tourism is also unevenly distributed, with most foreign visitors shunning the prairies of central Canada, and concentrating their attention on Vancouver and the Rockies in the west, and Toronto or Montréal in the south-east. In economic and cultural terms Canada tends to be overshadowed by its powerful neighbour, and this together with a more northerly location, has resulted in an image problem.

About 80 per cent of this vast country is classified as wilderness, mainly coniferous forest and tundra, while Canada boasts some of the world's largest lakes and 15 per cent of its freshwater resources. Not surprisingly the promotional literature highlights the unspoiled scenery and the great outdoors; but since most Canadians are city dwellers, the 'Discover Our True Nature' campaign also emphasised the sophistication of Canada's cities, contrasting the traditional appeal of Québec with the contemporary attractions of Montréal. Canada's separate identity is demonstrated by its political institutions, strict gun control laws, and by a number of heritage attractions commemorating French and British rule, including resistance to United States expansion in the War of 1812. Even so, Canada's quest for national unity is made problematic by the existence of two official languages, representing two different cultural traditions.

Domestic and international tourism together account for 5 per cent of Canada's gross domestic product and around 7 per cent of employment. As early as 1929 tourism was a major earner of foreign exchange, and in 1934 the Canadian Travel Bureau was established under the Department of Commerce to carry out promotion abroad.

The demand for tourism

Domestic tourism

As in the United States, domestic tourism is far larger in volume and expenditure than inbound or outbound tourism. British Columbia and Prince Edward Island are the destinations most favoured by Canadian holidaymakers.

Outbound tourism

The Canadian winter partly explains why Canadians have a high propensity to travel outside their own country, with around one-third of the population taking a trip abroad in any one year. This, combined with a high travel frequency, results in a massive deficit in Canada's international tourism account. The American border states of New York, Vermont, Michigan and Washington are the most visited destinations. Florida is also popular with Canadians, particularly in winter, with many retired people spending several months either there or in Hawaii. This exodus of 'snowbirds' may well increase with the general ageing of the population, while the open skies agreement between the US and Canadian governments will favour a greater use of the airlines rather than travel by private car. Other destinations include Mexico, the Caribbean islands, Europe and East Asia. Most of the expenditure on foreign travel, especially to Europe, is generated by the more prosperous and urbanised provinces, such as Ontario, British Columbia and Manitoba.

Inbound tourism

The majority of Canada's 16 million foreign tourists come from the United States, and less than 10 per cent arrive from European countries. Americans also account for the large volume of excursionists whose numbers fluctuate according to differences in prices on either side of the border and the strength of the two currencies. This does leave Canadian tourism vulnerable to a downturn in the US economy. The great majority of American tourists arrive by car, return frequently, and are attracted mainly by the recreational facilities of the Canadian countryside. Canada's cities are also perceived to be safe compared to those of the USA, the language and culture are familiar, and crossing the world's longest undefended border is an easy matter for Americans. Overseas visitors tend to spend much more per head than the Americans, the leading markets being the UK, France, Germany and Japan. Most overseas visitors arrive by air at Toronto or Montréal, and almost half of these stay primarily with friends and relatives.

The supply side of tourism

The resource base

Canada does not have such a wide range of resources for recreation as the USA, since it lies entirely outside the warm climate zone. Foreign tourists are attracted to the country's mountains, lakes and forests rather than its extensive coastline. Most of the national parks are situated in the more scenic western part of Canada. The Canadian Pacific Railway (CPR) was largely instrumental in their creation specifically as tourist attractions. The national parks, together with a large number of National Historic Sites (NHS), are administered by a federal agency – Parks Canada. In Canada's national parks the emphasis is on conservation rather than outdoor recreation, and, due in part to the shorter season, visitor impacts are less than in the parks of the USA. Each of the provinces and territories has an agency responsible for the conservation of natural resources, with a remit for recreation and tourism. The provincial parks are widely distributed, and while some provide a variety of recreational facilities, others are less developed than the national parks.

The severity and length of winter – even southern Canada is snow-covered for three months of the year – is seen as a challenge, rather than a constraint on tourism development. Canadians invented the snowshoe and snowmobile, and regard winter as a time for participation in a wide range of recreation activities. Snowmobile trails thread the countryside, and many ski resorts have developed to meet domestic demand within reach of all the major cities. Snowfall is heavier in southern Québec than in the Prairies, where temperatures are lower. Some of the resorts in the Laurentian Mountains of Québec and the Canadian Rockies attract a growing international market. Canadian cities are well equipped to deal with winter, and in some, underground shopping centres provide full protection from the weather.

Summers, at least in southern and western Canada, are warm enough for a wide range of outdoor activities, including beach tourism and water sports. Transport and equipment for fishing and hunting trips is provided by specialist *outfitters* in even the most remote areas of Canada. Boating and canoeing are especially popular in the many lakes and rivers of the Canadian Shield – the vast expanse of forest lying to the north of the Great Lakes and the St Lawrence River. Canada's waterways played a crucial role in the early development of the country. Unlike the French *voyageurs* and the Hudson Bay Company fur traders, today's canoeists have the advantage of lightweight equipment. The old canoe trails form the basis for a system of 'heritage rivers'. This is a good example of co-operation between the public and private sector in resource management; stakeholders include the federal government, provincial or territorial governments, the local communities – especially those of the 'First Nations' or native Indians – and tour operators. The activities of the users – anglers, campers and ecotourists as well as canoeists – are carefully monitored to avoid environmental damage.

Transport

In most of Canada winter poses problems for vehicles and road maintenance. As in the USA, the railways played a major role in opening up the western part of the country to settlement, and the scenic mountain areas to tourism. After the 1950s they faced severe competition from domestic air services. In 1972 the passenger services of the CPR and the state-owned Canadian National Railways (CNR) were combined under the banner of VIA Rail, an independent Crown corporation that is subsidised by the federal government. By the late 1980s scheduled train services had been drastically reduced on most routes with the exception of the Toronto–Montréal corridor. VIA Rail still provides a trans-continental service, but at a frequency of only three trains a week in either direction; while sightseeing tours by train are available in the Rocky Mountains in the summer months. The great majority of domestic trips are now undertaken by private car. Most of the major cities, from Vancouver to Halifax, are linked by the world's longest national road – the Trans-Canada Highway. Domestic air travel is dominated by Air Canada, which ranks as one of the world's leading airlines. There are a number of regional carriers and air charter companies serving the vast areas that are virtually inaccessible by surface transport.

Accommodation

At the end of the nineteenth century, the Canadian Pacific Railway was responsible for the development of luxury hotels across the country, including the impressive Chateau Frontenac overlooking the St Lawrence in Québec, and at scenic locations in the Rocky Mountains such as Banff and Lake Louise. Canada offers a wide range of accommodation, including the popular holiday homes known as 'cabins' or 'cottages'. In remote areas fly-in camps and eco-lodges serve adventure-seekers.

Organisation

Since the late 1960s the federal government in Ottawa has become directly involved in tourism promotion. Marketing is carried out by the Canadian Tourism Commission (CTC), created in 1995 as a partnership between the federal government and the domestic travel industry. The governments of the ten provinces and the three territories are also involved in product development and overseas promotion with all levels of government in Canada having tourism responsibilities.

The regional distribution of tourism resources

Ontario

Ontario accounts for over half of Canada's industrial production, and has a number of cities, apart from Toronto and Ottawa, that rank as major business centres. It is the most visited province, containing Canada's largest English-speaking city, is easily reached by road from New York in the south and Michigan to the west, and has a third of Canada's hotel capacity. Many holiday homes are located in the Muskoka Lakes area north of Toronto. Most of the population of Ontario is concentrated in the fertile peninsula lying between three of the Great Lakes – Huron, Erie and Ontario. Relatively few live in the Canadian Shield to the north of Lake Superior – a vast area of granite outcrops separated by lakes and *muskeg* (swamps), and covered with forests of spruce and fir.

- Toronto is Canada's most cosmopolitan city, with a vibrant nightlife and cultural scene – a far cry from its staid reputation in the 1950s, when it was known as 'Toronto the Good'. Attractions include Ontario Place – a major waterfront recreation area; the CN Tower; the Ontario Science Centre – one of the first interactive museums; and the Hockey Hall of Fame, celebrating Canada's national sport.
- Ottawa as the federal capital attracts sightseers to its impressive Gothic-style Parliament Buildings, the National Gallery of Canada and other important museums.
- The Niagara area includes not only the famous waterfalls, but also the resort of Niagara-on-the-Lake, famous for its theatre festival, and a popular wine route.
- Stratford is famed throughout North America as a theatrical centre.
- Kingston is important for its historical associations and as a base for visiting the scenic Thousand Islands.

- Georgian Bay and the Algonquin Provincial Park offer large areas of unspoiled lake and forest scenery on the southern edge of the Canadian Shield.

Québec

Québec Province is culturally distinct from the rest of Canada, an 'island' of French speakers in an English-speaking continent. Until the 1960s it was predominantly rural and traditional in outlook, but since that time there has been rapid economic growth, based largely on the province's huge resources of hydro-electric power. The great majority of the population live in a relatively narrow strip bordering the St Lawrence River. The influence of Catholicism remains strong, as shown by the popularity of pilgrimages to the shrine of St Anne de Beaupré.

- Montréal is Canada's largest city and the world's second largest French-speaking metropolis, with restaurants and *boites de chanson* (nightclubs) to match those of Paris. It vies with Toronto as the gateway to Canada, with two international airports – Dorval and Mirabel – and is a port on the St Lawrence Seaway linking the Atlantic to the Great Lakes. This has made Montréal a major financial centre. The 1967 World Exposition and the 1976 Olympic Games did much to improve the city's transport and recreation facilities. This includes Le Souterrain – an underground shopping area served by an efficient metro system, centred on Place Ville-Marie. The city also hosts the annual Canadian Formula One Grand Prix.
- Québec City is less cosmopolitan than Montréal and its historic core has preserved the ambience of eighteenth century France. Most of the tourist attractions are in the fortified Upper Town. Québec is also famous throughout Canada for the ice sculptures and exuberance of its Winter Carnival, and is the home of the *Cirque de Soleil*.
- Downstream from Québec City are two scenic areas – the fjord-like Saguenay River – increasingly popular for whale-watching – and the picturesque Gaspé Peninsula with its fishing villages.
- Ski resorts in Québec Province include Mont-Tremblant in the Laurentian Mountains and Mount Orford in the Notre Dame Range.

The Atlantic provinces

The provinces along the Atlantic seaboard of Canada are relatively poor, due to the decline of traditional industries such as fishing. International tourism is handicapped by the region's peripheral location and an indifferent climate.

Newfoundland, consisting of the island of that name and the coastal areas of Labrador, typifies these conditions. The climate is influenced by the cold Labrador Current, and for this reason the Atlantic coast is called 'Iceberg Alley'. This results in the late arrival of spring, frequent fogs, and a short, cool summer. Scores of small fishing villages cling to the rocky coastline, where ecotourism in the form of bird-watching and whale-watching may provide an alternative livelihood. The capital, St John's has an interesting heritage, while the interior offers opportunities for hiking and adventure tourism.

Newfoundland is the nearest part of North America to Europe and this was significant in the early days of trans-Atlantic communications; in the pre-jet era Gander Airport was an important staging point, and as 9/11 showed, it continues to play an important role as a diversionary airport. Coastal shipping services are a lifeline for many isolated communities, and Labrador's rugged 'Ghost Coast' is featured on summer cruises.

St-Pierre and Miquelon

These two small islands off the south coast of Newfoundland are not part of Canada but an overseas territory of France, all that remains of her once vast territories in North America. As such they have curiosity appeal, attracting American and Canadian day-visitors on shopping trips.

Prince Edward Island, the smallest of the three Maritime Provinces, enjoys a warmer climate and a flourishing tourism industry, although this caters mainly for the domestic market. The island's resources include fine sandy beaches, attractive countryside, golf courses and its literary associations – the town of Cavendish is the setting for *Ann of Green Gables,* which makes it popular with Japanese tourists. The island is now linked to the mainland by the Confederation Bridge.

Nova Scotia offers a variety of coastal scenery, and an interesting French and Scottish cultural heritage. Tourism is based on a number of touring routes such as the Evangeline Trail, but some communities might well benefit from a greater influx of long-stay visitors. The capital Halifax is a major seaport with a marine heritage that includes its association with the *Titanic.* Louisbourg on Cape Breton Island is a former French fortress that has been restored as a 'living history' attraction.

New Brunswick is less orientated toward the sea, although the Bay of Fundy is famous for its tides, and there are beach resorts such as Shediac Bay. The extensive forests and rivers of the interior attract hunters, anglers and canoeists. The main tourist centres are Fredericton, which has an impressive museum of art, St John and Moncton.

The prairie provinces

The heartland of Canada consists of two provinces – Manitoba and Saskatchewan – that are mainly known for their vast wheat-growing prairies. Winters are comparable with those of Siberia, but Lake Winnipeg is a major focus for water sports during the short hot summers. Further north the prairies give way to forests, where fly-in camps and lodges provide accommodation for anglers. Although the scenery may be low-key, the region is culturally diverse, with large communities of Ukrainians, Germans and Icelanders that have retained the traditions of their homelands. Winnipeg is the main business and cultural centre of the region, followed by Regina, home of that world famous national institution, the Royal Canadian Mounted Police.

The isolated community of Churchill on Hudson Bay (it can only be reached by air, or train from Winnipeg) is an example of how ecotourism can revive a local economy. A one-time fur trading post and grain exporting port, it is now visited by tourists in summer for whale-watching, and in October to view polar bears from the safety of 'tundra buggies' – four wheel drive all-terrain vehicles.

The West

The provinces of Alberta and British Columbia offer some of the most spectacular scenery and wildlife to be found in North America. The Rocky Mountains contain no less than seven of Canada's national parks. Most of the tourism development is on the Alberta side, and includes the following attractions:

- Banff National Park is the most popular area, attracting 4 million visitors a year, mainly in the months of July and August. It contains two world famous resorts – Banff and Lake Louise. Banff was originally developed as a spa by the CPR on the basis of its hot springs and attracted a wealthy international clientele in the early part of the twentieth century. With the development of skiing after the Second World War it became an all-year resort, with a winter sports season lasting from November to May. It is now a major urban centre with attractions, restaurants, golf courses, and other facilities that may seem inappropriate to the setting and the national park ethos. Banff also offers major cultural events, such art and film festivals.

- Jasper National Park lies close to the Yellowhead Pass, the route across the Rockies followed by the CNR. Major attractions include the Columbia Icefield and Maligne Lake, both superb examples of glacial scenery. Outside the park boundaries, heli-skiing and heli-hiking allow access to the most remote mountain areas.

- Calgary is the gateway to the Canadian Rockies. It is also the centre for the ranching industry of south-western Alberta, hence the significance of the 'Stampede' – a world famous event attraction celebrating the cowboy lifestyle. The winter climate of this area is often affected by warm, dry *chinook* winds – similar to the *föhn* of the Alps – that can raise temperatures by as much as 25°C. This would be disastrous for the ski resort operations were it not for the availability of computerised snow-making systems covering most of the pistes. Waterton Lakes near Calgary was the venue for the 1988 Winter Olympics.

- Edmonton has long been regarded as the gateway to the Canadian North. Its modern prosperity is largely based on the oil industry, and the city boasts the largest shopping mall in North America – Edmonton West – offering a range of themed attractions.

- The arid landscapes of the Alberta Badlands are unlike any other part of Canada. They are noted for their dinosaur fossil beds and the landforms resulting from wind erosion known as *hoodoos*.

The coastal region of British Columbia offers many attractions, including:

- A climate characterised by the mildest winters of Canada – with temperatures 20°C higher than in Labrador at the same latitude – and in the south, warm summers with abundant sunshine.

- A spectacular coastline backed by mountains, deeply indented with fjords, and with many offshore islands.

- Diverse ecosystems, including the rainforests of Vancouver Island, and rivers teeming with salmon. An extensive area including the Queen Charlotte Islands (Haida Gwaii) has been designated as Canada's largest marine reserve.

- The Indian heritage. The abundance of natural resources allowed the Haida and other coastal tribes to develop a sophisticated culture. This was severely disrupted by contact with Europeans, but the totem pole survives as the best known example of traditional skills.

The main tourist centres are Vancouver and Victoria:

- Vancouver is Canada's third largest city and a major gateway to the East Asia–Pacific Region. This makes the city particularly appealing for visitors from Japan, Hong Kong and other Asian countries. The superb natural setting means that sailing, golf and skiing can be enjoyed on the same day.

- Victoria, on Vancouver Island, is a major holiday resort and retirement area, with a strong English ambiance that makes it appealing to American tourists from the West Coast.

The interior of British Columbia comprises high mountain ranges, broad plateaux, and deep, canyon-like valleys. The climate is much drier than the coast, with cold winters but very warm summers. This is particularly true of the sheltered Okanagan Valley, where sailing and water skiing are popular at the lake resorts of Penticton and Kelowna. On the Fraser River visitors can experience white-water rafting or pan for gold near former mining towns. Excellent winter sports facilities are available in the Selkirk Mountains at Kimberley, and at Kamloops, heart of British Columbia's cattle-ranching country.

Discussion point

Much of British Columbia is impossible to reach except by air transport. These mountain and forest areas are nevertheless sought-after destinations for hikers, skiers and nature-lovers. Proponents of heli-hiking and heli-skiing downplay the environmental impact of helicopters and claim that with improved technology they are now much safer than in the past. Road-building, they argue, would produce much more pollution, while hiking to the destination would be a feat of endurance given the trackless terrain, and anyway, such hikers would produce waste, light fires and scare wildlife. Discuss the pros and cons of heli-touring, heli-hiking and heli-skiing in remote areas of North America.

The North

Southern Canadians perceive James Bay, Churchill on Hudson Bay, Labrador, and northern Québec (Nunavik) with its Inuit population, as being part of the North, but although these places experience a rigorous sub-arctic climate, in latitude they are no further north than Scotland. The Canadian North is generally defined as comprising the territories of Yukon, NWT and Nunavut which lie north of 60° latitude. Here tourism development is constrained by the high costs of transport and construction.

The Yukon Territory is more accessible than other parts of the Canadian North, and although winters are just as severe, summers are much warmer than in Nunavut to the east. The Yukon's tourism industry is mainly based on the heritage of the 1898 Gold Rush, Canada's equivalent of the 'Wild West' – at Dawson City and Whitehorse. The Kluane National Park provides limited facilities for adventure tourism.

The North-west Territories (NWT) have substantial indigenous communities, belonging to the Dene Indian and Inuit (Eskimo) cultures. Although there is road access to Yellowknife, and to Inuvik on the Mackenzie delta, most of the NWT can only be reached by air, while in winter ice roads on the frozen waterways serve some communities. The problems caused by even a limited amount of tourism are becoming evident in the region's main natural attraction – the Nahanni National Park Reserve. This World Heritage Site includes the spectacular Virginia Falls and an extensive karst limestone system – unusual in such high latitudes. Although this remote area is only accessible by air, it is already experiencing severe impacts, resulting from the growth of white-water rafting on the South Nahanni River.

Nunavut covers most of the Canadian Arctic, and was created by the federal government in 1999 specifically for the Inuit people. Visits to the region are part of the growing ecotourism movement, and this is a sector in which Inuit guides and outfitters, with their intimate knowledge of the country are playing an important role, sustaining both their economy and culture. Nunavut's rigorous climate, the vast distances between the few settlements, and the forbidding terrain are obstacles to tourism development and discourage independent travel. The resource base includes:

- the spectacular glaciated mountain and fjord scenery of Baffin Island, culminating in the Auyuittuq National Park;
- the pristine lakes and rivers of the Barren Grounds, the tundra plains extending from Hudson Bay north-westwards to the Arctic Ocean;
- the marine wildlife of Hudson Bay and Lancaster Sound; and
- Inuit handicrafts based on their hunting traditions.

Case study 23.3

The North-west Passage

The impact of climate change on the Arctic regions has revived interest in the idea of a commercial shipping route linking the Atlantic and Pacific oceans. As explorers such as Franklin and McClure found to their cost, in the past navigation was not feasible, due to the year-round pack ice blocking the channels between the islands of Canada's Arctic archipelago.

As with the North-east Passage to the north of Russia (see Chapter 18), such a route would greatly reduce shipping costs between Europe and the Far East, but also increase the risk of polluting an already fragile ecosystem. A North-west Passage also raises questions of international law, as Canada claims the sector from Lancaster Sound to Coronation Gulf as part of its territorial waters, which is disputed by the USA. The use of the route for cruising and yachting as well as commerce is problematic, given the unpredictability of ice and weather conditions, and the fact that supply and rescue facilities in Arctic Canada are few and far between.

Greenland (Kalaallit Nunaat)

A permanent ice cap thousands of metres thick covers 84 per cent of Greenland, so that the mainly Inuit population live in scattered communities along the western and south-eastern coasts. To the north and east, a barrier of pack ice prevents circumnavigation of the world's largest island. A self-governing Danish territory and a member of the Nordic Council, Greenland has nevertheless shunned incorporation into the European Union. Greenland's economy remains highly dependent on Denmark, and it is more accessible by air services from Copenhagen and Iceland than from Canada. The exploitation of rare minerals, now accessible due to climate change, may encourage Greenlanders to seek greater autonomy and closer links with their Inuit neighbours in Nunavut.

Greenland's main tourism resource is its fjord and mountain scenery, culminating in Disko Bay, where glaciers reach the sea to spawn myriad icebergs (the ice here is claimed to be the world's purest). Narsarsuaq in the extreme south is the main focus for activities such as hiking and mountain climbing, while the ruins of Viking farms and churches are evidence that Greenland was warmer early in the last millennium than it is now. Dog-sledding is offered by Inuit communities on the south-east coast. Prospects for tourism development are limited by the high costs of accommodation and transport. Even in summer, the coastal ferries and the system of air services (mainly using helicopters) are likely to be disrupted by a sudden deterioration in weather conditions, including fogs and strong winds.

Summary

- North America is a vast continent of scenic and climatic contrasts.
- With the exception of northern Canada and Greenland it is highly developed economically.
- Urban landscapes, lifestyles, transport systems, and tourist facilities are broadly similar throughout both the United States and Canada, and there is a considerable volume of travel between the two countries.
- The main problem for the overseas visitor is the great distances involved, but this has been largely overcome by excellent highways and an extensive network of air services, with rail transport now playing only a minor role.
- Tourist facilities have been developed mainly to serve the enormous domestic market, and it is only recently that federal, state and provincial governments have become directly involved in encouraging inbound tourism.
- North Americans spend heavily on travel abroad, with the result that Canada continues to have a large deficit on its international tourism account.
- Overseas visitors to the United States and Canada are attracted to the cities for cultural and business reasons, and there is a large VFR market. Florida on the other hand is regarded mainly as a beach and theme park destination.
- Both the United States and Canada have realised the importance of conservation and their state-controlled national parks and forest reserves are probably the world's finest.
- The native peoples of North America, marginalised in the past, are now taking a more active share in tourism development.
- The private sector of tourism is very much larger than the state sector, and is responsible for all profit-making enterprises; sports facilities and theme parks are particularly important.

Assignments

1 A group of students is planning a tour of the USA by Greyhound bus. They are particularly interested in places that are associated with the nation's musical heritage. Suggest a suitable route for the tour, giving brief descriptions of the places to be visited.
2 Describe how the dominance of the private car has influenced the pattern of domestic tourism and the landscapes and townscapes of North America.
3 Justify the statement that the USA is a 'land for all seasons', by satisfying the demands for many forms of outdoor recreation and tourism.
4 Compare and contrast Las Vegas and Disneyworld, Florida as tourist destinations.
5 Discuss the achievements of the conservation movement in the USA and Canada, and identify the ways in which natural resources are being put at risk by developmental pressures.

THE AMERICAS

24 CHAPTER

The tourism geography of the Caribbean Islands

Introduction

The islands of the Caribbean are often considered to be part of Latin America, but in fact this is strictly true only of Cuba, The Dominican Republic and Puerto Rico, which are Spanish-speaking, along with most of the countries on the mainland of South and Central America. Although Columbus 'discovered' and named most of the other islands and claimed them for Spain, these were later colonised by the British, the Dutch and the French. The colonists imported slaves from Africa to provide labour, and their descendants contribute a major ingredient in the cultural make-up of the Caribbean. The cultural heritage reflects the colonial past; most of the region is at least nominally Roman Catholic in religion, but some of the Commonwealth Caribbean islands are strongly Protestant with traditional views on moral behaviour.

Physical features

The islands of the Caribbean form a chain, extending for some 4,000 kilometres from Florida to the northern coast of South America. The Caribbean Sea is almost enclosed, and has been called, with some justification, 'the American Mediterranean'. However, it is warmer and less polluted than its Old World counterpart, with a greener coastline and finer beaches.

The islands are generally healthier than most tropical destinations, although this is due to medical advances since the nineteenth century rather than any climatic advantage. The north-east trade winds do moderate the rather high temperatures and humidity, bringing heavy rainfall to the windward coasts; this means that locations on the sheltered side of a mountainous island, and low-lying islands generally, have a much drier climate, as evidenced by cacti and other drought-resistant vegetation. The best time for visiting the Caribbean is from December through April when the weather is pleasantly warm, sunny and relatively dry. This has long been the high season for winter sun-seekers, arriving mainly from North America. Summer temperatures are appreciably higher and there is a greater probability of rain. Hotel prices are generally lower in summer, and this attracts a younger, less affluent type of holidaymaker, including many from Europe. In fact the Caribbean is no longer primarily a winter destination, as over 60 per cent of its visitors now arrive during the summer months. From July to November there is the risk of hurricanes occurring in some parts of the region, and these tropical storms can cause immense damage to the tourism infrastructure of the islands and the Caribbean coast of Central America.

While climatic conditions are fairly uniform throughout the region, there are considerable differences between the landscapes of the various islands. There are also great disparities in size – from tiny Saba, with little over a thousand inhabitants, to Cuba which is comparable in area and population to a medium-sized country in Europe. The Greater Antilles – Cuba, Hispaniola, Puerto Rico and Jamaica – could be described as 'continents in miniature'. The smaller islands or Lesser Antilles tend to fall into two categories:

- the 'low islands' of limestone formation, (these are scenically less interesting, but boast fine beaches of white coral sand); and
- the 'high islands' of volcanic origin in the eastern Caribbean. These are mountainous and often densely forested, but have fewer beaches and a wetter climate, while rugged terrain makes road building and airport expansion difficult. There have been few volcanic eruptions in recent centuries – Mont Pelée in Martinique (1902) and Montserrat (1995–1997) are notable exceptions – but there are significant geothermal resources in most of these islands.

Cultural features

The islands are a mosaic of different races, languages and religions, with a cultural heritage resulting from successive phases of European colonisation namely:

- **The age of discovery.** The arrival of the Spanish under Columbus had a fatal impact on the native Amerindians, particularly the Taíno of the Greater Antilles. They have left few physical traces, but the words barbecue, canoe, hammock, tobacco and hurricane are reminders of Taíno language and culture. The Caribs of the eastern Caribbean put up a longer resistance, and a small community still survive in Dominica.
- **The age of piracy.** The buccaneers of the seventeenth century used the smaller islands abandoned by the Spanish as bases for their expeditions, which were directed mainly against the Spanish treasure fleets from Mexico and South America.
- **The plantation era.** The plantation economy developed in the eighteenth century when sugar was a valuable commodity, and the islands a prize to be acquired by even minor European powers, such as Denmark (the US Virgin Islands) and Sweden (St Barts). In the course of the next century slavery was abolished, but the legacy of the plantation is still evident in the attitude of many Afro-Caribbeans toward tourism.

Development of tourism in the Caribbean

English is the most widely spoken language in the Caribbean, and this, together with proximity to the USA has been a factor encouraging the development of tourism. The region is however highly fragmented politically. The islands collectively known as the West Indies or the Commonwealth Caribbean retain cultural ties with Britain, but comprise no less than ten independent nations and five British colonies. Nevertheless, there is an increasing awareness of the advantages of co-operation in the fields of tourism planning and promotion. Most of the remaining islands retain close links with France, the Netherlands and the United States. Cuba, the Dominican Republic and Puerto Rico have strong cultural ties with Spain and the other Spanish-speaking countries of Latin America. There has been some progress toward economic integration through Caricom (The Caribbean Community), while the Caribbean Tourism Organisation (CTO) carries out joint promotion with member countries in Europe and North America.

Most of the Caribbean islands are over-populated in relation to their limited resources for economic development. Tourism is encouraged by most governments in the region who perceive that beaches, sunshine and scenery are more marketable assets than sugar or bananas. Since 1997 agriculture has become even less profitable, as islands are no longer guaranteed a market for their produce in the European Union, thanks to the ruling of the World Trade Organisation. Tourism has the advantage of creating jobs in a region where unemployment is high, where emigration to Europe and the USA is no longer an option, and where manufacturing industry is generally not viable. Tourism is now the major earner of foreign exchange, the fastest growing sector of the economy, contributing a considerable percentage of the region's GDP, and a major employer, accounting for over a third of the workforce in many of the islands.

Since 1985, the Caribbean's hotel capacity has grown rapidly, exceeding 150,000 rooms in the new millennium. However the region is highly dependent on the North American market, which supplies the majority of all staying visitors and over 90 per cent of cruise passengers, and is therefore vulnerable to the affects of recession in the USA. Most national currencies are tied to the US dollar, and resort accommodation is designed and priced to meet North American expectations. Foreign tour operators also tend to regard the islands as offering an interchangeable holiday product, disregarding the considerable cultural differences that exist within the Caribbean and national aspirations.

The dependence on tourism does mean that the islands are highly vulnerable to negative publicity on crime. Much of this is linked to drug-running, since the Caribbean Sea lies between some of the world's major suppliers and the world's largest market for narcotics. The many harbours and airfields are difficult to patrol effectively, with under-resourced police forces helping the US Coast Guard to intercept the traffickers. This is another area where greater co-operation between island governments would be an advantage.

An island's success as a tourist destination depends to a large extent on its accessibility to air and shipping services. Inter-island ferry services tend to be less reliable than air transport, making 'island hopping' problematic. There are many small regional airlines in the Caribbean but only a few international airports with the capacity to handle a large volume of long-haul traffic. Barbados for example acts as a regional hub, providing services to the less developed islands such as St Vincent and Dominica. The vital air links to North America and Europe are dominated by airlines based outside the

Caribbean, although BWIA (the national airline of Barbados and Trinidad) and Air Jamaica are gaining a larger share of the market.

Tourism in the Caribbean has had negative as well as positive impacts on host communities. This is particularly true of two holiday types which have been encouraged by most governments as a means of maximising income from visitors, namely cruising and all-inclusives:

Cruising. The Caribbean has maintained its position as the world's most popular cruise destination, due largely to competitive pricing by the shipping lines, aimed particularly at middle-income groups in the USA. Although Canada and the UK are important markets, they each account for less than 10 per cent of cruise tourists in the Caribbean, and the great majority are Americans. Cruising has shown a faster rate of growth than stayover tourism, from less than a million passengers in the early 1980s to about 5 million in the 2000s, while the ships boast a far higher occupancy rate than most resort hotels. In winter the Caribbean has unrivalled natural advantages, but in summer it faces strong competition from other destinations leading some cruise lines to reposition their vessels in Alaskan or Mediterranean waters. Both the number of ships and their overall size is increasing, with the largest accommodating more than 2,500 passengers and over a thousand crew. Size is an advantage for cruise operators in terms of yield, while stricter environmental and safety regulations also discourage the use of smaller, older vessels. Although providing terminal facilities is costly for island governments, an equivalent number of staying tourists would require a much greater investment in hotel building. Nevertheless the economic benefits of attracting the multi-billion dollar cruise market have been disputed, and there are also negative environmental and cultural impacts (Pattullo, 1996). We can summarise the objections to cruising as follows:

- Cruise lines offer unfair competition to Caribbean hoteliers, as they pay little in the way of taxes to island governments.
- Cruise lines provide few employment and business opportunities to island communities. They source most of their food requirements from outside the Caribbean, claiming that local farmers cannot provide supplies to the quantity or quality required.
- Cruising is high volume but low-spend tourism. With increasingly sophisticated on-board facilities for shopping, leisure and gambling, there is less incentive for passengers to spend in the ports of call. Duty-free goods – most of which have to be imported – account for half the spend ashore, which puts the smaller, less developed islands at a disadvantage.
- The sheer volume of passengers is difficult for some communities to handle, given the limited number of taxis and buses available.
- Cruising is 'convenience travel'. In contrast to the Mediterranean and other cruise destinations, the Caribbean attracts 'sun and fun' holidaymakers rather than those interested in sightseeing, while the ship is often promoted as the primary attraction. With just a few hours ashore, passengers receive only a stereotyped impression of the Caribbean, and the commercialisation of the ports of call can be demeaning to both the visitors and the host community.
- Cruise ships generate an enormous amount of waste, and island governments are ill-equipped to carry out clean-up operations on the scale required.

All-inclusive resorts. Although Club Méditerranée pioneered the all-inclusive principle in their villages in the French islands of Martinique and Guadeloupe, the idea did not spread to the rest of the Caribbean until the late 1980s, following the example of the Sandals group in Jamaica. All-inclusives have the following advantages:

THE AMERICAS

Photo 24.1 The harbour at Gustavia, Saint Barthelemy (©istockphoto.com/ Robert Cocozza)

- for tourists, they offer value for money holidays, as there is no need to budget for 'extras' such as drinks and the use of sports facilities;
- for tour operators they boost profits by stimulating sales; and
- for the hotelier they improve occupancy rates, allowing more staff to be employed year-round.

On the other hand, all-inclusives have been accused of widening social divisions between the tourists, who see little need to venture beyond the security of their hotels, and the host community. Also most are owned by multinationals, which reduces their benefits to the local economy.

Leakages of the earnings from tourism to import goods which the foreign tourist demands are a feature of most destinations, but they are problematic in islands lacking a diversified economy. Some forms of tourism allow more of the visitor spend to be retained locally, by encouraging *linkages* with suppliers in the islands. They include:

- **Yachting.** Whereas only a small number of harbours in the Caribbean can accommodate 100,000 tonne cruise ships, yachtsmen from Europe and North America have an almost unlimited choice of natural anchorages. Purpose-built marinas are available in many islands, providing facilities for both bareboat charter and crewed vessels. Nautical tourists are predominantly from the upper-income groups, but tend to be more informal in their dealings with local people than their counterparts in the luxury resort hotels, and are likely to buy supplies from local farmers and businesses.
- **Diving.** Some of the world's finest coral reefs fringe the Caribbean islands. The invention of the self-contained underwater breathing apparatus (scuba) in the 1950s revolutionised diving and opened up a new frontier for tourism. With more than 5 million practitioners in the USA alone, scuba diving is one of the world's fastest growing sports, and divers are among those campaigning against the depletion of the reef ecosystem by over-fishing and marine pollution. A number of resorts provide facilities for divers, but the best sites tend to be in areas which can only

be accessed by *live-aboards*, boats specially designed and chartered for diving expeditions.

- **Ecotourism.** Columbus was the first European visitor to describe the Caribbean islands, with their profusion of plant and bird life, as a 'paradise on earth'. Although the original forest cover has long since disappeared on most of the low islands, the Greater Antilles and volcanic Windward Islands retain much to attract nature lovers.
- **Cultural and heritage tourism.** Most Caribbean islands can offer an interesting colonial heritage and a vibrant contemporary culture, expressed particularly in music and dance (most 'Latin' rhythms are in fact Caribbean in origin), and to a lesser extent in the visual arts. The colourful Carnivals staged by many islanders, and other event attractions such as *Reggae Sunsplash* in Jamaica, *Junkanoo* in the Bahamas, *Cropover* in Barbados, and *Pirates Week* in the Cayman Islands – are showcases of national identity, giving tourists the opportunity to interact with the host community. We will now look at some of the islands in more detail, starting with the English-speaking countries of the Commonwealth Caribbean.

The Bahamas

Of the 700 islands that make up the Bahamas only 14 are inhabited. Poor soils and a lack of surface water mean that only 5 per cent of the land is suitable for agriculture, forcing the islanders to find alternative sources of income. Nassau became fashionable as a winter destination for wealthy Americans in the late nineteenth century, but it was not until the 1960s, in the aftermath of the Cuban Revolution, that mass tourism developed. Proximity to Miami has ensured that the Bahamas are the most popular ports of call for cruise ships, including a number of private islands, where passengers are free of the unwelcome attentions of the beach vendors and hustlers prevalent in many Caribbean resorts. Most of the hotels and other facilities are concentrated on two islands:

- New Providence contains the capital Nassau, and the resort areas of Paradise Island – which boasts casinos and the Atlantis hotel and leisure complex among its attractions – and Cable Beach, lined with expensive hotels; and
- Grand Bahama offers two purpose-built resorts – Freeport and Lucaya, based on golf, duty-free shopping and gambling.

In contrast, the 'Family' or 'Out Islands' are less developed, but provide for a range of outdoor activities and low impact eco-tourism. Abaco has a long established boat building industry and is a yachting centre; Eleuthera and Bimini are noted for game fishing, while the exceptionally clear waters around Andros are ideal for scuba diving

Discussion point

It is proposed to develop one of the Out Islands, which contains large areas of mangrove swamp, as a luxury resort with a marina and golf course. Most of the labour for the hotels will be imported from other Caribbean islands and from South America. The project is opposed by most local people and pressure groups such as Tourism Concern. Present arguments for supporting as well as opposing the project.

THE AMERICAS

The Turks and Caicos Islands

These islands to the south of the Bahamas are flat and rather arid, but upmarket tourism has developed on Providenciales, which offers fine beaches and world class diving, and is easily accessible with frequent air services from the USA.

Bermuda

We feel justified in including Bermuda as part of the Caribbean in view of the cultural and physical similarities. Nevertheless you should be aware that this small British colony is situated in the North Atlantic, well outside the tropics, and is much closer to North Carolina than to the Bahamas. A group of interlinked coral islands, Bermuda offers world class beaches of pink sand, facilities for sailing and diving, as well as golf, cycling and riding among its attractions. Bermuda was originally developed as a winter resort for wealthy Americans from New York and Boston, but since beach tourism became fashionable summer has been the preferred season. The islands have retained their exclusive appeal, primarily by careful resource management. For example:

- hotel capacity is limited to 10,000 bed spaces;
- cruise arrivals are restricted, to protect the hotel sector from competition and Hamilton's shopping and port facilities from congestion; and
- the environment is safeguarded by a ban on rental cars and roadside advertising.

To reduce its dependence on beach tourism Bermuda is also promoting its naval heritage and music festival scene.

Jamaica

Jamaica is located in the centre of the Caribbean, and is the largest of the English-speaking islands, with a more diversified economy and a higher international profile than most countries in the region. Elite tourism was well established before the Second World War, with writers such as Ian Fleming taking up residence near Port Antonio. However large-scale development did not take place until the 1960s. Jamaica's image has since been damaged by internal political strife and drug-related crime. The government has countered the effect of negative publicity with infrastructural improvements, event attractions, and currency devaluation to attract foreign visitors, while domestic tourism has also been encouraged. Outside Kingston, which is a major business centre for the Caribbean, most of the hotel development is concentrated along the north coast, at Montego Bay, Ocho Rios – a major port of call for cruise ships – and Negril. Here the fine beaches are backed by forest-covered mountains, the best known attractions being Dunns River Falls near Ocho Rios, and rafting on the Rio Grande near Port Antonio. Jamaica can offer excellent sports facilities, particularly at Negril which was developed in the 1970s to cater for the younger, more active type of holidaymaker. Much of the accommodation is in all-inclusives, but most of these are Jamaican-owned. Market segmentation is evident, with different hotels catering for young singles seeking a hedonistic lifestyle, couples, and families with young children. Jamaica can also offer the following alternatives to beach tourism:

- ecotourism in the Blue Mountains and the karst limestone Cockpit Country based on small resorts such as Discovery Bay and Mandeville;
- the colonial heritage, including the great houses built by wealthy plantation owners, the old pirate stronghold of Port Royal in Kingston harbour and the Seville Heritage Park; and
- contemporary West Indian culture, particularly the musical legacy of Bob Marley.

The Cayman Islands

These small islands lying to the west of Jamaica are the best-known of a number of Caribbean territories that provide offshore financial services to the international business community. Grand Cayman is also a developed up-market holiday destination, while the islands offer world class diving, including the 'drop-off' known as Bloody Bay Wall off Little Cayman.

The Leeward Islands and the Windward Islands

The islands of the eastern Caribbean fall into two major groups:

- the Leeward Islands, clustering around Antigua; and
- the Windward Islands to the south, forming a chain from Dominica to Grenada.

The two groups share a common currency – the East Caribbean dollar – and belong to the Organisation of Eastern Caribbean States (OECS).

Antigua is the most developed of the Leewards, in contrast to its dependent island, Barbuda. It has an international airport handling direct flights from London and North America, as well as a network of regional services. Most of the island is low-lying and suffers from chronic water shortages, and has few natural attractions other than a coastline indented with coves and harbours, and boasting many fine beaches. Tourism dominates the economy of this small island-nation and with tourist arrivals greatly outnumbering the resident population, has been a mixed blessing. For example:

- most jobs in tourism are low status, with managerial posts usually filled by expatriates – Antiguans have been criticised for their attitude to service work;
- Antiguan popular culture has been stereotyped to meet tourist expectations; and
- the island's ecosystems have been damaged by beachfront development.

Antigua offers a major heritage attraction in English Harbour, an attractive yachting centre where Nelson's Dockyard is a reminder of the island's former importance to the British navy.

The other Leeward Islands can offer a greater variety of scenery than Antigua, and have not embraced mass tourism to the same extent, retaining a mix of small hotels, inns and guest houses. **Anguilla**, with its pink and white sand beaches, **Nevis** and **Montserrat** are small-scale upmarket destinations reflecting a more traditional Caribbean lifestyle. **St Kitts** in its Frigate Bay development has sought the middle income market, particularly from Canada, and the island is a venue for a number of cultural events such as music festivals.

St Lucia is the most developed of the Windward Islands, and for many visitors it represents the ideal holiday destination. Fine beaches of coral sand, as at Marigot Bay, contrast with the mountainous interior. The twin peaks of volcanic origin known as the

Pitons must rank among the most spectacular attractions of the Caribbean and provide St Lucia with a unique selling point (USP) which few other islands can offer. However the international airport is inconveniently located at the southern tip of the island in relation to the capital Castries. Tourism developed rapidly during the 1990s and most of the resort hotels are now all-inclusives.

Ecotourism and adventure tourism have been promoted by the governments of Dominica, St Vincent and Grenada, on the basis of similar resources. **Grenada**, known as the 'Spice Island of the Caribbean', does have the attraction of white sandy beaches, coral reefs and the fine harbour of St Georges, which is a major yachting centre. For **St Vincent,** cruise excursionists are almost as important to the economy as stayover tourists, while the chain of small coral islands known as the Grenadines offer a number of small resorts catering for divers and yachtsmen, and hideaways for the rich and famous.

Case study 24.1

Ecotourism in Dominica, 'Nature Island of the Caribbean'

Dominica was a latecomer to tourism, with its lack of white sand beaches, rugged terrain, rainy climate and relative inaccessibility. This small island has set out to attract nature-loving tourists to its mountainous interior, which offers pristine rainforest, waterfalls, sulphur springs and a 'boiling lake' of volcanic origin. There are two marine reserves, and two national parks which attract hikers, nature-lovers and bird watchers. Accommodation is in small hotels and guest houses that are locally owned and managed, with strong linkages to the island's farms and craft industries. Dominica was the first country in the world to be officially benchmarked by Green Globe 21 as an ecotourism destination. However, tourism growth since the 1990s – including a tenfold increase in cruise passenger arrivals in Roseau, the capital – has put the more accessible sites such as Trafalgar Falls under severe pressure. Some would argue that cruise tourism on this scale is incompatible with ecotourism, and that Dominica's unique appeal as the 'nature island of the Caribbean' is at risk. The island could also do more to reduce its dependence on imported fuels by making more use of renewable energy sources – at present the island's water resources supply half its demand for electricity.

Barbados

Barbados is the easternmost of the Caribbean islands, with a long established tourism industry. This is one of the few destinations in the region where British visitors outnumber those of North American origin, and the legacy of over three centuries of uninterrupted British rule is evident. The appeal of Barbados lies in its cultivated countryside – 'the garden of the West Indies' – its sporting attractions, notably cricket, and the superb beaches. Most of the resort development is on the west coast near the capital Bridgetown, where land prices are among the highest in the world, fuelled by the influx of 'new money'. The rugged east coast, exposed to the Atlantic surf, is protected from development. Tourism has to compete with other land uses in this small densely populated island. To meet the challenge, the government has an effective coastal zone management plan to prevent beach erosion, and is reducing the country's dependence on fossil fuels by encouraging solar energy use. The tourist authorities have tried to maintain the exclusive appeal of Barbados while at the same time encouraging middle income holidaymakers on air inclusive charters.

Trinidad and Tobago

The large island of Trinidad lies outside the hurricane belt close to the mainland of South America. It has a fairly developed economy based on petroleum, and a vibrant culture in which Asian as well as African and European influences are evident. The capital Port of Spain is an important regional gateway and business centre. The collapse of oil prices in the 1990s has induced the government to place more emphasis on tourism. Trinidad is famed for its steel bands, calypso singers and limbo dancers, and its Carnival must rank as one of the most spectacular event attractions in the Caribbean. The island also boasts a geological curiosity – Pitch Lake – and the Caroni Swamp with its wildlife resources. The much smaller island of Tobago offers a more relaxed lifestyle than Trinidad and an environment that is better suited to beach tourism and water sports.

The Virgin Islands

This cluster of islands is divided between Britain and the USA. **The US Virgin Islands** have the advantage of free access to sources of investment in the USA, and in the case of St Thomas, frequent air and shipping services from the US mainland. The port of Charlotte Amalie is thronged with American cruise passengers seeking duty-free shopping bargains. St John's marine resources have been given National Park status. **The British Virgin Islands** (BVI) are much less developed in terms of hotel capacity and although Tortola and Virgin Gorda are on the cruise circuit they receive far fewer visitors than St Thomas. The sheltered waters between the islands provide an ideal environment for flotilla sailing.

The French Antilles

The former French colonies of Martinique and Guadeloupe have opted for closer association with France, as overseas *départements*, instead of independence. This has advantages in guaranteeing a higher standard of living than their Commonwealth Caribbean neighbours, and frequent flights to and from Paris. The influence of French culture is apparent in the cuisine and architecture, and the islands cater mainly for French holidaymakers. Of the two main islands, **Martinique** is scenically the more attractive, with its volcanic peaks and lush vegetation, and Fort de France is one of the most sophisticated cities in the Caribbean. **Guadeloupe** is less popular as a destination, despite the fine beaches along its eastern coast. The outlying island of St Barts (St Barthélémy) has become a 'jet-set' resort.

The Dutch Caribbean

Six Caribbean islands were former Dutch colonies known as the Netherlands Antilles. In 2010 Curacao and St Maarten became independent states, following the example of Aruba, leaving Saba, St Eustatius and Bonaire under Dutch administration.

Saba, St Eustatius and St Maarten are situated among the Leeward Islands. Of these St Maarten (St Martin) is by far the most developed, and it is a major port of call for cruise ships. Part of the appeal lies in the fact that this small island is divided between the Netherlands and France, so that the visitor has the choice of shopping in either Philipsburg or Marigot (on the French side).

The southern group, known as the 'ABC Islands' (Aruba, Bonaire and Curaçao) lie outside the hurricane belt, close to the South American mainland and the oilfields of Lake Maracaibo in Venezuela – hence the oil refineries on Curaçao and Aruba. The inhabitants speak a language – Papamiento – which is a mixture of Dutch and Spanish. The main attraction to tourists lies in the excellent beaches, facilities for water sports and duty-free shopping, rather than the rather arid landscapes. Aruba has set out to attract the mass market in the USA with casinos and non-stop entertainment, whereas Bonaire is much less developed, being mainly known for windsurfing and world-class diving. Curaçao has more diversity although it attracts far fewer visitors than Aruba. Its capital, Willemstad is a vibrant cosmopolitan seaport, with a townscape of picturesque canals and Dutch-style buildings, very different from the pastiche development that characterises most Caribbean resorts. Curaçao appeals to visitors from Europe and South America as well as the USA.

Hispaniola and Puerto Rico

The Dominican Republic and Puerto Rico – along with Cuba – share a heritage from the time of the Spanish Empire in the Americas. During the twentieth century they followed very different political paths, and this has affected the type of tourism that has developed.

Puerto Rico, not yet a state, although a former US territory, is associated with the USA as a self-governing commonwealth. With the advantage of ready access to markets and sources of finance in the USA, a large manufacturing and service sector has developed in an island that, prior to 1950, was one of the poorest in the Caribbean. The capital San Juan is a major business centre and one of the main gateways to the Caribbean. With a number of beaches within easy reach, it is also an important holiday destination with hotel accommodation geared to a clientele that is 80 per cent North American. Another major source of visitors is the large number of Puerto Ricans resident on the US mainland, but these usually fall into the VFR category. Puerto Rico's major attractions include:

- Old San Juan, the fortified colonial city, showcasing the Spanish heritage;
- El Yunque National Park, an area of rainforest in the eastern highlands; and
- cultural events such as the Pablo Casals music festival.

The large island of **Hispaniola** is divided on cultural as well as political lines between the Spanish-speaking Dominican Republic and French Creole-speaking Haiti, where African influences are predominant. Between 1980 and 1995 the fledgling tourism industry of the two countries took a very different course; the Dominican Republic experienced a phenomenal rate of tourism growth, to become the most popular holiday destination in the Caribbean, while arrivals in Haiti declined considerably during the same period.

The Dominican Republic has been much more successful than Haiti in attracting foreign investment, in a bid to become a low-cost beach destination catering primarily for West Europeans. The country is served by a large number of charter airlines, with international airports at Puerto Plata, Punta Cana and Santo Domingo. Development is mainly in tourist enclaves on the 'Amber Coast' in the north and in the south-east, with all-inclusives dominating the accommodation sector. However, tourism growth has tended to outstrip the provision of adequate infrastructure, and the country's vulnerability to the mass market was shown in 1997, when British tour operators dropped it from their programmes following a health scare. The Dominican Republic's cultural attractions are largely overlooked by most tourists, apart from an introduction to sensual *merengue* rhythms, but the country has much to offer besides fine beaches, golf and water sports. The Ministry of Tourism stresses the key role of the capital, Santo Domingo, in the Spanish conquest of the Americas; the city boasts the first cathedral in the New World and other early sixteenth-century buildings. This was given further emphasis in 1992, with the inauguration of the controversial Faro á Colón (Columbus Lighthouse) commemorating the great explorer's achievement. The interior offers scope for adventure tourism with a landscape that includes the highest mountain in the Caribbean, rainforest and desert. Although there are no less than nineteen national parks, conservation measures are largely ineffective, and there is a shortage of quality accommodation away from the coastal resorts.

Haiti is the poorest country in the Western Hemisphere, and has suffered more than other Caribbean destinations from misgovernment, political instability, and negative publicity – including an AIDS scare in the early 1980s, that had a severe impact on its tourism industry. Prospects for recovery have not been improved by a major earthquake in 2009 that devastated the capital, Port-au-Prince. Haitian emigrants provide much of the labour for tourism developments in the English-speaking Caribbean, and this has led to social problems, as in the Turks and Caicos Islands. Population pressures have resulted in ecological disaster, and only 1 per cent of the original forest cover now remains. All this has tended to overshadow the fact that Haiti was the first country in the region to win independence from colonial rule, and the skill displayed in the locally-made paintings and handicrafts, in contrast to the imported souvenirs available elsewhere in the Caribbean. The rituals of voodoo – an alternative African religion – used to attract the more intrepid type of tourist. Most of the limited hotel capacity is located in Port-au-Prince and Cap Haitien in the north. The latter is visited for the remarkable citadel built by Henri Cristophe, one of the leaders in the war of independence against the French. Cruise ships on the eastern Caribbean circuit tend to use the private island of Labadee, with its fine beaches, in preference to calling at Port-au-Prince or Cap Haitien – yet another example of 'enclave tourism'.

Cuba

Cuba, with the only centrally-planned economy in the Western Hemisphere, is a unique destination. Separated from the USA by only the 150 kilometre wide Florida Strait, this large island is far more than a beach destination and can appeal to a wider range of markets than most Caribbean countries. It has a vibrant Spanish and African cultural heritage, and Cuban dance rhythms – notably salsa – have done much to promote the country's image in Europe. Half a century of trade sanctions imposed by the United States government has resulted in a '1950s time-warp' with American cars of that era still in use on the streets of Havana. Cuba has nevertheless achieved a high reputation for health care, and this attracts visitors from a wide range of countries seeking medical treatment.

The demand for tourism

Tourism has gone through the following phases, in response to political changes.

- **'Elite tourism'.** From 1902 until 1959 Cuba's economy was controlled by United States interests. Tourism was concentrated, as it is today, in Havana and the beach resort of Varadero, which largely developed in the 1920s with American investment. Havana was renowned for its uninhibited nightlife and casinos, catering for a wealthy and predominantly American clientele. In the 1950s Cuba was the leading destination of the Caribbean.

- **'Socialist tourism'.** Fidel Castro's revolution in 1959 was followed by an exodus of middle class Cubans to the USA. Subsequently Cuba lost 80 per cent of its international tourist market as a result of the trade and travel embargo imposed by the United States government. Castro turned to the USSR for economic aid, and tourism subsequently followed a similar pattern to the countries of Eastern Europe, with the state ownership of hotels, an emphasis on social tourism for the domestic market, and cultural exchanges with other members of the Soviet Bloc. Visitors from Western countries were largely restricted to group tours, organised by specialist tour operators who were broadly in sympathy with the regime and its achievements in education and health care.

- **Incipient mass tourism.** During the 1980s the government modified its attitude to international tourism. Joint ventures between Cubanacán, the state-owned tour operator and foreign companies, such as the Spanish Meliá group were encouraged, with the aim of expanding and modernising the hotel sector. Cuba became popular as a low-cost winter sun destination for Canadians. With the collapse of the Soviet Union, Cuba was deprived of cheap oil imports and a guaranteed market for its sugar, so that tourism was increasingly seen as a lifeline for the economy. Cuba was now offered as a package holiday destination by the leading tour operators of Western Europe, and the US dollar, later replaced by the convertible peso (CUC), became the only acceptable currency for most transactions involving tourists. Small business enterprises were allowed limited participation in the tourism sector, such as the *paladares* (restaurants in private homes).

There is an apparent contradiction between the government's socialist principles and its support for a free market which benefits tourists, not the Cuban people (Pattullo, 1996, 85). Western-style tourism has created divisions in Cuban society between those with access to hard currency – in effect those in direct contact with tourists – and the 95 per cent of the population who are paid entirely in almost worthless Cuban pesos. Sex tourism, which was rife in pre-1959 Havana, and prohibited after the Revolution, is now evident in places frequented by foreign tourists. In 2008 some of the restrictions preventing domestic tourists from staying in hotels used by foreign visitors were relaxed, but Cubans wishing to travel abroad continue to face many obstacles.

Tourist arrivals grew from 30,000 in the late 1970s to 2.3 million in 2008. Canada is Cuba's main source of tourists, accounting for a third of arrivals, followed by the UK, Italy, Spain and Germany. In Latin America, Argentina and Mexico are important markets. A surprising number of US citizens find ways of getting round the embargo. Foreign visitors are mainly concentrated in tourist enclaves such as Varadero – located on a sandpit with restricted access and which has its own international airport – and Cayo Largo, a beach resort that has been developed on a small offshore island. Tourism receipts now exceed those from sugar exports, but the net gain to the economy is much less, due to the need to import materials that Cuban industry and agriculture cannot provide, and the repatriation of profits by foreign investors. Tourism developers also have to cope with a deteriorating infrastructure – including power cuts, poor roads and inadequate public transport – and an inefficient bureaucracy. On the other hand, Cuba has one of the best-educated workforces in Latin America.

Tourism resources

Cuba's resource base includes extensive sandy beaches, coral islands for scuba diving and picturesque mountain scenery. The best-known scenic area is the Sierra Maestra in the south-east of the island. The province of Pinar del Rio, closer to Havana, also offers attractive landscapes, and, as the main tobacco-growing area, supplies Cuba's most famous export. Heritage attractions include the colonial cities of Trinidad and Santiago de Cuba. The latter is almost 1,000 kilometres from Havana, and is best reached by air rather than the unreliable rail service.

Havana can offer ballet, art galleries and other cultural attractions comparable with those of Europe, and is arguably the most sophisticated city in the Caribbean region. One of Havana's biggest attractions is the Tropicana floorshow, a relic of pre-Revolution Cuba that has been revived for tourists.

Case study 24.2

Tourism and cultural heritage in Old Havana

In the eighteenth century Havana became the wealthiest city in the Spanish empire, thanks to its exports of sugar and tobacco, and the plantation owners had the means to build magnificent town houses, as well as endowing convents, churches, theatres and universities. However, in the course of the twentieth century the capital expanded to the west to accommodate its growing population, while the historic core of Old Havana declined through lack of investment.

When the historic core of Havana was declared a World Heritage Site in 1982 most of its buildings were run down and occupied by impoverished families, while the Plaza Vieja, the market square of the colonial city, was derelict. Once-elegant mansions, with their airy balconies, wide vestibules and interior patios showed the effect of decades of neglect, with peeling plasterwork and crumbling facades. With part-funding from UNESCO, a team of architects and planners has embarked on a systematic programme of restoration and reconstruction, using old plans, paintings and photographs to ensure that the end result is an authentic version of nineteenth century Havana. Since the old city covers an area of 5 square kilometres and has about 100,000 residents this is a major undertaking.

In 1992 the Cuban government set up the state agency Habaguanex to provide goods and services for tourists that were largely lacking in the old city. The income from tourism was intended to finance the restoration work, but it soon became expedient to allocate some of the proceeds to improve housing and infrastructure for the local community.

Old Havana is no museum piece, but a place full of vibrant activity. Former mansions have been converted to a variety of uses, such as art galleries, dance academies, gymnasiums, craft shops, bars and restaurants. El Floridita, the bar frequented in the 1950s by Ernest Hemingway and famous in the history of cocktails, has become a popular tourist attraction. Tourism has brought new opportunities to local artists and craftsmen, who display their wares in the cathedral square. Tourism may also have trivialised Cuban culture, with Che Guevara appearing as a tourist icon on a wide range of souvenirs.

THE AMERICAS

The future of tourism in Cuba depends on improved relations with the USA and a peaceful transition to a more liberal regime, in which the Cuban exile community in Miami is bound to play an important role. The lifting of the US embargo would undoubtedly have an impact on the type of tourism on offer, as the long-suppressed demand from ordinary Cubans for consumer goods becomes effective demand.

Summary

- The Caribbean is well endowed with tourism resources, making the region one of the world's most important destinations.
- On many islands tourism has replaced agriculture as the main source of income.
- The English language is widespread throughout the islands, so there are few language barriers to English-speaking tourists.
- The islands cater mainly for beach tourism and recreation rather than cultural tourism.
- The USA dominates the market, particularly for winter sun tourism and cruising.
- An island's success as a destination depends largely on its accessibility to air and shipping services.
- On many of the smaller islands tourists and cruise passengers outnumber the local population, and this has significant environmental and social consequences.

Assignments

1. Explain why the Caribbean has become the world's premier cruise destination.
2. Identify the features that make Cuba different from other Caribbean islands. Discuss how this situation might change in the near future.
3. Apart from beach tourism, what other tourism products can the smaller Caribbean islands offer, and what are their prospects for success?
4. Explain why leakages significantly reduce the economic benefit of tourism to the islands. Suggest solutions to the problem, such as developing linkages between tourism and other sectors of the economy.

THE AMERICAS

CHAPTER 25

The tourism geography of Central and South America

The countries south of the US border share many social and economic features, and while Mexico is part of North America in its physical geography, culturally it has more in common with its neighbours in Central America. Mainland Latin America contains 16 Spanish-speaking countries and Portuguese-speaking Brazil. Belize in Central America and the Guianas in South America were colonised later by the British, the Dutch and the French, and are culturally similar to the Caribbean islands. Most of the countries in the region have Amerindian communities practising a traditional, rural way of life, while the majority of the population are *mestizos* of mixed European and Amerindian origin. As in the Caribbean islands, the Spanish and Portuguese colonists imported slaves from West Africa to provide labour, and their descendants contribute a major ingredient to the cultural mix, particularly in Brazil. The total population of Latin America is about 550 million and includes two of the world's mega-cities with 20 million inhabitants – São Paulo and Mexico City. Most of the region is Roman Catholic, and religious festivals play an important role in the culture, although evangelical movements are challenging the dominance of the Church in parts of Latin America. In many countries the indigenous peoples are increasingly finding a voice in determining their destiny, including the management of tourism in their communities.

Most Latin American countries are at the emerging market stage of economic development. During the 1990s governments throughout the region adopted free market and privatisation policies in place of the protectionism of earlier decades, to stimulate economic growth and reduce dependence on the export of minerals or cash crops. With the new millennium most of Latin America experienced an economic malaise more severe in its impact than the Asian currency crisis of 1997–1998. Some blame this on globalisation, but much can be attributed to excessive borrowing by the public sector. Governments have been forced to adopt austerity measures and divert a high proportion of their resources to repay huge debts to foreign creditors. Since 2005 a number of countries in the region, particularly Brazil, have achieved substantial economic growth, but social inequalities remain evident, with over half the population living below the poverty line. There are usually great disparities in wealth between the major cities, that resemble those of Europe or North America, and the more remote rural areas where pre-industrial lifestyles persist. Rural poverty in turn has led to a massive exodus to the cities, where most migrants live in crime-ridden shanty towns on the periphery, deprived of basic services.

In 2010 the region accounted for just over 3 per cent of the world total of international tourist arrivals. Latin America includes four of the world's biggest spenders on international travel – Brazil, Mexico, Argentina and Venezuela – as well as some major destinations, while in a few countries tourism is in its infancy. However we can make the following generalisations about tourism in the region:

- The wealthier socio-economic groups often prefer to travel abroad, particularly to the USA, rather than take holidays in their own countries.
- Visitors from other countries in the region, usually short stay, make up the bulk of arrivals.
- The USA provides the majority of tourists from outside the region to Mexico and Central America, but some South American countries attract a large proportion of their tourists from Europe.
- Tourism is much less significant as a source of foreign exchange in South America than it is to the Caribbean islands.
- The region's airlines have suffered as a result of 9/11. They were already struggling against competition from US carriers, which now account for two thirds of the Latin American market. Unlike their North American competitors they can count on little support from their governments, and few are able to meet the stringent safety standards required by the US government in the aftermath of 9/11.

There is a great variety of tourism resources in a region which includes some of the world's highest mountains and which is greater in latitudinal extent than either North America or Africa, where climates range from the equatorial to the sub-antarctic. Products include beach tourism, adventure travel and ecotourism in the mountains and forests of the interior, and cultural tourism in the Andes of South America and the 'Maya Route' of Central America.

Mexico

The heartland of Mexico is a high plateau – the Meseta Central – separated by the mountain barriers of the Sierra Madre from the tropical coastlands to the east and west. To the north are semi-desert landscapes similar to those of the south western USA, whereas central and southern Mexico, along with the countries of Central America, forms part of the much more diverse region known to anthropologists as Meso-America.

Mexico is the second largest economy in Latin America and the world's most populous Spanish speaking country, with important publishing and film producing industries. Unlike most countries in the region it has experienced political stability since the 1920s, after one of the few Latin American revolutions that resulted in lasting social and economic change. The Revolutionary Party (PRI) had a near monopoly of political power in all 26 states of the federal republic until the Presidential elections in 2000, when the more conservative Nationalist party (PAN) won control. The nationalist and socialist aspirations of the Mexican Revolution remain largely unfulfilled, in part due to Mexico's situation in the economic shadow of the USA. Moreover, Mexico's impressive economic development scarcely keeps pace with rapid population growth, and there are regional disparities in wealth distribution. This has caused a massive flow of emigration – much of it illegal – to the USA, where the economic opportunities are so much greater. Mexico's membership of NAFTA has opened up the economy to foreign investment, and stimulated business travel to and from the United States and Canada.

Mexico's appeal to North Americans is partly based on its beaches and sunny winter climate, but the cultural contrasts which the country offers to the USA are equally important. Although the majority of Mexicans are *mestizos* (of mixed Spanish and Amerindian origins), the Amerindian heritage, as expressed in cuisine, folklore and handicrafts, is regarded as central to the national identity. There is a contradiction here, as the majority of present-day Amerindians are socially and geographically marginalised in the poorer southern states. The most significant features of this rich cultural heritage are:

* The pre-Columbian heritage, represented by the impressive remains of advanced Amerindian civilisations which flourished in Mexico before the Spanish conquest. The best known of these are Teotihuacán and Tula in central Mexico, and the cities of the Mayas in Yucatán and Chiapas in the south. These form part of the Ruta Maya tourist circuit, which also takes in neighbouring Belize, Honduras and Guatemala.
* The legacy of the Spanish colonial period, particularly the numerous Baroque churches, and picturesque towns such as Quéretaro, Morelia, San Miguel Allende and Guanajuato in central Mexico. These are associated with the Mexican struggle for independence, and have been meticulously preserved. Most of the colonial *haciendas* (country estates) on the other hand were destroyed during the Mexican Revolution (1910–1920). Other legacies of Spanish rule, such as the bullfight and the fiestas of the Catholic Church continue to flourish in the popular culture.
* The artistic legacy of the Mexican Revolution, as expressed by painters such as Frida Kahlo (now a feminist icon), Diego Rivera and many others who are noted for their murals decorating public buildings that celebrate Mexican folk traditions and the pre-conquest civilisations.

Tourism demand and supply

Mexico is one of the world's leading travel destinations, attracting just over 20 million foreign tourists in the early years of the twenty first century, with tourism supporting 1.7 million jobs and contributing over 7 per cent of GDP. However, the tourism industry is highly dependent on the United States and Canadian markets; less than 5 per cent of visitors originate from other countries, and this leaves it vulnerable to 'shocks' to tourism demand such as 9/11.

While traditional Mexico provides the tourist image, modern Mexico – particularly the wealthier northern states – has adopted many aspects of the lifestyle of the USA. A substantial middle class generates a considerable demand for domestic tourism and for international travel – despite a number of economic crises that have resulted in the devaluation of the peso against foreign currencies. The majority of Mexicans do not have sufficient disposable income to take holiday trips. There is some development of social tourism, including holiday villages for industrial workers such as those employed by PEMEX, the state-owned petroleum corporation.

In an attempt to improve the economic situation the federal government has given tourism a prominent role in national planning since the 1950s. Foreign developers are encouraged to participate in large hotel projects that will stimulate job creation, especially in the less developed regions. There is a strong Ministry of Tourism (SECTUR) that is responsible for policy-making. The federal government has also taken a direct role in tourism development through the FUNATUR funding agency. This has been responsible for a number of comprehensively planned resorts such as Ixtapa on the Pacific coast and Cancún.

As in most Latin American countries, domestic air services and long distance bus travel are more important than rail transport. The major cities are linked by modern highways to the USA, but east–west communications are less adequate. Water supplies and sanitation are defective in many rural areas, falling far short of those considered acceptable in the United States. Drug-related organised crime has spread in recent years from its focus in Sinaloa to Monterrey, Mexico's second city and the towns on the US border, particularly Ciudad Juárez. Many see this as a major threat to the country's stability and well-being.

Tourism resources

Mexico can offer a great variety of colourful traditions – showcased by the Ballet Folklórico in the capital – as well as contrasting landscapes. We can divide the country into the following regions.

The north and west

The northern part of Mexico is basin and range country with large areas of desert, similar to those across the US border in Arizona. The Barranca del Cobre (Copper Canyon) is the best known natural attraction, accessed by the spectacular Chihuahua–Pacific railway. Spending by United States visitors in the border towns, particularly Tijuana has accounted for over half of Mexico's receipts from tourism; such visitors are however cost-conscious and numbers vary according to the strength of the dollar against the peso. Also liberal attitudes to gambling and sex tourism are a less important motivator for young Americans now that such attractions are widely available nearer home, and drug-related violence has deterred visitors in recent years. Monterrey is the major city of northern Mexico, with an important manufacturing base and rivalling the capital as a business centre.

The **peninsula of 'Baja'** (Lower California) in the north-west is separated from the rest of Mexico by the Gulf of California, otherwise known to the travel industry as the Sea of Cortéz. The peninsula is largely desert, but temperatures along the Pacific coast are moderated by the cold California Current. The beaches and game-fishing attract large numbers of Americans, thanks to an excellent highway running the length of the peninsula from the border town of Tijuana. Ensenada and La Paz have become major tourist centres and cruise ports, while the federal government has developed purpose-built resorts at Loreto and Los Cabos.

The **'Mexican Riviera'** further south has a tropical climate with a long dry season corresponding to winter in the USA. This has made this stretch of Pacific coast popular with North Americans as a winter sun destination and retirement area. Acapulco is the most important centre, with good air and road communications to Mexico City. The historic seaport is now overshadowed by a vast agglomeration of hotels and condominiums surrounding the famous bay. Other resorts have developed from fishing ports, such as Puerto Vallarta and Mazatlán.

The Gulf coast of Mexico, with its more humid climate, is less popular as a holiday area, but offers the historic port of Veracruz among its many cultural attractions.

Central Mexico

The area richest in cultural attractions is the southern part of the Meseta Central, which is dominated by volcanoes such as Popocatepetl. These include the archaeological sites and colonial cities mentioned earlier, and many others such as Puebla – noted for fine ceramics, and Taxco – which grew rich on its silver mining industry. All of these are easily reached from the capital.

Mexico City, situated at an altitude of 2,700 metres, is the world's fastest growing metropolis, although this growth has been accompanied by severe air pollution, depletion of water supplies, and acute traffic congestion. Whilst few traces remain of the Aztec city of Tenochtitlán destroyed by Cortéz, the central square or Zocalo adjoined by the cathedral and Presidential Palace, occupies the site of its most important temples. The capital's attractions include:

- the National Museum of Anthropology, celebrating the achievements of the Aztecs and other Indian civilisations;
- the Basilica of Guadalupe, one of the world's most visited shrines; and
- the floating gardens of Xochimilco, popular for Sunday excursions. This is all that remains of the lake that once surrounded the former Aztec city, but the attraction is increasingly threatened by a lowering of the water table.

Southern Mexico and Yucatán

Southern Mexico, particularly the states of Chiapas and Oaxaca, is also noted for its Indian heritage. Along with the Yucatán Peninsula, this region forms part of the area covered by the *Mundo Maya* (World of the Maya) tourism development plan, which also embraces four Central American countries – Belize, El Salvador, Guatemala and Honduras. This is an example of regional co-operation between governments, tour operators and the local communities, with the aim of achieving sustainable development. There are also plans for an 'ecological corridor' giving more adequate protection to the rich biodiversity of southern Mexico and Central America.

Tourism is mainly focused on the fine beaches of the Yucatán Peninsula facing the Caribbean. The interior of Yucatán is a low limestone plateau dotted with *cenotes* (sinkholes) that have yielded much archaeological evidence of the ancient Maya civilisation. The region was isolated from the rest of Mexico until the 1970s, when the federal government improved the infrastructure and developed facilities, notably at Cancún. This part of Mexico can be included in the western Caribbean cruise circuit and also has the advantage of greater proximity by air to Miami and the cities of the eastern USA. Cancún is a good example of both mass tourism and 'enclave tourism', a self-contained 'mega-resort' where holidaymakers and conference delegates have little contact with the indigenous Maya population. South of Cancún, development is taking place along the so-called Mayan Riviera, but on a smaller scale and with more respect for traditional values. The hinterland, with its impressive Mayan cities of Uxmal and Chichen Itza, is of more interest for cultural tourists.

Central America

Central America is a mountainous neck of land linking the continents of North and South America. The region is prone to natural disasters such as earthquakes, volcanic eruptions and hurricanes, and also has a reputation for political instability. It consists of three main physical divisions:

- the coastal lowlands along the Caribbean, often densely forested, and sparsely inhabited by Afro-Caribbean and Amerindian communities, many of which are English-speaking;
- the central volcanic highlands, that contain the majority of the population and much of the cultural heritage; and
- the Pacific coast, which has better beaches and a drier climate than the Caribbean lowlands.

Central America consists of six Spanish-speaking republics and English-speaking Belize, which is culturally and economically part of the Commonwealth Caribbean. The majority of tourists – other than those from neighbouring countries – come from the United States. Most of these use air transport, especially from Miami, rather than the Pan-American highway system. Much of the region – notably Guatemala, El Salvador and Nicaragua – has only recently recovered from a long period of violent political strife, and this has held back the development of tourism. During the 1990s Central America experienced a higher growth rate in tourist arrivals than either the Caribbean or South America, but from a very low base. Costa Rica and Belize have concentrated on the development of eco-tourism while in Guatemala cultural tourism is dominant, but other countries in the region have been arguably less successful in defining their tourism product. In most of these countries the capital city is a major destination for business travel rather than leisure tourists.

While Central America attracted 8 million visitors in 2009, only 11 per cent came from Europe. Co-operative marketing by the seven national governments is expected to increase the demand from Europe and Asia, particularly China, which is already a major investor in the region. The main obstacle is the lack of direct flights to Europe and Asia, and the high cost of intra-regional travel.

Guatemala

Guatemala has a legacy of ethnic division between the Ladinos (Spanish-speakers) who are the dominant group, and the Amerindian majority speaking Mayan languages, who still live in traditional communities where the value systems are quite different. Guatemala has great scenic and cultural diversity for such a small country, and this is its strength as a tourist destination. Attractions include:

- The colonial heritage. This is based mainly on Antigua, the former capital, which has become an important centre for Spanish-language tuition.
- Traditional Amerindian culture. Each Mayan community has its own distinctive costume, which makes their markets exceptionally colourful, the best-known example being that of Chichicastenango in the northern highlands. Here ancient Mayan beliefs coexist with the Catholicism introduced by the Spanish.
- The volcanic mountain scenery around Lake Atitlán, and the Cuchumutanes range.

* The Tikal National Park in the Petén rainforest, protecting one of the most important Maya sites in Central America. This city, with its stepped pyramid-temples and ceremonial plazas was abandoned to the jungle centuries before the Spanish conquest, and was only rediscovered in the nineteenth century.

Belize

Belize can also claim large tracts of pristine forest, important Mayan sites, and the world's second largest barrier reef. The policy of the government is to encourage 'community-based ecotourism' but also to use it as a means of earning foreign exchange to finance economic development. In other words Belize is an excellent example of how a country can use the notion of sustainability to promote the development of new types of tourism (Mowforth and Munt, 2008). Much of the tourism industry is owned by expatriates, mostly US citizens, and although some reefs have been designated as marine reserves, others are likely to develop as exclusive resorts.

El Salvador

This small country is the most densely populated in Latin America, and one of the most developed. Salvadorcans are renowned for their business enterprise, and El Salvador has been at the forefront in attempts at regional economic co-operation, including Grupo TACA – a consortium of five national airlines. While little of the original forest cover remains, the landscape of coffee plantations in a setting of volcanic mountains is attractive, and is now promoted as a tourist route – La Ruta de las Flores. The Pacific coast offers world class surfing, while El Salvador's spas and beach resorts cater mainly for the domestic market and the large number of Salvadorean emigrants living in the USA.

Honduras

Honduras is better known for the banana plantations around San Pedro Sula than for tourism. The interior is rugged mountain country, making air transport almost essential. The country is one of the poorest in Latin America and its plans for economic development were dealt a heavy blow by Hurricane 'Mitch' in 1998. Honduras has significant wildlife resources, while Comayagua, the former capital, offers heritage attractions. The Bay Islands in the Caribbean Sea have good diving facilities, while Copán is one of the most important Maya sites in Central America.

Nicaragua

The international spotlight fell on Nicaragua in the 1980s, when the USA sought to bring down the left wing Sandinista regime through economic sanctions and support for the 'Contra' rebels. The present government has given generous tax breaks to foreign investors, and the country is becoming a retirement haven for US citizens, following the examples of Costa Rica and Honduras. Nicaragua's attractions include:

- the spectacular scenery of Lake Nicaragua, studded with volcanic islands; and
- the cities of Granada and León with their fine colonial heritage.

There is some small scale development of beach tourism along the Pacific coast, catering mainly to middle class visitors from other parts of Central America. Nicaragua is also promoting its attractions for ecotourists along the River San Juan and in the northern highlands around Estelí.

Costa Rica

Costa Rica has a well-developed infrastructure and accommodation sector, and unlike other countries in the region, has a long-established reputation for democracy and political stability. The country boasts an ecotourism industry with a worldwide reputation. The capital San José attracts 'health tourists' from the USA – mainly from the older age groups – with its low cost medical services. Beach tourism, dolphin-watching and diving are important, and Costa Rica now forms part of the international surfing circuit.

Case study 25.1

Costa Rica as a model for sustainable development

This small, mountainous country is exceptionally rich in biodiversity – for example there are no less than 1,200 kinds of orchids – not to mention a great variety of birds, reptiles, amphibians and butterflies. This is due to the country's location at the meeting-point of the ecosystems of North America and South America, its altitudinal range and a coastline fronting two oceans. Since the 1960s the government has designated national parks and reserves to include a range of ecosystems and a number of volcanoes such as Irazú. Many rural communities now see ecotourism as a viable alternative to cattle farming, mining and commercial logging. As a result, the damage to wildlife habitats that occurred between 1950 and 1987, when Costa Rica lost 25 per cent of its forest cover, has been stemmed to a large extent.

In addition to its natural resource base, Costa Rica has the following advantages for ecotourism:

- most hotels are small, with less than 20 rooms, are locally owned, and are examples of good practice in resource conservation;
- the Institute of Tourism (ICT) which is a public agency, encourages sustainable development by a voluntary programme of certification for all types of tourist enterprise;
- there is a strong environmental lobby supporting the government's conservation policies; and
- Costa Rica has technical and financial support from the IMF and the US government for its conservation programmes.

Furthermore, Costa Rica has ambitions to become carbon-neutral by 2021, starting with its domestic airlines.

However, tourist numbers have grown rapidly since the early 1990s to reach around two million international arrivals in 2008. With improved road access from San José and the port of Puntarenas, which receives a growing number of cruise passengers, some of the most popular national parks now receive a thousand visitors a day during the high season. There is a real danger that environmental capacities will be exceeded, resulting in disturbance to wildlife. With this rate of growth, the drive for profit in the short term may lead to a relaxation of conservation rules by national park staff. Other concerns include the following.

- The development of golf courses and a large resort complex in the Nicoya Peninsula has been criticised by environmentalists as being incompatible with Costa Rica's image as a destination for ecotourism. This is driven by the government's need for a higher yield type of tourism to service the country's large foreign debt.
- Although 25 per cent of the country is designated for protection, most of the land remains in private ownership so that enforcement of conservation measures can be problematic.
- The certification scheme has been criticised as 'greenwashing', where for example, a large hotel can be awarded the same environmental rating as a small jungle lodge, by complying with waste management and recycling targets (Dasenbrock, 2002).
- The growth of adventure tourism, which includes activities such as bungee-jumping, mountain bike riding and canyoning, as well as kayaking, white-water rafting and horse riding. Although most of these activities take place outside national park boundaries, some eco-tour operators view adventure tourism as a threat to their business. Zip-wires enable tourists to cross fast-flowing rivers but cause disturbance to wildlife, while developments such as a 'nature theme park' including an 'Indian village' are not really compatible with a nature-based tourism claiming it has 'no artificial ingredients'. On the other hand some tour companies combine adventure with nature study, and work closely with local communities. It is claimed that if the young people of the community are involved in these activities they will be more inclined to conserve the natural environment for future generations.

Panama

This country owes much of its importance as a tourist destination to the famous Canal, which passed from United States to Panamanian control at the end of 1999, along with the surrounding territory known as the Canal Zone. Some 40 to 50 ships pass through the Canal each day. The locks at Gatún, where the Canal crosses the Continental Divide, must count as one of the world's major feats of engineering. The city of Panama, with its mixture of high rise modern buildings and Asian bazaars is a major centre of international commerce, encouraged by the country's liberal banking laws and use of the dollar as the national currency. The free port of Colón, at the western (Caribbean) end of the Canal is another important trading centre. However Panama has yet to realise its full potential as 'the crossroads of the Americas', due to the jungles of Darien only 200 kilometres to the east. These pose a formidable barrier to the completion of the Pan-American highway system and any projected route must respect the land claims of the local Amerindian tribes.

Panama's holiday attractions mainly lie in the offshore islands. Of these the Pearl Islands have received the most attention from tour operators. The most important of these – Contadora – is a luxury resort and conference venue. The San Blas Islands are noted for game-fishing, but here the local Kuna tribe have kept development at arms length – tourism has to be on their terms.

It is likely that the former Canal Zone will be developed to yield maximum revenue, with marinas, hotels and timeshare apartments. The Canal itself is too restricted for the largest cruise ships, and a third set of locks will be needed to increase capacity – but this could have an adverse environmental impact, affecting water supplies to the city of

Panama. In contrast eco-tourism is being encouraged in other parts of the country, along with projects to restore the old Spanish seaport of Portobelo – a reminder that the isthmus was an important transit corridor for trade centuries before the opening of the Canal.

South America

South America receives around 2.5 per cent of the world's international tourist arrivals. The high cost of airfares and the lack of charter flights partly explains why this continent remains a destination for the wealthy or adventurous traveller. There is also a shortage of suitable hotels for the inclusive tour market. Long-term planning and investment in the tourism industry have been discouraged by political instability and inflation.

Climatic conditions, dense vegetation and rugged terrain have been a great obstacle to road and railway construction in many areas. In the west, the Andes – the world's longest mountain range, and second only to the Himalayas in altitude – pose a formidable barrier. Most of South America lies within the tropics, and the continent includes the world's largest rainforest in the Amazon Basin. Water transport is still widely used wherever there are navigable rivers – such as the Amazon and the Paraná – but the shipping services are usually slow and uncomfortable. Transport infrastructure is gradually improving with the expansion of the Pan-American highway network and the development of internal air services. Rail systems in South America tend to be rudimentary, but some of the world's most spectacular lines are to be found in the Andes, and these have become tourist attractions in their own right.

A number of countries in South America are undergoing rapid industrialisation, with a resulting increase in business travel from Europe and the USA. As regards the holiday market, national tourist offices in South American countries are generally underfunded, so that overseas promotion has been left to the national airlines or to specialist tour operators in the tourist-generating countries. Closer international co-operation, as among the Andean Pact countries and those belonging to MERCOSUR (the Common Market of the South) should facilitate travel within the region and bring about more effective tourism promotion.

Brazil

Brazil occupies almost half of South America and is a leading member of MERCOSUR. Unlike most Latin American countries, Brazil has a well-defined image, based on its beaches, the Rio de Janeiro carnival, and the Amazon rainforest. The country is comparable in size to the USA – spanning three time zones – and is the world's sixth most populous country, with almost 200 million inhabitants, who are mainly concentrated along the Atlantic seaboard. Brazilians are essentially the result of a fusion of three cultures – Portuguese, African and Amerindian. Since the nineteenth century the country has also attracted many millions of immigrants from all over the world, including Germany, Italy and Japan, but it has arguably been more successful than the USA in blending different races and cultures.

Brazil's market potential for tourism is closely linked to the development of the economy, now the largest in Latin America, which has grown rapidly since 2001. Brazil is now one of the four leading 'emerging market' economies, but it remains to be seen whether the 'boom and bust' cycle, so evident in the past, has been resolved. Most of the country's industrial wealth is concentrated in the Rio de Janeiro–São Paulo–Belo Horizonte triangle, while other regions, notably the North-east, remain poor and underdeveloped.

Demand for tourism

Inbound tourism

Brazil received 6.8 million tourist arrivals in 2009 and tourism ranks fifth in the country's foreign exchange earnings. Nevertheless, Brazil has a substantial deficit on its tourism account. There is a strong business travel sector, and São Paulo, Rio de Janeiro and Brasilia are among the world's leading cities for international conferences. The demand for holiday travel tends to be seasonal, with the greatest tourist activity taking place during the months of Carnival, which is also the hottest and most humid time of the year in most of Brazil. Nature, ecotourism and adventure are the motivators for 20 per cent of foreign tourists.

Domestic and outbound tourism

The growth in the economy has swelled the ranks of the Brazilian middle class who now have the discretionary income for both domestic and international tourism. Brazilians took 68 million domestic trips in 2010. Under the country's labour laws employees are guaranteed a 48 hour week and an annual paid holiday of 20 days, but many are excluded from becoming tourists by low incomes, especially in the rural areas. However, recreational facilities are provided by the state governments in city areas, while the beaches are freely available to rich and poor alike. Domestic tourists tend to use small hotels and campgrounds, or stay with friends and relatives. Currently the majority of tourism trips are by car due to the high cost of air transport, however this may change as a result of competition between the airlines and domestic tour operators. Although Brazilians are beginning to travel widely in their own country, they tend to be far more interested in beach holidays than in trips to the Amazon, as the beach and the cult of the 'body beautiful' occupies a central place in the nation's hedonistic lifestyle. Television through the popular *tele-novelas* (soap operas) plays an important role in opening up new coastal areas for the domestic market.

Outbound travel has doubled since 2002 to approach 3 million trips in 2010. For many Brazilians it is their first experience of travelling abroad, so group tours are preferred to independent travel, and with the advantage of a strong currency, spending levels (particularly on shopping) tend to be high. While the USA remains the most popular destination, more Brazilians than before are travelling to European countries and Asia, taking advantage of the competitive fares offered by Emirates and LATAM, South America's leading airline.

Transport

Lacking petroleum, Brazil pioneered the use of biofuels, with most of its motor vehicles using ethanol derived from sugar cane produced in the state of São Paulo. Environmentalists fear that production will spread north into Mato Grosso, causing destruction of forest, and widespread air and water pollution.

The vast size of Brazil poses a major problem for overland transport, especially during the rainy season from December to May. The Amazon and its tributaries provide

20,000 kilometres of navigable waterways, but these are far from the major populated areas and port facilities are inadequate. The national transport strategy is to construct a number of major highways through the rainforest to improve access to the Amazon and eventually link up with the road system of neighbouring countries. However the road network has not opened up the interior for development to the extent the government envisaged; rather it has facilitated rural out-migration, and contributed to the decline of Brazil's antiquated railway system. On the other hand Brazil's internal air network is well-developed, with nine international airports and hundreds of airfields allowing access to even the most remote areas. Facing a financial crisis, the national airline VARIG was acquired by the low-cost carrier GOL in 2007, and its competitor TAM now provides a greater choice of domestic and international services. There is a frequent shuttle service between São Paulo and Rio de Janeiro for business travellers.

Organisation

Tourism development since the 1960s has been the responsibility of Embratur, a federal government agency, but until 2003 Brazil did not have a Ministry of Tourism with dedicated funding. Previously the sector had been the remit of the Ministry of Sport and before that, to the Ministry of Foreign Trade. The federal government now recognises the central importance of tourism to the economy with more effective marketing, investment in training to improve professionalism, and expanding the infrastructure. National tourism plans should ensure that the country is well prepared to host the football World Cup in 2014 and the Olympic Games in 2016. There has also been considerable investment by state governments and the private sector in hotels, theme parks and other attractions.

Tourism resources

Brazil has five tourism regions, each offering a different appeal.

Amazonia forms the major part of the world's greatest river basin that covers 5 million square kilometres and contains 20 per cent of the planet's freshwater resources. The region's rainforests hold a fascination for foreign visitors as an ecological resource threatened with destruction. This is a good example of a change in perception, contrasting with the earlier view of the Amazon as the 'green hell' vividly described by Colonel Fawcett and other explorers. In Brazil itself there is a growing environmental movement, following the Rio Summit in 1992, to prevent further exploitation of the region for large-scale cattle grazing, mining and road-building, but this faces opposition from powerful vested interests. Most tourists to Amazonia arrive by air at Manaus or Belém. Both cities have fine buildings dating from the rubber boom of the 1890s, particularly Manaus with its magnificent opera house. After a long period of decline, this city has been revitalised with its development as a free port. Santarem, at the confluence of the Amazon and the Tapajoz, is another important tourist centre. Ecotourists seeking a closer encounter with the rainforest are accommodated in a number of lodges, some of which are built in the tree canopy, while others use 'floatels' moored at the river bank. Sustainable tourism is aimed for in the following ways:

- by restricting lodge capacity to a small number of guests;
- by keeping facilities simple, using solar power and local food supplies wherever possible, and dispensing with air-conditioning;

- by maintaining remoteness, with the journey from say, Manaus being undertaken by boat and canoe rather than by air; and
- visits to Indian villages are controlled by FUNAI, the Indian Protection Agency. Tourists are taken to visit local families but no family is visited regularly, so minimising impact. As a result of these policies the natural resources are protected and the quality of the experience for the visitor is also maintained.

The North-east consists of a fertile coastal belt and the semi-arid scrublands in the interior known as the *sertão* or backlands, an area often described as the 'Triangle of Thirst'. This is a poverty stricken region that has traditionally exported millions of rural migrants to the cities of southern Brazil. The coast is very popular with Brazilians, as it offers many fine beaches. Former fishing villages are 'discovered' and then cease to be fashionable in the never-ending quest for the 'perfect beach'. The coast is the subject of a tourism development programme, resulting from an agreement between the state governments of the region and the Inter-American Development Bank (IDB). International hotel groups have moved in, particularly along the 'Golden Coast' south of Recife, creating tourist enclaves. In contrast accommodation is in short supply and often substandard in the sertão, which has an important place in Brazilian folklore as former bandit country. The major tourist centres of the North-east include:

- Salvador de Bahia, one of the major cultural centres of Brazil, famed for its attractive colonial architecture, and as the birthplace of the samba, hosting a carnival that rivals the more famous one in Rio de Janeiro;
- Fortaleza, noted for its fine beaches; and
- Recife the international gateway to the region, known as the 'Venice of Brazil' on account of its many waterways.

The remote island of Fernando do Noronha, located in the Atlantic Ocean 400 kilometres from Recife, has become a fashionable destination, with world-class resources for surfing and diving. Designation as a national park means that the number of visitors is strictly limited, with each visitor paying an entrance fee, and the island remains difficult and expensive to reach.

The Centre-West is Brazil's underdeveloped heartland, although it received a major boost in the 1960s with the establishment of Brasilia as the new federal capital. Most of the region consists of savanna grassland, with extensive wetlands near the Paraguayan border. This area, known as the Pantanal, is rich in wildlife that had previously co-existed with cattle-ranching. This unique environment is now under threat from the activities of poachers and loggers, the expansion of agriculture, and projects to improve navigation on the Rivers Paraná and Paraguay that interrupt the annual flood cycle. The government-sponsored National Environment Agency has designated a number of natural reserves in the region, but these are relatively small and under-funded. In contrast, Brasilia is noted for its freeways and the visionary architecture of Oscar Niemeyer, epitomised by the Palace of Congress and the National Museum of the Republic. Although the capital is attractively landscaped, it lacks the vibrancy of other cities, particularly at night, as most workers have to live in dispersed suburbs.

The South is the only region of Brazil to experience a temperate climate, with occasional frosts during the winter months. It is home to many migrants from Europe, including a large German-speaking community. Florianopolis is a popular beach resort for domestic tourists and well-off Paraguayan visitors, while Curitiba is one of the most progressive cities in the Americas. The major attraction for foreign tourists is Iguaçú Falls on the border with Argentina. This is actually a series of cataracts three times larger than Niagara. Walkways have been built in the Garganta de Diablo gorge at the edge of the biggest waterfall. The resort of Foz de Iguaçú has good communications by air and is a major conference venue.

The South-east receives the most foreign tourists, largely because it contains Rio de Janeiro. This is one of the world's great tourist cities, for the following reasons:

- Some 80 kilometres of fine sandy beaches, the best known being Copacabana and the more fashionable Ipanema. These are ideal for people-watching (but not for bathing due to the heavy Atlantic surf).
- The uninhibited dance rhythms and extravagant costume parades of the Rio Carnival, which is a showcase for Brazilian creativity. There is the official Carnival, a sponsored event held in the Sambadrome, in which only the members of the top 'samba schools' participate, and then there are the popular street parties and parades which last for five days. Carnival attracts five million visitors, of whom 10 per cent are foreign tourists.
- The spectacular beauty of Rio's setting, on one of the world's finest harbours, backed by the granite peaks of Sugarloaf and Corcovado, which is crowned by the iconic statue of Christ the Redeemer.

To complement these resources the city has a good transport infrastructure, including two major airports, and world-class hotels that are concentrated in the Copacabana area.

Case study 25.2

Tourism and poverty alleviation in Rio's *favelas*

Mud-slides following exceptionally heavy rains in May 2010 caused hundreds of deaths in the *favelas*, the shanty towns spilling down the hillsides and overlooking the wealthiest neighborhoods of the city. Their inhabitants may have some of the best views, but they are deprived of basic sanitation and other services. About 20 per cent of Rio's population live in these slums. In response to the disaster, the government has undertaken a programme of relocating the slum-dwellers. Many residents suspect this is being used as a pretext to clear prime sites for redevelopment in readiness for the football World Cup and the Olympic Games.

Contrary to popular belief, the vast majority of their inhabitants are not criminals, but work in low-paid jobs in the city, mainly in the informal sector of the economy. Roçinha, the largest of the *favelas* with an area of 144 hectares and a population estimated at 150,000, supports many small businesses, cybercafes, bars and even a local TV station, all provided by local initiative. The city authorities are unable to control tax evasion, the setting up of businesses without legal permit, and the illegal tapping of electricity from the municipal grid. A semblance of order and social aid for those in need is provided by well-organised gangs involved in the illegal drugs trade. So far tourism has done little to benefit the people of the *favelas*, but Roçinha has been the subject of a private initiative to train local guides to show tourist groups the hidden face of Rio and help regenerate the area.

This policy is now being adopted by the city authorities, but only in those *favelas* that have been 'pacified' by removing them from gang control. It has become imperative to reduce the high levels of street crime for which Rio is notorious and provide a secure environment for foreign tourists arriving for the World Cup. A special police force, the UPP, has been deployed for this purpose, using less draconian methods than in the past. This policy has had some success, even in Cidade de Deus, a *favela* made internationally famous through the movie *City of God*. However some critics allege that the problem of criminal gangs is simply removed from the south and west of the city, the areas most visited by tourists, to *favelas* on the outskirts.

Photo 25.1 Rio de Janeiro receives the majority of Brazil's foreign tourists (©istockphoto.com/ Luoman)

The coastline between Rio and Santos, backed by the lush mountain scenery of the Serra do Mar, has been designated for major tourism development. A number of beach resorts are increasingly popular with foreign visitors, such as Buzios, Angra dos Reis and Sepetiba. However development poses a threat to the Atlantic rainforests, already under severe pressure. The interior of this part of Brazil also has much to attract the cultural tourist, including the picturesque colonial towns of Mariana and Ouro Preto, which grew rich from the silver and diamond mining boom of the eighteenth century. Business travellers gravitate to the big modern cities of Belo Horizonte and São Paulo.

• São Paulo diversified from coffee production to become one of the world's great manufacturing and financial centres during the twentieth century. Until recently the city was primarily a business destination and leisure tourism was of little significance. Brazil's largest city vigorously promotes its sporting, cultural and entertainment attractions, with the result it is now the country's leading destination, although only 10 per cent of its visitors are international tourists. The city typifies the contrasts that exist in Brazil between private wealth and social deprivation; it has South America's highest car ownership and a major pollution problem, which is now being addressed.

Northern South America

We could include the northern countries of South America as part of the Caribbean region; in fact Venezuela and Surinam belong to the CTO while Guyana and Surinam are members of Caricom. Colombia and Venezuela share an extensive coastline on the Caribbean, and the cities of Cartagena and Caracas feature prominently on some cruise itineraries. Guyana, Surinam and French Guiana have cultural similarities with the West Indies and retain close links with Britain, the Netherlands and France respectively. Moreover, the music of the tropical coastlands of Colombia, Venezuela and the Guianas is African rather than Amerindian in origin.

THE AMERICAS

Colombia

Colombia has the dubious distinction of being the country most threatened by terrorism since 9/11, while the prevalence of drug-related crime has made Bogotá one of the world's most dangerous cities. Although the political and economic situation has improved considerably in recent years, kidnappings are a feature of the long-running conflict between the army, paramilitaries and Marxist guerrillas – notably the FARC – that afflicts large areas of the country. Another, more romantic image is provided by the novels of García Márquez, epitomised by Mompox on the River Magdalena. Nowadays the town is a picturesque backwater, but in colonial times it was a major commercial centre. In fact Colombia has made considerable progress in industrial development as well as being the world's chief exporter of coffee and emeralds. The national airline – Avianca – was among the first to pioneer domestic air services in the Western Hemisphere; this was largely in response to the difficult topography. Colombia is compartmentalised by the Andes which here form a triple chain of mountains, acting as a formidable barrier to east–west communication. Not surprisingly, small regional airlines – often employing robust DC3 aircraft that can use short runways – are the lifeline for many communities.

Tourism development is the responsibility of the Corporación Nacional de Turismo (CNT) which has built a network of *paradors* along the main tourist routes. Most visitors arrive overland from Ecuador and Venezuela, attracted by shopping bargains. Promotion is mainly aimed at the US market, although growing numbers of tourists are coming from Germany and France.

Although Colombia has an extensive share of the Amazon rainforest and a long Pacific coastline, factors of climate, accessibility and security determine that the most popular tourist area is the Caribbean coast, where tropical beaches are backed by the snow-capped mountains of the Sierra Nevada. The beach resort of Santa Marta and the historic seaport of Cartagena de Indias – the key fortress of the 'Spanish Main' in colonial times – offer vibrant *cumbia* rhythms and beauty pageants among their attractions. The outlying islands of San Andrés and Providencia in the Caribbean Sea attract domestic tourists with duty-free shopping.

In the interior of Colombia, Medellin and Cali are major business centres, while the main tourist attractions are smaller cities such as Popayán, located in beautiful mountain valleys, that still retain much of their Spanish colonial heritage. Bogotá is noted for its Gold Museum, a collection of artefacts from the pre-conquest Indian civilisations, while San Agustin is one of the largest archaeological sites in the Americas.

Venezuela

As a major oil producer, Venezuela enjoyed the highest per capita income of any Latin American country prior to the fall in oil prices in the early 1990s. Middle-class Venezuelans travelled abroad in large numbers, particularly to Miami, leaving a substantial deficit in the international tourism account. The subsequent financial crisis has led the government to impose strict exchange controls and take a greater interest in encouraging inbound tourism. Venezuela has the reputation of being an expensive destination, despite the devaluation of the bolívar against foreign currencies. In contrast to the situation in other South American destinations, most of Venezuela's visitors do not come from neighbouring countries, but from Europe and the United States. About half are visiting for business reasons and many are VFR tourists – the result of substantial immigration from Spain and Italy. The private car is the dominant mode for domestic tourism, thanks to cheap petrol and an excellent highway network. Air transport is facilitated by a large number of airports throughout the country, and the many regional airlines.

Hotel capacity is mainly concentrated in the capital and the beach resorts of the Caribbean coast. Timeshare apartments are an important part of the accommodation sector, particularly for domestic tourists. Venezuela's tourism resources include:

- The capital Caracas, one of South America's great cities and a major gateway to the continent. It is primarily a business destination, but it does have historic significance as the birthplace of Simón Bolívar, who liberated six South American countries from Spanish rule. Unfortunately for its tourism image, Caracas is one of the world's most violent cities.
- The beach resorts of the Caribbean, the most important being Porlamar on the island of Margarita, and Puerto La Cruz.
- A section of the Andes, including the colonial city of Mérida, which also boasts the world's highest cableway.
- The vast grasslands known as the Llanos, and the Guiana Highlands south of the River Orinoco, offer many possibilities for ecotourism. Fly-in camps in this remote, sparsely populated region provide a base for exploring the strange landscapes of the *tepuys* – sheer-sided, flat-topped mountains that inspired Conan Doyle's *Lost World* – and viewing the world's highest waterfall – Angel Falls.

The Guianas

This region is isolated from the rest of South America, and in Guyana, Surinam and French Guiana tourism is in its infancy. Throughout the Guianas there is a contrast between the low-lying coast, with its plantation economy, and the forested interior, where Amerindian tribes maintain their traditional way of life. The majority of the population live on the coast and are mainly of African or Asian origin. The lack of beaches and poor infrastructure means that ecotourism is often the only viable form of tourism. A coastal highway linking the three countries was only completed in 1998, while the rivers and internal air services provide the only access to the interior.

- **Guyana** has some of South America's finest rivers and one of its highest waterfalls – Kaieteur – as yet barely exploited as a tourist attraction. The few hotels are found mainly in Georgetown, and elsewhere forest lodges provide accommodation. The Rupununi region in the south-west of the country is an example of sustainable development, integrating eco-tourism and forest management for the benefit of the local Amerindian communities.
- **Surinam** has strong cultural and business ties with the Netherlands, and the capital, Paramaribo is one of the most cosmopolitan cities in South America with its blend of African and Indonesian cultures.
- **French Guiana** benefits from direct flights between Paris and Cayenne, due to its status as an overseas *département* of France, and as the base for the European Space Agency's 'Ariane' programme. Ecotourism is being promoted, but the country is better known for its former role as a penal colony, including the infamous 'Devil's Island'.

The Andean Republics

Peru, Ecuador and Bolivia share a similar physical environment, dominated by the Andes mountains, and a similar cultural heritage, in which the Indian influence is more prominent than elsewhere in South America. The region consists of three major physical divisions, namely:

- The Pacific coastal lowlands of Ecuador and Peru, where there is some development of beach tourism.
- The High Andes – actually two mountain chains separated by a series of intermontane basins and high plateaux. Here cultural tourism and more recently, adventure tourism are important.
- The forested lowlands to the east of the Andes, forming part of the vast Amazon Basin, where ecotourism is being developed.

The majority of the attractions are to be found in the Andes, where there is a great variety of climates and landscapes due to differences in altitude. The arrangement of zones is similar to that of Mexico and Central America, but there are also extensive areas above 4,000 metres altitude, known as *puna* where the climate is bleak and dry, or as *páramo*, where it is cold and damp year-round. Although *soroche* (mountain sickness) is a distinct possibility due to the altitude, climbers from all over the world are attracted to the challenge of peaks such as Chimborazo, Huascarán and Illimani, while the spectacular scenery attracts growing numbers of trekkers from Europe and North America. There is also much to interest the cultural tourist. Intricate cultivation terraces on steep mountainsides, and the remains of temples and fortresses bear witness to the achievements of the Incas who ruled this part of South America prior to the Spanish conquest. The Amerindian influence is also evident in the artistic heritage of the colonial period in cities such as Quito, Cuzco and Sucre, and in the folklore and plaintive music of the Andes.

Due to the difficult terrain road transport in the Andean republics is inadequate. However air travel within the region has been facilitated since the early 1990s under the terms of the Andean Pact. Accommodation varies widely in quality, standards of service, and cost. There is a large informal sector of hostels, often with very basic facilities, that cater for the backpacker market.

Peru

Peru is the largest of the Andean republics and has the most developed tourism industry. Its capital Lima is the major gateway to the region. Since 1990 tourism has grown rapidly as a result of greater political and economic stability and the demise of the 'Shining Path' terrorist movement. However Peru continues to have many social problems, not least the marginalisation of its Quechua-speaking rural communities.

Tourists from Western Europe and the United States each account for about a quarter of all arrivals. Peru appeals both to the luxury tour market, which has proved resilient to the effects of recession, and to the young traveller on a budget who sees the country as an adventure destination. The Peruvian government has been involved in developing tourism with the Ministerio de Commerco Exterior y Turismo co-ordinating agencies such as Enturperu – now privatised – which runs a chain of hotels, and Copesco which is concerned with restoring historic sites. Tourism promotion is carried out by Promperu, with private sector backing. Most of the hotel capacity is concentrated in Lima and Cuzco – which is close to the major archaeological sites. The government's open skies policy has attracted foreign airlines, including European carriers. The rail system – primarily developed for conveying minerals from the Andes to coastal ports – is important for tourism, as it includes the highest narrow-gauge railway in the world (from Callao to Huancayo – reaching 4,800 metres), and the line from Cuzco to Machu Picchu – Peru's best-known tourist attraction.

Most of the tourist attractions of Peru are located in the Andes, although Lima is the usual starting-point for cultural tours. The Peruvian capital is less appealing to foreign visitors than Cuzco, which is said to be the oldest continuously inhabited city in the Americas. Here Spanish buildings have been erected on Inca foundations. Cuzco and the 'sacred valley' of the Urubamba provide the best examples of the heritage of this advanced Amerindian civilisation. These include:

- The Inca fortresses of Sacsahuamán and Ollantaytambo, built of intricate masonry without the use of mortar or iron tools; and
- The 'lost city' of **Machu Picchu,** abandoned for centuries in the forest and rediscovered by an American archaeologist in 1911. During the late 1990s the site attracted 300,000 visitors a year, a few arriving by helicopter, the majority making the journey by rail and road along the Urubamba Valley. Some 20 per cent of visitors followed the classic 'Inca Trail' – actually one of three trekking routes, originally used by Amerindian couriers and llama pack trains. This popularity has had a negative impact in the form of widespread erosion, discarded toilet paper and other refuse; and damage from illegal campfires. In 2001 the authorities closed the trail to all but authorised trekking companies employing local guides and porters, and imposed an upper limit of 500 trekkers a day.

Discussion point

Some argue that the ban on independent hikers, most of whom are environmentally aware, is indiscriminate. Another controversy concerns the transport of tourists from the hotels in Aguas Calientes, the service centre for Machu Picchu, to the actual site. In class, debate the pros and cons of replacing the diesel minibuses that are currently used with a high-capacity aerial cableway, taking account of visitor safety, the economic advantages and the impact on the environment.

Alternative attractions to Cuzco and Machu Picchu include:

- the attractive city of Arequipa with its colonial architecture and the nearby Colca Canyon;
- the Callejón de Huaylas in the north of the country with its spectacular mountain scenery; and
- Lake Titicaca – at almost 4,000 metres altitude, the world's highest navigable body of water.

The Peruvian coast is mainly desert, although fogs are a feature of the climate of Lima and El Niño episodes bring about dramatic changes. The capital has many cultural attractions as a reminder of its historic role as the power base for Spanish rule of South America and the region's beaches now feature on the international surfing circuit. The coastal desert has yielded many relics of ancient Amerindian civilisations, epitomised by the mysterious Nazca Lines and the Moche culture, celebrated for its pottery and advanced irrigation systems. This heritage is increasingly at risk from treasure seekers and the illicit trade in pre-Columbian artefacts.

Ecuador

Ecuador has many natural advantages as a tourist destination, containing a range of attractions within a relatively compact area, and the national tourism organisation CETUR has done much to promote the country in recent years. To an extent Ecuador is South America in miniature, characterised by a high rate of population growth and a high rate of urbanisation – both Quito and Guayaquil have grown tenfold since 1957. Tourist arrivals increased from 158,000 in 1980 to just over one million in 2010, but many of these are low-spending backpackers who perceive the country to be a safe destination compared to others in the region. The USA accounts for a quarter of arrivals, followed by Colombia, Peru, Chile and Venezuela.

Ecotourism is the largest growth market, and 17 per cent of the country has national park status. However conservation is threatened by under-funding and the lack of trained guides. The Cotopaxi National Park, centred on South America's most famous volcano, is under pressure from tourism development. Adventure tourism is also important, and the upmarket holiday options available include stayovers on colonial-style *haciendas* in the Sierra, the Andean region of Ecuador.

Within the Sierra are the series of intermontane valleys known as the 'Avenue of the Volcanoes'. An attractive countryside, framed by mountains and eucalyptus trees, along with picturesque markets selling a variety of handicrafts, explain the Sierra's appeal. The cities have a rich cultural heritage, especially the following which are both World Heritage Sites:

* Quito, known as 'the city of eternal spring' is celebrated for the number of Baroque churches and convents in its historic centre. However the capital is suffering from runaway growth, air pollution, and the consequences of the economic crisis that has afflicted Ecuador since the early 1990s.
* Cuenca, Ecuador's third largest city has similar cultural attractions, but fewer social and environmental problems. This is the main centre for the Panama hat trade, using toquilla fibre from Ecuador's coastal lowlands.

Domestic tourists visit spas such as Baños or the beach resorts of the Pacific coast. The coastal lowlands offer a very different environment to the Sierra, with a plantation economy geared to export markets, which explains why the seaport of Guayaquil is Ecuador's main business centre.

Ecuador's section of the Amazon Basin is known as the Oriente, an area of rainforest that was undeveloped prior to the discovery of oil in the 1950s. Adventure tourism, including canoeing on the River Napo, is organised by tour operators based in Quito, who also promote the region for ecotourism. However, much of this co-called ecotourism is merely another form of exploitation that fails to benefit the local Amerindians. The exceptions are the Cuyabeno Reserve and Yasuni National Park which are partly under the control of indigenous tribal communities. Here tourist groups are limited in numbers, and sustainable forms of transport and accommodation are used. Nevertheless the region's ecosystems continue to be under threat from oil spillages and its indigenous people from diseases against which they have little resistance.

The **Galápagos Islands** are situated in the Pacific Ocean some 1,000 kilometres west of Guayaquil. Despite their remoteness they are probably the best-known part of Ecuador and generate much of the country's revenue from tourism. They are volcanic and rather barren, but the unique wildlife is a world-class attraction for eco-tourists, and this has been given international recognition as a World Heritage Site and Biosphere Reserve. Most of the animals have no fear of human beings, as there are no natural predators. Although the islands are situated on the Equator, penguins and sea lions flourish alongside tropical species, due to the cold ocean currents offshore. The best-known animals are the giant tortoises and marine iguanas, with fourteen distinct species on the different islands. This provided the inspiration for Darwin's theory of evolution by natural selection, and the value of the islands as a 'living laboratory' has long been recognised. About 97 per cent of the Galápagos is designated as a national park, and stringent regulations are in force to protect the wildlife from the impact of tourists. Nevertheless this unique environment faces a more insidious threat from the growing number of Ecuadorian settlers from the mainland. As a result, introduced plant and animal species may soon outnumber those native to the islands.

Bolivia

Tourism in Bolivia is handicapped by the country's land-locked situation, inadequate communications, and a poorly developed accommodation sector. Yet the country has as great a variety of landscapes as any in South America, including vast salt lakes in the south-west, lush subtropical valleys on the northern flanks of the Andes, and tropical rainforests, swamps and savannas in the eastern part of the country. Here Santa Cruz has a booming economy, based on the region's oil and natural gas resources. The remote village of La Higuera, where Che Guevara met his death, is now on the tourist trail, thanks to the iconic status of the revolutionary leader. Although a number of national parks and trekking routes have been designated, the number of tourists is small compared to those using the Inca Trail to Machu Picchu.

The Altiplano, at an average altitude of 4,000 metres is Bolivia's heartland, a bleak plateau characterised by intense sunshine during the day and sub-zero temperatures for much of the year at night. The majority of the population are Amerindians, speaking the Quechua and Aymará languages rather than Spanish. The mysterious ruins of Tiahuanaco near Lake Titicaca are a reminder of a pre-Columbian civilisation that flourished here many centuries before the Incas. Mining was historically the basis for Bolivia's economy, as shown by the Baroque architecture of the city of Potosi. This was made possible by the silver mines of the mountain known as the Cerro Rico overlooking the city, and the backbreaking labour of untold millions of Amerindians. Bolivia also boasts the world's highest capital city and international airport – La Paz, and what surely must be the world's highest ski resort nearby. With its upper slopes at the breathtaking altitude of 5,500 metres, Chacaltaya is suitable only for skiers who are fully acclimatised, and its viability is in doubt due to climate change.

Temperate South America

Argentina, Chile, Uruguay and Paraguay are in the part of South America lying outside the tropics. Due to its triangular shape, with the Patagonia peninsula tapering toward

THE AMERICAS

Antarctica, this region is known as the 'Cono Sur' (Southern Cone) by Spaniards and Latin Americans. Distance from the main generating countries in both Europe and North America has been a major disadvantage for the development of international tourism. Nevertheless – with the exception of Paraguay – these countries share a relatively high level of economic development and educational attainment. Since the nineteenth century they have attracted large numbers of immigrants from Europe – particularly Italy and Germany – as well as Spain, and this has strongly influenced the culture, while the Amerindian heritage is less evident than elsewhere in Latin America. Tourism industries are well established, and there is a substantial middle class providing a large domestic market.

Paraguay

Paraguay is an enigma; one of the poorest, least developed and least publicised countries in the Western Hemisphere. Despite having a central location in South America, it is an isolated 'backwater', with few border crossings. Paraguay is also the only nation in Latin America where an Amerindian language – *Guaraní* – has the same official status as Spanish. West of the River Paraguay lies the Gran Chaco, an expanse of scrubland characterised by drought, extreme summer heat, and occasional winter cold associated with the *Pampero* winds from the south. Not surprisingly the great majority of the population live in the eastern part of the country. Here the scenery is also much more luxuriant, and attractions such as Lake Ypicaraí are popular with tourists. An important part of Paraguay's appeal lies in the music and handicrafts of the Guaraní people, a legacy of the Jesuit missions that flourished here in colonial times. Paraguay's membership of MERCOSUR provides access to funding from the wealthier South American countries for much-needed infrastructural improvements. At present there are few hotels outside the capital Asunción and the border town of Ciudad del Este, which has developed largely as a result of the Itaipú Dam project, and which offers shopping bargains to Argentinian and Brazilian visitors. Prospects for ecotourism are limited by poor infrastructure and lack of promotion.

Assignment: River cruising in South America

South America contains many rivers which are potentially first class waterways – the Paraná and the Paraguay are just two examples. Yet this resource has been barely exploited for transportation and tourism, and even the Amazon carries only a fraction of the shipping that uses Europe's much smaller rivers. Investigate why are there so few cruises on other major rivers such as the Magdalena, Orinoco, and the São Francisco in Brazil – is it lack of demand for the product, due to a lack of awareness, or are there problems with the resource? You might consider these factors among others in your investigation:

- climate, resulting in low water levels at certain times of the year;
- accessibility, with poor external and internal transport links by air and by road;
- lack of terminal facilities;
- the capacity and standard of the shipping available.

THE AMERICAS

Uruguay

Uruguay's position as a small country between two big neighbours – Argentina and Brazil – and its reputation for political stability, explains why it has become an important venue for international conferences. In colonial times it was fought over by the Spanish and the Portuguese, a heritage preserved in the historic town of Colonia del Sacramento. Almost half the population now live in the capital Montevideo, which is said to be the safest big city in Latin America. Uruguay is best known for sport (it was the first country to host the football World Cup – in 1930), but it also shares much of the cultural heritage of Argentina, including gauchos and tango rhythms. The *estancias* or country estates in the interior are developing rural tourism in response to the fall in beef and wool prices on the world market. Uruguay's main tourist asset however is 500 kilometres of fine beaches, many of which offer opportunities for surfing. Punta del Este is one of South America's most important holiday resorts, attracting the 'jet set' to its casinos, luxury hotels, boutiques and sports facilities between December and February. Other resorts along the Atlantic coast cater for large numbers of domestic tourists of modest means and Argentinians from Buenos Aires on the other side of the Rio de la Plata.

Argentina

Traditionally Argentina has looked towards Europe rather than the rest of South America for trade and cultural inspiration. The financial crisis of 2001 devastated the middle class and dealt a severe blow to the country's self-image. Yet the country has vast natural resources, including cheap energy supplies and the fertile farmlands of the Pampas. These resources made Argentina one of the world's richest countries prior to the Second World War, when Buenos Aires was known as the 'Paris of South America', but much of this wealth was squandered as a result of the social and economic projects of the Perón regime, and the decades of political strife that followed. One of the country's main problems is outdated infrastructure – most of the road and railway system was built in the early twentieth century; another is the imbalance between Buenos Aires – which has a disproportionate share of the wealth and population – and the provinces, which are deprived of political and financial influence despite a federal system of government.

Until the 1980s incoming tourism was of little importance to the country's economy and better-off Argentinians spent as much on travel abroad – particularly to neighbouring Chile, Uruguay and Brazil. Inbound tourism is a now an important earner of foreign exchange and employs over 10 per cent of the workforce. Hotel accommodation is mainly concentrated in Buenos Aires and the second city of Argentina – Córdoba, but there is a tendency for new projects to be located in outlying regions such as the Andes. Domestic air services are improving as a result of privatisation, but the same cannot be said of the Argentinian rail network, once one of the largest in the world. It now carries only a small volume of passenger traffic compared to road or air transport. The National Tourism Secretariat have promoted Buenos Aires both as a destination in its own right and as the gateway to the rest of Argentina. The latter role is problematic, due to the great distances separating the capital from the main tourist regions in outlying parts of the country:

- The **north-east** offers Iguazú Falls and former Jesuit missions that are now World Heritage Sites.
- The **north-west** is characterised by landscapes similar to those of neighbouring Bolivia. In the cities of Salta and Jujuy the colonial heritage of Spain is much more evident than in Buenos Aires.
- The **west** includes the vineyards around Mendoza, the important ski resort of Las Leñas in the foothills of the Andes, and the Argentine Lake District around San Carlos de Bariloche, which is both a summer and winter resort for domestic tourists. Here the Andes form a formidable barrier between Argentina and Chile. The only major route linking the two countries is over the Uspallata Pass, with its famous statue of 'Christ of the Andes'. Nevertheless, cross-border traffic forms a large percentage of the tourist arrivals in both countries.
- Argentina's share of **Patagonia** extends from the Rio Negro south to the island of Tierra del Fuego. This vast, sparsely settled region lies in the rain shadow of the Southern Andes and is mostly a wind-swept semi-desert. Here ecotourism is growing in popularity based on the wildlife resources of the Valdés Peninsula and the mountain, lake and glacier scenery of Los Glaciares National Park. All-terrain vehicles provide access for tour groups to Tierra del Fuego, reaching as far south as the Beagle Channel and Ushuaia, Argentina's gateway to Antarctica.

The **Pampas** are the heartland of Argentina, but these featureless grasslands are of little interest to foreign visitors, except as the setting for the gaucho (cattleman), who plays an important role in national folklore. Some of the *estancias* do provide visitors with accommodation, an *asado* (barbecue), as well as displays of horsemanship and other traditional skills. In contrast Buenos Aires is a cosmopolitan city displaying architectural styles from France, Italy, Spain and Britain. The waterfront district known as La Boca was the birthplace of the tango, while the Teatro de Colón rivals Milan's La Scala as one of the world's great opera houses. The beaches of Mar del Plata offer relief from the city's humid summers.

Chile

Chile must rank as one of the world's most remote destinations. It is a narrow expanse of territory between the world's largest ocean and the Andes, and further isolated by the world's driest desert – the Atacama – to the north. As part of the 'Pacific Ring of Fire', the country is prone to devastating earthquakes. Nevertheless, Chile is one of the most successful economies in Latin America, with a good infrastructure. Tourism is a major growth sector, promoted by SERNATUR, the national tourist organisation.

The latitudinal extent of the country results in striking differences in climate between the north and the south. Most of the population is concentrated in the central region which enjoys a Mediterranean climate.

The desert **North** was the setting for an important mining industry for nitrates and copper in the early part of the twentieth century, which brought prosperity to cities like Antofagasta. Many former mining communities have since become 'ghost towns' amid a landscape of geysers, salt lakes and sand dunes. There has been some development of beach tourism around ports such as Iquique, and eco-tourism in the Lauca National Park.

Central Chile can be compared to California, with a fertile central valley lying between the Pacific coastal ranges and higher mountains to the east. Here Santiago is one of the major gateways to South America. The ski resorts of Portillo and Los Nevados are within easy reach, and these attract skiers from the USA during the Northern Hemisphere summer. The vineyards of the Maipo Valley provide Chile's best-known export. The Pacific coast offers fine beaches – although heavy surf and strong currents discourage bathing. Viña del Mar is Chile's major beach resort and is also an important cultural centre. Valparaíso has a similar setting to that of San Francisco, but its prosperity declined with the opening of the Panama Canal, and the port needs urban regeneration.

The **Lakes Region** around Temuco has a cooler, wetter climate that supports extensive forests of Araucaria pine. It boasts some of the world's most spectacular lake and mountain scenery, culminating in the active volcano of Osorno. The region is also the homeland of a substantial Amerindian minority that has been in dispute with the government over land rights since the return of democracy to Chile in the 1990s.

Southern Chile. Puerto Montt is the gateway to the south, with shipping services linking this port to Punta Arenas, and from here the gravel-surfaced Carretera Austral provides a road link to the new frontier of settlement in Chilean Patagonia. The island of Chiloé in contrast was settled early in the colonial period, and due to its former isolation, the fishing communities here are different in their timber architecture and cultural traditions from the rest of Chile. Further south is one of South America's most challenging environments, a wilderness of fjords, forests of evergreen beech, and the largest glaciers in the Southern Hemisphere outside Antarctica, while the islands on its western fringes are exposed to the full force of the 'Roaring Forties' and 'Furious Fifties'. Between these rain-swept islands and the mainland is an intricate network of relatively sheltered channels that provide a route for summer cruises. To the east, the Southern Andes are dissected by a number of valleys that have a much drier climate. Here in the Aisén region are a number of national parks and wildlife reserves, but conservation efforts are threatened by commercial logging, mining and a vast hydro-electricity project which aims to solve Chile's pressing energy problems. Nevertheless, despite its rigorous climate and remoteness, southern Chile offers considerable scope for adventure tourism. This is particularly true of the Torres del Paine National Park which contains some of the most spectacular peaks in the Andes. Tourism has led to the revival of Punta Arenas, once a major port on a world shipping route through the Strait of Magellan, which became obsolescent with the opening of the Panama Canal. Although strong winds rather than warm sunshine characterise the weather here, the UV Index is frequently high, due to the depletion of the ozone layer over Antarctica.

Case study 25.3

The island territories of Chile

Chile owns a number of islands in the Pacific Ocean, including the Juan Fernández archipelago almost 700 kilometres west of Valparaiso, and the much more distant Easter Island. The main island of Juan Fernández is famous for its associations with the castaway Alexander Selkirk, the historical inspiration for Robinson Crusoe. Uninhabited at the time of its discovery by Europeans, the archipelago has been designated a national park and World Biosphere Reserve, due to the unique character of its plants and bird life. As yet there is insufficient infrastructure for tourism.

Easter Island (Isla de Pascua in Spanish, and Rapa Nui in the Polynesian language), is the most enigmatic of all Pacific destinations. Since 1969 scheduled air services by

LAN-Chile have crossed the 3,500 kilometres of ocean separating this remote island from mainland Chile and provide a link to Tahiti, which lies an equivalent distance to the west. Although there are world-class opportunities for surfing and scuba diving, tourists are attracted by the *moai*, mysterious stone statues serving as mute reminders of a vanished civilisation. It is now thought that these monuments were erected centuries ago as a form of competition between rival clans, and in so doing the inhabitants of Rapa Nui exploited the natural resources to the point of ecological collapse. The island was once covered with palm forest, but is now treeless and windswept.

The future of Easter Island is tied to the growth of international tourism. In 1990 this small island received 6,000 visitors; but with the extension of the airport to accommodate the largest jets (carried out by the US military), arrivals had increased to 45,000 in 2007. Tourism has brought economic benefits, but not without social tensions between the native Polynesians and the growing number of immigrants from mainland Chile. Without effective visitor management, historic sites are under threat, notably the Orongo crater associated with the 'Birdman' cult.

Discussion point

Small, formerly isolated islands are especially vulnerable to introduced species of plants and animals that wreak havoc with their ecosystems. Here tourism is both part of the problem and also part of a solution. In class, debate this statement with reference to the Isla del Coco (which belongs to Costa Rica), the Juan Fernández Islands, Easter Island and the Galápagos, explaining the differences between these four destinations and the approach to conservation by the authorities concerned.

The Falkland Islands

The Falklands are a group of islands in the South Atlantic some 500 kilometres east of Patagonia. Since 1833 they have been a British colony, but Argentina has a long-standing claim to the territory it calls 'Las Malvinas', and has also been in dispute with Britain over South Georgia and the sector of Antarctica lying to the south of Drake Strait, where the Atlantic meets the Pacific. In scenery, climate and lifestyle the Falklands more closely resemble the Scottish Hebrides than mainland South America. The wildlife – including penguins and sea mammals – is representative of the sub-Antarctic zone, and is of great interest to eco-tourists. The opening in 1985 of a modern airport near Port Stanley made the islands much more accessible to Europe, but they remain a remote and expensive destination. South Georgia, lying south of the Antarctic Convergence, has a much colder climate than the Falklands, and its mountains are heavily glaciated. The Falklands and South Georgia are included in the itineraries of many cruises to the Antarctic.

Antarctica

The most accessible part of the 'white continent' is situated 1,000 kilometres south of Cape Horn. This is the Antarctic Peninsula, held by geologists to be a southern continuation of the Andes, so it is not surprising that Britain's claims to the region's offshore mineral resources have been strongly contested by Argentina and Chile. However, Antarctica differs from other parts of the world in having no indigenous communities to be affected by tourism. Unlike the Arctic regions of Europe, Asia and North America, Antarctica is much less accessible, as it is separated from the nearest populated areas by vast expanses of stormy ocean, and is moreover ringed by a barrier of pack ice for most of the year. It is therefore unlikely that Antarctica was visited by man long before its recorded discovery by American, British and Russian explorers in the early part of the nineteenth century.

In the 1970s this was tourism's last frontier; now there are guide books to the Antarctic, feature films such as *March of the Penguins* have sparked popular interest, and the number of visitors arriving during the summer months (November through February) far exceeds the resident population of scientists and supply personnel at the research stations. Yet, aside from space, Antarctica is probably the most hostile environment known to mankind. Over 98 per cent of its 14 million square kilometres of land surface (larger than Australia or Europe) is permanently ice-covered. The continent is now thought to be two geologically distinct landmasses beneath the ice sheet – West and East Antarctica, separated by the Transantarctic mountain range. Many sub-glacial lakes are known to lie beneath 3,000 metres of ice; investigation of these poses a dilemma for scientists, because of the risk of contamination to an unknown ecosystem that has been isolated for many millions of years. Because of its high altitude, the interior of Antarctica is extremely cold and very dry, while the coast is swept by pitiless winds. Under the terms of the 1959 Antarctic Treaty the territorial claims of seven of the signatory governments are in abeyance, so that the continent serves as a vast international laboratory for scientific research. Environmental protection is given priority – for example, dogs, widely used by earlier polar expeditions, are prohibited by the Madrid Protocol – and there is a moratorium on mineral exploitation.

Tourism to Antarctica began in the late 1950s with the first charter flights from Chile and New Zealand, followed by the first Lindblad cruise in 1966. As a result of competition between tour operators and technological advances, tourism has grown rapidly from less than a thousand arrivals a year in the 1980s, to around 37,000 during the 2009–2010 summer cruising season.

The great majority of tourists in Antarctica are sea-based, with the ship providing the accommodation and all other facilities. This includes a small number of commercial yacht expeditions emanating from Ushuaia, but cruise ships carrying between 50 and 200 passengers account for over 90 per cent of tourist activities in Antarctica. Ushuaia is the starting point for most cruises, followed by Punta Arenas, Puerto Madryn and Port Stanley. Passengers are predominantly from the older age groups. Only 20 per cent of the demand for Antarctic tourism is from Southern Hemisphere countries, although Australia is among the top five generators. The USA accounts for a third of all tourists, followed by Britain, Germany and Japan. Such tourists are motivated to undertake a long air and sea journey by an interest in nature, the awe-inspiring glacial scenery and the history of polar exploration, while there is also the prestige of adding a sixth continent to an already extensive world travel portfolio. In fact many visitors do not actually set foot in Antarctica, being content to view the coast from the deck of a cruise liner, or from the air on a flight-seeing tour based in Australia or Chile. In contrast, a few cruise operators cater for adventure tourism, including sea kayaking, scuba diving, and longer shore excursions.

The west coast of the Antarctic Peninsula north of latitude 65° and the South Shetland Islands is by far the most visited part of Antarctica, and this relatively small area also contains many of the research stations. Cruise tourists are usually welcome visitors as they provide a break in routine for workers at the bases and (in the case of those run by less wealthy countries) some much-needed revenue. The number of sites on cruise itineraries has remained almost constant since the 1990s, with some receiving as many as 8,000 visitors in a season. Zodiac landing craft carry visitors ashore, accompanied by a naturalist-guide, to view penguin rookeries, the volcanic caldera of Deception Island, and Port Lockroy, a former British Antarctic Survey (BAS) base which is now a heritage attraction.

Some coastal locations in East Antarctica are now more accessible, thanks to ice-breaker ships formerly used by the Russian government for survey work. A few cruises, departing from Fremantle and Hobart in Australia, and from Christchurch and Bluff in New Zealand, undertake the long voyage to the Ross Sea. This is much closer to the South Pole than the Antarctic Peninsula, and has a shorter cruising season. Here the attractions include:

- Cape Evans – with its relics of Scott's ill-fated expedition to the South Pole;
- the colony of Emperor penguins at Cape Adare; and
- the Mount Erebus volcano.

Even the interior of Antarctica has been opened up for adventure tourism. Since 1985 a tour operator based in Punta Arenas has flown wealthy clients to a tented camp at Patriot Hills in the Ellsworth Range, where activities include mountain climbing and ski touring. 'Blue ice' landing strips are used for flights to the South Pole and the spectacular mountain peaks of Queen Maud Land, rising above the continental ice sheet.

Tourism in Antarctica is controlled by strict codes of conduct laid down by the International Association of Antarctic Tour Operators (IAATO). Cruise passengers during their few hours ashore are kept under constant surveillance, for their own safety, and to minimise contamination and disturbance to wildlife. Nevertheless, tourists are concentrated in a relatively few sites during the short summer season, and many believe this has an adverse impact on the breeding patterns of seals and penguins. There is also the possibility of pollution due to accidents, highlighted by the sinking of the veteran cruise ship *MS Explorer* in November 2007. A much greater potential threat to the environment is posed by the demand for land-based tourism, if we consider the impact already made by the permanent research stations. Ironically, it was the negative publicity generated by returning cruise tourists about the garbage at one American base that forced the authorities to clean up their act.

Assignment

Many people have a confused mental image of the two polar regions, assuming for example, that polar bears and penguins inhabit the same part of the globe. Draw up a chart that clearly identifies the differences between the Arctic and Antarctica, using categories such as the following:
- major geographical characteristics;
- climate (extent of ice cover, mean temperatures of the warmest and coldest months);
- ecology (terrestrial plants and animals, as distinct from marine life);
- the timescale of human occupation;
- economic development;
- external and internal transport links for tourism;
- the countries exercising political control; and
- the range of tourist activities available (some activities that are promoted in Alaska, northern Canada, Greenland and Lapland are prohibited in Antarctica).

Discussion points

1 In class, debate the proposition that the growth of tourism in Antarctica will help to protect its unique natural environment by raising public awareness, as against the view, held by many scientists, that the existing environmental guidelines are inadequate and more severe constraints are needed on any human activity there.

2 How environment-friendly is ecotourism in Antarctica, compared to the Galápagos Islands? Estimate the carbon footprint of a British or a Japanese cruise tourist to Antarctica, including air travel to South America as well as the cruise itself.

Summary

- The countries of the Western Hemisphere south of the United States border form a cultural entity where, for historical reasons, the Iberian culture and languages are dominant.
- The USA dominates the market for tourism to Mexico and Central America, but tourists from Western Europe are of growing importance to most South American countries.
- Beach tourism is of major importance in Brazil and Mexico, but elsewhere cultural tourism, based on traditional lifestyles and heritage sites is of more significance.
- Ecotourism is growing in importance, particularly in the more remote areas of central and South America, but it has often failed to benefit indigenous communities.
- 'Soft' and 'hard' adventure tourism are other growth markets, mainly in South America, based on spectacular scenery and vast areas of wilderness.
- Business tourism is also likely to increase in those countries which are undergoing rapid economic development, such as Brazil.
- Political instability, inadequate infrastructure, and ineffective marketing have held back tourism in most of the region.
- Although incomes are generally low throughout Latin America, domestic tourism is significant and there is a considerable demand for outbound tourism to Europe and the USA from a growing middle class.

Assignments

1 Identify the opportunities for ecotourism in Central America, South America and the Antarctic Peninsula and explain why these natural resources may be at risk.

2 Describe the pre-Columbian Amerindian cultures of Central and South America and explain the importance of this heritage to certain countries for domestic and international tourism.

3 Analyse the strengths and weaknesses of Brazil as a destination for business and leisure tourism.

4 Investigate the role of sport and water-based recreation in attracting tourists to Central and South America.

5 Compare and contrast Chile and Venezuela as destinations for beach tourism and adventure tourism.

THE AMERICAS

CHAPTER

Tourism futures

Learning objectives

After reading this chapter, you should be able to:
- Appreciate the need for a disciplined approach to predicting the future of tourism
- Understand the geographical impact of crises and shocks to the tourism system
- Appreciate the role of technology in shaping the future geography of travel and tourism
- Understand the changing behaviour of tourists
- Recognise the importance of the environmental movement in tourism
- Understand the changing nature of tourism destinations
- Recognise the trend towards the globalisation of the tourism sector

Introduction

The twenty first century has witnessed severe shocks to the tourism system – 9/11, terrorist bombings in holiday resorts and cities, evidence of climate change, a number of natural disasters such as earthquakes and tsunamis, and revolutions against long-established regimes in North Africa and the Middle East. These 'wild card' events emphasise the fact that we cannot manage tourism if we do not understand how it reacts to change. Making predictions is fraught with problems, especially with a sector as fickle as tourism; but if we are to successfully manage tourism in the future, that is what we must do. This means identifying the drivers of future trends, recognising that while some forces of change such as demographics and technology are already clearly evident, others have yet to emerge. We therefore set out to identify the key trends and issues that will reshape the geography of travel and tourism through the twenty first century under the following headings:

- changing markets;
- changing destinations;
- developments in transport and the tourism sector; and
- globalisation and the new world order.

Common to each of these themes are other agents of change such as technology, the search for sustainability in tourism allied to responses to climate change, and changes in consumer behaviour. These trends are interlinked and are combining to accelerate the pace of change. For example, tourists are increasingly knowledgeable and sophisticated, and can now be catered for by a tourism sector which is firmly embracing marketing and research strategies, facilitated by technological developments such as the Internet and mobile commerce – where the mobile phone becomes the medium for guiding and visitor information. At the same time, the sector is becoming truly global as larger organisations operate across different cultures and time zones. In combination with continued shifts in the world economic and political situation, these trends will influence tourism flows, as new generators and new destinations emerge. Underlying all of these trends are two imperatives. Firstly, the pressure for sustainable development and solutions to climate change will ensure that destinations are better planned and managed, and will show more concern for their environment and host community than did their earlier counterparts. This is supported by annual UN meetings on climate change and the UNWTO's global code of tourism ethics. Secondly, since 9/11 the tourism sector has recognised the imperative to develop crisis management response strategies covering all sectors of the tourism industry to anticipate future 'shocks' to the system, and ensure that tourism can recover from any future crises.

One of our consistent themes is that we can only understand tourism if we recognise the interrelationships between the various elements in the system. This is equally true in attempting to understand the future. Here the concept of 'product markets' is helpful; these recognise the relationship between the changing demands of tourists, and the need to develop tourism products to meet their needs. For example, we know that the 'new tourist' demands low impact tourism, active involvement and environmentally and socially acceptable tourism – hence the development of ecotourism products and companies specialising in carbon off-setting. At the same time there is a trend towards greater market segmentation and the development of a vast range of different products to meet specialised demands.

Markets

Patterns of demand

There is no doubt that since the 1950s a wave of leisure and travel has broken across the globe pushing the frontier of tourism further outward as more and more people have enjoyed access to both domestic and international travel. This trend will continue, despite financial crises, as the global economy expands, with international arrivals already exceeding the one billion mark. However, forecasters also suggest that both demand and supply side constraints may slow the growth of tourism:

FUTURES

- On the demand side, some countries are reaching ceilings of airport capacity and available leisure time that will constrain further growth. The UNWTO study on leisure time, for example, has shown that leisure is under threat from the pressures of changing work practices, technology and competition.
- On the supply side, the threat of terrorism, political instability, ethnic strife, health risks, climate change and capacity ceilings in transport infrastructure may also discourage tourism growth in some areas.

As we saw in Chapter 2, there is no doubt that the distribution of tourism by the year 2020 will therefore be different from that of the early years of this century. The countries of the East Asia and Pacific (EAP) region are emerging as important generators of tourism and as major tourist destinations. China and India in particular will become major generators of both domestic and outbound tourism, changing the nature of travel across the globe. The EAP region will rival Europe and North America in its significance for tourism. To some extent, the success of the EAP region is at the expense of Europe's traditional dominance. Europe's share of international tourism will continue to erode as more long-haul destinations grow in popularity. The principal long-term factors affecting demand for tourism are demographic changes, the amount of leisure and holiday time available, consumer preferences, and the economic performance of the main generating countries. In the short term, as well as the potentially drastic impact of wars and further terrorist incidents, other factors such as relative prices and exchange rates affecting the cost of travel and effective marketing and promotion will also be important. Although forecasters say that long-haul travel will continue to increase, short-haul travel – especially to neighbouring countries – will still account for a very high proportion of international trips; furthermore, responses to climate change may slow the growth of long-haul flights. Business tourism will remain an important segment of the market but developments in communications – such as video-conferencing and videophones – may reduce the need, at least in the West. The evidence here is inconclusive, suggesting that unless travel becomes prohibitively expensive, face-to-face meetings will remain an important reason for business tourism in some cultures at least.

Changing market demands

While there is no doubt that social and economic trends will encourage the growth of tourism, the nature of the market will change, with consequent implications for the type of development at the destination. The tourists of tomorrow will be more discerning, seeking to 'co-create' a quality experience and, in the developed world, increasingly drawn from an older age group. They may subscribe to the principles of sustainable development, but they also know their rights and, as an empowered group, will complain and seek compensation if their travel experience is disappointing. Demographic changes can be forecast to an extent – we know, for example, that as the baby boom generation ages, there will be a large 'grey tourism' market. Yet it is conceivable that larger families may become fashionable in the West and this, along with the consequences of massive migration from the Third World, would increase fertility rates and halt further population decline. It is also difficult to track the influence of changing values among the travelling public. For example, motivations for travel are moving away from passive sunlust towards active participation and curiosity about other cultures. As everyday life and work becomes safer, more predictable and less physically demanding, there will be a greater demand, at least in the youth market, for extreme sports, 'hard adventure' and other high-risk activities. More leisure should be available through flexible working practices, sabbaticals, study leave and early retirement. On the other hand, if the USA is any guide, the corporate workplace could become the chief provider of recreation opportunities for many employees, thus blurring the boundaries between work and leisure. Lifestyle changes such as the growing numbers of 'singletons' (young single person households), and 'downshifting'– where an individual changes from a highly paid, high pressure job to one with less income but more free time – will have an impact on the demand for tourism. Travel will also be tailor-made to suit other groups in society such as single parents. Intensive marketing research on consumer preferences, allied to technology, will increasingly allow more sophisticated market segmentation of tourists, so that product development can be engineered to deliver quality experiences. Use of the Internet is already allowing modularisation of the elements of travel packages so that consumers can co-create and customise their own holidays by trading direct with suppliers – an innovation with significant implications for the way travel has traditionally been distributed. As a consequence, travel intermediaries are re-inventing their role in the tourism system in order to survive. In short, tourism is becoming less passive and less dominated by the mass market, and more geared to active involvement, individual preferences and direct purchase of tailor-made products.

Destinations

Hand-in-hand with market changes is the realisation by tourism developers that destinations are unique, special and fragile places that have to be carefully managed if they are to retain their appeal. The destination of the future will use sustainability and product differentiation – based on a unique selling proposition (USP) – to remain competitive. Attitudes on the part of both consumers and suppliers are changing as the result of pressure from the environmentalist movement, media exposure of bad practices, and a more mature tourism industry. In particular, we are only just beginning to understand how destinations can adapt to climate change. Sustainability has been publicised through high profile conferences, initiatives from representative bodies for the industry such as the World Travel and Tourism Council (WTTC), and by tour operators themselves. In particular, the realisation of the negative impacts of tourism upon host environments, societies, and developing economies has prompted the search for alternative forms of tourism – such as ecotourism – and a critical attitude towards mass tourism (although we must recognise that mass tourism will remain a very substantial part of the market). Sustainable tourism ensures that the tourism sector is sympathetic to host environments and societies. An increasing number of public agencies are drawing up guidelines for the reduction of tourism impacts and there is no doubt that the consumer of the future will shun destinations that are not 'environmentally sound'. Increasingly, this will include concerns for basic infrastructure, for example potable water and electricity supply, as well as indicators such as biodiversity and changes in land use. In essence, we are seeing a move towards the responsible development and consumption of tourism through:

- more local control of tourism development, as recommended by the Agenda 21 initiatives of the Rio Earth Summit and the World Summit for Sustainable Development in Johannesburg in 2002;

FUTURES

- translation of the *principles* of sustainability into *practice* through codes of conduct, accreditation schemes, eco-labelling, best practice guidelines and industry self-regulation;
- proactive adoption of professional approaches to the integrated management of visitors, traffic and resources at tourist destinations, instead of reacting to problems as they arise;
- use of marketing and information management to influence the behaviour of visitors at destinations;
- initiatives such as the UNWTO's drive to use tourism as an agent of poverty alleviation, and its global code of tourism ethics;
- initiatives by destinations to respond to climate change by diversifying their products (from *beach* to *beach plus* for example); and
- an enhanced awareness of the impacts of tourism.

Discussion point: Destination response to climate change

As the evidence for climate change grows, many destinations are considering how to respond – traditional beach destinations are adding other products such as theme parks, and winter sports resorts are developing summer products to compensate for poor snow cover and a shortened season. Looking at a destination of your choice, how might it be affected by climate change, and how should it respond?

It is perhaps inevitable that these ideas will find more fertile ground in the developed world than in most developing countries, where the short-term imperatives of obtaining foreign exchange and job creation will still dominate and may eclipse the longer-term objectives of sustainable development. Destinations are responding to these demands in a variety of ways.

- Resource-based destinations, i.e. those based on elements of the natural or cultural heritage, are adopting sophisticated planning, management, and interpretive techniques to provide both a welcome and a rewarding experience for the tourist, while at the same time ensuring protection of the resource itself. It is felt that once tourists understand why a destination is significant they will want to protect it. Protection here may be not only in terms of changed behaviour but also through *enhancive sustainability* initiatives where the visitor 'leaves the destination in a better condition than before'. These initiatives include:
  - 'visitor payback' where visitors become financial supporters of a site;
  - voluntary 'eco-taxes' to protect and repair tourist destinations suffering environmental and social damage; and
  - new products publicised as 'working holidays', voluntourism to aid poor communities, and 'volunteer tourism' to 'clean up' degraded destinations.

  Good planning and management of the destination lies at the heart of providing the tourism consumer of the future with a high-quality experience. To achieve this, it may be that tourists of the future will have to accept increasingly restricted viewing times at popular sites, comply with destination 'codes of conduct', be content with replicas of the real thing (as at the caves of Altamira and Lascaux), or even a 'virtual' substitute in cyberspace using computer technology.
- As resource-based destinations come under increased pressure, we are seeing greater emphasis on purpose-built, demand-led attractions that merge tourism and

entertainment. The trend to more frequent trips taken closer to home will demand 'synthetic' attractions such as artificial ski slopes and those which combine leisure, entertainment, retailing, accommodation, and quality catering in a single setting. The emergence of totally enclosed and controlled tourist environments such as theme parks, mega-cruise ships, and vacation islands will be promoted as a 'market-oriented' alternative to the real, and increasingly fragile, 'resource-based', non-reproducible attractions of natural, historic, or cultural destinations. Such artificial settings have many advantages and can provide the safe and secure environment sought by most tourists – already destinations such as Dubai, Las Vegas and Alton Towers are bringing these trends to life.

In the future, destinations will be affected by climate change, with rising sea levels creating problems for coastal resorts, the erosion of the ozone layer modifying the traditional beach holiday to 'beach plus' tourism, and the generally more volatile weather conditions worldwide affecting the profitability of the sector. There is also a real threat that climate change will destroy some tourism icons, such as Australia's Great Barrier Reef and the Alpine glaciers. But a more insidious threat could be posed by the growth of tourism itself. In the 1950s the polar regions and the Himalayas were the ultimate frontier for tourism; nowadays they are exposed to the assault of thousands of adventure-seeking tourists, and climbers have to 'book' Everest several years in advance. Having visited most of the world's wild places and cultural sites, the well-heeled tourist is seeking new horizons and challenges. The frontiers of tourism will therefore expand ever-outwards, with new destinations being created under the oceans and in space. In fact we know less about the ocean depths than we do about the surface of the Moon or Mars, and this knowledge is vital if we are to combat marine pollution, which poses a threat to the entire planet. The development of submersibles capable of withstanding the immense pressures would enable tourists to view the *Titanic* wreck site and the strange life-forms of the ocean floor. On the continental shelves projects for undersea hotels are already underway. Yet it is space that is much more likely to appeal to the imagination of future tourists.

Discussion point: Travel in cyberspace as an alternative to real travel?

Virtual reality (VR) sparks controversy between futurists – some argue that it will never replace the real experience of travel, whilst others foresee the home becoming the centre for all leisure activities – a total immersive cave or experience chamber – with VR discs available for tourism destinations as 'tasters', the ultimate replacement for the travel brochure or DVD. In some respects, this is the perfect form of tourism – the destination receives a royalty for the disc, but receives none of the negative impacts of tourists actually on site. The *cybernaut* would have the advantage over a real tourist in being able to view an historic building, for example, Spain's Alhambra in its entirety, without the intrusive presence each day of this attraction's 9,000 visitors. He/she can also receive the sensory experience of a destination, for example the sounds, humidity and aromas of the rainforest, without irksome transport and border delays, or the risk of crime and disease. Crude versions of virtual destinations already exist and clearly the diversion of visitor pressure away from the real thing is important. The trend to substitute VR for real life experiences is already evident in the popularity of virtual worlds such as 'Second Life', where players create *avatars* or alternative personalities to act out their fantasies in cyber-space.

Discuss whether virtual journeys represent tourism in the true sense, any more than a 'second life' can be a surrogate for social interaction.

FUTURES

Case study 26.1

Our future lies in space?

Space is the destination of the future, and simulated space travel experiences and tours of space research centres are already popular. Although NASA first landed astronauts on the Moon in 1969, space tourism – as distinct from space travel for scientific or military reasons – did not become a reality until 2001, when an American millionaire became the first space tourist, visiting the International Space Station as a paying passenger on a Russian space mission. Space tourism has been defined as the 'taking of short pleasure trips in low earth orbit by members of the public' (Collins and Ashford, 1998). Until recently tourism in near space was prohibitively expensive, because of the high cost of launches. This situation is set to change as a result of international competition between two rival companies, namely 'Space Adventures' and 'Virgin Galactic' to produce a re-usable space vehicle. Of course, passenger safety will be a real issue for space tourism; however, space-planes would pose a much lower risk than the existing space shuttles that use ballistic missile technology (Ashford, 2003). Health risks are perhaps less significant. The condition of weightlessness, due to zero gravity in space, offers recreational opportunities as well as challenges to would-be tourists. Long-term health issues such as a loss in bone density, as well as exposure to cosmic and solar radiation, are unlikely to affect tourists – as distinct from astronauts or crew members – on a sub-orbital flight lasting only a few hours, but those staying at a 'space hotel' would need to have adequate protection. Inter-planetary voyages in outer space are some decades in the future, awaiting new technology that will overcome the tyranny of time and distance.

Developments in transport

We have already touched on some of the future developments in transport (see Figure 5.1). These are notoriously difficult to predict, and forecasts made in the 1950s have proved to be wide of the mark half a century later. Technology and changing business practices will have a major impact on transport systems. The hydrogen fuel-cell has been hailed as the answer to our energy problems, but as of now the production of hydrogen results in as much pollution as the burning of fossil fuels. However, by mid-century hydrogen and new types of biofuels should replace petroleum as the main source of motive power, with zero emissions of pollutants.

In civil aviation long-haul airline operations will be characterised by the use of a new generation of aircraft with a capacity for as many as 700 passengers. The application of space technology will enable these aircraft to achieve hypersonic speeds and a much greater range, so that the flying time between London and Tokyo could be reduced to two-and-a-half hours, without stops for refuelling. Nevertheless speed is not the only consideration, and many long-haul travellers may opt for the greater comfort provided by improved aircraft configurations, so that the journey itself becomes a pleasurable experience rather than a cramped ordeal. For short-haul operations the use of VTOL (vertical take-off and landing aircraft) would provide more flexibility. The trend toward deregulation will continue across the world. In the USA and Europe deregulation has led to domination of the market by a few major airlines and the forging of strategic alliances, a trend which is emerging in other sectors of the tourism industry. In such an environment competitive advantage will not come from government protection. On regional and short-haul flights 'budget' airlines already dominate, competing from a different business model based on Internet reservations, ticketless travel procedures and 'no frills' service. The major airlines will concentrate on hub and spoke operations. Airlines based at a 'hub' airport in a prime geographical location will co-ordinate their schedules, enabling travellers to make onward connections between flights on routes radiating from the central hub. This gives the hub airline a strong competitive edge and leads to a system of 'fortress hubs', keeping out newcomers. However, this could result in some communities having less choice in their travel arrangements than was the case hitherto.

Although VTOL aircraft and new versions of seaplanes could eventually take some of the pressure, airports will need to be built on a major scale to cope with the anticipated growth in air traffic; this will be greatest in the East Asia-Pacific region. Local communities and environmentalists from different countries will launch co-ordinated protest campaigns through the Internet, but these will largely be ineffective. However, governments, particularly in the West, will increasingly be faced with the dilemma of balancing the benefits of economic growth against the environmental damage, and climate change will become the new watchword for protestors. Government policies favouring airport expansion can be criticised for the following reasons:

- The predicted growth rate for air traffic is based on the rapid increase since the 1970s, but the demand for air travel will slow down as the market matures.
- The growth in demand for cheap air travel cannot be sustained indefinitely as the true cost in environmental terms is not borne by the airline or the passenger.

In surface transport the desire for personal mobility will have to be reconciled with the need for an efficient form of mass transit, one that truly responds to public demand. Throughout the world car ownership is growing inexorably, as suppressed demand becomes expressed demand as a result of economic growth and democratic structures of government that allow freedom of choice. Even in the USA the market has not reached saturation, as the demand for sports utility vehicles (SUVs) has shown. We can expect developments in automotive technology to make driving safer and more environmentally acceptable, including satellite navigation systems and improved fuel efficiency. We can be sure that the car of the future will be quite different from the vehicle that has evolved with the internal combustion engine in the course of the twentieth century, but until the infrastructure is in place, cars powered by hydrogen or electricity will be slow to capture the market. Highway networks will continue to develop around the world and the capacity of busy routes could be greatly increased with the use of computer controlled guideways; this will make motoring safer but at the cost of the driver's independence.

As the century unfolds, it is likely that car use will decline for inter-city travel and for trips within large cities for the following reasons:

1. Within the world's major cities rapid transit systems will reduce car use, as is now occurring in some Asian countries.
2. The development of high speed inter-city rail links could result in the train being preferred over the car – or air transport for journeys of less than 500 kilometres – due to the following:
   (a) congestion on the roads and airways;
   (b) the train is perceived as a 'greener' form of travel;
   (c) a range of new rail-based leisure and business tourism products will be developed;

(d) 'green' taxes will penalise car users; and

(e) the application of innovative technology, such as magnetic levitation or repulsion in which the train 'flies' above a track at speeds of up to 500 kilometres/ hour. This will transform the image of rail travel and bring it firmly into the twenty-first century.

On the world's oceans high speed vessels and passenger-carrying submarines will be developed. Mega-cruise ships carrying over 5,000 passengers will cater for the mass market, possibly with 'satellite' vessels for diving and shore excursions. A variety of much smaller ships would provide nature-based cruises to island destinations such as the Galápagos, linking up with local hotels on a 'cruise and stay' programme. Some experts predict that the tourists of the future will stay in prefabricated mobile 'pods' which can be set up in the most remote locations, such as Antarctica, with minimal impact on the environment.

The tourism sector

As the tourism market matures, the sector is striving for acceptability not only in terms of environmental practices such as auditing and total quality management, but also in business ethics and social responsibility as short-term, profit-driven operations become less acceptable. There will be an increasing consideration for all stakeholders involved in the business, including the well-being of the destination and its residents. For example, it makes increasing commercial sense for tour operators to invest in destinations and their facilities as evidenced by the 'Tour Operator's Initiative for Sustainable Tourism Development' representing 25 companies worldwide, whilst the accommodation sector is developing environmentally sound units such as eco-lodges.

In response to these trends, the tourism sector is rapidly becoming more professional and embracing developments in technology. Indeed, technology is being employed to improve the management of tourism businesses and has allowed the industry to move towards a marketing philosophy of anticipating consumer needs and ensuring that they can be supplied. Technology facilitates this through 'database marketing' allowing direct contact with the consumer. The Internet and computer reservation systems (CRS) are particularly important here. Use of the Internet, combined with a more knowledgeable tourist market, is driving the emergence of a growing number of independent travellers who bypass intermediaries in the tourism distribution chain. Suppliers will target their products more closely to the desires of their customers and, increasingly, new tourist destinations will be created.

Globalisation and the new world order

The tourism sector does not operate in a vacuum and is affected by globalisation – the trend for markets and production to become inter-dependent worldwide, regardless of government policies in any particular country. Smeral (1998) has identified the key drivers of globalisation in tourism as:

- the adoption of free trade agreements, removing barriers to international transactions;
- computer and communications technology encouraging 'e-business';

- worldwide-acting suppliers utilising CRS and global distribution systems (GDS); examples here include the major airlines, hotel chains and tour operators, as well as their strategic alliance partners in the supply chain;
- decreasing costs of international travel allowing access to most markets in the world;
- increasing levels of income in the generating countries, allied to the 'new tourist' who is experienced and discerning; and
- the emergence of 'new' destinations, fuelling the demand for more international travel.

The consequences of globalisation for the tourism sector include:

- standard procedures and quality control (as in the accommodation sector); there are concerns that this could result in a worldwide homogenisation of tourism products;
- increased competition;
- head office decisions on marketing and technology in the larger companies;
- forging of strategic alliances (as in the airlines sector);
- adoption of global brands (such as American Express, Sheraton and Disney);
- changing management approaches;
- adoption of new ways of doing business, such as use of e-mail and the Internet (already effectively used by budget airlines);
- adoption of global distribution systems and yield management; and
- more difficult trading conditions for small- and medium-sized tourism enterprises (SMTEs).

Discussion point: Global, local or 'glocal' tourism?

There is a danger that globalisation creates uniform landscapes, cultures and brands of tourism; for example Hilton, Coca-Cola, Starbucks, Avis rental cars and carriers such as British Airways can become ubiquitous with the spread of tourism around the world. But is this a good thing? Whilst the global brands and companies certainly provide quality assurance and service, they may erode the special 'sense of place' and cultural identity of a destination. And this is the challenge: how can we deliver a quality-assured, top-class tourism experience to international standards at the local level? Here we encounter the hybrid word 'glocal', combining global standards of expertise with the best in local products and skills. How might this be achieved at the destination of your choice?

On this latter point, there is scope in tourism for both the large organisation and the small independent operator supplying niche markets. However, the medium-sized enterprises have neither the power of the large firms, nor the opportunities to specialise, and will therefore struggle to survive in a globalising sector. In fact, the competitive dominance of larger corporations in tourism will continue through their strict quality control and global branding which is designed to reduce the perceived risk of a tourism purchase. This has implications for tourism destinations that may become increasingly dependent upon decisions made by such corporations. Nonetheless, we must never lose sight of the fact that tourism will continue to be delivered at a destination by local employees, within the context of a local culture.

The future of tourism cannot be divorced from political events and trends. Initiatives at different geographical scales are changing the world order and these will impact

FUTURES

upon tourism. At the national level, a major shift has been the way that the role of government in tourism has changed since 9/11. Until then the trend had been for tourism to be seen as a private sector activity and governments were gradually withdrawing support and subsidy. However, with the impact of 9/11 potentially devastating whole tourism economies and national airlines, the public sector's role has revived, with assistance to businesses through state funding and rescue packages, as well as the co-ordination and promotion of tourism at ministerial level.

At the international level, tourism in the future will be facilitated by the free trade agreements under the umbrella of the General Agreement on Trade in Services (GATS) signed in 1994. GATS is based on the principle that free market forces are the best means of providing consumers with the best products at the best prices. The role of GATS is controversial, since:

- on the one hand supporters of GATS point to the elimination of barriers to tourism growth, removing restrictions on hiring staff from other countries, establishment of management operations and franchises in other countries, easier transfers of currency and other payments; but
- on the other hand, opponents of GATS maintain that freedom for companies to operate where they wish, to hire non-local staff and to franchise their products flies in the face of the development of sustainable tourism, as there will be few controls on the activities of companies in the tourism sector.

There are two opposing trends to the world order implied by GATS. First, the formation of a number of trading blocs across the globe as country groupings come together in economic alliances is evident. Notable here are the North American Free Trade Agreement (NAFTA), the creation of the European Union (EU) under the 1992 initiative, the Association of South East Asian Nations (ASEAN), and MERCOSUR covering most of South America.

Secondly, regional and national politics are also at variance with the spirit of GATS. The rise of regionalism and a search for cultural identity – particularly amongst ethnic minorities – has led to conflict in some parts of the world (as in the regions of the former Yugoslavia), but elsewhere the trend is less sinister. In the midst of this contradiction 'city states' are emerging as major tourist destinations, whether it be as cultural centres, or simply competing with others to stage mega-events such as the Olympic Games or the soccer World Cup.

As the millennium unfolds, the new world order and the global tourism industry will continue to be threatened by terrorism. This, along with natural disasters, epidemics and inter-communal violence will particularly affect developing countries who can ill-afford the loss of foreign exchange. It is likely that tourists themselves will be a primary target for terrorists rather than being incidental victims. Security efforts after 9/11 have concentrated on protecting air travellers, but as the *Achille Lauro* incident showed as long ago as 1983, and the Madrid and London bombings since 9/11, cruise ships and rail systems can be vulnerable to attack. The effect of 9/11 and subsequent disasters has been to tighten security and immigration procedures, and for crisis and risk management plans to be developed for many destinations and the tourism sector generally. Crisis and risk management recognises that we must be prepared for man-made and natural disasters and lays down a response pattern to such events. The most significant risks are determined and strategies implemented to deal with them. Although international organisations will be important, as the World Health Organisation has shown by its role in managing the potential threat of an avian flu epidemic, the onus will be on individuals, private businesses and governments to be vigilant concerning future crises, but not to the extent of being risk-averse.

Trends toward a new tourism?

A number of commentators have attempted to synthesise the trends identified above. Poon suggests that the future will see a flexible, segmented, customised, and diagonally integrated tourism sector rather than the mass market, rigid, standardised, and packaged tourism of the 1970s (see Figure 26.1). Poon (1989, 92) identifies the key trends leading to this new tourism as:

- the diffusion of a system of new information technologies in the tourism industry;
- deregulation of the airline industry and financial services;
- the negative impact of mass tourism on host countries;
- the movement away from sunlust to sun-plus tourism;
- environmental pressures;
- technology;

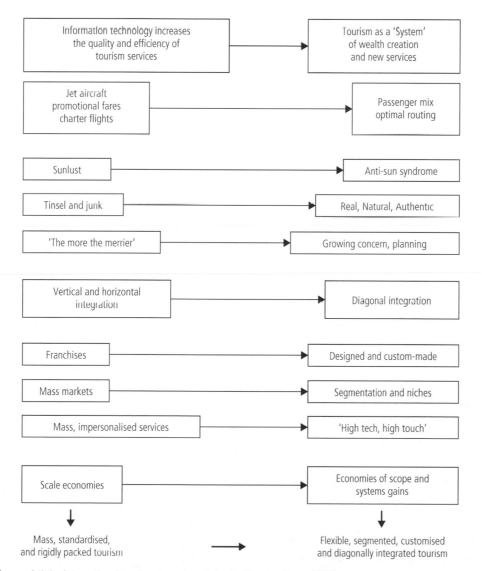

Figure 26.1 International tourism in metamorphosis (*Source:* Poon, 1989)

FUTURES

- competition; and
- changing consumer tastes.

There is no doubt that the maturing and changing tourist market will have major implications for the geography of travel and tourism. This will manifest itself in changing patterns of tourism around the world as new destinations emerge and older ones decline. The nature of the impact at the destination will increasingly depend on the type of tourism, and those charged with planning for the industry will respond more positively to the needs and desires of visitors. Above all, the challenge for this century, taking climate change into account, will be the balancing of the environmental and social impacts of tourism against its perceived economic gains. It is here that geography will continue to play a valuable role in providing us with:

1 an holistic approach to tourism; and
2 the specialised knowledge needed to plan and manage low-impact tourism.

Summary

- The future geography of travel and tourism will be influenced by a number of inter-related trends. These can be summarised as the changing tourism market place, new trends at the destination, the changing world situation, and the effects of globalisation on the tourism sector.
- In line with these forces for change are other influences such as technology, consumer behaviour, crisis management and the rise of environmental awareness, particularly climate change.
- Technology is forcing the pace of change in the transport sector, mobile commerce and the Internet. This is linked to changing consumer behaviour, particularly in the ageing markets of the developed world. Here knowledgeable, discerning tourists are seeking independent travel and active involvement.
- Destinations will respond through positive planning, showing more concern for the environment and host community, and by providing a quality experience.
- Finally, the world is changing and tourism will be affected by the developing economies of the East Asia-Pacific region, the rising number of signatories to GATS, and the expansion of the tourism frontier into space.
- There is no doubt that the skills of geographers and their understanding of these global issues will be a valuable contribution to the 'knowledge-based' management of the tourism sector in the twenty-first century.

Assignment

'Leisure landscapes of tomorrow'

Put forward your own ideas (not those derived from the writers of science fiction) on the 'ideal resort community' that will meet the environmental and social requirements of the mid twenty-first century. This should include considerations of transport infrastructure, public utilities and waste disposal, the form of accommodation, and the types of recreation, shopping and entertainment on offer. Your planning brief should take account of the needs of individuals and special interest groups as well as the demands of society as a whole.

FUTURES

Maps and spatial awareness

Maps should be an essential part of the study of geography, world affairs and tourism. This guide to using maps will enable you to:

- locate places of importance for travel and tourism on a world map, and on maps of different destinations at a variety of scales;
- select alternative routes to a destination, using the information provided by maps;
- interpret information on the natural resources, climate and population of a country or region from a variety of maps; and
- draw simple sketch maps of a destination to provide relevant information.

Position-fixing

There is a sure-fire method of finding a place on the map. You are probably familiar with global positioning systems (GPS). These pocket-sized traveller's aids are linked to a space satellite, enabling the user to establish their position with remarkable accuracy. Like GPS, maps and atlases use *coordinates of latitude and longitude*, angular measurements of the Earth, to determine position. The advantage of this system is that it is applicable to any part of the world and is internationally recognised for the purposes of navigation by air or by sea. As an example, Christchurch, an historic town in southern England, is at latitude 51° N (north of the Equator) and longitude 2° W (west of the Greenwich Meridian). Its 'twin town' is Christchurch, New Zealand, in the Southern Hemisphere and on the opposite side of the globe at latitude 44° S (south of the Equator) and longitude 175° E (east of the Greenwich Meridian).

You can usually identify latitude as the first set of numbers after the page entry in the index of a standard atlas, which are expressed in degrees (°), ranging from 0 (the Equator) to 90 (the North and South Poles), followed by minutes (″), a minute being one sixtieth of a degree. Lines of latitude called *parallels* cross the map from east to west, with a selection of numbers for degrees of latitude appearing in the left or right hand margins. Longitude refers to the second set of numbers in the index, ranging from 0 to 180°. The lines of longitude called *meridians* cross the map from north to south, converging at the Poles. There is a selection of numbers for degrees of longitude in the lower margin of the map. Once you know both the latitude and longitude of a place, you can then determine its location in any atlas. For most purposes we can ignore the minutes in the index, and round off the numbers to the nearest degree – this still gives a tolerance of at most 50 kilometres (30 miles) from the true position.

Understanding scale

All the general reference maps in an atlas have a ratio scale, shown as 1:x000,000, and a graduated linear scale (usually found in the lower margin of the map). A ratio scale of 1:5,000,000 means that one centimetre measured on the map represents 50 kilometres in reality. By marking two places, A and B, on the edge of a sheet of A4 paper you can measure the air distance between them from the linear scale. The actual distance by road and rail may be much longer, particularly in mountainous countries such as Switzerland.

You could describe a map as a two dimensional representation of a three dimensional part of the Earth's surface. Most of the maps in a standard atlas are **small scale**, showing the major features of the topography of a large area, such as a country, at scales of say, 1:5,000,000. Such maps have to be very selective in the range of information that they can show, and only the most important towns, rivers, summits, roads and boundaries are included. A map at a scale of 1:1,000,000 would provide a truer picture as more detail can be shown. To study a particular locality, such as a holiday resort, you need to consult a **large scale** map. These maps cover a small area, but in great detail.

Britain's Ordnance Survey maps, such as the 'Landranger' series at a scale of 1:50,000, are good examples of large scale **topographic maps**, and these are ideal if you're interested in hiking, cycling and outdoor adventure. Architects and planners use maps at much larger scales (1:1,250) that show individual buildings. Here the width of linear features such as roads is true to scale, in contrast to other maps and street guides such as London's A–Z.

Direction-finding

Navigators use bearings, angular measurements from the north point on a compass. From the associated *locagram* you can work out simple directions and distances from a central point, in this example, London. A compass rose is not just a decorative feature, as in many cases 'due north' is not at the 'top' of the map!

Understanding symbols on maps

Symbols are the language of topographic maps, representing natural and man-made features. They include:

- Area symbols that depict the size and shape of a feature, using shading, stippling and colour to depict land use and vegetation cover.
- Point symbols that mark the location of a prominent feature in the landscape. They can be pictograms resembling the feature they represent, or geometric shapes. With a reduction in scale, area symbols are generalised and become point symbols.
- Line symbols that indicate rivers, roads, railways or some other linear feature.
- Contours, which show the shape and elevation of the land surface.

Although water features are conventionally shown in blue, and forested areas in green, this is by no means a hard and fast rule. As symbols vary from country to country, and between maps at different scales, an explanatory key is always essential.

Relief, the third dimension, is usually shown by successive contours, lines that join points on the Earth's surface at the same height above sea level (or in the case of Death Valley and the Dead Sea, below sea level). It takes skill and imagination to visualise the lie of the land from contours, but it's worth the effort. If the contours are spaced far apart on a large scale map, this indicates that the land is quite flat and the gradients are gentle – ideal for cycling! Where the contours are very close together the land is rugged, with pronounced ridges and deep valleys, while gradients are steep, making travel difficult. In mountainous regions such as the Alps sophisticated forms of shading supplement the contours to achieve a '3D' effect. Although they are not true to scale, the panoramic maps produced for ski resorts use similar techniques to give a 'bird's eye' view.

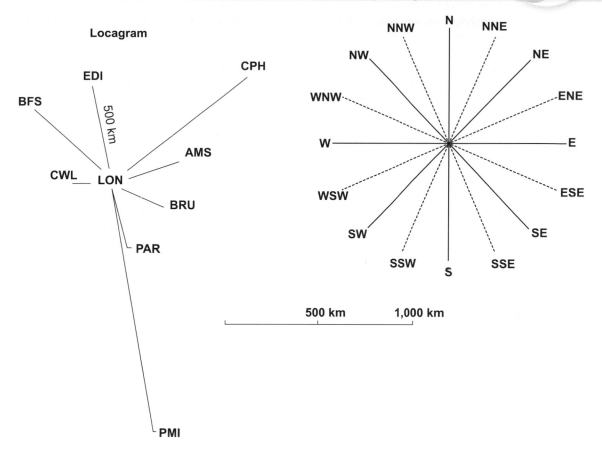

On small scale maps a graduated colour scheme is sometimes used between selected contours to show increasing elevation or altitude. This can be misleading, and it is difficult to see whether the land is rugged or gently sloping. The new breed of atlases dispense with contours in favour of shading techniques that emphasise particular landforms such as mountain ranges and volcanoes.

Thematic maps

Some of the maps in the atlas are for a special purpose, manipulating statistical data in a visual form. *Choropleth* maps use a graduated colour scheme, dots or circles of varying size to show distributions, such as population characteristics that may influence the demand for tourism. Only the outlines of countries or their administrative divisions are normally featured on the map. Sometimes pictograms or pictorial symbols are used to make visual comparisons, for example the number of people employed in hotels in different countries. *Flow-line* maps show the volume of movement between places, such as the numbers of tourists travelling from country 'A' to destination 'B'. *Isopleth* maps are characterised by lines joining points with the same numerical value, and can be used to give climatic information, for example, *isotherms* of the temperature for a particular month (usually January and July). A graduated colour scheme makes it easier to identify areas with freezing conditions (less than 0°C or 32°F) and areas that are hot (over 25°C or 77°F).

Topological maps

A topological map or *cartogram* deliberately distorts real distances and true directions to illustrate different relationships and patterns. If for example we wish to compare the countries of the world in terms of their population and per capita income, we let these criteria determine the scale of the map, rather than area and distance. The map still retains contiguity with respect to national boundaries. Topological maps are also used to visualise a route network without the mass of distracting information that appears on a conventional map. The best known example is probably the map of the London Underground.

Map projections

A globe is the only true map of the world, and it is in fact impossible to show a large part of the Earth, for example Asia or North America, on a flat surface without some form of distortion, in terms of shape, relative size, and directions. Most world maps fail to show the Pacific Ocean in its entirety. Instead they show Alaska (part of the USA) and Siberia (part of the Russian Federation) at opposite ends of the Earth, whereas in reality they are separated only by a narrow stretch of water known as the Bering Strait. World maps on the **Mercator** projection were – and probably still are – the most widely used way of representing the Earth in classrooms and boardrooms. The Mercator has the advantage over other projections since it allows a constant compass bearing to be shown as a straight line on the map, and this makes it ideal for the purpose of navigation. On the other hand these maps are not true to scale and show a gross distortion in the size of countries the further they are from the Equator. Thus Canada with its Arctic islands appears to be bigger than Africa, and Greenland larger than Australia, while the Russian Federation seems even vaster than in reality. This has had an important effect on how the West perceives various parts of the world, particularly Africa and the developing countries of the tropics generally. As for Antarctica, it only appears as a strip at the foot of a Mercator map, and not as a continental landmass around the South Pole, which is how you would see it from a space satellite.

World maps drawn on the **Peters** equal area projection are nowadays increasingly used to show Africa and other parts of the developing world in their correct size relative to Europe and North America, although this involves some distortion in the shapes of continents and countries.

Self-assessment questions

(i) Identify and describe the location of a popular holiday resort situated at 38° 32″ N and 0° 08″ W.

(ii) (a) Calculate the air distances between London and the other cities shown by their IATA codes in the locagram in kilometres (km) and miles. Although the USA is the only important country where the metric system is not in official use, this fact alone makes it essential to be able to convert from one system to the other. (To convert from kilometres to miles, multiply by 5 and then divide by 8.) (b) When flying between London and Copenhagen, in which direction would you be travelling? (c) How would you calculate the road distance from London to Edinburgh?

(iii) In your atlas identify the well-known holiday destination situated in mid-ocean at latitude 22°N and longitude 160°W, the name of this ocean, and the approximate distance of the islands from the mainland of North America.

(iv) Identify the famous mountain situated near the southern edge of the largest continent at latitude 28°N and longitude 87°E, the mountain range of which it forms part, and its altitude.

(v) Identify a group of islands that are situated the same distance south of the Equator as Birmingham, England is north of the equator. (The penguins and sea lions found here are an attraction for nature-lovers.)

(vi) Identify the world famous scenic attraction, one of the deepest valleys in the world, situated at latitude 36°N and longitude 114°W, and name the nearest large city.

(vii) A group of British musicians are planning a trip to Senegal, Mali, and Burkina Faso to collect fresh material for their forthcoming album. Ouagadougou is the first place on their itinerary, but they have no idea where it is. Describe as clearly as you can the location of Ouagadougou, (a) in relation to Britain and (b) in relation to the other countries to be visited on their tour.

(viii) Draw a simple sketch map of the River Rhine, and find out (a) the direction in which the Rhine flows where it forms the boundary between France and Germany, and (b) on which side of the river – east or west – is the left bank of the Rhine at Cologne (Köln).

(ix) Which direction would you be travelling, entering the Panama Canal from the Caribbean Sea and exiting the Canal into the Pacific Ocean?

(x) Which of these two islands is furthest west in Europe – Iceland or Ireland?

And which of these two capital cities is furthest east – Athens or Helsinki?

Answers to self assessment questions

(i) Benidorm, situated midway on Spain's Mediterranean coast, between the cities of Valencia and Alicante.

(ii) (a) Clockwise from north: London to Edinburgh 500 km (310 miles); Copenhagen 900 km; Amsterdam 360 km; Brussels 300 km; Paris 340 km; Palma (Majorca) 1,300 km; Cardiff 200 km; Belfast 540 km. (b) North-east. (c) From the mileage chart in a road atlas.

(iii) Hawaii in the north Pacific Ocean, 4,000 km (2,400 miles) from Los Angeles.

(iv) Everest in the Himalayas, 8,848 metres (29,000 feet) above sea level.

(v) Falkland Islands in the Southern Hemisphere at latitude 52°S and longitude 60°W in the South Atlantic Ocean.

(vi) The Grand Canyon of the River Colorado. The nearest large city with an international airport is Las Vegas (LAS).

(vii) Ouagadougou is situated in West Africa at latitude 12°N and longitude 2°W, due south of Britain and some 4,000 km nearer the Equator. Bamako and Dakar, the capitals of Mali and Senegal, lie to the west of Ouagadougou, which is the capital of Burkina Faso.

(viii) The Rhine flows from south to north, so the left bank of the river at Cologne, facing downstream, would be on the west side.

(ix) From west to east, although on a world map it would appear to be from north to south. Examination of a larger scale map shows that Colón at the Caribbean entrance to the Canal actually lies to the west of Balboa at the Pacific exit.

(x)   Iceland is situated furthest west at longitude 22°W, compared to Ireland at 10°W. Helsinki is situated further east than Athens, at longitude 25°E compared to 23°40″E.

References

Ashford, D. (2003) *Spaceflight Revolution*. Imperial College Press: London.

Ashworth, G. J. and Tunbridge, J. E. (1990) *The Tourist-Historic City*. Belhaven: London.

Bruner, E. (1996) Tourism in Ghana: the representation of slavery and the return of the Black diaspora, *American Anthropologist* 98 (2): 290–304.

Butler, R. W. (1980) The concept of a tourist area cycle of evolution, *Canadian Geographer* 24 (1): 5–12.

Butt, T. (2002) The Cape doctor, *Surfers Path* (December-January), 48–51.

Chubb, M. and Chubb, H. (1981) *One Third of Our Time: An Introduction to Recreation Behaviour and Resources*. John Wiley and Sons: London.

Clawson, M. and Knetsch, J. (1966) *The Economics of Outdoor Recreation*. Johns Hopkins University Press: Boston.

Cohen, E. (1972) Toward a sociology of international tourism, *Social Research* 39 (1): 164–183.

Collins, P. and Ashford, D. (1998) Space tourism, *Ada Astronautica* 17 (4): 421–431.

Dasenbrock, J. (2002) The pros and cons of ecotourism in Costa Rica, *Trade Environment Database Case Studies* 648: 1–12.

Defert, P. (1967) Le taux de function touristique mise au point et critique, *Les cahiers du tourisme*. Centre des Etudes Touristiques: Aix en Provence.

Fáilte Ireland (2007) *A New Strategy for Irish Equestrian Tourism*. Fáilte Ireland: Dublin.

Faulks, R. W. (1990) *The Principles of Transport,* 4th edn. McGraw-Hill: New York.

Gómez Martín, M. (2005) Weather, climate and tourism, *Annals of Tourism Research* 32 (3): 571–591.

Graburn, N. (1976) *Ethnic and Tourist Arts: Cultural Expressions from the Fourth World*. University of California Press: Berkeley.

Gray, H. P. (1971) *International Travel – International Trade*. Heath Lexington Books.

Jezovit, A. (2010) Sustainable Stockholm, *Leisure Management* 2: 46–49.

Kotler, P., Makens, J. and Bowen, D. (2003) *Marketing for Hospitality and Tourism*. Prentice Hall: New York.

Lansing, J. B. and Blood, D. M. (1960) *The Changing Travel Market*. Institute for Social Research.

Lavery, P. (ed.) (1971) *Recreational Geography*. David and Charles.

Lee, D. and Lemons, H. (1949) Clothing for global man, *Geographical Review* 39: 181–213.

Leiper, N. (1970) The framework of tourism, *Annals of Tourism Research* 6 (4): 390–407.

Mathieson, A. and Wall, G. (1982) *Toursim, Economic, Physical and Social Impacts*. Longman: Harlow.

Mieczkowski, Z. (1985) The tourism climatic index: a method of evaluating world climates for tourism, *Canadian Geographer* 29 (3): 220–233.

Moreno, A. and Amelung, B. (2009) Climate change and tourist comfort on Europe's beaches in summer: a reassessment, *Coastal Management* 37 (6): 550–568.

Mowforth, M. and Munt, I. (2008) *Tourism and Sustainability*, 2nd edn. Routledge: London.

Patmore, J. A. (1983) *Recreational Resources*. Blackwell: Oxford.

Pattullo, P. (1996) *Last Resorts: The Cost of Tourism in the Caribbean*. Cassell: London.

Poon, A, (1989) Competitive strategies for a 'New Tourism', in C. Cooper (ed.), *Progress in Tourism, Recreation and Hospitality Management,* Belhaven, London, 91–102.

Potier, F. and Terrier, C. (2007) *Atlas des mobilités touristiques*. Autremont. Paris.

Smeral, E. (1998) The impact of globalization on small to medium sized enterprises. *Tourism Management* 19 (4): 371–380.

Smith, V. L. (1978) *Hosts and Guests: The Anthropology of Tourism*. Blackwell: Oxford.

Swarbrooke, J. (2002) *The Development and Management of Visitor Attractions*, 2nd edn. Elsevier Butterworth-Heinemann: Oxford.

Terjung, W. H. (1966) Physiological climates of the conterminous United States: a bioclimatic classification based on Man, *Annals of the Association of American Geographers* 56: 144–179.

Trewartha, G. (1954) *An Introduction to Climate*. McGraw-Hill: Chicago.

Ullman, E. (1980) *Geography as Spatial Interaction*. University of Washington Press: Washington.

UNWTO (2001) *Tourism 2020 Vision*. UNWTO: Madrid.

UNWTO (2007) *Tourism Market Trends*. UNWTO: Madrid.

Waugh, D. (2009) *Geography: An Integrated Approach,* 2nd edn. Nelson Thornes.

Wheeler, D. (1996) Spanish climate: regions and diversity, *Geography Review* (September); 34–40.

Williams, A. V. and Zelinsky, W. (1970) On some patterns in international tourism flows, *Economic Geography* 46 (4): 549–567.

Winter, T., Teo, P. and Chang, T. C. (eds) (2009) *Asia on Tour: Exploring the rise of Asian Tourism*. Routledge: London.

World Tourism Organisation (2008) *Climate Change and Tourism. Responding to Global Challenges*. WTO: Madrid.

Useful sources

Sources to support work on worldwide destinations

This section is designed to support your work on this book. Whilst we have provided a set of relevant sources in this section, there is also a range of other material that you will find useful. These include abstracting services, handbooks and dictionaries of tourism and the academic tourism journals. We have not provided a listing of trade publications (such as *Travel Trade Gazette*) for two reasons; first, there will be different trade journals and newspapers available to you depending upon which part of the world you live in, and secondly, in our view, the material tends to date rapidly.

The World Wide Web is now a major source of information about tourism and destinations. Of course, the Web is disorganised and lacks any form of information quality control, but the official tourism sites in particular provide instant access to countries, cities and resorts. Other sites are now available that provide destination accounts, photographs and statistics. However, we would not recommend that you use only Internet sources, but use the Web to supplement print sources.

This list of sources is organised to cover the following types of reference material:

- general texts on tourism and the geography of travel and tourism;
- reports, dictionaries, yearbooks and encyclopaedias;
- abstracting services;
- statistical sources;
- tourism journals.

Books on tourism and the geography of travel and tourism

Airey, D. and Chong, K. (2011) *Tourism in China: Policy and Development since 1949*. Routledge.

Andrews, H. (2011) *The British on Holiday: Charter Tourism, Identity and Consumption*. Channel View.

Aramberri, J. and Butler, R. (2004) *Tourism Development*. Channel View.

Ashford, D. (2003) *Spaceflight Revolution*. Imperial College Press, London.

Ashworth, G. (1984) *Recreation and Tourism*. Bell & Hyman.

Ashworth, G. J. and Tunbridge, J.E. (1990) *The Tourist-Historic City*. Belhaven, London.

Ateljevic, I., Pritchard, A. and Nigel, M. (2007) *The Critical Turn in Tourism Studies*. Elsevier.

Baggio, R. and Klobas, J. (2011) *Quantitative Methods in Tourism: A Handbook*. Channel View.

Ball, S., Horner, S. and Nield, K. (2007) *Contemporary Hospitality and Tourism Management Issues in China and India*. Elsevier.

Beech, J. and Chadwick, S. (2005) *The Business of Managing Tourism*. Pearsons.

Bierman, D. (2003) *Restoring Destinations in Crisis*. Allen and Unwin.

Borsay, P. and Walton, J. K. (eds) (2011) *Resorts and Ports: European Seaside Towns since 1700*. Channel View.

Buckley, R. (2008) *Environmental Impacts of Ecotourism*. CABI.

Buhalis, D. and Darcy, S. (2010) *Accessible Tourism: Concepts and Issues*. Channel View.

Bull, A. (1998) *The Economics of Travel and Tourism*. Longman.

Burke, M., Towner, J. and Newton, M. T. (1996) *Tourism in Spain: Critical Issues*. CABI, Oxford.

Burkhart, A. J. and Medlik, S. (1991) *Tourism, Past, Present and Future*. Heinemann.

Burns, P. M. and Holden, A. (1995) *Tourism: A New Perspective*. Prentice Hall.

Burns, P. M. and Novelli, M. (2007) *Tourism and Politics*. Elsevier.

Burton, R. (1995) *Travel Geography*, 2nd edn. Addison Wesley Longman.

Buswell, R. J. (2011) *Mallorca and Tourism: History, Economy and Environment*. Channel View.

Butler, R. W. and Pearce, D. G. (1993) *Tourism Research*. Routledge.

Callaghan, P. (1989) *Travel and Tourism*. Business Educational.

Chubb, M. and Chubb, H. (1981) *One Third of Our Time: An Introduction to Recreational Behavior and Resources*. John Wiley and Sons, London.

Church, A. and Coles, T. (2006) *Tourism, Power and Space*. Routledge.

Clawson, M. and Knetsch, J. (1966) *The Economics of Outdoor Recreation*. Johns Hopkins University Press, Boston.

Cleverdon, R. (1979) *The Social and Economic Impact of Tourism on Developing Countries*. Economic Intelligence Unit, London.

Coltman, M. (1989) *Introduction to Travel and Tourism*. Van Nostrand Reinhold.

Conlin, M. V. and Baum, T. (1995) *Island Tourism*. Wiley, London.

Connell, J. (2010) *Medical Tourism*. CABI, Oxford.

Cooper, C. and Hall, C. M. (2008) *Contemporary Tourism*. Elsevier.

Cooper, C. P., Fletcher, J., Fyall, A., Gilbert, D. and Wanhill, S. (2008) *Tourism Principles and Practice*. Pearson.

Cristopherson, R. (2005) *Geosystems*, 6th edn. Prentice Hall, New York.

Crotts, J. C. and Van Raaij, W. F. (1993) *Economic Psychology of Travel and Tourism*. Haworth Press.

Daher, R. (2006) *Tourism in the Middle East*. Channel View.

Davidson, A. (1994) *Business Travel*. Addison, Wesley and Longman, Harlow.

Daye, M., Chambers, D. and Roberts, S. (2008) *New Perspectives in Caribbean Tourism*. Routledge.

De Kadt, E. (1979) *Tourism: Passport to Development*. Oxford University Press.

Deuschl, D. (2006) *Travel and Tourism Public Relations*. Elsevier.

Dove, J. (2004) *Tourism and Recreation*. Hodder & Stoughton, London.

Dow, K. and Downing, T. (2006) *The Atlas of Climate Change*. Earthscan, London.

Dowling, R. (2006) *Cruise Ship Tourism*. CABI.

Drakakis-Smith, G. and Lockhart, D. (1997) *Island Tourism: Trends and Prospects*. Pinter.

Dredge, D. (2006) *Tourism Planning and Policy*. Wiley, London.

Dumazedier, J. (1967) *Towards a Society of Leisure*. Free Press.

Duval, D. T. (2007) *Tourism and Transport*. Channel View Publications, Clevedon.

Dwyer, L., Forsyth, P. and Dwyer, W. (2010) *Tourism Economics and Policy*. Channel View.

Dwyer, L., Edwards, D., Mistilis, N., Scott, N., Cooper, C. and Roman, C. (2007) *Trends Underpinning Tourism to 2020: An Analysis of Key Drivers for Change*, STCRC, Gold Coast, Australia.

Fagan, B. (2000) *The Little Ice Age: How Climate made History 1300–1850*. Basic Books.

Faulks, R. W. (1990) *The Principles of Transport*, 4th edn. McGraw-Hill, New York.

Fennell, D. (2006) *North America*. Channel View.

Fennell, D. A. (2007) *Ecotourism*, 3rd edn. Routledge.

Frechtling, D. (2001) *Forecasting Tourism Demand*. Elsevier Butterworth-Heinemann.

Frost, W. and Hall, C. M. (2008) *Tourism and National Parks: International Perspectives on Development, Histories and Change*. Routledge.

Fyall, A. and Garrod, B. (2004) *Tourism Marketing*. Channel View.

Gee, C. Y., Choy, D. J. L. and Makens, J. C. (1997) *The Travel Industry*. Van Nostrand Reinhold.

Getz, D. (2005) *Event Management & Event Tourism*. Cognizant Communication.

Gibson, C. and Connell, J. (2005) *Music and Tourism*. Channel View.

Glyptis, S. (1993) *Leisure and the Environment*. Wiley, London.

Goeldner, C. R. and Ritchie, J. R. B. (2008) *Tourism: Principles, Practices, Philosophies*, 11th edn. Wiley.

Graburn, N. (1976) *Ethnic and Tourist Arts: Cultural Expressions from the Fourth World*. University of California Press, Berkeley.

Gray, H. P. (1971) *International Travel–International Trade*. Heath Lexington Books, New York.

Guichard-Anguis, S. and Moon, O. (2008) *Japanese Tourism and Travel Culture*. Routledge.

Gunn, C. A. (1997) *Vacationscape: Developing Tourist Areas*, 3rd edn. Taylor & Francis, London.

Gunn, C. and Var, T. (2002) *Tourism Planning*. Routledge.

Hall, C. M. (1994) *Tourism and Politics*. Wiley.

Hall, C. M. (2007) *Tourism Planning: Policies, Processes and Relationships*, 2nd edn. Pearson.

Hall, C. M. and Higham, J. (eds) (2005) *Tourism, Recreation and Climate Change*, Channel View Publications, Clevedon.

Hall, C. M. and Jenkins, J. M. (1994) *Tourism and Public Policy*. Routledge.

Hall, C. M. and Lew, A. (2009) *Understanding and Managing Tourism Impacts: An Integrated Approach*. Routledge.

Hall, C. M. and Page, S. (2002) *The Geography of Tourism and Recreation*. Routledge.

Hall, C. M. and Williams, A. (2008) *Tourism and Innovation*. Routledge.

Hall, C. M., Müller, D. K. and Saarinen, J. J. (2009) *Nordic Tourism: Issues and Cases*. Channel View.

Hanley, K. and Walton, J. K. (2010) *Constructing Cultural Tourism: John Ruskin and the Tourist Gaze*. Channel View.

Hannam, K. and Knox, D. (2010) *Understanding Tourism: A Critical Introduction*. Sage.

Hara, T. (2008) *Quantitative Tourism Industry Analysis*. Elsevier.

Harrison, D. (1994) *Tourism and the Less Developed Countries*. Wiley.

Harrison, D. (2002) *Tourism in the Less Developed World*. CABI.

Hayllar, B., Griffin, T. and Edwards, D. (2008) *City Spaces – Tourist Places*. Elsevier.

Heeley, J. (2011) *Inside City Tourism: A European Perspective*. Channel View.

Henderson, J. C. (2007) *Tourism Crises*. Elsevier.

Henson, R. (2002) *The Rough Guide to Weather*. Rough Guides, London.

Holden, A. (2008) *Environment and Tourism*, 2nd edn. Routledge.

Holdridge, L. R. (1967) *Life Zone Ecology*. Tropical Science Center, San José, Costa Rica.

Holloway, C. Davidson, R. and Humphreys, C. (eds) (2009) *The Business of Tourism*, 8th edn. Pearson.

Horner, S. and Swarbrooke, J. (2003) *International Cases in Tourism Management*. Elsevier Butterworth-Heinemann.

Howell, D. W. (1993) *Passport: An Introduction to the Travel and Tourism Industry*. South Western.

Hsu, C. H. C. (2008) *Tourism Marketing*. Wiley.

Hudman, L. E. (1980) *Tourism: A Shrinking World*. Wiley.

Hudman, L. E. and Jackson, R. H. (1999) *The Geography of Travel and Tourism*. Delmar.

Hudson, S. (1999) *Snow Business: A Study of the International Ski Industry*. Continuum.

Inskeep, E. (1991) *Tourism Planning: An Integrated Planning and Development Approach*. Van Nostrand Reinhold.

Ioannides, D. and Debbage, K. G. (1998) *The Economic Geography of the Tourist Industry*. Routledge.

Ioannides, D. and Timothy, D. (2009) *Tourism in the USA: A Spatial and Social Synthesis*. Routledge.

Jeffries, D. (2001) *Governments and Tourism*. Elsevier Butterworth-Heinemann.

Jennings, G. (2001) *Tourism Research*. Wiley.

Kelly, J. R. (1990) *Leisure*. Prentice Hall.

Kolb, B. (2006) *Tourism Marketing for Cities and Towns*. Elsevier.

Kotler, P., Makens, J. and Bowen, D. (2003) *Marketing for Hospitality and Tourism*. Prentice Hall, New York.

Kozak, M. and Andreu, L. (2006) *Progress in Tourism Marketing*. Elsevier.

Kozak, M. and Decrop, A. (2008) *Handbook of Consumer Research in Tourism: Theory & Research*. Routledge.

Lavery, P. (ed.) (1971) *Recreational Geography*. David and Charles.

Laws, E. Prideaux, B. and Chon, K. (2006) *Crisis Management in Tourism*. CABI.

Leiper, N. (1990) *The Tourism System*. Massey University Press.

Lenček, L. and Bosker, G. (1999) *The Beach: The history of Paradise on Earth*. Pimlico Press.

Lennon, J. and Foley, M. (2002) *Dark Tourism: The Attraction of Death and Disaster*. Continuum.

Lennon, J. J. (2003) *Tourism Statistics*. Allen and Unwin.

Leslie, D. (2008) *Tourism Enterprises and Sustainable Development: International Perspectives on Responses to the Sustainability Agenda*. Routledge.

Lew, A., Hall, C. M. and Williams, A. M. (2004) *A Companion to Tourism*. Wiley.

Likorish, L. and Jenkins, C. L. (1997) *An Introduction to Tourism*. Butterworth-Heinemann.

Löfgren, O. (1999) *On Holiday: A History of Vacationing*. University of California Press, Berkeley.

Lundberg, D. E. (1975) *The Tourist Business*. Van Nostrand Reinhold.

Lundberg, D. E., Stavenga, M. H. and Krishanmoorthy, M. (1995) *Tourism Economics*. Wiley.

Maitland, R. and Newman, P. (2008) *World Tourism Cities: Developing Tourism Off the Beaten Track*. Routledge.

Mason, P. (2008) *Tourism Impacts, Planning and Management*. Elsevier.

McCabe, S. (2007) *Marketing Communications in Tourism and Hospitality*. Elsevier.

McCabe, S., Minnaert, L. and Diekmann, A. (2011) *Social Tourism in Europe: Theory and Practice*. Channel View.

Medlik, S. (1995) *Managing Tourism*. Butterworth-Heinemann.

Mercer, D. (1980) *In Pursuit of Leisure*. Sorret.

Middleton, V. T. C. and Hawkins, R. (1998) *Sustainable Tourism: A Marketing Perspective*. Elsevier Butterworth-Heinemann.

Middleton, V. T. C. and Lickorish, L. J. (2007) *British Tourism*. Elsevier.

Mill, R. C. (1990) *Tourism: The International Business*. Prentice Hall.

Mill, R. C. and Morrison, A. (1992) *The Tourism System: An Introductory Text*. Prentice Hall.

Morgan, M. and Moran, J. (1997) *Weather and People*. Prentice Hall, New York.

Morgan, M., Lugosi, P. and Brent Ritchie, J. R. (2010) *The Tourism and Leisure Experience: Consumer and Managerial Perspectives*. Channel View.

Morpeth, N. D. (2007) *Religious Tourism and Pilgrimage Management: An International Perspective*. CABI, Oxford.

Mowforth, M. and Munt, I. (2008) *Tourism and Sustainability*, 2nd edn. Routledge, London.

Mowforth, M., Charlton, C. and Munt, I. (2007) *Tourism and Responsibility*. Routledge.

Muller, D. K. and Jannson, B. (2006) *Tourism in Peripheries*. CABI.

Murphy, P. E. (1991) *Tourism: A Community Approach*. Methuen.

Newsome, D., Moore, S. and Dowling, R. (2001) *Natural Area Tourism*. Channel View, Clevedon.

Nordin, S. (2005) *Tourism of Tomorrow – Travel Trends and Forces of Change*. European Tourism Research Institute, Ostersund.

Orams, M. (1999) *Marine Tourism*. Routledge.

Page, S. (1996) *Urban Tourism*. Routledge, London.

Page, S. (2007) *Tourism Management*. Elsevier.

Page, S. (2008) *Tourism Management: Managing for Change*. Elsevier Butterworth-Heinemann.

Page, S. (2009) *Transport and Tourism: Global Perspectives*, 3rd edn. Pearson.

Page, S. (2011) *Tourism Management*, 4th edn. Routledge.

Page, S. J. and Connell, J. (2006) *Tourism: A Modern Synthesis*. Cengage Learning.

Patmore, J. A. (1983) *Recreational Resources*. Blackwell, Oxford.

Pattullo, P. (1996) *Last Resorts: The Cost of Tourism in the Caribbean*. Cassell, London.

Pearce, D. (1989) *Tourist Development*. Longman.

Pearce, D. (1992) *Tourist Organisations*. Longman.

Pearce, D. (1995) *Tourism Today: A Geographical Analysis*. Longman.

Pearce, D. and Butler, R. (1993) *Tourism Research: Critiques and Challenges*. Routledge.

Pearce, D. and Butler, R. (1995) *Change in Tourism: People, Places, Processes*. Routledge.

Pearce, D. G. and Butler, R. W. (2001) *Contemporary Issues in Tourism Development*. Routledge.

Pearce, E. A. and Smith, C. G. (1990) *The World Weather Guide*. Hutchinson, London.

Pearce, P. L. (2011) *Tourist Behaviour and the Contemporary World*. Channel View.

Poon, A. (1993) *Tourism, Technology and Competitive Strategies*. CAB.

Prideaux, B., Timothy, D. and Chon, K. (2007) *Cultural and Heritage Tourism in Asia and the Pacific*. Routledge.

Pritchard, A., Ateljevic, I., Morgan, N. and Harris, C. (2007) *Tourism and Gender: Embodiment, Sensuality and Experience*. CABI.

Reid, R. D. and Bojanic, D. C. (2005) *Hospitality Marketing Management*, 4th edn. Wiley.

Reisinger, Y. and Dimanche, F. (2008) *International Tourism*. Elsevier.

Ritchie, J. R. B. and Crouch, G. I. (2003) *The Competitive Destination*. CABI.

Robinson, H. (1976) *A Geography of Tourism*. Macdonald & Evans.

Ross, G. F. (1996) *The Psychology of Tourism*. Hospitality Press, Melbourne.

Rostow, W. W. (1959) *The Stages of Economic Growth*. Cambridge University Press, Cambridge.

Royal Meteorological Society (1970–) *Tables of Temperature, Relative Humidity and Precipitation for the World*. HMSO, London.

Ryan, C. (2002) *The Tourist Experience*. Continuum.

Ryan, C. (2003) *Recreational Tourism*. Channel View.

Ryan, C. (2007) *Battlefield Tourism*. Elsevier, Oxford.

Ryan, C. and Aiken, M. (eds) (2005) *Indigenous Tourism*. Elsevier, Oxford.

Ryan, C. and Huimin, G. (2008) *Tourism in China: Destination, Cultures and Communities*. Routledge.

Scott, N., Baggio, R. and Cooper, C. (2008) *Network Analysis and Tourism*. Channel View.

Shackley, M. (2001) *Managing Sacred Sites*. Thomson, London.

Sharpley, R. (1994) *Tourism, Tourists and Society*. Elm.

Sharpley, R. and Telfer, D. (2002) *Tourism and Development*. Channel View.

Shaw, G. and Williams, A. (1994) *Critical Issues in Tourism*. Blackwell.

Sinclair, T. and Stabler, M. (1991) *The Tourism Industry: An International Analysis*. CAB.

Sinclair, T., Stabler, M. and Papatheodorou, A. (2009) *The Economics of Tourism*. Routledge.

Smith, M. (2003) *Issues in Cultural Tourism Studies*. Routledge, London.

Smith, M. and Robinson, M. (2006) *Tourism in a Changing World*. Channel View.

Smith, M. MacLeod, N. and Hart Robertson, M. (2010). *Key Concepts in Tourist Studies*. Sage.

Smith, S. L. J. (1983) *Recreation Geography*. Longman.

Smith, S. L. J. (1996) *Tourism Analysis: A Handbook*. Addison Wesley Longman.

Smith, V. L. (1978) *Hosts and Guests: The Anthropology of Tourism*. Blackwell, Oxford.

Smith, V. L. (1989) *Hosts and Guests*. University of Pennsylvania Press.

Smith, V. and Brent, M. (2003) *Hosts and Guests Revisited*. Cognizant.

Smith, V. L. and Eadington, W. R. (1995) *Tourism Alternatives: Potential Problems in the Development of Tourism*. University of Pennsylvania Press.

Stronza, A. (2008) *Ecotourism and Conservation in the Americas*. CABI.

Su, X. and Teo, P. (2008) *The Politics of Heritage Tourism in China: A View from Lijiang*. Routledge.

Swarbrooke, J. (2002) *The Development and Management of Visitor Attractions*, 2nd edn. Elsevier Butterworth-Heinemann, Oxford.

Swarbrooke, J. and Horner, S. (2007) *Consumer Behaviour In Tourism*. Elsevier.

Telfer, D. J. and Sharpley, R. (2007) *Tourism and Development in the Developing World*. Routledge.

Terrell, S. (2004) *The Geography of Sport and Leisure*. Hodder & Stoughton, London.

Theobald, W. F. (1994) *Global Tourism: The Next Decade*. Butterworth-Heinemann.

Thomas, R. and Augustyn, M. (2007) *Tourism in New Europe*. Elsevier.

Timothy, D. J. (2011) *Cultural Heritage and Tourism: An Introduction*. Channel View.

Timothy, D. J. and Boyd, S.W. (2003) *Heritage Tourism*. Prentice Hall, New York.

Timothy, D. J. and Nyaupane, G. (2008) *Cultural Heritage and Tourism in the Developing World*. Routledge.

Towner, J. (1994) *An Historical Geography of Recreation and Tourism*. Belhaven.

Trewartha, G. (1954) *An Introduction to Climate*. McGraw-Hill, Chicago.

Tribe, J. (2011) *The Economics of Recreation, Leisure and Tourism*, 4th edn. Routledge.

Tribe, J. and Airey, D. (2007) *Developments In Tourism Research*. Elsevier.

Turner, L. and Ash, J. (1975) *The Golden Hordes: International Tourism and the Pleasure Periphery*. Constable.

Ullman, E. (1980) *Geography as Spatial Interaction*. University of Washington Press, Washington.

Urry, J. and Larsen, J. (2011). *The Tourist Gaze 3.0*, 3rd edn. Sage.

Van Egmond, T. (2007) *Understanding Western Tourists in Developing Countries*. CABI.

Veal, A. J. (2011) *Research Methods for Leisure and Tourism*, 4th edn. Pearson.

Vellas, F. and Becherel, L. (1995) *International Tourism*. Macmillan.

VisitScotland (2005) *Our Ambition for Scottish Tourism: A Journey to 2025*, VisitScotland, Edinburgh.

Wahab, S. (1993) *Tourism Management*. Tourism International Press.

Weaver, D. (2008) *Ecotourism*, 2nd edn. Wiley.

Weaver, D. and Lawton, L. (2006) *Tourism Management*, 3rd edn. Wiley.

Weed, M. (2007) *Olympic Tourism*. Elsevier.

Wilks, J., Pendergast, D. and Leggat, P. (2006) *Tourism in Turbulent Times*. Elsevier.

Williams, S. (2004) *Tourism, Critical Concepts in the Social Sciences*. Routledge.

Williams, S. (2009) *Tourism Geography*. Routledge.

Winter, T., Teo, P. and Chang, T. C. (eds) (2009) *Asia on Tour: Exploring the Rise of Asian Tourism*. Routledge, London.

Witt, S., Brooke, M. Z. and Buckley, P. J. (1995) *The Management of International Tourism*. Unwin Hyman.

Woodside, A. and Martin, D. (2008) *Tourism Management: Analysis, Behaviour and Strategy*. CABI.

World Tourism Organisation (2001) *Tourism in the Least Developed Countries*, WTO.

World Tourism Organisation (2001) *Tourism 2020 Vision*, WTO, Madrid.

World Tourism Organisation (2002) *Enhancing the Economic Benefits of Tourism Through Poverty Alleviation*, WTO.

World Tourism Organisation (2002) *Making Tourism More Sustainable*, WTO.

World Tourism Organisation (2002) *Sport and Tourism*, WTO.

World Tourism Organisation (2002) *Tourism and Poverty Alleviation*, WTO.

World Tourism Organisation (2003) *Global Code of Ethics for Tourism*, WTO, Madrid.

World Tourism Organisation (2003) *Worldwide Cruise-ship Activity*, WTO.

World Tourism Organisation (2005) *City Tourism and Culture*, WTO.

World Tourism Organisation (2005) *Tourism's Potential as a Sustainable Development Strategy*, WTO.

World Tourism Organisation (2007) *A Practical Guide to Destination Management*, WTO.

World Tourism Organisation (2007) *Policies, Strategies and Tools for the Sustainable Development of Tourism*, WTO.

World Tourism Organisation (2007) *Tourism Market Trends*, WTO, Madrid.

World Tourism Organisation (2008) *Climate Change and Tourism. Responding to Global Challenges*, WTO, Madrid.

World Tourism Organisation (2008) *The Impact of Rising Oil Prices on Tourism*, WTO.

Yeoman, J. (2008) *Tomorrow's Tourist*. Butterworth Elsevier Heinemann, Oxford.

Reports, dictionaries, yearbooks and encyclopaedias

In addition to books, journals and trade press coverage of tourism destinations and cases, there are a number of useful sources to be found in consultant's reports (including those on-line such as www.euromonitor.com), tourism dictionaries, yearbooks and encyclopaedias. Some of the key sources include:

Beaver, A. (2002) *A Dictionary of Travel and Tourism Terminology*. Oxford University Press.

Cooper, C. and Lockwood, A. (1989) *Progress in Tourism, Recreation and Hospitality Management*. Vols 1–6. Belhaven and Wiley.

Economic Intelligence Unit publications.

Euromonitor publications.

Europa Publications (annual) *The Europa World Yearbook*. Europa Publications.

INSIGHTS, English Tourist Board.

Jones, I. and Mason, P. (2008) *Routledge Dictionary of Leisure and Tourism*. Routledge.

Jafari, J. (2000) *The Encyclopedia of Tourism*. Routledge.

Khan, M., Olsen, M. and Var, T. (1993) *Encyclopedia of Hospitality and Tourism*. Van Nostrand Reinhold.

Luck, M. (2008) *The Encyclopedia of Tourism and Recreation in Marine Environments*. CABI.

Medlik, S. (2002) *Dictionary of Transport, Travel and Hospitality*. Butterworth-Heinemann.

Page, S. and Connell, J. (2010). *Tourism*. Sage.

Paxton, J. (annual) *The Statesman's Yearbook*. Macmillan.

Ritchie, J. R. B. and Hawkins, D. (1991–1993) *World Travel and Tourism Review*. Vols 1–3. CAB.

Ritchie, J. R. B. and Goeldner, C. R. (1994) *Travel, Tourism and Hospitality Research: A Handbook for Managers and Researchers*. Wiley.

Seaton, A., Wood, R., Dieke, P. and Jenkins, C. (eds) (1994) *Tourism: The State of the Art: The Strathclyde Symposium*. Wiley.

Weaver, D. (2001) *The Encyclopaedia of Ecotourism*. CABI.

Witt, S. F. and Mountinho, L. (1995) *Tourism Marketing and Management Handbook*. Student edition. Prentice Hall.

World Tourism Organisation (2001) *Thesaurus on Tourism and Leisure Activities*, WTO.

World Travel and Tourism Council, *Special Country Reports*, WTTC.

Abstracting services

Using electronic searching and abstracting services is a very effective way of searching the available literature and a great way to begin a case. The key services include:

Articles in Tourism (monthly) Universities of Bournemouth, Oxford Brookes and Surrey.

International Tourism and Hospitality Data Base CD-ROM. The Guide to Industry and Academic Resources. Wiley.

Leisure, Recreation and Tourism Abstracts (quarterly). CAB.

The Travel and Tourism Index. Brigham Young University Hawaii Campus.

Tour CD – Leisure Recreation and Tourism on CD-ROM.

Statistical sources

There is still a limited range of sources that draw together tourism statistics and trends. Nonetheless, the UNWTO's increasingly user-friendly reports are well worth consulting for both global and regional trends – but beware the distinctions between travellers, tourists and day visitors in the tables. The key sources are:

Organisation for Economic Co-operation and Development (annual) *Tourism Policy and International Tourism in OECD Member Countries*. OECD.

Pacific Asia Travel Association (PATA) (annual) *Annual Statistical Report*. PATA.

Pacific Asia Travel Association (PATA) (2008) *Asia Pacific Tourism Forecasts 2008–2010*. PATA.

World Tourism Organisation (annual) *Compendium of Tourism Statistics*. WTO.

World Tourism Organisation (annual) *Tourism Highlights*. WTO.

World Tourism Organisation (annual) *Yearbook of Tourism Statistics*. WTO.

World Tourism Organisation (monthly) *World Tourism Barometer*. WTO.

World Tourism Organisation (1994) *Recommendations on Tourism Statistics*. WTO.

World Tourism Organisation (1999) *Observations of International Tourism Volume I*. WTO.

World Tourism Organisation (1999) *Observations of International Tourism Volume II*. WTO.

World Tourism Organisation (2004) *International Tourism. The Great Turning Point*. WTO.

World Tourism Organisation (2006) *Tourism Market Trends*, 6 volumes. WTO.

Journals

The growth in tourism journals has brought with it a rich source of case study and statistical material. In addition, the geographical and leisure journals are increasingly publishing tourism-related papers. Journals with content relevant to the geography of travel and tourism include:

Ada Astronautica

American Anthropologist

Annals of Leisure Research

Annals of Tourism Research

Annals of the Association of American Geographers

ASEAN Journal of Hospitality and Tourism

Asia Pacific Journal of Tourism Research

Australian Journal of Hospitality Management

Canadian Geographer

Current Issues in Tourism

China Tourism Research

Coastal Management

Economic Geography

e-Review of Tourism Research (http://ertr.tamu.edu),

Event Management

Festival Management and Event Tourism

Geography Review

Geographical Review

Hospitality and Tourism Educator

International Journal of Contemporary Hospitality Management

International Journal of Hospitality and Tourism Administration

International Journal of Hospitality Management

International Journal of Service Industry Management

International Journal of Tourism Research

Journal of Air Transport Geography

Journal of Air Transport Management

Journal of Convention and Exhibition Management

Journal of Ecotourism

Journal of Heritage Tourism

Journal of Hospitality and Leisure Marketing

Journal of Hospitality and Tourism Research

Journal of Hospitality, Leisure, Sport and Tourism

Journal of Hospitality Marketing & Management

Journal of Information Technology & Tourism

Journal of International Volunteer Tourism and Social Development

Journal of Leisure Research

Journal of Quality Assurance in Tourism & Hospitality

Journal of Sport Tourism

Journal of Sustainable Tourism

Journal of Teaching in Travel and Tourism

Journal of Tourism and Cultural Change

Journal of Tourism Consumption and Practice

Journal of Tourism History

Journal of Tourism Studies

Journal of Travel and Tourism Marketing

Journal of Travel Research

Journal of Travel and Tourism Research

Journal of Vacation Marketing

Leisure Futures, Henley Centre for Forecasting

Leisure Management

Leisure Sciences

Leisure Studies

Les cahiers du tourisme

Managing Leisure

National Geographic Magazine

Pacific Tourism Review

Progress in Tourism and Hospitality Research

Progress in Tourism, Recreation and Hospitality Management

Scandinavian Journal of Hospitality and Tourism

Service Industries Journal

Social Research

Surfers Path

The Tourist Review

Tourism Analysis

Tourism and Hospitality Research

Tourism Culture and Communication

Tourism Economics

Tourism Geographies
Tourism in Focus
Tourism Management
Tourism Recreation Research
Trade Environment Database Case Studies
Travel and Tourism Analyst
World Leisure and Recreation Association Journal

Website

http//www.spacetourismsociety.org

Selective place name index

Page numbers in *italics* refer to illustrations

Subject index

Page numbers in *italics* refer to illustrations.